Real Research
Conducting and Evaluating Research in the Social Sciences

Loreen Wolfer
University of Scranton

PEARSON
and

Boston   New York   San Francisco

Mexico City   Montreal   Toronto   London   Madrid   Munich   Paris

Hong Kong   Singapore   Tokyo   Cape Town   Sydney

Senior Series Editor: Jeff Lasser
Series Editorial Assistant: Erikka Adams
Senior Marketing Manager: Kelly May
Production Supervisor: Karen Mason
Editorial Production Service: Publishers' Design and Production Services, Inc.
Composition Buyer: Linda Cox
Manufacturing Buyer: JoAnne Sweeney
Electronic Composition: Publishers' Design and Production Services, Inc.
Interior Design: Joyce Weston
Photo Researcher: Annie Pickert
Cover Administrator: Kristina Mose-Libon

For related titles and support materials, visit our online catalog at www.ablongman.com.

Between the time website information is gathered and then published, it is not unusual for some sites to have closed. Also, the transcription of URLs can result in typographical errors. The publisher would appreciate notification where these errors occur so that they may be corrected in subsequent editions.

Cataloging-in-Publication data is not available at this time.
ISBN 0-205-41662-4

Text and photo credits appear on page 644, which constitutes a continuation of the copyright page.

Printed in the United States of America

10 9 8 7 6 5 4 3 2 1 RRD-VA 10 09 08 07 06

Contents

6. Experimental Research   228

7. Survey Research   276

8. Field Research   332

9. Unobtrusive Research Methods   380

10. Evaluation Research   425

Preface

As the word *science* implies, the social sciences of sociology, criminal justice, psychology, political science, and their related subfields are research-based disciplines. And since they are "sciences," that means that the research is systematic. True, it does not take a "scientist" to ask whether muckraking political campaigns are an effective campaign tool or if playing violent video games causes violence among children. Nor does it take a scientist to wonder why some people manage to pull themselves out of poverty while others do not.

What distinguishes social scientists from other people asking these questions is that scientists follow a prescribed, systematic method when examining these issues. Hence, social scientists are somewhat unique creatures in that, like the rest of the world, they have their own "pet" concerns, their own views of society or social processes, and their own social experiences that may at least direct the types of questions they ask. However, as scientists, they try to step outside of their personal views and perspectives to look at social issues more objectively. Are they always successful? Probably not, but the systematic nature of scientific research means that others can copy or build on individual scientists' investigations, and that helps detect any potential bias that may have crept into an analysis. You will learn that systematic way of examining the world as you read through the chapters of *Real Research*.

At the very least, I hope what you learn in this book will lead you to question the social "facts" that have pervaded our society. When you hear the latest poll or the latest dire social statistic, I hope you will start asking yourself how that information was gathered. How did the researchers define the problem? Who did they sample to obtain the information? How did they collect their sample? These are just a few of the questions that distinguish the general person interested in social issues from a social scientist who is interested in the same.

Of course, at the very most, I hope that you will be as intrigued about how to use the research process to examine your social world as I am! Like most things, research only seems "hard" when it's new and you're still figuring out what to do. With practice, you will be able to use your curiosity and the skills learned here to continue your scientific examination of society in the future.

Goals of This Book

This book has two general goals. Obviously, the first is to help you learn the various systematic steps social scientists take when examining the social world in which they live. Although I use the word *systematic*, you will soon learn that systematic does not necessarily mean that one proceeds neatly from Step A to Step B to Step C when doing research. Instead, *systematic* means that there are set issues that social scientists need to consider when examining their social world and when deciding *how* to examine their world. Therefore, this book is loosely organized to follow a basic research process from start to finish and to teach you the considerations and techniques in each stage of the research process. However, it is important to keep in mind that sometimes what happens in a later stage of the process may lead a researcher to go back and rethink decisions made at an earlier stage.

That being said, by the time you finish reading this book, you will have a basic understanding of how to formulate and organize a research question (including a hypothesis), how to establish a causal connection between variables, how to select a sample, how to conduct various forms of research design (e.g., surveys compared to experiments), and how to do some basic analysis of the resulting data. Along the way, you will also learn about methodological issues such as research ethics, reliability, validity, and generalizability. Remember, although all of this may seem somewhat intimidating now, with some practice, you will be able to distinguish easily between these concepts, so don't give up!

Despite my hope of hopes that I mentioned earlier, most of you reading this book are probably not going to *do* much social science research after you leave college. However, it is increasingly likely that you will have to read, understand, and be able to evaluate the research of others. In order to do this, you must first understand and be comfortable with the methods of social research; therefore, the first goal of the book still applies to you.

So, the second goal is to help you learn how to realistically evaluate the research of others. The key word in the previous sentence is *realistically*. Most research methods books, the present one included, tend to take an "ideal type" approach to the social sciences; the methods described are what researchers should *aspire* to incorporate in their research. However, most researchers are bound by time, money, skill, and other resources that prevent them from being able to conduct research in the ideal way.

For example, think of something as seemingly obvious as studying college students in the United States. To truly study college students, one would need access to a list of *all* the college students in the United States and then one would have to draw a sample of students from that list. Or one would need a list of all the colleges in the United States and one would then draw repeated samples of colleges from that list until one could obtain a smaller, but still prohibitively large, list of all college students at these selected colleges. Possible? Of course. Feasible? Less so. In reality, many researchers don't have the time or money to put together either list, but they can still study college students by focusing on college students at one particular school or a small list of schools.

The key is for the researchers to be careful about how they word their findings and what types of conclusions (e.g., about "college students") they draw. Yet, students frequently overlook the nuances of how research is presented and instead criticize researchers for not using larger, broader samples. Or sometimes they err in the opposite direction and assume that if something has been published, then it *has* to be good research. This is why I say that the second goal of the book is to teach you how to *realistically* evaluate the research of others.

At the end of each chapter are some guidelines for evaluating the written descriptions of individual parts of a research report. These guidelines are just that—*guidelines*. There is no magic formula for evaluating research, because even though science is systematic, there is some flexibility and creativity inherent in it. The guidelines are simply meant to get you started thinking more deeply about the research you read, and, hopefully, to also get you to think more carefully about any research you, in turn, may do.

Research Navigator

Research Navigator™ is an online, searchable research database, available exclusively through Pearson Education in partnership with EBSCO Information Services. Research Navigator is a subscription service, requiring a Login Name and Password. Every new copy of this text comes with a Research Navigator Guide, containing an access code that will allow you to subscribe to six months of free, unlimited access to thousands of articles from leading scholarly journals, popular magazines, and newspapers.

Research Navigator offers four exclusive databases of credible and reliable source content. The database used primarily in this text is **ContentSelect,** consisting of articles from leading, peer-reviewed academic journals, organized by academic discipline. Using ContentSelect, you can conduct searches in single or multiple disciplines simultaneously using either simple or sophisticated search strategies, such as keywords, article numbers, exact matches, or Boolean operators. Articles include abstract and citation information and can be cut, pasted, emailed, or saved for later use. Many of the examples in this text are from articles that can be easily retrieved with your Research Navigator subscription, and there are assignments that can be carried out using the wealth of published research literature in ContentSelect.

ContentSelect is a dynamic database. Older articles drop out after several years, and newer articles from the most current research literature are added on a regular basis. We have attempted to use more current articles that will remain available throughout the life of this edition. However, depending on when you use this text, you might occasionally try to retrieve an article that is no longer in ContentSelect. In those cases, one option might be to access that article through another service available to you through your college or university. Please notify Allyn & Bacon if you discover articles that are no longer in ContentSelect, and we will do our best to support your use of this text by directing you to suitable alternatives.

Acknowledgments

Professors frequently lament that existing textbooks do not exactly meet their teaching needs or pedagogical preferences. I am no exception. As a professor who tried to actively incorporate both the skills for conducting research and the tools for evaluating the existing research published by others, I continually searched for one book that would allow me to do both and that would serve as a reference for my students. Little did I expect that an early conversation with a book representative from Allyn and Bacon when I first began teaching almost ten years ago would lead to the opportunity to put together the kind of book I always wanted in my classroom. That book representative, Brandon Hight, is now an editor with another division of Allyn and Bacon/Longman, and I would first like to thank him for remembering our conversation all those years ago and for mentioning my name to my current editor, Jeff Lasser, when Allyn and Bacon was interested in developing a research methods textbook that used their Research Navigator search engine. Without his memory of our conversation, this book may very well never have been written.

I would also like to recognize my editor that I just mentioned, Jeff Lasser. His attention to detail and his comments regarding earlier chapter drafts were incredibly valuable and deeply appreciated. Although, of course, I take the responsibility for any limitations in this text, Jeff's comments definitely made each version of this book stronger than the previous.

Jeff is not the only member of the Allyn and Bacon team who was instrumental in putting together this book. I would also like to thank Erikka Adams for answering my numerous questions about the details of book publication; Lynda Griffiths, who had to painstakingly read through each word and detail during the editing process; Karen Mason, the production supervisor who kept track of the jumble of our e-mails and notes, in addition to handling various other administrative responsibilities; and Annie Pickert, who compiled a great set of photographs for this book. I'm sure there are numerous others at Allyn and Bacon who I did not have personal contact with but who helped make this book possible, and they deserve thanks as well.

I also recognize the valuable input of the following reviewers who have taken the time to read, evaluate, and comment on different chapter drafts: Carol A. Bailey (Virginia Polytechnic Institute and State University), Marian A. O. Cohen (Framingham State College), Keith Durkin (Ohio Northern University), Karen Honeycutt (Keene State College), Christine O'Neil (University of Montana Western), Bob Peck (University of Oklahoma, Norman), and Lesley Reid (Georgia State University). They often saw issues in the text that I did not, and their insightful comments and concrete suggestions were, whenever possible, incorporated into the book. I am grateful for their time and effort.

Last, I thank my family. I started writing this book soon after the birth of my first child. Had it not been for the support and time given by my family, I believe that this book would probably never have been completed. Thank you to my parents, especially my mother, who unselfishly devoted a huge portion of her time to watching and playing with her granddaughter while I was diligently writing the chapters of this book. Although this time undoubtedly helped my mother and daughter form a tight, unique bond (one that I know both cherish), the amount of time, patience, and love that my mother shows deserves special mention.

My mother is not the only one, however, who has helped with this book. Last, but not least, I thank my husband. He understood how important it was to me to write this book; and he too provided the love, support, and time to help my desire come to fruition. If he wasn't such a terrific husband and father, I would have felt guiltier about pursing this book while raising a young child.

Too all of you—thank you.

Chapter 1

The Role of Social Research

Courses in research methods and statistics are probably the two most dreaded courses in the social sciences. Students usually approach a research methods class with apprehension, fear, and general resistance. When I talk with students about research methods, they frequently ask questions such as Why do I need this? and Will I ever use it? When I ask students why they think we do research, they usually respond that people do research just to gather information that, in their (limited) opinion, is more academic than practical. For example, they cannot see how questions such as What leads teenagers to shoot teachers and fellow students? Do drug treatment courts help drug abusers overcome their addiction? and How does divorce affect women's labor force behavior? possibly have to do with their career aspirations of police officer, social worker, or attorney. Students frequently argue that they enter social science fields such as sociology, criminal justice, and social work to "help people" and can't even remotely understand why they would need to do something as seemingly academic or esoteric as research.

Well, let's stop and think about this for a moment. How do people in these fields know that what they are doing really is working? How do they even know what to try? If people don't have an idea of the cause of a problem, such as school violence or drug addiction, how can they possibly "help" prevent these behaviors? If we create a plan of action, say, to minimize school violence, how do we know where to start? How do we know if what we try is successful? After all, school murders, for all their publicity, still are not that common. Simply saying that "a murder did not occur this year" is not a strong indicator of program success, because even without any intervention, a school murder in any particular school at any particular time is generally unlikely. So the bottom line is this: How can we really *help* people if we don't understand the nature of the problem and have a means of evaluating any approach to intervention? The answer is, we can't. We need research to either fuel or evaluate any course of action that affects people's lives.

When I finally get students to grudgingly recognize that *maybe*, just *maybe*, they might need research at some point in the future, someone inevitably asks, "But why all the hoopla of research *methods*? Why can't we just go out and observe what we see or base programs on our expertise?" The implication behind these questions is that students are in college to become "experts" in their discipline. So why can't they just use the knowledge that they acquire in college to create meaningful and successful programs? To answer that question, let's look at the next section.

Avenues of Knowledge

Let's do a little experiment. When you are done reading this sentence (not before!) look at the photograph at the bottom of this page for 3 to 5 seconds. (Do **not** continue reading until you have looked at the photo for 3 to 5 seconds.)

Now turn the page and check your answers. Chances are that you were able to answer only a few of the questions correctly. Why? Because, left to our own devices, humans are notoriously poor at observation. You might say, "Well, if I knew what I had to look for in the picture I would have been better able to find it." Perhaps. But observation is not just what people see, but how they interpret what they see as well. All too often people are not sure about the interpretation of their observations until long after they make them, and once that occurs, people are not always so sure about what they actually saw anyway. People frequently redefine their observation to fit their interpretation of an event instead of the other way around. A classic study by Solomon Asch (1952) illustrates this. Asch conducted an experiment with seven students where five students (called "confederates" because they are part of the experiment and are playing along with the researcher) are already seated when a sixth (the real experimental subject) enters. A seventh confederate enters after the experimental subject. Asch uncovered a card with a single line and then uncovered a second card with three lines, like you see in Figure 1.1. Ache then asked each student, in turn, which of the three lines matched the line in the first card. All of the first five answer incorrectly, as does the seventh, even though the answer is clear. Asch repeated the experiment numerous times, each time with a new and different test subject (sixth student). Asch found that 33 percent of the experimental subjects (the sixth student) responded incorrectly, like the first five students, at least half of the time; another 40 percent also gave wrong answers, although less frequently than the first third. Only one-quarter (25 percent) of the

Now, without looking back at the picture, try to answer the following questions: How many people were in the crowd? Did they look American? Did you notice the one man who was bald? How many women were there?

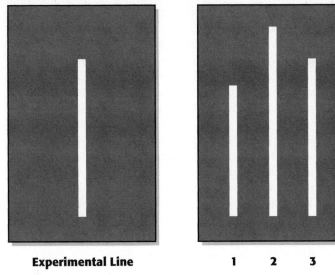

Experimental Line 1 2 3

Figure 1.1 The Lines in Asch's Experiment

experimental subjects consistently gave the clear right answer, regardless of the answers of the other students. Do you think you'd be different? Perhaps you would—perhaps you *would* be part of that 25 percent; however, Asch's experiment is the most consistently replicated study than any other, and the findings are always similar (Levine, 1999). Asch's study shows that people are vulnerable to the perception of others, and that we will adapt our view of an event to fit the perception of others. In a similar fashion, how we gather knowledge is shaped by a number of different factors. In this section we will discuss those factors, or avenues, of knowledge and make an argument for why scientific research, the kind you will learn in a research methods class such as this, is usually more accurate and reliable.

■ Tradition

Traditional knowledge is based on custom and habit. It's "true" because that's the "way it's always been" or because that's what we learned from our parents. How many of you have mothers or grandmothers who feed you chicken soup when you are sick? My mother never took notice of scientific research, but she "knew" that chicken soup was good for a cold because she learned it from *her* mother who, in turn, learned it from *her* mother. In fact, it is only relatively recently that some people even bothered to scientifically test whether this "knowledge" was true (Rennard et al., 2000). And guess what? The researchers found that—just as generations of mothers instinctively knew—chicken soup *does* have some healing properties. It not only keeps nasal passages moist and prevents dehydration but it also provides nourishment (Rennard et al., 2000). But moms already knew that. So, traditional knowledge is not necessarily bad. After all, being able to base some knowledge on the past frees us from continually having to reprove or search for patterns of behavior.

However, traditional knowledge can be limiting and distorting. For example, this form of knowledge would suggest that children benefit most, intellectually and socially, when their mothers are not employed. After all, nonemployed mothers have more time than employed mothers to read to children, to take children on educational trips, and to be a consistent emotional presence. Because this is the way mothers' roles were organized for much of the twentieth century, many people take the link between maternal unemployment and child development to be true. However, this form of traditional knowledge is flawed. Many nonemployed mothers do not necessarily spend more time with their children, as one would assume. Children spend a lot of time in front of television—otherwise known as the "electronic babysitter." Furthermore, some evidence suggests that employed mothers substitute quantity of time for quality of time (Aulette, 2002). Other studies suggest that the difference in care hours between nonemployed mothers and employed mothers is not as great as presumed because employed mothers spend less time on other home activities such as cooking and cleaning in order to make sure they still have plenty of time with their children (Aulette, 2002; Bianchi, 2000). However, traditional knowledge is very resistant to change, consequently the biases toward employed women remain. These biases may limit work–family policy, hurt the relationship between spouses in dual-earner families (for example, if one spouse has a very traditional view of women's roles even if a wife has to work to help support the family), or justify other social issues such as pay inequalities between men and women. The point is that traditional knowledge is very limited and actions based on this knowledge can have far-reaching, but misguided, consequences.

Traditional knowledge can also be distorted. Because traditional knowledge may apply in some instances, many assume it applies in *all* instances, regardless of whether the context of the situation changes. Although some children undoubtedly benefit from exclusive maternal care in early childhood, others benefit from a wider social experience. Day care may not be for all children, but it may help some children learn important social lessons such as sharing and taking turns at an earlier age than others.

■ Experience

The most frequent form of knowledge acquisition is **experience.** The old saying "Seeing is believing" has some merit. After all, if someone has been mugged by a seemingly low-income individual, that person is more likely to believe that low-income people have more criminal tendencies than middle-class people. Or if, as a man, I see a female hired for a job that I applied for, I may conclude that Affirmative Action leads to reverse discrimination. So what's the problem? Well, as I illustrated earlier with the "crowd" photograph, as a group, humans are notoriously poor observers of their world. How we interpret an experience is likely to be influenced by our social location (for example, our race, gender, and social class). Although the person who mugged me may have appeared to be of low income, how would I really know? Would I just have assumed that, based on the nature of the offense or the perpetrator's dress? If you look at teenagers, it can be very difficult to tell their social class background. Adolescents living in inner-city neighborhoods are frequently just as likely as suburban kids to wear $200 sneakers. Likewise, how do I know that a woman who got hired over a man was less qualified and hired due to Affirmative Action? Did I have access to her application, recommendations, and personnel files? Probably not.

There are many other problems with personal experience acting as a wider knowledge base. First, people frequently overgeneralize. We assume that one experience represents an entire class of experiences. The previous example of hiring a woman instead of a man illustrates this. If a man learns that an employer hired a woman rather than him, that man may assume that all or most women are hired due to Affirmative Action—not necessarily because a woman was the better person for the job.

Another example of overgeneralization is that we tend to assume what worked in one instance will work in all. For example, a colleague of mine once failed a student on a test. The student visited this professor to plead her case and ended up breaking down in tears. My colleague told me that he felt so bad for her that he allowed her to take a make-up exam to offset the original poor grade she received. Two semesters later, I had the same student and she failed an exam with me. She came to my office to plead her case and, like with my colleague, she broke down in tears. Based on her past experience, the student concluded that crying was one way to earn a second chance on an exam. She was wrong, however. I was not as moved by her tears and although I offered to tutor her extra hours to help her in future exams, I insisted that this exam grade stood unchanged. The student was surprised by my reaction. Apparently this student generalized her past experience (or "knowledge") to a different situation and expected a similar result. Similarly, if we base our scientific knowledge on our personal experience, we are vulnerable to the same mistake.

Second, not only do people overgeneralize but they also exhibit selective observation. In April 1999, in Columbine, Colorado, two students, Eric Harris and Dylan Klebold, opened fire at their school and shot and killed 13 people. They injured 21 more people before they turned the guns on themselves. This was a newsworthy event not just because of the sadness of it all but also because it was at that time the most devastating school shooting in U.S. history. The boys responsible for the Columbine shootings came from wealthy families with employed mothers. At the time of the shootings, this led to a lot of commentary that children with employed mothers are more likely to be deviant because they do not have adult supervision when they come home from school. However, this statement overlooks the millions of children whose mothers work but who do *not* open fire on a school full of students.

Furthermore, our experiences are vulnerable to selection bias. At the sake of continually repeating trite phrases, the saying "Birds of a feather flock together" is appropriate here. In other words, people tend to socialize with those who are similar to them. However, the people in service occupations such as law, policing, and social work frequently are of different social backgrounds than the clients they serve. If an attorney who never had a drug addiction is part of a treatment court team designed to help addicts, he could not make judgments about clients based on his experiences because they are likely to be very different. This attorney would need to rely on the expertise of others and on information learned from reading research relevant to drug courts.

Last, people have a vested interest in perceiving a situation in ways that benefit them. Take an unfortunate example where a college student dies from drinking too much alcohol. From the college's perspective, this is another example of how students are irresponsible and need to curb their drinking practices. The college may claim that students have many forms of entertainment—such as comedy nights, athletic events, dances, and plays—that make the need for alcohol-related parties unnecessary. Hence, from the university's perspective, any alcohol problem on campus is the result of student irresponsibility and unwillingness to utilize university resources. Consequently, the university is unlikely to accept much of the blame for the incident. On the other hand, students may say that these university activities are too infrequent (say, perhaps two nights a month), they are in an inconvenient location, or that they start too early. Hence, students place responsibility with the school rather than themselves. The point is that each party has a vested interest in placing blame elsewhere. The problem is that if the school alone creates solutions, then, as an institution, it is likely to overlook the real cause of the problem. Likewise, if a solution is based solely on the student view, it is likely to be cost-prohibitive with no better probability of success. Consequently, in order to address the issue of college drinking, one has to devise a way of studying the problem that includes *both* perspectives in addition to alternate views not addressed here. That's where scientific research comes into play.

Some of what we think of as **common sense** is supported by research, as we would expect. However, some of what we consider to be common sense is not, and that is one reason why we need research to examine human behavior. See if you can identify which of the following statements are scientifically supported and which, although you think are true, in fact are not. Just answer "true" or "false" to the following statements. The answers appear below, but don't read them until you've answered all seven questions.

1. Suburbs are a more dangerous place to live than are the inner cities. ❏ **True** ❏ **False**

2. The majority of people in poverty are racial minorities. ❏ **True** ❏ **False**

3. People who cohabit (live together) before marriage are less likely to divorce than are people who do not cohabit before marriage. ❏ **True** ❏ **False**

4. For people with a college degree, the gap in pay between men and women has disappeared. In other words, college-educated women now earn about as much as college-educated men. ❏ **True** ❏ **False**

5. Most rapists are mentally ill. ❏ **True** ❏ **False**

6. Fifty percent of all marriages end in divorce. ❏ **True** ❏ **False**

7. The life expectancy in Guam, Martinique, and Greece is higher than that in the United States. ❏ **True** ❏ **False**

Answers to Research or Common Sense

So how do you think you did? The first and last questions are true; the five in the middle are false. Let's briefly look at each of these in more detail.

1. **True.** Technically this statement is true; however, it is also an illustration of why it is important for people to understand how statistics were gathered and what studies measure. It is true that the rates of violent crime and property crime are higher in the inner city than in the suburbs; however, it is also true that more people are injured and killed in automobile accidents than by violent crime.

Furthermore, most automobile accidents happen relatively close to the victims' homes. Therefore, because more people are killed by automobiles than by violent crime and because those who live in the suburbs drive almost three times as often and drive much faster than urban dwellers, one can argue that the suburbs are a more dangerous place to live (Durning, 1996). Again, this is a matter of measurement.

The dependent variable, or outcome, is death or injury in both instances. However, what is causing the death or injury varies (violent crime or automobile death). If one looks only at violent crime, then the inner city is more hazardous to people's health. If one looks only at car accidents, then the suburbs are more dangerous. If one compares the death and injury rates due to violent crime and due to automobiles, the suburbs are still more dangerous because more people die from automobiles than from violent crime.

2. **False.** According to the U.S. Bureau of the Census (2002), 285,317,000 people were in poverty in 2002. Of that number, the overwhelming majority, 230,376,000 were what are categorized as "White alone," meaning that the respondents selected the "White" category and did not check any other additional races. Only 35,678,000 were Black alone, 11,541,000 Asian alone, and 39,216,000 Hispanic. The remainder selected combinations of races.

The point is that the majority of people who are poor are White. This should not be surprising since the majority of the people in the population are White; however, we tend to overlook this fact when we discuss the poor. Research reminds us of who the poor really are.

3. **False.** The statistics are actually the opposite. Couples who cohabit before they marry are generally *more* likely to divorce than couples

BOX 1.1   **Research or Common Sense?, continued**

who do not cohabit before marriage (Waite & Gallagher, 2000). Why? The reasons are many, but some involve less favorable attitudes about marriage. less negative attitudes about divorce (especially the longer they live together), and the challenge of fitting a nontraditional arrangement (cohabitation) into a traditional one (marriage), meaning that even if the couple does not have traditional attitudes about marriage, once the couple is labeled "married," other people have traditional attitudes that they impose on the couple, creating stress (Waite & Gallagher, 2000).

4. **False.** Many people are unaware that the gap in pay between men and women remains. Furthermore, many of those who know it persists frequently think that the gap only *appears* to persist because researchers do not consider possible intervening variables such education and age. In other words, some believe that the overall gap persists because researchers look at *all* women and *all* men as one group and ignore factors such as age or education (older women are more likely to have lower levels of education, which lead to lower-paying jobs).

However, using secondary sources such as the Current Population Survey, which we will discuss more in Chapter 10, we find that for full-time, year-round workers, women ages 25 to 44 with a college degree or more have median earnings of $44,615, whereas men with the same characteristics have median earnings of $57,333. This means that women ages 25 to 44 with *at least* a college degree earn 78 cents for every male dollar earned. For men and women ages 35 to 44 with at least a college degree, women earn about 61 cents for every male dollar (*Statistical Abstracts,* 2003).

5. **False.** Traditionally, people thought that rapists were "sick" and that they could not control overwhelming sexual urges. However, feminists have long theorized that rape is an issue of power. If men feel their power is threatened,

some will act physically aggressively in order to reestablish their dominance, and somehow these men have learned that rape is appropriate in certain circumstances.

Diana Scully and Joseph Marolla (1985) interviewed 98 men convicted of rape to test the theory that rape is a learned behavior, not a biological or psychological sickness. They found that the context in which men rape varies. Some rape on the spur of the moment; some rape with friends; some rape regularly and others irregularly; and some rape for revenge. However, they found a prevailing theme of power. Many of the convicted rapists they interviewed expressed some form of establishing power as the motivation behind their rapes.

Scully and Marolla also compared convicted rapists with 75 nonrapists convicted of other crimes and they found that the rapists were more likely to subscribe to rape myths, such as a woman's style of dress caused the rape. Consequently, the researchers found that many men who rape do so because of socially learned behaviors—lessons that taught them to use physical force to establish power and to justify nonconsensual sex as not rape (Scully & Marolla, 1985).

6. **False.** This 50 percent statistic has been quoted so often in the popular media that people now take it as fact. However, the statistic is incorrectly used. It is true that each year there are half as many divorces granted as there are marriages, but this does not mean that the divorce rate is 50 percent. Why not?

For starters, these two figures are almost like comparing apples and oranges—one has little to do with the other. For the most part, people who marry in a given year are also not divorcing in that same year; therefore, these statistics are not appropriate comparisons. Couples who divorce are from the entire group of married people, which is much larger than the number of couples marrying in a particular year!

According to the 2000 U.S. Census, there were 54,493,232 married-couple families in

BOX 1.1   **Research or Common Sense?, continued**

that year (U.S. Census Bureau, 2000), and according to the National Vital Statistics Bureau (2002), there were an estimated 953,704 divorces that year. This leads to a divorce rate of about 1.8 percent—a far cry from the 50 percent that is commonly cited.

7. True. Life expectancy information is available for 225 countries. The United States ranks 47 after Andorra (the highest at 83.49 years), Japan, Australia, Sweden, France, Italy, Spain, Guam, Martinique, and Greece—just to name a few (Index Mundi, 2003).

■ Authority

The pace in which new knowledge becomes available is astonishing. Most of us rely on the experts—those with education, training, and experience in specific fields—to keep us up to date. And in many instances, we benefit from those in **authority.**

However, even knowledge from the experts cannot be blindly accepted. There are many examples where new information made previous expert knowledge obsolete. For example, according to the medical experts 30 years ago, infant formula was believed to be better for babies than breast milk, and millions of mothers followed this advice. Now, expert knowledge suggests that breast milk has many more health advantages for children than formula. The American Academy of Pediatrics now contends that breast-fed babies are less likely to be obese, are less likely to develop ear infections, and are less likely to get sick within the first few months of life than are formula-fed babies; hence, it recommends breastfeeding for the first year of life. Perhaps 30 years from now the pendulum will swing back in favor of formula again.

Likewise, there are many examples of how experts have misinterpreted statistics or have twisted statistical findings to suit specific agendas. For example, anorexia nervosa is a dangerous disease in which a person, usually young women although the disease is not limited to them, eats dangerously little in order to be thin. Activists trying to increase public awareness about this disease note that about 150,000 American women are anorexic and that anorexia can lead to death (Lawson, 1985). Feminists argue that the pressures of a male-dominated society have led to the prevalence of this disease and that this 150,000 statistic was reinterpreted as 150,000 deaths of young women occur in a year due to anorexia (Sommers, 1994). Clearly, hearing that 150,000 people die from a disease is much more dramatic than learning that 150,000 suffer from a disease. The media quickly picked up on this statistic and it was erroneously reported in a number of different areas for quite some time. However, a critical reader should wonder about such a high number: 150,000 *young* women? Women who are supposed to be in the prime of their lives? Around this time (the late 1990s), about 8,500 women between the ages of 18 and 24 died a year from *any* cause, not just anorexia (U.S. Bureau of the Census, 1997). Even if the definition of "young" was questionable, according to the *Statistical Abstracts of the United States* (U.S. Bureau of the Census, 1997), 47,000 women between the ages of 24 and 44 also died in a given year at that time. That totals 55,500 women *if all of them died from anorexia*, which clearly they did not. Therefore, this 150,000 statistic is way too high, and that should tip off a critical reader that the statistic was either incorrectly calculated or incorrectly used.

Why would people, especially experts, do this? First, because they may not know that they are misusing or misinterpreting the statistics. In other words, it's an honest mistake. Second, if the goal of research is to generate public support regarding an issue, clearly one can see how 150,000 deaths among young women versus 150,000 instances of a disease among young women will generate more public support for a cause. If enough *uncritical* sources adopt the statistic, it becomes seen as a "fact" in its own right, simply because it's quoted so many times.

When authority figures speak outside their realm of expertise, the quest for unbiased knowledge is muddied. This frequently happens during political campaigns when actors speak out in favor of various candidates, or in commercials when athletes discuss the effectiveness of various products from sneakers to over-the-counter drugs. Stop and think. What does a basketball player really know about cough syrup? Yet, because many everyday people see sports figures as role models and aspire to be like them, these athletes have authority. Consequently, advertising agencies clamor to get athletes and actors to endorse products because they know that average people want to be more like these celebrities and they trust them; therefore, people may buy a product these authority figures endorse.

You may be asking yourself But don't social scientists consider themselves "experts" in social behavior? Why should we believe their research when I just illustrated that even medical research could be outdated easily? What's the point of it all? The point is that knowledge based on authority is not bad; it's just that one cannot blindly accept knowledge posed by those in authority simply *because* they have authority. Furthermore, just because research is done does not mean that it is done well. And *that*, folks, is the moral of the story! Why do people devote a whole course to learning how to gather research? Two reasons. First, one has to know how to do good research in order for it to be useful and effective. Second, people need to know how to distinguish between good and not-so-good examples of research so they can make intelligent decisions based on research. Just because a study is published does not mean that it is good. In other words, you can't necessarily believe everything you read.

This book is going to address both of these issues. By the time you reach the last chapter, you will have a basic idea of how to conduct scientific research. You will also have an idea of how to evaluate the research done by others. After all, many of you may be thinking that you won't ever do research once you are out in the "real world." True. Many of you won't. However, some of you will—whether you realize it or not. Many professions are getting increasingly statistical, and in order to calculate or interpret statistics correctly, it is helpful to have some information about how those numbers were achieved. Even if you do not do research yourself, you are likely to have to read the research of others at some point and make decisions based on what you've read. Hence, learning how to discern good research from bad is an increasingly important professional tool. Therefore, whether you realize it or not, many of you may encounter research even if you don't plan on it. So let's talk about why scientific knowledge is better, from a social perspective, than the other forms of knowledge I have covered.

■ Scientific Knowledge

Acquiring **scientific knowledge** is really not all that mystical. It simply is a more organized and rationalized way of observing the world than people ordinarily do on their own. The natural sciences—the disciplines of biology, chemistry, and physics, for example—focus on observing the *material* world of animals, chemicals, and atoms. The social sciences—such as sociology, criminal justice, political science, psychology, and social work—focus on understanding the *social* world of human interaction. Regardless of whether one is a chemist or a sociologist, scientific knowledge has some characteristics that generally help it be less biased than the other forms of knowledge I've discussed.

First, and foremost, scientific knowledge is empirical and theoretical. It is *empirical* in that it is based on direct observation of the world. This is an important issue because it means that science can document only what *is*. It cannot make judgments based on value or what people think *ought* to be. In other words, scientific research can document the financial costs of the death penalty compared to life in prison; however, it cannot settle the debate as to whether a state should *have* the death penalty. Likewise, scientific research can describe the emotional effects of abortion on the women who have one, but it cannot draw any conclusions about whether abortion should be legal.

Without *theoretical* scientific knowledge, which puts observed facts into a context to explain *why*, science would just be a glorified way to document the world around us. Theory takes the empirical facts from observation and organizes them to help people understand the facts, to explain the cause behind the facts, and/or to predict future occurrences of them. In the next chapter I discuss the relationship between research and theory in more detail; however, this book generally focuses on the empirical aspect of research—on how to accurately gather the facts that will be further interpreted by theory.

Second, science is *systematic*. It is based on generally agreed-upon steps that are organized, publicized, and recognized by other scientists. The specific steps of the scientific method will be discussed in Chapter 2. Why is being systematic important? It is important because it allows research to be replicated, which, in turn, is important because if a study is repeated many times and similar results are found, then social scientists have more confidence in the results.

In an infamous study about arrest and domestic violence, Sherman and Berk (1984) found preliminary evidence that in Minneapolis, men arrested for suspected domestic violence were less likely to commit future assaults than were men who were not arrested. Even though Sherman and Burke urged caution in interpreting their results, many law enforcement agencies quickly adopted a policy of arresting men suspected of domestic violence because the research was done by well-known researchers (in other words, they had authority in this area), was widely published, and made sense (knowledge related to tradition). However, when the U.S. National Institute of Justice funded replication of the study in six other cities, the deterrent effect of arrest in domestic violence became *less* clear. In some cities arrest had no deterrent effect on future domestic violence, and in other cities researchers found that the propensity for violence actually increased (Sherman, 1992). If police agencies waited for the results of other studies (replication) before they implemented the findings of one study, they would have saved the time and cost of implementing a questionable program. Because the scientific method outlines specific steps researchers follow, replication is possible. Consequently, as I stated previously, when more than one study finds similar patterns among variables, our confidence in those patterns increases.

Third, science is *probabilistic*, which means that it describes what is *likely* to occur in most instances when certain factors are present, but it recognizes that this is not necessarily going to occur in *all* instances. For example, it is now common knowledge, based on many replicated studies, that cigarette smoking leads to a higher risk of cancer and can cut years off of a person's life. Empirical studies also suggest that cigar smoking can be more

BOX 1.2   Scientific Knowledge versus Other Knowledge

When nonsocial scientists read research or articles that present research findings, they rarely read the information critically. Consequently, people tend to accept questionable information as true, or they misinterpret an author's argument. Following is an excerpt from a *New York Times* article on poverty. Read it and then answer the critical thinking questions that follow.

> The number of black Americans under 18 years old who live in extreme poverty has risen sharply since 2000 and is now at its highest level since the government began collecting such figures in 1980, according to a study by the Children's Defense Fund, a child welfare advocacy group.
>
> The Children's Defense Fund has been a consistent critic of the vast overhaul of the American welfare system carried out during the 1990's. "The study shows that in the first recession since the welfare law took effect, black children who have the fewest protections are falling into extreme poverty in record numbers," Ms. Weinstein said.
>
> *Source:* Sam Dillon, "Report Finds Number of Black Children in Deep Poverty Rising," *New York Times*, April 30, 2003.

Critical Thinking Questions

1. What type of knowledge does the information in this *New York Times* article cover?

2. What are some pieces of "knowledge" that can be interpreted from this article?

Critical Thinking Discussion

1. If you answered scientific *and* traditional knowledge, you'd be correct—or at least partially. This article *is* a form of scientific knowledge since it was gathered using the scientific method (as implied by the term *study* used in conjunction with Child Defense Fund, a reputable organization that studies children's issues).

A quick, uncritical read would also suggest that it is scientific knowledge that supports traditional "knowledge" about welfare—namely, that the majority of individuals who are on welfare are racial minorities—more specifically African Americans. However, news blurbs frequently cover only part of a story, which can result in misleading or misinterpreted information. A person reading the beginning of this story may reach a conclusion consistent with traditional knowledge, but a more thorough reading makes it clear that the author's point is different, as I discuss next.

2. One common interpretation would be that the majority of individuals who are on welfare are of a racial minority. There are some problems with this interpretation, however. First, this article is *not* claiming that the majority of individuals in poverty are Black, or even that the percentage of Blacks in poverty is increasing. It is saying that *among Blacks* under age 18, individuals are increasingly falling into poverty. What is the problem?

Well, the first assumption, the one that I tagged as "traditional" knowledge and that was worded as "individuals who are on welfare," uses the number of individuals on welfare as the reference group. The article, which states, "The number of black Americans under 18 years old," uses the number of Blacks—an entirely different group of individuals—as the reference group. So what? Well, depending on the reference group, we get a different look at who is on welfare.

Scientific research reveals that about 24 percent of those in poverty are African American and an additional 21.8 percent are Hispanic (U.S. Census Bureau, 2002). This means that over half of those in poverty—the clear majority relative to these other groups—are White. However, if we look at the poor another way—by using the proportion of a group in society as the reference point for comparison—we get a different picture. African Americans make up 24 percent of the poor, as we just mentioned, but they constitute about 12 percent of the total population (U.S. Census Bureau, 2001). This means that African Americans are overrepresented among the poor, given their representation in the United States.

Second, like many new sources, what is presented here is only a small excerpt of the

BOX 1.2   Scientific Knowledge versus Other Knowledge, continued

article. Conservatives can read these two paragraphs and argue that there is a problem in the Black community, as indicated by the rising number of Black youth in welfare. However, a liberal can look at these paragraphs and argue for the very same reason, that there is a problem with the current welfare program.

General Commentary

Keep in mind that even scientific knowledge has to be read carefully, critically, and in its entirety in order to avoid drawing inaccurate conclusions. Otherwise, scientific knowledge can be distorted to the degree that it essentially sheds no light on a situation.

Note: Incidentally, if you look up this article on Research Navigator and read it in its entirety, you will see that the writer uses scientific research to argue that there is a problem with the current welfare reform. Again, however, only looking at an excerpt may mask the intent and conclusion of the research.

---

dangerous than cigarette smoking. However, George Burns reportedly smoked 10 to 20 cigars *a day*, even past age 84 and after heart problems; yet, he lived to be 100 years old. Does this exception invalidate the research? No. People are highly varied and no "fact," biological or social, is going to apply to all people at all times. Scientific research that aims to establish a causal connection between variables never claims to explain all instances of all behavior; it merely states what is likely (or *probably*) going to happen in most cases if certain conditions are met.

That last part of the paragraph—"if certain conditions are met"—is important. This means that the more information researchers consider at the time, the more likely they are to be able to predict a behavior. Think of it this way: I discussed before that traditional knowledge argues that children benefit most from exclusive maternal care, which means mothers do not participate in the labor force. Yet, studies show evidence for both arguments—the benefit of having exclusive maternal care and the benefit of having an employed mother. How can this be? Ignoring variations in research design, a simple answer is that maternal employment may benefit children *when certain conditions are met*. For example, when mothers want to work, have support (both emotional and in terms of sharing practical tasks) from a significant other, and/or have jobs that they find personally fulfilling, many children benefit from maternal employment (Kalmijn, 1994; Bianchi, 2000). Likewise, the effects of maternal employment vary by race and social class (Wolfer & Moen, 1996). Granted, this is an oversimplified explanation to prove a point (for example, other issues such as child temperament, family social class, and child gender also influence the effects of maternal employment on children's development); however, the point remains. When researchers establish certain conditions for the research, they are more likely to achieve a deeper and reproducible understanding of a situation.

Related to the probabilistic nature of research is its *provisional* nature. Research conclusions are also tentative and subject to change, primarily

George Burns illustrates how even traditional scientific knowledge does not apply to everyone. He smoked cigars and drank alcohol frequently, yet he lived to be 100 years old.

because social conditions change. Hence, in social science research, experienced researchers rarely use the word *proved*. Researchers recognize that their findings merely support or refute a claim, and that a claim is subject to reinterpretation until it is replicated a number of times.

In summary, science is merely a more vigorous means of collecting knowledge—one that is designed to encourage replication as people search for meaningful patterns in their social world. To this end, there are steps we can take to improve the likelihood of replicated findings. Teaching those steps is what this book is dedicated to doing.

Uses and Purposes of Social Research

What are the experiences of men who reverse gender roles by dropping out of the labor force to care for children while their wives (the children's mothers) work for pay? How do children whose parents divorced when they were young view the institution of marriage? What characteristics predict whether men or women will reverse gender roles with mothers working and fathers staying at home? What is the probability that adult children whose parents divorce when they are young will get divorced themselves as adults? These four questions are all viable research questions. The first two are generally qualitative research questions, whereas the latter two address the same general topic (gender roles and divorce) but are posed as quantitative research questions.

Qualitative research is aimed at a more in-depth understanding of a research issue. This type of research usually involves small sample sizes because the researcher is not interested in generalizing to a wider population, but instead is focused on a more detailed exploration of a topic. Therefore, examining what adult children of divorced parents think of marriage and what men's experiences are if they stay home and raise children are topics that lend themselves to small, in-depth examinations.

Quantitative research, on the other hand, focuses on finding statistical trends that researchers can use to generalize to larger groups or populations. Quantitative research, as you probably guessed since is sounds like "quantity," is more mathematical in nature than qualitative research (which sounds like "quality"). Consequently, these studies usually involve larger sample sizes and statistical analyses that try to establish patterns of variables in a population based on what researchers observe in a sample. Establishing a probability, such as the probability that adult children whose parents divorced when the children were young will get divorced themselves as adults, is a mathematical calculation; it is therefore quantifiable. Prediction also implies a quantitative analysis because prediction frequently involves statistical analysis, which again, is mathematical. Therefore, the research question, What characteristics predict whether men or women will reverse gender roles with mothers working and fathers staying at home? is also an example of quantitative research.

However, as I stated earlier, students initially associate research with a somewhat arbitrary collection of facts just for the sake of knowledge. Some of it is, and there is nothing wrong with this because all facts have their place. However, research can be used for much more than just collecting data. What follows are some uses and purposes of social research.

■ Exploration

Given our information-driven world, it may seem unlikely that there are still a lot of social experiences about which we know little. In these instances, **exploration** research is appropriate. For example, in the 1980s, social scientists knew very little about gangs. Who joined them? Why? In what types of activities were they involved? Did people ever leave gangs? If so, how? What was the social hierarchy within the gangs? How did one earn respect and power? Researchers who do exploratory research are interested in gathering large amounts of relatively unstructured information in order to piece together a preliminary understanding about a subject. The design for this type of research is frequently qualitative. However, exploratory research does not *have* to be qualitative. Cummings and Kraut (2002, **AN 7075143**) wanted to explore how Internet usage has changed from 1995 to 2000. To do this, they used a survey research firm to survey over 4,000 people in 1995, 2,000 people in 1998, and over 3,500 people in 2000 about how much and why they use the Internet. With such large sample sizes, their research was definitely quantitative instead of qualitative. Cummings and Kraut argued that researchers have been documenting the increasing use of the Internet since the 1990s, but they understood little about *how* the Internet was being used. Exploring that topic, Cummings and Kraut found that the use of the Internet became increasingly domestic in this five-year span, meaning that people were more likely to use the Internet for personal and pleasurable experiences than for paid employment in 2000 than in 1995.

Exploratory research is also common when people are considering a type of policy change. Prison overcrowding is currently a public concern, and one explanation for it is the high concentration of individuals incarcerated for drug-related offenses. Officials began to question whether incarceration was an effective response to behavior ultimately caused by an addiction. As a result, people began to experiment with alternatives to imprisonment for offenses that seemed to stem from drug addiction; thus, drug treatment courts and home detention programs were born. Officials interested in changing local problems such as prison overcrowding frequently look to research for ideas about what types of programs worked in other areas. They then use this research to help them organize and pilot their own policies and programs.

■ Description

Almost all research has a descriptive component aimed at defining or describing the sample and social situation being studied. However, some research is solely for description. A good example of **description** research is the U.S. Census. Every 10 years the U.S. government embarks on a major descriptive study of the country, cataloging such issues as race, gender, marital status, employment experiences, income, and housing among American residents. Consequently, unlike exploratory studies, descriptive studies are frequently concerned with counting or documenting information.

Cummings and Kraut's research (2002) also included a descriptive component. One of their goals was to see the change in the percent of the population on the Internet on any given day from 1995 to 2000. They found that the percent of the population on the Internet on any given day in 1995 was 8 percent, but by 2000, this figure more than tripled to 29 percent. These percentages document, or *describe*, a count of people on the Internet at two time points.

Other questions answered in descriptive research are ones such as What percentage of Americans is married? What percentages of teenagers who use drugs are from single-parent homes? What is the most common crime committed in the United States? Researchers for the Pew Research Center for the People and the Press conducted research that described

Internet use among college students. Among their findings, researchers learned that 85 percent of college students have gone on-line compared to 59 percent of the general population and that almost three-quarters of college students (73 percent) use the Internet for finding information more so than the library (Gordon, 2003, **AN 8850286**). These statistics do not explore a problem; rather, they simply document what is happening without any other context. Hence, they are descriptive.

For descriptive research, issues such as measurement (Chapter 4), sampling (Chapter 5), survey construction (Chapter 7), and agency data (Chapter 9) are important considerations.

Explanation

Explanation research is concerned with answering *why* or *how*. It is frequently associated with establishing a causal connection between variables; therefore, it requires a more vigorous approach to research methods than the other two types previously discussed, because establishing causation is more challenging than simply showing an association. Descriptive research may ask what percentage of teenagers who use drugs are from single-parent homes; explanatory research, however, asks Why does family structure affect drug use? or Why are children from single-parent homes more vulnerable to drug use than are children from two-parent homes? Another example of explanatory research would be asking Why do women use the Internet to search for health information, as opposed to just relying on more traditional methods such as doctors? Is it because with the common use of the Internet today, women can see it as a proactive means of obtaining health information that can supplement other avenues of information, or it is because women who already have specific health needs use the Internet to learn more? Or, is it a third reason—namely, that the Internet can reduce high information search costs? Pandey, Hart, and Tiwary (2003) examined these three explanations for women's heath-related Internet use and, although they found some support for all three explanations (meaning that women were likely to use the Internet to serve each of these health needs), they found the strongest support for the proactive information explanation. In other words, the researchers found that, of these three explanations, women were most likely to use the Internet for health-related issues to proactively supplement the information they learn from more traditional sources.

Explanation frequently requires establishing hypotheses or cause/effect relationships (Chapter 3), having clear measures (Chapter 4), and vigorous sampling (Chapter 5).

Evaluation

As mentioned earlier, applied research is becoming increasingly common in the social science fields. Social workers, law enforcement officials, and sociologists, to name a few professions, increasingly have to do research to get funding and to justify (evaluate) a funded policy's effectiveness. **Evaluation** research generally takes one of two forms. The first approach, known as *program evaluation*, assesses policy effectiveness and focuses on whether a policy "works." For example, Do drug treatment courts reduce recidivism for drug abuse cases over the traditional policy of incarceration? Does community-oriented policing reduce residents' fear of crime? Does no-fault divorce encourage divorce?

Scheidet (2003, **AN 11951186**) did an evaluation research when he studied whether the Web-enabled computer technology from the Internet would help history students to

BOX 1.3   Purposes of Research

There are four main purposes behind research: exploration, description, explanation, and evaluation. In many instances, more than one purpose of research will appear in the same article. Following is an excerpt from an article on eating disorders by Zabinski and colleagues (2001). Read the excerpt and then answer the critical thinking questions. Once you have answered the questions, read on to see my comments in the Critical Thinking Discussion section.

Assessment

Acceptability

Acceptability was assessed through a 20-min. interviewer-based questionnaire at post treatment. The satisfaction survey consisted of 17 close-ended questions and 26 open-ended questions regarding the intervention. Participants were asked to comment on the time commitment, their experiences with the computer and technological difficulties, their level of comfort with group participation, and any suggestions for improvement. Interviews were conduced by a research assistant unknown to the participants.

Evaluation of Intervention Effects

Due to the small sample size, only descriptive analyses and effect sizes are reported.

Results

Four female students from a public West Coast university participated. They completed all three assessments. Participants included 3 freshmen and 1 sophomore with a mean age of 19.4 (ranging from 18 to 20 years). The group comprised 2 Caucasians, 1 Asian and 1 Hispanic/Latina.

Acceptability

In general, participants rated their satisfaction with the program very highly. None reported difficulty following the flow of the conversation. Participants believed that it was easier for them to be honest on the computer compared with face-to-face discussions because there was less focus on physical appearances. Further, 3 of 4 participants reported being very satisfied with the moderator and 1 participant reported being moderately satisfied (2 on a 7-point scale). All participants preferred chatting to posting to the news group (Table 2).

Table 2 Participant Ratings of Satisfaction with the Chatroom Program

	Raw Score / Response
Overall satisfaction with the program (1–7): 1 = very satisfied, 7 = not at all satisfied	1, 3, 2, 2
Overall, how satisfied were you with the moderator? 1 = very satisfied, 7 = not at all satisfied	1, 1, 1, 2
Did you prefer to post messages to the newsgroup or chat with members during the sessions?	Chat, Chat, Chat, Chat
Have you ever chatted before?	No, Yes, No, Yes
Did you have difficulty following the conversation?	No, No, No, No
Overall, did you like or dislike the moderator?	
Was the moderator helpful in keeping the flow of the conversation going?	Yes, Yes, Yes, Yes
Did you feel that you got a chance to participate enough in the group?	Yes, Yes, Yes, Yes
How would you feel about having photos of yourself and other members posted on-line?	Don't care, Would be cool, Wouldn't like, Fine
Would you like a photo of the moderator?	Don't care, Yes, Yes, Yes

BOX 1.3   Purposes of Research, continued

Participants also believed that the intervention helped them to improve their interpersonal relationships (outside the group) and their ability to recognize and challenge negative thought about their shape and weight. Specifically, all participants reported that the intervention helped them to prevent negative attitudes about their weight and shape from making them feel badly, and to recognize the thoughts and situations that trigger negative feelings or behaviors (4 or higher on 7-point scale). Three participants also reported that the intervention helped them to challenge negative though patterns (5 or higher on a 7-point scale). Behaviorally, all participants reported that the intervention helped them to eat at regular intervals during the day and allowed them to eat a variety of foods. . . .

Source: Marion Zabinski, Denise Welfley, Meredith Pung, Andrew Winzelberg, Kathleen Edlredge, and C. Barr Taylor, "An Interactive-Based Intervention for Women at Risk of Eating Disorders: A Pilot Study," *Eating Disorders, 9* (3) (2001). Reprinted by permission.

Critical Thinking Questions

1. Based on the excerpt presented, what purpose(s) does this research address? The information about "Assessment" is included to help give you some idea of the goal of the research. Support your answer with evidence from the article.

2. If you were doing a similar study, how would you tailor your questions and/or information gathered to address the purposes of research *not* captured by this study?

Critical Thinking Discussion

1. This research is both descriptive and evaluative. One might be able to make the argument that this research is also exploratory.

With regard to the claim that the research is descriptive, the section "Evaluation of Intervention Effects" specifically states that only descriptive analyses are presented (due to small sample sizes). Furthermore, the information in Table 2 is descriptive, as it describes only what respondents said to individual questions (what researchers call univariate statistics). In other words, the information in Table 2 does not examine how variation in the chat room (one variable) varies by, say, race (a potential second variable).

The research is evaluative in that the program is designed as an intervention—again based on information presented in the title. Interventions can be interpreted as a type of program. Furthermore, the goal of the research is to see whether the Internet is a useful tool in addressing eating disorders. Consequently, it is evaluative—with some cautions.

Only four people participated in this study. Be clear: Four is an exceptionally small sample size! No definitive conclusions can be made from four observations, especially in an evaluative framework; therefore, at best, this study can be described as an exploratory attempt to see if this program works. In fact, the title of the article makes it clear that this is an exploratory attempt when it states that this work is a "pilot study."

2. These questions are up to you and the possibilities are endless. However, here are some points to consider. The only purpose of research left to address would be explanation. To do this, one would need (1) a much larger sample size and (2) a clear idea about the different aspects of the program/intervention so a researcher can determine which parts (or whether the effect is only noticed as a whole) of the program influence eating disorder behaviors.

become more motivated in their study of history and to better master that information. Scheidet studied students in the Mount Sinai School District in New York and used the New York Regents as the assessment of mastery of history. He found that test results from the Global History Regents exam and survey results from parents and students indicated that students in classes that completely integrated Web-enabled computer technology were both more motivated to learn history and had better mastered the material than their peers who did not have Web-enabled technology in their classrooms. Hence, this evaluation research suggested that the program (the Web technology) was a success.

The other evaluation approach is *policy analysis*, which focuses on policy considerations from an implementation perspective. Policy analysis is concerned with if a program is operating as designed or what potential administrative changes are necessary instead of focusing on whether a program works. For example, this approach asks a question such as How many counselors would have to be hired if a battered women's agency tracked clients every month for two years after they left an abusive environment? or How many random drug screens a month are effective yet cost efficient?

Consequently, evaluation research can be both descriptive and explanatory. It is descriptive because it first has to describe the general policy and/or its outcomes. It is explanatory because it examines what factors of the policy work most effectively. However, evaluation research is different from descriptive and explanatory research in that it exclusively deals with social policy and not just general social phenomena.

An important point is made here. None of these four general uses of research (exploration, description, explanation, and evaluation) are mutually exclusive. In fact, most studies will have a descriptive component in addition to an explanatory or evaluative one. For example, if you were interested in seeing whether an on-site day-care facility was an effective means of help working families balance their professional and personal lives, you would first describe the nature of the program and who is using it (in terms of professional position, demographics, children's age, etc.). You might also compare whether worker productivity, work hours, and/or job satisfaction was higher after the institution of the program compared to before. The latter part would be evaluative research. Thus, researchers frequently use more than one purpose of research within one particular study.

Evaluating Written Research: Titles

Just because someone does a study, does that mean that the study is useful? Obviously, a study seems important to the people who are conducting it; however, we have all heard the jokes about the amount of money the government has spent investigating the consequences of cow flatulence! A major goal of this book is to help you evaluate the merit and design of written research. Remember, as many of you are probably thinking to yourself, you may not *do* your own research once you graduate. However, professionals, especially in the fields of sociology, social work, criminal justice, education, and business, are increasingly expected to improve skills, implement programs, and make decisions that are based on the research of others. Surprisingly, there is very little training in *how* to do this. People seem to assume that if research is printed, then it is "good" and appropriate for any social situation. This is far from true! Before I discuss some considerations for evaluating research titles, I would like to discuss some general issues in being a critical reader of research.

■ Being a Critical Reader

Part of learning how to evaluate research involves clarifying the reasons we are reading something and altering our approach to thinking about a topic. For example, some people have clearly defined beliefs and disbeliefs. These people automatically reject any unaccepted belief regardless of information presented to the contrary. According to Milton Rokeach (1960), these people are "close-minded" or "dogmatic." On the other hand, some people automatically believe anything an "expert" tells them without evaluating the information or authority of the so-called expert. For instance, all one has to do is turn on the television to see a doctor promoting some new diet drug that is "guaranteed" to take off the weight without any exercise or sacrifice by an individual. Millions of people rush to buy these weight-loss drugs only to later find that they, at best, don't work and, at worst, cause serious health risks. On the other hand, people trained in critically evaluating information would ask themselves questions such as What are the credentials of this doctor? What research shows that this pill works and documents any possible side effects? Is this doctor any good? and perhaps even more telling, Is this doctor being paid for his endorsement? Medicine is not the only field vulnerable to this trend; social science is as well. Earlier I presented the confusion over the interpretation of statistics relating to anorexia nervosa. Another example, which I will discuss in more detail in a moment, is the erroneous belief that 50 percent of U.S. marriages end in divorce.

People who too eagerly accept the word of "experts" are vulnerable to the following errors in thinking:

1. If statistical outcomes support a research hypothesis, that finding must automatically be correct.
2. If data produce statistically significant findings, those findings must have real meaning—or be what we call of substantive importance.
3. Findings of short-term, cross-sectional studies would also hold in long-term situations.
4. Findings in one geographical location would automatically apply to another geographical location.

Regarding the first point, if a study is poorly designed, the statistical outcomes need to be interpreted very cautiously—that is, if they are useful at all. Plus, we have all heard that statistics can be "manipulated" or that people can get statistics to say anything they want. To some degree this is true—but it only works if people do not read statistics and research methods critically. One statistic estimates that 2.3 million people in the United States are homeless at some point in a given year (Urban Institute, 2000). Another source states that the homeless number around 600,000 each night (U.S. Department of Health and Human Services, 2003). What accounts for the difference? The first statistic, posed by the Urban Institute, is the number of people who are homeless at some point in a *given year*. The second is the amount homeless in a given *night*. An uncritical reader may ignore these subtle differences and assume that the 2.3 million and 600,000 are directly comparable, when in fact they are not. You may have caught the distinction, but that may be because I am already sensitizing you to read for the details. Many people miss the distinction and then get accused of "lying with statistics." In reality, it is very difficult to lie with statistics or manipulate them and get away with it when someone is critically reading those numbers.

Another example of how statistics can be misinterpreted and taken as "fact" if someone does not read them critically is the divorce rate. It is now common "knowledge" that 50 percent of all marriages in the United States end in divorce. But this isn't true! A critical reader should have taken a step back and said, "Whoa! That percentage is *huge!* Could it be that the statistic is misinterpreted?" People who bothered to ask themselves this question actually found that, yes, this statistic *is* misinterpreted, and a lot of the confusion stems from not understanding how the statistic was generated. In other words, confusion is created by not understanding the research methods that led to that statistic. The 50 percent statistic *is* true in that if one looks at the number of marriages in a given year and the number of divorces in the same year, there are half as many divorces as marriages. Because 50 percent is such a shocking statistic, it quickly caught the attention of the media and has been taken as "fact" ever since. However, how many couples do you know who marry and divorce *in the same year?* Obviously, some do—but *half* of all the marriages? No way.

Furthermore, this method of calculation is problematic because it overlooks the length of marriage relative to a single event—divorce. Divorce is a once and done event, whereas marriage can endure for decades; consequently, the unit of time is not comparable either. In other words, these numbers are not really related to each other at all. So what *is* the correct way of measuring the divorce rate? There are a few, but the method most accepted by those familiar with research and statistics is to consider the percentage of divorces in a given year relative to the *entire* pool of married couples—not just those who get married in the same year. Based on this calculation, the United States has roughly 59,000,000 married couples in any particular year and about 1,135,000 of them obtain a divorce that same year (Henslin, 2003). This means that only 1.9 percent of marriages end in divorce—a figure *a lot* less than 50 percent!

The second point from the list of errors in thinking, which notes that findings of statistical significance do not necessarily mean substantive significance, requires a basic understanding of statistics. Although a detailed statistical discussion is beyond the scope of this book, there are some basic points that do not require much statistical knowledge. Essentially, there are three types of statistics: descriptive, inferential, and association. *Descriptive* statistics are just what the name implies: They simply describe the sample (for example, sex, race, age) and/or what the respondents answered for specific questions. *Inferential* statistics test hypotheses and are basically what many researchers mean by "statistical significance" or "statistics" when they use the term generally. The last form of statistics is the measure of *association*, or how strongly two or more variables are related, and these essentially refer to the substantive significance mentioned earlier. In other words, it is possible for a hypothesis to be supported by the data, and consequently to have statistical significance, but for the degree of association—or substantive significance—to be very small. Therefore, even though findings are statistically significant, meaning that they are not likely to occur by chance, if the relationship between two variables is very small, researchers generally consider the two variables to be unrelated.

Social scientists also may fail to achieve substantive significance if the findings from their data have very little practical meaning. For example, a researcher may do a study of drug users and find that drug use and month of birth are statistically related. The data may show that people who are born in December are more likely to be drug users than are people born in other months. So what? Are researchers about to declare that people should try to avoid giving birth in December for fear of their children being drug users? That's ridiculous. We couldn't explain this result with a theory even if we tried; therefore, this is also a good example of the importance in linking theory and research. If researchers can't link statistical findings to a theoretical explanation for those findings, then they need to be suspect of the substantive significance of those results. This also holds true for people reading the research.

You may be asking yourself, How can something be statistically significant, but not have any substantive significance? This can happen for a number of reasons that I will discuss more closely in Chapter 12.

The last two errors in thinking have to do with issues of interpretation. Many studies are cross-sectional, meaning that they capture a social situation at one point in time. But what holds at one point in time may not hold over a longer period. For example, does research that was done 10 years ago hold today? Maybe. Maybe not. Or a study of the effects of a community policing program on crime may show no program effect at one point, but if the same study was done at a later point (say, for example, after residents became more aware of the community policing program), we may see a change in the crime rate. The time consideration is an important one, and I will discuss it in more detail in Chapter 3. Last, a policy change in an urban youth center may not have the same effect as the same policy change in a rural one because the two communities are likely to be very different. Consequently, taking in the geographical location of a study is also an important critical point in evaluation.

On the other hand, people can be *too* critical of research as well—to the point that any research under scrutiny would fall short and be discounted. Some common mistakes the overly critical reader makes are:

1. Assuming that quantitative methods are always better than qualitative ones
2. Believing that the only good samples are ones that were drawn randomly
3. Thinking that large sample sizes are always necessary
4. Thinking that if a researcher identifies limitations to his or her own research, then the research should be discounted as flawed and weak.

In the next chapter, I will discuss the research process. One component of that process is choosing which research design is most appropriate for the research question. Quantitative research designs, such as mailed surveys, are more appropriate for some questions, whereas qualitative designs, such as personal interviews, may be more appropriate for others. For instance, surveys frequently involve large, randomly selected samples. If someone wanted to research the life of teenage prostitutes, doing a large randomly selected mailed survey is not only almost impossible, but it won't provide the depth of responses that smaller, more personal interviews would. In this instance, qualitative research is preferable.

Likewise, random samples are not always possible. For a sample to be truly random, someone cannot simply stand on a sidewalk and "randomly" select who he or she wants to study. Think about it: A petite, female researcher is not likely to "randomly" select passersby who appear intimidating, dirty, deranged, or in a bad mood. Because of this, all people walking by do not have an equal probability of being selected for a study; therefore, true random sampling does not take place. Random sampling requires obtaining a complete list of all possible people who fit the study criteria and using a table of random numbers (or a computer with one) to select participants. This way, *everyone* who fits the study criteria has an equal probability of selection—regardless of their physical features, state of mind, or personal hygiene. If you think such lists can be hard to come by, you're right!

Consequently, not all study situations lend themselves to random sampling. For example, it is almost impossible to find a list of all teenage prostitutes in an area—but without that list, random sampling cannot occur. Does this mean that we can never study teenage prostitutes? Of course not. We just have to use a different sampling technique—one that isn't random but nonetheless will still provide some useful information.

Tied to the previous point, samples do not always have to be large to be useful. Remember, one purpose of research is exploration. If we know little about a topic, it does not make sense to invest tons of money into a large research project because we wouldn't know where to start—and money is too hard to obtain to spend much of it on a fishing expedition. Instead, doing a small, more qualitative, study will provide some information that may possibly serve as a starting point for a larger study. In this sense, that small study is very informative.

The key to addressing all of these issues—nonrandom samples, small samples, real-life constraints of time, money, skill, and so on, or any other unforeseen glitch that can arise in the course of research—is to be honest and not to overstate the importance of one's findings. In other words, no research is perfect. Publicly identifying the limitations of one's own research helps prevent mistakes in interpretation by others and shows that a researcher recognizes that his or her research provides only one piece of any puzzle. Furthermore, no one person—or even a team of people—can adequately study a topic in all possible settings. Therefore, researchers commonly focus on only one part of a problem, a problem in a specific setting, or a combination of these. This is okay—in fact, it's the most common research scenario. That is, it is okay and standard operating procedure, so long as one does not overstate the importance or generalizability of one's findings. For example, let's say I did a study of teenage prostitutes in Littletown, New York, population 250,000. So long as I did not word my findings and conclusions to imply *all* teenage prostitutes in Littletown (remember, I did not do a random sample of teenage prostitutes in this town) or in the United States (unless I did a random sample of prostitutes in the United States, I can't apply my findings to prostitutes in general), having a small, nonrandom sample is perfectly acceptable.

Previously, I said that learning to evaluate research involves altering our approach to thinking and examining our motivation to read. Unless one is an academic, most people do not read research just to become better informed about a discipline. Most people read research with a specific purpose in mind—primarily to find research that supports a view or that specifically refutes someone else's view. If you are reading an article with one of these motivations in mind, you need to be careful. Although scientists are supposed to try to remain objective in research, that is not always the case, and objectivity is even harder for the average reader. Furthermore, everyone should strive to approach research with an open mind, especially if you are reading research as a means to develop a policy or program. However, we are human; sometimes total objectivity is just not possible. Still, if you approach an article with a predesired outcome in mind, your ability to critically and accurately evaluate that material is compromised. We can often learn more about a topic from research that does not fit our preconceived beliefs than one that does. After all, in order to make sound, logical, and empirically supported arguments, we must fully understand the logic and empirically supported arguments of the other side. Otherwise, our discourse results in little more than the equivalent of a child's "Because my Daddy says so" response.

The rest of this chapter and all of the following ones will provide guidelines, relevant to the material in each chapter, for evaluating written research articles. Frequently, I will illustrate these points in boxed research excerpts from articles found in Research Navigator, which you have access to with the purchase of this book. These exercises (expressed as Critical Thinking Questions at the end of the boxed article excerpts) appear both in the context of a chapter to practice chapter points and in the Evaluating Research section to practice evaluating written research, while students can still have some guidance by me in the form of my answers to the same evaluation questions (expressed as Critical Thinking Discussion immediately following the Critical Thinking Questions). While I will only present and discuss article excerpts in these boxes, the citation and location of the article will always be provided so that you are able to refer to the full article if you so choose.

The guidelines in each of the chapters are meant to help you organize your thoughts and approach in order to make research evaluation more systematic. That being said, there is no one way to accurately evaluate a research report. The questions for consideration that will be included at the end of each Evaluating Written Research section are meant only to get you started. They are general questions; as you learn more about a topic, more specific questions may occur to you. You may disagree with my evaluations or my reasoning; after all, such evaluations are to some degree subjective. However, regardless of whether you agree or disagree, make sure your arguments are methodologically sound and be prepared to support your stance with concrete information from the article.

Furthermore, a specific component of a research report does not have to adequately answer all relevant evaluation questions. Remember, no research is perfect, and any article, even one that is exceptionally designed and reported, is going to have some flaws. Therefore, when evaluating an article in its entirety, the goal is to see whether you give favorable responses to most of the evaluation questions. To that end, how you want to rate sections or specific components is up to you. You can answer "yes" or "no" or "strong," "medium," or "weak." Or you can answer the individual questions with a 5-point scale, with 5 meaning you think a component is as good as it gets and 1 meaning you think the researcher completely missed the boat regarding a component. The choice is yours.

Last, not all evaluation questions are created equally. An article may have a wonderfully informative title and receive high evaluation ratings regarding that title, but it might have a poor sampling design. Sampling design is more important than the wording of a title in judging the strength of a study; therefore, problems with sampling should make you more cautious about the merit of research than should a poorly worded title. The second part of research evaluation is seeing whether the components you do not give favorable responses to are important enough to invalidate the entire study.

So, what do you look for in each section of a research report? Let's begin at the beginning by discussing how to determine if an article is relevant to your specific interests by evaluating the article's title. However, I want to mention a cautionary note. In this instance, evaluating a research title is not necessarily an issue of deciding whether the research conducted was done well. Instead, I begin with evaluating research titles because the title of a research report acts as the gateway in your decision as to whether that particular report is or is not relevant to your interests. Therefore, evaluating written research has two goals: (1) to see if a particular article is relevant to your needs (which is why I am beginning with the evaluation of titles) and (2) to assess the merit of the research conducted, and therefore, how much weight you should give that particular study to your considerations (which I will address in later chapters).

■ Evaluating Research Titles

The beginning of this Evaluating Written Research section mentioned the studies of the effects of cow flatulence and the ozone. Much to the joy of comedians and the chagrin of the general public, the government has spent thousands of tax dollars on this topic. Although I haven't discussed much about specific research design in this chapter, I did mention the usefulness of various studies. I will therefore begin with a discussion about how to evaluate the usefulness of a research topic to your needs. The first place to identify the utility of a research topic is the title of the corresponding article. Remember, in this instance, I am not using the evaluation of research titles as a means for evaluating the quality of the research presented. I am only fulfilling one of my goals of research evaluation: the evaluation of the usefulness of a specific article to your purposes.

Research topics go by a number of names: problem statements, research questions, research topics, and research orientations, to name a few. A good title will give the reader an idea of the article's research problem so that the reader can quickly assess whether he or she should investigate the article further. The following guidelines will help you evaluate the usefulness of an article for your needs by its title.

1. Is the title specific enough to differentiate it from other related topics?

Unlike novels, which rely on catchy titles to encourage people to purchase the book, the titles of research reports are not aimed at encouraging people to read the article out of general interest. Instead, research titles should encourage people to read the article based on its relevance to the reader's specific research interest. Consequently, a research title's goal is to briefly orient the reader to the research problem. Therefore, good titles are direct and are aimed at giving the reader a quick idea as to whether the article's focus is relevant to him or her. However, titles can be too broad, which may cause a reader to spend unnecessary time reading further only to find that the research focus is not really relevant to the reader's interests. Take the following title, for example:

The Effects of Divorce on Adult Children

What does it tell us? It tells us that the article studies divorce and adult children. But what about divorce? What "effects" are the researcher's focus? Is the researcher interested in these adult children's own marital behavior? Is the research in this article about depression among these adult children? Does it refer to adult children whose parents divorced when they were younger or adult children whose parents divorced when the children were already adults? Clearly, this title produces more questions than it answers. The following examples are stronger titles related to the same topic:

The Effects of Childhood Divorce on the Marital Behavior of Adult Children

Longitudinal Gender Differences in Depression among Adult Children of Divorce

Differences in Marital Behavior among Adults whose Parents Divorced in Adulthood as Opposed to Adults whose Parents Divorced in Childhood

In the second set of examples, the researcher's specific focus is much clearer. Consequently, someone who is interested in depression among adult children of divorce would know to read only the second article, not the first or third.

2. Do subtitles, if present, provide important information regarding the research?

Remember, research articles are not novels. Most of you are not likely to read research for "fun" reading; therefore, catchy titles are unnecessary. Sometimes researchers use catchy subtitles to grab the reader's attention, but, face it, how many of you are really going to decide whether to read an article because the title sounds fun? This is not to say that subtitles cannot be beneficial, however. If a subtitle includes information that further specifies the research problem—thereby providing the reader with more tools to see whether the research problem is relevant to him or her—then it is appropriate. For example:

A Tale of Two Cities: A Comparison of Drug Treatment Courts in Easternville and Midville, U.S.A.

Are you likely to read this article because you like the main title? Probably not. So what if we are comparing two cities? What about the title gives the reader any information as to *why* these two cities should be compared? A more useful title would be something like:

The Effects of Drug Treatment Programs on Drug Usage Recidivism: An Urban and Suburban Comparison

In this title, the main title tells the reader that the article is about drug treatment programs and future drug usage—important information. The subtitle further clarifies that the article is comparing an urban program with a suburban program—also important because a person looking for information about a rural program would know that this article might not be useful for that purpose.

3. Are the main variables expressed in the title?

Frequently researchers will mention the main variables studied in the title. Let's go back to one of the titles I first discussed:

Longitudinal Gender Differences in Depression among Adult Children of Divorce

The variables in this title are *gender* and *depression*. "Adult children of divorce" is *not* a variable; it refers to the study subjects. In other words, the title does not imply that the study compares depression among adult children whose parents divorced to those whose parents are still married. The only people studied are the adult children whose parents divorced. Thus, since this trait does not vary (e.g., divorced parents and nondivorced parents), it cannot by definition be a variable. However, *gender* can vary. One is either a male or female. Likewise, the level of depression can vary as well.

4. Are the terms in the title easily understood by most people?

Sometimes in an attempt to sound academic or smart, or simply to conserve space, researchers use jargon, undefined acronyms, or unnecessarily complicated wording in titles. This is as if to say: "If you don't understand the title, then this article is too complicated for you." What purpose does that serve? Good titles let the reader make the decision as to whether an article is appropriate based on the study content, not based on some filtration device imposed by the researcher. That being said, violating this suggestion is occasionally appropriate under very specific circumstances such as when the researcher is writing to communicate only with his or her direct peers or when the acronym is well known to most readers (e.g., AA for Alcoholics Anonymous). However, these instances are very rare.

BOX 1.4   **Evaluation of Titles**

Article titles are supposed to give readers a quick idea of what the authors address in the paper. The following titles serve as practice for evaluation. You may want to rate the titles on a scale of 1 to 5 (with 5 being a high rating) and use that rating as one piece of information when evaluating an entire journal article. In other words, if you rate each aspect of a journal article (the title, the abstract, the literature review, etc.) on a scale of 1 to 5, it may be easier for you to reach an overall rating or decision of an article simply by looking at the holistic ratings of the individual parts. However, since these ratings *are* subjective, the discussions of the critical thinking questions do not include them.

These discussions are meant to serve as the basis for your own evaluations. You may think of more questions or have different opinions of the answers than I. Just remember to be able to support all of your conclusions with concrete and realistic reasoning.

General Critical Thinking Questions for Titles

1. Is the title specific enough to differentiate it from other related topics?

2. Do subtitles, if present, provide important information regarding the research?

3. Are the main variables expressed in the title?

4. Are the terms in the title easily understood by most people?

5. Does the title avoid any reference to the study's results?

6. Overall, is this a good title? Why or why not?

> **Title 1**
> Whitfield, Gary W. (1999, July). Validating school social work: An evaluation of a cognitive-behavioral approach to reduce school violence. *Research on Social Work Practice, 9* (4), 399. 28 pp.

Critical Thinking Discussion of Title 1

1. It is specific enough for a reader to know that the article addresses reducing school violence.

2. The main title is that which appears first. In this instance, it is "Validating School Social Work." Ask yourself, Does this title give you an idea of what the paper is about? Not really. What about school social work is being validated? Academic counseling? Family counseling? Both of those could lead to school violence. Or is it validating the means of measuring school social work? This is unclear.

    The second half of the title—technically the subtitle—is much more informative. It tells the reader that the article will evaluate one specific approach to reducing school violence—a cognitive-behavioral approach. However, if you are asking *what* cognitive behavioral approach and feel that the title is lacking because this is so vague, you are not completely off base. The article does not need to specify the approach, although it would be nice *if* the approach can be succinctly described (for example, in less than five words). *If* the approach cannot be succinctly described, then this somewhat vague reference is all that should appear in the title.

3. We know that one variable is school violence and that the other is a cognitive-behavioral intervention; however, we do not know *what* that intervention is. However, technically, both variables are presented.

4. Yes, the terms are basically easily understood.

5. There is no reference to the study's results.

6. This would be a fairly decent title to an article *if* the first part of the title were omitted. What is currently the main title does not provide any information about the study; however, the current subtitle does address the topic and the two general main variables. Furthermore, it avoids jargon and is easily understood (even if we do not know what the specific approach entails).

BOX 1.4   Evaluation of Titles, continued

Title 2

Paolino, Philip, and Shaw, Daron R. (2001, September). Lifting the hood on the straight-talk express. *American Politics Research, 29* (5), 483. 24 pp. (*AN 6220378*)

Critical Thinking Discussion of Title 2

1. This title is catchy, but it really doesn't give any idea (in and of itself) what the article addresses. Does the article research teenage slang? How about how people talk in circles when they have little to say? Or is it about how politicians present themselves during campaigns? The answer is the last one, but that really isn't clear given the title.

2. There is no subtitle, so this question is not relevant. Remember, articles do not *need* subtitles; however, if one is present, it needs to add information to the title.

3. We have no clear idea what the variables are because we don't really know what the article is about (based on the title alone).

4. The English words are easily understood, but the context in how they are being used is not. Again (notice a theme?), we are not clear as to what this article is about.

5. There is no reference to the study's results.

6. Overall, this is a very poor title. It sounds catchy, but the goal of research is not to make it to the

top of the New York Times Bestseller List. People read research because they need to find information. This title gives the reader no clear idea about what type of information the article contains.

Title 3

Baytan, Ronald. (2000, October). Sexuality, ethnicity and language: Exploring Chinese Filipino male homosexual identity. *Culture Health & Sexuality, 2* (4), 391. 14 pp. (*AN 3959623*)

Critical Thinking Discussion of Title 3

1. The purpose of this article is clearly expressed in the title. The article examines the identity of homosexual (sexuality) Chinese Filipino (ethnicity and language) men.

2. There is no subtitle, so this question is not relevant.

3. We know the variables are homosexual identity (first variable) and how that is affected by ethnicity (second variable) and language (third variable). So there are three main variables.

4. All words in this title are easily understood. There is no jargon present.

5. There is no reference to the study's results.

6. This is a very good title. The purpose and variables are clearly expressed and there are no references to findings or unnecessary jargon present.

---

5. *Does the title avoid any reference to the study's results?*

Putting study results in a title is poor practice for a number of reasons. First, it may bias the reader to accept the results without critically examining the methods behind them. Second, it may bias the reader to accept the results without critically evaluating their interpretation. Third, it unnecessarily inflates a title. Titles should be as short as possible, mentioning only the main variables and perhaps who was studied. For example:

Census Data Reveals that Divorce Rate Continues to Hover around Fifty Percent

Why is this title problematic? It sounds catchy and it definitely would get people's attention. However, as we covered in our discussion of accepting information too easily, there is a big risk of doing that here. One would have to continue reading the article to see how the divorce rate was calculated and then banish that surprising "50 percent" statistic from their thoughts long enough to realize that the methods generating that statistic are questionable. More appropriate titles would be:

Longitudinal Examination of U.S. Divorce Rates

or

U.S. Divorce Rates from 1900–2003: An Analysis of Census Data

Just as a quick note: The first title does not mention that the data are from the Census. This information, although nice, is not really necessary. If one wants to keep the title short, the first example suffices. If one can have a slightly longer title, then the second one is appropriate because both the title and the subtitle provide useful information regarding the study.

■ Putting It All Together

I can't reiterate enough that these points, and the ones I present in later chapters, are only guidelines for evaluating journal articles. Based on your expertise, you may come up with additional criteria. Furthermore, I also want to stress that there is no one *right* way of evaluating research. These points serve as guidelines to orient your thoughts and approach in order to evaluate research systematically. As I said, you may choose to answer these questions with a "yes" or "no" response or you may want to rate each item with perhaps a 5-point scale to capture the differences between what you consider to be good, neutral, or poor studies. Whichever way you choose, remember that you need to examine all ratings, across all parts of the article, as a whole. No research is perfect, and even the best articles are likely to be weak in specific areas. You must decide whether those weaknesses are important enough to question the validity of the findings. In some later sections, I will provide loose suggestions on how to do this; however, your skill and expertise will still be an important tool.

To summarize, here is what to look for in a good title:

1. Is the title specific enough to differentiate it from other related topics?
2. Do subtitles, if present, provide important information regarding the research?
3. Are the main variables expressed in the title?
4. Do most people easily understand the terms in the title?
5. Does the title avoid any reference to the study's results?

As I said, I begin with the evaluation of research titles because when you read research, you have to first decide whether a specific article is relevant to your needs. The title is the first piece of information that you will use to determine this. Once you think an article may be relevant, based on the title, then you may read other sections, such as the abstract (addressed in the next chapter) to further determine whether a piece of research is relevant to you.

Key Terms

Authority (knowledge) (8)
Common sense (6)
Description (research) (14)

Evaluation (research) (15)
Experience (knowledge) (4)
Explanation (research) (15)

Exploration (research) (13)
Scientific knowledge (9)
Traditional knowledge (3)

Review Questions and Exercises

1. What are the four uses of research? Create a research question that illustrates each of the four for the following topics: worker flextime, social networks, political identification, student mentoring, and self-esteem.

2. Use Research Navigator to find an example of a study that combines descriptive and evaluative purposes of research. What type of evaluation research, policy analysis, or program evaluation does the study undertake? How could the research focus of the study be changed to be an explanatory form of research?

Research Process and Considerations

Why do I hear more now about children using violence as a means to settle disputes than I did 15 years ago? Why is there a small, but growing, trend for professional women to leave the labor force and raise children? Why do politicians spend so much time belittling the other candidates instead of discussing the issues?

All of these questions focus on "why" and are therefore the precursors to theory. If you ask a friend or your parent why he or she thinks children appear to be increasingly violent, this person may answer that it is because of the high rate of violence in television or movies. Or this person may attribute the apparently high violence rate to violent video games or working mothers who are not home supervising children. Perhaps your friend or parent will say that violence among children has *not* increased, it just appears to have done so because of its increasing visibility (thanks largely to the media). Believe it or not, all of these explanations are a type of "theory," even if people do not generally think of them as such. People use theories all the time to explain social phenomena. However, it appears that once someone calls an explanation a "theory," then people, especially students, feel that the explanation is beyond them—that it is too academic.

Social Theory and Ideology

I used the word *theory* in quotes when I applied that term to the possible explanations for violence by children because although the explanations are theories in the sense that they try to explain a phenomena, they really are not "theories" in the scientific sense because they are just short attempts at explanation. Instead, what I loosely called theories in the introduction to this chapter are really ideologies. *Ideologies* offer explanations with absolute certainty. The belief that video games cause violence among children is such an ideology. People who subscribe to this view are so convinced that video games, especially violent ones, are the cause behind aggressive behavior in children that various states are considering legislation to ban or seriously limit the distribution of violent video games, beyond the mere labeling of a rating such as "M" for "mature players."

Ideological explanations also tend to be rather fixed. People treat these explanations as complete, and, consequently, often ignore evidence that may contradict the explanation. Although there are many studies that show an association between viewing violent video games and aggressive behavior (Anderson & Dill, 2000; Griffiths, 1999; Anderson & Ford, 1986), others question the strength of this association (Dill & Dill, 1998; Emes, 1997). Yet, when people (including researchers) subscribe to an ideology, they tend to ignore studies that question the research methodology and data interpretations of studies that contradict or weaken the ideological argument.

Also, ideologies become immersed in moral debates. Consequently, various messages, including those from the media, imply that "good" parents are the ones who worry excessively about the content of the video games their children are playing and, consequently, will join the lobby to restrict the production of such video games.

As Figure 2.1 indicates, scientific theories share some characteristics with ideology. Both scientific theory and ideology try to explain the social world and people's behavior in it. Furthermore, both provide relationships between concepts and link these relationships to wider groups of ideas. However, scientific theories aim at a deeper understanding of *why* a relationship exists than an ideology does. For example, in response to why children appear to be increasingly violent, a response rooted in social ideology would simply theorize that the "cause" is the high popularity of violent video games.* As I said, many people are content with this explanation because it makes sense. If children copy what they see—and anyone around a child for a few hours understands children's entertainment at copying behavior—then it makes sense that if children see violence, they will copy violence. It also offers an easy cure: Change videos and one can work to minimize violence among children.

Scientific theory, on the other hand, would go deeper and seek to find the reasons behind the reasons. Scientific theory would ask *why* violent video games are associated with violence among children. After all, children frequently see violence—Bugs Bunny cartoons are notoriously violent with Elmer Fudd's gun frequently blowing up another cartoon character's head, or Wile E. Coyote trying to exterminate that rascally Road Runner with explosions and pranks. One may say that Bugs Bunny is only a cartoon—just make-believe. Yet, video games are also make-believe and, for all of their high-quality graphics, still somewhat cartoonlike. Furthermore, television shows, such as *COPS* and *Homicide: Life on the Street,* that are in the family time slot of 8:00 to 9:00 p.m. also show violence. So, how can researchers isolate the effects of violent video from other social influences, such as violent television, on children's behavior? There's no easy answer to this, because isolating these effects is difficult and most studies do not successfully do it. Likewise, gen-

---

*I am not going to debate whether children are more violent today than in the past. My discussion here focuses on explanation and theory; therefore, the relevant point is that many *believe* violence among children has increased, and therefore they are trying to explain why. Those explanations are the foundation of theory or ideology, which is why I am discussing them here.

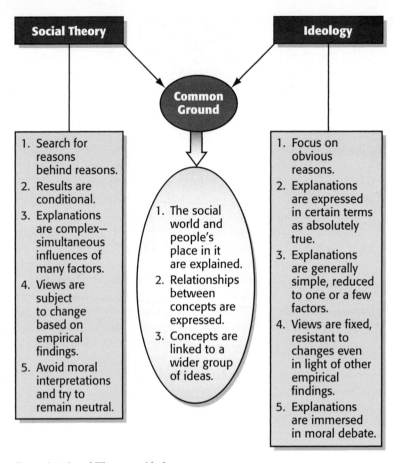

Social Theory

Ideology

Common Ground

1. Search for reasons behind reasons.
2. Results are conditional.
3. Explanations are complex—simultaneous influences of many factors.
4. Views are subject to change based on empirical findings.
5. Avoid moral interpretations and try to remain neutral.

1. The social world and people's place in it are explained.
2. Relationships between concepts are expressed.
3. Concepts are linked to a wider group of ideas.

1. Focus on obvious reasons.
2. Explanations are expressed in certain terms as absolutely true.
3. Explanations are generally simple, reduced to one or a few factors.
4. Views are fixed, resistant to changes even in light of other empirical findings.
5. Explanations are immersed in moral debate.

Figure 2.1 Social Theory vs. Ideology

erations of children played Cops 'n' Robbers or Cowboys and Indians—both relatively violent forms of pretend that frequently involved guns and shooting. Yet, in both instances—of cartoons and Cops 'n' Robbers—children were able to distinguish between make-believe and reality.

Finally, some researchers found that any time a new form of media enters our cultural realm, people fear it. Ancient philosophers such as Plato warned people that telling stories to children will distort their ability to distinguish between fantasy and reality. Furthermore, when radio became more popular in the early 1900s, studies linked listening to the radio with an inability to distinguish reality from fiction (Glassner, 1999).

So the theoretical question remains: If violent video games lead to violence, then *why* are children no longer able to make the same distinctions? What is different now than in the past when similar fears were present with other forms of media? A social theory would go beyond the merely ideological response and try to ascertain a deeper explanation for social phenomena.

Do violent video games lead to violent behavior? What kind of evidence would you need to gather to answer this question?

Consequently, social theories differ from ideologies in a number of ways. Theories are conditional, meaning that they recognize that a relationship between variables is often more complex than an ideology suggests; and, in order to explain a behavior, one needs to examine multiple factors. For example, when examining violent behavior by children, theory would examine parenting styles, socioeconomic status of children, the effects of other forms of media such as television and movies in addition to videos, and children's personality prior to video playing, just to name a few variables. Furthermore, theories welcome empirical tests and are amenable to change based on the findings of those tests. Theories also try to consider all possible sides of an issue so as to avoid narrow interpretations and "quick" fixes that are not necessarily the most appropriate fixes. Finally, theories try to remain neutral. Remember, science aims to be objective and can study only what is. When moral elements or judgments enter the equation, the ability to impartially interpret findings (including those that do not support an individual researcher's personal views) becomes hindered.

It is important to keep in mind, however, that theories themselves do not provide the answers to these questions. Instead, they provide a direction of study; they give researchers somewhere to look to see if they can empirically observe a relationship between two or more factors.

Social theory differs from ideology in some other ways. Scientific theories are empirically testable—in other words, by design, they fit with the goals of research methods. Scientific theory is not static; it can be adapted and edited as new empirical observations become apparent. Ideology, however, tends to be enduring and it morphs into the "traditional" form of knowledge that I discussed in the last chapter.

Theory also helps research in two other ways. First, it prevents people from being duped by random observations. For example, if a researcher finds that people born in February are more likely to be financially successful, but he or she can't find a theoretical explanation to explain why, then this finding is likely to be a fluke—or just due to random chance. Second, theories also help direct our research efforts. This means that theories give us a direction in which we are likely to empirically observe interesting and useful patterns in social behavior.

To summarize, an ideology would argue that violent videos cause violent behavior in children. A theory, on the other hand, would perhaps recognize an *association* between viewing violent videos and violent behavior. A theory would elaborate this relationship perhaps stating that watching violent videos leads to violent behavior for children who (for example) have aggressive tendencies even without videos and who watch violent television (in addition to playing these video games). A theory would then argue that violent videos are one of many simultaneous social influences that desensitizes a child to the consequences of behaving violently.

Theory and Its Parts

Like research, which has multiple components such as hypothesis formation, sampling design, observational design, data analysis, and so on, theories have various components as well. Since social class is such an important factor in our society—affecting everything from children's educational opportunities, to the types of treatment one receives for drug use, to one's experiences with the criminal justice system, and lots of other experiences—let's talk about social stratification from a theoretical viewpoint.

In a society as wealthy as ours, why does poverty still exist? Why haven't people managed to create a social system that divides wealth more equitably? Kingsly Davis and Wilbur Moore (1945) tried to explain the U.S. stratification system with their Functionalist Theory of Stratification, which very basically argues that some positions in society are more important for the overall functioning of society. These positions require more personal investment, whether it is talent or education, and in order to encourage people to fill these positions, members of society need to offer these individuals greater rewards. The difference in position importance and its corresponding reward structure leads to the different social classes we observe.

Let's look at some of the main components of social theory and relate them to the example of Kingsley and Davis's Functionalist Theory of Stratification.

■ Concepts

Concepts are abstract tags social scientists use to describe observations, ideas, and social life. Concepts are also the fundamental building blocks of theory. Prejudice, discrimination, crime, age, race, gender—all of these are examples of concepts. However, these terms themselves are abstract and vague because, while we all have a sense of what many of these concepts mean, creating an exact definition can be difficult. For example, we all have an idea of what "crime" is, but how would you explain it, for instance, to a child? To say that a crime is simply doing something wrong is inaccurate, because that, in and of itself, is not criminal. You can't necessarily say that a crime is "breaking a law," because then you also have to explain the concept of law. *Crime* is a word that most of us use to explain a whole host of behaviors—killing another person, robbing a house, spray-painting hate comments on the side of a church, and many other examples. All of these, and many more, are crimes. Hence, the word *crime* refers to an abstract idea that has no inherent meaning of its own. I will discuss the issue of concepts more in Chapter 4, when I explain how researchers actually measure concepts. For now, it is enough for you to understand that concepts are abstract terms researchers use to describe social phenomena, and that theory is frequently expressed as the relationship between concepts.

Theoretical concepts frequently appear as clusters. For example, the concept "crime" can entail white-collar crime, street crime, and hate crime. These three types of crime are still conceptual in that if I ask you what you think "hate crime" is, you and I may still have different definitions. Perhaps you think that beating someone up because he or she is gay or a minority is a hate crime. I may or may not agree. I think that etching a racial slur in the side of a car with a key is also a hate crime. You may or may not.

In our example of stratification theory, stratification is usually further defined as "social class." Different people may think of different definitions or categories of social class. Some people just use the clusters of upper, middle, and lower class. Others, such as Karl Marx, cluster social class into the bourgeois and proletariat. Still others cluster social class into upper class, middle class, lower-middle class, working class, working poor, and underclass clusters (Gilbert & Kahl, 1993).

■ Dimensions

Some concepts are complex, and researchers can more easily examine and understand them if they look at the concepts in smaller subclassifications, called **dimensions.** Essentially, dimensions are groupings of like concepts that define broader more complex concepts.

These classifications can fall into two types: ideal types and typologies. **Ideal type** is a phrase coined by Max Weber and it refers to descriptions of abstract characteristics that, taken together, create a complete ideal definition or description of a concept. Researchers frequently use Weber's concept of ideal type to describe, for example, the concept of "bureaucracy." Most people have an idea of what a bureaucracy is; however, when pushed to give a description of one, people's descriptions are likely to differ. This is because, in reality, bureaucracies can look very different, even if people still understand that *generally* they are bureaucracies. For instance, according to Weber (1913), an ideal type description of a bureaucracy has the following characteristics:

1. Clearly defined levels
2. Assignments that flow down levels and accountability that flows up levels
3. Clear divisions of labor
4. Written rules
5. Written communication and records of most actions within the bureaucracy
6. Impersonality

However, not all bureaucracies fulfill these characteristics to the same degree. A specific organization may be high on one trait and low on another, but I still call that organization a bureaucracy. So why use ideal types if, in reality, few entities fit their rigid descriptions? Because most entities have most or all of the characteristics of ideal types—just in different degrees, and these types allow us to form a uniform base understanding of what I mean by specific concepts such as "bureaucracy" and "the wealthy."

Typologies involve intersecting two or more simple concepts to create new concepts. The concept of "social class" is a good example of this. Most of us have a general idea of what social class means; however, it is a very broad concept, and if I asked you what it means to be "middle class" versus "working class," you probably could not give me a clearly observable distinction. However, social class is an immensely important concept for social research, so social scientists need some clear way of identifying it. Functionalist Theory of

Stratification explains why people are in different social classes; however, to do so, I must first define what I mean by social class. Frequently, "social class" is used interchangeably with "socioeconomic status," a concept coined (once again!) by Max Weber that examines the intersecting dimensions of class, status/prestige, and power. From a research point of view, these three concepts are indicated by an interaction of income (class), education (status), and occupation (power). Table 2.1 illustrates how these three individual concepts combine to form the new concepts of social class.

Dimensions are useful because they serve as a bridge between broad concepts and theories, making it easier for researchers to design manageable research questions to test theories. In other words, research cannot address all components (or all concepts) of a theory at once, but, by specifying dimensions of concepts, researchers can break large research topics into more manageably observable designs.

■ Relationships

Not only do theories discuss concepts but they also—more importantly—relate concepts to each other. Theories, as I have stated, explain why a relationship exists by first telling us whether concepts are related and, if so, explaining how. Remember my earlier example of

TABLE 2.1 Dimensions of Social Class

Social class is a concept that is based on the intersection of three dimensions: education, income, and occupation. Gilbert and Kahl (1993) use these three dimensions to identify six different social classes.

Social Class =	Education	+ Income	+ Occupation
Capitalists	Prestigious university	$620,000+	Investors, heirs, some top executives
Upper Middle	College/university, usually postgraduate study	$112,000	Professionals, upper managers
Lower Middle	High school/college, maybe apprenticeship	$50,000	Semi-professionals, lower managers, foremen
Working Class	High school	$37,000	Factory workers, clerical, low-paid retail, craftspeople
Working Poor	Some high school	$25,000	Laborers, service workers, low-paid sales
Underclass	Some high school	Under $13,000	Part-time and unemployed people

Source: Adapted from Dennis Gilbert and Joseph A. Kahl, *The American Class Structure: A New Synthesis,* 4th ed. (Homewood IL: Dorsey Press, 1993). Income statements are from Christina Duff, "Superrich's Share of After-Tax Income Stopped Rising in Early '90s Data Show," *Wall Street Journal,* November 22, 1995, p. A2, but are updated to 2004 dollars.

people who were born in February as being more financially secure than people born in November or December? If I cannot find a theory that would suggest why birth month is associated with financial stability (that is, whether I would *expect* these two concepts to be related), then I am also not likely to be able to explain how or *why* I found the results I did—at least not from a theoretical perspective. In other words, *why* I found the results I did is likely to be due to random error, or chance—not because there is any real relationship between birth month and financial security in the real world.

Consequently, theories often make causal connections between concepts and explain why we would expect these causal connections. When theories link concepts together causally, researchers call these statements **propositions.** When researchers try to make a causal connection between concepts to test with data they gather through observation, they call that statement a **hypothesis.** The different terminology relates to whether the relationship is theoretical or empirically observed. There are many areas in research and statistics where researchers use different terminology to make distinctions between what they can empirically observe (research) and whether those findings will fit the wider population or a broader theoretical context.

Remember, Functionalist Theory of Stratification tries to explain why our society (and all others so far) is organized in such a way as to lead some people to be poor. I can describe this theory in a series of relationships that can be empirically tested:

1. In order to function smoothly, society must make sure that its positions are filled.
2. Some positions are more important to the functioning of society than others.
3. More important positions require greater personal resources, such as talent, education, or dedication.
4. In order to motivate people to invest or make available these necessary resources for these positions, society needs to offer them greater rewards.
5. The more important a role for social functioning, the greater the offered reward.
6. People who fill these positions will therefore have more resources and be higher in the social stratification hierarchy (here defined as having a higher social class).

Levels of Theory

Generally there are three categories of theories that classify social theories. These categories are macro-level, micro-level, and meso-level theories. **Macro-theories** focus on how the wider social structure affects groups. For example, macro-theorists try to explain how a group's experiences in social institutions, such as the family or education system, affects its occupational opportunities (the economic institution). Other examples include how economic factors influence marital stability, reasons why drug use may be higher for men or for women, or whether different racial groups are more likely to get the death penalty. Macro-theories also explain interaction between very large groups. Examples of this include theories of cooperation and conflict among different countries or different political systems. Davis and Moore's Functionalist Theory of Stratification, which I have been using as an example throughout this chapter, is an example of a macro-theory.

Micro-theory, on the other hand, explains the social experience of individuals, smaller social groups, small segments of time, or small instances of space. For example, micro-theory would try to explain individual decisions to divorce, reasons for drug use, and reasons behind jury deliberations. Theories are overwhelmingly macro- or micro-oriented; however, there is clearly a gap here. Institutional experiences not only affect groups but they also affect individuals. Furthermore, individuals can mobilize to influence institutions.

The third level of theory, **meso-theory,** tries to link macro- and micro-levels of theory. However, because these theories are more difficult to formulate than you may imagine, they are relatively rare. A discussion of the specific reasons why meso-theory is difficult to formulate and rarely used is beyond the scope of a research methods course or book; however, some general topics in which people have tried to develop meso-level theories to explain issues involve social movements or issues at the community level.

The Link between Theory and Research

Although I have addressed the general components of theories, it is not appropriate in this book to go into a detailed explanation of the main theories of all the different social science disciplines. However, I will take an example of each from sociology and criminal justice to illustrate the theory-research connection explaining people's career choice. But before I begin, let me clarify the distinction between a paradigm and theory. **Paradigms** are essentially loose models that organize our thoughts about some phenomena—a general point of view, so to speak, of concepts or assumptions relevant to a theory. A *theory*, then, is a more systematic, detailed explanation of phenomena. Groups of theories constitute paradigms. For example, symbolic interactionist theory is really a paradigm in sociology that, in its simplest terms, argues that people learn social behavior through their interaction with others. Within this paradigm are more specific theories, such as labeling theory, differential theory, and social learning theory. These three theories have the same basic argument—that people learn social behavior from others—but they differ slightly in arguing *how* others teach behavior.

Now let's use these theories to explain career choice. The functionalist paradigm generally argues that all elements, which include institutions and social roles, exist because on some level they contribute to the smooth functioning of society. Functionalist Theory of Stratification is a specific theory under the functionalist paradigm, which I just discussed in some length with social class. Applying it to whether someone pursues a legitimate career, Functionalist Theory of Stratification argues that some jobs, such as surgery or corporate law, require many years of education and even continuing education after a person obtains a degree and a job. Why? Because these occupations require special skills that need to be learned. I couldn't do brain surgery and I wouldn't want someone who has a doctorate in sociology doing brain surgery on me. Sorry, but the two doctorates are *not* the same. I find brain surgery fascinating—but not enough to invest the time required to obtain and maintain the necessary skills.

Functionalist Theory of Stratification argues that although interest in a topic is important, it is not necessarily enough to encourage people to invest in that career. Therefore, to encourage people to commit to the training required to be, for example, a brain surgeon, there needs to be more social rewards (e.g., money and prestige) than for other occupations such as a store cashier. How might a researcher test this theory? He or she could form a hypothesis that argues that people in occupations that require higher levels of education will receive more pay and prestige than people in occupations that require little education or skill.

In fact, studies do support this hypothesis. Being a physician requires more years of education than does being a college professor, a telephone operator, or a taxi cab driver (and all of these other occupations require decreasing levels of education in the order I presented them). According to the U.S. Census Bureau (2002), the median (middle) hourly earnings of each of these four occupations, respectively, is $51.66 per hour, $39.97 per hour, $13.23 per hour, and $8.41 per hour. So, as you can see, with decreasing years of education necessary for these careers, the pay (and the prestige) of these occupations declines as well.

But what about people who become drug dealers? For some, this is very profitable; but, clearly, people (we hope) do not go to college to learn how to be drug dealers. So if drug dealing can be profitable for some people, why do we make it so? Functionalist Theory of Stratification may be able to explain how becoming a drug dealer is functional, but a different theory, one that falls under the symbolic interactionist paradigm, may be more appropriate.

Differential association theory is a theory under the symbolic interactionist paradigm, like Functionalist Theory of Stratification fits in the functionalist paradigm. Differential association theory argues that behavior is learned in the context of primary groups and that people in our primary groups teach us how to behave and how to justify our behaviors to be normative or acceptable. Research suggests that there is an association between gang membership and drug use (Bureau of Justice Statistics, 1994), and differential association theory would argue that young people learn how to use drugs and how to justify that use as normative, or acceptable, in these gangs (their primary group). Therefore, if researchers wanted to take this argument one step further and argue that, according to differential association theory, peer groups or gangs may teach young people how to sell drugs and how to justify the selling of drugs as socially acceptable. Such a hypothesis may be: "Gang members teach other members that selling drugs and adopting a violent attitude is an acceptable means of gaining money and prestige."

Clearly, these two issues are more complex than I have presented here. I just took two different examples (legitimate and illegitimate) of career choice to illustrate that no one theory can explain all behavior and that theories can lead to hypotheses that can be empirically testable with research. I made these examples basic to illustrate a point, and this illustration is summarized in Table 2.2. The "empirically testable prediction" mentioned in Table 2.2 is essentially a hypothesis, which is a key element in research. Hypotheses are simply empirically testable statements, and I will discuss them in more detail in Chapter 3.

Let's take a different example. Downey (2005, **AN 16832435**) examined whether environmental hazards are more likely to be in areas where there is a high proportion of racial minorities and low-income individuals. Downey draws on spatial mismatch theory, which argues that since World War II, the shift in industry from the urban core to the suburban and more rural areas has hurt African American workers more than it has hurt White workers. This is because residential segregation prevented African Americans from moving away from the central cities, thereby creating a spatial mismatch between the location of jobs and the location of African American neighborhoods. Furthermore, since African Americans more heavily relied on these manufacturing jobs than did Whites, they were essentially doubly affected (by their greater reliance on these jobs and by the decreasing availability of these jobs given the changing location) (Farley, Danziger, & Holzer, 2000).

TABLE 2.2 Functionalist and Symbolic Interaction Paradigms and Their Explanations for Career Direction

	Functionalist Paradigm	Symbolic Interactionist Paradigm
Paradigm Assumptions	All elements of society exist because, on some level, they fulfill a role (function) that allows society to run smoothly.	Through interaction with others, people learn the symbols of their culture, which enables them to learn how to act within that culture.
Theory Description	*Functionalist Theory of Stratification:* Different occupations correspond to different levels of rewards (such as money, power, prestige) based on the occupation's importance to the functioning of society. Occupations that are more important require greater investment in terms of talent, education, experience, and so on, and therefore have to be compensated more in order to encourage people to pursue them.	*Differential Association Theory:* Behavior is learned in the context of primary groups (those groups to which we have strong ties). People in our primary groups teach us how to behave and how to justify our actions as acceptable.
Empirically Testable Prediction (Research)	Occupations that require high levels of education (e.g., neurosurgeon) or talent (e.g., athlete) will receive more pay and prestige than occupations that require little education or skill (e.g., grocery clerk).	Youth who become involved in gangs (a primary group) are taught by other gang members how to successfully complete a drug sale. Gang members also teach other members that selling drugs and adopting a violent attitude are acceptable ways of gaining money and prestige.

Downey (2005) argues that if this argument is correct, then contrary to what many researchers maintain, we would expect African Americans and low-income people to be *less* affected by manufacturing facility pollution, not more, since these jobs (and the pollution they create) have moved away from these neighborhoods. Downey uses data from the Detroit metropolitan area's U.S. Census for the years 1970, 1980, and 1990 as well as data from the Michigan manufacturing facilities directories for those same years to assess four different models of whether race and manufacturing pollution are related: an economic model, a racist intent model, a segregation model, and a racial succession model. Using data from these two sources, across these three specific years, Downey conducted statistical tests to assess these four views of race of pollution.

I am not going to go into the full statistics and findings of Downey's (2005) research (you can find the full article on Research Navigator, however, if you are interested), but, in order to illustrate the theory-research connection, suffice it to say here that Downey's research found that only the racial succession model had any statistical influence on environmental inequality. However, he also found that this model operated in a way that supported spatial mismatch theory and not common perceptions of environmental racism. In other words, Downey found that, at least in the Detroit metropolitan area, racial segregation prevented the African American ghetto from expanding along the region's manufacturing areas, which led to environmental income inequality in terms of job availability, but not in terms of bringing African Americans closer to manufacturing pollution.

Downey's research is a good example of the theory-research connection. He started with a problem (inequality between African Americans and Whites), moved to a theory explaining that problem (spatial mismatch theory), and then used research to test the strength of that theory (analysis of U.S. Census and manufacturing data from Detroit, Michigan).

■ Inductive versus Deductive Research

One additional word about research and theory addresses the difference between inductive and deductive research. The classic research model (the one that is the focus of this book) is one of deduction, where the researcher moves from theory to hypothesis to observation to conclusion (see Figure 2.2). Hence, in deductive research, researchers review the literature to find out what social scientists already know about a problem; they fit that knowledge into a theory; they develop a hypothesis to fill in the gaps; they proceed to test that hypothesis by observation; they make conclusions based on what the data reveal; and, finally, they relate those conclusions to future theory and research formation. This is essentially what Downey (2005) did in his research about race and environmental inquality.

On the other hand, sometimes, especially when researchers are doing explorative research, the researcher begins with observation and then forms some type of general explanation (a theory) to account for the observations. Hence, rather than starting with a theory and moving toward observation (like deductive research), inductive research starts with observation and then moves to form a theory. Frequently, researchers doing inductive research don't even have a specific research question in mind when they begin; they allow the questions to emerge from the data. This is why exploratory research is frequently a good example of inductive reasoning.

A classic example of inductive research is William Foote Whyte's study of male gangs in the 1950s that he published in his book, *Street Corner Society* (1955). The gangs in *Street Corner Society* are vastly

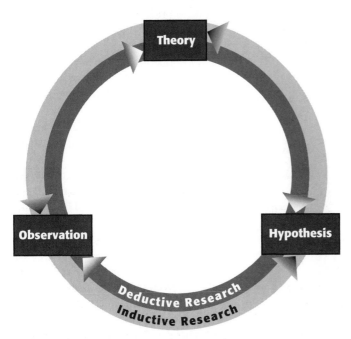

Figure 2.2 Inductive Deductive Wheel

different from the groups people call gangs today. At the time Whyte did his research, social scientists knew little about such clusters of adult men. Using a form of observation called *field research,* also known as *participant observation,* Whyte observed the economic, political, and social networks of a group of adult men and made some of the field's earliest statements about gang behavior. Through his research, social scientists learned, contrary to the opinion held at the time, that social life in the slums is very structured and organized. This knowledge helps fuel other research on gangs and helped form theories about social organization.

Whether one chooses to do deductive or inductive research largely depends on one's research problem, the level of information currently available, and one's research expertise. As I previously mentioned, in this book I will largely focus on deductive research because it is the most common form of research conducted and published.

The Research Process: An Overview

As Figure 2.3 illustrates, the research process is not a linear one. Furthermore, one does not necessarily progress neatly between various stages. Instead, much of the process is in flux, where operationalizing the terms in the hypotheses may lead one to reexamine the existing literature and reformulate the problem. On the other hand, the process of coding data may cause one to reexamine the measurement and perhaps combine data to form more complex variables for analysis. Furthermore, researchers do not approach these steps in isolation. Researchers must have a sense of what they can realistically do in later steps, such as sampling or measurement, when they are working on earlier steps, such as hypothesis formation. For example, if a researcher wants to study attitudes toward campus athletes (problem formation), and the researcher has the means to do a probability sample (data gathering), he or she may choose to do surveys (method of observation) administered to a sample of 200 students selected from the entire university. If a probability sample is not feasible—say, because of time constraints or bureaucratic issues—then the same researcher may decide to interview a small select subgroup of students, such as 20 seniors. Whatever research design he or she selects, in turn, will affect the types of questions that the researcher can ask and, therefore, the type of measurement that the researcher can design. Thus, thinking about problem formation requires some thought about measurement, sampling, and the mode of observation as well.

Even so, one has to begin research somewhere and have a general idea of a path to follow. To that end, Figure 2.3 is very informative, and this book is, with some

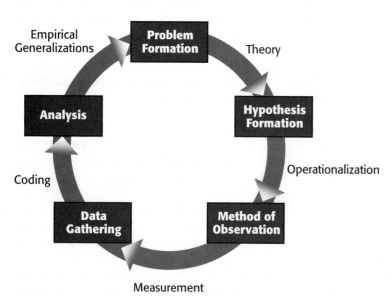

Figure 2.3 An Overview of the Deductive Research Process

exceptions, generally organized to follow the research process in the same direction. Let's briefly look at each stage of the research process to get an overview. Individual chapters will go into more detail about the specific nature of each stage.

■ Problem Formation

The deductive research process begins with *problem formation*. This frequently involves identifying a research question—essentially, what the researcher wants to study. This is harder than it seems. The difficulty does not lie in creating interesting or socially useful questions; the problem lies in selecting research questions that are manageable. A researcher may aspire to study the social dynamics of gangs, but the researcher needs to understand that not all gangs are alike, that he or she may have difficulty gaining access to a gang, that not all members of a gang may want to be studied, and, if they do, that the activities a researcher may witness could be difficult to report. Furthermore, as I will discuss in Chapter 5 on sampling, probability samples (ones where every relevant person has an equal probability of being selected for a study) are usually methodologically preferred, but they are not always possible. For example, it is impossible to get a list of all gang members in a city and then randomly select which ones to study.

Consequently, it is important to remember that when forming a research problem, a researcher has to be realistic about what he or she can feasibly accomplish, given financial, ethical, political, and time constraints (to name a few) present in the real world. It is better, instead, to study a small part of a problem. The key is to document clearly what part of an issue will be your focus and then not to overstate the scope or generalizability of your findings.

Furthermore, no one expects you suddenly to pull full-blown, feasible research questions out of your head. Nor do people want to waste time completely reinventing the wheel, so to speak. Instead, when forming a research question, social scientists always begin with a review of the existing research literature, called a **literature review.** Researchers use it to see what is already known about a topic, what research gaps need to be filled, and where conflicting findings might exist. All of these give you direction in how to word and proceed with the formation of your research question. Chapter 3 will discuss what to look for in a literature review in more detail. After a researcher formulates a research problem, he or she is ready to examine various theories to explain this problem. Remember, as I discussed before, researchers do not specifically test a research problem; they test/research a theory that explains that problem.

For example, there are competing explanations as to why residential patterns remain racially segregated. Some argue that this segregation results from discrimination in the real estate market, where Whites choose not to live near minorities, especially Blacks (Goering & Wienk, 1996). Others argue that residential segregation persists because of the opposite reason—that Blacks choose to live away from Whites (Patterson, 1997; Thernstrom & Thernstrom, 1997). Consequently, Krysan (2002, **AN 6394847**) was interested in examining in more detail why racial residential segregation persists even in light of all the gains of the Civil Rights movement. This was the general problem or question Krysan used as the basis for her research.

In conducting a literature review, Krysan found that there is a lot of research that examines African American–White residential patterns. However, the findings of various studies contradicted each other or were inconclusive. Krysan believed that these issues resulted from a gap in the research—namely, that no one was studying the nuances behind Black preferences and the reasons behind those preferences. Hence, Krysan focused her research on studying the underlying social, psychological, demographic, and socioeconomic reasons behind Blacks' choices of residential patterns. To do this, she created a qualitative and quantitative research approach.

Applying a theory to discuss a social issue is also frequently part of the problem formation. I discussed the role of theory in the previous section, so I won't cover it again here. However, be aware that even researchers sometimes justify their research in ideology instead of theory. This is a problem with much of the published research—it essentially skips an important component of the research process. Krysan's research falls prey to this. She spends quite a bit of time in her literature review discussing the causes behind racial residential segregation that are established by other researchers, but she never discusses the deeper meaning behind those causes from a formal theoretical point of view. To be fair, Krysan herself argues that part of the goal of her research is to discover why these preferences occur; however, she still does not support her hypotheses with formal theory. Since omissions like this unfortunately are common, it does not discredit Krysan's research; however, it is a notable oversight.

■ Hypothesis Formation

A hypothesis is a statement that researchers can empirically test. Notice the choice of words here: A hypothesis is a *statement* about how two variables are related. It is not a question and, to that end, it is different from a research question that is usually broad and does not specifically link two or more specific concepts. Hypotheses consist of independent and dependent variables. The dependent variable is the outcome you are interested in studying—the effect. The independent variable is the variable that is producing a change in the dependent variable—the cause.

Students are frequently hesitant to word hypotheses as statements because they are afraid of being wrong. Being wrong is okay because, so long as the research is well designed, having hypotheses refuted can be just as informative as having them be supported. Chapter 3 discusses hypotheses in more detail; however, I can illustrate them here by discussing Krysan's racial residential segregation research.

One of Krysan's (2002) hypotheses is "Blacks who believe there is a great deal of both institutionalized and individual discrimination will find integrated neighborhoods less attractive and will be less willing to move into all-white neighborhoods" (p. 945). The dependent variable, the behavior Krysan is interested in trying to predict, in this hypothesis is whether Blacks will be willing to move into an all-White neighborhood. The independent variable, or the variable that Krysan believes will influence Blacks' willingness to live in an all-White neighborhood, is twofold. One independent variable is the participants' perception of institutionalized discrimination, and the other independent variable is the participants' perception of individual discrimination.

■ Operationalization

Talk to five of your friends and ask them what the term *juvenile delinquency* means. One person might respond that juvenile delinquency is acts such as skipping school; another might answer that it is participating in gangs, and a third might say that juvenile delin-

How would you define a "racially integrated" neighborhood? Would you consider the people in the photo to be living in such a neighborhood?

quency is actions such as minor vandalism by youths. The point is, if you ask five different friends what a term means, you are likely to get five different responses. That can be a problem when trying to study social phenomena! In order to avoid this, researchers have to be very clear as to what they mean by various concepts. The process of defining concepts, or saying exactly what you mean when using terms such as *juvenile delinquency,* is **operationalization,** and it is the first step in determining how to measure (or observe) social phenomena.

Frequently, the terms that need to be operationalized are those that appear in a hypothesis or research question. Even with these definitions, the process of measurement is not complete. Once researchers clearly define their concepts, they have to devise some way of conveying them to other people—in other words, they have to actually observe these concepts with other people. This means that the researcher has to be fairly sure that the people participating in the study share the same definitions or understandings of a measure with one another and with the researcher.

In Krysan's (2002) hypothesis, she will have to operationalize what she means by *institutional discrimination, individual discrimination, integrated neighborhood,* and *attractive.* For example, "individual discrimination" can range from side verbal comments to throwing rocks through a person's windows. Likewise, what is the racial composition of an "integrated neighborhood?" Fifty-fifty? Forty-sixty? Krysan approaches this dilemma by using a continuum where she shows cards depicting five racially different communities. These communities are all Black, 10 Black and 4 White, 7 Black and 7 White, 2 Black and 12 White, and all White. Consequently, there is no question about what the racial composition is of the communities under study. For the measures of discrimination, Krysan defines institutional discrimination as "respondents' assessments of the extent of discrimination against blacks in the job market as the degree to which they attribute poor quality housing for blacks to discriminatory treatment by real-estate brokers and lenders" (p. 945). Furthermore, individual discrimination focuses on Blacks' belief "that individual whites are more difficult to get along with than blacks and the degree to which they think individual white property owners discriminate against blacks when blacks search for housing" (p. 945).

■ Method of Observation

Researchers have many choices for how to observe people and collect data. They can do experiments, quasi-experiments, surveys, interviews, field research, and secondary research (to name a few). Which method a researcher chooses depends largely on the research question, the concepts being studied, and real-life considerations such as time and money. Some methods are better suited for some topics than others. For instance, sending surveys to gang members sounds somewhat ridiculous—and for good reason. Obviously, if someone is interested in studying gangs, a face-to-face interview or some type of field research is probably more appropriate than a mailed survey.

However, this does not mean to imply that interviews and field research are the only ways to study gangs. Depending on your research question and/or hypothesis, if you are interested in the criminal behavior of gang members, you might use police records to study the crimes associated with gang members. Alternatively, if you are interested in the public's glorification of gangs, you might choose to do content analysis of popular songs that involve gang references. The point is that there are many different forms of research available and this book will address how to do many of them.

How to decide which research design to use depends on a variety of factors. One is the nature of the research question, as just discussed. The second consideration is resources. Doing surveys, especially large ones that will involve sophisticated data-gathering or sampling techniques, is very expensive—so much so that they are frequently beyond the means of the average individual researcher. Consequently, instead of doing a survey, a researcher may decide to do a smaller study that involves interviews or use the data collected by someone else, like Krysan did for the racial segregation study (which I will discuss in more detail in a moment). A third consideration is one's access to the subjects. As I mentioned earlier, random sampling is methodologically preferred whenever possible, but sometimes it simply is *not* possible, as in our discussion of gangs. In order to do a random sample, a researcher has to obtain a list of all possible subjects and each subject has to have an equal probability of selection for the study. Obviously, it is impossible to obtain a comprehensive list of all gang members in an area in order to randomly select some for study participation. Last, a researcher's own training is important. Some researchers are more comfortable with quantitative data analysis and the statistics that go along with that form of research, whereas others are more comfortable with qualitative data analysis and the designs that correspond to those techniques.

Krysan's (2002) study of racial residential segregation used information from the Multi-City Study of Urban Inequality (MCSUI). The MCSUI consists of face-to-face interviews with approximately 9,000 randomly selected adults from four cities—Atlanta, Boston, Detroit, and Los Angeles—in the mid-1990s. So, the research design here was interviews, which is a type of survey research that I will discuss in more detail in Chapter 7. However, technically, Krysan's study is secondary analysis of primary data because she is using data that other people gathered. In other words, Krysan is a "second" person using the data, but since she is using it in its raw form (as opposed to studying the original results of the study), she is using the primary data. This isn't considered cheating. In fact, it's a very realistic and respected form of research design that enables individuals who do not have the time or money to undertake large studies (like the MCSUI) to analyze massive organized research. By having other researchers examine existing data, new findings may emerge.

■ Measurement

After a researcher has chosen a design and operationalized the concepts, it is time to decide exactly how to convey the operationalized concepts to the people he or she is studying. If the researcher has done a good job with the operationalization, this step is relatively simple. The step simply involves taking the operationalized concept and putting it into the form of a question. A good way to tell whether a concept has been fully operationalized and is ready for **measurement** is to ask yourself, What do I mean? until you get to an answer that is universally understood by everyone and does not require further elaboration.

For example, suppose I wanted to survey children between the ages of 10 and 17 in Smallville, Pennsylvania, regarding juvenile delinquency. As said earlier in our discussion of operationalization, there are many definitions—or answers to the question What do I mean?—of juvenile delinquency. I just have to choose one. Let's say I decide to define juvenile delinquency as "petty vandalism." Am I done? No. There are many examples of "petty vandalism" and I need to be clear as to which is my focus. So if I continue to ask myself What do I mean? and I answer, "Acts such as graffiti, breaking windows, and toilet papering houses," I am one step closer. In this instance, I happen to be done because "graffiti," "breaking windows," and "toilet papering houses" are all easily understood and empirically observable. Can someone else choose different definitions? Absolutely. I just have to be clear as to the definitions I am using. I will discuss this a bit more in Chapter 4.

Now that I have clear, identifiable definitions for my concepts and I've selected a research method (survey), all I have to do is put those three definitions into questions, such as, "Have you ever toilet papered someone's house?" I can then decide whether I want to give respondents answer choices, as I would in *closed-ended questions,* or whether I want to leave the question as is and let the respondent fill in what she or he wants, as in *open-ended questions.* I will discuss question formation and measurement more in later chapters. Measures are also frequently called **variables** because they are free to vary. In other words, for each measure, there is more than one possible response that people may select; consequently, what people can say varies (hence the name, variable).

Instead of creating measures from scratch, I can also borrow the measures other people have used. Krysan (2002) did this when she used the Multi-City Study of Urban Inequality, but researchers can also borrow just the measurement or variable definition of others without having to use their data per se. The method of observation will also strongly influence how researchers choose to measure their concepts. Regardless of whether you create your own measures or borrow someone else's (without using his or her specific data), you must clearly specify to anyone reading your research what a measure entails. For example, Krysan discusses a concept called "residential preferences"—admittedly vague—and goes into great detail describing how such a vague concept is measured:

Residential preferences were measured with a hypothetical neighborhood technique. African Americans were handed a set of five cards depicting neighborhoods containing fourteen homes each. They were asked to imagine that they had been looking for a house and found a nice one they could afford. They were told it could be located in any of the neighborhoods shown on the five cards, which ranged from all-black to all-white with three racially mixed neighborhoods in between. . . . Respondents were asked to arrange the cards in order from the one they found most attractive to the one they considered least attractive. After interviewers recorded their preferences, respondents were given the neighborhood cards a second time, and were asked "Are there any of the five neighborhoods you would not want to move into?" In asking this, I determined the preferences of African Americans for neighborhoods with different degrees of integration and the important related issue of their views about which neighborhoods they would be willing to move into if they found an affordable, attractive home there. (p. 942)

After reading this description, there is no doubt about what Krysan means by "residential preference" or how it is measured. A well-defined measure is one in which someone reading a research report can copy, or replicate, the measure easily on his or her own.

■ Data Gathering

The next step in the deductive research process is data gathering—or actually going out and somehow using the research design you've created to gather the information. The big issue here is how to identify your sample. In a perfect world I would study everyone who fits our research interest. However, that is frequently impossible, so researchers content themselves with a study of a small group, called a *sample,* which represents the larger group, called the *population.* This is a deceptively detailed step in the research process and it will be discussed in more detail in Chapter 5.

However, Krysan's (2002) study provides a good example. Krysan mentions that the MCSUI studies people in Atlanta, Boston, Detroit, and Los Angeles. Obviously, she did not study *everyone* in those four cities—trying to do so would very likely make someone insane and would be a futile effort to boot, since it would be impossible to accurately identify all people who live in these four cities. Instead, Krysan states that the MCSUI is a study of 9,000 individuals *randomly* selected from these four cities. As I will show in Chapter 5, "random" from a methodological point a view does not mean the same as "random" does in our everyday lives. What people generally think of as random in our daily lives really is not. But, again, that is a point that I will discuss in Chapter 5. For now, it is enough for us to realize that Krysan's study actually uses a very sophisticated form of random sampling called *multistage probability sampling,* which means that the researchers sampled smaller and smaller units until they reached the individuals who eventually ended up participating in the study.

■ Coding

Much data analysis, especially quantitative data analysis, which is the next step, involves computers. Since statistics are mathematical calculations, the answers respondents give in English (or whatever written language is used) need to be converted to numbers. Researchers call this process *coding*—where each written response is given a numerical code that is readable by a computer. This important step frequently does not appear in written research reports, primarily because it is important only to the researcher conducting the study. I will discuss coding in Chapter 12.

■ Analysis

Now the researcher is *finally* ready to get some answers! It isn't until the researcher completes all of the previous steps that she or he is finally able to see what respondents say about his or her research questions and to test whether the hypotheses are correct. This section, sometimes called a *results section,* may involve a simple description of what people responded to each question, or it may be more elaborate and look for patterns in aggregate responses by a specific characteristic such as sex, marital status, or education. The list of possible comparisons and analyses is as long as the number of variables included.

Analysis frequently involves two parts. The first is some type of table, chart, or graph that visually summarizes or presents statistical findings. These visual depictions are quick snapshots of the findings so people can look at them in detail and form their own interpretations. This also serves the indirect purpose of double-checking what the researcher purports to find. In presenting the findings in tables so that others can see exactly what the researcher is using as a basis for his or her conclusions, other people reading the research are not limited to blindly accepting the researchers' conclusions. This helps ensure against mistakes in interpretation and application.

This double-checking, so to speak, addresses the second component of a results section, which is a written summary of the findings that follow and it elaborates on and explains the tables or charts. This is so that those who are less comfortable with statistical techniques or with reading tables also can learn about the researcher's findings.

Remember, though, that there are three purposes of research in addition to description. These are evaluation, explanation, and exploration. The *analysis section* is where you fulfill the purpose of your research. Consequently, this section may include both description and explanatory information, for example.

Krysan's (2002) study includes both tables and written interpretation of those tables. Some of her tables are descriptive in that they visually describe the aggregate trends of what respondents said. Other tables are explanatory in that they involve statistical tests to see which factors explain the variation in the dependent variables the most. Krysan's articles include six tables, which are too many to present here. You may look up Krysan's article in Research Navigator and read the results section to see the match between the tables and Krysan's discussion of the findings in those tables.

■ Empirical Generalizations

The last stage of the research process involves taking your results and putting them into a wider context. In written reports, researchers typically present this in a *discussion* or *conclusion section*, and they start with a brief recap of the research goals and the main findings. Here, researchers remind readers of the goals and general trends found in the research. Numerical findings, such as statistics, are rarely present in this section. That would be a repeat of the previous section, so researchers discuss their findings in terms of their patterns, not the numbers that led to those patterns. Furthermore, in this section, researchers frequently tie their findings to theory (hence the reason the diagram in Figure 2.3 is circular). Without any theoretical or practical context, research findings are little more than numerical documentation of our social world.

During this section, researchers often remind readers of the limitations of the research and any research flaws that may unavoidably exist. Students frequently read these limitations and automatically discount the entire study. Don't fall into that trap. No research is perfect—no matter how hard a person tries to cover all the bases. Furthermore, nothing is ever indisputably proven. In fact, it is worse for a researcher to ignore or gloss over the limitations of a study than to be up front about them in the discussion section. Stating limitations and/or making suggestions for future research are important parts of the research process. This allows readers to evaluate how important a particular study is to their own research questions, and it provides direction for future research involving the same topic. In short, one researcher's discussion section may fuel another researcher's literature review, and hence the research method cycle continues.

BOX 2.1   **Theory and Research Practice**

Global terror, the fight for civil rights, political participation, marital instability—all of these, and many other examples, are social dilemmas that require cooperation in order to be resolved. Consequently, many researchers have studied how people cooperate to deal with social dilemmas. However, according to Simpson (2003), researchers cannot reach an agreement about how gender affects cooperation to resolve social dilemmas, even though there is a strong theoretical basis to expect specific differences in how men and women deal with these issues.

According to Simpson (2003), most research regarding cooperation is done with a Prisoner's Dilemma model. In its classic sense, the Prisoner's Dilemma is a game theory in which two players can either cooperate or "defect."

The Prisoner's Dilemma got its name from a hypothetical situation where two criminals were arrested under the suspicion of having committed a crime together. However, the police do not have enough proof in order to have them convicted. The two prisoners are isolated from each other, and the police visit each of them and offer a deal. The one who offers evidence against the other one will be freed. If neither of them accepts the offer, they are in fact cooperating against the police, and both of them will get only a small punishment because of lack of proof. They both gain. However, if one of them betrays the other one, by confessing to the police, the defector will gain more, since he is freed; the one who remained silent, on the other hand, will receive the full punishment, since he did not help the police, and there is sufficient proof. If both betray, both will be punished, but less severely than if they had refused to talk. Hence, the dilemma: Choose to cooperate, hoping the other person will as well, or defect and maximize your payoff at the expense of the other.

Simpson (2003) argues that in a Prisoner's Dilemma, females would be more likely to defect out of fear (fear that one's cooperation would be exploited), whereas males would be more likely to defect out of greed (wanting the higher payoff). Consequently, the Prisoner's Dilemma contains both fear and greed in the same scenario,

thereby making it impossible to discern gender differences in behavior.

An excerpt from Simpson's article tries to empirically test three different theories of gender behavior in cooperation: feminist theory, social role theory, and evolutionary psychology theory. This excerpt focuses on his discussion of social role theory. To test these theories, Simpson conducted two studies (with minor differences between the studies) of undergraduate students at a large university and told them to decide on an action based on different dilemmas.

Simpson arranged the dilemmas so that some would provide an incentive to defect out of fear, another out of greed, and a third type out of a combination of both. Simpson told participants that they would not be interacting with other people more than once or face to face; all interaction was via a computer. This way, they could not really discuss the scenario with their "partner," so cooperation, if it was going to occur, would have to be on faith. The first study consisted of 33 male and 49 female undergraduates; the second study had 32 males and 38 females. For purposes of brevity and because the results were similar, only the concrete results for the second study are included in the excerpt.

Read the following excerpt and then answer the critical thinking questions below. If you need more information, the full text is available on-line in Research Navigator.

"Eagly's [social role theory] views behavioral differences between males and females as a result of their performance of different sex roles . . . that apply to individuals on the basis of their socially identified gender" (1987:12). The *theory* maintains that actors "seek to accommodate sex-typical roles by acquiring the specific skills and resources linked to successful role performance and by adapting their social behavior to role requirement" (Eagly & Wood 1999:412–13). . . . Eagly and associates have identified several features of sex roles relevant to behavior in social dilemmas. First . . . the male role includes norms that encourage com-

BOX 2.1   **Theory and Research Practice, continued**

petition and aggression. . . . The female role not only de-emphasizes aggression but also emphasizes an avoidance of aggression from others or harm to oneself. Applied to cooperation in social dilemmas, the argument that male roles encourage competition suggests that males will be more likely than females to defect out of greed . . . [and] females will be more likely to defect out of fear.

Hypothesis 1: Given equal levels of greed and fear in a social dilemma, females and males will be equally likely to cooperate.

Hypothesis 2: Given fear but no greed in a social dilemma, females will be less likely than males to cooperate.

Hypothesis 3: Given greed but no fear in a social dilemma, females will be more likely than males to cooperate.

Results: Study 2

The results are remarkably consistent with those of Study 1. Hypothesis 1, which predicts equal rates of cooperation from males and females in Prisoner's Dilemma, is supported: 34% of males and 37% of females cooperated . . . .

Results do not support [the second] hypothesis. Cooperation rates of males (41%) and females (42%) were virtually identical . . . .

Finally, [for] hypothesis 3 . . . the results are consistent with the results of Study 1 and with the hypothesis. . . . Females (47%) were more than twice as likely as males (22%) to cooperate in the Greed Dilemma . . . .

Discussion

The findings of Study 2 suggest that the Study 1 findings are quite robust. . . . As greed increased (from nonexistent in the Fear Dilemma, to intermediate in Prisoner's Dilemma, to the maximum in the Greed Dilemma), fewer and fewer males cooperated. . . . [However, the] results did not support the argument that females would respond more strongly than males to the fear component. The findings are therefore only partly in line with the reasoning of social-role theory. . . . The . . . results suggest that if social-

role *theory* and evolutionary psychology are to guide our understanding of the issue, alternative specifications are needed. . . .

As noted earlier, social dilemmas codify a wide range of situations that pose conflicts between individual and collective interests. . . . Consider, for example, how these findings might inform *research* on the mobilization of collective action. . . . These findings should also have import for a more commonplace phenomenon: everyday social and economic exchanges. . . . [As] discussed earlier, many types of exchanges entail high levels of greed. The *theory* and results reported earlier suggest we should expect more opportunistic acts from males . . . [which] may provide one micro-mechanism through which sex-based resource inequalities persist.

Source: Brent Simpson, "Sex, Fear, and Greed: A Social Dilemma Analysis of Gender and Cooperation." From *Social Forces,* Volume 82. Copyright © 2003 by the University of North Carolina Press. Used by permission of the publisher.

Critical Thinking Questions

1. What are the main components of social role theory presented in the excerpt?

2. Would you categorize social role theory as a macro-, meso-, or micro-level theory? Why?

3. This is an example of deductive research. The theory–research link is clear here because Simpson clearly identifies the hypotheses stemming from the theory and the results correctly refer back to the hypotheses. Has Simpson, however, completed the theory–research connection by discussing the theoretical implications of his findings and future theoretical direction? Why or why not?

Critical Thinking Discussion

1. First, let's identify some main concepts. These include (but are not necessarily limited to) social dilemmas, sex roles, successful role perfor-

BOX 2.1   **Theory and Research Practice, continued**

mance, role requirements, and social behavior. Sometimes concepts are complex and are more easily understood by examining specific subde-finitions or dimensions.

Simpson considers fear and greed to be dimensions of the broader idea of "social dilemma." A third aspect of concepts, typolo-gies, does not appear present here. The second main component, relationships, can be sum-marized as follows:

a. Specific roles are associated with different genders.
b. Specific skills and resources are necessary to successfully enact these gender roles.
c. People adapt their social behavior to exhibit these skills and resources.

Simpson then goes on to try to empirically test these relationships by defining what roles are associated with males (aggression) and females (fear), and how men and women enact them in a Prisoner's Dilemma.

2. Social role theory is a micro-level theory because it tries to explain the actions of individ-uals. Try not to get confused: Even though the theory is discussing the differences in behavior between men and women, which may appear to be two large groups—and therefore a macro-theory—it is examining the *individual choices* that men and women make; therefore, it is a micro-theory.

If you used the previous argument, a com-parison of men and women, then *all* social theory would be considered macro because, by definition, social science looks for patterns of behavior across aggregates. So the issue here isn't that you are comparing men and women, but instead *what* are you explaining about men and women? If you are explaining decisions that individuals make, this is a micro-process, even if you are looking at many indi-viduals and you want to see whether there is a *pattern* in those individual decisions for men and women.

3. Yes, Simpson has completed the theory–research connection. In his discussion, he eval-uates how the findings fit with the hypotheses and what the implications for social role theory are. He states that the data only partially support social role theory (and evolutionary theory, which is not part of the excerpt presented), which implies that the theory needs further development to adequately explain gender dif-ferences in behavior. Future research can aid theoretical development if it can empirically identify specific conditions where men and women may and may not cooperate. Simpson even goes as far as to suggest some different scenarios (those involving collective action or everyday social and economic exchanges) for researchers to examine men's and women's cooperation behavior.

Ethics in Social Research

If a professor told you to administer an electric shock to another person simply because that person answered a question incorrectly, would you? What about if the person telling you to administer the shock was a doctor? A police officer? A military general? You might *think* you wouldn't administer a shock to another person simply because he or she gave a wrong answer, but as Stanley Milgram found, chances are you actually *would*. And you're not alone.

In the mid-1970s, Stanley Milgram, intrigued by the atrocities of the Holocaust, wanted to see how "normal" people could come to commit such acts. At the time of Milgram's experiments, many people felt that blind obedience to authority, like the Nazi soldiers illustrated, was a trait common only to the Germans. After all, Americans were pretty sure that *they* would never have committed these acts. Milgram, on the other hand, wasn't so sure.

Milgram hypothesized that the behavior exhibited during the Holocaust had something to do with authority—that these people were responding to orders of others who had more authority than they did. To study the process of how everyday people can come to commit heinous acts, Milgram recruited a group of people to act as students and to express discomfort when people Milgram paid to be teachers asked them questions. The students were confederates in that they were aware of the experiment; the real subjects were the teachers. Milgram instructed the "teachers" to administer gradually more painful electric shocks every time the "students" answered a question incorrectly. Now remember, the students were part of the experiment—they were not really being shocked and any discomfort they expressed was acting. The teachers, however, did not know this.

Surprisingly, Milgram found that the teachers were generally willing to administer levels of voltage for the shocks that they believed to be dangerous—despite protests and expressions of "pain" from the "students." Remember, these "teachers" were everyday people like you and me. To be fair, many of them expressed personal unrest at these actions, but when "lab assistants" (also confederates) assured them that these shocks were scientifically necessary, the "teachers" generally continued giving them. After the experiment, when researchers asked why the "teachers" were generally willing to hurt subjects, the "teachers" responded that they complied because the lab assistants, who the "teachers" perceived as having scientific authority, told them to do so.

Milgram learned some very valuable information about human behavior from this experiment. First, he learned that Americans' obedience to authority was not so different from that of German scientists and soldiers; therefore, there was nothing peculiar about the German culture that led to the atrocities of the Holocaust. Second, Milgram learned that authority means power. Those who have authority can generally get others to do what they want, even if these people are initially resistant.

The experiment is now considered a classic in the social sciences. However, was the cost too high? Is it fair, or ethical, to cause research participants distress in the name of science? Milgram conducted debriefing sessions, where he explained the goals of the study—after it was completed—with participants. The point remains, however, that many subjects still experienced turmoil during and immediately after the experiment. Therefore, some social scientists questioned the ethical nature of the study.

Milgram is not alone. Philip Zimbardo (who, incidentally, was a high school classmate of Stanley Milgram) also conducted a now-classic study of authority but within a simulated prison instead of a student–teacher setting. In his experiment, Zimbardo paid male undergraduate volunteers to act as guards or prisoners in a mock prison setting. To make the roles more realistic, "guards" had uniforms, mirrored sunglasses, and nightsticks; "prisoners" wore prison clothes and were identified by numbers. Zimbardo instructed the "guards" not to use violence; however, Zimbardo found that the "guards" quickly exhibited aggressive and dehumanizing behavior toward the "prisoners" and the "prisoners" quickly became both passive and hostile toward the "guards." Therefore, in one sense, the experiment was a huge success. Zimbardo did show, as did Milgram, that authority can lead "normal" people to exhibit abnormal behavior. An article from the Stanford University New Service (1997) notes:

In his classic experiment, Zimbardo found that it does not take much for people to willingly follow those in authority.

From the perspective of the researchers, the experiment became exciting on day two when the prisoners staged a revolt. Once the guards had crushed the rebellion, "they steadily increased their coercive aggression tactics, humiliation and dehumanization of the prisoners," Zimbardo recalls. "The staff had to frequently remind the guards to refrain from such tactics," he said, and the worst instances of abuse occurred in the middle of the night when the guards thought the staff was not watching. The guards' treatment of the prisoners, such things as forcing them to clean out toilet bowls with their bare hands and act out degrading scenarios, or urging them to become snitches, "resulted in extreme stress reactions that forced us to release five prisoners, one a day, prematurely."

In fact, as the quote suggests, the experiment may have been *too* successful. Even though Zimbardo designed the experiment to last two weeks, he ended it after six days because he was concerned about the potential harm to the participants.

Even though Zimbardo tried to minimize the harm to participants by ending the experiment early, his study (like Milgram's) was still widely criticized at the time for how it treated human subjects. Although Zimbardo did follow guidelines of the Stanford human subject ethics committee—and had the experiment approved—studies like Zimbardo's and Milgram's (and there are many more to cite in addition to these two) made it clear to some that a code of ethics for social science research had to be more clearly defined. This leads us to a discussion of the evolution of ethical guidelines in the social sciences.

■ Brief History of Ethics in the Social Sciences

There are no universally defined ethical guidelines for all the social sciences to follow—each discipline generally has its own code of ethics. However, this does not mean that the ethical codes across the social sciences are not similar.

Historically, the Department of Health, Education and Welfare (HEW) established a code of ethics for those agencies or groups receiving federal funding for social research. Most basically, the HEW's guidelines focus on informed consent and review by an Institutional Review Board (IRB) before any research begins. **Institutional review boards** are responsible for making sure that the benefits to society outweigh any potential costs to the participants and that the procedures used in the research methodology include adequate safeguards to protect the identity, safety, and general well-being of participants. According to some, however, weighing the costs and benefits is problematic because potential costs cannot always be anticipated. For example, in the article for the Stanford University News Service mentioned earlier, Zimbardo notes that his study passed the human subjects ethics committee because the committee, as well as the researchers, never anticipated the reaction exhibited by the test subjects.

Informed consent is the other main element of the HEW's ethical guidelines. The HEW's original 1971 guidelines list six elements for obtaining informed consent, which, according to the guidelines, had to be obtained in writing (Code of Federal Regulations, 1975, pp. 11854–11858). These are:

1. A fair explanation of the procedures to be followed, and their purposes, including identification of any experiment procedures
2. A description of any attendant discomforts and risks that can be expected
3. A description of any benefits reasonably to be expected
4. A disclosure of any appropriate alternative procedures that might be advantageous for the subject
5. An offer to answer any inquiries concerning the procedures
6. Instructions that the person is free to withdraw consent and discontinue participation at any time without prejudice to him or her.

However, in some social science instances, especially, for example, when doing field research of the homeless or field research of subjects engaged in deviant or illegal behavior (such as gangs), such a rigid informed consent guideline is almost impossible. First, people may be hesitant to sign forms of any kind, especially if the subjects are being studied *because* of their criminal or deviant activities. Second, in the cases of homeless individuals, or similar groups of people, the subjects may be semi-literate. Consequently, not only may the subjects be suspicious of legal forms but they also may not be able to understand them enough to truly provide informed consent. Therefore, much of the dissatisfaction with the HEW's guidelines among social scientists stems from the HEW's tendency to make no distinction between social science and biomedical science. The HEW's guidelines apply equally to both broad disciplines, even though the research conducted among these disciplines is frequently very different.

In response to concerns like these, the National Research Act of 1974 was passed. This act created the National Commission for the Protection of Human Subjects, which, in turn, published the *Belmont Report,* which altered the ethical guidelines in such a way as to distinguish between social science and biomedical research. The Belmont Report broadly outlines three general ethical guidelines:

1. Respect for persons
2. Principle of beneficence
3. Principle of justice

The **respect for persons** recognizes that people are autonomous individuals and have the right to make decisions for themselves. Essentially, this guideline is referring to informed consent; however, it adds that if individuals, for whatever reason, cannot fully make informed consent (e.g., either through their own inabilities or through the design of the research), they are entitled to protection, and it is the researcher's responsibility to make sure that these individuals *are* protected. The **principle of beneficence** entails making sure that the research does not harm participants and that the researcher works to maximize the social, individual, and/or scientific benefits of the research while minimizing any potential harm. Last, the **principle of justice** requires that the benefits and burdens of research be distributed equitably through the selection of subjects. This means that no one group of subjects should be unduly rewarded or encumbered relative to another group.

If you are saying to yourself that these three guidelines seem very vague, you are right. However, they are purposively designed that way because the various social sciences deal with different research questions and therefore different ethical concerns. Consequently, as part of the changes from the Belmont Report, the role of the government in ethical decisions is lower than in the past, whereas the role of IRB is stronger. This makes the monitoring of ethical standards more localized to the researcher's home institution, which (theoretically) has a better understanding of the details of the researcher's project.

This section began by stating that there is no universal code of ethics across the different disciplines in the social sciences. This is true. However, if you peruse the websites for the national organizations in each discipline (the links are available at the end of this chapter), you will see that they all deal with similar issues such as professional and scientific standards, informed consent, confidentiality, research planning/implementation, and dissemination—just to name a few. As the codes of ethics for each individual social science discipline suggests, social scientists have ethical responsibilities to science and to society as well as to the people who participate in their studies. Let's examine some of the ethical responsibilities in each of these three areas.

■ Ethical Responsibility to Science

People do research to find answers to questions. As stated previously, researchers try to avoid "reinventing the wheel" every time they embark on a research project. To avoid this, they conduct the literature reviews I mentioned earlier in this chapter. However, the fundamental assumption regarding literature reviews is that the published research is as accurate as possible—in terms of the research design, study implementation, and interpretation of results. Consequently, any research project or implementation of findings relies, to some degree, on the quality of the research that comes before it. If you looked up the code of ethics for your discipline, you will notice that in all the social sciences, there are explicit expectations about the relationship between the researcher and the researcher's responsibility to science (see Figure 2.4). I will focus on only four ethical issues pertaining directly to science here. These are the issues of research fraud, plagiarism, the role of values in research, and the roles of organizations in research.

Research Fraud

Cyril Burt was a famous British educational psychologist who studied the genetic intelligence of twins. However, soon after Burt's death in 1971, two psychologists, Leon Kamin and Arthur Jensen, independently began to question Burt's work. The concern among these two psychologists centered on the nature of Burt's data. Briefly, Burt studied monozygotic twins who were reared apart. In his first study in 1943, he reported 15 sets of monozygotic twins. In 1955, he added 6 sets of twins to the study for a total of 21 sets, and by 1966, he more than doubled that number by reporting on 53 pairs of monozygotic twins. Both

Sociology: The full code of ethics is available at the American Sociological Association webpage under the "Resources for Sociologists" subsection. www.asanet.org/members/ecoderev.html.

Psychology: The full code of ethics is available from a link at the American Psychological Association homepage. www.apa.org/ethics/code2002.html.

Political Science: The full code of ethics is available under the "Publications" subsection of the American Psychological Association homepage. www.apsanet.org/pubs/ethics.cfm.

Social Work: The full code of ethics is available from a search for the word "ethics" from the National Association of Social Workers homepage. www.socialworkers.org/pubs/code/code.asp.

Figure 2.4 Code of Ethics Websites

Kamin and Jensen noted that 53 was an unusually high number of monozygotic twin pairs—especially those reared apart. In fact, in 1955, Burt himself noted that his sample size of 21 (at that time) was unusually high (Plucker, 2003). Tucker (1997) further questioned this number when he examined all the research studies on twins between 1922 and 1990 and found that the *total* number of twins studied across these studies still did not reach 53—the number that Burt claimed to have in just one study.

Although some people support Burt's work and argue that he did not violate ethical standards (Joynson, 1989), most cite it as an example of **research fraud.** Research fraud is believed to be relatively rare, but it occurs when researchers invent or intentionally distort information. Many believe that Burt committed research fraud by fabricating twin sets (thereby boosting his numbers). Some also argue that Burt made up research assistants (Plucker, 2003; Tucker, 1997). However, the last point is more debated because it can be convincingly argued that Burt used pseudonyms to protect the identity of his research assistants (and since the controversy started after his death, he cannot explain his reasons for this if it indeed is what he did). Either way, research fraud is problematic because anyone reading a study and using its information as a basis for his or her own research, or even more directly as a foundation for a program or policy, would base decisions on lies or misinformation. At the very least, fraud can involve a waste of time and money as researchers and practitioners follow an incorrect path. At the very most, research fraud can be problematic if it potentially puts researchers, participants, or clients at undue risk for harm by providing false information.

An important note is that not all mistakes or inconsistencies in research are fraudulent. Social scientists are people doing research on people, so errors somewhere—whether it is in coding, how a sample was drawn, or how findings are interpreted—are possible. Social scientists have the responsibility to do their best to minimize errors, and those who do not run the risk of committing fraud. However, just because some errors may be present in a study does not automatically mean that that researcher was dishonest.

Most research articles appearing in print are peer reviewed, which means that other researchers in the field with similar expertise critically read and evaluate a researcher's work before the study gets published. This process weeds out many, but not all, of the studies with obvious errors. However, some error may be unavoidable, as research (in any discipline, including the traditional sciences) is designed by fallible people in an imperfect world. Consequently, readers still have the responsibility to critically read and question any findings or methodologies that do not make sense or that do not fit with the current theoretical explanations. In fact, this is why I have included the sections for evaluating research at the end of each chapter in this book.

Even scientists sometimes fall prey to unethical behavior. Cyril Burt was a British researcher who faked data on twins to support his theories.

Plagiarism

Another responsibility researchers have to science is to avoid **plagiarism.** Many of you are probably familiar with the concept of plagiarism from writing papers in high school and college. The idea is the same for research articles. Researchers, like students, have the ethical responsibility to give credit to the ideas or work that they borrow from other people. Failure to do so means that the researcher is basically taking credit for these ideas, even when they are not the researcher's—and that is plagiarism. Even excessive paraphrasing can be considered plagiarism if the researcher doesn't give credit to the original author of the ideas.

Perhaps the most extreme form of plagiarism by a professional is the case of Elias A. K. Alsabti. Alsabti, an exceptionally prolific medical student, allegedly plagiarized some 60 complete papers between 1977 and 1980 (Barber, 2002). Alsabti would copy the entire article, changing only the title and substituting his name for the name of the original author. The fact that his "articles" were published illustrates the fallibility of the peer review system—which is why individual readers also bear responsibility to read articles critically.

The role of values in research

Researchers have the responsibility to remain value free during their research. This is more challenging than it sounds. Researchers obviously choose topics that have some interest to them; going through all the steps of research would be almost painful if one had absolutely no interest in the topic. Furthermore, researchers, especially those designing or evaluating programs, plan on *using* the findings in the real world. Hence, a researcher may have a personal interest in interpreting findings in a way that supports her or his personal views as opposed to remaining value free, as the goal of science requires.

Not only can it be very tempting to focus only on the parts of a problem or on interpreting findings in a way that correlates to personal or social goals, but researchers may be tempted to give into political pressure as well (after all, some people's jobs may depend on the nature of the research findings). This trap is hard to avoid and there is no magic bullet for doing so. A researcher's only defense is to remember that his or her primary responsibility is to science. However, even I recognize the weakness of this suggestion.

The roles of sponsoring organizations in research

Since most researchers are not wealthy enough to fund their own research, part of their ethical responsibility to science is to be clear about the role of funding organizations.

When researchers team with organizations or agencies to conduct studies on their behalf, these agencies obviously hope for very specific results. No organization wants to hear that its program or product has negative consequences, is ineffective, or is so full of problems that it is unsalvageable. Consequently, organizational leaders may decide that if they do not like the research findings, they do not want the findings to be published. Essentially, they may want to "bury" the report. The behavior of the tobacco industry is an example of this.

Research has clearly documented an association between smoking and specific health problems such as lung cancer and emphysema. For years, the tobacco companies sponsored research to determine the effect of tobacco on smokers' health. Some critics argue that, like other researchers, the tobacco companies found a link between smoking and poor health, but they did not like the findings and, consequently, allegedly suppressed the negative findings (Hirschhorn, 1999).

Clearly, a funding source's desire to produce specific results and a researcher's desire to have the findings used appropriately or publicized can conflict. In a purely academic view, negative findings, unanticipated findings (even if negative), or statistically insignificant findings can be just as informative as findings that support research hypotheses or goals. Therefore, a researcher may feel an ethical responsibility to science to publish any findings. On the other hand, if it wasn't for the sponsor, the research is not likely to be done in the first place. Hence, the researcher is in a difficult position: Follow the rules of the party paying for the research or follow the rules of the research community.

The only real way to prevent this problem is to have a contract with the funding agency prior to any research. In this contract, the researcher needs to clearly specify that the researcher has control over the findings of the study, or at least that the researcher can publish findings in relevant academic journals. Sometimes if the problem of publishing the study's results comes after the researcher and funding agency signed a contract, the researcher may be concerned about personal or professional relations with the funding organization, who is partially responsible for the researcher's ability to put food on the table. In these instances, the researcher should at least state specifically who the funding agency is in any written reports. Critical readers then have the responsibility of evaluating whether they think the funding source had any bearing on the nature of presented findings.

To summarize, this section addressed four main responsibilities researchers have to science: responsibility to avoid research fraud, responsibility to avoid plagiarism, responsibility to remain value free, and responsibility to be mindful of the role of organizations. Following are the summary guidelines for how to practically fulfill one's responsibility to science.

1. Be vigilant and thorough in designing research.
2. Make all research steps clear and public by mentioning them in written reports.
3. Give credit where credit is due. Make sure that all borrowed information is properly cited.
4. Consciously avoid the tendency or temptation to become attached to specific outcomes.
5. When working with the public or with specific agencies/programs, researchers need to ensure that they do not assume—or even appear to assume—any nonresearch roles.
6. Make it clear in any contracts that the researcher has control over the dissemination of findings. If full control is not possible, try to negotiate the right to publish findings

in academic journals. (These are not as frequently read by the general public; however, other researchers interested in the topic will still have access to the study's findings.)

7. When research is funded by an outside agency, always make it clear in any written reports who funded the research.

■ Ethical Responsibility to Participants

In the beginning of this section, I described Milgram's and Zimbardo's experiments and mentioned that each of them caused some psychological distress to the participants. Consequently, some researchers argue that although the studies were informative, this information came at the cost of some ethical considerations—that is, the responsibility to do no harm to participants. Institutional Review Boards have the responsibility to oversee the ethical treatment of individuals; however, researchers still have the initial responsibility to make sure that their designs comply with ethical guidelines. What follows are some of the main ethical considerations researchers need to address when studying individuals.

Voluntary participation

Most social science research intrudes into people's lives to some degree. Not only do research participants have to donate time to participate in studies but also social scientists frequently ask personal questions—questions that participants may not be willing to discuss even with their closest friends. Furthermore, social scientists can't even justify this intrusion by arguing that the information gathered will directly benefit the participants—it likely won't. At best, researchers can tell participants that this information will benefit humanity, but "humanity" is such a huge and vague concept that most people can't even concretely grasp its scope.

Therefore, like other research, such as medical research, participation in all social science studies must be voluntary. **Voluntary participation** means that people will allow researchers to intrude on their lives on their own free will. This may not be as simple as it sounds. If a sociology professor wants to study college students and asks members of his classes to complete surveys, these students may feel obligated to do so in order to make a good impression on the professor (or, perhaps more accurately, avoid standing out as a "trouble maker"). Is this voluntary? Or a coordinator of a drug treatment court may require program graduates who are checking in for quarterly reports to complete a survey about their drug and employment information in order for the coordinator to study success of the program three, six, nine, and twelve months after clients leave it. Is this voluntary?

Some would argue that neither of these examples is purely voluntary, much in the same way that some could argue that research that offers a cash incentive may not be voluntary because low-income individuals may be more attracted to a cash incentive than middle-class individuals. On the other hand, one can argue that using only willing participants may threaten research generalizability. Much like a high school reunion, where only the class members who feel content with their lives attend (therefore, they are similar on this one trait—contentment), one can argue that those who choose to participate in studies may share general traits that predispose them to participating.

So how do researchers truly establish voluntary participation without biasing results? They probably can't. To some degree, voluntary participation is more easily achieved in theory than in practice. However, from an ethical point of view, a researcher has adequately fulfilled this requirement if she or he tells the respondent the general topic or nature of research, makes it clear that participation is perfectly voluntary (meaning that there are no special rewards for participating or punishments for not participating), and makes it clear to that participant that he or she can stop participation in the study at any time. However, even these are just general guidelines. For example, we will see with survey research that researchers frequently offer incentives, such as coupons or small cash payments ($1 or $5) to participate. So long as the rewards are very small—really only tokens—one can be more confident that those who choose to participate in the survey are doing so voluntarily. To some degree, the next ethical responsibility, achieving informed consent, also addresses the issue of voluntary participation.

Informed consent

Researchers have the ethical responsibility to make sure that participants have a clear idea of what they are getting into when they agree to participate in a study. In other words, researchers need to tell individuals any information that might influence that person's decision to participate in the study. To achieve *informed consent*, researchers have to make sure they specify:

1. The purpose of the research
2. Any potential risks or harms the participants may experience
3. Any benefits the participants may experience
4. The procedures used in the research
5. Who is funding the research
6. Incentives/payments for participation (if any)
7. That participation in the research is voluntary
8. That confidentiality or anonymity is guaranteed

After participants are told the parameters of the research, if they agree to participate, scientists can assume that this participation is informed and voluntary.

Specifying the *purpose of the research* does not mean that researchers must tell the respondents their hypothesis. In order to avoid having participants alter their behavior to fit what they think is the researcher's hypothesis, some deception in research is allowed—and frankly, common. For example, in Zimbardo's prison experiment, Zimbardo was really studying people's conformity to authority. However, all he had to tell participants was that he was studying the dynamics between prisoners and guards in a pseudo-prison setting. Technically, conformity to authority is part of prisoner–guard dynamics, so, at least with this aspect of informed consent, Zimbardo was well within his ethical limits to tell the participants only as much as he did. Remember, Zimbardo (and his university's human subjects ethics committee) never anticipated the mock prisoners and guards to behave as they did; therefore, Zimbardo could not even warn potential participants of this behavior in order to achieve informed consent.

One point I do want to make clear, and I'll briefly cover this again in Chapter 6 when I discuss the ethics involved in experiments: Just because some deception may be necessary does not mean that researchers have carte blanche to deceive. The deception has to be handled carefully, wherein the researcher may tell participants part of the truth, just not the complete truth. Furthermore, even with some allowable deception, the researcher cannot deceive the participant regarding any foreseeable harm—physical, social, legal or psychological. This leads me to the next responsibility.

BOX 2.2	Example of Cover Letter

It is no secret that Americans are overweight. Our culture is one of indulgence and our food practices are no different. Recognizing this, many seek to change this aspect of our culture and to live a healthier lifestyle. Below is the cover letter for a survey where the researchers were interested in trying to figure out how the workplace environment could encourage a healthier lifestyle. Read the cover letter and answer the critical thinking questions.

To All Employees;

You may have heard talk about how eating less fat and more fruits and vegetables, and being more physically active can help people feel healthier and more productive.

The hard part is making the changes. We have to find time in our day for a walk, or take extra steps for a healthier snack or meal when fast and easy is the first concern.

The Tompkins County Health Department (TCHD) is looking at how people can address these concerns at their worksite. The goal is to help employees with an interest in healthy eating and physical activity find *encouragement and support* at work.

TCHD is looking to worksites for ideas and we've been invited to participate. If you have ideas about how to make our worksite more supportive of a healthy lifestyle, jot them down! We'll take 3 or 4 ideas and actually try them out here at our worksite. The more suggestions the better, so please join in! Staff members from the Health Department's Health Promotion Program will be working with us on this.

For a start, look over the *[attached] survey*. The questions will give you a better sense of the kind of ideas we want. Your answers will help us understand where your interests lie. Please take a minute to complete the survey today and give it to your supervisor. To keep your answers anonymous please do not sign the survey. Write your ideas and suggestions on the back of the page.

Thanks for your interest and input!

Source: www.co.tompkins.ny.us/wellness/worksite/survey/surveyex1.html.

Critical Thinking Questions

1. Is the purpose of the research clear?

2. Does the letter address any potential risks or harms the participants may experience?

3. Are there any benefits the participants may experience?

4. What are the research procedures?

5. Who is funding the research (if applicable)?

6. Are there any incentives/payments for participation? If so, what?

7. Did the researcher state that participation in the research is voluntary?

8. Has the researcher expressed how he or she will guarantee anonymity or confidentiality?

9. Is this a good example of a cover letter?

Critical Thinking Answers

1. Yes. The survey is designed so people at this particular worksite can get ideas on how to make a healthier workplace (in terms of eating and physical activity).

2. No. This is just a survey; it is not a survey about behaviors or experiences that most people find threatening

3. No benefits are directly stated; however, an indirect benefit may be that it gives workers a say in organizing their worksite and in finding "encouragement and support."

4. The research procedure is a survey and there is a link to it.

5. This is not clear. It may be that Tompkins County Health Department is funding the researcher since the TCHD is mentioned; however, this is not explicitly stated.

| BOX 2.2 | Example of Cover Letter, *continued* |

6. No incentives or payments are mentioned.

7. No, the researcher did not explicitly state that participation is voluntary. However, the entire tone of the cover letter is casual and it may be that the implication is that it is voluntary.

8. The researcher directs people not to put their names on the survey in order to protect anonymity. However, anyone completing the survey has to submit the survey to his or her boss. This means that the boss could feasibly match responses to identity; however, unless the boss is a member of the research team,

technically this does not violate anonymity since the *researcher* cannot match identities to responses.

9. This is an adequate example of a cover letter. There is some information that could be more explicitly stated (benefits to participation, whether the Tompkins County Health Department is funding the research, that the survey is voluntary) and the issue of anonymity may be questionable in some circumstances. However, overall, the cover letter addresses the main elements for informed consent.

The second issue in informed consent is *informing subjects of potential harms and benefits*. There are a multitude of ways that research can harm participants. Harm can be individual (such as psychological distress), legal (such as getting arrested), or social (such as being stigmatized by family and friends or losing one's job). Researchers can easily prevent most of these with safeguards in the research design so that the issues do not merit discussion for informed consent.

When the research design, for example, cannot avoid some level of potential distress, researchers have the ethical responsibility to be truthful about the risks. In surveys, for example, informing subjects of potential harm in the informed consent process generally means warning participants that some questions may be of a personal nature and/or may cause discomfort. Simply telling respondents that they have the right to skip any questions that they do not want to answer usually fulfills this ethical responsibility.

However, if the research could cause more serious psychological issues or if there are any potential physical or legal risks to participation, the researcher has the responsibility not only to bring those to the attention of the participant but also to inform the participant of any help that may be provided. For example, if interviewing rape victims, the researcher may warn potential participants that they will be asked some detailed questions about the rape event and that they can refuse to answer any questions. However, since rape is a traumatic event, the researcher should also mention some resources available to the participants if dredging up memories of the event causes them particular distress at the end of the interview. This may be as basic as providing a hotline number or more concrete such as a providing the phone number of a counselor who the participants can contact if needed.

Stanley Milgram tried to address this issue by having a debriefing session after individual experiments when the researchers informed the "teachers" (test subjects) of the real purpose of the study and assured them that no individuals were actually harmed. Furthermore, Zimbardo tried to minimize the unforeseen harm to his subjects by ending the study early once he realized that the "prisoners" and "guards" were too closely identifying with their roles and he became worried about their psychological and physical well-being.

Just as the researcher has a responsibility to tell participants of potential harm, the researcher also has the responsibility to discuss *potential benefits* (the third component of informed consent). For example, if a researcher is interviewing residents about the local police, he or she may state that this research is going to be used to help the police better serve the neighborhood. Informing participants of any incentives to participate (e.g., a small cash payment) may also be considered informing them of the study benefits; however, as incentives are used almost as a form of bribery for participation and not a general benefit of the research itself (whereas the potential harm is harm that may arise from the research itself), incentives really deserve their own mention independent of any benefits that may arise out of the research itself.

Fourth, participants need to know the *general design of the research* in which they are being asked to participate. Is it a survey? One or more interviews? An experiment? Participants may be willing to participate in a "once-and-done" survey (otherwise known as a *cross-sectional survey*), but they may not want the researcher intruding in their lives on a regular basis for a longitudinal survey. Likewise, participants may be willing to participate in an interview, but they may feel less comfortable with participating in an experiment.

Not only do the participants need to know the general research design but they also need to know the details of the particular study itself. How long will it take? What does the participant have to do? Potential participants may be perfectly fine with participating in an experiment, until they learn that they will need to deliver an "electric shock" to another human being. Although they may not mind being in an experiment, they may not want to be a part of that *particular* experiment.

Informing possible participants of the *agency funding the research* is the fifth component of informed consent. Knowledge of the funding agency helps give participants the opportunity to decline participation based on their own ethical values. For example, a person who is strongly against abortion may be unwilling to participate in a study sponsored by Planned Parenthood because that person may feel that the findings will be used to further the cause of a social issue that he or she does not support. On the other hand, that same person may choose to participate because it is a way to have the funding agency consider his or her views. Either way, the point is that the individual gets to decide whether he or she wants to participate in the study, and knowing the funding agency may be a factor in that decision.

As I mentioned previously, since *incentives* for participation (the sixth criterion for informed consent) are a type of bribery, they may negatively affect the voluntary nature of research. A college student, for example, may be more enticed to participate in a study that pays $10 than would a middle-aged person. However, if the incentive is small and a mere token at best, the risk for this can be minimized. Some researchers, especially when doing surveys, get around this problem by giving the incentive with the solicitation, so that everyone approached receives the incentive regardless of each person's decision to participate. The hope is that even those who may not ordinarily want to participate (thereby making sure that participants are not necessarily of a specific personality trait) may still do so out of a sense of obligation. Is this voluntary? Not completely, of course, but as you've probably already guessed, achieving pure voluntary participation is problematic no matter what the instance.

The studies that do rely purely on volunteers (no incentives) may be attracting a certain personality type that may influence findings; studies that offer incentives may not be perfectly voluntary in that some people will participate out of a sense of obligation. Whichever approach you choose, whichever view you take, largely depends on the nature of the research questions you are asking. The bottom line is this: If you are going to offer any incentives to encourage participation, individuals need to know that up front in order to decide whether they want to be a part of your study.

Seventh, I've already discussed the *voluntary* nature of research to some extent, so I won't go into much detail about it here. For the purposes of achieving informed consent, just keep in mind that the researcher has the responsibility to tell individuals that they are not required to participate in the study, that they can decline to answer any questions, and that they can decide to end their participation at any time. And, of course, the researcher has to honor these wishes if they do arise during the course of a study.

Last, *guaranteeing confidentiality or anonymity* is an ethical responsibility to individuals independent of informed consent, just like having voluntary participation. I will discuss this in more detail in the next section. The point here is that a respondent's identity should not be linked to his or her comments at any time in a published report. Therefore, the researcher has the ethical responsibility to tell the respondent how his or her identity will be protected.

To summarize, obtaining informed consent means telling an individual about any aspect of the study that may affect that person's decision to participate. It does not mean telling the person your research hypotheses. Nor does it mean confusing the individual with technical jargon or the minute specifics of your research design. It simply means highlighting the general purpose of the research (with a little deception as to not bias participants' behavior), any potential risks and benefits to the individual, the general procedures, the funding source, how the researcher intends to protect this person's identity, and, if present, any incentives for participation.

This is not necessarily as easy as it sounds. Subjects need to be able to understand these issues before they can give informed consent. Therefore, the language must be clear and simple. Furthermore, you may need to think of alternative ways of presenting the information. For example, you might need to read the information to participants who cannot read or, for subjects who do not speak English, you will need to make sure that you or someone else can describe the research procedures in the person's native tongue.

Achieving informed consent helps ensure that the research is voluntary. It also helps ensure that the benefits of the research outweigh its costs by giving the participants some power over that decision. If individuals do not feel that the benefits outweigh the costs of the research, they generally will not choose to participate. If enough people decline participation, that is a signal to the researcher that there is something fundamentally wrong with the risks associated with the research as designed.

Protection from harm

When you think of protecting your research participants from harm, physical harm is probably what you think of first. True, researchers have to protect their subjects from physical injury that is directly related to the research design. For example, if another researcher wanted to replicate Zimbardo's experiment, this person would definitely not give the "guards" weapons such as knives (knowing that Zimbardo found that the subjects will too eagerly grasp their roles), but the researcher may not want to give the "guards" batons (nightsticks) either, because a "guard" could potentially use it to harm an "inmate." Technically, researchers call this responsibility the **principle of nonmaleficence,** which simply means the responsibility to do no harm.

Physical harm is a risk with other types of observation, too. Field research of criminal behavior can lead to physical harm to subjects if other people find out about the research and are against the subjects' participation. For example, what if a researcher decides to study the influence of teen peer groups on violent behavior? Some teens may be willing to participate in the study, but some of their friends may not and may resent having those who do participate reveal information about their actions. As a result, the teens who do not want their behavior revealed to the researcher may threaten (or worse) the teens who are participating in the study.

Researchers also must protect their subjects from psychological, social, and legal harm (see Table 2.3). *Psychological harm* usually refers to various forms of emotional distress. *Social harm* can include embarrassment, ostracizing, job loss, and problems with interpersonal relationships that result from participation in the study. For example, if a researcher

TABLE 2.3 Potential Harms Relevant to Social Science Research

Type of Harm	Effect on:	
	Individual	Wider Society
Physical injury	Physical pain, personal cost of treatment; fear; diminished trust	Cost of treatment; diminished trust
Psychological injury	Damaged interpersonal relations; personal discomfort	
Legal	Investigation by authorities; arrest	Person or groups in question are stigmatized regardless of guilt or innocence; cost of criminal justice proceedings
Social	Loss of job, damaged interpersonal relations; stigmatization	Scapegoating, stereotyping, or vilifying certain groups
Loss of privacy, anonymity, or confidentiality	Reduced control over how one presents self to others	Reduction of general privacy; concern that continually watched
	Public exposure that may lead to other psychological, physical, legal, or social harm	

is doing a study on workplace morale and a boss recognizes the identity of a disgruntled worker (even if the researcher tries to maintain confidentiality) and the boss fires that worker as a result, this researcher has violated the ethical responsibility to do no harm. The worker received negative social consequences as a result of participation in the study.

Research can also lead to *legal harm* if, through the research, authorities learn of criminal behavior and prosecute the participant. If you are studying inner-city gangs and you describe a criminal act of a gang member with enough detail that the police can identify this individual and, as a result, the police put that person under surveillance and he or she gets arrested, that's a legal harm to the participant. Now, you may be thinking that if a person commits a crime, then that person deserves to be arrested. This could be a valid argument. However, if it was *your research* that either provided evidence for the police or in some other way led to this individual's arrest, you are now in a fuzzy ethical area. Is your ethical responsibility to the individual or to the wider society? There is no easy answer to this; similar situations will be discussed later in the chapter.

Legal harm does not just refer to catching individuals in criminal acts they may do regardless of your research. Research may lead to potential harm of participants by the authorities, as Latané and Darley (1970) found when they staged "crimes" to study the instances when witnesses would intervene. One of the staged "crimes" was a liquor hold-up; however, one of the witnesses called the police, who arrived with drawn guns. The potential for physical and legal harm to both researchers and participants here is clear.

Confidentiality and anonymity

Perhaps the best way to protect an individual from harmful ramifications for participating in research is to protect that person's identity. This is generally done by guaranteeing the subject either confidentiality or anonymity. Researchers protect subjects' **anonymity** when the researchers themselves cannot link a piece of information to a subject's individual identity. Mail surveys that have no identification numbers are a good example of this. Researchers who use mail surveys have no way of matching individual surveys with names selected in their samples if they do not have identification numbers matching the surveys and names. This can be especially useful when surveying deviant behavior. People may be more willing to reveal their behavior if they understand (and believe) that there is no way that the information can be individually linked to them.

Many people mistakenly use the term *anonymity* when they really mean **confidentiality.** Unlike anonymity, where the researcher cannot match information to a person, with confidentiality, the researcher *can* identify the information with a specific person, but promises not to reveal that person's identity to others. With confidentiality, the researcher assures the participants that he or she will not reveal their identities publicly. The researcher usually accomplishes this by using pseudonyms, or fake names, when he or she needs to publicize a person's information. The key to confidentiality is for the researcher to make sure that she or he does not use too much description or does not mention unique characteristics that would enable those familiar with the research or geographical area to identify the participants. For example, in his work *Street Corner Society*, William Foote Whyte (1955) studied the social dynamics of a group of young men in the West End of Boston. He used pseudonyms such as "Doc" and "Chic" to describe his participants; however, another researcher, Herbert Gans, later studied the same area of Boston and noted that one of the candidates in an election that occurred during the course of his study was a person who Whyte included in his book. Because Whyte provided a detailed description of the person in his book, even though Whyte used a pseudonym to protect this person's identity, members of the community were able to identify the individual and voters responded to him negatively based on what they read in Whyte's study (Gans, 1962). Therefore, by violating confidentiality, Whyte's research also indirectly led to social harm for that participant because this person lost an election, in part, because of information others learned about him from Whyte's work.

Confidentiality can also be appropriate for survey research. One drawback to anonymous surveys is that longitudinal study may be difficult because individuals cannot be tracked across time and researchers have no way of telling which sample members actually participated in the study. Researchers who intend to track individuals over time or monitor specific returns may decide to match survey responses to sample members by an identification number. If this is the case, any identifying information (such as on an envelope) should be destroyed as soon as it is received and a master copy linking the identification numbers with the names and addresses of the respondents should be kept under lock and key and should be accessed only by the primary researchers for legitimate purposes.

Even though potential subjects need to be apprised of any potential harm they may experience by participating in research, this notification does not alleviate the researcher from the responsibility of preventing the harm in the first place. For example, some social research may involve very personal information that may produce psychological or social distress or embarrassment to participants. Questions about drug use, sexual orientation, sexual behavior, or other deviant behavior that is stigmatized may make respondents uncomfortable and/or cause them embarrassment if their answers were ever revealed. The best way to avoid this problem is to be vigilant about protecting anonymity or confidentiality and to provide resources for participants to contact if they need help.

Reciprocity

Without willing participants, there would be no research. The very least researchers can do is to keep any promises or agreements with subjects made during the course of the study. This is the ethical responsibility of **reciprocity.** If researchers promise an incentive to participate, they have the ethical obligation to deliver that incentive as soon as possible after a subject's participation. When researchers promise confidentiality, they have to do their best to fulfill that promise and not let the role of science get in the way of that fulfillment.

In the course of field research, researchers become more than just casual observers. They participate in the lives of those they are studying. As part of that participation, they have the ethical responsibility to help or assist their subjects in any legal way possible during the course of the study. The ethical responsibility of reciprocity is obvious; it is also very important. Reciprocity establishes the foundation of trust that is important in all research, but especially in the social science. In the social sciences, researchers rely on individuals to express their views and experiences. The biomedical sciences, on the other hand, can gather their data by mechanical medical tests that rely less on the goodwill of participants.

Summary

To summarize, researchers have the following ethical responsibilities to individuals:

1. Ensure voluntary participation.
2. Obtain informed consent.

3. Protect anonymity/confidentiality.
4. Avoid harm (the principle of nonmaleficence).
5. Ensure reciprocity.

To be sure, more ethical responsibilities to individuals exist. These are just five of the main responsibilities that are present in all social science research. The websites for the national organizations for specific social science disciplines also outline the ethical responsibilities that each discipline finds important. Checking out those sites will give you a more detailed description of the responsibilities to individuals in your discipline.

■ Ethical Responsibility to Society

Because most of social science occurs within a natural setting (as opposed to a laboratory), researchers cannot always control all the elements affecting their research. Researchers do have the responsibility to protect not only the participants from harm but also innocent bystanders who are not directly involved in a study but who may still be affected by it. Sometimes participants behave in undesirable and, frankly, illegal ways. As I described with the hypothetical gang situation in the discussion about the principle of nonmaleficence, sometimes the ethical guidelines are confusing. Does a researcher protect the participant or protect the wider society? Here, the researcher has to use his or her own judgment, recognizing that there is little legal protection for people in their role as researchers. Unfortunately, I cannot provide more concrete guidance here. All I can say is that in a life or death situation, or other similarly serious situation, the researcher's responsibility to society may outweigh the researcher's responsibility to an individual participant. For example, if a research participant plans a murder and the researcher knows about it but does nothing to prevent the act, the researcher may be legally liable—not to mention that the researcher may have the death of another human being on his or her conscience.

■ Problems with Ethical Responsibilities

As you can probably tell by the example I just represented, ethical issues are not always easy to follow, nor are they always clear. In fact, there have been times in this chapter where I illustrated that ethical responsibilities in two or more areas sometimes directly conflict. So I think it is useful to discuss some concrete areas in which ethical responsibilities may be unclear or conflicting.

Legal issues

Social scientists are like priests and lawyers in that people may confess behaviors that are not only deviant but also illegal. However, unlike priests and lawyers (or other client-oriented practitioners), social scientists have no legally recognized privilege of confidentiality. This means that, technically, even though you try to guarantee your research subjects confidentiality, if subpoenaed, you might not be able to uphold this promise. In other words, if legal authorities demand a social scientist to discuss information, researchers have a choice. They can break their promise of confidentiality or they can keep their promise and go to jail. However, we need to look at this in context. Although these legal limitations are true, a study by Soloway and Walters (1977) found only one instance of where a scientist was subpoenaed (and in this instance the subpoena was later dropped). Therefore, these concerns do not appear to be a great risk.

Also, legal issues relate not only to what subjects may tell researchers but also to what researchers may observe in the course of their research. For example, if a researcher is studying gangs and the gang commits a drive-by shooting, under criminal law the researcher could be charged with obstruction of justice or with being an accessory to a crime.

In reality, some of the practical risk of these issues is low because since the mid-1990s researchers have had more protection than in the past. According to the National Institute of Justice, research information, in most circumstances, is protected from the legal process and cannot be admitted as evidence in any judicial proceeding without the consent of the person involved. However, this applies only if the researcher has some evidence that she or he promised participants confidentiality *prior* to the beginning of the research.

Lack of clear definitions

Some ethical problems also stem from the disagreement over the meaning of an ethical issue or the lack of clear definitions. For example, does doing no harm to participants mean that it is unethical for participants to feel *any* psychological distress or anxiety during research? Or does it mean that participants shouldn't feel lasting distress after the study ends? If participants are allowed to experience some distress—after all, talking about deviant behavior or victimization experiences may cause *some* distress—how much is allowable? Should the possibility of any harm, even a little, prevent social research?

Furthermore, although researchers have an ethical responsibility to protect respondents' identities, what about instances where, if the context was different, reporting would be mandatory? What if during the course of a study a researcher realizes or suspects that a child she or he is interviewing is experiencing abuse? Doesn't the researcher have an ethical responsibility to the child to try to help him or her? Or would reporting the incidence in the name of "help" violate confidentiality and create more problems for the child?

Clearly, ethical guidelines are just that—*guidelines*. They are purposefully vague to provide researchers some flexibility. Obviously, no study is going to be completely voluntary, and obviously, there may be instances where confidentiality may have to be violated for legal reasons or to protect the participant in other ways. Consequently, ethical guidelines, to some degree, specify what "ought" to happen in the course of social science research. The term **ethical relativism** recognizes that ethics stem from social values, and, as such, a behavior that is ethical in one context may not be in another. In the example where a researcher suspects child abuse among one of his or her research subjects, violating confidentiality may be viewed as unethical; however, not getting the child help may be viewed as unethical as well.

The bottom line is that researchers need to make every possible effort to foresee any possible potential ethical problems in their research and then to address those problems so they either disappear or are minimized. In the case of minimizing ethical dilemmas, researchers must continually evaluate whether the benefits resulting from their research outweigh the potential ethical costs of conducting it. If, at any time, the costs of the research outweigh the benefits, researchers have the ethical responsibility to redesign their study in such a way that this is no longer the case.

One of the goals of this book is to introduce you to realistic social research. The methods I will discuss are the methods to which researchers should aim to achieve; however, actually being able to accomplish or include the "best" strategies for all research is not always feasible. Therefore, in understanding realistic social research, one has to know which concessions—due to time, design, resources, or other reasons—are acceptable.

■ Evaluating Your Selection of Research Topics

This selection does not directly address evaluating the research of others, but instead addresses evaluating the topic *you* plan to research and report. In accordance with some of the issues I presented in the first chapter of this book, there are some guidelines for budding researchers to remember when designing their own research projects.

1. *Be cautious of studying topics for which you have a strong personal identification or interest.*

Obviously, research topics that relate to people's individual interests are more attractive to them. Just like students find it hard to sit through a class that does not interest them, researchers are not going to want to study topics in which they have little or no interest—especially since research frequently involves an investment longer than an academic semester! However, it isn't wise for researchers to study topics for which they already have strong beliefs. Remember, as I discussed in Chapter 1, one of the reasons scientific research is better than some other forms of knowledge is that it is objective. If researchers study topics that are close to their hearts, their objectivity is questionable. Researchers are human. They may focus only on data interpretations that support what they already "know" or believe to be true. This weakens the benefits of research, as opposed to other avenues of knowledge.

2. *Try to at least loosely follow the research design wheel.*

In Chapter 1 I also stated that science was stronger than other forms of knowledge because it was systematic. Following the research design wheel in Figure 2.2 as closely as possible ensures that your research is systematic. However, it is not always possible to follow the research design in a unidirectional, step-by-step fashion. Sometimes new research becomes known that causes people to redefine their concepts, or an unexpected cut in resources occurs that changes the selected research design and leads people to redefine research goals and hypotheses. Furthermore, sometimes researchers start creating their research measurements before they fully develop the research design. This is expected. However, trying to follow the general design steps as closely as possible, especially thinking carefully about how to formulate your research question and hypotheses and the best way to test them, helps you organize your research systematically and enables others to better replicate it.

3. *Be realistic in what you can study and in what you have found.*

It is impossible to study all aspects of a social issue; therefore, it is important to be explicit about what specific aspects you are studying. It doesn't matter if someone else reads your research and decides that he or she would not have made the same topic or variable choices—that is an individual's prerogative. Your only obligation is to be explicit about what it is *you* are studying. However, in doing so, make sure that you do not overstate your findings. If you are studying divorced children's attitudes about marriage, for example, resist the temptation to make conclusions about their likelihood of marrying as adults—that is not what you studied. Even though attitudes about divorce may influence marital behavior, if that is not what you explicitly studied, then you should not comment on that topic.

4. Clearly document all your research steps.

As stated in Chapter 1, research needs to be reproducible. If researchers omit steps, such as wording of questions, operational definitions, or sampling techniques, then others cannot reproduce the research in different settings to help validate it. Researchers should write their reports in enough detail to allow others to copy even bits and pieces of the research if they do not choose to replicate your study in its entirety. Including operational definitions for concepts is especially important, since different readers may have different definitions and need to be clear regarding your specific focus in order to interpret and evaluate your findings.

5. Approach all research and scientific knowledge critically but realistically.

Two hundred years ago, the leading scientific knowledge supported the use of bloodletting to release the bad "humors" in the body that caused sickness. Systematic research later revealed that this practice actually did more harm than good. The moral here is that society is constantly changing; therefore, knowledge about what is happening in society also has to change. Looking at research critically helps lead to new research that can improve the social condition. However, as the guideline says, your critical review of research also has to be realistic. Remember, imperfect beings do research in an imperfect world—researchers are constrained by real-world issues such as time, money, public ideology, and personal constraints.

6. Search for patterns in data.

Social science is interested in the aggregate, or the group. Although individual deviations are interesting—and may provide another avenue of research—much of the social sciences focuses on finding patterns among groups of people. Perhaps this is most true in evaluative research. No research conclusions will apply to all people. Similarly, no program is going to benefit all people. The goal of evaluative research, for example, is to see which programs benefit the most. Deciding whether the findings are "acceptable" or not from a public point of view is the role of politicians, social workers, and the like—not researchers.

Evaluating Written Research: Abstracts

In this chapter I briefly discussed an overview of the research process. When researchers write research reports, they frequently provide an overview of their research process in an *abstract*. Usually an abstract appears at the very beginning of an article, right under the title and name(s) of the author(s). The abstract is a very brief summary of the research that is usually 100 to 150 words long, although some journals may require more or allow less. Abstracts generally include a summary of the research problem, a brief description of the sample and sampling techniques, the general research design, and a basic overview of research findings. Writing an abstract is harder than it sounds; in fact, in the Critical Thinking Questions section at the end of this chapter are some links to articles in Research Navigator for which you can practice writing abstracts. There is a lot of information to cover in a very short amount of words; therefore, researchers have to be selective about what they present. Consequently, abstracts are not overly detailed; however, they do serve as a better indicator to a reader than a title does as to whether the content of the article is relevant to the reader's interests. Here are some general guidelines for evaluating abstracts:

1. Is the purpose of the research clear?

Researchers do not have to state explicitly the purpose of their study. In other words, researchers do not have to come right out and say, "The purpose of this study is to . . ."; however, they should at least clearly imply their study purpose. For example, "The effects of weather on voter turnout were assessed . . ." lets the reader indirectly know that the research focuses on the variables of weather and voter turnout.

2. Does the researcher highlight the main details of the methodology?

Obviously in 100 to 150 words researchers cannot go into detail about their research methods. However, a good abstract will at least mention who or what the researcher studied and the general method of observation (e.g., survey, experiment, etc.). If space permits, researchers should also include information regarding the sample size and how they selected their sample. This does not necessarily take a lot of space. For example:

The researchers surveyed a stratified random sample of 2,434 college students . . .

This partial sentence of only 11 words lets the reader know who was studied (college students), how many were studied (2,434), how the participants were selected (a stratified random sample), and what the research design was (a survey). There's a lot of information packed in those very few words!

3. Does the researcher highlight the main findings?

The researcher should mention the main findings in the abstract. Generally, the abstract is not the place to discuss numerical findings or statistical tests (such as tests for statistical significance or strength of association), but, if space permits, there is nothing wrong with mentioning a few if the researcher mentions them briefly and if the findings are important.

Whether an abstract mentions specific measures used (for example, a standardized scale that is common in a particular field) or mentions implications for future research are additional pieces of information that are not required in a good abstract and should be handled carefully if they are included. Standardized or specialized measures should be mentioned only if they are the focus of the study and easily recognizable by many in the field. Otherwise, they take up valuable word space. Implications for future research should be included only if they are concrete—for example, if the researcher states who would be especially interested in the findings or how to use the findings. Otherwise, researchers should omit including implications for future research. Regardless, both of these—mention of standardized measures and implications for future research—should be included *only* if the previous three points have been adequately addressed. Researchers should not

| BOX 2.3 | Evaluation of Abstracts |

Following are abstracts from two studies. Try answering the critical thinking questions on your own before you read my feedback. Remember, you may want to rate each part of an article on a scale of 1 to 5. This is *your* subjective rating to help you decide an article's relevance to you. Therefore, I will present commentary on each evaluation point, but I will not provide a ranking because there is no "correct" ranking. Furthermore, my commentary on any evaluation of the parts of research should also not be taken as the only "correct" response. They are merely comments about points you need to consider when evaluating any aspect of research.

Abstract 1

This study investigated school psychology doctoral students' beliefs concerning their preparation for, and concern about, dealing with 12 ethical issues based on year in graduate school and whether they had taken an ethics course. Two hundred thirty-three doctoral students from 18 of the 44 American Psychological Association accredited programs in school psychology listed in the December 1996 issue of the *American Psychologist* completed ethical issues surveys. Results showed that students who had taken an ethics course and those with more years of graduate education said they felt more prepared to deal with ethical issues than students who had not taken an ethics course and who had fewer years of graduate education. Participants believed they were least prepared to deal with ethical issues involving child custody cases, possible ethical violations by colleagues, and potentially violent clients. Participants' concern about dealing with ethical issues was negatively related to their number of internship hours.

Source: Georgiana Shick Tryon, "School Psychology Students' Beliefs about Their Preparation and Concern With Ethical Issues," *Ethics & Behavior, 11,* (4) (October 2001).

Critical Thinking Questions

1. Is the purpose of the research clear?

2. Are the main points of the research methodology highlighted?

3. Does the researcher highlight the main findings of the research?

4. Overall, do you find this to be a strong abstract? Why or why not?

Critical Thinking Discussion Abstract 1

1. The purpose of this study is abundantly clear. In fact, Tryon directly states it in the first sentence. This study examined how prepared psychology doctoral students felt about dealing with 12 ethical issues of their field. It is perfectly okay that the abstract does not specifically mention what these 12 ethical issues are. Remember, abstracts are short—usually around 150 words (and this one is 151 words)—so specific details like that are not necessary.

2. Remember, here the two main questions to ask are: Who was studied? and How were the data gathered? Any extra information is a bonus. In this abstract, Tryon mentions that the study examined doctoral psychology students (thereby answering the "who") and that these students completed surveys (the "how"). Technically, this is enough; however, Tryon also mentions how the doctoral students were identified and how many participated in the study. There were 233 students selected from "students from 18 of the 44 American Psychological Association accredited programs in school psychology listed in the December 1996 issue of the *American Psychologist.*" Consequently, this abstract does an excellent job at briefly describing the main points of the methodology.

3. Again, here Tryon does a good job. He mentions that participants were "least prepared to deal with ethical issues involving child custody cases,

BOX 2.3 **Evaluation of Abstracts, continued**

possible ethical violations by colleagues, and potentially violent clients." No percents or concrete statistics are mentioned, nor should they be. These are just the main findings described in everyday language. Furthermore, Tryon adds highlights of some findings from more sophisticated analyses (in that this analysis looked at the relationship between at least two variables) by stating, "Participants' concern about dealing with ethical issues was negatively related to their number of internship hours." Again, no statistics are mentioned; however, it is clear that Tryon examined the relationship between ethical issues (one variable) and internship hours (a second variable).

4. Overall, yes, this is a very strong abstract. Each of the three components is well described, and some extra information is also provided without making the abstract overly long.

Abstract 2

[This research] examines influence of religion on the number of years of schooling of an individual using data from 1987–88 National Survey of Families and Households in the United States. Role of religious affiliation in schooling decisions; Differences in educational attainment by religion; Importance of religion in education.

Source: Evelyn L. Lehrer, "Religion as a Determinant of Educational Attainment: An Economic Perspective," *Social Science Research, 28,* (4) (1999): 358.

Critical Thinking Discussion Abstract 2

1. The purpose of this study is also fairly clearly stated. It is to examine the relationship between religion and number of years of schooling—specifically, the influence of religious affiliation, educational attainment, and the importance of religion in education.

2. Here, the abstract presents information only for half of the two main questions relevant to

methodology. We know that the method of choice was a survey because the abstract states that the author used the 1987–1988 National Survey of Families and Households in the United States (NSFH). However, we do not know *whom* the authors used from that survey. The NSFH is a huge dataset and it is very likely that the author did not use every possible person who participated in that study. Therefore, this aspect of the abstract is only mediocre.

3. Absolutely no information on the results of the study is stated. We have no idea what the researcher found; consequently, this section is very weak.

4. Overall, this is a fairly weak abstract. It addresses only one and a half of the three main questions abstracts should answer. Now, you might be tempted to state that this was a poor abstract simply due to its obvious short length (it is only 47 words); however, that is not a strong decision-making criteria to use.

Abstract 3

This paper explores the gender differences in achievements at a variety of levels in secondary schools in New Zealand. Gender differences are shown in relation to English, mathematics and science, but the pattern is not consistent across year levels in the senior school. The relative achievements of girls in single-sex and coeducational schools are explored in detail, with careful controls for the student population differences at the two types of school. When such controls are exercised, the apparent differences between the two types of school reduce to nonsignificance. Data from a longitudinal study of 37 schools and from the Ministry of Education national database are used.

Source: Richard Harker, "Achievement, Gender and the Single-Sex/Coed Debate," *British Journal of Sociology of Education, 21,* (2) (June 2000): 203.

BOX 2.3   **Evaluation of Abstracts, continued**

Critical Thinking Discussion Abstract 3

1. As with the other two abstracts, the purpose of this paper is clearly stated in the first sentence. It is to explore "the gender differences in achievements at a variety of levels in secondary schools in New Zealand."

2. The abstract implies that secondary school students will be examined, since the author is studying achievement at secondary schools. Furthermore, we know that the author will be comparing boys and girls. However, that is about all we know. We do not know how the author is examining achievement—in a sense, we do not know his methodology. Is the author studying grades (hence, the method would be an unobtrusive type of research) or did he survey students about their grade-point averages?

   Furthermore, we do not know how many students are examined. True, the author states "37 schools and from the Ministry of Education national database" are used, but looking at differences among schools (single-sex and coeducational) is only part of the analysis. The author also states that he is studying the achievement of *girls and boys* at schools—hence, we need to know how many girls and boys participated in

the study. This is clarified when the author discusses the results. He notes that differences were found across subjects, not necessarily across schools. Hence, his discussion of the research methodology is mediocre—it has some key information, but not enough.

3. The author's discussion of results is better. He states that there were gender differences across subjects and that the differences across the two types of schools are statistically insignificant after controlling for certain factors. Technically, this is enough, although it might be useful to note what those gender differences in the subjects are. The first few sentences could be reworded to accomplish that without adding undue length to the abstract.

4. Don't let the length fool you. Even though the abstract is 106 words, and looks as if it *should* cover all the relevant information, overall, this is a relatively mediocre abstract. The purpose is clearly stated and some key findings are alluded to in general terms; however, at least half of the relevant methodology is missing and the results are glossed over in such a way that they provide little specific information (which is possible even without mention of statistics).

---

unnecessarily shorten—to the point of being confusing or incomplete—the description of the study, methods, or findings in order to insert these additional features.

To summarize, the main questions to ask when evaluating abstracts are:

1. Is the purpose of the research clear?
2. Does the researcher highlight the main details of the methodology?
3. Does the researcher highlight the main findings?

To this list you can add a fourth question:

4. *Overall, do you find this to be a strong abstract? Why or why not?*

You should ask yourself this last question, or a version of it relevant to specific individual sections of the research report, at the end of each research section. That way, when you evaluate an article in its entirety, you have a sense of your overall view of each component.

For all of the lip service paid to making sure that social science research is ethical, researchers rarely discuss the ethical components of their research in their published work. It is almost as if adhering to ethical guidelines is an assumption. It is important for readers to evaluate whether they think the researcher has fulfilled his or her ethical obligations to both science and the participants. However, in order to do so, they may have to read between the lines. These questions may help to do this.

1. Are the steps the researcher took to honor ethical responsibilities to individuals clear? Are they appropriate? Are they enough?

Readers are more equipped to evaluate whether a researcher has fulfilled his or her ethical responsibilities to the subjects; they are less equipped to evaluate whether the researcher has fulfilled his or her responsibility to research or society. Sometimes researchers will mention that a survey was "anonymous" and leave it at that, assuming that by simply using the term *anonymous* they have fulfilled their ethical obligation. Essentially researchers are telling readers just to believe them and that if they state that a study was anonymous, then it truly was. However, as you have learned, people—including researchers—frequently use the term *anonymous* erroneously when what they really mean is *confidential*. Readers have the responsibility to read between the lines; they must ask themselves, Based on the information the researcher provided, did the researcher really protect anonymity or confidentiality?

By the same token, not all research topics require lengthy ethical discussions. Although replicating Zimbardo's prison experiment may involve both a discussion of how researchers protected the subjects from harm and how they guaranteed confidentiality, surveying working mothers about their child-care choices and work experiences may not require a discussion of how the researchers protected these participants from harm. Regarding a study of working women, the real issue is for the researcher to be clear as to whether she or he guaranteed anonymity (or confidentiality) and whether the participation of the respondents was voluntary. A lengthier discussion of ethical issues is unnecessary.

Consequently, readers need to ask themselves, Given the nature of the topic being studied, has the researcher done everything possible to protect all of the relevant ethical concerns for participants? At the very least, readers should be convinced that the subjects are participating voluntarily and that the researcher is adequately protecting their identities. If the researcher claims that he or she is protecting anonymity, then it needs to be clear to the reader *how* this was done so the reader can verify that anonymity was indeed protected, as opposed to really protecting confidentiality and mistakenly calling it anonymity. If, given the research topic or design, it is clear to readers that there may realistically be some potential harm to the subjects, then the researcher has to have clearly explained what he or she did to prevent that harm.

Remember, however (and this cannot be stressed enough), that to some degree what is important to see in an article is defined by the nature of the research topic and data-gathering strategy. It is unreasonable to expect a researcher studying maternal employment to provide information regarding where employed mothers may find help in case completing the survey caused them distress. Although some mothers may ultimately feel some anxiety about balancing work and family relationships, for the most part, this type of anxiety (especially anxiety that may result from answering survey questions) is not likely or serious enough to require some type of intervention. Consequently, readers have to be realistic about what they expect researchers to reveal.

2. If there were any findings (based on readings of tables or other means of data presentation) that refuted the researcher's hypothesis, did he or she address these findings?

With regard to ethical responsibilities to science, to some degree the peer review board of a particular journal is responsible for identifying research that it suspects to be fraudulent or mistakenly interpreted. However, even the editorial review process is not foolproof, and poor research does get published. Therefore, readers have the responsibility to critically evaluate what they are reading.

Earlier I mentioned that mistakes in interpretation are not necessarily fraudulent and unethical in and of themselves, but there are some "red flags" that indicate that a researcher is not mistaking an interpretation but instead is trying to imply that findings are more important or accurate than they are; this behavior borders on the unethical.

There are three main pitfalls readers need to be able to identify. The first is when researchers discuss only those findings that support their hypotheses. Researchers are at times tempted to discuss or present findings that only support their hypotheses, perhaps thinking that a reader will then see that a researcher was "right." However, findings that refute hypotheses can be just as informative as findings that support them. How can a reader tell if a researcher is selectively reporting results? Usually by reading the data tables. I will talk more about how to evaluate the presentation of results in written research in Chapter 12, but for our purpose here it is enough to understand that research findings are generally presented in two ways. The first is in some type of table or graphical form—essentially a picture that provides a quick snapshot of the findings. The second is a written discussion that walks the reader through what the researcher finds to be important. Sometimes it is clear by reading a table that there are findings that do not support the hypothesis, and that the researcher does not discuss in the written section of the report. It is only natural to want to report findings that fit your carefully designed and refined research questions, but limiting your discussions to this presents a biased view of the research.

3. If any results were unexpected, did the researcher acknowledge this? Did the researcher discuss any explanations for the unexpected effects?

The second pitfall that may indicate borderline unethical behavior is when researchers try to pass off unexpected findings that result from a carefully preplanned research approach. Sometimes a researcher believes that if he or she did not anticipate a relationship that was found in the data ahead of time, then readers may think that the researcher was unprepared. This is silly. No one can possibly anticipate all possible relationships between variables prior to a study. If an unanticipated relationship that is both practically and theoretically important emerges, so be it. Instead of spending time making this unanticipated relationship seem anticipated, the researcher should spend time fitting the finding into a theoretical context so others can more fully explain and examine the findings in the future.

4. Did the researcher adequately acknowledge the limitations of the research?

Last, researchers need to identify the limitations of their own research. Students frequently incorrectly assume that if researchers are finding fault with their own studies, then

BOX 2.4   **Evaluating the Ethics in Research**

Although ethical considerations are important elements in any research, they are frequently the most underreported sections in research reports. In the excerpt below, Soukup uses participant observation research to study gender patterns in computer chat room conversations. Use the questions for ethical evaluations to determine whether Soukup adequately addressed the main ethical issues of research we discussed.

Introductions and Methods

This study explores the gendered discourse of social-based computer-mediated contexts. Specifically, the critical ethnography explicates the patterns of discourse of both a sports-related (masculine-dominated) chatroom and a female-based (feminine-dominated) chatroom. . . .

In order to study two chatrooms, I participated in the interaction and submerged myself in the group dynamics of two chatrooms. Furthermore, I became a complete member of the chatrooms. Because informed consent would sacrifice the participants' anonymity (and be a logistical impossibility), I entered the scene as if an "ordinary" member of the chatroom. Ethically, due to the public nature of chatrooms (like radio talkshows) and the anonymity of the participants, this choice was appropriate. The complete participant role allowed me to interact with the members of the scene with limited disruption. Because the members of the chatroom were unaware of my researcher role, quite naturally occurring behavior emerged.

. . . The participants were the members of the *chatrooms*. Because the members of the groups used screen names (virtually always pseudonyms), the specific characteristics of the participants were unknown. Beyond cursory information (e.g., probable sex, probable income level, and interests and hobbies), due to the anonymity of the Internet, the detailed characteristics of the participants will never be known. . . . For this research, I was primarily concerned with the gendered patterns of discourse, not the "actual" physiological characteristics of the participants.

Results

. . . [In female based chatrooms] . . . the public discourse seemed to be a way of finding common interests and screening for appropriate interactional partners. The emphasis of the feminine-based discourse seemed to be relationship building.

Occasionally, intimate discussions occurred in public:

Simion2: lauf why did you get in the fight?
lauf: she was talking about my family, especially my dad, he died 6 months ago
Simion2 how did he die?
lauf: car accident
fuzzy32: thats too bad, my dad just died of cancer
fuzzy32: pretty scary what life can throw at you huh?

. . . This quotation shows the significant shift from the competitive and aggressive communication styles of the sports chatroom. The communication, traditionally feminine, was far more relationship based. Much like the traditional feminine role, participants were "expressive and person oriented" (Tavris, 1992, p. 247).

Conclusion

This research project suggests that [chatroom] users tend to follow the traditional conceptions of masculinity and femininity. . . . Particularly, gender-based norms were established, negotiated, and maintained via sanctions. Unfortunately, the complex process of group norm maintenance through sanctioning was outside the scope of this study. Although this research was able to delineate a few general characteristics of the sanctioning process, due to the focus of the study, the complex intricacies of the sanctioning process were not considered. Future research should certainly consider the process of social sanctioning in CMC. For instance, how do sanctions help users learn group norms? How do members move from "being sanctioned" to "doing the sanctioning" (i.e., in- and

BOX 2.4   Evaluating the Ethics in Research, continued

out-group membership)? How does the sanctioning process impact on and adapt to changes in group norms?

Source: Copyright 1999 from "The Gendered Interactional Patterns of Computer-Mediated Chatrooms: A Critical Ethnographic Study" by Charles Soukup, *Information Society, 15,* (3). Reproduced by permission of Taylor & Francis Group. LLC., www.taylorandfrancis.com.

Evaluation Questions

1. Are the steps the researcher took to honor ethical responsibilities to individuals clear? Are they appropriate? Are they enough?

2. If there were any findings (based on your readings of tables or other means of data presentation) that refuted the researcher's hypothesis, did he address these findings?

3. If any results were unexpected, did the researcher acknowledge this? Did the researcher discuss any explanations for the unexpected effects?

4. Did the researcher adequately acknowledge the limitations of the research?

5. Overall, has the researcher adequately fulfilled his ethical obligations?

Critical Thinking Discussion

1. Remember, the main ethical considerations of individuals are informed consent, anonymity/confidentiality, nonmaleficence, beneficence, and reciprocity. Let's look at each of these in turn.

    Soukup claims that informed consent was not possible to obtain because it would compromise anonymity. Is this true? Couldn't Soukup note that he was a researcher in the beginning of his involvement in the chat room (essentially the beginning of his study) and let others choose to participate in that chat room? If he participated in the chat room over a period of time, then participants would be used to his identity and, consequently, their behavior would less likely be affected by it.

On the other hand, chat room participants are not always the same people, and if Soukup had to obtain informed consent from every new participant, then people may not have gotten used to his presence and may have behaved differently because they were being "observed." There is no right answer here; however, the point is that one *can* make an argument that Soukup may have been able to obtain informed consent.

Regarding anonymity, his reasoning is sound. First, most people in chat rooms have self-appointed pseudonyms that protect their identity (and since the researcher never knows people's true identity, he can guarantee anonymity). Second, the point that chat rooms are like radio talk shows is valid—essentially these are public arenas.

There is no evidence of maleficence or harm to participants, nor is there any clear evidence of any benefits to them. However, since harms are absent, the absence of benefits—which primarily would counteract any possible harm—is acceptable.

Likewise, reciprocity isn't an issue because Soukup is not requesting anything from those participating in the chat room. Since he isn't requesting any favors of them (even their time—these people have decided to participate in the chat room on their own, therefore their participation is voluntary and unsolicited), he has no favors or obligations to make sure are fulfilled.

Consequently, many of the ethical responsibilities to individuals are not relevant to this study. Although Soukup has fulfilled the responsibilities of anonymity and not doing harm to participants, whether his failure to obtain informed consent is justifiable is less clear.

2. All of the findings presented (for a full view of the findings, you can access the article on Research Navigator) fit the data presented. You may be thinking that the data presented are selective because they are transcriptions of chat room conversations. This is true; however, given the nature of the research methodology cho-

BOX 2.4   **Evaluating the Ethics in Research, continued**

sen—participant observation—edited transcriptions are the standard means of data presentation. We will cover this in more detail in Chapter 12.

3. No results appear unexpected.

4. Soukup acknowledges that other research issues, such as how norms were maintained, were "beyond the scope" of the present study. This is fair. No piece of research can study all aspects of a social issue well; drawing attention to the points *not* considered is not a problem with the study itself. In fact, it is good practice. That being said, it is the only limitation that

Soukup really mentions. Can you think of other important (meaning, not an issue of "I would have done this differently," but instead an issue of "this *should* have been done but was not") limitations? If not, then Soukup has adequately addressed this issue. Given the purpose of this research and the parameters he clearly establishes for it, there are no other significant methodological limitations.

5. Overall, Soukup did a fairly good job at discussing the relevant ethical issues of his research. Although the issue of informed consent can be debated, it is the only real potential ethical limitation possibly present.

the studies themselves are problematic. This couldn't be farther from the truth! No research is perfect—you can only use the techniques you will learn in classes and books like this one to design the best possible research you can—but it still will not be perfect. No one knows the limitations of a study better than the person who conducted it. Consequently, researchers have a responsibility to clearly identify the limitations of their own research so those reading the material, who may be less familiar with the topic, do not overstate the importance of the research and are aware of some issues that they may want to work to minimize in their own research.

When evaluating the ethics presented in research, the following questions are relevant:

1. Are the steps the researcher took to honor ethical responsibilities to individuals clear? Are they appropriate? Are they enough?
2. If there were any findings (based on readings of tables or other means of data presentation) that refuted the researcher's hypothesis, did he or she address these findings?
3. If any results were unexpected, did the researcher acknowledge this? Did the researcher discuss any explanations for the unexpected effects?
4. Did the researcher adequately acknowledge the limitations of the research?
5. Overall, was this researcher ethical?

Key Terms

Anonymity (67)
Concept (34)
Confidentiality (67)
Dimension (35)
Ethical relativism (70)
Hypothesis (37)
Idea type (35)
Informed consent (55)
Institutional Review Board
  (54)

Literature review (43)
Macro-theory (37)
Measurement (47)
Meso-theory (38)
Micro-theory (37)
Operationalization (45)
Paradigm (38)
Plagiarism (58)
Principle of beneficence (56)
Principle of justice (56)

Principle of nonmaleficence
  (66)
Proposition (37)
Reciprocity (68)
Research fraud (57)
Respect for persons (55)
Typology (35)
Variables (47)
Voluntary participation (60)

Review Questions and Exercises

1. *Evaluate the abstracts for the following articles found in Research Navigator. (Note: You can easily see the abstract provided by clicking the title of the article that appears in blue.)*

a. *Ainsworth, James W. (2002, September). Why does it take a village? The mediation of neighborhood effects on educational achievement. Social Forces, 81 (1), 117. 36 pp. (AN 00377732).*

b. *Coburn, David. (2004, January). Beyond the income inequality hypothesis: Class, neoliberalism, and health inequalities. Science & Medicine, 58 (1), 41. 16 pp.*

c. *Marcus, Robert F., and Reio, Jr., Thomas G. (2002 August). Severity of injury resulting from violence among college Students: Proximal and distal influences. Journal of Interpersonal Violence, 17 (8), 888. 21 pp.*

d. *Kusz, Kyle W. (2001 November). "I want to be the minority": The politics of youthful white masculinities in sport and popular culture in 1990s America. Journal of Sport & Social Issues, 25 (4), 390–407.*

e. *Kempinen, Cynthia A., and Kurlychek, Megan C. (2003, October). An outcome*

evaluation of Pennsylvania's boot camp: Does rehabilitative programming within a disciplinary setting reduce recidivism? Crime & Delinquency, 49 (4), 581. 25 pp.

f. *Powers, Rebecca S., and Livermore, Michelle M. (2003, Fall). Will unwed new mothers seek employment?: The role of government and social support. Gender Issues, 21 (4), 31–49.*

2. *Evaluate the ethical steps the researchers have taken in the following studies:*

a. *Soukup, Charles. (1999). The gendered interactional patterns of computer-mediated chatrooms: A critical ethnographic study. Information Society, 15 (3), 169–177. (AN 2223837)*

b. *Dowsett, Gary W., Bollen, Jonathan, McInnes, David, Couch, Murray, and Edwards, Barry. (2001). HIV/AIDS and constructs of gay community: Researching educational Practice within community-based health promotion for gay men. International Journal of Social Research Methodology, 4 (3), 205–224. (AN 5171695)*

c. *Blair-Loy, Mary, and Wharton, Amy S. (2002, March). Employees' use of work-family policies and the workplace social context.* Social Forces, 80 (3), 813. 33 pp.

d. *Horodynski, Mildred A., and Stommel, Manfred. (2005, September/October). Nutrition education aimed at toddlers: An intervention study.* Pediatric Nursing, 31 (5), 364–372. (AN 19222803)

Getting Started

I began this book by asking questions such as What leads teenagers to shoot teachers and fellow students? Do negative political campaigns affect voter turnout? and How does divorce affect women's labor force behavior? These are examples of social science research questions because they are interested in studying behavior in groups, the relations of individuals to social institutions, or the results of social processes. In fact, there are so many different viable social science research questions out there that listing what can be a research question in a textbook like this is impossible.

This chapter will examine what I will arbitrarily call the beginning of the deductive research process known as *problem formation*. More specifically, I will discuss how to select a research problem, the development of a specific research question, and the definition of research terms. A multitude of potential research questions is available, but creating well-constructed and meaningful research questions can be surprisingly challenging.

Selecting a Research Problem

I remember being in class and complaining when a professor would assign research papers but would provide very little guidance regarding the specific topic of the paper. These professors usually said something like, "Write a paper on group behavior." "My word!" I would think. "There's so many possibilities!" Selecting an appropriate research question can be surprisingly challenging, whether it is for a class or a scientific study (see Figure 3.1). All of the questions that began this chapter are viable research questions, but many others are not. For example, a question such as In the criminal justice system, should children be tried as adults? or Should we create more limits on divorce? is not an appropriate research question. Why? Because as I stated in the beginning of this book, science can answer only questions that can be empirically

Poor Research Questions

1. What affects children's views of gender roles? (Too vague)
2. Disabilities and workplace discrimination (Variables, not a research question)
3. How do peers affect behavior? (Too vague)
4. Racial discrimination (General topic, not a research question)
5. What factors help low-income individuals obtain better-paying jobs? (Too vague)
6. Do we need to classify crimes as hate crimes? (Value question, not empirically observable fact)

Good Research Questions

1. How does father involvement in child care affect children's views of men's roles?
2. Do people with disabilities experience subtle discrimination in the workplace?
3. Are adolescents whose mothers are employed more likely to have friends who exhibit deviant behavior than adolescents whose mothers are not employed?
4. Do racial minorities discriminate against each other?
5. Does having an associate's degree help low-income individuals obtain better-paying jobs?
6. What proportion of people support the federal government tracking the incidence of hate crimes?

Figure 3.1 Good and Bad Research Questions

observed firsthand. The two questions about children in the criminal justice system and divorce, on the contrary, are value questions—they do not address an observable phenomena, but instead ask what *should* be done. Questions like these do not involve observable facts. Therefore, science cannot answer them.

So how do people select research topics? Well, the logical first place to begin is with personal experience. Look to your own life for ideas. Do you belong to a church? Do you wonder how people of different religions view abortion, the death penalty, or divorce? Do you have siblings? Perhaps you see similarities in your experiences with friends who are of the same birth order as yourself. Or maybe you see differences based on gender—in other words, perhaps you notice that first-born boys have different experiences with their families than do first-born girls. What types of jobs do your parents have? Do you think their jobs (e.g., white collar, blue collar, etc.) affect the types of values your parents reinforced in you and your siblings? You are a social being; therefore, your personal experiences are a rich starting place to develop research questions.

Be careful, however. There is a strong temptation to interpret findings a particular way if people choose to research a topic that not only is part of their personal experience but is also one in which they have strong beliefs. If you feel particularly strong about an issue—perhaps the homeless because you were once homeless yourself—you need to be especially conscientious about maintaining your objectivity during the study. If you are unsure of your ability to do this, you are well advised to select a topic that interests you but one in which you are less personally invested.

The selection of a research topic may also depend on outside social, political, and economic consideration. For example, bosses may ask researchers to study a topic for administrative needs—such as to see whether a particular police precinct is handling crime calls efficiently and effectively. Or perhaps you are volunteering at a women's shelter and the agency wants to learn more about client needs. These are more pragmatic reasons behind research—the research topic evolves to fulfill a specific social or administrative need.

Also, topics may depend, at least to some degree, on the economic resources available to the researcher and/or the political climate of the researcher's environment. I might be interested in studying the longitudinal effects of individuals who graduate from a drug treatment program, but this is a costly endeavor and without some outside funding, I may not be able to do the study. Or, if the community has a generally negative view of the treatment court, I may not have the support from local agencies, such as drug treatment providers or the police, to do the study. This will impede my ability to gather data, and, consequently, to adequately examine my chosen research problem.

Developing a Research Problem

Choosing a broad research topic is only part of the challenge. After researchers choose the topic, they need to clarify or specify the *specific* research problem relating to that topic that will be the focus of their study. The real issue here is narrowing a general research topic to a specific problem of manageable size. For example, studying the homeless is a broad research topic. There are many issues related to homelessness. A researcher who wants to study the homeless can study the demographics of the homeless in a community. Or the researcher can compare the homeless across different communities. Maybe the researcher wants to evaluate the shelters that serve the homeless. Or perhaps he or she is interested in the public's perception of the homeless problem. The list about possible research topics relating to the homeless are endless, and any one researcher obviously can't study them all. Consequently, developing a research problem allows a researcher to clearly state the specific aspect of the phenomena that will be the focus of his or her research.

So how do researchers go about doing this? The main way is to review the published research that documents what other researchers have found; this is, rather appropriately, called a **literature review.** A literature review will help you define your problem by giving you ideas of when researchers have found conflicting findings (and then you can design your research to help resolve the conflict), where there are gaps in the research (for example, you may find that some research creates more questions than answers), whether your planned design is appropriate for the topic, and if your particular topic has already been adequately studied. Although replication is important, when many studies agree about a particular topic, there is little to gain by studying it again, unless you have a very strong theoretical reason for expecting to add to the existing knowledge. I will discuss how to evaluate a literature review in the Evaluating Research subsection at the end of this chapter. For now, however, let's talk about how to put together a literature review.

Homelessness is a serious problem in our society, and researchers have tried to study it in many different ways. If you were interested in studying the homeless, what would your focus be?

Conducting literature reviews are relatively easy in today's electronic world. Begin by drafting a working research problem—for example, How does welfare receipt affect individuals? You might need to revise this research question as you learn new information or as you realize that you cannot find any relevant research (although the latter, in reality, is somewhat rare, since research questions are usually very broad). After researchers have a research question, they make note of key words that appear in that question. In your example, you may want to note "welfare" or perhaps "welfare receipt." These key words are where researchers will begin their search, which is likely to begin at a local library (university or community) with either an on-line catalog to search for relevant books or an electronic index (like Research Navigator, which you are using in conjunction with this book) to search for research articles appearing in professional or academic journals.

Many beginning researchers frequently turn to books for their material, but don't get worried if you cannot find any books about your topic. In fact, although books can be useful, some would argue that research articles found in academic or professional journals are of greater use because they are usually more recent, more directed, and shorter. Both sources of research, books and academic journals, may be useful in building a literature review; so don't be discouraged if you can find information in only one avenue.

Once you are at your local library and are using either an on-line catalog or an electronic index, you are likely to begin your search by using the key words you identified in your research question. Sometimes, you might get lucky and find enough relevant information simply with the keywords you started with in your research question. However, sometimes you need to refine your search either because your terms are too broad or, the exact opposite, too specific. Again, do not be discouraged. Simply think of similar words or different phrases with the same meaning and keep an ongoing list of what phrases you are using and what databases you are looking in for research. For example, if I am interested in studying negative political campaign tactics but I cannot find any information on negative campaign advertisements, I might also try searching by keywords such as "campaign strategies," "campaign news clips," "mudslinging and campaigns," and "politician debates."

Some caveats when using electronic databases are noteworthy. First, many electronic indexes have a variety of media, such as newspapers and popular magazines, represented in addition to academic or professional journals. Not all of these sources are created equally. Professional and academic journals are usually the best bet for literature reviews because the material in them have usually been peer reviewed, whereas this is not likely to be the case in newspapers or popular magazines (such as *Newsweek* or *Time*). *Peer reviewed* means that each article published has been critically evaluated by two or three people who are familiar with the topic and who are in a position to be able to evaluate the quality of the research used. Although this is not a perfect system because reviewers are people too and have their own niches, level of skill, and attention to detail, peer review more adequately filters and evaluates material than your typical newspaper or popular magazine article does.

Second, sometimes the terms in research questions are so broad that the number of "hits" is enormous. For example, if you wanted to study the effects of welfare receipt on people's self-esteem and you searched for the word *welfare* in Research Navigator, you would receive 395 hits for articles with "welfare" mentioned from the sociology databases alone. If you included other social science databases, such as those for criminal justice, social work, political science, and general interest, in your search you would receive 1,237

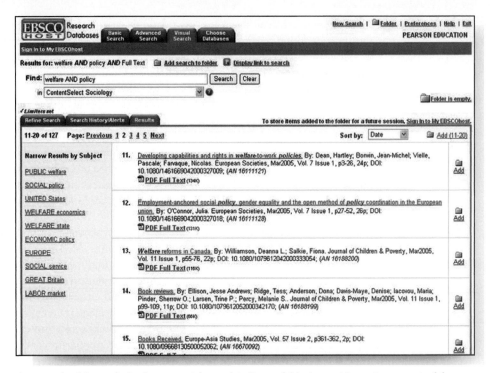

An example of the results list from an article search in Research Navigator. Narrowing your search by using more than one keyword can reduce the number of "hits" and help you focus in on the most relevant articles.

hits! Obviously that is a lot of articles to peruse! When this occurs, you need to limit your search; you can do this in a number of ways.

You can look for multiple keywords simultaneously. This way, you get hits only for articles that contain all of your keywords. You can also limit your searches by specifying the search engine to look only in specific journals (such as *American Sociological Review* or *Crime and Delinquency*) or for specific publication date ranges (e.g., only for articles published after 2000). If you limited your search to "welfare" and "self-esteem," you would have only two hits—a far cry from the 1,237 hits previously! In fact, two hits is probably too little to be truly informative, so you would still have to think of other keyword combinations to search for your topic. This is a common process. Reviewing the literature is a back-and-forth operation until you have identified and read enough articles to truly grasp your research topic and form a meaningful research question.

The third caveat when using electronic databases is that sometimes students look only for articles that address exactly what they are studying. Be careful here. You want articles that are topically relevant, but you do not want to cite 10 different studies that *exactly* address your research interests, unless they differ or disagree in some significant way. If you find a noticeable number of articles with research that is exactly like what you wanted to study (and similar findings), you need to refine your research problem in a different way. You need to make it unique. As I will discuss in the next chapter, replication of studies is important—it helps researchers be more confident that a particular study's findings are not a "fluke"—but, in reality, few studies should be exactly alike. All research should aim to further existing knowledge. Therefore, a portion of your research may replicate earlier studies, but a portion should also move your understanding of the topic to a higher level. Consequently, you want to find articles that look at a similar problem in different ways (and then you can think of another way to examine the problem) or that look at various aspects of the same problem (and then you can either unify these aspects or add another specific aspect to consider).

As a side note, even though you are likely to do your searches using an electronic index, this does not mean that the information found via other avenues of the Internet is not informative. For example, if you know the uniform resource locator—more commonly known as the URL—which is the Internet address for a specific site, you may be able to find useful information there or links that will connect you to other potentially useful sites. For example, if I want statistics about the poor, I may start by looking at the U.S. Census website at www.census.gov. This website will, in turn, contain links to other websites that have information relating to poverty. However, as I stated earlier, when you are getting information from the Internet, you need to be conscious of its source. Just like newspaper and magazine articles, there is no peer review on the Internet. Consequently, it is the reader's responsibility to ensure that the site is unbiased or, at the very least, that any information from a site with a particular stance is clearly documented to that site so that readers are able to determine how much weight they will give a particular piece of information.

Once you have identified possible articles to read, you can frequently save time by reading the titles and abstracts to determine if a particular article really has information that is relevant to your interests. In the Evaluating Research section in Chapter 1, I discussed what to look for in a good title, and in that section in Chapter 2, I discussed what good abstracts should entail. Once you read the title and abstract, if the research sounds relevant to your needs, then you need to take the next step and read the article in its entirety. This is important! Don't try to save time by reading just the abstract and then formulating your problem around the abstract information only. Many important details about methodology, findings, limitations, and implications are found only in the body of the article. Therefore you need to read the entire article itself.

Furthermore, once you identify some articles that are particularly relevant to your research, you can expand your literature review by reading the bibliographies of *those* articles. This is not cheating! In fact, it's good, efficient practice. You can then read the articles listed in these bibliographies to see if they contribute any knowledge to your research problem. Continue this process of article and bibliography searching so long as the process provides useful and new information.

When you have enough literature to serve as the background for your own research, you are ready to continue defining your research problem. Remember, you are looking for issues or variables not covered by existing research, conflicting findings across various studies, or questions posed by researchers themselves at the end of their reports. All of these pieces of information can help you narrow your broad research topic into a more manageable piece.

Incidentally, just because you think you have created a manageable and meaningful research question at the end of this process, the process itself isn't really over. In fact, reviewing the literature should continue with the rest of the research process. New information is constantly appearing in research articles and other sources. Furthermore, as you do your research, you might develop questions that previous researchers have already

| BOX 3.1 | Identifying Research Problems |

Below is an excerpt of a literature review that discusses how ethnic-based social networks influence immigrants' abilities to find employment in our society. Read the excerpt to see how many research questions you can develop.

The contemporary sociological study of immigrant labor markets is indebted to Granovetter (1973,1985), who points to the importance of interpersonal ties in getting jobs and the advantage of examining economic action with regard to how it is embedded in networks of interpersonal relations. Acquaintances serve as bridge ties that link people to social networks to which they previously had no connections. New social connections encourage information diffusion and expanded opportunity. In this way, interpersonal ties play a role in expanding employment opportunities. For Granovetter (1973), it is usually weak ties (acquaintances rather than family or close friends) that serve as bridges between networks because strong ties such as family members are thought to be connected to the same networks. But Burt (1992) contends that focusing on the strength of a bridge tie misses the point. According to him, the essential structural element is the hole between networks. Once a hole is bridged, information flows and opportunities increase. The strength of the tie that makes a bridge has little or no bearing on the benefits that result from the bridging.

Burt's (1992) point simplifies matters for those who study how people get jobs. Our experience suggests that the social connections that result in a job seeker gaining new sources of information can be difficult to attribute to a specific weak or strong tie. Such information often moves along a chain of actors, some of whom are weakly tied and some of whom may be strongly tied to the job seeker. The precise details of the information exchanged along the various points of the chain can be difficult to document. And sometimes two actors do not agree on the strength of their relationship. Therefore, attributing the bridge tie to a particular individual, and measuring the strength of the tie, can be more difficult than observing that access to a new social network has occurred.

Waldinger's (1996b) account of why African Americans are underrepresented in the construction trades in New York City illustrates the importance of bridge ties and structural holes in affecting the diffusion of employment-related information. Access to training and employment in these trades is governed by access to particular social networks. Job-related information is passed along chains of ties within these networks. These chains often include both weak and strong ties. The disadvantage of African Americans is that they have few interpersonal ties that can bridge the structural holes between themselves and the social networks that control access to employment in the construction trades.

Source: Sanders, Jimy, Nee, Victor, and Sernau, Scott. (2002, September). Asian immigrants' reliance on social ties in a multiethnic labor market. *Social Forces, 81* (1), 281. 34 pp. *(AN 7513773)*

Critical Thinking Question

1. What types of research questions can you create from this excerpt of a literature review? Make sure that they can be feasibly studied. In other words, do not create research questions that are so large as to be unmanageable.

Critical Thinking Discussion

1. Some sample research questions are:

- How can holes between social networks be bridged?
- How can social networks be better measured?
- How do social networks differ for members of Asian Americans and African Americans?
- How do social networks differ for men and women?
- Are social networks more important to finding employment for members of different groups (e.g., more important for men or for Asian Americans)?

answered. Literature reviews are also useful in defining and justifying variable choices, in selecting a research methodology, and in fitting the results of your study into a theoretical framework.

The last point I want to make before moving on to causality is how to organize your literature review so it is useful to both you and other readers. Probably the most common mistake beginning researchers make is including every article that they examined in the literature review. Perhaps this stems from practices in high school or college, where students try to achieve a certain page length as an indicator of completion. Or perhaps it comes from a desire to document every step of the research process. Either way, reporting on every single article read is unnecessary.

In writing your own literature review, think of the entire research report as a story. The literature review sets the scene whereby at its conclusion, the reader should have a very clear idea of what you will specifically study. The other parts of the report—the methods, results, and discussion sections—will continue the story by answering how you did the research, what you found, and what the broader social implications of your findings are. Therefore, write the literature review so that it concretely contributes to your research goals. Start with a broad discussion of the research question, explain and evaluate the articles that will help direct the reader to your specific research problem, and then state the problem or hypothesis concretely at the end. Some of the articles you read will be highly relevant to the development of your research problem; some will not. Those that are not very relevant should not be included in the literature review. In other words, the literature review should be organized like a funnel that starts broad and progressively narrows until it specifically identifies your research problem. Only the information that allows you to do this is relevant and should be included in your literature review.

Hypotheses and Causality

Problem specification frequently results in hypothesis formation. Not all research is aimed at explanation, and therefore does not work to establish causality; however, much deductive research frequently involves hypotheses and tries to establish a casual connection. If your research goal is exploration, you are unlikely to need hypotheses and you are even less concerned with establishing causality. If your research purpose is description, you may have hypotheses, but you are not interested in taking those hypotheses to the next level and establishing causality. However, if your research goal is explanation or evaluation, then you are likely to not only have hypotheses, but your aim is to take those hypotheses to the next level and try to establish causation. Consequently, in this section I will discuss both hypotheses and the criteria for causation in detail.

■ Hypotheses

I discussed hypotheses briefly in Chapter 2 when I outlined the research process. To review, a **hypothesis** is an empirically testable statement. That means that it is not a question and that it has to involve concepts that can be directly observed.

Hypotheses generally have two components—an *independent variable* and a *dependent variable*—and some will have a third component, which is a *direction of effect*. Take, for example, the following hypothesis: The likelihood of voting increases with income. There are two concepts present: the likelihood of voting and income. Both of these are called

BOX 3.2   Hypothesis Formation

Which of the following are hypotheses? When you find a hypothesis, identify its independent and dependent variables and the direction of effect (if present).

1. "Migrants with social ties to other migrants in their place of settlement will have a greater risk of investing their remittances and savings on a productive activity or a home than of spending them on consumption."

2. "Compared to marriages in which both partners are happy and the wife is not employed full-time, marriages in which the wife is employed full-time are at a significantly greater risk of marital dissolution only when one or both spouses are not happy."

3. "Deviants must neutralize moral prescriptions prior to committing a crime."

4. "Level of education and occupational status are positively related to the number of musical genres a person appreciates."

5. "This study attempts to identify factors that single out junior and senior high school students as victims of campus theft and violent crime."

Discussion

1. This is a hypothesis. The dependent variable (the outcome you are interested in predicting or studying) is whether migrants invest their remittances and savings on a productive activity or for a home. The independent variable is the migrants' social ties. There is a direction of effect and that is a *greater* risk for those migrants with social ties than those without them.

2. This is also a hypothesis. The dependent variable is risk of marital dissolution. What is going to predict that, and is therefore the independent variable, is the wife's employment status. Being happy is *not* really part of the independent variable because it is an assumption for both families with employed wives and families without employed wives. There is also a direction of effect here and that is a *greater* likelihood of marital dissolution.

3. This is not a clear hypothesis. Although it *is* a statement of what the author is studying, there is no clear independent or dependent variable because there is no clear comparison. Comparisons imply variation and variation is part of the word *variable*. Hence, what we have here is more of a research thesis, which is often (but not always) treated differently than a traditional hypothesis.

4. This is a hypothesis. The dependent variable is the number of musical genres a person appreciates. There are two independent variables. Level of education is one and occupational status is the second. Could the author have written these as two distinct hypotheses? Absolutely. However, researchers frequently won't when they have multiple independent variables for the same dependent variable or vice versa to save space.

5. This is not a hypothesis. It is a research goal, but there is no attempt at establishing causality and explaining *what* causes campus theft and violent crime. Consequently, this research is essentially a fact-finding mission — or more formally expressed as exploratory or descriptive research (not explanatory or evaluative which frequently involve hypotheses).

Citations (correspond to the hypothesis number)

1. Mooney, Margarita. (2003, June). Migrants' social ties in the U.S. and investment in Mexico. *Social Forces, 81* (4), 1147. 24 pp.
2. Schoen, Robert, Astone, Nan Marie, Rothert, Kendra, Standish, Nicola J., and Kim, Young J. (2002, December). Women's employment, marital happiness, and divorce. *Social Forces, 81* (2), 643. 20 pp.
3. Cromwell, Paul, and Thurman, Quint. (2003, November). The devil made me do it: Use of

BOX 3.2   Hypothesis Formation, continued

neutralizations by shoplifters. *Deviant Behavior,* *24* (6), 535. 16 pp.

4. Van Eijck, Koen. (2001, March). Social differentiation in musical taste patterns. *Social Forces,* *79* (3), 1163. 23 pp.

5. McMahon, Jennifer, and Clay-Warner, Jody. (2002, September). Child abuse and future criminality: The role of social service placement, family disorganization, and gender. *Journal of Interpersonal Violence, 17* (9), 1002. 18 pp.

variables because they can vary across individuals. One individual may choose to vote, another may not—hence, whether one votes varies. Likewise, one person can earn $45,000 a year, whereas another earns $150,000.

Among these two variables, the likelihood of voting and income, the **independent variable** would be the one that causes the change in the **dependent variable.** In other words, the value a person has for the dependent variable is *dependent* on or determined by whatever value that person has for the independent variable. Some students find it easier to think of the dependent variable as the one in which they are interested in predicting or explaining. To that end, the likelihood of voting is the dependent variable and income is the independent variable. Sometimes, in a pinch, you can distinguish between the two by asking yourself, Which makes more sense: that income will influence one's likelihood of voting or that one's likelihood of voting will influence how much one earns? If you think about it for just a millisecond, it is clear that it makes more sense that one's income will influence one's likelihood of voting—after all, it's a stretch to argue that whether one votes or not is going to determine how much a person earns! If it were that simple, there would be no need to go to college—everyone would just make sure that he or she votes in order to earn money!

Although is it perfectly acceptable for a hypothesis to simply state that two variables are related, the last, somewhat optional, part of a hypothesis is the direction of effect. A strong hypothesis will say whether the independent variable increases/decreases, is higher/is lower, or is more/less than the dependent variable. This addition makes a hypothesis stronger in two ways. First, from a theoretical point of view, it clarifies exactly what the researcher is hoping to find. This makes evaluating the researcher's interpretation of the data a little easier. The second way a direction of effect strengthens a hypothesis is from a statistical point of view. The statistical threshold for accepting a hypothesis is lower when there is a direction of effect. In other words, statistically it is easier to support a hypothesis that has a direction than it is for one that does not. This second point, however, involves the discussion of one- and two-tailed statistical tests and is beyond the scope of this book. The hypothesis in our previous example argued that the likelihood of voting *increased* with income, hence it did have a direction of effect.

One last word about hypotheses: Sometimes they are expressed as the specific value of the variable and not as the general concept, such as "income." An example of this would be if the previous hypothesis was reworded as "People who earn more than $100,00 are more likely to vote than are people who earn less than $40,000." Here, the dependent variable is still "likelihood of voting" and the independent variable is still "income." The only difference is that the hypothesis blends into the next aspect of research, which is measurement.

◼ Causality

As you already know, social science is interested in examining how social factors affect people's behavior. This implies that how people behave is influenced by social factors external to them—in other words, people are not acting completely on their free will. People make choices within the constraints of their social experiences, which sometimes provides little real choice. For example, suppose you want to examine the causes behind teenage pregnancy. The obvious cause is that a young girl had unprotected sex with some man. The deeper questions are *Why* did they have sex? and *Why* did they not use some type of contraception? After all, many people believe that having a child while young hurts women's future economic and social opportunities. So why risk it?

Social scientists could argue that if this young woman lives in an economically depressed area and is from a lower-income family, she may not perceive any benefits of a high school degree. From her view, even if she gets a degree, she is unlikely to go on to college due to lack of finances, and the types of jobs available with a high school diploma are not very lucrative. From this point of view, why should a woman with few economic opportunities delay having children until she is more economically stable, when (from her perspective) she is *not* likely to *ever* be economically stable? It is true that this hypothetical young woman chose to have unprotected sex and run the risk of getting pregnant, but, from her view, there was really little to choose from—there was no real benefit to delaying this transition.

The point I am trying to make is that most science takes a deterministic view of people's behavior. This means that science assumes that people do not have much individual freedom of choice; consequently, they will behave in somewhat predictable ways in specific situations. This view allows scientists to find patterns in individual behavior that can be used to explain behavior and to create policy aimed at changing behavior.

That being said, determinism—and those who generally believe in determinism, like social scientists—do not believe that all human actions are determined. They just believe that the choices peo-

Many people believe that having a child while young hurts women's future economic and social opportunities. Scientists frequently take a deterministic view when studying human behavior; therefore, they would study what conditions lead a young person to risk getting pregnant, even in light of the possible consequences.

ple make are influenced and limited by the social experiences those people have. Consequently, you might be more likely to find instances of teenage pregnancy among lower socioeconomic groups than among upper–middle-class groups.

The deterministic view does not imply that causal patterns are simple. In general, I discuss causal relationships involving one independent and one dependent variable, but I do this for simplicity and to facilitate learning. Most causal relationships are very complex and require the simultaneous examination of many variables to disentangle the relationship between any two main variables. Whereas one teen mother may have a child because she does not see any benefit in delaying parenthood while she invests in her economic future, another may have a baby in order to "keep" her boyfriend, a third teen might become a parent in order to obtain love she felt was missing from her life, and a fourth teen mother may have had a child for a combination of these reasons. The point is, the causal explanation behind the decision to become a teenage mother is very complex; consequently, the research designed to address this issue also needs to be complex.

Also, the deterministic view does not imply that a researcher will be able to predict or explain all the reasons why people behave a certain way, nor does it mean that all people will behave in the same manner. Remember, as I stated in Chapter 1, science is provisional and probabilistic. Consequently, given that researchers can identify certain conditions or independent variables (the provisional side), people are *likely* to behave in a specific manner, but not everyone will (the probabilistic side). That being said, let's examine hypotheses and the issues behind establishing causality in more detail.

In the beginning of Chapter 2, I mentioned that the role of theory is to provide a deeper explanation of *why*. For example, based on differential association theory, a theory under the symbolic interactionist paradigm, which argues that people learn their behavior (both normative and deviant) in the context of their primary groups, such as friendships, I may theorize that peers have a strong influence on whether a teen would participate in property crimes such as graffiti. Consequently, I hypothesize that the stronger an adolescent's tie to his or her friends, the more likely he or she is to participate in property crime if they do. In other words, theories aim to explain social phenomena; and, to that end, hypotheses frequently test theories.

In order to accurately argue that friendship groups cause property crime among adolescents, my research would need to fulfill three very stringent criteria: (1) an empirical association between two variables is shown, (2) the cause must precede the effect in time, and (3) any observed relationship between my independent and dependent variable is nonspurious. The first two criteria are fairly straightforward; the last, however, is rather involved. I will illustrate all three by looking at the relationship between adolescent peer groups and property crime.

Empirical association

The criterion of empirical association is pretty direct. It basically argues that if there is going to be a causal relationship between two variables, then a change in one variable (empirically, the independent variable) has to be associated with a change in the other variable (the dependent variable). Sometimes people refer to this criterion as a *correlation*, in that there has to be a correlation between the two variables. Essentially, correlation and association are the same idea; a correlation is really a statistical means of measuring an association.

Statistically, teenagers are more likely than people of other age groups to commit property crime. Teenagers are also more likely to have strong friendships groups. So, does it stand to reason that teenage friendship groups cause property crime? Can all the criteria for causality be met?

Establishing the first rule of causality for my example of whether adolescent friendship groups cause property crime seems pretty obvious. After all, parents are concerned about their children getting involved in the "wrong crowd" because they worry about the influence of friends on their children's behavior. Beginning researchers may be tempted to conclude, then, that friendship groups, which I will designate as F, lead to property crime, which I will designate as PC. This relationship is illustrated as: $F \rightarrow PC$.

However, keep in mind that correlation alone does not equal causation. If you read other social sciences texts, you may hear this warning, which reminds researchers and readers that establishing a correlation, or association between two or more variables, is only the first part of establishing causality. In and of itself, it is not enough. As I will illustrate with the other two criteria of causality, my ability to causally link adolescent peer groups to juvenile crime may not be as easy as you think.

Time order relationship

Like association, the time order relationship is a pretty obvious criterion. All it means is that the cause (independent variable) has to clearly precede the effect (dependent variable) in time. Obviously, an effect can't occur after a cause.

That being said, although the time order relationship is clear in theory, in reality it can be harder to establish. Take, for example, the relationship between mental illness and homelessness. Which comes first? One can make an argument that mentally ill people are more likely to be homeless, especially with the deinstitutionalization of mental hospitals; however, one can also argue that the stresses of living on the streets can lead some people to exhibit behaviors associated with mental illness. In this instance, establishing a causal connection would be very difficult.

Going back to our previous example, it may seem logical that making friends proceeds any deviant or criminal behavior such as property crime. It is less logical to argue the opposite (i.e., as an individual, Jim will vandalize property on his own because "he feels like it" and then ask others if they vandalize property in order to determine whether Jim want to be friends with them). Therefore, the time order of vandalism as the independent variable (which comes first) and friendship groups as the dependent variable (which comes second) does not make sense. (Even if Jim vandalized property in order to prove himself to a group of people who he wanted as friends, the friends are *still* the independent variable because Jim's desire for their friendship is the motivation behind the vandalism, therefore it still comes first.)

Nonspurious relationship

A **nonspurious relationship** is perhaps the most complicated and frequently overlooked aspect of establishing causality. Showing that a relationship between variables is nonspurious means establishing that the observed relationship between two variables is not due to (or caused by) a third variable. Researchers frequently call these causal variables, which are extraneous to the original independent/dependent relationship, **rival causal factors** because they are rival explanations for the association noticed between the original two variables.

In my example, not only can I show an association between friends and property crime but I can also make a logical argument that juveniles who are from lower economic backgrounds (which I will call E) may be more prone to committing property crime than middle-class children because they may lack money to buy items they want, or they may be less likely to have a job and/or participate in after-school activities (which provides them with more available time to commit deviant acts such as property crime). I can summarize this relationship as: $E \rightarrow PC$.

Furthermore, social scientists are more likely to associate specific types of friendship groups, such as gangs, with criminal behavior, and we are also more likely to see gang membership among lower-income groups than among middle-income groups. Consequently, $E \rightarrow F$.

All of these relationships can be summarized as follows:

1. Friendship groups are associated with property crime: $F \rightarrow PC$
2. Economic background is associated with property crime: $E \rightarrow PC$
3. Economic group may be associated with friendship groups: $E \rightarrow F$

If I take these three possible relationships and combine them, I see that economic background may be directly related to property crime or it can be indirectly related to property crime via an effect on friendship groups. Furthermore, friendship groups can be directly related to property crime independent of economic background. I can depict these potential relationships as such:

Sound confusing? It should. What causes property crime is a very complex issue—much more so than I even present here. You should be getting the idea, however, that arguing that friendship groups cause property crime is inaccurate. All I have done here, and what the bulk of the research has really shown, is that there is an association between friendship groups and property crime. As soon as researchers can theoretically and empirically show that other variables may be producing the observed relationship between their first two variables, they cannot establish causality.

BOX 3.3   **Correlation or Causation? Establishing Causality**

It seems that barely a few months goes by when we do not hear about some form of adolescent violence. Since the 1990s, fear surrounding school shootings and other violent crimes committed by teenagers has spurred a lot of research and discussion about the influence of popular culture on teens' behavior. Below is an excerpt that links teen violence (i.e., school shootings) to video games. Read the excerpt and then answer the critical thinking questions to determine whether we can make a causal connection between violent videos and violent behavior or whether this relationship is merely a correlation.

Marching through a large building using various bombs and guns to pick off victims is a conventional video-game scenario. In the Colorado massacre, Dylan Klebold and Eric Harris used pistol-grip shotguns, as in some video-arcade games. The pools of blood, screams of agony, and pleas for mercy must have been familiar—they are featured in some of the newer and more realistic kill-for-kicks games. . . .

Did the sensibilities created by the modern, video kill games play a role in the Littleton massacre? Apparently so. Note the cool and casual cruelty, the outlandish arsenal of weapons, the cheering and laughing while hunting down victims one by one. All of this seems to reflect the style and feel of the video killing games they played so often.

. . . But there is a cultural problem here: We are now a society in which the chief form of play for millions of youngsters is making large numbers of people die. . . . A widely cited survey of 900 fourth- through eighth-grade students found that almost half of the children said their favorite electronic games involve violence.

. . . The conventional argument is that this is a harmless activity among children who know the difference between fantasy and reality. But the games are often played by unstable youngsters unsure about the difference. . . . Adolescent feelings of resentment, powerlessness, and revenge pour into the killing games . . . [which] can become a dress rehearsal for the real thing.

. . . More realistic touches in video games help blur the boundary between fantasy and reality—guns carefully modeled on real ones, accurate-looking wounds, screams, and other sound effects, even the recoil of a heavy rifle. Some newer games . . . invite players to blow away ordinary people who have done nothing wrong—pedestrians, marching bands, an elderly woman with a walker.

. . . [T]he bottom line is that the young are being invited to enjoy the killing of vulnerable people picked at random.

. . . "We have to start worrying about what we are putting into the minds of our young," says Grossman. "Pilots train on flight simulators, drivers on driving simulators, and now we have our children on murder simulators." If we want to avoid more Littleton-style massacres, we will begin taking the social effects of the killing games more seriously.

Source: John Leo, "When Life Imitates Video," *U.S. News & World Report,* May 3, 1999, p. 14. (***AN 1767562***). Copyright © Chloe Consulting, Ltd. Reprinted by permission.

Critical Thinking Questions

1. Is there an association between the two variables, video games and adolescent violence (school shootings)?

2. Does the independent variable precede the dependent variable in time?

3. Has the researcher established that the relationship is nonspurious?

4. Has causality been established?

Critical Thinking Discussion

1. The author cites only one piece of anecdotal evidence of a direct association—the Littleton school shootings. The other evidence he presents—the survey of 900 fourth- to eighth-grade students which found that most students like violence in their video games—is not really

BOX 3.3   **Correlation or Causation? Establishing Causality, continued**

evidence of an association. Why? Because it does not even mention the dependent variable—namely, the committing of violent acts.

All this study said is that these children prefer violence in their video games. There is no mention of whether any of these children have exhibited violent behavior themselves. Furthermore, just because the author cites that the makers of video games devote a lot of attention to making their games realistic, that, too, never directly links viewing those games with violence on behalf of the viewers. So again, this is an interesting piece of information, but it does nothing to fulfill the first criteria of causality.

2. One can pretty much argue that it makes sense that watching precedes acting. However, even the author muddies this view by saying that adolescents who are feeling "resentment, powerlessness, and revenge" turn to video games. If this is the case, the temporal relationship is actually the opposite—those who are already prone to violence are more likely to *choose* violent video games. In this instance, the temporal relationship is the opposite of that necessary to argue that violent videos lead to violence.

3. Remember, nonspurious means that the relationship between two variables cannot be explained by another, third variable. Well, here we have a number of possible alternative explanations for the observed relationship between violent video games and subsequent violent actions. This relationship may be due to some preexisting violent tendencies on behalf of the individual (which we just discussed and which the author even recognizes may be present); it

may be due to a society in which guns are too easily obtainable (after all, have you never wondered about *where* these teens obtain the guns that enable them to shoot others?); or, most likely, it is due to a number of different factors that coexist simultaneously. The point is that most studies have not accurately addressed all the possible topical rival causal factors that could explain why a very small minority of children who watch video games act violently. This study is no different.

4. It should be clear that a causal link between watching violent video games and consequently behaving violently remains elusive. All we have generally been able to establish is a correlational relationship. However, this excerpt illustrates an important point. Much of what we read in the popular media—and even in some academic research, which should know better—argues causal connections when, in fact, none has been established. This example further illustrates the need to adopt a critical view of information learned.

The nation has devoted millions of dollars to added security in schools when, in reality, school violence is exceptionally rare. Furthermore, the country has devoted a lot of time and money on harsher legislation regarding video games, when, in fact, the overwhelming majority of people who play violent video games do not act violently. Designing policy on misperceived conclusions only wastes time and money but it can also misdirect efforts to search for and address the real causes behind social problems.

These rival causal factors can be variables related to the topic that researchers fail to include in their designs, such as with my example of adolescent property crime, or they can be problems that arise in the design of the research itself. For clarification, I'd like to call the other topical influences that can interfere with a causal relationship *topical rival causal factors*. Researchers can statistically address the problem of topical rival causal factors so long as they anticipate these additional factors and include them in their design.

For example, if I interviewed adolescents about their friends and about their behaviors, I may also want to include information that addresses the economic background of an adolescent's family, whether the adolescent participates in after-school activities, whether the adolescent has a job, or any other factors that my review of the literature suggests may be important. If I have information on these factors, when I get ready to analyze my data, I can see if friendships groups have an effect on property crime *while controlling* for these other potential rival causal factors. In other words, I can see whether friendship groups have an effect on behavior while I am *simultaneously* recognizing the effect of these additional variables. Although this is not necessarily difficult to do, the statistics behind it are beyond the scope of this book. I just wanted to let you know that social behavior is too complicated to be causally explained by two variables, and failure to control for other topical rival causal factors is a common, but not insurmountable, problem with some research.

Rival causal factor problems that stem from the design of the research itself are a bit more difficult to resolve. In my hypothetical study, a design rival causal factor would have occurred if I was studying adolescent crime in a community in which a large local business recently closed. Did the property crime I noticed stem from adolescent friendship groups or did it stem from the business leaving which created indirect issues such as decreased family income or some other home life stress that led these children to behave deviantly? These potential rival causal factors affect the overall validity of my research, not just my ability to make causal connections, although that is affected, too. When researchers discuss issues of study validity, they are often referring to evaluations of this third causal criteria. Hence, it is appropriate here to introduce the discussion of validity now. I will revisit this discussion in the next chapter when I talk about measurement validity.

Study Validity

In its most basic sense, *validity* refers to the accurateness of research. A variety of issues can threaten research validity, and different research designs are better at minimizing different validity threats. Part of choosing an appropriate research design for a topic involves a preliminary consideration of potential threats to validity and the consequent selection of a design that minimizes the most of those potential threats. Let's discuss each of these threats to validity in more detail.

■ Statistical Conclusion Validity

Sometimes validity is threatened when a researcher cannot find a relationship between two variables that he or she has a strong theoretical reason to believe should be present. This means that the researcher is unable to fulfill the first criteria of causality. For example, research has long suggested (so much so that it is now a common stereotype) that upper–middle-class people are more likely to be registered as Republicans and working-class people as Democrats. However, if you wanted to study how educational attainment (which is associated with social class) affects political party affiliation, but more working-class respondents were Republicans and more upper–middle-class respondents were Democrats, you might have a problem with **statistical conclusion validity.** You cannot find an association between these two variables, education and political party affiliation, even though the research you reviewed suggested that there should be a relationship because of the strong association between social class and educational attainment. You might fail to establish statistical conclusion validity for a number of reasons, but the two most common reasons are that you did a poor job at conceptualizing and measuring your concepts and that your sample size is too small to make accurate conclusions.

On the other hand, you could also have a problem with statistical conclusion validity if you find an association between variables and are tempted to make a causal connection, when in fact, no causal connection exists. For example, have any of you played or watched someone play a slot machine? People at casinos frequently stake out a slot machine and when they start playing one, they become very territorial. Even if they are losing continually, the more they lose, the more likely they are to feel that "the Big One" is right around the corner. Why? Because after losing for so long, they think that they are "due" for a win. However, games such as slot machines, roulette, and card games are games of chance, which means that there is no pattern as to when someone will start winning or start losing. The erroneous belief that a pattern exists, and that someone is "due" for a change simply because they have been in a specific state for so long, is called the **gambler's fallacy.** If someone wins at a slot machine, she or he might be tempted to conclude that the win was due to the way he or she pulled the handle just so or because the machine didn't have a win for a while and was "due"; in reality, neither explanation is appropriate. The only reason someone wins at a slot machine in pure blind luck, and thinking otherwise is falling prey to the gambler's fallacy.

To summarize, statistical conclusion validity is a threat to causality because the first criteria for causality cannot be fulfilled. Researchers either cannot observe an association you theoretically believe should be present, or the opposite, researchers *are* observing a relationship that has no corresponding theoretical explanation. This threat to validity illustrates the importance of the theory–research connection. Research and theoretical expectations need to match. Findings that theory cannot plausibly explain should be suspect, as should the lack of findings when researchers have a theoretical reason to believe they are present.

■ Internal Validity

Internal validity refers to whether some factor other than the independent variable produced the observed change in the dependent variable. Most commonly, threats to internal validity are other topical issues related to the research that a researcher failed to take into account. When I discussed the difficulty establishing a causal connection between viewing violent videos and aggressive behavior in Chapter 2, I was referring to problems of internal validity because many variables, rarely included in these studies, affect violent behavior.

However, other design issues can also threaten internal validity. Some common threats to internal validity include the following:

1. History effects
2. Maturation
3. Testing
4. Instrumentation
5. Selection bias
6. Contamination
7. Experimental mortality

History effects

History effects are events external to the research that can affect the results obtained. History effects can be seasonal fluctuations, newsworthy events that influence people's perceptions, or even natural disasters. For example, suppose you did a study of the use of shelters in January by homeless people and you noticed that shelters were incredibly understaffed and underequipped to deal with the amount of homeless individuals trying to gain entry. Can you conclude that the homeless population in this particular city is so large that it is unmanageable? Not necessarily. It may be that a city's shelters are inadequate to deal with that city's homeless only in the winter, when colder and harsher weather force more people to seek shelter. Furthermore, there may be fewer work opportunities in the winter, which may seasonally influence the number of homeless in a particular area.

Let's look at a second example. If you compared prejudicial attitudes toward various minority group members in 1992 with attitudes in 2002, you might notice more prejudicial attitudes in 2002. Why do you think this is the case? One explanation could be that the events of September 11, 2001, were still fresh enough in people's minds at that point to alter their views of specific minority groups. Once the shock and horror of that event calmed, prejudicial attitudes may return to the levels noticed in 1992. Consequently, researchers need to remember that social lives do not occur in a vacuum; therefore, they need to be conscious of any potential external influences that may affect study participants' behavior.

Unfortunately, there is little that researchers can do to prevent history effects, since these threats to validity are frequently beyond the researcher's control (for example, no one foresaw the events of September 11). If a researcher suspects that a history effect occurred during the course of the study, then the researcher has an obligation to make this suspicion known in his or her write-up. On the other hand, a little common sense on behalf the researcher when designing research may minimize seasonal history effects.

Maturation

Maturation effects are possible in longitudinal research when participants' behavior changes occur due to the simple act of aging or the length of the study (e.g., the participants grew bored) instead of the independent variable. Take the hypothetical example where I study the effects of a year-long juvenile counseling program on drug use among 40 boys ages 14 to 18 and I follow each of these boys for 10 years after the completion of the juvenile counseling program. If I notice that the percentage of boys using drugs continues to decline a few years after the program and then levels off as the boys reach their mid- to late twenties, can I conclude that the juvenile counseling program has long-term negative effects on drug use? As in the previous example, not necessarily. Studies show that criminal behavior, including drug use, generally decreases as people age because as people mature, they assume jobs, perhaps get married, or even have children, all of which serve to stabilize individuals (especially men). Because employed people have less time for acts such as drug use and because married people, especially those with children, have more social costs (e.g., the threat of losing one's job or family) for being deviant, as people mature and assume these roles, drug use declines.

Again, researchers can do little to prevent maturation effects—after all, it's not as if researchers can prevent individuals from growing up! If maturation is a suspected threat to causal validity, then, as with history effects, the researcher has the responsibility to mention this potential threat when reporting the study. That is really all a researcher can do.

Testing

Testing threats to validity, sometimes called *pretest bias*, or **pretest effects,** occur when the administration of a pretest or a survey affects a later test or survey because participants have now been sensitized to the research information as a result of being tested. This is primarily an issue when the pretest and posttest are close together; however, sometimes this cannot be avoided. Consequently, the main way to minimize this threat to is design observation points that are sufficiently spaced apart. However, what is "sufficient" is not easily defined and is pretty much determined by the topic, the research design, and any information gleaned from previous studies found in the literature review. I will address this issue in much more detail in Chapter 7 when I discuss experiments.

Instrumentation

Instrumentation is another potential threat to validity that occurs when the measures used to observe concepts change during the course of the study. This can occur due to changes in concept definition, question wording, and/or data-gathering strategies. An excellent example of this threat to validity is when researchers try to use sources such as the Uniform Crime Reports to make longitudinal comparisons of crime rates. Any time a law changes the definition of a crime, researchers may see a change in crime rates. For example, when rape laws changed to include forcible sexual intercourse by husbands to wives as rape, it appeared to the casual observer that rapes were becoming more frequent because the reported incidence of rape increased. However, rapes were not necessarily becoming more frequent. The broader definition of rape meant that more acts that previously were not defined as rape were now defined as such, which increased the number of rape incidents reported.

When using secondary data, data produced by other people, instrumentation may be difficult to avoid because the secondary researcher does not have control over the definition of terms. In this case, researchers should make comparisons cautiously, if at all. When designing one's own research, this is much easier to avoid simply by making sure that the research design is consistent across the different time periods. If any questions are added to the analysis, they should not be added as a replacement for a preexisting variable. They should simply be added to the existing survey, leaving the original variable present in its original form.

Selection bias

Selection bias occurs when characteristics of the experimental and control groups differ. This can occur in a number of ways: comparing the effectiveness of a family leave policy in a medium-sized business (experimental group) to a corporation (control group), examining the effects of community-oriented policing in a rural town to a suburban town that does not have this program, or comparing an experimental group of children who are from middle-class families to a control group of children who are from primarily working-class families. Be careful, however. Students frequently misinterpret study and control groups in and of themselves to be illustrations of selection bias under the argument that since one group (the experimental group) receives a treatment and the other group (the control group) does not, these two groups are not equivalent and therefore bias is present. This is not so. In studies, researchers *want* the experimental and control group to differ on the independent variable (essentially what the treatment is). They just do not want them to differ on *other* variables relevant to the study, such as age, race, sex, education, or any other obvious topical variable related to the dependent variable.

Researchers can estimate this type of selection bias by using a pretest that includes measures of concepts, other than the independent variable of interest, that may affect the behavior of interest (dependent variable). In this case, statistical tests can estimate whether the comparison groups are significantly different on any variables of interest, and the goal is to have them not be. I will discuss this more thoroughly in Chapter 6.

Contamination

Contamination may be a threat to internal validity when members of the experimental or control group learn of each other and this knowledge affects their behavior in the posttest. For example, if members of a control group learn that they are being denied some treatment that they perceive as advantageous, they may increase their efforts to compensate or they may become demoralized and perform worse than expected on the posttest (Cook & Campbell, 1979). This internal threat to validity results when researchers do not adequately control their experimental and control groups by either letting the groups learn too much about the study (for example, a newspaper article on the experiment while the experiment is still in progress) or have contact with each other (as in the case where the experimental and control groups are two neighboring cities or towns).

The main way to prevent contamination is to ensure that the experimental and control groups have no contact during the course of the study and that the treatment time is relatively brief. To the degree that these conditions are not achieved, and that contamination is therefore suspected, the validity of the findings become suspect.

Experimental mortality

Experimental mortality is a common threat in longitudinal studies, especially studies known as *panel studies* in which the same people are studied at multiple time points. This occurs when members of an original sample drop out of a study as time passes. Some loss of study participants over time is expected and does not automatically mean that experimental mortality is a problem. Experimental mortality becomes a threat to validity when large percentages of participants drop out or if participants who have similar characteristics or behaviors stop participating. There is not much one can do to prevent experimental mortality, other than the typical tactics used to elicit participation in any study, longitudinal or cross-sectional. Even with these tactics, however, experimental mortality is a risk of longitudinal studies and needs to be monitored.

Summary

In summary, internal threats to validity are threats to the research design that interfere with a researcher's ability to fulfill the third criteria of causality — the elimination of rival causal factors. I will revisit these validity threats in Chapter 6 when I discuss experiments, the classic method (but not the only method) for establishing causality.

■ External Validity

Research is not just vulnerable to threats that jeopardize the ability to draw causal connections within a study. There are also threats to validity that inhibit the ability to argue that the causal connections found among a sample in one study also apply to larger or different populations. When researchers are unsure whether cause/effect relationships will hold for other groups, different settings, or different times, they are concerned with external validity. According to Campbell and Stanley (1963), some issues of **external validity** are

1. Testing effects
2. Selection bias
3. Reactivity/Hawthorne effect

Testing effects

As I mentioned in the previous section on internal validity, testing effects occur when the administration of a pretest sensitizes participants and therefore affects their answers at a later test point. Not only can a pretest be a rival causal factor for any observed relationship between independent and dependent variables but it can also affect the generalizability of findings to other populations that have not been pretested. In other words, if a pretest affects the measurement of a dependent variable in a particular study, then others will be unsure how to apply the findings of that study to a group that was not part of the original study and that did not receive the pretest.

Selection bias

Selection bias can hinder not only internal validity but also external validity. This type of validity threat occurs when researchers draw samples that are not representative of the population about which researchers hope to make conclusions. If I want to study Americans' views of the president's education plan and I draw a sample of 5,000 people of whom only 5 percent are African American, I cannot make conclusions about "Americans'" views of this plan because I have selection bias. African Americans constitute approximately 12 percent of the U.S. population; any sample that has noticeably less (or more) than that 12 percent is vulnerable to selection bias.

Researchers can minimize the likelihood of this type of selection bias by using random sampling or random assignment. I will discuss this more in Chapter 5.

Reactivity/Hawthorne effect

Roethlisberger and Dixon (1939) conducted a now classic study of worker efficiency in the Hawthorne plant of the Western Electric Company in Chicago. The researchers created experimental treatments that were aimed at increasing and decreasing worker efficiency, but they found that the treatment consistently increased efficiency—even those treatments designed to *decrease* worker efficiency! What was going on? Roethlisberger and Dixon discovered that the workers were not actually responding to the researchers' experimental treatments; rather, they were reacting to the experiment itself! In other words, these workers were reacting to being studied. Happy to be part of an important study, the workers tried to behave in a way that they thought the researchers wanted.

The concern that subjects will act differently, or *react* to being studied (or exhibit the **Hawthorne effect,** as frequently dubbed in reference to that study) is a very real one. Juveniles who think acting aggressive is part of being "cool" may act more aggressively when studied than they would otherwise because they want to impress the researcher. Or bosses who might otherwise be very derogatory to women and minorities may be on "good behavior" during a study because they know that such behaviors are socially unacceptable and they do not want to appear prejudiced in front of other educated individuals. It is obvious that findings based on atypical behavior may not be applicable to different settings where people are not aware that they are being observed.

Students frequently ask whether any research is truly free of the Hawthorne effect—after all, people have to voluntarily agree to participate in a study, they therefore know they are being studied, and, consequently, may alter their behavior as a result. In this very rigid view, the answer is no—all research may be vulnerable to the Hawthorne effect. However, there are steps researchers can take to minimize this validity threat or make it so negligible that it does not, in reality, threaten validity.

For example, surveys can be anonymous, which gives people a sense of protection and security when revealing personal information. Interviewers can observe any subtle changes in body language among respondents that may suggest a **reactivity** effect and decide what to do with the information from those particular respondents. Much like the popular MTV show *The Real World,* which advertises that it is a show about "what happens when people stop being polite and start being real," field researchers stay in the field with participants for extended periods of time so that participants "stop acting polite and start acting real," which minimizes the threat of reactivity. Finally, having sufficiently large sample sizes also can help ensure that those who, despite other attempts on behalf of the researcher, are still influenced by the study will be a statistical minority and therefore have little real effect on the findings.

■ Measurement Validity

How do researchers know that their measures, or variables, are accurately measuring what they think they are? In other words, if you want to study the effects of watching violent movies on people's aggressive behavior, how do you know that the ways you define and measure "aggressive" behavior really do assess the issues you're interested in studying? Will someone who uses a different definition be able to find similar results as you do? Does this mean that one measure is "correct" and another is not? These questions address issues involving measurement validity. The next chapter focuses on how researchers define and measure the concepts in hypotheses; therefore, I will postpone the discussion of measurement validity until then.

Bringing It Together: A Summary of Hypotheses, Causation, and Validity

This chapter began with the seemingly easy job of choosing a research topic—I say "seemingly" because research topics are difficult to select because there are so many potential topics available. Because topics are so varied and broad, social scientists frequently examine only one or two specific aspects of any one research topic. Doing otherwise would require more time, money, and energy than most people have. Literature reviews help researchers narrow their specific line of inquiry by educating them about what is already known about an issue, where studies are producing contradictory findings, and where gaps in knowledge remain. Researchers can use this information to narrow their general research problems into more specific and manageable research hypotheses. These hypotheses are statements about social phenomena that researchers can directly observe and, therefore, empirically test.

Many, but not all, hypotheses aim to build on existing theory by establishing some type of causal relationship between two or more variables. More specifically, hypotheses aim to illustrate how one variable, the independent variable, produces a direct change in another variable, the dependent variable. Once again, on the surface, this seems easy because two of the three criteria for establishing causality are relatively straightforward. These two criteria are (1) establishing covariance, or an empirical association between the independent and dependent variables; and (2) showing that the independent variable precedes the dependent variable in time—or establishing the appropriate temporal association between the independent and dependent variables.

The third criteria for causality, making sure that any observed relationship between the independent and dependent variables is nonspurious (or not explained by a third variable)—is the one that involves more forethought and vigilance on behalf of the researcher. These other variables that can get in the way of establishing causality are frequently called rival causal factors (creatively enough!) and they threaten the validity of the conclusions that researchers can reach.

These threats to validity fall into three main categories. The first category, threats to internal validity, threaten a researcher's ability to make causal conclusions within his or her specific study. These threats include history effects, maturation effects, testing effects, instrumentation effects, selection bias, and experimental mortality. The second group of validity threats, external validity, threatens a researcher's ability to generalize her or his cause/effect relationships to other times, people, and places. This group includes testing effects and selection bias again, but also involves participant reactivity. Finally, the third group of rival causal factors, or threats to validity, are threats to measurement validity, which will be discussed in the next chapter.

Needless to say, establishing causality is very difficult and needs to be treated very carefully. To some degree, researchers can minimize these threats to validity by how they design their research; however, the difficulty of truly establishing causal connections between variables remains. That is why researchers take such pains to design research methodologies that are as carefully planned as those I will discuss in this book. The next sections look at two other issues researchers consider when getting started on a research project: the time dimension of the research and the units of analysis.

Time Dimensions

Suppose you wanted to evaluate whether student mentors helped other students learn to read. To do this, you decided that you were going to use sixth-grade students who had grades of A in reading serve as student mentors to third-grade students who were having trouble reading. How would you know if the mentoring helped? You couldn't just look at reading scores, say, three months after the mentoring started because you wouldn't know if the scores changed if you didn't first examine reading scores *prior* to the mentoring program. Essentially, if you wanted to evaluate this program, you would need to do **longitudinal research**—or research that occurs at more than one time point.

Interestingly, for reasons we'll discuss shortly, most research is cross-sectional, meaning that it occurs only at one point in time only. A marketing survey you receive in the mail, complete, and never hear from again is an example of **cross-sectional research.** A study about college students' views on homosexuality that occurs at one time only is cross-sectional. Essentially, think of cross-sectional research as a snapshot

—it is as if the researcher is freezing a moment of time by studying a phenomenon at one point in time.

Cross-sectional research is frequently used for exploratory and descriptive studies. For example, a police department may survey community members to determine their view of the police and what they think the police need to address. This would be an exploratory study that may be useful in designing program changes that will later be evaluated. Sometimes cross-sectional research can also be used for explanatory purposes if the researcher is interested in explaining people's attitudes or behaviors at one point in time. For instance, the previously mentioned survey about college students' views on homosexuality may also include questions designed to try to explain why college students have the views that they do. However, one has to be cautious. Remember that one aspect of establishing causality is making sure that the cause precedes the effect in time. This is difficult to ascertain with cross-sectional studies. In other words, a researcher can never be truly sure that student responses to the independent variables truly occur prior to the formation of students' views on homosexuality (the dependent variable). Nevertheless, cross-sectional studies are frequently cheaper and easier to conduct than are longitudinal studies; consequently, for better or for worse, they are frequently the time design of choice.

Longitudinal studies, on the other hand, are better suited for explanatory and for evaluation studies because they permit observation over a longer period of time. Longitudinal studies can therefore establish change. They can also help clarify the time criteria for establishing causality when which comes first, the independent or dependent variable, might otherwise be unclear. In longitudinal studies, researchers can document the dependent variable at various time points and then see if it changes *after* the independent variable is introduced. By introducing the independent variable at a specific date and by having details about the dependent variable before and after the inclusion of the independent variable, researchers are better able to fulfill that second criteria of causality: establishing a time order relationship. Three types of longitudinal studies that are relevant for our purposes are trend studies, cohort studies, and panel studies. Figure 3.2 summarizes the different time dimensions.

Trend studies examine the changes in a general population over time. If I studied members of my local community in 2002, drew a new sample of community members in 2004, and collected a third sample of members in 2006, I'd be doing a trend study. Hamilton and Form (2003, **AN 9426181**) used trend study data when they examined how introductory sociology textbooks' use of categorical descriptions of race, ethnicity, and religion compared with social trends noticed in academic research that use more detailed classifications of these three issues (race, ethnicity, and religion). To establish social trends, Hamilton and Form used the 1972–1998 waves of the General Social Survey (GSS). The GSS selects a new sample of noninstitutionalized adults every time the survey is done, which was yearly from 1972 to 1993 and biannually after 1994. Because data were gathered over many different years, it is a longitudinal dataset. Because the people selected for the sample are different each time a study is done, it is trend data.

Cohort studies examine, over time, a group of individuals who share some type of time-related characteristic. If I study 100 college students in September at the start of their school year, draw a new sample of 100 students from the same college in January at the start of the new semester (no longer using the original sample of 100 students), I'd be doing a trend study. Similarly, if I studied a sample of 500 people born in 1987 across four different years, drawing a new sample of 500 people born in 1987 each time, I'd also be doing a

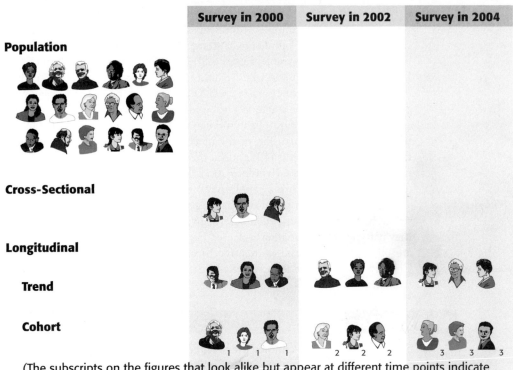

	Survey in 2000	Survey in 2002	Survey in 2004

Population

Cross-Sectional

Longitudinal

Trend

Cohort

(The subscripts on the figures that look alike but appear at different time points indicate that there are three different people at the different time points, but they share the same characteristics as those in the other time points—for example, an elderly woman in the 2000 survey ($_1$) a second, different elderly woman in the 2002 survey ($_2$), etc.)

Panel

(The subscripts indicate that the *same people* are being interviewed at the different time points—for example, an elderly woman in the 2000 survey ($_1$) is the same elderly woman in the 2002 survey ($_2$), etc.)

Figure 3.2 Time Dimensions in Research

cohort study, as all the people participating across the four time spans have their birth year in common (even though I am using separate individuals). Smit, de Zwart, Spruit, Monshouwer, and van Ameijden (2002, **AN 6933937**) did a cohort longitudinal study when they used the Dutch National School Survey to assess the survey's ability to monitor substance use and putative risk factors among adolescents. This survey is done every four years, so it is longitudinal, and it is always done on adolescents, a specific cohort of people. These adolescents are not going to be the *same* people from one survey period to the next because, by definition, the adolescents in one wave will no longer be adolescents in school by the next wave, simply due to biological aging.

Panel studies take trend and cohort studies one step further by examining the *same* individuals across the different time spans. In other words, instead of drawing an entirely new sample each time I conducted a study, in panel studies, I just use the same people over and over again. For example, I used the 1972–1990 waves of the Panel Study of Income Dynamics (PSID) to assess whether and how mothers' jobs throughout their daughters' childhood and adolescence affect these daughters' early adult fertility and marital patterns (Wolfer, 1998). As the name implies, the *Panel* Study of Income Dynamics follows the same people at each point of the survey process. Therefore, I was able to piece together the employment information of the mothers for the daughters in my sample *each year* from the daughters' births (1972) until they reached the age of 18 (1990). In other words, my dataset contained yearly information (hence, it was longitudinal) on the same people for 18 years (hence, it was a panel study).

As you may guess, panel studies are particularly informative when doing evaluation research, as the researcher can detect any change in behavior among individuals before they participate in a program and after. However, panel studies are also very expensive (as are all longitudinal studies, relative to cross-sectional studies) and, as we will see in Chapters 6 and 7, have some specific methodological challenges that researchers may need to address.

Units of Analysis

Suppose a researcher examined the SAT scores of 50 private and 50 public universities and found that the SAT scores in private universities were not statistically different from the SAT scores in public universities. Can the researcher then conclude that individual students in private schools are no smarter than individual students in public schools? No. Doing so would be committing what researchers call **ecological fallacy,** which occurs when researchers draw conclusions about *individuals* when they really study *groups*. This is a common and easy mistake to make. In order to avoid incorrect inferences such as this, researchers must continually keep in mind their units of analysis.

Simply put, **units of analysis** are the people or things that a researcher is studying. There are generally four units of analysis: individuals, groups, organizations, and social artifacts. Probably the most commonly used type of unit of analysis is individuals. If I took a random sample of 200 college students from Smithtown College to examine their attitudes about school sports, I would be studying individuals. If I compared the responses of male and female college students, based on this study, I would *still* be studying individuals, even though I would be aggregating this information into group comparisons. Why? Because in collecting the data, I just approached individuals and asked them questions that might later categorize them into groups. I did not first decide to include a person in the study *because* he or she was a member of a specific group I was going to later compare.

For example, Yang and Lin (2004, **AN 12670781**) wanted to study thinking styles, such as critical thinking, among high school students. To conduct their analysis, they surveyed 1,119 male senior high school students from six senior high schools in Taiwan. Even though they selected students from different schools, their purpose was not to *compare* students in the different schools; they simply needed more than one school to reach their desired sample size and representation among high school seniors. In other words, they just wanted to examine thinking among the entire pool of 1,119 students, regardless of the school from which they came. Hence, Yang and Lin were studying *individuals*.

If, on the other hand, I surveyed all the campus groups—both sport oriented and non-sport oriented—and compared the views of sport groups (e.g., football, basketball, etc.) to nonsport groups (e.g., student government, drama club, etc.), then my units of analysis would be *groups*. Why? This may sound confusing because obviously a sports *team* itself cannot answer questions—individuals who belong to that team would be answering questions, making the units of analysis appear to be individuals. However, this is not the case. In this instance, I am not selecting individuals, asking them what groups they belong to and then making group comparisons (that would be an individual level of analysis). Instead, I am identifying groups, then selecting the individuals *from* those groups, and then lumping those individual responses back into a group identity to compare the groups. Figure 3.3 further illustrates the difference between individual and group units of analysis relating to the photo below.

Essentially, the order and purpose of data collection is the opposite for groups than it is for individuals. Some examples of units of analysis at the group level are teams, classrooms, gangs, households, cities, and states. A comparison between racial, ethnic, national, and religious groups can also be group-level units of analysis, provided that the people were first identified based on group membership and then selected. This is what McBride, Xiang, Wittenburg, and Shen (2002, **AN 667756**) did when they selected 218 American physical education students and compared them to 234 students from the Shanghai Institute of Physical Education in terms of how they approach critical thinking in their discipline. The purpose of their study was to compare American and Chinese students—two differently selected groups of students—within the same field. Contrary to Yang and Lin's (2004) study, which only wanted to study students, as a wide pool regardless of where the students were selected, McBride and colleagues specifically selected their participants to facilitate the comparison of groups—American and Chinese students. Therefore, even though they had to ask questions of individual students, their unit of analysis was groups, since their subjects were first, and purposely, identified by their group membership.

The third unit of analysis is organizations. This unit of analysis usually refers to formal organizations—political or social. Formal organizations can frequently be characterized in terms of who belongs, who they serve, what they do, how they are organized, and so on. If, for example, I wanted to compare the student composition of Smithtown College to Jonestown University, my units of analysis would

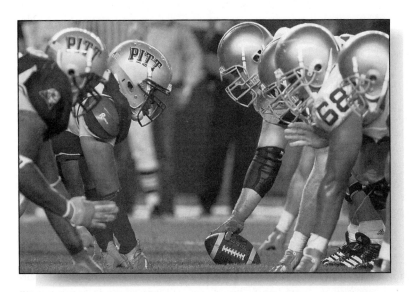

If a researcher selects college students and uses, for example, a survey question to determine who among these students is on the football team and who is on the baseball team in order to compare these athletes' views, then that researcher's unit of analysis is individuals. If that researcher, however, purposefully selects students from the football team in order to compare them to students selected from the baseball team, then that researcher's unit of analysis is groups.

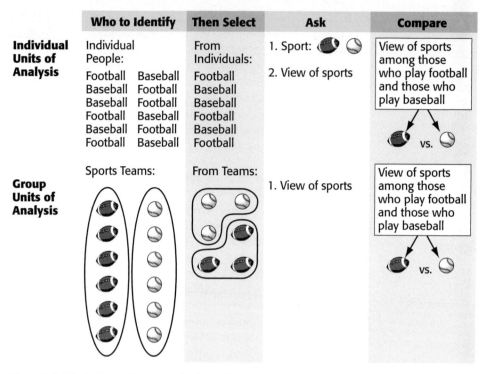

	Who to Identify	Then Select	Ask	Compare
Individual Units of Analysis	Individual People: Football Baseball Baseball Football Baseball Football Football Baseball Baseball Football Football Baseball	From Individuals: Football Baseball Baseball Football Baseball Football	1. Sport: 2. View of sports	View of sports among those who play football and those who play baseball
Group Units of Analysis	Sports Teams:	From Teams:	1. View of sports	View of sports among those who play football and those who play baseball

Figure 3.3 *The Difference between Individual and Group Units of Analysis and Comparisons*

be organizations. Again, the characteristics being examined may be related to the characteristics of individuals who belong to these organizations, but it is important to keep in mind that I am not looking for trends among these individuals; rather, I am looking for trends on a more aggregate level—among the organizations to which these individuals belong. For example, Gould (2001, **AN 5909202**) examines whether political party size in a legislature affects the tax revenue collected by a state. In Gould's analysis, he is considering political parties, which are organizations.

Studies can also be done on things like laws, songs, books, crime reports, newspaper articles, political speeches, and court cases. None of these are people, but they all were produced by people. Hence, the last type of unit of analysis is social artifacts. Consequently, a researcher can study what percentage of legal cases went to trial compared to what percentage were settled out of court. Or, one can examine crime rates to see whether crime was increasing or decreasing over a specific span of time. Or, as Brasher (2003, **AN 11309167**) did, one can study campaign messages to assess a political party's campaign setting agenda during an election year.

Given all these possibilities among units of analysis, it is easy to see how researchers can make incorrect causal connections between their units of analysis and the population that those units represent. This is even the case when studying social artifacts. For example, let's say a researcher is studying property crime by looking at the property crime rates of different neighborhoods and notices that reported incidences of property crime are higher in low-income neighborhoods. The researcher may be tempted to conclude that

BOX 3.4 **Units of Analysis Practice**

Below are some excerpts from the abstracts of articles found in Research Navigator. Identify the units of analysis of each study.

1. "Despite some progress, women remain under-represented in the boardrooms of Corporate America, a recent study found. Women currently account for 779, or 13.6%, of board seats at Fortune 500 companies, according to the census conducted in research firm Catalyst."

2. "Children with special health care needs (CSHCN) often require more extensive services than children without special needs. The State Children's Health Insurance Program (SCHIP) in many states typically provides less extensive benefits and services than do state Medicaid programs. To design SCHIP to address the needs of CSHCN adequately, it is important to measure the degree to which children who enroll in SCHIP have special health care needs and to assess their health status and unmet health care needs. Little is known about the characteristics or pre-enrollment experience of CSHCN who enroll in SCHIP.

   Objectives. To use data from the Child Health Insurance *Research* Initiative to measure the prevalence of CSHCN in SCHIP in 4 states, describe their demographic and health care features at enrollment, and compare their socio-demographic characteristics, health status, prior health care experiences, and unmet needs versus children without special health care needs."

3. "Organizers of the [Third International Mathematics and Science Study] TIMSS wanted to go beyond simple comparison of mathematics and science achievement to consider the contextual factors that may help to explain international achievement differences. Three supplementary studies were conducted with this aim in mind: Case studies of the educational systems in each country (Stevenson & Nerison-Low, 1999); an analysis of curriculum materials from the TIMSS countries (Schmidt, McKnight, & Raizen, 1997); and the TIMSS video study. The TIMSS video study was carried out in three countries: Germany, Japan, and the United States. Germany and Japan were chosen because they are viewed as economic competitors to the United States. The goals of the study were to create a portrait of eighth-grade mathematics teaching in the three countries and to assess the effects of reform policies on U.S. mathematics teaching practices.

   Videotaping procedures were standardized so that all videographers followed the same decision rules. Only one camera was used in each classroom, and in general it focused on what an ideal student would be focusing on—the teacher. After taping, the teacher filled out a questionnaire describing the goal of the lesson, its place within the current sequence of lessons, and so on."

4. "The purpose of this study is to explore how antisocial content in televised wrestling is represented in match–nonmatch time and in three different television time periods: prime time, after midnight, and weekend morning time. Based on previous television violence studies, the antisocial content (aggressive acts, rule violations, and glamorization of violence) important in evaluating televised wrestling was analyzed. The results indicate that national televised wrestling programs (World Wrestling Federation, World Championship Wrestling, and Extreme Championship Wrestling) frequently show more antisocial content than locally oriented ones (National Wrestling Alliance and International Wrestling Union). The antisocial content is also frequently represented in nonmatch time as well as match time. There is no significant difference of frequency of antisocial representation among prime time, after midnight, and weekend morning time periods, so this study suggests that children might be exposed to similar amounts of antisocial behaviors regardless of time period."

BOX 3.4   **Units of Analysis Practice, continued**

5. "The ongoing war on terrorism has apparently taken a toll on the First Amendment. A new poll shows that nearly half of Americans surveyed believe the First Amendment goes too far in protecting rights, and increasing numbers believe the government should be able to monitor some religious groups.

   The poll, "State of the First Amendment 2002," was issued last month by the First Amendment Center, an arm of the Freedom Forum in Nashville. In the survey, 49 percent said the First Amendment goes too far in protecting the rights it guarantees—a jump of 10 points since 2001."

6. "This paper examines heterosexual adults' attitudes toward bisexual men and women using data from a 1999 national RDD *survey* (N = 1,335). Ratings on 101-point feeling thermometers were lower (less favorable) for bisexual men and bisexual women than for all other groups assessed—including religious, racial, ethnic, and political groups— except injecting drug users. More negative attitudes toward bisexuals were associated with higher age, less education, lower annual income, residence in the South and rural areas, higher religiosity, political conservatism, traditional values concerning gender and sexual behavior, authoritarianism, and lack of contact with gay men or lesbians. White heterosexual women expressed significantly more favorable attitudes than other women and all men. A gender difference was observed in attitudes toward bisexuals and homosexuals: Heterosexual women rated bisexuals significantly less favorably than they rated homosexuals, regardless of gender, whereas heterosexual men rated male targets less favorably than female targets, regardless of whether the target was bisexual or homosexual."

7. "To determine gender role stereotyping based on the presence or absence of female characters and the types of clothing those characters were wearing in video games, a content analysis was conducted. A population of video games was constructed by compiling a list of the Nintendo 64 and PlayStation games available for purchase at the time of the study, except for adult-only titles. The game titles were supplied from a major national toy store. By listing only those games still available for purchase from the manufacturer's supplier, discontinued titles were not included in the population. The population of video games consisted of 227 PlayStation games and 114 Nintendo 64 games. A random sample was taken from this population—every seventh game beginning with the fifth game in the list of games compiled from the store was selected. These numbers were randomly selected from a list of random numbers. A total of 48 games was selected for the sample—32 PlayStation games and 16 Nintendo 64 games."

Critical Thinking Answers

1. Organizations: The researcher examined the structure (board seats) of Fortune 500 companies, which are formal organizations.

2. Groups: The sample is selected from children with special needs (a group) and is compared to behavior of children without special needs (a second group).

3. Groups: This is a little tricky. The research is studying teaching styles in classrooms across three different countries. What the researchers are observing is the classroom setting, which is a group setting.

4. Social abstracts: The researchers are analyzing televised wrestling, which is something created by people.

5. Individuals: The hint is that this excerpt polled Americans. However, since it does not compare Americans to people of other nationalities, this is just an individual unit of analysis.

BOX 3.4 **Units of Analysis Practice, continued**

6. Individuals: The study states that a survey analyzes the attitudes of heterosexual adults. These are individuals within the same group.

7. Social artifacts: Clothing is created by people. Therefore the researcher is studying social artifacts.

Citations (correspond to the excerpt number)

1. Women make poor showing on boards. *Investor Relations Business, 8* (24), 5. (***AN 11748989***)
2. Szilaagyi, Peter, G., Shenkman, Elizabeth, Brach, Cindy, LaClair, Barbara J., Swigonski, Nancy, Dick, Andrew, Shone, Laura P., Schaffer, Virginia A., Col, Jana F., Eckert, George, Klein, Jonathan D., and Lewit, Eugene M. (2003). Children with special health care needs enrolled in the state children's health insurance program (SCHIP): Patient characteristics and health care needs. *Pediatrics, 112,* supplement 2, 508–521. (***AN 11654910***)
3. Stigler, James W., Gallimore, Ronald, and Hiebert, James. (2000, Spring). Using video surveys to compare classrooms and teaching across cultures: Examples and lessons from the TIMSS video studies. *Educational Psychologist, 35* (2), 87–101. (***AN 3140574***)
4. Woo, Hyung-Jin, and Kim, Yeora. (2003, November). Modern gladiators: A content analysis of televised wrestling. *Mass Communication & Society, 6* (4), 361. (***AN 11463322***)
5. Poll shows support for government monitoring of religion. (2002, October). *Church & State, 55* (9), 16. (***AN 7552890***)
6. Herek, Gregory M. (2002, November). Heterosexuals' attitudes toward bisexual men and women in the United States. *Journal of Sex Research, 39* (4), 264. (***AN 8894129***)
7. Beasley, Berrin, and Standley, Tracy Collins. (2002, August). Shirts vs. skins: Clothing as an indicator of gender role stereotyping in video games. *Mass Communication & Society, 5* (3), 279. (***AN 7195817***)

lower-income individuals are more likely than their middle-income counterparts to rob others because they lack the financial means to obtain goods from legitimate sources (buying them). However, this conclusion is another example of the ecological fallacy. The researcher has no idea why robbery rates are higher in low-income areas—and he or she definitely did not study individuals arrested for robbery to see whether these people were robbing simply because they wanted goods they could not buy. The only thing the researcher studied were the rates—no links to individuals. Consequently, the only conclusions the researcher could viably make is that property crime is higher in low-income areas. The explanation of *why* needs to be answered by a different study whose units of analysis are individual robbers.

Furthermore, although individual-level data can be aggregated to study groups (e.g., using race information individuals supply to make comparisons about different racial groups), doing so can run the risk of **reductionism.** This is essentially the mirror opposite of the ecological fallacy. It occurs when researchers are overly limited, either in terms of their variables or their units of analysis to make conclusions about a broad range of human behavior.

William Julius Wilson, a noted sociologist whose expertise lies in examining race issues, notes that reductionism is a common problem among studies of race. Wilson claims that the association between race and likelihood of being arrested for a crime is usually based on individual-level data. But doing so obscures the fact that poor Blacks are much more likely to live in very poor areas than are poor Whites—over five times more likely (Wilson, 1987). Consequently, the real reason for the higher rates of violence among African Americans may be their higher concentration in very poor areas—not their race per se. Studying the relationship between crime and race at the community level (where the unit of analysis is groups) may be more accurate in establishing a causal relationship than is studying the problem from the individual level, since community characteristics (high concentration of African Americans in very poor communities) may be more relevant to crime than individual characteristics (here, race alone).

Evaluating Written Research: Literature Review

In this chapter, I discussed how to conduct a literature review and how the literature review can help you refine your research problem. However, I also stated that not all of the research you read should be included in your literature review; the same holds for the research of others. Furthermore, your evaluation of a study's literature review hinges on how relevant that review is to your problem. Therefore the best criteria, and first question to ask, when evaluating a literature review is whether it has information in it that is relevant and useful to your research needs. If the answer is yes, then there are additional considerations that will further help you assess the quality of that literature review. This section provides some of those criteria that will not only directly help you evaluate other researchers' literature reviews but will also indirectly help you write effective literature reviews yourself.

1. Is the specific problem area identified in the first paragraph or two of the report?

Somewhere along the line, students learned that, like titles, introductions had to be "catchy" in order to attract readers. However, as I stated in previous chapters, people do not read research because they find it relaxing beach reading. That being said, one can still write an interesting beginning to a literature review that specifies a particular problem area. Take the following hypothetical example:

> Many consider the right to an education as a basic tenant of U.S. society. Many researchers have evaluated the effects of educational attainment on future earning capabilities, family formation, and self-esteem. Furthermore, many feel that the problems teachers face are among the most serious in society.

Sounds interesting, right? But what does it really tell us? The hypothetical article that may follow could involve the broad issue of education, but what about education? How, contrary to the basic belief in our society, people really do not have equal access to education? Educational attainment and future earning? Educational attainment and family formation? Or the problems teachers and administrators have in educating students? The paragraph was way too broad to be useful. An improved version could read something like:

> Although many may consider the right to an education a basic tenet of U.S. society, the education that many young people are receiving is substandard. This hurts their future earning potential and may even affect their adult family practices. Common explanations for substandard education include limited tax money, gang activity, and behavioral problems in the classroom.

The second example is still broad; however, a reader has a clearer idea that this research is going to involve examining substandard education—not attainment per se or good examples of the education system or whether people agree with the assumption that everyone deserves an education.

2. Does the researcher establish the importance of the research problem?

The studies about cow flatulence are a good example of this. Obviously, the researchers who did that study believed that the topic was important, and perhaps if they clearly explained the importance to the public, the jokes would not exist. Although this is a bit of a tongue-in-cheek example, the point still holds.

Researchers may believe that their topic is important to study, but they still need to convey the importance to the people who are reading their research. They can do this by citing statistics to illustrate how widespread a problem is or that a problem is increasing. For example, researchers can cite statistics comparing the different median earnings for college-educated individuals compared to high school dropouts. Or researchers can compare the average educational budget for an inner-city school with the amount of money middle-class people spend on entertainment for a year. The first establishes the importance of an education; the second illustrates how little money some schools really do have.

Any evidence, statistical or otherwise, presented to establish the importance of a topic needs to be directly related to that topic. Presenting statistics about the percentage of minorities in high school is not directly relevant to an examination of substandard schooling. (It may be indirectly related if I wanted to make the argument that members of certain minority groups were more likely to receive substandard educations, but that is not how the previous example was presented.)

3. Has the researcher been appropriately selective in deciding what studies to include in the literature review?

The main criteria for inclusion in a literature review is a study's relevance to the topic. However, some topics are very broad and can, feasibly, require many pages to summarize and evaluate the work of others. Remember, though, that professional and academic journals (as well as other media sources) frequently have a limited amount of pages available for the description of research. Therefore, a researcher does not want to fill up all available space with the summary of other people's work, leaving very little room to discuss his or her research goals, observation methods, findings, and conclusions. Long strings of citations, simply to illustrate to a reader that the researcher has read a lot of other research, is unnecessary. If you notice a researcher using long strings, that means that he or she has not been appropriately selective. Although it may be accurate that 10 different articles reached a similar conclusion or recognized a social problem, researchers need only to cite those articles that are the most directly relevant to their own focus or that are the most recent.

4. Is the research cited recent?

Given the plethora of research people are doing, you need to be skeptical when you encounter a literature review that cites only older studies. As I stated earlier, with the speed in which new information is being generated, researchers must do frequent reviews of the literature to learn of new developments in their area. Researchers who have not done this (which may be the case if the literature review overly relies on older research) are not aware of new findings regarding their topic, new methodologies, or new interpretations. This weakens the contribution of their research to the specification of *your* research problem.

This does not mean that research that is 10 years old is no longer relevant. It does mean, however, that that 10-year-old studies should be included only if they are directly important or influential. Reliance on primarily older work is also acceptable is when there has been little recent research on a topic (although the author needs to state this and speculate as to why that is the case) or when an author wishes to establish historical links involving the research on a topic.

Furthermore, make sure you evaluate whether research is recent based on the publication year of the article. You cannot feasibly expect an article published in 1995 to cite research conducted in 2000 (five years *after* the publication date). You can, however, expect that most of the research cited in an article published in 1995 is from the 1990s or late 1980s.

5. Is the literature review critical?

Some literature reviews read as if they are book reports; they are interested only in summarizing what researchers have found about a particular topic. Other literature reviews are more critical; besides summarizing some main findings, they also evaluate the methodological procedures or findings of other studies. Although the noncritical reviews have their place and can be informative if the researcher is using the reviews as a type of data from which to draw conclusions, I believe that reviews that have a critical element are more useful in designing other research studies. Not every study mentioned in a literature review needs a discussion evaluating its methods or findings, but when studies use very different methodologies or contradict each other, researchers usually should draw attention to these differences and evaluate which methodologies or studies are more dependable (with a justification, of course).

In fact, be leery of literature reviews in which all or most of the studies reach the same conclusions. Literature reviews that present only one side of an issue are biased and are designed to lead the reader to a specific conclusion (usually one that supports the data that will be presented in the results section). Sometimes researchers do this because they want to pad your interpretation of their findings (although, as I discussed in Chapter 2, this type of manipulation is borderline unethical). Other times, researchers unconsciously are too attached to an issue or have lost some of their objectivity and are looking at an issue in only one way. Although this is more innocuous than the researcher who is purposely trying to manipulate the reader, it is still problematic because it violates the premise of objectivity that sets science apart from other avenues of knowledge. If you notice a one-sided literature review, as a reader, you need to raise some questions about that research and be more critical of any findings and conclusions the researchers draw. You also have to decide whether you want to give any weight to this research at all.

However, being "critical" does not mean that researchers only mention the weaknesses of other research in their literature review. Researchers can also draw attention to methodologies or findings they find particularly strong, especially if these methods or findings are very influential to the design of the current research.

6. Is the researcher clear as to what is research, theory, and opinion?

Not all research cited or comments made in literature reviews are factual results of studies. Researchers frequently cite theoretical comments and opinions of other researchers as well. This is perfectly fine and is frequently common. However, the researchers need to make it clear to the reader what they are repeating as research and

BOX 3.5   **Evaluation: Literature Reviews**

Below is an excerpt of a literature review from an article found in Research Navigator. As the material presented here is just an excerpt, I encourage you to go to Research Navigator to read this literature review in its entirety. Furthermore, remember, my comments are just guides. You may reach different conclusions than I do. The important point to keep in mind is that you need to support your opinions or conclusions with evidence and concrete reasoning from the material.

Do birds of a feather stick together when it comes to delinquent behavior? This seems to be the case initially. Many researchers, such as Elliott, Huizinga and Ageton (1985), asked delinquent adolescents whether their friends had committed offenses and were given an affirmative answer. However, the research methods could be criticized because socially desirable answers are not unlikely in this type of research. Adolescents are likely to make their peer groups seem more homogeneous than they really are (for instance, see Aseltine 1995). Nevertheless, recent social network studies measuring delinquent behavior and friendship relations independently show that the delinquency rates of adolescents are related to the rates of their friends (Baerveldt & Snijders 1994). These results indicate that significant correlations between friends' delinquent behavior exist. Nevertheless, the question of whether a causal relationship actually exists between friendship and delinquency is left unanswered. It remains unclear to what degree friends influence each other's delinquent behavior, or whether delinquent youths select each other on the basis of the other's delinquent behavior, or both. One reason for this ambiguity is that, in order to make causal interpretations on the subject, adolescent social networks should be studied over time, which is a difficult and time-consuming procedure. As a consequence little research is done on this subject (also see Reed & Rountree 1997).

Although friendship is therefore generally regarded as an important factor in the forming and persistence of delinquent behavior, the role of this friendship-factor remains unclear in several studies. A review study by Marcus (1996) suggests that the friendships of delinquent adolescents are less intimate than those of non-delinquents. If this is the case, the conclusion that the rate of delinquency correlates with the existence of friendship ties is not sufficiently informative. As a consequence it is crucial whether the type of relationships adolescents have with their peers differ when these adolescents behave in a (more) delinquent fashion. Stating that delinquent adolescents would not have the same intimate relationships as their peers could imply that they are not capable of forming and maintaining such bonds with their peers, and therefore lack the appropriate social skills. Is deviant behavior a sign of a lack of social abilities in general? The main question is therefore whether deviant, criminal behavior is an indicator of an overall individual lack of social skills, or whether it is simply the consequence of relating to other deviant peers.

Earlier Research

Several researchers have dealt with the question of social deviancy in friendships and delinquent behavior. In his review of delinquent friendships, Marcus (1996) concludes that in general little evidence has been found in favor of the superior quality of friendships with delinquents compared to friendships with non-delinquents. Whether friendships with delinquents are of a lesser quality remains unclear. Do adolescents who are prone to delinquent behavior lack the normal social skills compared to non-deviant peers? In fact, the studies show contradictory results. For instance, Giordano, Cernkovich & Pugh (1986) present evidence for the fact that delinquent youths do actually have intimate friendships, despite the fact that they experience more conflicts in their friendships compared to their peers. However, Dishion (1990) states that

BOX 3.5   **Evaluation: Literature Reviews, continued**

deviant youths are rejected by their peers and therefore committed to the deviant peer group. In this group, negative transactions are enhanced and their social interactions are therefore of limited quality. Pabon, Rodriguez & Gurin (1992) found comparable results, namely that involvement in delinquent behavior is mainly associated with a lack of emotional closeness typical of adolescent friendships.

The main reason for the contradictions seems to be methodological. The mere comparison of the three studies presented above poses a variety of problems. While the population investigated by Dishion and by Pabon, Rodriguez & Gurin consisted only of boys, Giordano, Cernkovitch & Pugh examined both sexes. Additionally, Pabon, Rodriguez & Gurin measured delinquent behavior of both the subject and his friends, so that their statements concern friendships specifically with delinquents, while those of Giordano, Cernkovitch & Pugh concern friendships of delinquent youths in general (with both delinquent and non-delinquent friends). In Dishion's study, for example, delinquency is measured by police reports of delinquent acts, while Giordano, Cernkovitch & Pugh and Pabon, Rodriguez & Gurin use measures of self-reported delinquency. Moreover, Dishion uses the judgement of parents and peers concerning the social abilities of the subjects, while the other two studies use the opinion of the subjects themselves when it comes to the qualitative aspects of their friendships.

Source: B. Houtzager and C. Baerveldt, "Just Like Normal: A Social Network Study of the Relationship between Petty Crime and the Intimacy of Adolescent Friendships," *Social Behavior & Personality: An International Journal, 27* (2) (1999). Reprinted by permission.

Evaluation Questions

1. Is the material presented in the literature review relevant to your research interests?

2. Is the specific problem area identified in the first paragraph or two of the report?

3. Does the researcher establish the importance of the research problem?

4. Has the researcher been appropriately selective in deciding what studies to include in the literature review?

5. Is the research cited recent?

6. Is the literature review critical?

7. Is the researcher clear as to what is research, theory and opinion?

8. Overall, do you think this is an adequate literature review? Why or why not?

Evaluation Question Discussion

1. Most of the research cited deals with the dynamics of friendships, how friendships affect behavior and, more specifically, how friendships affect deviant behavior. Therefore, if your research interests relate to adolescent friendships and deviance, then this literature review would be very relevant to the formation of your research problem.

2. Yes. The specific problem area is the effect of friendships on deviant behavior. Incidentally, the researchers begin the paper with a bit of a hook by starting with a common saying in the first sentence, and then implying that there is more to the story than common belief suggests in the next sentence. Since I know that the paper is going to focus on the same topic (based on the title), this introduction is an example where the researchers can grab people's attention with relevant information.

3. This is less clear. I assume that the importance of studying friendship groups is so, as a reader, I can make some connections between friendship groups and deviant behavior among adolescents, but the authors are unclear as to why they are interested in making this link.

BOX 3.5   Evaluation: Literature Reviews, continued

4. There are no long strings of research citations. Furthermore, the researcher weaves all the citations together so they flow logically, suggesting that they are all appropriate selections.

5. This research was published in 1999 and the oldest study in the excerpt is from 1985. Furthermore, few studies are from the late 1980s, most are from the 1990s; therefore, the recent cited is generally fairly recent relative to the publication date of the article.

6. The literature review is critical. The first paragraph notes that even though research has been done linking friendships to deviant behavior, a causal connection is still unclear. The review also notes that "several studies" have the role of friendships unclear. Furthermore, the issue of the quality of friendships is unclear and there are conflicting findings about friendship quality (which the authors later speculate is due to methodological differences). Therefore, the literature review not only summarizes key information but it also lets the reader know where questions in the research remain, where there

are conflicting findings, and what some cause of the conflicting findings may be.

7. Most of the research the authors cite is factual, as indicated by the authors' wording of phrases such as "Studies show . . . ," "Pabon, Rodriguez and Gurin (1992) found . . . ," and "Results indicate that. . ." However, opinion is also clear when the authors note that "Marcus concludes . . ." (concluding is an interpretation of material, therefore, opinion) and the phrase "adolescent networks *should* [italics added] be studied over time. . . ." The next section, which is not shown here, has "theory" in the title and would distinguish the theoretical views from the facts of the research and opinions of the researchers.

8. In my opinion, this is a very good literature review. The only weakness present is that it does not clearly state the importance of the study. It may be that the authors felt that the significance of studying the relationship between friendship groups and deviance was obvious. I disagree; however, this is a minor limitation given the strength of the other parts.

---

what they are repeating as fact or theory. Expressions such as "Smith (2000) argues that . . . ," "Some researchers feel . . . ," and "Common assumptions are . . ." all indicate an opinion. On the other hand, phrases such as "The data suggest . . . ," "Smith (2000) found that . . . ," or "Surveys reveal . . ." all indicate some type of factual claim. Readers know that researchers are discussing a theory when they use terms such as *theory* and *paradigm*.

To summarize, when reading literature reviews, ask yourself the following questions:

1. Is the material presented in the literature review relevant to my research interests?
2. Is the specific problem area identified in the first paragraph or two of the report?
3. Does the researcher establish the importance of the research problem?
4. Has the researcher been appropriately selective in deciding what studies to include in the literature review?
5. Is the research cited recent?
6. Is the literature review critical?
7. Is the researcher clear as to what is research, theory and opinion?
8. Overall, is it a strong literature review?

Key Terms

Cohort study (108)
Contamination (104)
Cross-sectional research (107)
Dependent variable (93)
Ecological fallacy (110)
Experimental mortality (104)
External validity (105)
Gambler's fallacy (101)
Hawthorne effect (105)
History effect (102)

Hypothesis (91)
Independent variable (93)
Instrumentation (103)
Internal validity (101)
Literature review (86)
Longitudinal research (107)
Maturation (102)
Nonspurious relationships (97)
Panel study (110)
Pretest effects (103)

Reactivity (106)
Reductionism (115)
Rival causal factors (97)
Selection bias (103)
Statistical conclusion validity
  (100)
Testing (103)
Trend study (108)
Units of analysis (110)
Variable (93)

Review Questions and Exercises

1. *Read the following articles and decide whether the researchers present a hypotheses or not. (Note: Just because a researcher identifies a sentence as a hypothesis does not in fact mean that it is one. Just because an article is published does not automatically mean that it is good research. We will discuss this further in the next chapter.)*

a. Van Eijck, Koen. (2001, March). Social differentiation in music taste patterns. Social Forces, 79 (3), 1163. 23 pp.

b. Blair-Loy, Mary, and Wharton, Amy S. (2002, March). Employees' use of work-family policies and the workplace social context. Social Forces, 80 (3), 813. 33 pp.

c. Kempinen, Cynthia A., and Kurlychek, Megan C. (2003, October). An outcome evaluation of Pennsylvania's boot camp: Does rehabilitative programming within a disciplinary setting reduce redicivdism? Crime & Delinquency, 49 (4), 581. 25 pp.

d. McMahon, Jennifer, and Clay-Warner, Jody. (2002, September). Child abuse and future criminality: The role of social service placement, family disorganization, and gender. Journal of Interpersonal Violence, 17 (9), 1002. 18 pp.

2. *Find the following articles in Research Navigator and identify the independent and dependent variables in the hypotheses presented.*

a. Kelly, Kathleen J., Slater, Michael D., Karan, David, and Hunn, Liza. (2000, Fall). The use of human models and cartoon characters in magazine Advertisements for cigarettes, beer, and nonalcoholic beverages. Journal of Public Policy & Marketing, 19 (2), 189. 12 pp on Research Navigator.

b. Eitle, David, D'Alessio, Stewart J., and Stolzenberg, Lisa. (2002, December). Racial threat and social control: A test of the Political, economic, and threat of black crime hypotheses. Social Forces, 81 (2), 557. 20 pp.

3. *Identify the time dimensions in the following studies. If the time dimension is longitudinal, identify whether it is a trend, cohort, or panel study. Support your conclusions with evidence from the article.*

a. Cummings, E. M., Goeke-Morey, M. C., and Papp, L. N. (2004). Parental conflict creates aggressive response in youth. Brown University Child & Adolescent Behavior Letter, 20 (6), 4–6. (AN 13266868)

b. Isralowitz, Richard E. (2004, April). Cultural identification and substance use. Journal of Social Psychology, 144 (2), 222–225. (AN 12905550)

c. Barnes, Sandra L., (2003). Determinants. Sociological Spectrum, 23 (4), 463–498. (AN 10719906)

d. Entwisle, Doris R., Alexander, Karl L., and Olson, Linda Steffel. (2004). Temporary as compared to permanent high school dropout. Social Forces, 82 (3), 1181–1206. (AN 13070401)

e. Shannon, David M., and Bradshaw, Carol C. (2002). A comparison of response rate, response time, and costs of mail and electronic surveys. Journal of Experimental Education, 70 (2), 179–193. (AN 6282924)

4. Identify the units of analysis in the following studies.

a. Eschholz, Sarah, Bufkin, Jana, and Long, Jenny. (2002, July). Symbolic reality bites: Women and racial/ethnic minorities in modern film. Sociological Spectrum, 22 (3), 299–265. AN 6885844)

b. Drago, Robert, Costanza, David, Caplan, Robert, Brubaker, Tanya, Cloud, Darnell, Harris, Naomi, Kashian, Russell, and Riggs, T. Lynn. (2001). The willingness-to-pay for work/family policies: A study of teachers. Industrial & Labor Relations Review, 55 (1), 22–42. (AN 5444993)

c. Ono, Hiroshi, and Zavodny, Madeline. (2002). Race, Internet usage, and e-commerce. Working Paper Series (Federal Reserve Bank of Atlanta), vol. 2002, issue 1, pp. 1–18. (AN 5936561)

Operationalization and Measurement

Suppose you and I are sitting in my office when another student, Jill, walks in. I tell you that I want to study prejudice. You say, "Great. That's an important topic. I always wondered why White people were afraid of African Americans." I give you a puzzled look and answer, "I'm not studying White attitudes about African Americans. I'm studying Asian American attitudes about Latinos." To which Jill pipes in and says, "Why are you focusing on race? Shouldn't a study of prejudice examine men's attitudes toward women?" What's going on? Why do we each have a different view of prejudice? We have all heard the term *prejudice* and have used it more than a few times. How, then, can three people have three different ideas of what "prejudice" entails?

The answer is because prejudice doesn't really exist in the same way, as say, a car exists. If I want to describe a car, I can talk about its make (a Subaru), its model (a Forester), its color (midnight blue with a gray running board), and its year (the 2004 model). Or we can play a guessing game by saying, "I am thinking of a box that seats one to four people comfortably, moves on four wheels, is steered by one person, and is frequently used to commute to places such as work, the mall, or Little League. This box has a blue and gray exterior and a gray interior. It has a CD player and radio, windshield wipers for when it rains, headlights for when it's dark, and a cargo spot in the back for our dog Fido. What am I?" There probably isn't anyone in the United States who would not know that we are describing a car. Objects such as cars we can see, we can touch, we can smell, and we can hear. Therefore, there is little confusion or disagreement about what we are observing. Therefore, we *don't* *need* to go into detail describing a car. Even if one person is thinking of a blue car and another green, when people use the word *car*, they are essentially in agreement as to what a car is.

Everyone knows what a house is, but if someone just says, "Think of a house," we would create a different mental image because, in itself, the word house *is just a concept. In order to conceptualize a house, we need to define it further so that everyone has a more similar mental image. For example, one would say, "I am thinking of a slate-blue, two-story house with a front porch that has two trellises on it and two windows on the upper floor in the front of the house." With this description, people are more likely to have similar mental images of what one means by "house." When we do this for research, it means that people participating in the research will have a clearer mental image of what the researcher is studying, thereby increasing the accuracy of the results obtained.*

This is not really the case when people use terms to describe social behavior, as I illustrated with the hypothetical example for prejudice. Like a car, people may know that prejudice exists, but unlike a car, they are less likely to agree that an attitude is an example of prejudice. Why? The reason is that prejudice is basically a made-up concept that we use to describe a whole bunch of possible attitudes. We all have our own ideas of what prejudice entails. A woman may primarily think of prejudice as negative attitudes about women; a member of a racial minority may think of different racial attitudes as prejudicial; a White person may think that prejudice no longer exists; an African American may think otherwise.

We call terms such as *prejudice, discrimination, delinquency, poverty,* and *life satisfaction*—to name a very few examples—**concepts.** Concepts are simply abstract terms social scientists use to summarize a set of mental images, observations, feelings, or ideas. Because these mental images are abstract, researchers frequently have to specify what they mean by them—a process called *conceptualization.* This chapter examines how researchers convert these mental images, or concepts, to empirically observable views or behaviors.

Conceptualization and Operationalization

The specific steps researchers use to define concepts varies a bit, depending on the source or research methods text people use. For example, some researchers move from conceptualization (the identification of concepts) to operationalization (which involves working definitions, otherwise known as operational definitions), to variables (Hagan, 1997). Others move from the abstract construct to conceptualization to conceptual definition to operationalization to indicators or measures (Neuman, 1991). Still others group some of these steps together into a simpler model that moves from concepts to variables to indicators (Schutt, 2001). Which specific path you follow is not as important as realizing that all of these paths are aimed at helping people move from abstract, multidefinitional ideas to specific, empirically understandable and observable questions.

In this book I will follow a model borrowed from Babbie (1995) that moves from conceptualization to conceptual definition to operational definition to measurement. The main point to remember in this framework (and in all of the others mentioned as well) is to keep asking yourself, What do I mean? until you get to an answer that has only one interpretation. In other words, you know you are done with the conceptualization and operationalization process when you ask yourself, What do I mean? and your answer can be unambiguously understood, without any other possible interpretations or explanation, by another person. Because some concepts are quite simple, when you ask yourself, What do I mean? you will be able to reach that last step fairly quickly. However, concepts such as "prejudice," "crime," "social class," and "economic opportunity" are quite complicated and require frequent rounds of "What do I mean?" until that last step is reached. These four steps—conceptualization, conceptual definition, operational definition, and measurement—will help you move through the conceptualization and operationalization process more easily for those complex concepts. Consequently, although not all concepts will necessarily have to move through these four stages, these stages are useful in focusing your definitions and inquiry for those concepts that are very complex.

Let's begin by looking at the first step in the process: conceptualization.

■ Conceptualization

An interesting *New York Time*'s article was entitled "Crime Wave with Shades of the Past" (*New York Times*, January 31, 2003). What does this mean? Does it mean that crime rates have decreased to earlier historic lows? Or does it mean that crime rates have matched a previous historical high? In fact, what does it mean by "crime wave"? Does the article discuss violent crime such as murder or rape? Or does it discuss white-collar crime such as fraud? Surprise! The answer is none of these! The article is about two new television crime shows that are competing against each other in the same time slot. Did you even think that this possibility was the focus? I didn't.

Even when titles are not as vague as the one just mentioned, concepts such as "crime" require some type of clarification before we can empirically observe them because different people may have different definitions. The process of **conceptualization,** quite simply, is the process of identifying and defining the concepts your research will address. For example, if you wanted to study people's reaction to crime, you need to specify what you mean by that reaction. Do you mean the relationship between people's perceptions of their risk for crime and their corresponding fear of it? Or do you mean whether people support some new type of policing tactic aimed at combating crime? Or do you mean whether people think crime is worse now than when they were children? The number of potential meanings is limited only by your (and your reader's) imagination. This is why it is so important for researchers to be explicit about what they specifically mean in a given instance.

Even researchers and experts may have different definitions, which is okay so long as these people are clear about what *they* mean by a concept. In other words, there is not necessarily one true definition of any concept. On the contrary, there is likely to be widely (if not unanimously) agreed-on definitions. This does not mean, however, that researchers have free reign to dream up just any definition they want. I cannot simply decide to define crime as "any act that goes against my personal code of honor" because I feel like it. Definitions need to be firmly rooted in social theory and it is also beneficial if they have been used by other researchers as well. So how do researchers know what are generally agreed-on definitions? They conduct a review of the literature to determine appropriate theoretical and methodological definitions.

Consequently, conceptualization may involve the use of dimensions and frameworks, which I discussed as part of theories in Chapter 2. For example, "violent" and "nonviolent" crimes are dimensions of the concept of "crime." Violent and nonviolent crimes are concepts themselves, since there are many types of crimes within each category; therefore, simply specifying these dimensions is not the end of this process. It is merely the bridge to the next stage, which is the development of a working definition. Figure 4.1 provides another example of conceptualization, this time of the concept "social capital."

■ Conceptual Definition

The **conceptual definition** is the working definition a researcher uses for a concept. If I wish to study people's fear of violent crime, and I ask myself, "What do I mean?" by "fear of violent crime," my conceptualization may involve specifying "fear" to be fear of victimization and specifying "violent crime" to be crimes against a person. The conceptual definition of *fear of victimization* may be fear of experiencing physical harm and the psychological fear of being alone. These conceptual definitions rule out other possibilities such as concern over economic loss. I may conceptually define *violent crime* to be assault,

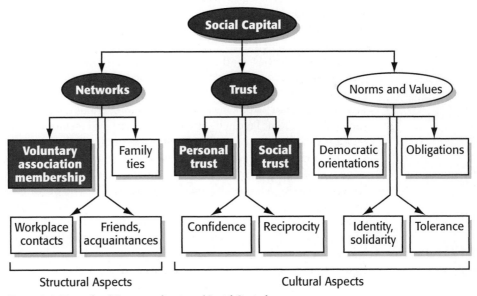

Figure 4.1 Example of Conceptualization of Social Capital

Social capital is an abstract term social scientists use to describe both the resources available within social groups (such as families, community, firms, etc.) and the networks of mutual support, reciprocity, reliance, and responsibility. Here is an example of how VanDeth (2003) conceptualizes and operationalizes the concept of social capital in an attempt to unify the various definitions for this concept that are common in the social sciences.

Source: Jan W. VanDeth, "Measuring Social Capital: Orthodoxies and Continuing Controversies," *International Journal of Social Research Methodology, 6* (1) (January 2003): 79. (**AN 9248158**). Reprinted by permission of Taylor & Francis Ltd. www.tandf.co.uk/journals.

battery, and rape. In choosing this definition, I rule out other types of violent crime, such as robbery and murder. Can a researcher select other conceptual definitions for fear of victimization and violent crime? Absolutely. However, all researchers want to make sure that the definitions they choose are grounded in theory and have been used by other researchers (unless the purpose of the research is to specifically assess using a new definition of a concept).

Specifying conceptual definitions are important because even if social scientists agree on a variety of definitions for a concept, it is usually not feasible (or desirable) to study *every* possible definition of a concept. Researchers are, after all, mere mortals, and due to issues of time, talent, and money, they really cannot study all aspects of a problem at once. Consequently, researchers study smaller, more manageable segments of a problem, and a conceptual definition helps them clearly identify to others what that small part is. To summarize, conceptual definitions are broad working definitions that help researchers focus their inquiry and allows others to follow the researcher's thought process as he or she moves from the abstract to the concrete.

■ Operational Definition

Now that I have specified my conceptual definitions to be fear of experiencing physical harm and the psychological fear of being alone, I need to continue asking myself, "What do I mean?" **Operational definitions** help social scientists continue to move from a broad but somewhat refined conceptual definition, to a more specific definition that they will use to form their research question. Consequently, operational definitions are also known as *indicators* because they are the definitions that indicate exactly what researchers mean by their concepts. *Fear of physical harm* is more specific than the idea of "fear of crime" or "fear of victimization," but it can still have multiple meanings. Do I mean physical harm such as a bruise on my arm, or do I mean something more serious that requires a hospital stay? The same applies to what I mean by *psychological harm*. Do I mean whether people need to sleep with a nightlight on because they are afraid to be alone? Do I mean that people are afraid to go outside at night unless they are with a large group of people? For my purposes, I'm going to define *fear of physical harm* as "fear of personal injury that requires medical attention." Although I am probably pretty close to a "What do I mean?" definition that most people understand without further explanation, I'm going to further narrow this to "personal injury such as suspected broken bones, cuts which require stitches, and swellings." Likewise, for *psychological fear of being alone*, I'm going to further define that as "being afraid to be home alone during the day, " "being afraid to be home alone during the night, " and "being afraid to go outside alone during the day."

These operational definitions seem fairly straightforward, so you might be wondering why I am not done. Why do I have this fourth step of "measurement" if I have adequately answered What do I mean? by the third step? The answer is because even though we now have a clear understanding of my terms, I need to word them in a way that enables me to move from theory to something that is statistically useful. Let's find out how to do that.

■ Measurement

Measurement is the process of observing concepts, as indicated by their operational definitions, and assigning some type of score or meaning to people's responses. This involves

Community attachment is relevant to a host of social issues including the likelihood of personal deviance, one's sense of safety, and one's level of life satisfaction. Consequently, many researchers have studied community attachment. However, according to Rachel Woldoff (2002), many of these studies are limited by an overly simplistic definition of community attachment. Drawing on theories of neighborhood attachment, Woldoff tests a more vigorous operationalization of community attachment using a 1988 survey of 51 micro-neighborhoods. Below is an excerpt from that article in which Woldoff explains her conceptualization and operationalization process.

Community attachment is not well understood because previous research has focused on one or two forms of attachment. . . . I analyze three major dimensions of neighborhood attachment: attitudinal attachment, behavioral attachment through neighboring, and behavioral attachment through problem solving

. . . I . . . make a distinction between attitudinal and behavioral attachment . . . [that] is consistent with the traditions of community studies, which tend to categorize community life into attitudinal and behavioral domains. . . . Then I separate behavioral attachment into neighboring interaction and problem-solving interaction to separate qualitatively how people behaviorally demonstrate attachment to their neighborhood by the type of interaction with others.

. . . Neighboring—or social interaction with neighbors . . . is a behavior that demonstrates a connectedness to the locale, and it may have different determinants than attitudinal forms of attachment. Neighboring captures the social vitality of the neighborhood without relying on sentimental or evaluative expressions. . . . Lee and Campbell (1997) find that a large proportion of urban residents define neighborhood in terms of friendliness or a shared sense of community.

. . . [N]eighborhood attachment is [also] residents' behavioral demonstration of commitment through problem-solving responses to local stressors. Researchers emphasize that neighbors must participate in efforts to maintain the community if a neighborhood is to remain vital (Sampson et al. 1989; Skogan 1990; Taylor 1995).

. . . To measure neighborhood attachment, I use six dimensions that form coherent constructs. . . . Drawing on Guest and Lee (1983), I include six items related to sentiment and evaluation. Sentimental attachment measures residents' emotional connection to the community and is grounded in whether residents would miss the area if forced to move, whether they have strong ties to the community, and whether they feel "at home" there. Evaluation is a general cognitive measure of satisfaction with the neighborhood environment. I measure evaluation with three items: a global community satisfaction item indicating the respondents' overall rating of their neighborhood as a place to live, an item indicating whether they would recommend their neighborhood to friends, and their assessment of their neighborhood as a good financial investment.

For behavioral attachment through neighboring, I include a set of items concerning routine and social neighboring activities. This approach distinguishes ordinary, civil acts of neighboring from more intense neighbor relationships. I measure routine neighboring using the proportion of neighbors whom respondents know by name, the frequency of greetings and long talks exchanged with neighbors, the frequency of borrowing small items from neighbors, and the frequency of "helping them out." More intimate, friendship-oriented neighboring has three indicators: residents' assessments of the degree to which they socialize with neighbors away from home, discuss personal problems with neighbors, and have dinner with neighbors.

Finally, I measure formal and informal problem solving, which are behavioral forms of

BOX 4.1   **Conceptualization and Operationalization, continued**

neighborhood attachment. My study evaluated formal problem-solving by using three questions probing attendance at crime-watch group meetings, neighborhood associational meetings, and other formally organized meetings that target local problems. I measure informal problem solving with two questions on residents' efforts to support each other and whether neighborhood problems are solved without the help of formal, structured organizations.

Source: Rachel A. Woldoff, "The Effects of Local Stressors on Neighborhood Attachment," *Social Forces, 81* (1) (2002): 87. **(AN 7513641)**

Critical Thinking Question

1. Apply the four stages of the conceptualization–operationalization process to Woldoff's research. If you do not think that a specific stage applies, explain why.

Critical Thinking Discussion

1. Remember, the four stages are conceptualization, conceptual definition, operational definition, and measurement. Woldoff's process can most succinctly be summarized in the following flowchart where the main concept is at the head or top of the chart and each stage of the conceptualization–operationalization process is as follows:

Concept		**Neighborhood Attachment**			
Conceptualization	Attitudinal Attachment	Neighborhood Behavioral Attachment		Problem Solving Behavioral Attachment	
Conceptual Definition					
Sentiment	Evaluation	Routine	Intense	Formal	Informal
Indicators					
—Miss area if forced to move —Have strong ties to community —Feel at home	—Rating of neighborhood as place to live —Whether recommend neighborhood to friends —Neighborhood sound financial investment	—Proportion of neighbors known by name —Frequency of greetings/ long talks —Frequency of borrowing small items —Frequency of "helping out"	—Socialize away from home —Discuss personal problems —Have dinner	—Attend crime watch meetings —Attend neighborhood association meetings —Attend other organizational meetings	—Efforts to support each other —Degree neighborhood problems are solved by neighborhood

Measurement

The discussion of this is not present in the excerpt, but Woldoff presents the survey questions and their answer choices in Appendix A of her article. These questions and their answer choices are the measurements that complete the conceptualization–operationalization process.

writing the actual questions that address the concepts and that others will answer. This is not as simple as it may sound. For measures to be useful, researchers need to count on them to produce reliable findings. Plus, researchers have to make sure that the measures are actually measuring what the researchers think they are measuring. To put these points another way, researchers need to make sure their measures are reliable and valid. Consequently, the last stage of the conceptualization–operationalization process may be the most difficult because it is the most detailed. Because of this, I will devote an entire section to discussing the issues around measurement.

Also, as I stated in Chapter 1, research methods do not necessarily proceed linearly through clean-cut steps; decisions in the early part of the process have important ramifications later in the research process. Measurement is a good example of this because it has important implications for statistical analysis, which happens closer to the end of the research process. I will soon discuss this in more detail.

■ Cautions

By the time researchers are done with the conceptualization–operationalization process, they are frequently lulled into thinking that their definitions have real meaning. They don't. Researchers' definitions are simply a means for researchers to clarify to others what *they* mean by a concept so that they can more easily discuss these concepts with others. Other people may not share a specific definition, and that is fine.

In a similar vein, this concern is even greater when people encounter experts who they consider to be more knowledgeable than themselves. As I discussed in Chapter 1, people are frequently tempted to believe what experts say, and therefore tend to believe the expert's definitions of concepts simply because they *are* experts. But it is important to remember that just like us, experts have also gone through this creative process of operationalization and deserve to have their work critically examined as well. It is not mandatory for people to agree with the so-called experts.

Measurement

The conceptualization–operationalization process helps social scientists move from very abstract ideas to specific and empirically observable ones. However, even after researchers go through all of these stages, they still have to convey their concepts' meanings to their study participants and they have to have a means of empirically recording participants' responses. Consequently, the last stage of the process involves creating observable measures (which will fall into one of four possible levels), and assessing the validity, reliability, and generalizability of these measures. So let's look at the issues involved in measurement in more detail.

■ Levels of Measurement

Let's continue with my example from the previous section where I operationalized the concept "fear of crime" until I reached the following operational definitions:

1. Afraid of personal bodily injury that requires medical attention—for example, suspected broken bones, cuts that require stitches, and swellings.

2. Afraid to be home alone at night
3. Afraid to be home alone during the day
4. Afraid of going outside alone during the day

What I have here are just potential indicators, which, if I put them into a question format, "How afraid are you to be home alone at night?" have easily begun the transformation from an indicator to a measurement. Researchers formally call this question a **variable** because the responses to it can vary. One person may be very afraid to stay home alone at night, another not afraid at all. The possible responses to a question or variable are called **attributes** or **values,** which formally are characteristics or qualities of something.

Gender is a variable, but the answer choices of "male or female" are attributes that measure the characteristics of gender. Likewise, the level of people's fear when home alone at night is a variable and the responses "very afraid," "somewhat afraid," "not very afraid," and "not at all afraid" are values that measure the quality of people's fear (as I've defined it). Whether an answer choice is an attribute or a value depends on its mathematical relationship. Answer choices that have no direct mathematical meaning are frequently called *attributes*, whereas those that do have some mathematical relationship are called *values*. Although the distinction is real, many researchers stick with one term and use it regardless of the mathematical relationship between answer characteristics.

The levels of measurement correspond to the different levels of mathematical precision values can possess when describing a variable. To illustrate the levels of measurement, let's just use the second indicator, fear of being home alone at night. I can measure this indicator four different ways, each one illustrating a different level of measurement. Let me start with the most basic level of measurement, which is the *nominal level*.

Nominal measures

There are two criteria that *all* levels of measurement must possess. All measures must have attributes that are exhaustive and mutually exclusive. Attributes that are **exhaustive** are those that have an answer choice for every possible characteristic of the variable. Put another way, there should be an answer choice for everyone. Attributes are **mutually exclusive** when there is *only one* answer choice for people, unless the respondent is specifically instructed in the question to circle or check all responses that may apply. Consider the following question with corresponding attributes as an example:

What is the general field of your first declared college major?

a. Traditional sciences (biology, chemistry, physics)
b. Social sciences (anthropology, criminal justice, economics, psychology, sociology, social work)
c. Humanities (English, communication, education)
d. Other (please specify) _____

Does this example fit the two criteria of being exhaustive and mutually exclusive? Yes. The example is exhaustive because there *is* an answer choice for everyone. Even if the academic majors presented among the answer choices do not include a specific respondent's major, then the respondent can circle option "d," the "Other" category, and write his or her major in the line provided. As a researcher, I can later decide whether that major fits one of the first three attributes (and then code that response accordingly), whether I want to create a new fourth response that is not "other" but refers to a fourth unique form of grouping of academic majors (for example, counseling and human services), or if I want to just keep that response as part of a vague "other" category. My decision depends on my research question, my level of necessary precision, and the pattern of responses. I will discuss what to do with information in "other" categories more closely in Chapter 12; but suffice it to say here that these answer choices are indeed exhaustive.

What about mutually exclusive? Is there only one answer choice for everyone? Yes. By wording the question to be "the general field of your *first declared* major," respondents who have more than one major know which major to which I am referring.

What about the next question:

Which sports have you played in the past month? Circle all that apply.

a. Football
b. Basketball
c. Soccer
d. Swimming
e. Other _____

This example is exhaustive, once again due to the "other" category. However, in this example, the requirement of "mutually exclusive" is loosened because of the directions to "circle all that apply." Questions are supposed to have only one answer option for each individual; however, if the researcher *wants* respondents to circle more than one value, all the researcher has to do is specifically direct the respondents to do so by saying "Circle all that apply."

So what makes this a **nominal** measure? Well, as I noted at the beginning of this section, attributes and values describe mathematical relationships. But can you see a mathematical relationship between college majors or sports? No. The question doesn't ask anything about which is one's favorite (which would imply a ranking) or about how many times one has played each sport in the past month (which is a count). These questions ask the respondent only to identify a specific quality, which has no corresponding amount. Therefore, there is no mathematical relationship here. Even though when researchers code these attributes (e.g., give football a "1," basketball a "2," soccer a "3," etc.) during the coding phase of the research process (because statistical programs recognize numbers only when doing calculations), these numbers have no inherent mathematical meaning. They are simply a way of coding written language into a mathematical language a computer can understand.

Because these attributes have no mathematical meaning, they are nominal levels of measurement. Nominal levels of measurement are the most basic and have only the following characteristics: To illustrate with my example of fear of crime, I can very easily word the question as:

Are you generally afraid to be home alone at night?

a. Yes
b. No

Technically this question is exhaustive (you either are afraid or you are not) and exclusive (you can't be both afraid and unafraid). However, you probably realize that this is somewhat of an overly simplistic view of fear of crime. Hence, even though it is technically correct, a higher level of measurement may be more informative.

In a study of frisbee players, a question asking the gender of two people playing a game of frisbee would be an example of a nominal level of measurement (answer choices: both female, both male, one of each gender) because there is no ranking implied. A question asking a person to rate the skill of the players (answer choices: very skilled, somewhat skilled, somewhat unskilled, very unskilled, no answer) would be ordinal because it involves ranking without directly quantifiable distinctions in ranks. A question asking people to compare playing frisbee to other outdoor activities (on a scale of 1 to 100 in increments of 10) would be an interval level of measurement. You can quantify the levels, but they have been arbitrarily created. A question asking how many successful passes of the frisbee between the two people before someone dropped it would be an example of a ratio level of measurement because it is quantifiable and nonarbitrary.

Ordinal measures

Ordinal measures are one step above nominal levels of measurement. Because all measures have to be mutually exclusive and exhaustive, ordinal measures also have these characteristics. However, in addition to these two criteria, in ordinal measures, the attributes, or values, can be logically ranked. This means that one value can be relatively more or relatively less than another; however, we do *not know how much* more or less each value is.

Opinion questions are frequently ordinal levels of measurement. For example, a researcher can ask:

What is your view of increased taxes to fund job training for welfare recipients?

a. Very supportive
b. Somewhat supportive
c. No opinion
d. Somewhat unsupportive
e. Very unsupportive

These values are mutually exclusive, as a respondent cannot simultaneously be very supportive and somewhat supportive. They are also exhaustive because there is a "no opinion" category. Sometimes people just do not have an opinion about a topic. This may be because they have never considered that topic and they may not want to take the time to do so while completing the survey, so "no opinion" is the most accurate response they can give. Therefore, when asking respondents about their opinions, this catch-all "no opinion" or "no answer" category is important in order to achieve exhaustiveness. Also, the answer choices are relatively ranked. I know that a person who responds "very supportive" is more in favor of the tax increase for job training than is someone who says "somewhat supportive," but I cannot concretely quantify how much more supportive this is.

Ordinal levels of measurement may also be useful when trying to quantify large numbers or concepts that people are apprehensive about answering. A good example of this is a question that deals with income:

What was your total household income the previous year?
a. Under $30,000
b. $30,001–$60,000
c. $60,001–$90,000
d. $90,001–$120,000
e. Over $120,000

Because people are frequently uneasy discussing their income, asking this question with broad relative categories may be less threatening than asking someone to estimate a more exact figure. If a person selects answer "d," the researcher still does not know the exact amount of income—only that it is somewhere between $90,001 and $120,000. This brings up a good point. Notice that each category begins with one dollar value higher than the end of the previous category. Since income is frequently measured in dollars, we are not violating the rule of exhaustiveness by not taking each category to the penny. Likewise, by starting with the next whole dollar amount, we are also not violating the criteria of mutually exclusive, which would be the case if, for example, our answer choices were as such:

What was your total household income the previous year?
a. Under $30,000
b. $30,000–$60,000
c. $60,000–$90,000
d. $90,000–$120,000
e. Over $120,000

In this example, people earning $60,000 and $90,000 would be compelled to answer *two* answer choices, thereby violating the mutually exhaustive rule.

I'll provide one last illustration by showing how I could word the fear of crime measure:

How afraid are you to stay home alone at night?
a. Very afraid
b. Somewhat afraid
c. No opinion
d. Not very afraid
e. Not at all afraid

This measure fits the criteria because there is a choice, and only one choice, for everyone, and we know that person who says "not at all afraid" is much less afraid than someone who says "somewhat afraid," but we do not know specifically how much less afraid that person is.

To summarize, ordinal levels of measurement are:

1. Mutually exclusive
2. Exhaustive
3. Ranked

Interval measures

Perhaps you can predict where the levels of measurement are heading. **Interval** measures have all the characteristics of ordinal measures with the additional feature that each value is a fixed, quantifiably observable unit. The only catch here is that there is no true zero point that has meaning in and of itself. Any zero point is arbitrary.

There are few examples of interval measures in the social sciences. A person's IQ score, however, is an example of this measure. Regardless of whether you put much stock in IQ tests (and the point here is not to argue the merits of these tests), the Stanford-Binet scale is the generally agreed-on test for intelligence. The average IQ score, according to this scale, is 100, where scores above 100 theoretically indicate higher levels of intelligence and scores less than 100 indicate lower levels. Theoretically, social scientists can go any amount above or below 100, but in practice they don't meaningfully go outside of a 50- to 150-point range (Audiblox, www.audiblox.com/iq_scores.htm). Think about it. When was the last time you ever heard of someone having a 0 IQ? I'm willing to bet that you haven't. Why? Because there really isn't a 0 IQ. Although it is a theoretical possibility, even those who use the scale recognize that the results are questionable for scores below 50. If zero had true meaning in a scale, questionable interpretations would not be an issue.

There are two other ways social scientists tend to use interval levels of measurement when they, in fact, do choose to use this measurement type. The first is to create a scale or index. Indexes that researchers create by combining multiple ordinal levels of measurement are frequently treated as interval levels of measurement. A second form would be a ranking question such as the following:

If stealing a bicycle has a value of "10," comparatively how serious are the following crimes? If you think a crime is more serious than stealing a bicycle, write an amount that reflects how much more serious (e.g., if a crime is twice as serious, you would write 20 for 10 × 2). If you think a crime is less serious, write 0 in the space.

_____ stealing an old lady's purse
_____ stealing someone's newspaper from his or her front porch
_____ stealing a ream of paper from the office
_____ stealing money from the company "slush" fund
_____ stealing money from your parents' wallet

In this example, if someone put a 40 in front of the choice "stealing an old lady's purse," I know how much more serious they think that behavior is, relative to stealing a bicycle. That person thinks stealing an old lady's purse is four times more serious. Hence, I can quantify the difference between levels, unlike in ordinal levels of measurement. However, even if a person wrote 0 for the first one, that 0 doesn't have real meaning. It only means that the person thinks that behavior is less serious than stealing a bicycle.

If I wanted to provide a similar example that follows our fear of crime illustration, I could word a question as follows:

If staying home alone at night has a value of "5," how much more afraid are you to do the following? Please express your answers in units of "5" with an answer of "0" meaning less afraid:

_____ staying home alone during the day
_____ going to the neighborhood park alone during the day
_____ going to the neighborhood park alone during the night
_____ taking a walk in your neighborhood alone during the day
_____ taking a walk in your neighborhood alone during the night

To summarize, interval measures have the following characteristics:

1. Mutually exclusive
2. Exhaustive
3. Ranked
4. Intervals that have quantifiably meaningful distances between them

Remember, though, that interval measures are relatively rare. Consequently, when doing statistics, researchers frequently combine interval levels of measurement with the next level, ratio measures.

Ratio measures

The last, and most detailed, level of measurement is a **ratio** measure. The only difference between variables measured at the ratio level and variables measured at the interval measure is that variables at the ratio level have a true zero point. In other words, for ratio measures, the zero is meaningful and real; it is not arbitrary. For example, if I did a survey and I asked participants how many years they have accepted welfare payments, if a respondent answers 0, that means that that person never received a welfare payment. That zero has real meaning. Likewise, if a second person said 4 years and a third person said 2 years, I also know that: (1) the second person accepted welfare for 4 more years than the first person, who said 0, and 2 more years than the third person, who said 2; and (2) the third person accepted welfare for 2 more years than the first person. What I'm trying to illustrate is that not only does the value of zero have real meaning for the first person, I can use that value to quantify the differences in years of welfare acceptance between the first person and the other two people. Likewise, I can still quantify the difference in years of welfare receipt between the second person and the third person.

There are many possible ratio levels of measurement. Age, years of education, years of experience, number of alcoholic drinks consumed in the past week, number of people who voted in the last election—the number of possibilities is, once again, limited only by your imagination and the nature of your research topic. If I wanted to finish my illustration of levels of measurement with my fear of being alone example, I could word a question as:

How many nights in the past week were you afraid to be home alone? _____

The person answering the question would very likely write in a number. If the person writes 0, I can suspect that he or she is not afraid to be home alone at night. If another person answers 4, I realize that this person is more likely to be afraid of being alone than the first person is.

Ratio levels of measurement are very powerful. For example, they allow for sophisticated statistical measures of association and hypothesis testing that produce results that are more intuitively understood. So, for example, in my fear illustration, I am probably going to be able to do more meaningful statistics if I ask a question such as the preceding one as opposed to asking the respondent how afraid she or he is to stay home alone at night and providing five answer choices that range from very afraid to very unafraid.

Likewise, ratio levels of measurement can be recoded, what some researchers call "collapsed," into lower levels of measurement; lower levels of measurement cannot, however, be inflated to higher levels of measurement. For example, I can take the responses to my question "How many nights in the past week were you afraid to be home alone?" and recode them into ordinal levels of measurement by combining answer choices to be 0–2 nights, 3–5 nights, and 6 or 7 nights. If one person answers the first category, 0–2 nights, and a second answers 3–5 nights, I know that the second person was afraid more nights than the first, but I do not know how many more nights because I do not know the exact number of nights that each person was afraid. I only know that the first person was afraid either 0, 1, or 2 nights and the second was afraid 3, 4, or 5 nights. This is an ordinal measure. Likewise, I can leave everyone who answered 0 alone and recode all those who answered 1–6 nights into a new category called "afraid" and given a value of "1." This would be a nominal level because people would either be afraid (value of "1") or unafraid (value of "0"). In a pure sense, there is no numerical difference in being afraid or unafraid; these are just characteristics now, and so this measure would be nominal.

However, take the flip side. What if I wanted to take an ordinal measure and move it up to a ratio measure? Well, let's go back to the question we used earlier:

How many nights were you afraid to stay home alone?

a. 0–2 nights
b. 3–5 nights
c. 6 or 7 nights

Can I make this a ratio level of measurement? No. If a person answered 0–2 nights, I do not know whether that person was afraid 0, 1, or 2 nights. I do not know the exact number; and, if I do not know the exact number, I cannot know the exact distance between values, nor can I decide whether zero has a true meaning or not. Therefore, I cannot move an ordinal level of measurement up to a ratio level.

To summarize, ratio levels of measurement have the following characteristics:

1. Mutually exclusive
2. Exhaustive
3. Ranked
4. Intervals that have quantifiably meaningful distances between them
5. Have a true zero point

Sometimes researchers provide the actual variables with their corresponding attributes as they appeared on the survey or other instrument in the research report (usually in an appendix toward the end of the report). More frequently, they will not. However, researchers still have an obligation to let the reader know what the variables of interest were and how they were measured.

Below is an excerpt from an article by Herek that examines the views of 1,335 heterosexuals in the United States toward bisexual men and women. The excerpt deals with how Herek measured attitudes and some of the other characteristics of his respondents. Read the excerpt and then answer the critical thinking questions. You can find the article in its entirety on Research Navigator.

This paper examines heterosexual adults' attitudes toward bisexual men and women using data from a 1999 national RDD survey (N = 1,335). . . . Attitudes toward bisexual men and women were measured with 101-point feeling thermometers. . . . Higher ratings (maximum = 100) indicate warmer, more favorable feelings toward the target whereas lower ratings (minimum = 0) indicate colder, more negative feelings. The instructions for the feeling thermometers were: "These next questions are about some of the different groups in the United States. I'll read the name of a group and ask you to rate the group on a thermometer that runs from zero (0) to one hundred (100). The higher the number, the warmer or more favorable you feel toward that group. The lower the number, the colder or less favorable you feel. If you feel neither warm nor cold toward them, rate that group a fifty (50)."

. . . Respondents were categorized into five geographic regions based on their residence in the 48 contiguous states: Northeast (New England and Mid-Atlantic states), South (Southeastern and Southern states), Midwest (Midwestern and Plains states), Mountain (Rocky Mountain and Southwestern states), and Pacific Coast (California, Oregon, and Washington).

. . . Respondents were asked whether they usually think of themselves as a political liberal, conservative, moderate, or something else. . . . Religiosity was assessed by asking how often respondents had attended religious services of any kind in the past 12 months and by asking about the importance of religion in their life: whether it is "very important," "somewhat important," "not too important," or "not at all important."

. . . Sexual attitudes were assessed with two items. Respondents were asked whether they believed that sex is acceptable (a) only for two people who are married, (b) for two people who are not married provided that they are in love, or (c) for two people who are not married even if they are not in love with each other. The response that sex is acceptable only for married people was coded as expressing traditional sexual morality. Respondents were also asked whether they agreed or disagreed with the statement "The main purpose of sex should be for having a baby." Agreement was coded as expressing traditional sexual morality.

. . . Although a formal measure of authoritarianism was not included in the survey, three items tapped attitudes associated with this construct. Respondents were presented with pairs of traits and asked to indicate which trait was more important for a child to have. The pairs were: (a) "respect for elders" versus "independence," (b) "obedience" versus "self-reliance," and (c) "good manners" versus "curiosity." . . . An authoritarianism score was computed by assigning respondents 1 point each if they selected "respect for elders," "obedience," or "good manners." This procedure yielded scale scores ranging from 0 to 3 (M = 1.79, sd = 1.11, α = .65). Higher scores reflect beliefs more consistent with authoritarianism.

Source: Gregory M. Herek, "Heterosexuals' Attitudes toward Bisexual Men and Women in the United States," *Journal of Sex Research, 39* (4) (November 2000): 264. (*AN 8894129*)

Critical Thinking Question

1. Identify each variable and its corresponding values in the excerpt. What level of measurement is each variable?

Critical Thinking Discussion

1. The variables, their attributes, and their levels of measurement are presented in the following table. Notes are sometimes made in parentheses for specific points that may help clarify the relevant issues.

Variable	Attribute/Value	Level of Measurement
Feeling thermometer (attitudes toward bisexuals)	Range from 0–100	Interval (Rankings can be quantified, but zero point is arbitrary.)
Geographic region	Northeast, South, Midwest, Mountain, and Pacific	Nominal (Any numbers assigned for coding purposes have no real mathematical meaning.)
Self-reported political attitudes	Liberal, conservative, moderate, or something else	Nominal (The "something else" category makes the attributes exhaustive.)
How often respondents attend religious services ("Religiosity is a concept, not a variable")	None presented; presumably the respondent wrote in a specific number	Ratio (When numerical counts are left for the respondent to write in, that is usually a good indicator that a variable measured at the ratio level.)
Importance of religion in their life	Very important, somewhat important, not too important, not at all important	Ordinal (Responses can be ranked, but they are not quantified. Also, for good form, a "no response" category should be included.)
Who respondents felt sex was appropriate for	Only for two people who are married, for two people who are not married provided that they are in love, or for two people who are not married even if they are not in love with each other	Nominal (There is no ranking here.)
The main purpose of sex should be for having a baby	Agree, disagree	Nominal
Authoritarianism score	0–3	Ordinal (This is tricky. Because the index is based pairs of traits, which are purely descriptive and not numerical, meaning they are measured at the nominal level, the index itself can only be boosted to the ordinal level. It does not combine differences in rank orders (ordinal distinctions), which would boost it to the interval level. Consequently, the next step from nominal is ordinal, which is what this score is.)

■ Considerations for Moving from Operational Definition to Measurement

There are two issues that are important when moving from your creation of the operational definition to your decision about the level of measurement. These two issues are the range of variation you desire among your values and the variation between the extreme ends of your values.

When researchers refer to the *range of values*, they are interested in the extent to which someone is willing to combine attributes or values into broader categories. For example, if I am interested in knowing people's income, as I said before, people are unlikely to report a specific amount for their total household income on a survey. Instead, I'm going to have to create values that group different income levels together. However, how do I know what amounts to group? Some people earn hundreds of thousands of dollars, but how many of them am I likely to get in my sample? Not many, unless I'm specifically doing a study of, say, upper-level managers and business owners. So it probably won't benefit me to have 15 different categories of income that move into the hundreds of thousands of dollars. Plus, even if I do have a respondent who earns, say, $350,000 a year and another who earns, $400,000 a year, in the real value of that money, do I care? A $50,000 difference in the higher income brackets has less real meaning in terms of what kind of goods and lifestyles people have than does a $50,000 difference between someone who earns a total household income of $30,000 compared to $80,000.

Take another example. Earlier I presented the question about fear of crime and I provided five different values that ranged from "very afraid" to "not at all afraid," with a neutral category in the middle. But couldn't I have just had three different values that were "afraid," "no opinion," and "not afraid"? Technically, yes. It would still be an ordinal level of measurement. However, it is feasible to think that some people might be mildly or occasionally afraid (for example, they watch a lot of scary movies and are afraid of any little bump only on those nights as opposed to someone who habitually sleeps with a nightlight). Likewise, someone may be afraid even less than our person who has a habit of watching a lot of scary movies (perhaps this person watches scary movies only once a month), but still recognizes that he or she is afraid now and then. To measure the full range of fear, I may want to operationalize fear in a way that gets at the nuances of the different levels of being afraid *and* of being unafraid. In fact, social science research frequently asks opinion questions and most opinions are not a clear-cut "yes," "no," or "maybe" issue.

So how do you know if you have adequately established a range of variation? Range of variation depends on (1) what you need for your research purpose and (2) what type of variation you expect from your research participants. If fear of victimization is not your main focus and you do not care about the distinctions between very afraid and somewhat afraid, don't use them. Keep the category as "afraid." If, however, you have reason to believe (based on what you know from your expertise and what you've read in a literature review) that there *might* be a difference, then go the extra mile and expand your range to a five-point continuum. What about a seven-point continuum? It's possible, but again, unless you have strong theoretical or practical reasons for expecting a seven-point continuum to give you more information, stick with the five-point continuum. In fact, the five-point continuum is commonly used in the social sciences.

Likewise, if a researcher is studying the population at large where an overwhelming majority of respondents earn more than $20,000 a year and less than $150,000 a year, that researcher can probably forget about including specific income values such as $10,000 or $400,000. The researcher can lump these values together as "under $20,000" and "over $150,000" and will probably not hurt his or her research at all.

The second consideration is the *variation between the extreme ends of specific values*. Essentially, I'm talking about how fine a researcher wants to make the distinctions between values. Again, income is a good example. I can narrow income down to the penny or the dollar. But do I really need to do this? Does it really matter whether someone earns $40,000 versus $42,000? Depending on my research question, it may; however, chances are that it does not. So the question remains, How fine (or broad) do I want to make the extremes of individual values? Since people are apprehensive about talking about their income and since small variations in income may not have significant real-life consequences, I may be able to argue for income ranges that are in increments of $30,000. Therefore, my values (or answer choices) for income might be "under $20,000," "$20,001–$50,000," "$50,001–$80,000," "$80,001–$110,000," "$110,001–$140,000" and "over $140,001." This measure is mutually exclusive (the low extreme of each new value is one dollar greater than the high extreme of the previous one), exhaustive (people who earn $200,000 still have an answer choice for them), ranked, and manageable. Again, how fine I want the distinctions to be will be determined by my research question and the characteristics of who I am studying.

However, one last point here. As with determining the level of measurement, when in doubt about range of variation and variation between extremes, it is better to go into more detail than less. You can always make broader categories and decrease your range of variation if you have specific data; however, if you start with broad and limited ranges of data, you cannot tease out more specific information from it.

■ Implications of Levels of Measurement

So why bother in selecting a level of measurement? The main reason is because the level of measurement has important statistical implications. Some analytic techniques require that variables meet certain levels of measurement in order for those statistics to be accurate. Therefore, in the beginning of the research process, scientists need to think about what types of statistics they want to run at the end of the research process so they can design their research accordingly.

Why can't you always use ratio levels of measurement to be safe? Sometimes these higher levels just are not possible or do not fit with a research question. For example, no matter how you define it, gender is never going to be a ratio level of measurement. A person is either a male or a female. There is nothing numerical about that categorization, nor will there ever be. Plus, gender is such an established question in research that we do not *want* to toy with that level of measurement because doing so would make it difficult to compare findings across studies. Furthermore, sometimes a researcher does not need a high level of measurement. If I am studying mothers' attitudes towards work–family policies, I may not need to know the ages of people beyond an ordinal level. Consequently, instead of asking a ratio-level question, knowing I will recode it into an ordinal one later, I can save myself some time and just word the variable on the ordinal level from the start.

Sometimes a research question does not naturally lend itself to higher levels of measurement. If I want to study people's attitudes toward abortion, for example, the most direct way to do this is either to ask them outright or to set scenarios depicting different conditions where people might accept abortion even if they generally do not and then ask them their opinion. If the research question is simply interested in a "do you agree" type of answer, an ordinal level of measurement may suit the researcher's purposes just fine. Plus, it is very difficult to make an opinion question an interval or ratio level of measurement unless I created a detailed index or scale. I will discuss this further in Chapter 11.

That being said, whenever a researcher is not completely clear about the overall research process, the general rule of thumb is to strive for the highest level of measurement possible when operationalizing a concept. The researcher can always bump these measures down to lower levels; however, as I illustrated earlier, the researcher cannot inflate lower levels of measurement to higher ones.

I cannot stress enough that the research process is not linear. When you begin to define the terms in your research questions or your hypotheses, you need to be clear about (1) what types of variables will best address your research question and (2) your minimum levels of measurement necessary for the statistics you plan to do after you collect your data. These considerations help researchers decide how to construct the measures for their research concepts.

■ Measurement Quality

Not only must researchers decide a variable's level of measurement but they also must make sure that their measures are meaningful and will lead them to the information that will accurately test their research hypotheses. Do you remember what I stated at the beginning of the conceptualization–operationalization process? The definitions social scientists give to their concepts really do not have true meaning. In other words, these definitions are what a *researcher* means when he or she thinks of a concept, or they define what a researcher *thinks* a concept means; however, these definitions are still somewhat subjective and fuzzy. That makes measuring them an imperfect science at best. Instead of getting frustrated, throwing your hands up in the air and saying, "If I'm trying to measure something that has no inherent definition, how can I ever know if I am truly measuring what I think I am anyway? What's the point?" researchers know that they are not flying blind in this process. Other researchers have developed ways of measuring the quality of measurements, and the higher the quality of a measure, the more faith researchers and others have in the findings the research produces. The keys to measurement quality are a measure's validity and reliability.

Validity

You might remember that in Chapter 3 I discussed issues of study validity in relation to threats to causality known as rival causal factors. When referring to measurement validity, validity refers to whether a measure is really measuring what the researcher thinks it is measuring. Since concepts have the meaning people attach to them, a concept's definition that leads to the development of a measure is an approximation of what that concept means. But how do we *really* know whether our definitions accurately measure our concepts? In other words, if, after I progress through the conceptualization–operationalization process, I decide to measure alcoholism among adolescents by the number of nights an adolescent has two or more alcoholic beverages, how do I know whether that measure truly captures the essence of "alcoholism" among adolescents? After all, the adolescent consumption of alcoholic beverages is illegal in all 50 states, so how do I know if my measure is restrictive enough? In reality, I will never completely be able to answer this question; however, by establishing the validity of the measure, I can have more confidence that the measure is, in fact, measuring what I intended. There are four types of measurement validity: face validity, content validity, criterion validity, and construct validity.

Face validity: **Face validity** is the most basic validity test and it literally means whether the measure appears valid "on the face of it"—in other words, whether the measure seems to make sense as a logical indicator of a concept. Let's continue with my study of alcohol addiction among adolescents. Suppose, as I said before, that I consider adolescents to be addicted to alcohol if they drink more than two alcoholic beverages a day at least four days a week. Looking at how much a person drinks alcohol makes sense when measuring alcoholism and therefore it is valid "on the face of it." You and I might disagree as to whether two alcoholic beverages a day at least four days a week is enough. For example, you might think that alcoholism is more than just the frequency someone drinks. You may think that it also involves the context in which someone does most of his or her drinking (e.g., alone), whether that person tries to hide the drinking (implying that there is something wrong with the behavior), or how often that person drinks in order to get drunk. You may also question whether my definition is enough. You may think that alcoholism is when a person has at least one drink every day. Your points may have merit; however, even with these disagreements, you would still have to agree that the amount a person drinks (even if you disagree with what I've defined as that amount) has *something* to do with alcoholism. Therefore, it still achieves face validity.

On the other hand, deciding to use a person's social class as an indicator of alcoholism does not achieve face validity. Even though people of lower socioeconomic backgrounds are more likely to have their drinking behavior labeled as problematic, thereby making them "alcoholics," that does not necessarily mean that people from lower socioeconomic backgrounds are indeed more likely to *be* alcoholics. All it means is that others are more likely to interpret their drinking behavior as indicative of alcoholism. Furthermore, clearly there are many lower-income people who are *not* alcoholics and there are many middle-class and wealthy people who are. Hence, social class as an indicator of alcoholism does not achieve face validity and is therefore a very poor measure of this concept.

Content validity: If you questioned my use of "number of nights a week a person has two or more alcoholic drinks" as a measure for alcoholism because you thought that there were other aspects of alcoholism in addition to the frequency a person consumes alcohol, then you would be questioning the content validity of my measure. **Content validity** refers to whether the measure covers the full range, or all of the dimensions, of a concept's meaning. How do researchers know what the "full range" is? The most frequent way to answer this question is to review the research of others. In other words, researchers do a literature review, like I discussed in Chapter 3.

In my example of adolescent alcoholics, the Adolescent Drinking Index (ADi) may be a better indicator of adolescent alcoholism because it contains more dimensions than simply how often an adolescent consumes alcohol. The ADi measures the severity of adolescent drinking using four dimensions: loss of control of drinking, social indicators of drinking problems, psychological indicators, and physical problems related to drinking (Harrell & Wirtz, 1985). This measure seems to be a more encompassing measure of adolescent alcoholism than my initial measure of "the number of nights an adolescent consumes two or more alcoholic beverages." Consequently, in addition to having face validity (each of these four dimensions "make sense" when referring to "adolescent alcoholism"), the ADi measure is higher on content validity than my original measure. So let's pretend I decide to abandon my original measure and go with this one instead. Let's see how the ADi meets the other two criteria of measurement validity.

Criterion validity: Criterion validity compares a researcher's chosen measure to some external criteria—whether it is another measure widely accepted in that particular field or whether it is a more directly observable criteria. For example, if I spoke with the two people an adolescent identifies as his two closest friends and their accounts of the drinking behavior of the adolescent in question matches the findings of the ADi, then I have a loose measure of criterion validity based on direct observation (the observation of the friends). On the other hand, if I do a study using the ADi and my findings are similar to findings of another study that used a different, but generally accepted scale of alcoholism, such as the Adolescent Diagnostic Interview (ADI) or the Adolescent Alcohol Involvement Scale (AAIS), then my measure would have established criterion validity.

There are two type of criterion validity. One, **concurrent validity,** researchers can measure during the course of their study. The other, **predictive validity,** researchers can use to validate their measure when the study is complete. Researchers can establish concurrent validity by using another, widely accepted measure at the same time the researcher is using the variable of interest. For example, if I included the Adolescent Alcohol Involvement Scale (AAIS) in my study that also had my main measure of interest, the Adolescent Drinking Index (ADi), and if the scores on the AAIS and the ADi are similar, then I have achieved concurrent validity for the ADi.

Predictive validity, on the other hand, is the ability of a measure to predict future behavior. For example, if adolescents who score high on the ADi and do not receive treatment for a potential problem with alcoholism develop drinking problems as adults, then the ADi has predictive validity.

Although establishing criterion-related validity greatly improves researchers' confidence that a measurement is truly measuring what they think it is, sometimes this type of validity is not feasible. For example, if I want to measure feelings of abandonment or isolation, what direct measure can I use to establish criterion-related validity? Likewise, if I want to study poverty, what type of direct confirmation can I get of a person's self-reported income? I can't look up his or her tax return because I do not have access to it. I also cannot contact the Department of Health and Human Services to see if that person is on welfare. Not only are those records unavailable to me, but many people who are in poverty do not apply for welfare. Furthermore, social scientists do not have established scales of poverty like they do for alcoholism. Therefore, I cannot really compare my measure to an otherwise validated measure. Thus, obtaining some concrete confirmation of a person's poverty status is very difficult. As a result, we have to trust what people report to us.

Many social science concepts are like this. Therefore, if researchers cannot establish criterion-related validity for a measure, that in itself does not negate the value of that measure. In fact, when criterion-related validity is not feasible, researchers are frequently content with a measure's validity if that measure fulfills the last type of validity: construct validity.

BOX 4.3   **Measuring Career Indecisiveness: Issues of Validity**

Are you having trouble deciding what you want to do with your life once you leave college? If so, you are not alone. Researchers have tried to understand the different reasons students are undecided about their career paths. The argument is that if researchers can identify reasons behind students' indecision, then career counselors can use that information to better help students develop a career path that suits their interests and needs.

Below is an excerpt from an article that tests the validity of the typology of different career indecision types. According to Kelly and Pulver (2003), the research involving career indecision has moved from an original dichotomy of decided–undecided to a more complex typology that recognizes that not all undecided students are alike. However, if counselors are going to be able to help these students, they need to know whether the different typologies are valid—in other words, whether they are accurately measuring differences between different types of undecided students.

In order to develop their typologies, Kelly and Pulver studied 566 first-semester freshmen at a large midwestern university who had not yet declared a major. These students were members of a career exploration class, and as part of that class, they completed the measures Kelly and Pulver describe in the excerpt. In fact, since the focus of this discussion is measurement validity, the following excerpt contains information on the career indecision and personality measures Kelly and Pulver used. Read the excerpt and answer the critical thinking questions. You can obtain the complete article using Research Navigator and searching either by the citation or the article number in parentheses at the end of the citation.

> Consistent with previous investigations, we used career indecision and personality variables to determine the types [of undecided students].
>
> Career indecision. The CFI [Career Factors Inventory] is a 21-item assessment that yields four scales. . . . The Career Choice Anxiety and General Indecisiveness scales reflect the affective component of career indecision. . . . The Need for Career Information and Need for Self-Knowledge scales reflect the cognitive component of career indecision. . . .
>
> Chartrand et al. (1990) also presented considerable evidence of the validity of the CFI scales. Evidence for the four-scale structure of the CFI emerged first in factor analysis and then in a subsequent confirmatory factor analysis. The test developers also presented information regarding the convergent validity of the individual CFI scales. The affective CFI scales are positively correlated with anxiety and negatively correlated with self-esteem and goal instability.
>
> Students scoring higher on the Career Choice Anxiety and General Indecisiveness scales tend to be more anxious and to report lower self-esteem and less goal stability. The cognitive CFI scales are correlated negatively with vocational identity; students expressing a greater need for career information and self-knowledge have a less stable vocational identity (Chartrand et al., 1990). The significant associations between the CFI scales and theoretically related career and personality variables constitute adequate validity evidence.
>
> *Personality.* The FFI [NEO Five Factor Inventory] . . . measures five aspects of personality: Neuroticism, Extraversion, Openness, Agreeableness, and Conscientiousness. . . . Participants use a 5-point Likert scale to describe themselves, higher scores indicating a greater tendency to display each of the five personality characteristics. There is a wealth of data documenting the internal consistency and stability of the FFI scales (Costa & McCrae, 1992). There are hundreds of studies supporting the validity of the Big Five model of personality assessment as well as the FFI scales (Piedmont, 1998) . . . .
>
> **Results**
>
> We labeled the first type [of student] well-adjusted information seekers. This type . . .

share[s] the focal need for career- and self-information and the absence of negative affect. . . . These students lack . . . anxiety or distress regarding their academic major and career choices.

We labeled the second indecision type neurotic indecisive information seekers. [This] type seems to experience considerable anxiety regarding the career choice as well as more general negative affect, as indicated by the elevated score on Neuroticism. This type indicated a strong need for career- and self-information. They also seem to be generally indecisive [about a variety of non-career issues].

The third type, low ability information seekers, . . . indicated a strong need for career information that seems to be related to their low verbal and math ability. The low ability information seekers . . . are more likely than their peers with higher ability to have difficulty in completing the baccalaureate degree.

. . . We labeled the fourth . . . uncommitted extraverts. . . . This type is . . . closed to new sources of self-knowledge, [has] low neuroticism, and [has] high extraversion and agreeableness. This type shows no signs of decision conflict or negative affect. [They] seem to . . . have significant personal strengths that can be applied in the search for a career.

Source: Kevin R. Kelly and Chad A. Pulver, "Refining Measurement of Career Indecision Types: A Validity Study," *Journal of Counseling & Development, 81* (4) (Fall 2003): 445. (*AN 11261432*)

Critical Thinking Questions

1. What types of validity do Kelly and Pulver establish for the measures they chose? Support each claim with evidence from the excerpt.

2. How would the authors' measures achieve predictive validity? Of what type of validity is predictive validity a subcomponent?

Critical Thinking Discussion

1. Let's begin by looking at the Career Factors Inventory (CFI). Does it make sense that a scale such as this may measure one's career indecision? Yes, therefore it achieves face validity. Furthermore, the authors note that the scale consists of four subscales: Career Choice Anxiety, General Indecisiveness, Need for Career Information, and Need for Self-Knowledge scales. The first two scales address the emotional (affective) dimension of career indecision and the latter two the cognitive dimension. Therefore, by recognizing various dimensions of career indecisiveness, this measure takes a step toward establishing content validity.

Are there other dimensions possible? Probably—for example, perhaps there is a social dimension (such as pressure from parents which is causing indecision among students); however, any one measure is unlikely to include *all* dimensions of a concept and including two is better than just including one.

The measure also has construct validity, or more specifically convergent validity, as the authors mention how the CFI scores correlate with similar, but distinct, measures such as vocational identity. We don't have any concrete evidence of criterion validity, although perhaps this type of validity was addressed by Chartrand and colleagues in their study that the authors cite (1990). We do not know this based on the information here.

So how about the personality measure, the NEO Five Factor Index (FFI)? Well, most of us have probably used adjectives such as *extroverted, neurotic,* and *conscientious* to describe someone, therefore the five factors the index uses (Neuroticism, Extraversion, Openness, Agreeableness, and Conscientiousness) all make sense as indicators of personality and, therefore, meet the requirements of face validity. Likewise, these five dimensions address different aspects of people's personality, therefore it has some level of content validity.

As with the CDI, we do not have any more concrete information about criterion-related validity, nor do we have information about construct validity; however, the authors claim that the validity of this test has been thoroughly examined by other researchers and they provide some citations that we can pursue if we are interested.

Are these omissions a problem? Do researchers need to document every aspect of validity on their own or is it sufficient that they cite the studies of others to establish this? Because researchers frequently have to be selective about how much material they put into a report (largely due to space limitations in many academic journals), for the most part, providing citations for other studies that document validity is enough if those studies exist.

Ideally the researcher will still discuss some highlights, as Kelly and Pulver did; however, if they do not and only provide the citation, that is still sufficient. It is the reader's responsibility then to look up those citations, evaluate their content, and determine if the material presented is convincing.

2. One way Kelly and Pulver would achieve predictive validity is to show that students who they classified as a specific type, such as neurotic indecisive information seekers, had less career indecision after they experienced specific counseling tactics aimed at that type of undecided student.

Construct validity: When researchers can show that their measure is related to other measures specified in a theory, then that measure has **construct validity.** For example, I can establish construct validity for the ADi if I can show that adolescents who score high on the ADi also exhibit behaviors such as discipline problems in school, low grades, and family conflict. Theoretically, all of these behaviors are related to alcohol abuse among adolescents; therefore, if my measure behaves as these other measures do, then my measure has construct validity.

Like criterion-related validity, there are two subtypes of construct validity. The first is **convergent validity.** When one measure shows the same characteristics as different types of measures of the same concept, we have convergent validity. In other words, the various measures *converge* to illustrate the same concept. On the other hand, when scores on a measure are compared to measures of different, but related, concepts and the measure of interest behaves differently, then we have **discriminant validity,** which is the complement to convergent validity. For discriminant validity, I want to show that the scores of my measure are not related to scores on a measure of something that indicates the opposite. Put another way, if Concept A and Concept B are different, then Measure A should not be the same as Measure B. If an adolescent scores *low* on the ADi, meaning that that adolescent is not likely to have an alcohol problem, then that person should not score *high* on the other measures of adolescent alcoholism. If all measures are valid, that person who scores low on the ADi should not have high scores on other measures indicating alcohol problems and/or he should not have friends saying that he is drinking a lot (if the friend measure is also valid).

Reliability

Establishing measurement validity is only part of the challenge to establish the quality of a measure. Measurement reliability is also important for determining measurement quality.

As the term **reliability** suggests, measures are reliable if they produce consistent results when they are repeatedly used. Hence, reliability tells researchers about a measure's dependency—in other words, how well researchers can depend on that measure to produce consistent results. For example, suppose I asked you to guess my age. You might look at me and guess "mid-thirties." Now suppose I asked you to guess the ages of 15 other people; and, unknown to you, I put on a wig that changes my hair from blonde to gray, I put on a cardigan sweater over my T-shirt, don glasses, and go to the end of the line of the people you are guessing. You come to me, look me over again, and guess 42. See? Your estimate of age is not very reliable. If a measure is reliable, it is less vulnerable to misinterpretation, random error, or chance variation. Hence, researchers have more confidence in it.

Although the example I gave is pretty obvious, reliability is not always easy to achieve. Suppose someone wanted to study the overall satisfaction of the student body with their collegiate experience. That researcher might do things like ask students whether they like their classes, whether they like their professors, how many times they cut class, or if they would recommend the school to other people. The researcher might also observe how frequently people laugh with friends on the quad.

There are some problems with this approach, however. The researcher might approach a student after he failed an exam, therefore that student might have a particularly negative view of a class or a professor at that point in time. Or a student might love a class because it is easy, but also report that she skips that class frequently (presumably because it is easy). Or there might not be a lot of people laughing on the quad because the researcher is doing her or his study during finals and students are in their dorms studying. Or perhaps the researcher is making observations near a weekend or vacation break and many people have left the campus. People might be happy with their campus, but they may simply not be around due to other external factors. The point is that these are not very reliable measures of college students' satisfaction with college life. These measures are likely to produce different findings based on a host of different personal and environmental influences.

So what would be a more reliable measure? How about calculating the percentage of the student body that transfers out of the school each year? You can obtain a count for all the students attending the university and you can obtain a list of all the students who have transferred to another school. No matter how many times you count the names on that second list, or calculate the percentage of people who have left, you will always get the same number or percent. Therefore, *that* measure is reliable.

There are three types of reliability and four ways of assessing reliability.

Types of reliability: The first type of reliability is **temporal reliability.** This type of reliability is reliability across time. In other words, will this measure produce the same results if measured at different time periods? For example, if I ask someone his or her gender, I would suspect that this person will give the same response regardless of whether I ask the person in the morning, evening, or a week later. Likewise, if a person scores high on an addiction probability scale and I readminister that scale a week later, if that scale is reliable, that person should still have a high score because addictions do not go away after a week.

The second type of reliability is **representative reliability** and this addresses whether an indicator produces the same results across different groups of people. If I asked people their weight and very thin people overstated their weight and very heavy people understated their weight, I would not have representative reliability. Both groups of people would have to accurately report their weight. As another example, the ADi I mentioned in the previous section will have representative reliability if, for example, it successfully predicts adolescent alcoholism for adolescents of different genders, social classes, and race.

Last is **equivalence reliability,** which occurs when several items are used to measure the same concept and they all produce the same result with all indicators. I will discuss the use of multiple measures in the next section; however, an illustration is given here. Let's say that I had several items on a survey ask about adolescents' drinking behavior (such as the number of nights they consume alcohol, the number of drinks per night, the number of friends they have who consume alcohol, and whether they drink with their friends). If a respondent answered similarly (it is not necessary that the answers be exactly the same, just similar) to all of those items, I would have equivalence reliability. You may be saying to yourself that equivalence reliability sounds somewhat similar to convergent validity. You are right, because reliability is a prerequisite for any measure of validity. We cannot really measure a concept if the measure we are using produces different findings each time we do use it. I will discuss the validity-reliability connection more in a bit.

Reliability tests: There are four possible reliability tests. A researcher does not have to do all of them to establish reliability. Which methods a researcher selects depends on the research question (notice how that part of the research process keeps popping up?) and the type of reliability he or she is trying to establish. The four methods are test-retest method, split-half method, using established measures, and interobserver reliability.

The **test-retest** measure of reliability is pretty much what it sounds like. Researchers administer a measure more than once. If there is no reason to expect people's answers to that measure to change, then the responses should be the same at both time points. If the answers vary, however, that may indicate that the researcher has a problem with measurement reliability. For example, if you take the SAT more than once and do not have a long span of time between tests and do not take a test prep class between the two test points, your score on the SAT should be fairly consistent. For instance, if the SAT is reliable, you should not have a combined math and verbal score of 800 the first time and a score of 1200 the second.

Can you identify which type of reliability the test-retest method addresses? It primarily addresses stability reliability because this type of reliability, as I mentioned earlier, is interested in seeing whether people provide similar answers to the same indicator across two different time points. Therefore, the test-retest strategy assesses temporal reliability. The SAT is the indicator in both instances and the two time points are the two different times you took the test.

Questions that ask about specific life events (such as whether a person got married, the number of children a person has) frequently have high reliability. However, questions that ask people about general past behavior (e.g., "In the past six months, how often did you go to church?") generally have low reliability. Researchers call questions that address past behavior *recollective questions* and researchers recognize that recollection questions are particularly vulnerable to reliability issues. If I asked you what you wore the first day of class *last year,* you probably can't remember the specific outfit. You might know that you wore jeans and a T-shirt, but which pair of jeans and which specific T-shirt? If I pushed you, you'd probably give me two different answers if I asked you at two different times. That illustrates people's poor powers of recollective observation.

The second type of reliability test is the **split-half** reliability test. Again, the term itself is very descriptive of the actual process. In split-half reliability tests, the researcher divides a survey into two smaller instruments by randomly (either by the unscientific, but still random, method of flipping a coin or by the more scientific method of using a table of random numbers) separating the questions. Instead of testing temporal reliability, this method assesses internal reliability because the two halves should produce similar results.

Usually researchers do this one of two ways. The first way is that if researchers have used some type of probability sampling to obtain their sample (I will discuss this in Chapter 5), then they may have randomly selected half of the indicators of a concept to be on one survey and the other half to be on a second survey. Then the researchers may give one survey to the first half of their participants and the other survey to the second half. If the participants were selected randomly (using a probability sampling technique, not a layperson's idea of "random"), there is no reason to expect that the participants will answer the different but related questions differently *if the questions are reliable* because there is no difference between the two sample groups (again, due to their random selection). However, if these people *do* answer differently, the measures are not going to be reliable.

For example, let's suppose I wanted to test prejudice, like I did in the beginning of this chapter, and I put 20 items about prejudice in my survey. I then selected a simple random sample of 200 college students and I used a table of random numbers to randomly separate the 20 prejudice questions into two groups of 10 questions. Then, 100 students received a survey with the first 10 questions about prejudice, the other 100 students received a survey with the second 10 questions. If my measures of prejudice are reliable, then the scores on the 10 questions for the first 100 students should be similar to the scores on the second 10 questions for the other students. Similar scores would indicate internal reliability because I am illustrating that my measures of prejudice are consistent regardless of which ones I am asking. In this case, each student is completing only one survey, therefore I am not looking for consistency in their responses across time (since there is no second time point for comparison). Thus, I am not interested in temporal reliability.

The second way of conducting a test-retest for reliability involves only one sample that is not subdivided. Let me alter my previous example to illustrate this second case. Let's assume I am still measuring prejudice and I still select 200 students to be in my study. In this second approach, I would keep all 200 students as one large sample (not subdividing them into two groups of 100 students) and I would keep all 20 questions in the same survey. Thus, there is one sample of 200 students and one survey. To assess split-half reliability, I can then see if the answers to the odd-numbered questions about prejudice are correlated, or associated, to the even-numbered questions about prejudice. If the odd-numbered answers are similar to the even-numbered answers, then I have reliability (Hagan, 1997).

The third type of reliability, using established measures, is fairly self-explanatory. In this instance, the researcher uses a measure that other researchers have frequently used alone or in addition to another measure. If the findings from the researcher's study, using the same measure, support the findings of other studies and/or support the findings of the additional measure, then reliability is established.

The fourth type of reliability is less common in self-report surveys but is still useful when the researcher, or research assistants, have to interpret the meaning of people's behavior (in other words, the subjects themselves are not reporting their own behavior or attitudes) or of the material being studied (such as newspaper articles). This type of reliability is called inter-observer reliability or **inter-rater reliability** or *researcher-worker* *reliability).* This technique simply involves having more than one researcher observe and code people, events, or environments. If the two researchers agree on their observations and interpretations, we are more confident that the observations really do reflect what occurred instead of the quirks or perspectives of the observers.

■ The Relationship between Validity and Reliability

Validity, reliability, and generalizability are all important and necessary indicators of measurement quality. However, achieving all three simultaneously is difficult. It is much easier, for example, to achieve reliability than it is to achieve validity. It is easier to show whether a measure will produce consistent outcomes than it is to determine whether those outcomes truly measure a particular concept. For example, I may weigh myself numerous times on my digital bathroom scale and get the same weight. However, if I go to my doctor's office and stand on his or her scale, which is recalibrated monthly, I might find that my scale is not calibrated correctly and is therefore consistently off by 4 pounds. Because my bathroom scale is consistently off, its estimate of my weight is still reliable; however, it is not correct and therefore is not valid.

Reliability is a criterion for validity because if an indicator truly does measure the concept under consideration, then it will consistently produce similar results. However, as I just illustrated, reliability is not enough for validity. Sound confusing? Figure 4.2 of a methodological "bulls-eye," borrowed from Babbie (1995), illustrates this idea. Each of the three pictures is a target where the center, or bulls-eye, is a perfect measurement of a concept of interest. Therefore, if all the points "hit" the bulls-eye, we have high reliability and high validity. In the first picture, we have low reliability and low validity because although the points are hovering around the bulls-eye, they are not dead center (therefore they are not valid) and they are not close together (therefore they are not reliable). In the second picture, we have high reliability but low validity because the points are all clustered together (high reliability); however, once again, they are not near the bulls-eye and therefore they are not measuring the concept of interest (low validity). The last picture is the jackpot where we have high reliability *and* validity. In the last picture, the observations are all clustered together to the point where they now make one fairly large black blob. That is high reliability. Notice that the points do not neatly converge to one point that perfectly absorbs all of the individual observations. Such a perfect fit is not necessary. As you also notice, the points are all within the center bulls-eye, which illustrates high validity.

Occasionally validity and reliability conflict because as one increases, the other may decrease. For example, the concept of *anomie* or, as it is sometimes better known, *alienation*, is very popular in social science research. Yet, this is a very complex concept that has been explored, debated, and analyzed in

 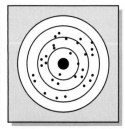 

Reliable But Not Valid   Valid But Not Reliable   Valid *and* Reliable

Figure 4.2 The Relationship between Validity and Reliability Using a Bulls-Eye Analogy

Source: From *Practice of Social Research,* 7th edition by Earl Babbie, © 1995. Reprinted with permission of Wadsworth, a division of Thomson Learning: www.thomsonrights.com. Fax 800-730-2215.

hundreds of books since Emile Durkheim published his first book on the subject in 1897. Why all the research? Because alienation is a very abstract and subjective concept.

Some social scientists define alienation as a deep sense of aloneness that transcends various areas of a person's life, such as his or her family relations, school relations, work relations, and so on. Others measure anomie or alienation like Durkheim did and count the number of suicides in a particular area during a particular span of time. Counting is fairly straightforward and if I give you a list of all the suspected suicides, you can count the names and reach the same number as I do. This would be a very reliable measure. However, because alienation is such a complex concept (remember, it has generated hundreds of books on this topic alone), I obviously am going to miss the deeper meaning behind the concept of alienation if I just count the number of suicides. Hence, my measure (the number of suicides) may have criterion validity (since my definition is accepted by many people in the social sciences), but it's still pretty obvious that that measure is limited in definition, and therefore it is limited in content validity (because many also argue that this definition only addresses one aspect of anomie).

At this point you may be getting frustrated by the complexity involved in achieving valid and reliable measures. That's understandable, but don't give up! Just remember that science, *any* science, is not perfect. After all, I began this chapter by saying that many social science concepts do not have inherent meaning in and of themselves. The only meaning a concept has is the meaning we give it. Therefore, no measure is going to be without some error, nor can we expect it to be perfectly valid at all times and in all situations. In other words, we must *expect some limitations*. However, even with these limitations, scientific observation is still a better, more meaningful, way of observing our social environment than are the informal methods of personal observation, tradition, and experience that I discussed in Chapter 1. The very fact that scientists *know* that their concepts are complex and difficult to define makes them try harder to produce measures that are as valid and reliable as possible; this conscious strife for validity and reliability is missing in less structured modes of observation.

So how do social scientists deal with this inherent limitation? Well, in any individual study, the validity and reliability of measures are frequently assessed after the fact—meaning after the data are gathered. This means that if a researcher determines that a measure is unreliable or invalid, then the study cannot be saved—and all that time and money in collecting the data are wasted. Therefore, researchers take many pains to try to develop valid and reliable measures *beforehand*, even though their success or failure cannot be assessed until the data have been collected.

There are a couple of suggestions for improving your chances of having reliable and valid measures. First, if there is no clear agreement about how to measure a concept (for example, the concept of "alienation or anomie"), then use multiple measures. Include different dimensions of a concept and measure those dimensions in several different ways. Second, use measures that have been used in other published research and that have already been validated and shown to be reliable. However, with this strategy, keep in mind that *your* study is likely to involve a different population, a different time, and/or a different location. Therefore, you still need to validate and test for reliability, but you have a little more confidence in measures that have worked for other people than in brand-new measures that have not been tested in the "real" world.

Although the importance of valid and reliable measures cannot be overstated, I do not want you to get the idea that social science research always involves tension and insecurity as researchers worry about every indicator they want to include in their studies. Many social science concepts are fairly straightforward. Gender is a good example. There are only two genders recognized in our society, and social scientists can measure that with confidence by just using one variable. Other times, concepts have such an agreed-on definition that researchers can use a relatively few number of indicators to measure it. The concept of "poverty" is an example. Although there may be many aspects of poverty worthy of research, one of the main ways of defining poverty is the government's calculation of the poverty line, which can easily be identified by looking at the United States Bureau of the Census website. Now, this does not mean to imply that everyone *agrees* with this definition; in fact, many researchers take issue with the government's means of calculating the poverty line. However, the point remains, that the government's calculation *is* a fairly standard calculation that, if used with some other indicators of poverty (such as those proposed by critics of the government's calculation method), can very likely produce a valid and reliable idea of poverty.

So don't be frozen by indecision regarding operationalization of a concept or by establishing a concept's validity and reliability. Most researchers do not start from scratch in either of these endeavors, and critically examining the research of others can be a useful tool in moving from concepts to measures on your own. To further help you with this, the next section of this chapter will focus on evaluating the measurement you see in published research.

Evaluating Written Research: Operationalization and Measurement

In this chapter I discussed the steps and challenges of operationalization concepts and creating meaningful indictors to measure those concepts. I'm going to follow a similar approach for my discussion of how to evaluate the operationalization, measurement, and validity of other research. Let me begin by discussing some questions to keep in mind when evaluating researchers' conceptual and operational definitions.

1. Is the conceptualization suitably specific?

Remember, concepts are just abstract tags on reality. Different people may have different definitions of a concept. It is important, then, for any researcher to clearly conceptualize and identify what he or she means by a concept. This way, a reader can better understand the researcher's perspective and the corresponding research. The following example from Schedler (2001, **AN 5367643**) illustrates the conceptualization process of the concept, "democratic consolidation":

> Thus, "consolidating" democracy may involve the "positive" tasks of deepening a fully liberal democracy or completing a semi-democracy. Or it may respond to the "negative" challenges of impeding the erosion of a liberal democracy or else, avoiding the breakdown of whatever minimal kind of democracy we have in place.

In this segment, you need to ask yourself if Schedler's conceptualization of democratic consolidation is suitably specific. I believe that it is because Schedler defines the general parameters of what he means by democratic consolidation. I know, for example, that it does not refer to how Democrats in our country try to gain votes to win an election. I also can tell by the general definition that this concept has multiple definitions. That is not unusual, as I stated previously.

2. Are conceptual/operational definitions presented and are they adequate?

Remember, some books have different terms for the conceptualization–operationalization process. The real issue is not the terms the researcher uses to define the process but rather whether the researcher moves from broad concepts and definitions to narrower, more specific ones. That is essentially what you are looking for when considering the second evaluation question. Later in the article, Schedler (2001) notes:

> Some students of regime [democratic] consolidation look at political actors' behavior, others at their attitudes, and still others at their structural environment. . . . [We] may comprehend behavioral, attitudinal, and structural data as operational indicators that refer to different levels of measurement.

This segment alone is not a sufficient operational definition. It needs more clarification as to what Schedler (2001) means by "behavior," "attitudes," and "structural environment." He specifies this a bit more in the following section:

> Some scholars focus on the "behavioral foundations" of regime stability. They think that democrats cannot lean back and relax unless they have proven their capacity to roll back antidemocratic challenges, or else, unless no major political actors violate basic democratic rules anymore. Others privilege the "attitudinal foundations" of democratic governance. They take democracy to be under risk unless all major political players develop the normative motives, strategic rationality, and cognitive perceptions required to sustain a liberal-democratic regime.

Further definition is likely to lead us to the measurement section of the process and I will discuss some criteria for evaluation of that shortly.

3. Are the definitions productive?

Productive definitions build on existing research, contribute to our understanding of the concept in the field, and are useful to our particular research needs. In other words, are the definitions likely to be useful to others interested in the same concept, or are the definitions too specific to this one research study at this one point in time? Good definitions have utility beyond the immediate study.

How do you know whether a definition has utility? A couple of ways. First, if a researcher borrows a definition from other sources, then you know that this definition (by default of being used before) has some utility to others in the field. Second, a researcher may explicitly state the utility of his or her definition by discussing its implications. The third criteria is purely subjective on your part. Does the researcher define the concept in a way that makes this article relevant for *your* purposes? Just because a definition may make the research incompatible with your needs doesn't mean that the research itself is necessarily bad—it just means that you can't use it and therefore it is not relevant for you. If this is the case, you simply do not focus on that particular study and instead move on to read the next article you've gathered.

The material in this chapter and the process of evaluating the conceptual and operational definitions of others may seem somewhat abstract and challenging, and that is because it is. Therefore, when reading the research of others, do not expect them to be able to do more than you could if *you* were conducting the research. This means that when evaluating the research of others, we need to keep a couple of points in mind that will help us be critical reviewers without expecting the impossible. I'll list these points for easy reference and then I will discuss each in a bit more detail.

1. No concept is going to ever be completely defined in a research article, nor can it be.
2. Even when a researcher *does* specify many possible conceptual definitions, no research can feasibly and adequately measure all of them. Researchers *must* limit their focus to one or two definitions.
3. Some concepts are very difficult to operationalize. Criticize a researcher only if you can produce or find a better definition and a stronger justification for using your alternate definition.

Let's discuss the first point. Many concepts have a variety of dimensions and indicators for those dimensions. Quite simply, it would take too much time and space for a researcher to detail all the possible definitions of a concept in a written report. Furthermore, doing so would detract from the direct presentation of the research and would result only in confusing readers rather than enlightening them. If there is particular disagreement in the field about how to measure a concept, the most a researcher is likely to do is recognize the disagreement, cite some researchers who support various sides of the disagreement, and then proceed with her or his specific focus. This is perfectly acceptable, but it does not release the researcher from an obligation to discuss how she or he operationalizes a concept. The only point here is that a researcher does not have to spend much time writing about operationalization that will not be used as the focus of his or her research. Any definition relevant to the researcher's particular study, however, still has to be presented.

Second, even if a researcher does discuss various dimensions and indicators, it is unlikely that the researcher can focus on all of them in his or her particular study. If a researcher is collecting his or her own data, there may be time and money limitations. Therefore, the researcher may focus only on the definitions and indicators that are most widely used and accepted by others in the field. If a researcher is analyzing data collected by someone else (e.g., a large national probability study by a research institute), then that researcher's operationalization of concepts is limited by the measures already available to him or her. Evaluating whether a researcher has selected the most appropriate definitions and indicators in this instance requires the reader to use his or her *own* expertise and understanding of a topic.

Once again, this does not mean that readers should just blindly accept researchers' decisions; however, it *does* mean that readers should think about whether there are more appropriate choices, why those choices are more appropriate, why the researcher may not have used those choices, and what affect the researcher's choice is likely to have on the study outcome. To put this another way, how did the researcher justify his or her choice of definitions and indicators and is the researcher's reasoning sound?

The third point addresses the issue I raised at the end of the discussion of validity and reliability. Some social concepts are just very difficult to adequately measure. You may disagree with a researcher's choice; however, unless you can discount her or his justification and provide a better reason to choose a different definition or indicator, then the researcher's choice is acceptable from a methodological point of view.

To summarize, when evaluating a researcher's operationalization, ask yourself:

1. Is the conceptualization suitably specific?
2. Are conceptual/operational definitions presented and are they adequate?
3. Are the definitions productive? (Keep in mind that it is not feasible to expect a researcher to do more than you would be able to do in similar circumstances.)

Once you have decided that a study has adequately addressed the first three issues for operationalization evaluation, you are ready to evaluate the measures used. Sometimes the researcher makes it easy for you by providing the actual study questions; other times the researcher does not, which means that you have to make some inferences. What follows are seven issues to ask when evaluating the measures in a study.

4. How many different dimensions are being measured at once? Are the various dimensions sufficient?

As previously discussed, many social science concepts have more than one dimension. Does the researcher recognize this? Does the researcher discuss the dimensions and explicitly state on which dimensions she or he will focus? Remember, it is okay if a researcher does not focus on all of the dimensions possible—in fact, it is frequently impossible due to limitations in resources. However, if the concept is very complex and multidimensional, the researcher should focus on more than one dimension (even if it is not all the possible dimensions) and explain, at least briefly, why the other dimensions are not included in the analysis. If dimensions are omitted, it is also important that the researcher remember to discuss only the concept, in the results and conclusion sections, in terms of the dimensions actually studied.

For example, let's pretend you want to study employee satisfaction. To do so, you would need to recognize that the various concepts of employee satisfaction may include satisfaction with their work conditions, satisfaction with their benefits, satisfaction with their pay, and satisfaction with their bosses. Perhaps, because of the nature of your research question or the amount of resources you have to do the research, you are going to focus only on employee satisfaction with their pay and benefits. That is fine so long as you (1) briefly recognize (perhaps in a literature review) the various dimensions of employee satisfaction, (2) explicitly state which dimensions will be the focus of your research, and (3) make sure that when you discuss your results and conclusions, you are clear that they refer to employee satisfaction with pay and benefits only and *not* the more general wording of "employee satisfaction."

5. Are the actual questions (or a sample of them) provided?

When researchers provide at least a sample of the questions they used in the research, this is very helpful from an evaluative point of view because now the reader knows *exactly* what the researcher asked participants. In other words, the reader knows the exact answer to the researcher's self-question of What do I mean? because the answer in included in the report. The research excerpt from Woldoff's article (2002) in Box 4.1 is a good example of this. In her article, Woldoff explicitly states what her questions were. Some researchers may present this information in an Appendix; others may indirectly present this material in a table of results. For example, in a study about people's attitudes toward banks, Gjertsen (2000, **AN 3545926**) presented the survey question as part of a table of results:

If banks sold homeowners' insurance, people would be expected to buy their homeowners' insurance there to get a loan.

Strongly agree	16%
Agree	19%
Probably agree	26%
Don't know	11%
Probably disagree	11%
Disagree	10%
Strongly disagree	7%

All of these are acceptable forms. By seeing the survey question, readers can also evaluate whether that question was worded in a methodologically sound manner or whether it was worded in a way that would "load the dice" and increase the chances of getting a particular response. The latter practice is poor design. I will discuss how to properly word questions in Chapter 7 on survey techniques.

6. **Is the response format clear or, when not already clear, does the researcher provide information on the response format? Is there any information on restrictions in the respondents' response?**

This basically asks whether you know how respondents could answer the questions. Were the questions open-ended, meaning that the respondent could write in any response and then the researcher had to code and compile the individual responses? Or were the questions closed-ended, meaning that answer choices were provided for respondents to select. If the latter was the case, what were those answer choices? Knowing the answer to the last question helps you assess Evaluation Question 7, since certain statistics can only be accurately done with certain levels of measurement. Sometimes when the researcher provides the entire survey, the answers are included, as in the following article from Garner (2002, **AN 7255477**):

EXPECTATIONS

- Six months from now, do you think business conditions in your area will be [better/same/worse]?
- Six months from now, do you think there will be [more/same/fewer] jobs available in your area?
- How would you guess your total family income to be six months from now? [higher/same/lower]

University of Michigan Survey Questions

PRESENT SITUATION

1. We are interested in how people are getting along financially these days. Would you say that you (and your family living there) are better off or worse off financially than you were a year ago?
2. About the big things people buy for their homes—such as furniture, a refrigerator, stove, television, and things like that. Generally speaking, do you think now is a good or bad time for people to buy major household items?

In this exert, Garner lets you know what the answer choices were in questions 3 through 5 and that the first two questions from the University of Michigan survey were open-ended (although they are worded in a way that most people are likely to give a similar level of response verses a long explanation).

Coding may also appear as it does in this excerpt from Gabris and Ihrke's (2001) study:

> Midwest County employees were found to experience lower than normal levels of burnout, as well as lower than average job satisfaction scores, as measured by Hackman and Oldham's motivating potential score (MPS). We next turn to a discussion of the independent variables in the study that measure various attitudes toward performance appraisal.
>
> The primary independent variables for this study were derived from an initial series of 26 attitude items utilized in our Phase I survey instrument. These items are reported in Table 3, along with their mean response scores, where a 1 through 5 scale was employed — with a 1 indicating "strong or intense disagreement" and a 5 indicating "strong or intense agreement."

Here, the authors give you the general idea of questions and the general ordinal ratings (1 to 5, with 1 being strong disagreement and 5 being strong agreement).

Other times, researchers may present the answer choices in a table of results, like Gjertsen (2000) did in Evaluation Question 4. Researchers should also describe any special instructions to respondents regarding their response format. For example, a researcher may note, "Participants were instructed to only pay attention to the questions and scenarios appearing on their computer screens. They were prohibited from discussing any scenarios with other participants in the room." This helps the reader determine whether any special instructions for the research may have produced rival causal factors, such as reactivity or other threats to validity.

7. If the researcher is using a published instrument, does he or she cite sources where additional information can be found?

One way for researchers to improve their chances of having a valid measure is to use measures that other researchers have already used and validated. If a researcher chooses to do this, he or she may not have enough space to go into a complete detailed discussion of the particulars of that measure or the results of others' validity and reliability test. However, a researcher *is* obligated to acknowledge that this information exists. The easiest way to fulfill the responsibility of describing an established measure and showing a reader that the particular measure is valid and reliable is to cite the research of others who have described and documented these relevant tests. In fact, some of these citations may be for research articles whose sole purpose *was* to illustrate validity and/or reliability.

For example, in the article by Kelly and Pulver in Box 4.3, the researchers cite an article by Chartrand and colleagues (1990) that validated the Career Factors Inventory (CFI) that Kelly and Pulver used in their study. This is an appropriate and, for Kelly and Pulver, space-saving tactic that directs the reader to the necessary information on the validity of the measure while still freeing valuable manuscript space that allows Kelly and Pulver to describe their study in more detail.

8. Has the researcher avoided overstating the preciseness of the measurement?

The level of precision of a measure is supposed to correspond to the level of precision the author needs to answer her or his research question. However, sometimes researchers have little control over their level of precision, especially if they use measures constructed by other people. Why would anyone choose to lose control of their research like this? Frequently, researchers trade some design control (like the creation of indicators) to use larger datasets they otherwise would not have the resources to collect on their own or to use measures that have been empirically validated elsewhere.

For example, I may be interested in charting the daily drinking practices of college students (e.g., How many alcoholic beverages do you generally consume in a typical weekday?); however, a dataset might only include a measure of the weekly drinking practices (e.g., How many alcoholic beverages do you generally consume in a typical week?). If this is the case, I need to make sure that I don't word my findings to imply daily drinking habits when the measure addresses weekly drinking habits, because weekly habits are a less precise measure since they refer to a longer span of time. The caution here is to make sure that researchers do not imply that they have achieved a finer degree of measurement than their instruments truly allow.

9. Does the researcher provide some measure of reliability? What type of reliability is established? Do the measures indicate adequate reliability for your purposes?

Remember, there are a variety of different reliability issues and therefore there are a variety of reliability tests. For example, if the coding of observations is subjective and more than one person was doing the coding, a researcher should provide some evidence of inter-rater reliability, usually indicated by the rate of agreement between the two researchers. Researchers can establish this by describing the percent agreement (for example, 68 percent agreement), specifying what he or she feels is an appropriate level of agreement, and then providing some justification for that threshold. Readers can then evaluate whether they agree with the researcher's threshold and justification. Alternatively, a researcher can statistically establish inter-rater reliability by measuring the association between the codlings of two different raters. These associations usually range from 0 to 1, where the closer the measure is to 1, the higher the agreement (or association) between the two raters and the more reliable the findings are believed to be.

To assess whether a measure has internal consistency—in other words, whether various measures were consistent with each other—again, researchers can explicitly describe how they did a split-half reliability test, like the one described in the chapter, or they may use a statistic called Cronbach's alpha as a statistical test of internal validity. Although a discussion of Cronbach's alpha is beyond the scope of this text, it too is a measure of association that ranges from 0 to 1. Social scientists generally accept a Cronbach's alpha of about 0.70 as an indicator of internal reliability.

If a researcher is interested in establishing temporal stability or reliability, he or she can administer the survey or other instrument to the same people at more than one time point. The researcher can then statistically compare their findings, and, as with the Cronbach's alpha, if the findings have a statistical association of 0.70 or greater on a scale of 0 to 1, then temporal reliability has been achieved.

How do you know if a researcher has adequately addressed reliability? The researcher has to explicitly discuss the reliability tests that he did and their corresponding findings or he has to cite other research that has established the reliability in a different setting. In the latter case, the researcher ideally should illustrate how his or her measure compares, and is therefore reliable, with the previous research of others that the researcher may have cited. For example, an article by Lefly and Pennington (2000, **AN 00222194**) notes a relationship between children's risk for reading disorders and a family history of reading problems. These researchers assessed the reliability and validity of an adult reading history questionnaire used to gather reading history information. Lefly and Pennington say:

> In terms of internal consistency, the questionnaire was evaluated in both samples independently, to ensure that the results were not driven by the highly selected familial sample. The Cronbach's alpha for the 23-item ARHQ was .94 in the familial sample and .92 in the longitudinal sample, indicating that the items were highly intercorrelated with one another and that this result was not sample dependent. So, the questionnaire clearly demonstrates internal consistency.
>
> To evaluate test-retest reliability, we correlated the scores of the earlier and later forms of the questionnaire in both samples. The correlation between the two questionnaires in the family sample was .87. Table 5 presents the means of the original and revised Adult Reading History Questionnaire scores by diagnostic group. The means and standard deviations on both versions of the questionnaire were very similar, just as was observed for the longitudinal sample in Table 2, even though the test-retest interval in that sample was much longer (9.7 years, on average).
>
> In the longitudinal sample, the test-retest interval was 3 years. The correlation between the two questionnaires in the longitudinal sample was .81 (n = 59) for mothers and .84 (n = 52) for fathers.
>
> In sum, these results demonstrate that the ARHQ had similarly high levels of both internal consistency and test-retest reliability in both samples. Because of the length of the test-retest interval, there is also evidence for considerable longitudinal stability of this measure in adults.

Therefore, Lefly and Pennington provide Cronbach's alpha statistics and correlation statistics to establish internal correlation and test-retest reliability.

10. *Does the researcher provide some measure of validity? What measures of validity are presented and are they adequate for your purposes?*

Remember, validity refers to whether a measure is really measuring what it is supposed to be measuring. How do you assess this? Since there are different types of measurement validity (like there are different types of measurement reliability), there are different ways of assessing validity.

If you are interested in assessing content validity, the researcher needs to illustrate how his or her measure matches with other commonly used indicators of that concept. You decide whether the researcher has adequately made his or her case for this match. Does the match make sense to you? Has the researcher clearly established the connection between his or her measure and other related indicators?

If you are interested in predictive, concurrent, criterion-related, and construct validity, then you are interested in whether the data using the instrument "make sense." In the methods section, researchers will frequently try to establish this validity by using the measures of others and citing studies that have established the validity. At the end of the research, a researcher may try to reaffirm this type of validity by presenting some type of correlation between the findings and other measures. For example, the study by Gabris and Ihrke (2001, **AN 4600767**) that I mentioned earlier notes that performance appraisal can cause a lot of stress among workers. Hence, how much validity employees think that their performance appraisals have may affect employee behavior and burnout. This makes sense, therefore it achieves face validity. Gabris and Ihrke (2001) conduct other validity tests and find the following:

> As evident in Table 3, most Midwest County employees exhibited a generally positive attitude toward the three major factors associated with the county's performance-appraisal efforts (Instrument Validity "IV," Distributive Justice "DJ," and Procedural Justice "PJ"). . . . Employee perceptions regarding the validity of the performance-appraisal instrument used by Midwest County are not significantly associated with levels of job burnout. Conversely, perceptions of both distributive and procedural justice were found to be significantly correlated with an employee's MBI phase level. In the latter case, the receptiveness toward the performance-appraisal system from an equity and procedural standpoint decreases the incidence of burnout for Midwest County employees.

Gabris and Ihrke discuss some statistical tests of validity in the first sentence and present those findings in Table 3 of their report. They discuss empirical validity by saying that the measure of employee-perceived validity does not correlate well with job burnout. In other words, they *invalidate* that measure that is frequently used in other studies.

11. Is the measurement appropriate and adequate, given the research purpose?

The researcher's purpose for the research is your most powerful piece of information when evaluating any aspect of the research itself. In this instance, you are asking yourself if the researcher's measure adequately addresses his or her research goal. Researchers who are diligent will actually try to convince readers that a measure is appropriate by providing an explanation for its selection. Researchers may explain why they selected one instrument over another or why they felt the need to modify an already existing (and frequently accepted) measure. For example, in a study of teachers' attitudes toward technology, Chambers and colleagues (2003, **AN 10954975**) describe the following about their reasoning for selecting the Myers-Briggs Type Inventory (MBTI) as a measure of teacher personality and a technology survey developed by another researcher:

> The MBTI is a widely used personality inventory with positive evidence of its construct validity (Thompson & Borrello, 1994). Mendelsohn (1965) reported that "an unusually large body of reliability and validity data" (p. 321) has been completed on the MBTI. Test-retest correlation of approximately 0.70 was obtained for three of the indices and 0.48 for the fourth. Further, Mendelsohn (1965) reported internal consistency reliabilities (split-half) for the indices ranged from 0.70 to 0.80.
> . . . The technology survey was developed by Smith (1993) and reported by Smith, Munday & Windham (1995). Background literature and similar studies guided the selection of questionnaire items (Dezell, 1989; Callister & Burbules, 1990; Cicchelli & Baecher, 1989). Content validity was established using a panel of six professional educators with expertise in the field of educational technology.

For the MBTI, Chambers and colleagues state that they selected this measure because it was "widely used" and there was a "large body of reliability and validity data." They even go so far as to document some of the reliability and validity data (which relates to Evaluation Questions 9 and 10). For the technology survey, the researchers argue that the ques-

Below are excerpts from two articles. The first is an article examining the relationship between women's dissatisfaction with their bodies and their corresponding self-image over the life span. The second article focuses on how teacher mentors view their experiences in a teacher training program. You can practice evaluating their operationalization and measures by applying the eleven critical thinking questions to these two excerpts.

Article 1

In the first article, Webster and Tiggemann (2003) study 106 women between the ages of 20 and 65. These women completed a survey that measured their body dissatisfaction, their perceptions of body importance, their perceptions of cognitive control, their self-concept, their self-esteem, and their age. Below is an except from their methods section, which discusses their measures of body dissatisfaction, body importance, self-concept, and self-esteem.

In the present study, we focused, not on body dissatisfaction per se, but on the potential consequences of body dissatisfaction for global views of the self—both on how women think of themselves (self-concept) and on their overall affective evaluation of themselves (self-esteem) . . . .

. . . Body dissatisfaction was measured with the use of a modified version of the 46-item Body Cathexis Scale (Secord & Jourard, 1953). The modified version listed 17 items of body image . . . (weight and lower body, physical skills and fitness, appearance, and body function). The participants rated their dissatisfaction with each body aspect on a 5-point Likert-type scale (1 = very dissatisfied to 5 = very satisfied). . . . Secord and Jourard's full Body Cathexis Scale had a reported reliability coefficient (Cronbach's α) of .83. The modified version of the scale in the present study returned a slightly lower but still reliable Cronbach's alpha coefficient of .72.

. . . Body importance was measured with the same 17 items that were used for measuring body dissatisfaction. . . . We again summed the scores to produce total scores that ranged from 17 to 85. Internal reliability was found to be moderate (α = .76).

. . . Self-concept was measured by the Tennessee Self-Concept Scale (Fitts, 1965). The participants are presented with a list of 100 statements (e.g., "I am a friendly person") describing possible ways that they may see themselves. The participants respond to each statement on a 5-point Likert-type scale (1 = completely false to 5 = completely true). The Tennessee Self-Concept Scale has been found to be a reliable measure of self-concept with reported reliability coefficients of .80 and .90 (Fitts) and test-retest reliability of .92 (Balogun, 1986). The present study returned a similarly high Cronbach's alpha reliability coefficient of .81.

. . . Self-esteem was measured by adapting the Bachman and O'Malley (1977) version of the Rosenberg Self-Esteem Scale (Rosenberg, 1965). The participants rated the accuracy of 10 self-statements (e.g., "I take a positive attitude toward myself") on a 5-point Likert-type scale (1 = never true to 5 = almost always true). . . . The Rosenberg Self-Esteem Scale has a reported internal consistency of .88 and test-retest correlation of .82 (Blascovich & Tomaka, 1991), which indicate that the test is a highly reliable measure of self-esteem. We found a similar high internal reliability (α = .92) in the present study.

Source: Jessica Webster and Marika Tiggeman, "The Relationship between Women's Body Satisfaction and Self-Image across the Life Span: The Role of Cognitive Control," *Journal of Genetic Psychology,* 164 (2) (June 2003): 241. (**AN 10313454**) Reprinted with permission of the Helen Dwight Reid Educational Foundation. Published by Heldref Publications, 1319 18th St., NW, Washington, DC 20036-1802. Copyright © 2003.

Critical Thinking Questions for Articles 1 and 2

1. Is the conceptualization suitably specific?

BOX 4.4   **Evaluation of Written Research, continued**

2. Are conceptual/operational definitions presented and are they adequate?

3. Are the definitions productive?

4. How many different dimensions are being measured at once? Are the various dimensions sufficient?

5. Are the actual questions (or a sample of them) provided?

6. Is the response format clear or, when not already clear, does the researcher provide information on the response format? Is there any information on restrictions in respondents' responses?

7. If the researcher is using a published instrument, does he or she cite sources where additional information can be found?

8. Has the researcher avoided overstating the preciseness of the measurement?

9. Does the researcher provide some measure of reliability? What type of reliability is established? Do the measures indicate adequate reliability for your purposes?

10. Does the researcher provide some measure of validity? What measures of validity are presented and are they adequate for your purposes?

11. Overall, is the measurement appropriate and adequate given the research purpose?

Critical Thinking Discussion

1. The main concepts in our except of the Webster and Tiggemann study are body dissatisfaction, body importance, self-concept, and self-esteem. Webster and Tiggemann provide conceptual definitions for self-esteem (evaluation of self) and self-concept (how one thinks of self). However, they do not provide any conceptual definitions for "body dissatisfaction" and "body importance." Perhaps they feel that these two

concepts are fairly clear on their own. This is arguable and a brief conceptualization would be beneficial.

2. When discussing body satisfaction and body importance, the authors consider a person's satisfaction/view of importance with their weight and lower body, physical skills and fitness, appearance, and body function. However, they say they use 17 items, but we do not know which 17 they use. Hence, even if we looked up the citations for the scales, we would not learn the necessary material because we still do not know *which* parts of the scales the researchers used.

This is not a problem with their measures of self-concept and self-esteem because the authors have used the complete (although somewhat modified) scales. Therefore, even though the researchers do not mention the specifics of the scales, since they have used the *entire* scale, we can look up the scale and find the relevant information. This is acceptable; therefore, only the conceptual definitions for body satisfaction and body importance seem to be weak.

3. The definitions for body satisfaction and importance are weak because without knowing what they entail, we cannot evaluate whether they adequately address the phenomena (what if important dimensions were omitted in the authors' selection? How would we know this?); however, the material for self-esteem and self-concept seem fine.

4. The dimensions for the bodily satisfaction and importance are the same as those mentioned in Question 2. They seem adequate. We can only tell whether the dimensions for self-concept and self-esteem are adequate if we look up the details of the original scales. However, given the wide use stated by the authors, we can indirectly surmise that they are adequate because so many other people have used the scales in their research.

BOX 4.4 **Evaluation of Written Research, continued**

5. The actual questions are not provided, although some samples (for example, for the self-esteem scale: "I take a positive attitude toward myself") are occasionally provided. However, again, even though other questions are not provided, the authors cite the creation of the scales so we can look up the questions on our own. This is helpful for the self-concept and self-esteem concepts, but not the body satisfaction and importance concepts, as I stated earlier (since we do not know what specific questions or items the authors decided to include from the broader scale).

6. The response format is clear. We know that the answer responses are coded using a five-point Likert scale. In this scale a score of 1 is low or a false measure, and a score of 5 is a high or true measure.

7. Yes on all four accounts.

8. We don't have the information for that here since the results are not included in the excerpt. However, if we look up the article on Research Navigator and read the results section, we would see that, no, the researchers do not overstate the preciseness of their measure. Being that most of their measures are scales, they are fairly precise interval levels of measurement to begin with.

   Furthermore, from a statistical point of view, interval measures are treated the same as ratio measures, allowing the researchers to do more sophisticated statistical analyses. Therefore, their statistical usage and discussion of the measures (and their preciseness) is appropriate.

9. The researchers provide a Chronbach's alpha both for the original scales and their subscale.

10. The Chronbach's alpha linked with the citations of other researchers or tests for validity combine to serves this purpose when the researchers use it as a comparison between their subscale and the original scales.

11. For the self-concept and self-esteem concepts, the measurement is clearly appropriate and adequate. This is less clear for the concepts of body satisfaction and body importance. However, given the high reliability and well-established validity of the original scale from which these two measures are derived, we have more (but not complete) confidence in them than we would have if the authors created their own measures from scratch and neglected to present the information regarding conceptual definitions and actual question wording/selection. Therefore, for these other two concepts, the measurement is weak but not necessarily to the point to negate the value of the article.

Article 2

In this article, Cornell (2003) examines an important component of teacher training: the field experience in a classroom. He argues that, unlike a typical student–teacher relationship, teacher mentors actually partner with the teacher-in-training, thereby allowing the teacher-in-training more hands-on experience in the classroom. Cornell's research stems from the call for ongoing evaluation of the mentor training field experience. Cornell notes that mentors' perceptions of their roles and relationships with others involved in the program are important aspects to program functioning. Consequently, he studied 66 (out of a possible 100) mentor teachers participating in one of seven collaborations between Texas A & M University–Commerce and local school districts in the northeast Texas area. Here is an except from his discussion of methods:

> **Data and Methods**
>
> A questionnaire involving 2 demographic questions and 13 perceptual statements was sent to every mentor in both districts. The 13 statements required a response according to the following Likert-type scale:
>
> 5 strongly agree; 4 agree; 3 am neutral; 2 disagree; 1 strongly disagree

BOX 4.4   **Evaluation of Written Research, continued**

. . . The five-number scale was later telescoped into three categories of "agreement," "neutral," and "disagreement" for each statement. A tally of percentages in both districts and in each individual district is shown in Figure 1. As an integral part of the study, volunteered comments were evaluated qualitatively and were found to supplement and add detail, clarification, and rationale to Likert scale responses, and to raise interesting questions and concerns regarding perceptions and relationships.

Results

Fifty percent of the entire sample agreed that the more years of teaching experience one has, the better mentor he or she will be.

. . . Sixty percent in both districts agreed that CPDT training is as good or better than the pre-service training they themselves had received.

. . . Seventy-two percent, in both districts, perceived their mentor role as satisfying and fulfilling, with a higher proportion in the new district holding this view.

. . . Seventy-one percent in both districts stated that becoming a mentor teacher had been their decision.

. . . Eighty-five percent believed their role critical to program success and all felt that an effective mentor teacher must possess outstanding classroom management and instructional skills.

. . . Combining districts, forty-eight percent stated they received adequate orientation, preparation, materials and guidance to function as a mentor teacher.

. . . Fifty-nine percent in both districts agreed they would not hesitate to be a mentor teacher in future field-based situations. The wording "I would not hesitate" in the question was designed to screen those who, though willing to be mentor teachers, might attach one or more conditions to their agreement to do so.

Source: Charles Cornell, "How Mentor Teachers Perceive Their Roles And Relationships in a Field-Based Teacher-Training Program," *Education, 124* (2) (Winter 2003): 401. (*AN 11984470*)

Critical Thinking Discussion

1. No clear concepts are identified in the methods section or in the literature review. (The latter is not presented but can be found by searching for *AN 11984470* on Research Navigator.) I assume that the concept is general satisfaction; however, that is never stated.

2. Since there are no concepts, there are no conceptual definitions.

3. No conceptual definitions means no evaluation of their appropriateness.

4. No information on dimensions.

5. It is unclear whether the actual questions are provided. They are not provided in typical question form, but the results are worded in a way that suggests that each paragraph corresponds to a question. For example, the first sentence in the edited excerpt is also the first sentence in that paragraph in the full article and states: "Fifty percent of the entire sample agreed that the more years of teaching experience one has, the better mentor he or she will be." The implication is that the original question was worded something like: "Does the more years of teaching experience one has lead that person to be a better mentor?" Consequently, by looking at each point in the results section, we can begin to piece together an approximation of the actual survey questions.

6. We do know the response format because we know that each question was originally coded as a five-point Likert response ranging from strongly agree (a code of 5) to strongly disagree (a code of 1) with a neutral category in the middle.

7. This is not applicable because we can assume that the researcher devised the questions since there is no reference or mention to a previously published scale.

BOX 4.4   Evaluation of Written Research, continued

8. This is just a standard 5-point scale that the researcher actually makes *less* precise by collapsing into three categories (agree, neutral, disagree) instead of the five. This move in itself is not necessarily problematic; if the measures were originally *too* precise and few people distinguished between, for example, strongly agree and agree, then having the 5-point continuum is unnecessary.

   Furthermore, all the researcher's results are presented as agreement or disagreement, without a finer distinction; therefore, his interpretation *is* consistent with his level of precision and therefore he adequately fulfills this requirement. However, we do not know the researcher's reasoning for reducing the precision. It would have been helpful for him to present just a quick sentence justifying his decision.

9. There is no discussion of reliability tests or considerations.

10. There is no discussion of validity tests or considerations (such as how he selected his measures).

11. Overall, these measures are inadequate. There are no clear concepts; therefore, there is no clear way of determining whether the measures adequately address the research purpose. The purpose may be evaluation and assessing mentors' views; however, views on what? Even though we have a rough idea of what the researcher's questions are and how they are measured (a Likert response), without a clear conceptualization–operationalization process, these measures have little foundation.

   Hence, the first article was stronger in the conceptualization–operationalization phase than the actual details of the measurement. The second article is the opposite. We know the "measures," but we do not know *what* they measure. Even with its faults, the first article is a much better illustration of the measurement process than is the second article.

---

tionnaire items were based on "background literature and similar studies" and they provide a citation that supports their claim. Here, too, they discuss a validity issue—namely, content validity. The whole purpose of their discussion is to convince the reader, you, that their measures are appropriate for their topic.

Summary

To summarize, there are 11 general questions readers of research need to ask themselves when evaluating the research of others. Not all questions are relevant in all situations, nor do they need to be. To recap, here are the questions to keep in mind:

1. Is the conceptualization suitably specific?
2. Are conceptual/operational definitions presented and are they adequate?
3. Are the definitions productive?
4. How many different dimensions are being measured at once? Are the various dimensions sufficient?
5. Are the actual questions (or a sample of them) provided?

6. Is the response format clear or, when not already clear, does the researcher provide information on the response format? Is there any information on restrictions in the respondents' response?
7. If the researcher is using a published instrument, does he or she cite sources where additional information can be found?
8. Has the researcher avoided overstating the preciseness of the measurement?
9. Does the researcher provide some measure of reliability? What type of reliability is established? Do the measures indicate adequate reliability for your purposes?
10. Does the researcher provide some measure of validity? What measures of validity are presented and are they adequate for your purposes?
11. Is the measurement appropriate and adequate, given the research purpose?

Sometimes researchers have to omit some of this information due to space limitations in journals. As a critical reader, it is up to you to decide whether the researchers included *enough* information for you to have confidence in their measures. Omissions may not be very important if a researcher managed to convey the main gist of the measures, but the more detail the researcher can provide, the more confidence a reader can have in his or her own evaluation of this material.

A later chapter, survey design, is the first in the section that examines the various methods of gathering data. I will examine issues of measurement again in Chapter 7 when I discuss survey formation.

Key Terms

Attributes (132)
Concepts (125)
Conceptual definition (127)
Conceptualization (126)
Concurrent validity (145)
Construct validity (148)
Content validity (144)
Convergent validity (148)
Criterion validity (145)
Discriminant validity (148)

Equivalence reliability (150)
Exhaustive (132)
Face validity (144)
Interval (136)
Inter-rater reiability (151)
Measurement (128)
Mutually exclusive (132)
Nominal (133)
Operational definition (128)
Ordinal (134)

Predictive validity (145)
Ratio (137)
Reliability (149)
Representative validity (149)
Split-half reliability (150)
Temporal reliability (149)
Test-retest reliability (150)
Values (132)
Variable (132)

Review Questions and Exercises

1. In Box 4.1 you read an excerpt from Rachel Woldoff's article on neighborhood attachment and practiced the conceptualization–operationalization process using her concept of neighborhood attachment. The article's full citation is Woldoff, Rachel, A. (2002). The effects of local stressors on neighborhood attachment. Social Forces, 81 (1), 87. It can most easily be found using the Research Navigator article number AN 7513641. Use this article to:

   a. Apply the conceptualization–operationalization process for her concept of "stressors."

   b. Examine the survey in Appendix A and determine the level of measurement for each question.

2. Using Research Navigator (AN 9248158) find this article: VanDeth, Jan. (2003, January). Measuring social capital: Orthodoxies and continuing controversies. International Journal of Social Research Methodology, 6 (1), 79–83.

   a. Apply each step of the conceptualization–operationalization process to VanDeth's concepts that appear in the flowchart in Figure 4.1

   b. Look up VanDeth's article and write questions that correspond to his measures. Make sure you have at least two representatives from each level of measurement in your examples.

3. Apply the 11 steps to measure evaluation to evaluate the operationalization and instrumentation in the following articles:

   a. Sciarra, Daniel T., and Gushue, George V. (2003, Fall). White racial identity development and religious orientation. Journal of Counseling & Development, 81 (4), 473. 10 pp. (AN 11261463)

   b. Dennis, Michael Robert, and Kunkel, Adrianne Dennis. (2004). Perceptions of men, women, and CEOs: The effects of gender identity. Social Behavior & Personality: An International Journal, 32 (2), 155. 17 pp. (AN 12803273)

   c. Dijker, Anton J., and Koomen, Willem. (2003, February). Extending Weiner's attribution-emotion model of stigmatization of ill persons. Basic & Applied Social Psychology, 25 (1), 51. 18 pp. (AN 9159422)

   d. Frey, Lawrence R., Adelman, Mara B., Flint, Lyle J., and Query, Jim L. (2000, January–March). Weaving meanings together in an AIDS residence: Communicative practices, perceived health outcomes, and the symbolic construction of community. Journal of Health Communication, 5 (1), 53. 20 pp. (AN 2882113)

Chapter 5

Sampling

D o you think most people are poor because they are lazy, or because they are content with their lives and therefore do not strive for more comfortable resources? How do you think the poor see themselves and their place in society? Do you think they *want* to be on welfare and see it as their right? Or do you think they feel that they are stigmatized by the rest of society, and that this stigma has a negative effect on their self-concept? The first question I asked is a common one; however, the others are not. Read the following description and account by "Suzette," a mother on public assistance.

Suzette describes the public shame she experiences as a welfare recipient. People look down on her for being on welfare. She feels in "hiding"—her real identity as a woman who has a strong work history (and had to stop working to take care of her sick mother) is unknown by the larger world. She is only seen as someone who is not "doing anything good." Suzette told the group a story about going to the supermarket with her adolescent daughter. Her daughter did not want to go into the store with her, as she was afraid one of her friends would see her mother using Food Stamps. Suzette assured her that no one would see them. However, at the checkout line, her daughter says, "Oh my God, Mommy, we have to get out of here. My friend is over there." Suzette was torn between having to do the shopping and wanting to protect her child from experiencing humiliation. She left the store without the groceries. [Suzette goes on to say:]

The welfare system is not working. You feel like you are hiding yourself. . . . You are not outside. You don't come out, because they don't know how you get to be there. . . . The only thing they see is because you're not the person that you're supposed to be. You know, you're not qualified. You can't be doing anything good, being there. And that's the way, you know, the public sees it. (Smith, 2002, pp. 58–59)

This excerpt is from a study by Smith (2002) of interviews with 14 mothers on public assistance. In Smith's research, these 14 women explain how they feel about the work mandate in the 1996 welfare reform known as Temporary Assistance to Needy Families (TANF) and about welfare in general. What do you think of this study? Do you think what "Suzette" said can be generalized to all poor mothers? Do you think Smith's findings from these 14 people can even be generalized to all the poor mothers in her specific area? Why would we care about the generalizability of a sample anyway? Is 14 people enough people to include in any study?

To answer the last question, you would have to know how Smith reached those 14 women. Did she randomly sample them from all the mothers on welfare at the time of her study, or did she obtain these women's names more conveniently, say from a social worker? Did the social worker recommend other names or were there only 14 women on that list? If there were other people on a hypothetical list, what is known about the women who were not willing to participate in the study? How do they compare with the 14 women that Smith interviewed? These are all important questions when considering the sample of a study.

Smith tells us the race, age, and education (among some other variables) of the 14 people she selected for her study; however, we do not know anything about those who are not members of her sample. Smith also tells us that her sample of 14 were what researchers call a *convenience sample* from a possible pool of 200 mothers with children under age 2 and who were on public assistance. Since Smith had a convenience sample, this means that she did not randomly select the 14 women to be in her study; instead, they volunteered or were otherwise willing to participate after being approached by mailings, meetings with caseworkers, or meetings with directors. This means that Smith's findings cannot be generalized to a broader group, or population, of mothers on welfare.

This lack of generalizability alone does not hinder the merits of Smith's research, however. Her research is qualitative, which means that it aims to achieve a greater understanding of an issue (here, the specific issue of how welfare mothers view the work requirement that is part of the welfare program Temporary Assistance for Needy Families). Smith's goal is not to see what *all* or even *most* welfare mothers think. Her goal is to describe what *these* 14 mothers think, because, as Smith states in her article, social scientists know little about what those who use welfare services actually think of the services. Her research educates other researchers about this issue, and her findings may serve as the foundation for a more quantitative study by someone else who *is* interested in assessing trends in attitudes and beliefs across a more comprehensive and representative sample.

How researchers decide who to study and how to obtain a sample has important implications for how others can use the results. In this chapter, I will examine the reasons why people draw a sample instead of study all the individuals who fit the researcher's criteria, the different methods of sampling, the advantages and disadvantages of the various methods of sampling, the implications of the sampling technique to the rest of the research process, how to assess sample quality, and how to determine how many people to include in a sample. As you can probably guess, selecting a sample is an important part of the research process.

Why Sample?

As you learned in the last chapter, researchers cannot study all aspects of a research problem. For example, researchers cannot study all dimensions of poverty. Similarly, social scientists cannot study all the people who experience an issue. This means that if I want to study poverty, I cannot study all the poor people who exist in the United States. Why? First, it would tremendously expensive, without very much additional payoff in terms of research quality. It's much cheaper for me to study a sample of 3,000 people currently qualifying as "poor" than it is to study 3 million of them. Furthermore, if I do the sampling well, I am not going to have to sacrifice research quality in the process. In other words, if I do the sampling well (and we will learn how to do this shortly), I can be pretty confident that the 3,000 people I actually do study will represent the 3 million people who really exist.

The trick is that I have to do my sample "well." I am not going to be able to pull off the same degree of accuracy if I only sample people to whom I have easy access or if I have a relatively small sample of say, 30 people. As I will discuss in a bit, if I use some type of mathematical random assignment and my sample is sufficiently large, given the size of the population, then it's cheaper and therefore more rational for me to study a small group of that population, rather than the population in its entirety.

Second, distributing a research instrument, receiving the returned instrument, coding it, entering the data, and analyzing the data for the 36.4 *million* people the government considers to be officially in poverty in the United States (U.S. Bureau of the Census, 2003) would probably take the rest of my natural life; and, as much as I enjoy research, I do have other interests. It doesn't require much explanation to see that it would take me much less time to sample maybe 9,000 individuals than 36,400,000 of them!

A third reason that researchers cannot study all aspects of poverty is that the individuals comprising a specific population may change over time. For example, since most people are not in poverty their entire lives, by the time I was able to identify the millions of people in poverty in a particular year and actually try to contact them individually, a good portion of my sample would no longer be in poverty. What would I do then?

Clearly, studying a sample, or smaller subgroup, of an existing population is faster, cheaper, and more manageable than studying an entire population. It is also just as accurate if it is done correctly. Therefore, the majority of this chapter is aimed at showing you how to draw research samples accurately and how to evaluate whether others have done so as well. But before I get to that, let me introduce you to the terms researchers frequently use when discussing sampling.

Sampling Terms

Most researchers hope to apply the findings of their research that involves a small (relatively) subset of a large group to make conclusions about that large group. To achieve this goal, researchers had to develop a very specific language for distinguishing between when they were referring to the people they studied and when they were referring to the larger group of people represented by those who are studied. Before I discuss the details of select-

If a researcher wanted to do a study of attorneys, like the ones in this picture, methodologically speaking, these attorneys would be called elements.

ing a sample, it is important for you to know the terms researchers use when referring to samples and the sampling procedure.

Elements

If I am interested in studying the attitudes of poor mothers toward the work requirement of TANF, methodologically, those poor mothers are my **elements,** or the units, about which I am collecting information. Very often, elements are people (poor people, people with addictions, young adults' views of a political candidate, community members' views of the addition of a prison in their neighborhood, etc.); however, they can also be groups of people (families, athletes, or gangs) or organizations (colleges, civic associations, or corporations). Elements are frequently the same entities as *units of analysis,* although elements are a sampling term and units of analysis refer to data analysis (Babbie, 1995). Similarly, look at the photograph on this page. The people are a small group of the attorneys practicing in this state. If I wanted to study what characteristics attorneys want in people serving on their jury if they are involved in a murder case, and I gave a survey to everyone in this photo, my elements would be individuals, the attorneys.

Population

Clearly, the people in this photograph do not constitute *all* of the attorneys in this state. If I am doing my study in Pennsylvania and Pennsylvania has 10,000 attorneys practicing criminal law, those 10,000 lawyers would be the **population** of criminal lawyers in the state. A population is the entire set of study elements. The goal of most research would be to study a sample of elements and use the information from that sample to generalize about the attitudes, behaviors, or experiences of the wider population.

Sometimes populations require specification. For instance, in my hypothetical attorney example, if I went to the Pennsylvania Trial Lawyers Association and got a list of all the 10,000 criminal attorneys in the state and drew a random sample from them, then my population would be criminal attorneys in Pennsylvania. However, attorneys prosecuting a murder suspect might look for different characteristics in potential jury members than attorneys defending murder suspects. Let's suppose I am interested in the views of attorneys who do criminal defense. Clearly, it would not make sense to include criminal attorneys who are prosecutors, because their litigation goals are different. Therefore, let's suppose I work with the Pennsylvania Trial Lawyers Association to obtain a list, called a *sampling frame*, of all criminal defense attorneys in the state for a specific year, say 2004. If I draw my sample from these attorneys, my population is no longer criminal attorneys because not all criminal attorneys were eligible for my study. My population is now criminal defense attorneys registered with the Pennsylvania Trial Lawyers Association in 2004.

Specifying specific populations to study is not a problem; in fact, it is a means of making research and samples manageable. However, when researchers narrow their population to a specific group, they need to make sure that they do not mistakenly overgeneralize to a broader population. In other words, now I can discuss my findings only with regard to "criminal defense attorneys," and I *cannot* generalize to "criminal attorneys."

Theoretically, researchers can specify an even finer distinction of population, called the **study population.** A study population is the population from where the elements were actually selected. In my example of criminal defense attorneys, I said that my population was criminal defense attorneys registered with the Pennsylvania Trial Lawyers Association in 2004. Some could argue that if my goal was to generalize my findings to "criminal defense attorneys" as a broad group, instead of generalizing just to "criminal defense attorneys in Pennsylvania," the criminal defense attorneys in Pennsylvania are really my study population because it is the population from which I will actually select my elements. Technically, this is true; in this purest sense, my "real" population would be all criminal defense attorneys in the United States, or even the world, in 2004. In reality, however, most researchers treat the population and the study population as the same, even if they pay lip service to recognizing that technically a "population" is a much broader group. In other words, researchers frequently decide to limit their populations to study populations; and many will still discuss their findings in generic terms such as "criminal defense attorneys" instead of "criminal defense attorneys in Pennsylvania," the latter of which would technically be more accurate.

Either way, it is important to realize that populations are very theoretical, abstract concepts. Researchers can really never know all the people, groups, or organizations in a population at a given period of time. Study populations are frequently (but not always) more concrete, and this is why many researchers use the term *population* generically, even though what they are really referring to is a study population.

■ Sampling Frame

You may notice that I snuck in a term, **sampling frame,** during my discussion of populations. A sampling frame is simply a list of all the possible elements from which your sample will be drawn. Researchers do not always need a sampling frame. Sometimes there are populations or groups where a list of all the people is unobtainable.

If you are studying a group, say the homeless, you will not be able to compile a reliable and complete list, or sampling frame, of all the homeless people, even if you restrict your examination to the homeless in a specific city. Sometimes researchers do not even need a sampling frame because their research goal does not involve generalizing to a wider population. In my example with the attorneys, however, I *do* want to generalize to the wider population and I have a potential population that is very large. Therefore, in this instance, a sampling frame would be useful, and it would be the list of all the criminal defense attorneys listed with the Pennsylvania Trial Lawyers Association in 2004. Sometimes researchers have sampling frames of the elements, like I just mentioned here; other times, they are of sampling units, which I will discuss next.

Sampling Units

What will I do if my study population is so large that listing all individual elements will be onerous and unwieldy? For example, 5,000 criminal defense attorneys are a lot of names! In instances like this, researchers might conduct multiple samples of groups of people that get increasingly more specific (and smaller in size) each subsequent time a sample is drawn. For example, if I want to sample 500 criminal defense attorneys from this list of 5,000, but I do not want a complete list of these 5,000 names, I might first sample a selection of counties. Then I would list all the cities within those counties that I selected and next get a list of all the criminal defense firms (including the public defender's office) that are present in the cities that I chose from the counties that I selected in the previous step. Finally, suppose I got a list of all the attorneys in the firms I selected and then drew my sample of criminal defense attorneys from this last list. Sound confusing? It really isn't.

What I outlined here is a type of sampling known as *cluster sampling*, which I will discuss later in the chapter. For now, all you need to be aware of is that the counties, the cities, and the firms that I selected from the previous groups are called **sampling units.** Sampling units are a group of elements, usually in decreasing size, that researchers select in multistage sampling. When researchers draw only one sample, the sampling unit is the same as the element; therefore, researchers don't really use the term *sampling unit.* The term is used only when social scientists draw more complex samples, like in the earlier example where I first selected counties, then I selected cities from the counties I selected in the previous step, then I chose the law firms from *those* cities, and it took a fourth round of sampling before I actually selected the individual elements, the criminal defense attorneys themselves.

Statistics and Population Parameters

To refresh your memory, *variables* are a set of mutually exclusive and exhaustive values that describe a social characteristic, attitude, or behavior. Researchers use samples of people from a population to collect information about variables that a researcher, in turn, will use to describe the characteristics or attributes of a population. The average age and the number of years of litigation experience of my sample trial lawyers are *statistics*, because I can calculate them based on what I can observe from the sample. Likewise, the percentage of the sample who prefer to have women in their juries is a statistic, as is the percentage of criminal defense attorneys who admit to using a jury consultant to select a jury. Any information researchers directly obtain from their sample, any sample, is a **statistic.** However, remember that the purpose of a sample is to make conclusions about the population. When researchers take statistics and use them to infer about the population, they call the value in the population the **population parameter.** For example, I may find that 70 percent of my criminal defense attorneys want women on their juries, and I can be 95 percent sure that the percentage of criminal defense attorneys in Pennsylvania who feel the same is between 66 and 74 percent.

Sampling Error

But wait! You may be wondering: Why is the statistic one exact percent and the population parameter is a range of percents? And why can't I be 100 percent sure of the percentage of the criminal defense attorneys who want women on their juries? These are both valid questions and I can answer them with the last few terms we need to discuss.

The only way we would know the *exact* percentage of criminal defense attorneys in Pennsylvania who want women on their juries is to study every criminal defense attorney in Pennsylvania. In other words, the only way to know the population parameter for certain is to study the population. However, at the beginning of the chapter, I discussed why studying the population is generally unfeasible and undesirable for the vast majority of research. Social scientists must accept that researchers will study only a sample drawn from any given population. Similarly, we must accept that even if researchers do probability sampling—the method of sampling that allows social scientists to make conclusions about a population based on a sample from that population—our sampling method will most likely never provide statistics that are exactly equal to the population parameter. In other words, researchers are almost always likely to have some type of **sampling error** even with the most carefully constructed sampling designs.

In my example, some people may not be correctly registered with the Pennsylvania Trial Lawyers Association, some people may have left the practice of law, some people may have joined since the list was last updated (and consequently would not even be eligible for the study because if their names are not on the list, I do not know about them), and some people may have switched sides. Therefore, even with the best possible sampling design, there is at least some possibility for error.

Confidence Levels and Intervals

Probability sampling allows researchers to get very close to the true population parameter; in fact, and more important, researchers can estimate the degree of sampling error, the range within which the true population parameter is likely to fall, and how confident they are of their estimations. The accuracy of researchers' estimations are the **confidence levels,** usually expressed as 95 percent and 99 percent in the social sciences (for mathematical purposes, 68 percent is also useful). The range of values within which researchers think the true population parameter (which we don't know for sure) lies is the **confidence interval.** The sampling error is reflected in the confidence interval. Sampling error, sometimes also called *standard error*, is usually expressed as some number following the symbol $\pm$, which means "plus or minus." Therefore, a sampling error that is $\pm$ 4 percent means that the true population parameter may be as much as 4 percentage points higher or lower than the reported statistic. This plus/minus sampling error in conjunction with the statistic creates a confidence interval.

BOX 5.1   Sampling Terms

Even though you might not be aware of it, it is very likely that you are familiar with some concept of sampling. You have probably heard of the Gallup Poll, one of our nation's most widely known polling services. What follows are two examples of sampling. One is from the March 26–28, 2004, Gallup poll; the second is an example of research focusing on gender stratification.

Example 1: Gallup Poll

The Gallup Poll is a probability sampling poll based on telephone interviews with a randomly selected national sample of 1,001 adults, age 18 and older. To conduct its sample, the Gallup

Poll starts with a list of all household numbers in the continental United States, which is partially created from a random digit dialing process that allows the inclusion of unlisted phone numbers.

For results based on the sample of 469 baseball fans, the maximum margin of sampling error is ± 5 percentage points.

Here is a sample statistic from the Gallup News Service about baseball fans' views of steroid use in the sport. This poll was done with 469 baseball fans who were part of the 1,001 sample of adults conducted during March 26 to 28, 2004. According to the Gallup Poll services, one can be 95 percent confident that the sampling error is ± 5 percentage points:

42. *Should major league baseball players be tested for steroids or other performance enhancing drugs, or not?*

	Yes, Should	No, Should Not	No Opinion
	%	%	%
2004 Mar 26–28	91	9	*
2003 Oct 24–26	92	7	1
2002 Jun 7–8	86	12	2
* Less than 0.5%			

Note: Based on 469 baseball fans.

Source: Mark Gillespie, *Baseball Fans Overwhelmingly Want Mandatory Steroid Testing,* April 6, 2004. http://poll.gallup.com/content/default.aspx?ci=11245.

Critical Thinking Questions

1. Identify the population, study population, sampling frame, and elements in the above example. How many people are in the sample?

2. For Question 42 about whether major league baseball players should be tested for steroids, what is the statistic, sampling error, confidence level, and confidence range for the percentage of people surveyed between

March 26 and 28, 2004, who felt that major league baseball players should be tested? What is the population parameter?

Critical Thinking Discussion

1. The population is all adults age 18 and older who were baseball fans between March 26 and 28, 2004. The study population is all the people who are age 18 and older who are baseball

BOX 5.1   Sampling Terms, continued

fans between March 26 and 28, 2004, and who have telephones (which most likely is not very different from the "population"). The sampling frame is the computer-generated list of all the possible phone numbers for the people in the study population. The sample consists of 469 baseball fans who were part of the original 1,001 probability sample.

2. The statistic is the 91 percent we see in the box. This is the answer we can directly observe from our sample. The sampling error is ± 5 percentage points. According to the Gallup organization, the confidence level is 95 percent, and if we combine the sampling error with the test statistics, we get a confidence interval of 86 to 96 percent (91% − 5% = 85% and 91% + 5% = 96%). Therefore, put together, we are 95 percent confident that between 86 and 96 percent of baseball fans in the nation (the population parameter) favor testing baseball players for steroids.

Example 2: Gender Stratification

It is widely known in the social sciences that for every level of educational attainment, women still earn less than men. The reasons for this are varied and range from overt discrimination on the part of employers (albeit creative discrimination since unequal wages based on sex are illegal in many industrialized countries) to different characteristics and attributes men and women bring to their employment experiences. Tanner, Cockerill, Barnsley, and Williams (1999, **AN1819964**) tested stratification theory and human capital theory as explanations for the differences in wages between male and female pharmacists in Ontario, Canada.

> The data for the study are drawn from a random mailed questionnaire survey of pharmacists in Ontario, Canada. All practicing pharmacists are required to be members of the Ontario College of Pharmacists, and the College's listing was used as the sampling frame. A systematic sample of 752 pharmacists was generated from the listing of 7,900 pharmacists. A total of 463 completed questionnaires were returned, 29 pharmacists were determined by mail and telephone contacts to be ineligible (moved, deceased, no longer practicing), for an overall response rate of 64 per cent. Response rates between male and female pharmacists, and among the different sectors of pharmacy (community, hospital and industry) did not differ statistically from population estimates, indicating a representative sample of licensed pharmacists.
>
> . . . From the perspective of supply side "human capital" theory, the occupational attainments and destinies of women are attributable to choices that have been made: choices that reflect differences in motivations and orientations/commitments to work. The theory suggests that men and women enter work for different reasons and evaluate the potential rewards from jobs differently. . . . Do women and men see in pharmacy different opportunities and rewards—such that, for instance, women are less interested in financial rewards than men, and more interested in fulfilling a health care giving role?
>
> To test the thesis that there are differences between male and female professionals in their motivations for entering pharmacy, respondents were asked to rate the importance of various potential influences on occupational choice. . . . As is readily apparent from [the table], there is little evidence to support either of these propositions. Overall, the similarities in motivation and orientation between the genders are more notable than the differences between them. Thus, helping people, job security and income potential were the top three ranked motivating influences to enter pharmacy for both males and females. Similarly, both male and female pharmacists stressed that paid employment was very important to them, that they put more into their job than was required, and that they would continue to work even if they won the lottery.

BOX 5.1   Sampling Terms, continued

	Male	Female
Importance of Factors in Considering Pharmacy as a Career		
(1 = Not at all important, 5 = Very important)		
Income potential	3.73	3.59
Job security	4.01	3.93
Desire to help people	4.11	4.18
Opportunity for self employment	3.58	2.51[a]
Opportunity for flexible work hrs	2.66	3.50[a]
Family encouragement	2.83	3.17[b]
Rec. from someone in profession	2.62	2.31[c]
Rec. from school counselor	1.63	1.80
Professional prestige	3.19	3.15
Agreement with Job Commitment Statements		
(1 = Strongly disagree 5 = Strongly agree)		
Paid employment is very important to me	4.24	4.20
I put much more effort into my job than what is required	4.07	4.13
I would likely continue to work even if I won the lottery	3.29	3.51

Note: [a] $= p < .001$; [b] $= p < .01$; [c] $= p < .05$.

Source: Julia Tanner, Rhonda Cockerill, Jan Barnsley, and Paul A. Williams, "Gender and Income in Pharmacy: Human Capital and Gender Stratification Theories Revisited," *British Journal of Scoiology*, 50 (1) (March 1999): 97. DOI: 10.1080/000713199358833 (**AN1819964**). Reprinted by permission.

Critical Thinking Questions

1. Identify the population, study population, sampling frame, and elements in the above example. What is the population size and what is the sample size?

2. Is this sample representative of the population? What is the evidence for your answer?

3. What are the statistics? What is the confidence level? What is the confidence interval?

Critical Thinking Discussion

1. The population and study population are all practicing pharmacists who are members of the Ontario College of Pharmacists. The sampling frame is the actual list of all practicing pharmacists that the researchers obtained from the Ontario College of Pharmacists. The elements are the individual pharmacists.

   According to the article, there are 7,900 pharmacists in the study population and the researchers selected a sample of 752 pharmacists. However, due to nonresponse and ineligibility, that 752 sample size dwindled to a study sample size of 434 people (the 463 returned surveys minus the 29 people the researchers deemed as ineligible to participate in the study).

2. According to the authors, the rates of response in the sample—or the percentage of responses—did not differ by gender or by sector of pharmacy from the population.

   This means that since the authors had the original list of 7,900 practicing pharmacists, they were able to identify the gender and sector of pharmacy for all 7,900 individuals in their

BOX 5.1   Sampling Terms, continued

sampling frame—meaning they knew race and sector for their population. They simply did a statistical test comparing the percentage of men and women pharmacists in their sample to that of the population and found no statistical difference.

This is one of the few areas in research where lack of statistically significant findings are desirable because if there is no statistical difference between the characteristics of the sample and the characteristics of the population, then we can conclude with some confidence that the sample and population are not different. To put it another way, we can conclude that the sample is representative of the population.

3. This question is a bit harder. Let me answer the last question first. No, there is no confidence interval given in the excerpt or in the original study. Instead, the authors did specific statistical tests to see whether there were statistically significant differences between men and women.

The table shows that there *are* statistically significant differences between the statistics noted for men and women regarding the importance respondents give to the opportunity for self-employment, flexible work hours, family encouragement, and recognition from someone in the profession. How do I know this? The last line of the table has what are called "p-values," otherwise known as "probability of error" values. If I want to be 95 percent confident of an estimation, how likely am I to be *wrong?* The answer is 5 percent (100 percent certain − 95 percent certain = 5% error). That 5 percent expressed as a probability is 0.05; therefore, if I see a probability of error expressed as $p < .05$, that means that the probability of error in this estimation is less than 5 percent—or that I am at least 95 percent confident of my findings.

Similarly, $p < .01$ means that I'm at least 99 percent sure of my findings, and $p < .001$ means that I'm 99.9 percent sure of my findings. This means that with regard to gender differences in the importance of opportunity for self-employment, the researchers are 99.9 percent sure that there is a difference between men and women (because if we follow the footnote for [a], we see $p < .001$). And since the researchers have established that their sample of pharmacists was representative of the population of pharmacists, then they can be 99.9 percent sure that there is a difference between men and women's importance of opportunity for self-employment in the population as well.

In other words, here the researchers did not use a sample to estimate the actual population parameter per se; they used the sample statistic to estimate whether there were differences in views among pharmacists based on gender in the population. Hence, the numbers in the table are the statistics observed in the sample, and the probability values the researchers present for some parts of the table indicate that for those issues, the researchers are confident (to different degrees based on the footnote letter behind the statistic) that this difference also exists in the population.

For issues in the table in which there is no corresponding letter or footnote, the researchers cannot say that there is a statistical difference between genders in the population. They have to conclude that even though the numbers for men and women may be different, the difference is not large enough for them to assume a real difference between men and women in the population.

Based on my data, I may find that 68 percent of the attorneys in my sample want women on their juries. If my **standard error** at a 95 percent confidence level is $\pm$ 4 percent, in our hypothetical study of criminal defense attorneys I can then say that I am 95 percent confident that between 64 and 72 percent of the criminal defense attorneys in Pennsylvania want women on the jury if they are defending a murder suspect. The 95 percent confidence is my confidence level, and the range 64 to 72 percent is my confidence interval, which is based on my observed statistic and my sampling error.

Probability Sampling

I began the chapter with an example of research that examined the views of 14 different welfare mothers toward employment and asked you whether you believed that what those women said could be generalized to most welfare mothers. I also said that to answer that question (and the others I raised), we had to know more about how the 14 women were selected. Basically I was referring to the distinction between probability and nonprobability sampling methods. If researchers want to use what they observe in a sample to make conclusions, or generalizations, about what the wider population would say, they need to do some form of probability sampling. In *probability sampling*, each member, or element, of the population has an equal chance (or probability) of being selected into the study, and because of this, researchers can estimate issues such as sampling error and confidence levels. However, nothing in research comes free; probability sampling is sometimes more time consuming, costly, and challenging than other forms of sampling that researchers, very creatively, call *nonprobability sampling*.

Whether a researcher decides to do a probability or a nonprobability sample depends on her or his research goal. If a researcher is doing only a pretest or an exploratory study, then the researcher probably will not choose to do the intricate steps involved with a probability sample because he or she is likely to be more concerned with gathering new information and less concerned with generalizing findings to a population. Likewise, if I am testing a policy, I may be unable to do a probability sample for political or ethical reasons. On the other hand, if a researcher is doing an opinion poll or some other type of research in which the researcher wants to estimate what is going on in a specific population, then that researcher has little choice but to do a probability sample.

In this section, I will discuss what probability and nonprobability samples are. I will also examine the theory that makes probability samples work as they do and the different specific techniques for selecting various probability and nonprobability samples. I'll conclude this section with a closer examination of how to decide which sampling technique is most appropriate for various research questions. Let's begin with a look at probability sampling and probability theory.

■ Central Limit Theorem and Probability Theory

Have you ever had trouble making a decision and decided to "let fate decide" by flipping a coin? Heads you choose option A; tails you choose option B. Even at many sporting events, the referee assigns one team to be "tails" and another to be "heads" and then flips a coin to decide who will get the ball first. Why? Because you and the sports referee both recognize that if the coin is "fair" (meaning equally weighted at all points), whether it lands heads or tails is completely random and completely equal. There is a 50-50 chance (or a .50 probability) that any one flip will land heads. Likewise, there is a 50-50 chance that any one flip will land tails. Because each side (heads or tails) has an equal probability of being selected, we consider a coin toss to be random.

Probability theory works much the same way. Like the coin toss, probability theory is based on the assumption that every person in the study population has an equal chance of being selected into the sample and that whoever is selected is simply due to chance. Why is this equal chance selection important? Because if everybody has an equal and random chance of selection, then the risk of selection bias (where one person or a group of people has a greater likelihood of being selected than another person or group) is minimized and researchers can then estimate how closely their sample resembles the population they are trying to study.

Remember, the fundamental goal of sampling is to select a sample that will mirror the population in such a way as to produce statistics that can accurately estimate the true population parameters. To this end, people often confuse "random sampling" from a scientific point of view with that of a layperson's point of view. Students frequently think that they can do scientific research by standing out on their campus quad and "randomly" asking people who pass them to complete a survey. This method of sampling is haphazard, not random. Why? Because in this method, everyone does not have an equal probability of being selected.

For example, suppose you see a professor you do not like walking in the quad when you are doing your study. You may decide not to ask that professor to participate simply because you don't want to interact with the professor or you think that that particular professor doesn't like you and wouldn't agree to participate anyway. Right there, random selection is violated because that professor does not have the same probability of selection that a friendly professor or an unknown professor might have. Even if you decide to be tricky and recognize your potential bias and make a special point to ask that professor to participate *because* you don't want to question whether you let him walk by simply due to your dislike of him, you *still* violate the equal chance of selection criteria. This professor *still* doesn't have an equal probability of selection for the opposite reason; in your attempt to make sure your personal biases don't get in the way of your research, you are now *more* likely to include him in the study than you otherwise may have if you didn't know him.

Similarly, if you see your friends you might be more inclined to ask them to participate because you think they will say "yes" due to your friendship; you might be less inclined to ask someone who you met at a party and neglected to call (even though you said you would); or you may overlook students who seem threatening because of their gender, acquaintances, reputation, disposition, and so on. The point is this: When people "randomly" select participants on their own, the participants really do not have an equal probability of selection because one's personal characteristics and experiences are likely to get in the way and alter the probability of an individual's selection.

The only true way to obtain a scientifically random sample is to use a table of random numbers or a computer program that can use a random method for selecting elements or sampling units. For populations that have a sampling frame readily accessible in electronic form, a computer-generated random selection is easiest. However, because researchers frequently do not have access to electronic sampling frames, a table of random numbers is still useful. Such a table is presented in Appendix C, but I will postpone a discussion of how to use it until I specifically discuss how to draw random samples.

The question remains: Why is random selection so important that researchers can't trust themselves or their instincts to accurately select their population? Why is all the focus on a purely equal probability of selection? Let's answer those questions by working through an example. The photograph on this page depicts 10 people in a business meeting. Let's make our example easier to see by supposing that these 10 people are the total number of people who work for this company; in other words, they are the population of employees. I understand that a population of 10 is incredibly small and that I said earlier that we usually do not know the characteristics of a population.

Let's assume that these 10 people were the entire population of employees for a company. If you wanted to study their work hours and selected only a few employees to represent all 10, how close would your approximations be? How can you improve your estimate?

However, I'm asking you to suspend disbelief in order to explain probability theory with numbers we can actually see.

Now let's ask each of these people to tell us how many hours they devote to their company in a week. Figure 5.1 illustrates each of the people from the photo with his or her corresponding work hours as symbolized by the number in the computer icon.

If we add up the number of hours and divide by 10, our population size, we know that the average number of hours a person in this company works is 40.5 hours. Since I said that I am pretending that these 10 people are the only people in the company, they are the population of workers and the 40.5 hours is the population parameter. Now, let's use random sampling to estimate the population mean without actually observing all 10 of the workers (remember, this is a fictitious population just to illustrate the ideas behind sampling). I am not going to discuss exactly how to do a random sample here (I will address that shortly); for now, assume that when I say "random," I have done the methodologically

41 Hours 42 Hours 40 Hours 43 Hours 39 Hours 44 Hours

38 Hours 45 Hours 37 Hours 36 Hours

Figure 5.1 Icon Symbols of the Weekly Work Hours for the People in the Photograph

approved means of random selection even though I have not yet discussed exactly what that is.

Suppose I decided to start by randomly selecting a sample of 1; in other words, I am going to randomly select 1 person from the 10 and I will use however many hours of work that person does to approximate the average number of hours that the population of employees works. Suppose I draw the person who works 44 hours. If I do this, my estimate of the hours these employees work is 3.5 hours higher than the true value. Now suppose I put that first person "back into the pot," meaning I pretend that I never drew the first sample and that first person's name is back in the sampling frame and that person is eligible for the second sample. I randomly draw a second sample of 1 and it is the person who works 38 hours. I am closer, but now I am 2.5 hours *lower* than the population parameter I am trying to estimate. Figure 5.2A, borrowed from Babbie (1995, pp. 198–199), illustrates this first attempt at sampling. The points you see are the values I select in 10 different samples with a sample size of 1. In other words, the dots represent the "sample mean" (even though here it technically isn't a mean because my sample size is only 1) of 10 different samples where I selected only one employee for each different sample. The graph of dots is called the *sampling distribution*

You can probably see that drawing a sample of 1 is a hit-or-miss shot at the true population parameter, and that I have no means of estimating how close I would be if this were a real population and I didn't know the true population value. Furthermore, I may be very far from the true population parameter, which essentially makes my sampling meaningless from a methodological point of view.

Now let's suppose I drew a larger random sample, say of 2 people. Figure 5.2B shows the sampling distribution of means that I would receive from drawing the 45 different possible combinations of two workers (with the people selected in any one sample being returned to the sample population before I draw any subsequent samples). You may notice that some 2-person worker combinations produce the same means (e.g., 41 and 40 hours; 39 and 42 hours; 37 and 41 hours). What else do you notice about the second graph relative to the first? The first graph is a straight line with all of the points evenly spaced; the second graph shows that the points are not evenly distributed in a straight line. Instead, the points cluster around the true population parameter of 40.5, with more sample means near the 40.5 (as indicated by the more dots) than further away from it.

Now I'm going to do two different samples. The first is 210 random samples of 4 employees (sample size = 4) and the last is 210 random samples of 6 employees (sample size = 6). What happened to the graphs in Figures 5.2C and 5.2D? They may be looking more like graphs you already know. These graphs are called *normal distributions* and result when information is randomly selected. You may also notice that as the sample size increases, more points are clustered around the true population parameter. In other words, the graphs form a point in the center that corresponds to the true population parameter. Furthermore, the graphs are getting narrower. This means that with increasing sample sizes, more of my samples are going to hit the true population parameter heads on (as indicated by the point) and the others are going to be closer approximates of the true population parameter (meaning that if they are "off," they will be off by less than if the sample size was smaller).

This phenomenon is fairly consistent when samples are truly selected randomly. In fact, the pattern becomes clearer as even larger samples, and more of them, are drawn. Mathematicians calls this phenomenon the **central limit theorem.** When a huge number

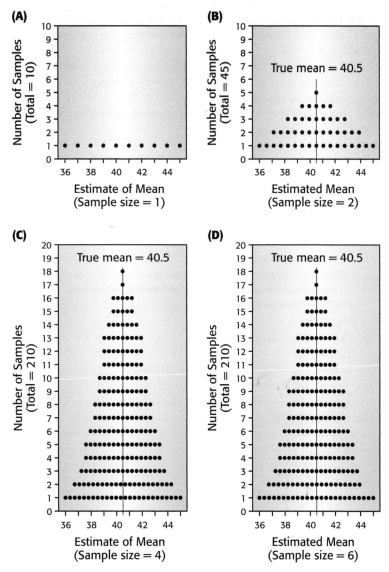

Figure 5.2 Four Graphs of Samples

of samples of sufficiently large size are drawn, the means of those samples will distribute themselves along the normal curve with the midpoint of this curve approaching the true population parameter. This is going to be true whether researchers are examining people's ages, people's incomes, the number of times people drink alcohol in a week, or the percentage of red marbles in a jar of red, white, blue, and green marbles. Whatever researchers are trying to estimate in the population, if they *randomly* draw many samples of sufficient size from that population, the means of the sample will distribute themselves along the normal curve with the midpoint of that curve approximating the true population parameter. Remember, researchers will rarely ever know the true population parameter in the real world; however, the reason I used our fictitious population of 10 workers was so that I could illustrate the central limit theorem and show you that it works.

Because of this consistency, when researchers draw samples randomly, they can also use the properties of the normal curve to predict how well their sample statistics approximate the true population parameter. This process is known as **probability theory.** Probability theory can be summarized as such:

1. If many independent random samples are drawn from a population, the sample statistics produced will be distributed around the population parameter in a known way. (This "known way" is the normal curve.)
2. Because of this predictability, we can estimate how closely the sample statistics are clustered around the true population parameter. This is the standard error.
3. We know that one standard error in either direction (plus or minus) of the mean of the sampling means will account for approximately 68 percent of the means of the samples drawn. Likewise, we know that two standard errors in each direction will account for 95 percent of the means of the samples selected. Three standard errors in each direction will account for 99 percent of all the sample means selected.

Let's look at this more closely. The central limit theorem addresses the first part of probability theory, which I've already addressed. The second part of probability theory argues that researchers can calculate how close their sample statistics (estimates) are to the true population parameter. Essentially, this means that there is a mathematical formula researchers can use to estimate how close their statistics (gathered from a sample) are to the true population parameter (which the researcher does not know in reality). For data that are measured at the interval/ratio level of measurement, the general formula for the standard error is:

$$\sigma = \sqrt{\Sigma\left(X - \bar{X}\right)/n}$$

where σ = symbol for standard error
Σ = Greek symbol "sigma" meaning the "sum of"
X = any one individual score (here, the mean)
$\bar{X}$ = the mean of the scores (here, the mean of the means)
n = the sample size

In English, to calculate the standard error, you first subtract the mean of the sampling distribution (essentially, the "mean" of the individual sample means or "mean of the means") from each individual sample mean, square those individual differences, and then add up all of the squared differences. You divide that sum by the sample size of the individual samples and take the square root of the result.

For data that are discrete, or measured at the nominal or ordinal level, the formula to use is:

$$\sigma = \sqrt{\left(P * Q\right)/n}$$

where σ = symbol for standard error

P = probability of being in any one state (e.g., a white marble, a Latino, a woman)

Q = probability of being in all other relevant states (e.g., all other colored marbles except white, a White/African American/Asian American/Other race, a man)

n = the sample size

Discrete variables are variables with a set number of answer choices. Gender is an example of a discrete variable because a respondent's choices are either male or female. If I use gender as an example, the probability of being male is represented by P and is 0.50 (the probability that corresponds to a 50 percent chance). The probability of being female, or Q, is also 0.50. On the other hand, if I had a bag of 100 marbles in which 25 where white, 25 were red, and 50 were blue, the probability of selecting a white marble, P, is 25 percent or .25, and the probability of selecting any other marble, Q, is 75 percent or .75. Notice that the sum of P and Q will always be 1.0. This is because if you put all the marbles in a bag, you have all the marbles—or the population—a value of 100 percent (a probability of 1.0).

Now let me get back to the third point, that social scientists can predict what percentage of samples fall within different degrees of the standard error. Let's suppose that I drew 100 samples of 6 employees from my fictitious population of 10 and the mean hours worked from the 100 different sample means (in other words, the mean of the means) was 41 hours and the standard error was 1.5 hours. The third part of probability theory tells me that plus and minus one standard error from the mean of means will account for 68 percent of all the sample means I've selected. This means that 68 percent of the sample means will have a value between 39.5 and 42.5 hours and that somewhere within that, the real population value will lie.

Remember: In the real world, we would not know the real population value. Even with my hypothetical example, the mean of the means of 41 was slightly off of the real value of 40.5, which we know only in this instance, but nonetheless *is* within the range of 39.5 to 42.5. I also know that about 95 percent of the same means will fall within a range of 2 standard errors, or within $\pm$ 3 work hours ($1.5 \times 2 = 3$). Put another way, 95 percent of the sample means will fall between 36.5 and 43.5 hours. Again, the true population parameter is within this range as well.

You may be reading all of this and asking yourself why you care what means fall within 68 percent of the 100 samples or 95 percent of 100 samples. After all, you never intend to draw 100 samples of anything, so what is the point? Well, researchers don't intend to draw 100 samples or even 50 or 20 samples of anything either. Just like you, researchers are interested only in drawing one sample. However, researchers understand that if 68 percent of sample means will fall within $\pm$ 1 standard error of the mean of a sampling distribution (or true population parameter), then *any one* sample has a *68 percent chance* of doing the same. In other words, there is a 68 percent chance that the true population parameter will fall between $\pm$ 1 **standard deviation** of the sample statistic.

Incidentally, a standard deviation is the same idea as the standard error; however, when discussing the variation in responses in one specific sample as opposed to variations in means in many different samples, researchers use different language. *Sampling error* is the variation between sampling means and the true population parameter when many samples are done. *Standard deviation* is the variation between any one observation in a sample from the sample mean. Like I said, essentially the two are similar, but standard error uses the population parameter as the reference measure (and since researchers rarely know this, it is more of a theoretical existence) and standard deviation uses the sample mean as the reference measure (which researchers do know and can calculate from their sample and can therefore use as the basis to estimate the population parameter). Likewise, *any one* sample has a 95 percent chance of falling within ± 2 standard deviations of the true population parameter and a 99 percent chance of falling within ± 3 standard deviations.

I know all of this sounds horribly confusing, but understanding the central limit theorem and probability theory are integral to understanding why researchers need to go through all of the steps I will describe shortly to draw a truly random sample. So let me summarize the main arguments and tie together some of the terms I've used previously, such as confidence interval and confidence level:

1. The goal of research is to draw conclusions or to estimate an incidence in the population (which researchers cannot directly observe) using a sample from that population (which researchers can directly observe).
2. If researchers randomly select a sample of people from a population, then everybody in that population has an equal probability of being selected, or, put another way, an equal chance of being in the sample.
3. If everybody has an equal chance of selection into the sample, then the responses for a particular variable (test statistic) will hover around the true value of that variable in the population (population parameter) researchers are trying to estimate in a known way: the normal curve.
4. When responses pattern themselves along the normal curve, I can use the sample mean and standard deviation to predict the range of values within which I think the true population parameter will fall (confidence interval).
5. Through the sample mean and standard deviation, researchers can also provide information as to how confident they are that the true population value will fall within the range of values (confidence interval) that researchers have established. This is the confidence level.
6. Therefore, if researchers draw a random sample from a population of sufficient size, researchers can use my sample mean and standard deviation to establish a confidence level and interval, which will be the estimation of the true population parameter, which researchers cannot directly observe. Hence, the research goal expressed in Step 1 will be fulfilled.

I hope that I have made it clearer as to why random samples, also known as probability samples, are so important and why people, not even scientists, can't trust themselves to select a truly random sample in their own. Let's move the discussion to the different types of probability sampling and how to do them.

■ Simple Random Sampling

The first method of sampling I'll describe is called **"simple" random sampling** for a reason. It is the most basic type of probability sample and it is also the simplest to draw. As with all probability samples, simple random sampling requires some type of procedure in which all the elements in a sampling frame have an equal probability of selection. This means that whether any one element is included in the sample is purely random.

In order to draw a simple random sample, a researcher obtains a sampling frame, numbers each element in that sampling frame (being careful not to skip any numbers), and uses a table of random numbers, either from a computer or in a book, to select elements from the sampling frame to include in the sample. Let's pretend that I want to study the views of the elderly in my community about teenagers. I visit a local seniors center and get a list of all the members in the community who they serve. This list totals 300 people who are age 65 or older. I decide to sample 30 percent of these elderly, for a sample size of 90 people. I obtain a list of all 300 people, which is my sampling frame, and number the names from 1 to 300.

Why can't a person just look at the list and "randomly" eyeball and select which elements to include in a sample? For the same reason I discussed in explaining probability theory: Human selection is rarely completely "random." Individuals may be drawn to specific numbers. For example, if an individual starts to "randomly" select numbers and notices that many of the numbers he or she "randomly" selected are rather low, the person might purposely try to "randomly" select more higher numbers to even out the numbers selected for the sample. However, remember, these numbers have no inherent meaning in themselves; therefore, purposely trying to select higher numbers to "balance" a selection violates the idea of randomness. Therefore, only through some use of a table of random numbers can a sample be truly randomly selected. If the bulk of the numbers selected from a table of random numbers are lower numbers in the range, so be it. They were truly selected randomly, so this is acceptable.

There are some rules and conventions when using a table of random numbers. First, although a person can read this table any way, many read these tables left to right, as you would a book. Below is an excerpt from a table of random numbers:

40480	15011	01536	02011	81647	91646
22368	46570	25595	85393	30995	89098
24130	48360	22527	97265	76393	64809
42167	93093	06243	61680	07856	16376
37570	39975	81837	16656	06212	91782

The numbers in these tables may be presented in a variety of ways. They may appear as one long string of numbers, or they may be separated into groups of numbers, such as into groups of five, such as in our example. The spacing has no inherent meaning; tables that group numbers simply do so to make the numbers easier to read. To select a random start, one can very simply shut one's eyes and drop a pencil somewhere on the table. When I did this, my pencil landed on 3, which is bolded and slightly enlarged so you can spot it, in the fourth column and second row. This means that when I read this table, I will read left to right starting at the 3 that I selected.

Another point about using random tables is that I am going to read or look at groups of numbers that correspond to the size of my sampling frame. In my hypothetical example of elderly people, there are 300 people in my sampling frame; therefore, using the table of random numbers I look at three-digit groups because there are three digits in the number 300. Furthermore, I am going to look only for numbers that range from 1 to 300. Any number over 300 isn't useful to me because I have only 300 possible people. Likewise, if I encounter a number twice, I need to skip it because I obviously will not distribute two surveys to the same person. When I reach the end of a row in the table, I simply use any numbers remaining in that row and wrap them around to the next row. Let's look at the table of random number excerpt to see how I would begin selecting this sample:

40480	15011	01536	02011	81647	91646
22368	46570	25595	85393	30995	89098
24130	48360	22527	97265	76393	64809
42167	93093	06243	61680	07856	16376
37570	39975	81837	16656	06212	91782

As I said, the 3 in the fourth column and second row is my starting point. If I am looking at blocks of three digits, that means that my first three-digit consideration is 330 (it is underlined in the above table). I can't use this number because I only have 300 possible names to select. The next number is 995, which is italicized. I alternate between italicizing and underlining the three-digit increments to make it easier for you to follow what I am doing in the table. I still can't use 995, nor can I use the next few numbers (890, 982, 413).

Reading this thread illustrates an important point. You will notice that after number 890, I have only two digits (98) left in the line. These numbers are italicized, as is the first number in the next line (2), and illustrates the wrapping practice I mentioned earlier. The 8 is the last number in the second row; however, I need to read the numbers in increments of three digits. Therefore, I "wrap" the number into the third row to get my third and I pick up the 2 for a three-digit increment of 982. However, this number is also too high and cannot be included in my sample. The next number, 048, I *can* use because it is between 1 and 300 and it means that the person who has the number "48" by his or her name is the first person in my sample.

This, too, illustrates a good point. Students frequently are confused as to how numbers that are low (for example, the number 5) could be selected for a sample when the sampling frame is large. The answer is because zeros are also part of the table of random numbers and it is very possible to have 005 be a set of digits, which would correspond to the fifth person in your sampling frame. You can read the rest of this table on your own, but the numbers I would select for the sample, based on this excerpt, are

48, 94, 216, 93, 62, 160, 007, 163, 039, 212

In order to select my full sample of 90 people, I would need to continue with the table of random numbers. I only stopped here because I did not include a complete table, but merely an excerpt for illustration. As I mentioned before, a complete table of random numbers appears in Appendix C. Figure 5.3 provides a complete summary and illustration of simple random sampling (and systematic, which I will discuss shortly) for further practice.

One interesting point about random samples is that because they *are* random, if another person picks a different starting point, that person is likely to end up with a sample that is totally different from the one I drew. This is fine because in both of the samples, the people in the sampling frame had the exact same probability of selection in both instances. The only point that varied was exactly who was selected.

As you may have noticed, drawing a simple random sample, although easy, can quickly become cumbersome if you have a large sampling frame and/or need to draw a large sample. If your sampling frame is available in an electronic form that can be read by a statistical package (even a very basic one), you can quickly select a random sample with a computer. Business and organizations also use a form of random sampling, called *random*

Suppose I wanted to study the views of high school teachers in my community about nationally mandated educational standards. There are three high schools in or near my community (which I'll simply identify as A, B, and C) that have a total of 60 teachers. I decide to sample 25 percent of these teachers, for a sample size of 15 teachers. I obtain a list of all 60 teachers, which is my sampling frame and appears below. Let's draw a simple random sample and a systematic sample of the students to illustrate these two sampling processes.

The steps for a simple random sample are as follows:

1. Obtain a complete list of your sampling frame.

2. Number all elements in your frame starting at the beginning of your list with 1 and moving to the end of your list with your last number being the size of your sampling frame. Here, I numbered from 1 to 60.

3. Decide on a sample size. Here, I will select 25 percent of the sampling frame, or 15 names ($60 \times .25 = 15$).

4. Using a table of random numbers, select a starting point from which you will select your sample (here, 15 names). Remember to:

   a. Read left to right.

   b. Read groupings of digits that correspond to the size of your sampling frame. I have 60 people in my sampling frame; 60 is two digits, therefore I look at groupings of two numbers at a time. If I had a sampling frame that was 100 to 199 people, I would look at three-digit groupings; if my frame was 1,000 to 9,999 people, I would look at four-digit groupings, and so on.

   c. Skip numbers that are larger than your sampling frame or that are repeated numbers. Here, I would ignore any number that is greater than 60 and any numbers that appear more than once in my selection.

   d. If necessary, wrap digits around to the next row when you reach the end of one row. Remember that any spacing of digits is merely to facilitate the reading of the table and has no inherent meaning in itself.

   e. Continue until you reach your desired sample size.

   f. *Practice:* My starting point was the 0 in the fourth column (columns read down) and the second row (rows read across). The elements selected have a Y in the column for SR (simple random) by their names. An asterisk (*) by a name means that the number corresponding to that name appeared twice and had to be ignored the second time.

The steps for a systematic sample are as follows:

1–3. Same as for simple random sampling.

   4. Decide on a sampling interval, k, that is equal to the size of your sampling frame divided by the size of your desired sample. Here, my sampling frame is 60, my desired sample size is 15, and therefore my interval is 4 (60/15).

   5. Pick a random start on the table of random numbers that is between 1 and k, your sampling interval. Here, I would look for a number from 1 to 4.

(*continued to next page*)

Figure 5.3 Simple and Systematic Sampling

a. Select a random start.

b. Read left to right, looking for digits that correspond to your interval size (*not* your sampling frame size). My sampling interval is 4, which is one digit, so I am reading for single digits.

c. As with simple random sampling, ignore any numerical groupings that are higher than your sampling interval.

d. As soon as you have a number between 1 and k, stop using the table of random numbers. This person that you have randomly selected is the first person in your sample. The rest of the sample will be selected by simply choosing every kth person in your sampling starting with the number you selected. If you get to the end of your sampling frame before you have the last person in your sample, simply circle around to the beginning of your frame and continue.

e. *Practice:* I shut my eyes and dropped my pencil on the 9 in the third column, sixth row. However, 9 is greater than my interval 4, so I read left to right starting with the number 9, looking at single digits. Three digits over, I come to a 4, which means that the person identified by number 4 (Almar, B.) is the first person in my sample. I now put aside the table of random numbers because I no longer need it, and I move down the list of my sampling frame marking every fourth person to be in my sample. Consequently, my second person would be person #8 (Bellmont, E.), my third person would be #12 (Donalds, W.), and so on, until I reach 15 people. The people selected by systematic sampling are indicated by a Y in the Sys (systematic) column.

No.	Name (HS)	SR	Sys	No.	Name (HS)	SR	Sys
1.	Ahrens, L. (A)			22.	Kipper, G. (A)		
2.	Aikens, D. (B)	Y		23.	Krause, S. (B)	Y	
3.	Aquilino, W. (A)	Y		24.	Kuntz, K. (B)		Y
4.	Almar, B. (A)		Y	25.	Landis, A. (C)		
5.	Ashton, C. (C)	Y		26.	Lavelle, O. (C)		
6.	Baker, R. (C)	Y		27.	Layton, D. (A)	Y	
7.	Bandis, Y. (A)	Y		28.	LeMark, F. (A)		Y
8.	Bellmont, E. (C)		Y	29.	Lewis, G. (B)		
9.	Candor, P. (B)			30.	Lewis, S. (B)		
10.	Cellis, C. (B)	Y		31.	Marks, J. (C)		
11.	Davis, D. (C)			32.	Marvin, R. (A)	Y	Y
12.	Donalds, W. (A)		Y	33.	Melvin, D. (C)		
13.	Evans, E. (B)			34.	Moore, W. (B)		
14.	Garing, L. (A)			35.	Moxy, L. (B)		
15.	Geevan, K. (A)	Y		36.	Nardo, J. (A)		Y
16.	Harris, H. (A)		Y	37.	Neevan, W. (A)		
17.	Hashem, B. (C)			38.	Newton, F. (B)		
18.	Hilkins, F. (B)			39.	Nickel, P. (C)		
19.	Irvine, S. (B)			40.	Noodes, L. (A)		Y
20.	Jones, L. (C)		Y	41.	Nuke, F. (A)	Y	
21.	Jones, T. (A)	Y		42.	Opie, O. (A)		

Figure 5.3 Continued

No.	Name (HS)	SR	Sys	No.	Name (HS)	SR	Sys
43.	Orzel, R. (B)			52.	Smith, F. (A)		Y
44.	Owens, T. (C)		Y	53.	Stevens, W. (A)		
45.	Patrick, P. (C)	Y		54.	Szukics, M (B)		
46.	Paul, B. (B)	Y*		55.	Taylor, L. (C)		
47.	Peters, K. (B)	Y		56.	Tomlinson, R. (A)		Y
48.	Rameses, K. (C)		Y	57.	Tretter, H. (C)		
49.	Reedy, P. (C)			58.	Vandell, B. (B)		
50.	Ruddy, T. (C)			59.	Wirth, J. (B)		
51.	Santos, W. (B)			60.	Wolf, E. (C)		Y

Excerpt from a Table of Random Numbers

48663	91245	85828	14346	09172	30168
54164	58492	22421	74103	47070	25306
32639	32363	05597	24200	13363	38005
29334	27001	87637	87308	58731	00256
02488	33062	28834	07351	19731	92420
81525	72295	04839	96423	24878	82651
29676	20591	68086	26432	46901	20849
00742	57392	39064	66432	84673	40027
05366	04213	25669	26422	44407	44048
91921	26418	64117	94305	26766	25940
00582	04711	87917	77341	42206	35126
00725	69884	62797	56170	86324	88072
69011	65795	95876	55293	18988	27354
25976	57948	29888	88604	67917	48708
09763	83473	73577	12908	30883	18317

Source: Earl Babbie, *The Practice of Social Research,* 7th ed. (New York: Wadsworth, 1995), p. A25.

Figure 5.3 Continued

digit dialing, where a machine randomly dials telephone extensions with phone prefixes that correspond to the geographical area the business or organization is interested in sampling. The benefit of random digit dialing is that it makes a sampling frame unnecessary. It makes studying households much easier because a researcher does not need a list of phone numbers for all of the households in a community—a list that is, quite frankly, likely to be very large and burdensome.

Very often, however, researchers do not have access to random digit dialing, nor do they want to take the time to conduct a simple random sample (especially if their sample or population is large). Therefore, they may opt to do a systematic random sample, which is a variant of simple random sampling.

■ Systematic Random Sampling

Systematic random sampling is usually more efficient than simple random sampling. Reading a table of random numbers to select each individual element to be in a sample can be time consuming and tedious. Systematic sampling tries to speed the process by choosing elements based on a uniform interval, *k*, that is appropriate for that particular population or sampling frame. Hence, by choosing every *k*th element, researchers "systematically" select their sample. For example, Pelzer (2001, **AN 8768342**) used a 1-20 systematic sample of a White urban area and a Black urban area to select 250 Whites and 250 Blacks in South Africa when they studied what leads these people to practice healthy lifestyles. The 1-20 systematic sample means that these researchers selected every twentieth person in the phonebook to be members of their study. Hence, "20" was their "*k*th element."

In the *k*th element, the *k* stands for the **sampling interval,** which is a value calculated using the population size (as represented by the sampling frame) and the desired sample size. Let me illustrate by returning to our hypothetical study of the elderly in a community. If you remember, I have a sampling frame size of 300 elderly individuals and I want to select a sample of 90 of them. The steps for a systematic sample begin much like the steps of a simple random sample. I would obtain a complete list of my study population (a sampling frame) and then number each element within my sampling frame beginning with 1 and ending with the size of the sampling frame. Therefore, like a simple random sample, I would assign each name on my list a unique number from 1 to 300. However, unlike a simple random sample, where I would now head for a table of random numbers, for a systematic sample, I am going to calculate a sampling interval, *k*. The sampling interval is the standard distance between each element in the sampling frame. I calculate *k* by the following formula:

$$\text{sampling interval} = k = (\text{population size/sample size})$$

The population size is really the size of my sampling frame, which is the list of all the people in the population who are eligible for inclusion in my sample. In my example of the elderly, my sampling interval, *k*, would be 300/90, or 3.33. Uh-oh. My interval does not come out to a nice neat number. How do I sample 3.33 people? Good question. It's true that researchers need to work with whole numbers, therefore researchers follow the rules of math and round *down* to the nearest whole number when they have a decimal value of .5 or below, and they round *up* to the nearest whole number when the decimal is .51 or higher. Therefore, since my decimal value is .33, I round down to the nearest whole number, or 3. Therefore, my interval is 3.

Once I have calculated my sampling interval, I am ready for the table of random numbers. Unlike a simple random sample, however, I am not going to use the table to select each individual element for my sample. I am only going to use it to get me started by selecting the *first* element. I will use my sampling interval after that to select everyone else. For example, if I go back to the excerpt of my table of random numbers I used for simple random sampling and selected a random starting point, suppose I landed on the third 6 in the fourth column and fifth row (it is bolded and enlarged so you can see where it is).

In a systematic sample, I read left to right until I find a number that is between 1 and *k*, my sampling interval size. In my elderly example, my sampling interval is 3; therefore, I am looking for a starting point between 1 and 3. Clearly, 6 is too high, therefore I have to read left to right in the number of digits that correspond to my sampling interval. Since my sampling interval of 3 is a single digit, I am looking at individual numbers. Reading left to right, starting at the bolded 6, I don't reach a number that is between 1 and 3 until I hit the 2 in the fifth column, fifth row (it is bolded and italicized so you can find it).

40480	15011	01536	02011	81647	91646
22368	46570	25595	85393	30995	89098
24130	48360	22527	97265	76393	64809
42167	93093	06243	61680	07856	16376
37570	39975	81837	16656	06212	91782

This means that the first person in my sample is person 2. Now I put away the table of random numbers because I do not need it anymore. I select the rest of my sample using the sampling interval that I calculated and sample every kth person from the first person I selected. In my elderly example, the first person in my study is person 2, whom I randomly selected. The other people are persons 5, 8, 11, 14, 17, and soon, until I reach my desired sample size of 75 people. How did I determine these numbers? I simply kept adding 3, my sampling interval, to the previous number: $2 + 3 = 5; 5 + 3 = 8; 8 + 3 = 11$, and so forth.

As you can probably see, systematic sampling is much faster and easier on the eyes than is simple random sampling—especially when you have large populations and large samples to select. Some researchers select a random start anywhere within the sampling frame (Neuman, 1997); however, most limit the random start to a start between 1 and the interval size, k (Hagan, 1997; Babbie, 1995; Schutt, 2001). Regardless of their different views on starting points, researchers overwhelmingly recognize that the results of simple random sampling are similar to that of systematic sampling, provided there are no patterns in the sampling frame which would violate the equal probability of selection, and therefore favor the simpler and faster method of systematic sampling.

However, this is only the case if there are no patterns in the sampling frame. When elements in a sampling frame are arranged in a cyclical pattern, researchers call this **periodicity,** and it may inhibit systematic sampling if the pattern coincides with the sampling interval. For example, suppose I want to do a study of a company and I get a list of all employees. Further suppose that this company is organized into 15 different divisions each with 10 different employees whose names are presented in descending order of tenure. In other words, the first name in each division is of the person who has been with the company the longest and the last name is that person who has been with the company the shortest. If I calculate a sampling interval of 10, only the people with the fewest years with the company will be in my study. Clearly, this is a biased sample that does not represent the population of employees.

Periodicity can be a problem in any population or sampling frame where people are listed via a specific pattern. Apartments listed by number may lead to a sample that includes, say, only the renters who live in a southwestern corner. Or when family members are listed with the father first, then mother, then children, samples may have only mothers in the study. The possibilities are numerous. To prevent a problem of periodicity, researchers must examine their sampling frames to make sure that there are no patterns in how the elements are listed. If there is a pattern, it is safer to do some other type of sampling, such as simple random sampling or stratified random sampling. Let's turn now to a discussion of stratified random sampling in more detail.

■ Stratified Random Sampling

In both simple random and systematic sampling, elements in the population, by definition, have an equal probability of selection, provided there are no patterns in the sampling frame; therefore, these samples are believed to be unbiased. However, by sheer chance alone, I may have many more men than women in my sample. Or, using Figure 5.3 as an example, in the population of teachers, the three schools are almost equally represented. There are 21 teachers in High School A, 20 in High School B, and 19 in High School C. However, when I selected a simple random sample, the number from each school selected was High School A: 7, High School B: 5, High School C: 3. Teachers from High School C are about one-third (31.7 percent) of my population of teachers but only 20 percent of my sample of teachers. Likewise, in the systematic sample, there is only one teacher who was randomly selected from High School B. You might remember that researchers call this mismatch *sampling error,* or the degree to which the sample does not represent the population from which it was drawn. **Stratified random sampling** tries to reduce sampling error by making the sampling process more efficient and also ensuring that there is adequate representation of key population groups in the sample.

How does stratified sampling accomplish this? There are three ways of reducing sampling error. The first is to do a probability sample, which is why I am devoting so much time to discussing the various techniques. However, as you saw with my example in Figure 5.3, this is not necessarily enough. The second way to reduce sampling error is to increase the sample size, which I will discuss later in the chapter. The third way to reduce sampling error is to make the sample more *homogenous,* or alike. This is what stratified random sampling tries to do. Stratified random sampling breaks the original population into smaller subpopulations that are alike on a specific variable of interest, called a **stratification variable.** For example, elderly women still outnumber elderly men, and the gap in representation increases with age. In my hypothetical study of the elderly's view of teenagers, 70 percent of that elderly population may be women, whereas only 30 percent are men. To minimize the risk of having too many men in my sample, I may decide to do a stratification sample.

Scherff, Eckert, and Miller (2005) recognized the risk of an imbalanced sample when they decided to study public school administrators' acceptance and use of three different suicide prevention programs in high schools. In order to identify their sample, they obtained a list of the American Association of School Administrators (AASA); however, they recognized that by sheer random chance alone, they might not draw a sample representative of the different regions of the United States. Therefore, when they selected their sample of administrators, they first divided, or stratified, their sample into five regions of the United States: northeastern, southeastern, north central, west central, and western. They then categorized the names of people in the AASA into these five regions and randomly selected participants accordingly.

To start a stratification sample, I would first choose a stratification variable, or a variable of interest that will divide my larger population into smaller homogenous subgroups. If I am studying police precincts in an area, I may use crime statistics to divide those precincts into those serving generally high-, medium-, and low-crime areas. If I am studying college students, I might ask the Registrar to organize the students into their academic year: freshmen, sophomores, juniors, and seniors. In my elderly sample, I am going to choose gender (male/female) as the stratification variable.

Once I decide on a stratification variable, I assign each element in my population to one and only one value of that strata. Think of it as literally separating your larger population into distinct groups (subpopulations) that you will treat as populations in their own right. In other words, once you divide your original population into subpopulations based on strata, you can "forget" about the original undivided population. In my wider population of 300 elderly, I have 210 women and 90 men. I am going to literally separate the men and women, so instead of one population of 300, I now have two populations. One population is of 90 men, and the other population contains 210 women. The original, broader population of 300 is no longer relevant to my sampling.

Once I have my subpopulations, I am going to number within them from 1 to the subpopulation size. Consequently, I will number my women from 1 to 210 and I will number my men from 1 to 90. Notice that I have two 1s. That is because these two groups are now distinct from each other. This is why I said for you to ignore the broader population of 300. It is no longer relevant.

After I have numbered my elements within the subpopulations, I need to decide how many people from each group I want to sample. I very likely have already decided what my total sample size is, but I have yet to decide how many people I am going to select from my various subpopulations to equal that total sample size. This decision is not as easy as simply taking half from each group. In my study of the elderly views of teenagers, if I took half of my total sample of 90 from each group, men will be overrepresented in my sample compared to their representation in the population, and, unless I correct for this, my sample will no longer be as representative as it could be. Consequently, researchers decide subpopulation sample size by deciding whether they want to do a proportionate or disproportionate stratified sample.

As the name implies, in a **proportionate stratified sample,** the proportion of each group in the sample corresponds to the proportion of that group in the population. Since women make up 70 percent of my study population, in a proportionate stratified sample they should make up 70 percent of my sample. If I have already decided that my total sample size is 90 and I want 70 percent of that sample to be women, I need to select 63 women from the subpopulation size of 210 (90 × .70 = 63). Likewise, I want 30 percent of my total sample to be men, therefore I will select 27 men. I can reach this number the same way I did for the women, which is 90 × .3 or I can simply subtract the sample size for women from my total sample size and reach 27 men.

On the other hand, there may be times when the proportionate representation of one of my groups in the population is very small. Consequently, if I do a proportionate sample, I am likely to have a resulting subpopulation sample size that is really too small to trust as unbiased. Remember, the second way to minimize sampling error is to have a larger sample size. For example, if I choose to stratify my elderly population in terms of age—such as 65–75 (55.5 percent of my population), 76–85 (34.5 percent of my population), and 86 or older (10 percent of my population)—the corresponding proportionate sample sizes would be 50, 31 and 9.

The number of elderly age 86 and older is very small, and it is very possible that those I select will not be representative of the 30 people who appear in the population simply due to random error. This will hinder my ability to estimate meaningful and accurate statistics later in the research process. If I am concerned that there may be bias in a sample due to small proportionate sample sizes, I would decide to do a **disproportionate stratified sample.** In this type of sampling, the researcher intentionally has the proportion of a group in the total sample *not equal* the corresponding proportion in the population. Instead, I may decide to have 50 percent of my sample be between the ages of 65 and 75, 30 percent of my sample between 76 and 85, and 20 percent of my sample be 86 or older. In this scenario, the representation of my oldest age group is double of what it would be in the population.

But wait! You may be asking yourself, "If I can just pick any proportion I want, why bother with a proportionate sample in the first place? I'll just select whatever proportion I feel like." No! Nothing in research comes without a price! Although it may initially appear easier to do a disproportionate stratified sample and just select a proportion you like, this sampling technique is actually more detailed than proportionate stratified sampling. Because the sample proportions are not representative of the proportions in the population, this type of sampling, as I've described it so far, is less representative than it could be; and, if you weren't going to worry about being as representative as possible, you would do a simple random or systematic sample and wouldn't have bothered reassigning people in the population to specific subpopulations. Because, by definition, disproportionate samples no longer proportionately represent the populations from which they are drawn, researchers have to add a step to the research process when they calculate results by *weighting* individual responses so the responses can be made to proportionately represent the population after the fact. Let me illustrate this with my elderly example.

Because I was worried about the small sample size of the oldest members of my population (remember, proportionately there would have been only 9 people from the oldest group in my sample), I decided to play with the proportions I selected from each group so that my sample sizes would be 45 (about 50 percent of the population), 27 (about 30 percent) and 18 (20 percent), respectively. However, these proportions (expressed as the percents after the sample sizes) are no longer representative of the population, which on the surface, seems to defeat the whole purpose behind probability and stratified sampling. However, because I know the true proportion in the population, and I know the proportion I used in my sample, I can create a mathematical weight that I will apply to the responses of each individual who participated in my study when I calculate the results later in the research process. The mathematical weights will bring the responses of my individuals back in line with the true representation of that person's group in the population.

There are many ways of weighting findings and a full discussion is beyond the scope of this book. However, a simple weight is to take the sample size for a specific group you would have used if you did a proportionate sample (since this reflects the proportion in the population) and divide it by the sample size for that group that you decided to use in a disproportionate sample (Schutt, 2001).

Suppose I am looking at the yearly income of my elderly population. I may therefore multiply (or weight) the income of each of my young-old elders (ages 65 to 75) by 1.11 (50, the proportionate sample size that reflects this group's representation in the population, divided by 45, the disproportionate sample size I chose). This number means that the response of any one person age 65 to 75 in the sample counts for (or represents) what 1.11 people aged 65 to 75 in the population would have said or experienced. Likewise, the income of each of my respondents who are between the ages of 76 and 85 will be multiplied by 1.15 (31/27), and for the oldest age group, which I purposely oversampled, I would multiply by .0.5 (9/18). Don't be worried that these numbers do not equal "whole" people. Weights are mathematical entities, therefore they do not really represent whole individuals or units. Therefore, do not round weights. Leave them in their decimal form.

Consequently, stratified random sampling further minimizes the amount of sampling error by dividing broad populations into smaller, more homogenous subpopulations. Believe it or not, at this point, I still have not selected my sample. Once I decide to do a proportionate *or* a disproportionate sample, which tells me the number of people I will select from each subpopulation, I am finally ready to actually draw my sample. Luckily, for us, this step is easier. All I have to do is either simple random sampling or systematic sampling *within* each subpopulation. Be careful! Although I said that this is easier, there is one trick you have to remember. Since you now have separate, unique (at least based on the stratification variable) subpopulations, you need to draw a separate simple random or systematic sample for *each* subpopulation. This means that in our study of the elderly, since I have two distinct subpopulations (male and female), I will draw two different simple or systematic samples.

For example, suppose I decide to do proportionate stratified sampling with simple random selection (essentially simple random sampling within the framework of proportionate stratified sampling). Remember, there are 210 women and they make up 70 percent of my total study population (of men and women combined). Since I want a total sample size of 90, then 70 percent of that sample should be women. Doing the math, I find that about 63 people in my total sample size of 90 should be women. Therefore, since I want to do simple random selection and I have 210 total possible women, I will use my table of random numbers to choose a random start and then read the numbers in increments of three (since 210 is three digits), looking for any unique numbers between 1 and 210, until I obtain 63 numbers. Those numbers correspond to my women, whom I numbered in the sampling frame. When I have 63 numbers, or women, I have selected my first sample.

Now I turn to the study population of men. Once again, I choose a random start. However, notice! This is a *new* random start because once I separated my sample into men and women, I treat the two groups as if they are unrelated (or what we mathematically call *independent*). Now I repeat the process, but this time I use this new starting point to look for two-digit increments between 1 and 90, my male subpopulation size. Based on previous calculations, I know that I need to select 27 men to be in my study. Notice that my total sample size will still be 90. It will include 63 women and 27 men and the proportion of men and women in my sample, which I actually selected using the simple random sampling technique, mirror the proportion of men and women in my study population. Figure 5.4 further summarizes and illustrates stratified random sampling by extending my hypothetical high school teacher study.

■ Cluster Sampling

Simple random, systematic, and stratified sampling are all methods of probability sampling that allow researchers to make conclusions about populations based on samples selected from them. However, as you may notice, all three of these techniques require lists of population members. But what if you wanted to do a probability sample of U.S. citizens? Do you really want a sampling frame with millions of names? I certainly wouldn't! Furthermore, can you imagine how expensive such a study would be? Even obtaining a sampling frame of all residents of a city can be daunting. Think about the number of people living in New York City or Los Angeles! Those sampling frames would be huge, even though they are referring "only" to a single city. Furthermore, there really aren't lists of all people who

This example builds from the example of high school teachers' views of nationally mandated educational standards presented in Figure 5.3. As noted in Figure 5.3, there are 60 teachers from three different high schools in the study population. As in Figure 5.3, I will select 15 teachers from this population of 60; therefore, my sample size is 15. Let's use this population to further summarize and illustrate the steps of stratified random sampling.

The steps for a stratified random sample are as follows:

1. Obtain a complete list (sampling frame) of your study population.
2. Decide on a stratification variable. Here, our stratification variable will be the high school: A, B, or C.
3. Assign each element in the population to one and only one value (strata) of the stratification variable.
4. Number from to *n*, which is the size of each strata, within each strata. This is done below with the list of teachers separated by their respective high schools. The names on this list are the same as appear in Figure 5.3; however, in Figure 5.3, the names are listed alphabetically with no respect to their particular schools. Now the names are listed *separately* by school, which means they are *stratified* by school.
5. Decide on whether to draw a proportionate or disproportionate sample.
   a. *Proportionate:* The proportion of each strata, or subgroup, in the sample is the same as that in the study population.
   b. *Disproportionate:* The researcher selects subgroup population sizes; however, the researcher needs to calculate a weight to apply to later results so that the results no longer reflect any purposeful imbalances in the sample and instead reflect the proportions on the population.

   In this example, 36.7 percent of all the teachers are from High School A, 33.3 percent are from High School B, and 30 percent are from High School C. These proportions are somewhat similar, therefore I will do a proportionate stratified sample. That means that the proportions from each high school in my total sample need to be the same as the proportion from each high school in the population. Since I want a total sample size of 15, that means that I need to select about 6 people from High School A ($15 \times .337$), 5 people from High School B ($15 \times .333$), and 4 people from High School C ($15 \times .30$).

   The sample sizes for High Schools A and C both have a decimal value of 0.5 (the "real" size for High School A was 5.5 and High School C was 4.5). I decided to round up for A and down for C, so the sample size for High School A would be greater than that for High School B (6 versus 5) and High School B would be greater than High School C (5 versus 4) to reflect the slight differences in population size.

6. Select the samples from each subgroup using either simple random sampling or systematic sampling. Follow the steps outlined in Figure 5.3 for whichever selection method you chose. However, remember to treat each subpopulation as unique; therefore, however many subpopulations you have is how many different, unique and independent samples you need to draw. Each sample has its own starting point on the table of random numbers.

   In this example, the table of random numbers from Figure 5.3 is reproduced here. If I do simple random sampling, my three samples are as follows:

   a. High School A: Random start at 1 in blocked column 1, row 2, reading for two-digit numbers between 1 and 22, the sample is 16, 22, 17, 3, 7, 2

Figure 5.4 Stratified Random Sampling

b. High School B: Random start at 0 in blocked column 6, row 5, reading for two-digit numbers between 1 and 20, the sample is 6, 9, 5, 16, 4 (*Note:* the 9 came up twice, so it is ignored the second time since it is already in the sample.)

c. High School C: Random start at 9 in blocked column 8, row 10 (end of second blocked row), reading for two-digit numbers between 1 and 18, the sample is 15, 14, 2, 5

High School A		High School B		High School C	
1. Ahrens, L.		1. Aikens, D.		1. Ashton, C	
2. Aquilino, W.	Y	2. Candor, P.		2. Baker, R.	Y
3. Almar, B.	Y	3. Cellis, C.		3. Bellmont, E.	
4. Bandis, Y.		4. Evans, E.	Y	4. Davis, D.	
5. Donalds, W.		5. Hilkins, F.	Y	5. Hashem, B.	Y
6. Garing, L.		6. Irvine, S.	Y	6. Jones, L.	
7. Geevan, K.	Y	7. Krause, S.		7. Landis, A	
8. Harris, H.		8. Kuntz, E		8. Lavelle, O.	
9. Jones, T.		9. Lewis, G.	Y	9. Marks, J.	
10. Kipper, G.		10. Lewis, S.		10. Melvin, D.	
11. Layton, D.		11. Moore, W		11. Nickel, P.	
12. LeMark, F.		12. Moxy, L.		12. Owens, T.	
13. Marvin, R.		13. Newton, F		13. Patrick, P.	
14. Nardo, J.		14. Orzel, R		14. Rameses, K	Y
15. Neevan, W		15. Paul, B.		15. Reedy, P.	Y
16. Noodes, L.	Y	16. Peters, K.	Y	16. Ruddy, T.	
17. Nuke, F.	Y	17. Santos, W.		17. Taylor, L.	
18. Opie, O.		18. Szukics, M		18. Wirth, J.	
19. Smith, F.		19. Vandell, B.			
20. Stevens, W		20. Wirth, E.			
21. Tomlinson, R.					
22. Tretter, H.	Y				

Same Excerpt from Table of Random Numbers as Shown in Figure 5.3

48663	91245	85828	14346	09172	30168
54164	58492	22421	74103	47070	25306
32639	32363	05597	24200	13363	38005
29334	27001	87637	87308	58731	00256
02488	33062	28834	07351	19731	92420
81525	72295	04839	96423	24878	82651
29676	20591	68086	26432	46901	20849
00742	57392	39064	66432	84573	40027
05366	04213	25669	26422	44407	44048
91921	26418	64117	94305	26766	25940
00582	04711	87917	77341	42206	35126
00725	69884	62797	56170	86324	88072
69011	65795	95876	55293	18988	27354
25976	57948	29898	88604	67917	48708
09763	83473	73577	12908	30883	18317

Source: Earl Babbie, *The Practice of Social Research,* 7th ed. (New York: Wadsworth, 1995), p. A25.

Figure 5.4 Continued

live in a city; therefore, if I wanted a probability sample of New Yorkers, I wouldn't even be able to obtain a sampling frame of individual names. So how do researchers do probability sampling of very large populations or populations for which there are no specific member lists?

The answer, as you may have guessed by the title of this subsection, is **cluster sampling.** Frequently, very large populations can be divided into smaller groups. The nation, for example, can be divided by states, states can be divided by counties, counties can be divided by cities, cities by city blocks, city blocks by houses and, finally, houses by the people who live within them. Essentially, cluster sampling involves dividing large populations into smaller "clusters" and repeatedly drawing samples of clusters of decreasing size until the researcher arrives at a sampling frame that is the list of elements in which he or she is actually interested in studying. These "clusters" are the *sampling units* that I mentioned in the terminology section of this chapter. The sampling method used to select clusters, or sampling units, can be simple random, systematic, or stratified. Consequently, cluster sampling simply involves the repetition of two steps: listing the sampling frames of units and drawing a sample of units.

For example, let's suppose I want to study college students' views of their professors at a very large state university I'll call Constitution University. Suppose Constitution University has a population of 40,000 students who live in 70 different dorms that actually resemble apartment complexes in size. Instead of obtaining a sampling frame of 40,000 individuals, I decide to use simple random sampling to randomly select 10 dormitories. The selection of 10 dorms will be my first stage of a cluster sample. In this instance, my dormitories are sampling units because they house about 575 elements within each of them. Now I've taken my list of students and reduced it from 40,000 to 5,750 (10 dorms × 575 students in each dorm).

I still think a list of 5,750 names is too long, so I decide to go even further. I do another stage of cluster sampling and select various floors (again, using simple random sampling within the cluster) from the dorms I selected in the previous stage in order to bring me one step closer to my elements of interest, the students. If each dorm has 10 floors (for a total of 100 floors from which to select my sample; 10 dorms × 10 floors), then there are about 58 people on each floor. By selecting 60 floors from the possible pool of 100, I've further reduced my possible population size to 3,840 people. In this instance my second sampling unit, or cluster, is the dormitory floors.

What you should be noticing is that I have so far repeated two steps: the listing of sampling units (dorms and then floors) and the selection, or sampling, of units within each of these clusters. In other words, so far I have drawn two samples—one of dormitories and a second of the floors within the dormitories that I selected from my first sampling—all to get to my original interest, which is the elements or the college students themselves. Now with a sample of 3,840 students, I can more easily obtain a list of 3,840 students than I can of 40,000 students, and it is easier to select my sample of 2,000 students. Or put it another way, in the third stage of sampling, I am finally selecting my elements—the individual college students.

Thorpe and colleagues (2004) did a cluster sample of elementary school children in New York City in order to study childhood obesity. Below is an excerpt from their article:

> A total of 736 elementary schools were listed and enumerated (all New York City public schools, excluding special education schools), and 70 schools were randomly selected by means of Microsoft Excel–generated random numbers. From

the sampled schools, classes were then selected for inclusion into the study. The process for classroom selection was designed to minimize the burden on schools and to ensure adequate representation across all 6 grades. For each of the 70 schools, 2 grades were selected, by means of systematic assignment of the following groupings: kindergarten and third grade, first and fourth grade, and second and fifth grade. These groupings were applied sequentially to the list of sampled schools. For each school, a list of all classes in the 2 grades was generated, and 1 class in each grade was randomly selected with the same random selection techniques described earlier. A total of 140 classes, 2 from each school, was selected. (pp. 496–497)

Clearly, there are thousands of elementary school-aged children in New York City, and trying to obtain a sampling frame of all of them would be very cumbersome. Thorpe and colleagues avoided this problem by breaking their approach into more manageable units that involved three stages, or three sampling units. The first unit was the elementary schools, the second was the grades, and the third was the class within the grades.

As you can probably see, cluster sampling is a highly efficient way of tackling very large populations. A sampling frame of 736 schools is more manageable than a list of all the students who attend those schools. Likewise, to refer to my earlier example, a sampling frame of 3,840 students that resulted from my repeated selection of sampling units is much more manageable than one of 40,000 students, which I would have used if I did not first select units of decreasing size. However, this efficiency comes at a price.

If I draw one simple random or systematic sample from a sampling frame of my elements, I will introduce sampling error only one time—because I am drawing only one sample. In other words, there is only one chance that I will, by sheer random bad luck, draw a sample that is not entirely representative of my population. Just by coincidence, I may have too many freshmen or too many men or too many Whites relative to the population of the campus. However, if I do a three-stage cluster sample where I first sample dorms (stage 1), then floors (stage 2), then elements/students (stage 3), then I am vulnerable to sampling error three times—one with each sample I draw. I may, by random chance, draw too many upper-class dorms in the first stage; then, by random chance, draw too many men's floors in the second stage; and, by random chance, miss many of the minorities who room together in the third stage. Now my sample is not really representative of the population of college students with respect to academic year, gender, and race.

But don't give up hope! There are ways to minimize the threat of sampling error in multistage cluster samples. Remember, in the discussion of sampling error, I said that there are two ways to minimize error. The first is to increase sample size and the second is to make the populations more homogenous, or the same. The first safeguard is easy. Researchers just have to make sure that they draw a large proportion of clusters in each stage. This will reduce the likelihood of omitting certain key characteristics. The second safeguard may also take care of itself to some degree because elements in a naturally occurring cluster (e.g., dormitories) are more homogenous that the broader population as a whole. In other words, if dorms are naturally organized by class year at Constitution University (meaning that there are dorms of all freshmen, dorms of all juniors, etc.), then the students in a particular dorm are more alike in terms of that characteristic (students in a dorm are all in the same academic year) than are the entire population of students (which comprise people of many different academic years).

Even though the 50 percent divorce statistic is a fallacy, the country's current divorce rate is higher than it was 100 years ago. Consequently, many researchers have devoted time to studying whether parental divorce has longitudinal effects on children. Wolfinger (2003) is one of those researchers. As Wolfinger notes:

> At least 25 separate studies have examined the impact of family structure on offspring marriage timing. Some find that parental divorce makes marriage more likely, while others show that it delays or deters marriage. . . . The extraordinarily varying results of prior studies can probably be attributed to change across two dimensions of time, individual life course and historical period. In 1973 parental divorce greatly increased the chances of marriage but by 1994 people from divorced families were slightly less likely to marry than were people from intact families. Furthermore, parental divorce raises the likelihood of teenage marriage, but if the children of divorce remain single past age 20 they are disproportionately likely to avoid wedlock.
>
> . . . This debate has important implications. Early wedlock greatly increases the chances of divorce (Bumpass, Martin & Sweet 1991; South 1995), while people who never marry report lower levels of overall well-being than their married peers (Waite 1995; Waite & Gallagher 2000).

Source: Nicholas H. Wolfinger, "Parental Divorce and Offspring Marriage: Early or Late?" *(AN 11233213).* From *Social Forces*, Volume 82, Issue 1. Copyright © 2003 by the University of North Carolina Press. Used by permission of the publisher.

In order to study the marriage rates of children of divorce, Wolfinger uses the General Social Survey (GSS), one of the most comprehensive social surveys available to scientists. Below is an excerpt of his use of the GSS and his findings:

> This research uses the 1973-94 *General Social Survey (GSS)* (Davis & Smith 1994), an ideal data set for studying trends because of its consistency over time. A national probability sample of English-speaking households within the continental U.S., the GSS has been conducted annually or biennially since 1972. The 1972 and post-1994 surveys omit key variables and are therefore not used. Analyses also exclude the black over samples in 1982 and 1987. The final sample size for the years studied is 23,195. Weighted and unweighted analyses produce almost identical results. . . .
>
> Although the sampling design of the GSS has undergone various changes over the years, one constant has been cluster sampling.
>
> Parental divorce has a significant effect on marriage timing, although the relationship varies greatly by respondent age and survey year. The children of divorce have high marriage rates through age 20, but if unmarried by this point they are disproportionately likely to remain so. Marriage rates also declined considerably over the course of the study, for both the over-20 and under-20 age groups. Together, these results can explain why prior studies produced conflicting results.
>
> Since people from divorced families experience both high and low marriage rates at different ages, all the arguments considered earlier may hold true. The children of divorce may marry as teenagers to escape unhappy home environments, as the inadvertent result of premature sexual activity, or simply to assuage psychic wounds. After the age of 20, interpersonal problems may get in the way of marriage, or people may opt for cohabitation. The only hypothesis that can be rejected is the notion that the socioeconomic well-being of single mothers leads to high levels of youthful marriage. Controlling for parental and respondent education did not affect marital rates, and so the children of divorce probably do not marry for lack of other opportunities. This result should be qualified on the grounds that educa-

BOX 5.2   Cluster Sampling, continued

tion taps only certain elements of socioeconomic well-being.

Source: Nicholas H. Wolfinger, "Parental Divorce and Offspring Marriage: Early or Late?" ***(AN 11233213).*** From *Social Forces,* Volume 82, Issue 1. Copyright © 2003 by the University of North Carolina Press. Used by permission of the publisher.

As Wolfinger notes, the GSS is a cluster sample. However, in order to be representative of the entire U.S. population, the sampling technique of the GSS is a complicated combination of probability and nonprobability sampling of about 1,500 people every two years. Here is a summary of how the sampling is done according to the GSS Codebook, Appendix A:

The sample is a multi-stage area probability sample to the block or segment level. At the block level, however, quota sampling is used with quotas based on sex, age, and employment status. The cost of the quota samples is substantially less than the cost of a full probability sample of the same size, but there is, of course, the chance of sample biases mainly due to not-at-homes which are not controlled by the quotas. However, in order to reduce this bias, the interviewers are given instructions to canvass and interview only after 3:00 p.m. on weekdays or during the weekend or holidays. This type of sample design is most appropriate when the past experience and judgment of a project director suggest that sample biases are likely to be small relative to the precision of the measuring instrument and the decisions that are to be made.

Selection of PSUs

The Primary Sampling Units (PSUs) employed are Standard Metropolitan Statistical Areas (SMSAs) or non-metropolitan counties selected in NORC's Master Sample. These SMSAs and counties were stratified by region, age, and race before selection.

Selection of Sample within PSUs

The units of selection of the second stage were block groups (BGs) and enumeration districts (EDs). These EDs and BGs were stratified according to race and income before selection. The third stage of selection was that of blocks. The blocks were selected with probabilities proportional to size. In places without block statistics, measures of size for the blocks were obtained by field counting. The average cluster size is five respondents per cluster. This provides a suitable balance of precision and economy.

Interviewer Instructions

At the block or segment level, the interviewer begins a travel pattern at the first DU (dwelling unit) from the northwest corner of the block and proceeds in a specified direction until the quotas have been filled.

The quotas call for approximately equal numbers of men and women with the exact proportion in each segment determined by the 1970 Census tract data. For women, the additional requirement is imposed that there be the proper proportion of employed and unemployed women in the location. Again, these quotas are based on the 1970 Census tract data. For men, the added requirement is that there be the proper proportion of men over and under 35 in the location.

These particular quotas have been established because past experience has shown that employed women and young men under 35 are the most difficult to find at home for interviewing.

Sampling Error

Past experience would suggest that, for most purposes, this sample of 1,500 could be considered as having about the same efficiency as a simple random sample of 1,000 cases.

Source: General Social Survey Codebook, "Appendix A: Sampling Design and Weighting," The National Opinion Research Center. http://webapp.icpsr.umich.edu/GSS.

BOX 5.2   **Cluster Sampling, continued**

Critical Thinking Questions

1. How many sampling stages does the General Social Survey sample entail?

2. What are the different sampling units?

3. What type of sampling within the cluster sampling in the early stages does the General Social Survey use?

4. Does the quota sampling prevent the generalizability of the General Social Survey to the U.S. population?

Critical Thinking Discussion

1. There are four sampling stages: Standard metropolitan statistical areas (SMSAs) were the first (they are identifiable from U.S. Bureau of Census information); block groups and enumeration districts were the second stage; actual blocks (as opposed to groupings of blocks or districts) were the third stage; and individuals were the last stage.

2. The different sampling units were SMSAs, blocks/enumeration districts, blocks, and individuals. Notice how each subsequent cluster is a smaller grouping than the previous one. That is the purpose of cluster sampling: to utilize smaller and smaller clusters of people until researchers get to a feasible cluster size from which to select their elements (here, individuals).

3. The GSS uses stratified sampling. The SMSAs were stratified by region, age, and race. The block groups/enumeration districts were stratified by race and income. The third stage, blocks, were proportionately stratified by size.

4. By definition, quota samples involve "eye-balling" to make sure that certain groups have appropriate representation in the sample as compared to the population. The only difference between quota sampling and proportionate stratified probability sampling is that the people who the researchers select for the sample were not obtained randomly. It is clear that the interviewers make a concerted effort to obtain accurate quotas, even going as far as making sure that the proportion of employed and nonemployed women in the sample mirror the proportion in the population according to the most recent U.S. Bureau of the Census information.

Consequently, because the General Social Survey utilizes a number of complex probability samples in the cluster process, many researchers consider the final sample to be a probability sample, even though the elements in very last stage do not have a truly equal probability of selection. This is largely because those who run the General Social Survey have done tests that show that their sample of 1,500 has the same accuracy of a slightly smaller sample (1,000 people) selected via simple random sampling. Therefore, by sampling more people with a combination of probability and nonprobability techniques, their sample is as accurate as a somewhat smaller sample that used only probability techniques.

In sum, the use of quota sampling at the very last stage does not threaten the generalizability of the General Social Survey, and researchers can, and do, treat it as a probability sample.

So, to some degree, the process of clustering is likely to create some homogeneity within the larger population. Careful, however. The goal of sampling is to make sure that you have as much representation in the population as possible, so don't confuse the point I just made about *homogeneity within* clusters to negate the importance of *heterogeneity across* clusters. In other words, within a cluster, sampling error can be reduced because people are likely to be similar within a cluster, but in order to make sure that representativeness is not compromised, researchers have to make sure that they have a variety *across* clusters. Therefore, researchers would have to make sure that they include many senior, many sophomore, many junior, and many freshmen dorms to get a representation of students from different collegiate years because the students *within* a dorm are likely to be from the same collegiate year. Essentially, I'm saying that the best way to avoid sampling error is to do a stratified sample within a cluster design.

Nonprobability Sampling

Not all research questions involve populations that can produce an accurate probability sample. For example, how can researchers obtain a random sample of homeless people? After all, it's not as if the homeless have addresses researchers can obtain or phone numbers that random digit dialing can call. Furthermore, the attendance of homeless people at shelters is spotty, and many homeless are distrustful of strangers. Consequently, there is almost no way to generate an accurate sampling frame from which to draw a random sample of homeless people. Or let's take another example. What if people wanted to study the networking support among prostitutes? Again, there is no way a researcher is able to compile an accurate sampling frame of prostitutes that would lead to a probability sample. The solution to this dilemma is to use a nonprobability sampling technique.

As the name *nonprobability sampling* may imply, in these samples people do *not* have an equal, or known, probability of selection. However, because of this, there are serious limitations to what researchers can do with their findings. Remember, the goal of much of research is to make accurate generalizations to a population based on a sample selected from that population. However, the key to being able to do this is to have a randomly selected sample. Therefore, if by definition, nonprobability samples do not involve equal chances of selection, the findings, also by definition, cannot be generalized to a broader population.

So why bother with this type of research? Well, just because it can't be generalized to a broad population doesn't mean that these samples don't produce useful information. For example, suppose a local social services agency wanted to reach out to prostitutes to offer them job training, hoping to lead these people to more legitimate means of earning a living. If you are a social worker in the area, you have a fairly good sense of who the prostitutes are. Likewise, you may be able to cooperate with the local police to obtain the names of some prostitutes. Once you identify some possible prostitutes to include in your sample, you may approach them about a pilot job-training project. If they agree, they are in your sample. If not, they are not. Those who agree will still provide information, based on their experiences in the job-training program, which will give those organizing the program ideas about operation, challenges, and outcomes that will inform a more vigorous application of that program in the community. In other words, the findings from this nonprobability sample would not be generalizability to the national population, or even the population of prostitutes in this specific community. However, it can still provide information that will be useful for perhaps a larger implementation of this project.

However, I do not mean to glamorize the usefulness of nonprobability samples. Although they are severely limited, they are not useless. Most people who use nonprobability samples have the research goal of exploration. This means that researchers who use nonprobability samples intend to test small pilot programs or find deeper qualitative understanding of a specific topic and do not intend to achieve more quantitative, generalizable data. The trick is to make sure that the researcher who uses these types of samples does not overstate the reliability of his or her findings. I will address the issue of generalizability in more detail when I discuss how to evaluate the sampling in published research. For now, I will focus on a discussion of four different types of nonprobability sampling: accidental, purposive, quota, and snowball.

■ Accidental Sampling

If you have ever watched a late-night television show host who has stopped people on the street to test their knowledge about current events, you have seen an accidental sample. **Accidental sampling,** sometimes also referred to as *haphazard* or *convenience sampling,* is just what the name implies: People are part of the study because they just "happen" to be in the right place at the right time (or wrong place and time, depending on their view). Hence, whether a person is part of a study is accidental or purely coincidental. Accidental samples are sometimes called convenience samples because whether a researcher includes someone in the study depends on if that researcher has convenient access to a person. An example of accidental sampling is when you hear news broadcasters or other television people asking viewers to "call in" their vote or views. Obviously, not all people in an area that that television station serves is watching the broadcast when the call goes out; likewise, only those with views on the extreme ends of the spectrum or very strong views about a topic are likely to be motivated enough to get off the couch, grab the phone, and dial in their vote. Hence, these types of samples are convenient but also haphazard.

Consequently, among the different nonprobability samples, accidental sampling is the weakest. The chances are very high that these types of samples will produce highly unrepresentative samples of the population that may, in turn, seriously misrepresent that population. Hence, researchers, even those doing nonprobability studies, frequently shy away from this sampling technique.

■ Purposive Sampling

Purposive samples are a little more methodologically sound than accidental samples because in this design, the researcher selects a sample based on her or his knowledge of the population and what type of sample would best suit her or his research goals. This is an especially useful technique if the population of interest is one that can be easily identified but not easily listed. For example, if I wanted to study powerful gang members in a community, I might *know* who these people are, but obtaining a list of them may not be feasible. Therefore, if I try to include all of the most powerful gang leaders, or at least the most visible ones, I may have a sufficient sample. Likewise, if I want to study the homeless, as I mentioned in the beginning of this section, I am not likely to have a complete list of the homeless in a particular city. However, if I speak with social workers or if I visit shelters, I will develop a sense of who the homeless are and I may be able to select specific individuals to study based on this observation.

Another example is a study by Dingy and Roux (2003, **AN 12164847)** of inner-strength among older Hispanic women who are chronically ill. Dingy and Roux studied five elderly Hispanic women who were recommended by their nurses. Among these five women, Dingy and Roux were able to identify various themes in how these women coped with a chronic illness. These themes involved a reliance on past experiences, support of family and friends, a sense of purpose, and a strong sense of spirituality. Obviously, if someone wants to study chronically ill patients who are racial minorities, one of the best places to begin would be with recommendations by the nurses who treat these patients. However, due to issues of time and funding, studying all or compiling a sampling frame of these individuals may not be desirable or feasible. Therefore, researchers such as Dingy and Roux use their expertise to select which chronically ill Hispanic patients among those identified by their nurses were appropriate for their study.

Even though purposive sampling involves some use of expertise, do not be fooled. This is still a nonprobability form of sampling; therefore, purposive samples are limited in terms of the types of conclusions researchers can draw. Purposive sampling is only appropriate when (1) researchers specifically want to limit their research to unique cases, (2) when researchers want to focus on specific cases for further in-depth examination, and (3) when population members are difficult to reach.

My earlier example of powerful gang leaders complies with the first appropriate scenario. In this instance, I was not interested in *all* gang members, but instead in a very specific type of gang member among a population that is hard to identify on its own. Dingy and Roux's (2003) research is an example of the second criteria. It also fulfills the third condition. Their sample size was only five women, because they wanted to conduct a small but intensive and in-depth study of this very specific subpopulation. Researchers who identify their sample as "case studies" also frequently are using this second criteria of justification for a purposive study. Last, my example of studying the homeless is an illustration of the third situation in which purposive sampling is appropriate. Clearly, I would not be able to mail a survey or conduct a survey over the phone to homeless individuals—and, perhaps more important, I would not be able to use addresses or telephone extensions as a means of identifying my population and selecting a sample. Therefore, in this instance, a purposive sample is completely appropriate.

Researchers using the purposive sampling technique, as I have said before (and I cannot stress enough), still need to be cautious about how they draw and word their research conclusions.

■ Quota Sampling

Quota sampling is an improvement over accidental sampling because, like probability sampling, quota sampling at least tries to create a sample that mirrors the wider study population. Hence, in most quota samples, the researcher tries to make sure that the proportion of each group of interest in the sample mirrors the same proportion that exists in the population. However, unlike probability sampling, quota sampling does not involve random selection; therefore, elements do not have a known, or equal, probability of selection.

For example, if I wanted to study college students and I wanted to make sure that the proportion of students from each academic year in my sample is the same as the proportion in the university, but I am not going to get a list of all the students, stratify that list by college year, and then do some type of probability sampling, I am probably going to do a quota sample. I may learn from the Registrar that 26 percent of the students are freshmen, 28 percent are sophomores, 23 percent are juniors, and 23 percent are seniors. If I want a sample size of 100, then I would select 26 freshmen, 28 sophomores, 23 juniors, and 23 seniors. To do this I might go to the campus quad and ask students walking by to complete a short survey. However, before I handed them the survey I would have to ask their academic year. If a particular student fit my criteria, I would hand him or her a survey; if a student fit the criteria of a category that is already filled, or has reached its *quota*, I would say thank you, inform that person that he or she is ineligible for the survey, and then *not* give that person a survey. I would continue this until I reached my desired quota, or sample size, for each specific category.

Let's take another example. Malmgren, Martin, and Nicola (1996) used a quota sample to study the health behaviors and the barriers to health care of 125 adults aged 62 and older who lived in public housing in Seattle, Washington. The researchers visited the 28 different public housing complexes and sampled elderly residents there until their sample mirrored the proportions of men and women in the total Seattle Housing Authority population according to an earlier survey documenting that amount. This is an example of a quota sample because these researchers based their sample sizes of men and women on the population representation for this specific group (elderly individuals living in public housing); however, the researchers admit that they continued sampling elderly residents until they reached their desired sample size. In other words, these researchers did not randomly decide who to contact; they asked individuals who were accessible to them and stopped when they achieved their desired sample size.

As I said previously, quota sampling is an improvement over accidental sampling; but after researchers fix their sample sizes of each category, they are likely to use an accidental technique to actually obtain their desired quota. Because of this, researchers are likely to approach only certain people. They may be more likely to approach those who appear happy or friendly, but not those who appear unhappy or mean or rushed. Consequently, bias is still likely. Another limitation of quota sampling is that in order to try to obtain a representative sample, researchers need to have information about the exact population in order to establish the right quotas. If researchers do not know what percentage of drug users in an area are addicted to heroin, crack, or cocaine, those researchers are not going to be able to select even a rudimentary quota sample.

■ Snowball Sampling

Let's suppose I want to do a study of teenagers who attend the types of parties known as "raves." Raves are dance parties that last all night and feature electronically synthesized music. These parties are commonly associated with drug use, and I want to study the actual prevalence of drugs at these parties. To do this, I don't want to go stand on a street corner at 3:00 a.m. and take an accidental sample of people who look like they might be looking for a drug party. Furthermore, although I might be able to identify some very specific individuals who frequently attend raves (based on conversations with the local police), because these parties are secret and change location nightly, it will be difficult to locate these parties or to find people who admit to attending them. Likewise, I am not likely to have accurate information about this population from which to draw a quota sample. So what would I do?

The answer is a **snowball sample.** This is a type of nonprobability sample in which a researcher identifies one member of a population, that person introduces the researcher to another member, those new members can introduce the researcher to additional people and, before you know it, the researcher's initial sample size of one has "snowballed" into a larger sample.

Hallstone's (2002, **AN 10226699**) research on marijuana users is an example of this. People are not born knowing how to use marijuana; they have to learn it. Becker (1953) first hypothesized about how people come to learn how to use marijuana for pleasure and found that there is a three-step process in which people learn how to (1) smoke the drug properly, (2) identify the signs that they are intoxicated from the drug, and (3) define that intoxication as pleasurable. Hallstone's research tested this widely accepted hypothesis more than 40 years after Becker first proposed it.

In order to identify people who used marijuana for pleasure, Becker (1953) relied on *chain-referral* (more technically called *snowball sampling*) to identify people he knew had easy access to marijuana and who fit his criteria for marijuana use. As a result, Hallstone (2002) obtained 15 people from college classes and 16 more people from user groups Hallstone knew in the wider community to participate in his study. Hallstone tentatively found that, with the exception of needing to be taught how to feel high (the second criteria in Becker's framework), Becker's framework for explaining how one learns to use marijuana still generally holds.

Note how I added the word *tentatively* and Hallstone implies the same restriction. Hallstone recognizes that without having a probability sample, he needs to be limited and cautious in the interpretations of his findings. However, this does not mean that Hallstone's research is not informative. It is technically impossible to obtain a complete sampling frame of all marijuana users in a community, because marijuana use is still deviant as well as illegal. Therefore, in order to be able to do *any* research on this group, researchers must relax some of the methodological standards, with the caveat that they need to be cautious about the manner in which they interpret their findings. Figure 5.5 summarizes the different sampling techniques.

Probability Samples

Simple Random: Uses a table of random numbers to select each element or sampling unit.

Systematic: Uses a table of random numbers to select the first element or sampling unit and then selects every *k*th element or unit based on a calculated sampling interval.

Stratified: Before sample selection, divides broad sample into subgroups called strata to improve the likelihood of adequate representation of these subgroups in the sample. Then uses either simple random or systematic sampling to select individual elements separately from the different strata.

Cluster: Addresses very large populations by randomly selecting sampling units of decreasing size until reaching sampling units from which manageable sampling frames of the desired elements can be obtained.

Nonprobability Samples

Accidental: Simply selects people who happen to be "in the right place at the right time."

Purposive: Selects elements who, based on the researchers' expertise, seem like they would be appropriate for study of the research topic; however, these people are not selected using a table of random numbers.

Quota: Like the stratified random sample, the researcher tries to make sure that the proportion of subgroups in the sample are the same as those in the population; however, unlike in a stratified sample, the elements are not selected using a table of random numbers.

Snowball: Sample elements are obtained by word-of-mouth or recommendation by other sample elements. As participants recommend other participants for the study, the sample size grows or snowballs.

Figure 5.5 Summary of the Different Sampling Techniques

By now your head may be spinning with all the possibilities for selecting samples. You probably wish to go back to the simpler times when you thought that standing out in a public place "randomly" selecting individuals was enough to do a methodologically sound study! In this section, I will present some brief considerations that will help you decide what sampling technique is appropriate for different situations.

Let's start broadly. The first consideration should be whether to do a probability or a nonprobability sample. In making this decision, the main criterion is what your research goal is. Do you want to be able to generalize your findings to a large population, or are you satisfied with describing what is going on in just your particular sample? If you want to make conclusions about college students at your university, you will want to do a probability sample. If you want to make conclusions about the college students in your sample, a nonprobability sample will work fine.

In addition to your research goal, you must consider whether you can obtain a comprehensive and complete sampling frame of your population. There are tricks to doing this. For example, perhaps you initially think that you want to study all people who live in a city. This sounds like a feasible endeavor, and in many cases it is. However, special subgroups such as homeless people, prison inmates, children, or college students may live in your selected city but may not be relevant for your research purposes or may be difficult to identify in a sampling frame. Therefore, in deciding between a probability and a nonprobability sample, it is perfectly acceptable to be more specific about the population in which you want to study.

For example, I may limit my study of people in the city to a study of noninstitutionalized adults who live in residential homes. This population definition excludes all of the cases I mentioned previously who may be difficult to identify and it allows me to use other sampling units (such as city blocks and homes/apartment buildings) to identify my elements (the individuals). The point is that if definitions are too broad, it may appear that a probability sample is not feasible, even though it may be appropriate for the research question at hand. Don't let this deter you. Simply specify your sample into a more manageable, identifiable subpopulation.

Last, in determining whether to do a probability or nonprobability sample, you want to consider your available resources. Probability samples can be more expensive and time consuming than nonprobability samples, depending on the population of interest. Even if you want to study only the students at your university, if your university has 20,000 students in its entire student body, that can be a daunting, expensive, and time-consuming sample to select. Luckily, if you have already decided that you can successfully address the second question and obtain a feasible sampling frame, you may be able to do a multistage cluster sample, which would allow you to break that large population into increasingly smaller units until you obtain a more manageable sampling frame of your desired elements, the college students. However, drawing many samples of sampling units can still be time intensive; therefore, your available resources remain a consideration when deciding to do a probability or nonprobability sample.

To summarize, when deciding which sampling technique to use, you should first decide whether you want to do a probability or a nonprobability sample. The following questions will help you with that decision:

1. To whom would you like to generalize your findings?
2. Can you obtain an accurate sampling frame of your sampling units or elements?
3. How much time and money are available to do the study?

After you decide to do a probability sample or a nonprobability sample, you want to consider your research question and resources in deciding among the specific sampling types within these two broad categories. Some questions that might help you determine the appropriate technique for your study are:

4. Are there any specific subgroups you want to assure are adequately represented in your sample?
5. What form is your sampling frame? Paper? Electronic?
6. How easily can you identify your elements?
7. What are the goals and uses of your research?
8. How much time and money do you have? (Some techniques within probability and nonprobability categories are more time and financially costly than others.)
9. Based on your skill and experience, what technique do you feel comfortable doing?

If you want to make sure specific subgroups are adequately represented in your sample, you might want to consider doing a stratified sample if you are doing a probability sample, or a quota sample if you are doing a nonprobability sample. If you can easily identify your elements, then simple random or systematic sampling may be appropriate for a probability sample or quota sampling may work for a nonprobability sampling. On the other hand, if your elements cannot easily be identified, then you don't want to do probability sampling at all and you might want to do the nonprobability snowball sampling technique. Likewise, if you are doing a probability sample and your sampling frame is on paper, you might want to do systematic sampling instead of simple random because it involves less use of the table of random numbers.

Again, these are just some questions for you to consider when deciding on your specific sampling technique. No one technique will always work in a specific instance; instead, all the questions have to be considered together to decide on the most suitable technique for any specific study. Even so, Figure 5.6 tries to illustrate one possible way of using these questions to select a sampling technique.

Sample Size

Earlier in the chapter when I discussed probability theory I said that the two main ways to reduce sampling error was to make the sample more homogenous (such as in a stratified sample) or to increase the sample size. If you are not interested in doing a stratified or quota sample, you may be tempted to just sample as many people as you possibly can in order to obtain a sample that is as large as possible. However, realistically, researchers cannot study huge samples because of the cost in terms of money and time. Also, what students usually think of as a "large" sample may not be large enough to adequately decrease sampling error.

So what do researchers do? The answer is not necessarily a simple one; however, selecting sample sizes are not too difficult once a researcher considers a couple of issues. Two general considerations researchers keep in mind when selecting sample sizes is how accurate the sample needs to be for their research goals and what the population's characteristics are.

	Probability Sampling	Nonprobability Sampling
General Selection		
Generalize findings to:	Population	Sample
Can you obtain an accurate sampling frame?	Yes	No
Amount of time	Moderate–A lot	A little–Moderate
Amount of money	Moderate–A lot	A little–Moderate
Specific Technique within Broad Category		
Do you want to study subgroups?	Yes: Stratified	Yes: Quota Purposive Snowball
	No: Simple random Systematic	No: Accidental Snowball
Can you easily identify elements?	Yes: Any probability technique	Yes: Accidental Purposive Quota
	No: Use a nonprobability technique	No: Snowball
Sampling frame form:	Electronic: Any probability technique Paper: Systematic	Does not matter
Time and money:	A lot: Simple random Stratified Little: Systematic	A lot: Quota Snowball Little: Purposive Accidental

Figure 5.6 Selecting a Sampling Technique

Researchers who are using their research for descriptive purposes may be able to use somewhat smaller sample sizes than those who plan on doing complex statistical analyses between many variables at once. For example, if someone wants to do a descriptive study of the national population, a person is likely to be able to use a sample of 1,000 to 1,500 people—much like the Gallup Poll that I discussed earlier. However, if a researcher wants to do more sophisticated statistical analyses of the national population, a sample size of 2,500 is preferred (Sudman, 1976).

Also, researchers can study populations that are more homogenous with smaller sample sizes than they can more diverse populations. If you think about it, the stratified sampling technique addresses this observation. The stratified sampling technique allows researchers to draw smaller subsamples (which, when combined, will equal the original total sample size) from a population because the original population is broken into groups based on a specific characteristic (such as race, income, or gender), which makes the members of that group more homogenous on at least one trait—whatever the stratification variable was. In other words, if I stratify a sample based on gender, I know that all of the elements who are in one subgroup (for example, women) have that subgroup's trait in common (here, their gender); therefore, each subgroup is more homogenous based on each value of the strata (here, gender). Hence, I can get away with using my original sample size (say 200) and selecting 100 men and 100 women with more confidence than I would by just selecting 200 people from the original, unstratified, sampling frame.

There are more concrete ways of deciding on sample sizes as well, once a researcher has considered the theoretical issues I just mentioned. The most basic is simply called the *rule-of-thumb method*. This method is actually based on historical observations of previously drawn samples that showed that larger populations can be adequately studied with smaller sampling ratios than smaller populations because as population size grows, the benefits in terms of accuracy for larger samples decreases.

Consequently, for populations that are roughly 1,000 elements or less, a researcher needs a larger sampling ratio of about 30 percent. For example, if I want to study people's satisfaction with a local congressman in a small town of 800 people, I would need to sample about 240 people in order to get an accurate representation of community members. However, for larger populations, those between 1,000 and 10,000 people, I need a sampling ratio of only about 10 percent. So if I wanted to do my study in a larger town that has 8,000 people, I'd need to study 800 people. Now before I go on, you may be thinking that a sample of 800 is a lot more people than a sample of 240, and you're right. However, remember that the relevant consideration is the percent of the total population, not the raw number of the corresponding sample size. Therefore, it is important to note that for smaller samples, I need to sample a larger *percent* of the population (30 percent) than I do for larger samples (10 percent). The percentage of the total population necessary for an accurate sample decreases as the sample size continues to increase. Therefore, for samples that are large (about 150,000 or more), researchers need sample sizes that are 1 percent of the total population size, and for very large samples (over 10 million), researchers need sample sizes less than 1 percent, about one-quarter of a percent (.25 percent).

An approach that is a little more complicated, but one that allows researchers to better control the degree of statistical accuracy, is to use a mathematical formula based on the calculation for a confidence interval. This works for random samples only. You have probably seen polls where the results are expressed something like this: "The President of the United States currently has an approval rating of 56 percent plus/minus 4 percent." If the result is written (as opposed to being broadcast on the news, for example), there is likely to be a footnote that remarks that this statistic has a 95 percent accuracy (or some similar accuracy) percent. This is a confidence interval, which I discussed earlier in this chapter. Expressed another way, the statistic could read: "We are 95 percent sure that the president's approval rating is between 52 and 60 percent." The 52 to 60 percent is the confidence interval that simply is the statistic (56 percent) minus the deviation (4 percent) and plus the deviation (4%). For data expressed as a percent, this statistic is calculated with the following formula:

$$ci = P_s + Z\sqrt{(P)(1-P)/N}$$

where: ci = the confidence interval you are trying to establish
P_s = the observed percent expressed as a sample probability
Z = a standardized Z score that reflects a standardized measure of sampling error (in this case)
P = the probability of any one value of a variable
N = the sample size

Through algebraic manipulation, this formula can be altered to decide what sample size is necessary to achieve a particular range (confidence interval) for a specific confidence level. I am not interested in the sample probability in the equation because I am only trying to see what sample size is necessary for a specific level of confidence and range, therefore that part of the equation is eliminated. Consequently, after the elimination of the mean and the algebraic manipulation, the formula becomes:

$$n = \frac{Z^2(P)(1-P)}{ci^2}$$

This allows researchers to decide what sample size is necessary for a specific level of precision. For example, suppose I am studying whether community members prefer a community-oriented form of policing. I want to be 95 percent sure of my findings and I want my range of error to be only 3 percent. The Z score is a standardized score that is based on the amount of error in a study, and its opposite refers to my confidence level. Therefore, what you need to know for the calculation of the sample size is (1) the two confidence levels that are the standard thresholds for statistical significance are 95 percent and 99 percent, (2) the Z score that corresponds to these confidence levels are constant, and (3) a Z score for a 95 percent confidence level is ± 1.96 and the Z score for a 99 percent confidence level is ± 2.58. Therefore, if I want to be 95 percent sure of my findings, the corresponding Z score is 1.95, and if I want to be 99 percent sure of my findings, the corresponding Z score is 2.58. For my example, I want to be 95% sure, therefore the Z score I am going to use is 1.96.

The P is the probability of being any one value of a variable. Suppose for my measure of community-oriented policing preference, I simply have my answer choices be support, neutral, and do not support. There are three choices and the probability of selecting any one choice, all else being equal, is 33 percent, or .33. I already said that I want my range to be plus/minus 3 percent, so that is my confidence interval. Hence, I can substitute the numbers into the equation to read:

$$n = \frac{1.96^2(.33)(1-33)}{(.03)} = \frac{3.84(.33)(.67)}{.0009} = 943.36$$

Hence, based on my calculations to be 95 percent sure of my findings and to have a range of plus/minus 3 percentage points, I need a final sample size of about 943 people. This is a little more specific way of calculating sample size than the rule-of-thumb method and is appropriate when researchers have very specific requirements for the degree of accuracy of their findings. However, when researchers do not have highly specific accuracy requirements, the rule-of-thumb method works just as well.

In conclusion, sample size relies on (1) the degree of accuracy a researcher wants, (2) the level of heterogeneity or diversity in the population, and (3) the number of different variables examined. Generally, for very specific levels of accuracy, very diverse population, and many different variables, larger samples are necessary. However, simply selecting as large a sample as possible is not necessarily beneficial or efficient. Much of research is descriptive or focuses on very specific populations (which tend to be more homogenous due to the specific specification of the population), therefore smaller sample sizes are possible.

Evaluating Written Research: Samples

So far in this chapter I have discussed how to select different types of samples and presented some considerations for deciding which sample is appropriate for different research goals. How a researcher selects his or her sample determines the degree of generalizability of that sample and therefore how relevant a particular study may be to your individual needs. How a sample is selected is also important for evaluating the appropriateness of the statistics a researcher chooses to do and how the researcher decides to interpret and apply those statistics. Much hypothesis testing relies on the assumption that the data used comes from a probability sample. Doing *inferential statistics* (which is what hypothesis testing is technically called) on data gathered using a nonprobability sampling technique needs to be cautiously interpreted, at best, and may simply be inappropriate at worst. Here are some questions to guide you.

1. ***Does the research goal lend itself to generalization? Is the broad sampling method appropriate for the research goal?***

   Just doing a probability sample does not necessarily ensure that the sample is high quality. To be able to evaluate the quality of the samples we read in research, first and foremost, we need to know what the research goal is. If the goal is to study a population that is hard to identify or to study an issue we know little about, then a probability sample may not be necessary. However, if the goal of the research is to make conclusions about a broader population (for example, college students, voters, or employees), in general, then a probability sample is very important.

2. ***Does the researcher provide information regarding the sample?***

   If a researcher *does* intend to generalize to a wider population, a reader cannot evaluate the quality of the sample if that reader does not know the specific population that that sample is supposed to represent. In other words, if we cannot identify the population, we cannot evaluate whether that sample adequately represents that population; therefore, be suspect of any conclusions we or a researcher makes. In order to evaluate this, the researcher needs to describe the relevant demographics of the sample at the very least (and the reader can decide whether those demographics fit the wider population) and, ideally, the demographics of the population as well. To be fair, researchers are unlikely to describe the demographics of the population; therefore, this is an added "bonus" if they do. However, no matter what, the demographics of the sample should be described.

3. ***Is the exact sampling method (e.g., simple random, purposive) specified? Remember, it is not sufficient for a researcher to simply state that a sample was selected "randomly."***

   As I've hopefully made clear in the beginning of this chapter, simply saying that a sample was "randomly selected" does not mean that it actually *was* randomly selected. Researchers need to specify what type of sampling method they used so that readers of articles can make their own conclusions about the appropriateness of the choice and the generalizability of the results. This applies to both probability and nonprobability samples. In probability samples, readers need to know, for example, whether a simple random sample or a stratified sample was used, because those techniques have important implications to deciding whether sample sizes are adequate. Since stratified random sampling breaks a population into smaller homogenous (at least with respect to the stratification variable(s)) subgroups, smaller sample sizes with stratified samples may be more acceptable than with simple random samples.

Likewise, doing a nonprobability quota sample may be more accurate than doing a nonprobability accidental sample, depending on the research question and goals. If a researcher shows that a nonprobability quota sample is at least as diverse as the true population for the main variables of interest, readers may have more faith (although not as much as if it were a probability sample) in those findings than they would if other types of nonprobability sampling were used.

4. Is the sample size sufficient, given the research goals, the degree of accuracy the researcher desires, and the nature of the population studied? Given the nature of the research, is the sample size sufficient?

The sample size is an important piece of information. Have the researchers described how they decided on a specific sample size? Have the researchers used a reasonable number of participants, given their research goals, the degree of accuracy they intend, and the nature of their population? A fourth question to consider within this wider issue of sample size is whether the sample size is sufficient, given the nature of the research. Research designs that require a lot of cooperation on the part of respondents or that would be costly (as in some experiments) might require smaller sample sizes. However, this last issue should be considered only in light of the other three issues mentioned; it is not a criterion that in and of itself negates the other three.

Furthermore, if the study examines different subgroups of people (such as different races, drug users with different drugs of choice, criminals with different ages), are there enough people in the different subcategories to report on them separately, if the researcher does so? For example, let's say that I am doing a study of 50 drug users and I want to make conclusions about different subgroups of users based on their drug of choice. If I have 30 heroin users, 15 cocaine users, and 5 crack users in my sample, clearly the number of crack users is too small to make any real conclusions about their behavior.

Because of the risk of small subgroups, you may see that some researchers have "over-sampled" for specific individuals. This is frequently done, for example, when people study race. Since African Americans make up roughly 12 percent of the population (U.S. Bureau of the Census, 2001) and mailed surveys have low response rates in general (a point I will address more in Chapter 7), some researchers may report that they "oversampled" African Americans to make sure that they would have adequate representation in the final sample. This is completely appropriate, and essentially it is a form of disproportionate stratified sampling because the researcher is selecting people based on race (the stratification variable) and is altering the proportion of a specific group in the sample so that it does *not* represent the actual proportion in the population. However, if researchers use this form of sampling, it is important for them to weight their findings, much like I discussed how to do in this chapter.

5. If the researcher uses a probability sample, does he or she generalize the findings to the appropriate population? If the researcher uses a nonprobability sample, does he or she refrain from generalizing to a wider population?

If the researcher makes generalizations about a population based on a sample, the reader needs to evaluate (1) whether any generalizations are appropriate and (2) whether

BOX 5.3   **Evaluating Research: Samples**

Below are excepts from the sampling and results sections of four studies. Apply the evaluation guidelines to evaluating the quality of the samples. In each of the cases, as before, I've presented the evaluation questions first and then my comments, so students can either read my comments directly or first practice the evaluation on their own and see how their responses match with mine.

Study 1

In this study, Pena and Sidanius (2002) examine the relationship between patriotism and feelings of group dominance among Whites and Latino Americans in Los Angeles. More specifically, they examine whether national pride leads to ethnocentrism whereby a strong sense of national pride by the dominant group (such as Whites) correlates with a strong sense of ethnocentrism for White values, and how this relationship holds for subordinate groups such as Latino Americans.

The data came from the Los Angeles County Social Survey (LACSS), conducted every year by the Institute for Social Science Research (ISSR) at the University of California, Los Angeles (UCLA). The survey assessed approximately 250 variables, including standard demographics and general attitudes regarding ethnicity, political ideology, job satisfaction, income distribution, and ethnic dispersal.

The 1999 LACSS total data set consisted of 791 respondents. We selected members of the two largest ethnic groups (Whites: $n = 290$; U.S. Latinos: $n = 265$). From these two groups, we then selected only those who were U.S. citizens. This left a total of 405 respondents (Whites: $n = 275$; Latinos: $n = 130$) for final analysis.

. . . The LACSS was drawn as a probability sample of adult residents of Los Angeles County. The computer-assisted telephone interviewing unit of ISSR conducted the survey, which used a random digit-dial telephone technique directed at households. To fully capture the views and opinions of Los Angeles County's large Latino population, the questionnaire was translated into Spanish for use with mono-lingual Spanish speakers and those who preferred to be interviewed in Spanish rather than English.

. . . Thus, results from this random sample of Los Angeles County adults confirmed the asymmetrical relationship between patriotism and social dominance orientation. . . . However, this asymmetrical relationship appears to be restricted to the subdimension of group dominance or the desire to actively subordinate inferior groups. . . . Although patriotism was positively related to affective preference for the racial in-group among Whites, the opposite was found among ethnic minorities (Sidanius & Petrocik, 2001). In other words, among all groups, U.S. patriotism was associated with the preference for White Americans over other U.S. ethnic groups (Blacks, Latinos, and Asian Americans).

. . . The present results suggest that U.S. patriotism means different things to members of different ethnic groups. U.S. patriotism shows a slight tendency to be associated with increased commitment to group dominance among Whites, but it has exactly the opposite implications for Latinos. For members of the Latino American community, greater patriotic commitment to the United States appears to be even more strongly associated with the rejection of group-based social dominance. However . . . we assert that these implied differences are tied to the hierarchical power relationships among the groups and the history of ethnic and racial domination within the nation.

Source: Yesilernis Pena and Jim Sidanius, "U.S. Patriotism and Ideologies of Group Dominance: A Tale of Asymmetry," *Journal of Social Psychology, 142* (6) (December 2002): 782. *(AN 8559160).* Reprinted with permission of the Helen Dwight Reid Foundation. Published by Heldref Publications, 1319 18th St., NW, Washington, DC 20036-1802. Copyright © 2002.

Critical Thinking Questions for Studies 1–4

1. Does the research goal lend itself to generalization? Is the broad sampling method appropriate for the research goal?

BOX 5.3   **Evaluating Research: Samples, continued**

2. Does the researcher provide information regarding the study population? The sample?

3. Is the exact sampling method (e.g., simple random, purposive) specified? Remember, it is not sufficient for a researcher to simply state that a sample was selected "randomly."

4. Is the sample size sufficient, given the research goals, the degree of accuracy the researcher desires, and the nature of the population studied? Given the nature of the research, is the sample size is sufficient?

5. If the researcher uses a probability sample, does he or she generalize the findings to the appropriate population? If the researcher uses a nonprobability sample, does he or she refrain from generalizing to a wider population?

6. Overall, is the sampling appropriate?

Critical Thinking Discussion

1. The general goal is description—to see how national pride is associated with feelings of ethnocentrism for two different racial groups: Whites and Latino Americans. Hence, this goal does lend itself to generalization. One cannot study all Whites and Latino Americans; however, the researcher hopes to make some conclusions about these broad populations based on a sample of them.

2. There is no information about the study population; however, since the researcher is very clear that the population comes from Los Angeles County, California, it is possible for the reader to obtain that information from Census information. Therefore, although it certainly would be easier if the researchers included this information, since they at least provide information (the location of the study) that would enable the reader to find the data, the omission of information is not a serious problem. Other than race, there is no description of the sample.

3. Here, the researchers do not specify what type of random sampling they used. However, random digit dialing is a common form of simple random sampling, and therefore readers can infer that simple random sampling was the specific technique these researchers used.

4. To answer this question, readers would need to know the population sizes of the two groups in Los Angeles. According to 2000 U.S. Bureau of the Census, Los Angeles County had approximately 3 million White people and 4 million Latino people. Consequently, applying a rule of thumb, the researchers would need to sample between 1/4 of 1 percent and 1 percent of the population. This means they would need to sample about 150,000 of each group.

However, remember that for national studies of the entire U.S. population (which is about 281.4 million people according to the 2000 U.S. Bureau of the Census), researchers usually sample about 1,500 people for a descriptive study (about .00005 percent); therefore, the sample size of 405 respondents (about .006 percent of the total population) is proportionally fine.

5. Yes, the researchers appropriately generalize. They state that their findings are from "Los Angeles County," which is who they can truly generalize their findings.

6. Overall, their sampling is very appropriate. In fact, with the exception of limited sample description, it is well done.

Study 2

Certainly the problems revolving around juvenile delinquency are not new; however, the value we, as a society, place on childhood and the concern about adult criminality has led to much research about what causes juvenile delinquency. The hope is that by identifying facts that lead to juvenile delinquency, we can better prevent this nonconforming behavior among children and, in the long run, prevent adult criminality as well. Preski

BOX 5.3 **Evaluating Research: Samples, continued**

and Shelton (2001) are among the many researchers who have tried to disentangle the causes of juvenile delinquency, more specifically by focusing on the link between childhood maltreatment and juvenile behavior.

> . . . A random sample of detained and committed juveniles ($n = 355$) was collected over a 4-month period in the summer of 1996. All females in the system at that time were included due to their small number ($n = 60$). Sixty percent of youth sampled were in committed programs, the remaining youth were in detention centers.
>
> . . . Similar to other juvenile offender populations, this sample can be profiled as African American (57%), adolescent (82%), and male (81%). These distributions led to the decision to control for age, sex, and gender in the exploration of variables contributing to the model. All episodes of criminal behavior over the child's lifetime were utilized as the unit of analysis. A logistic regression analysis was completed to answer the question, "Which individual, family, and community characteristics predict child maltreatment in a juvenile delinquent population?"
>
> . . . Variables remaining in the model allude to the issue of neglect. It can be imagined that children with a mother struggling with her own mental illness might not receive a lot of support or attention. For this sample, given that so many in the household are substance users, little appropriate support or attention can be received from these other sources. Additionally, the youth's own behaviors alienate him or her from school and other prosocial environments, activities, and individuals. Clearly, maltreatment begets poor outcomes. Victims become perpetrators in a vicious cycle that remains difficult to disrupt.

Critical Thinking Discussion

1. Here, the researchers are doing explanatory research. They want to see whether childhood maltreatment leads to (causes) juvenile delinquency. Explanatory research essentially requires probability sampling, especially if the researcher's goals is to explain such a broad topic as juvenile delinquency.

2. The researcher claims that the sample population is similar to the juvenile offender population; however, there is no description of the juvenile population presented in the article. The article states that this research is secondary data analysis of another study by one of the coauthors (which means that it is using data previously gathered for a different purpose) and provides a citation for this study (not shown in the excerpt); however, when a reader goes to the bibliography to find the study for further examination, the reader learns that it is an unpublished report. This means that an average reader cannot find the particulars of the original study without contacting the author or who received the report.

   Therefore, in essence, the reader has to accept the authors' word that their sample is representative, and, from an evaluation perspective, this is unacceptable. With regard to the sample description, gender and race are presented in the excerpt and other characteristics, such as forms of maltreatment, are presented in the full text.

3. The researchers claim that a random sample was used, but they do not specify what type of random sample. Since the original research is essentially unavailable, once again there is incomplete information to evaluate the sampling technique.

4. Again, because of the other issues, there is no way to evaluate this.

5. The researchers provide some description of their sample, but we cannot be sure whether

BOX 5.3   **Evaluating Research: Samples, continued**

we can generalize it to a wider population of juveniles because we do not have the information necessary to evaluate whether this sample accurately represents that wider population.

6. This sample may be appropriate; it may not be. We cannot evaluate this effectively based on the information provided and available. Therefore, we have to err on the side of caution and assume that the technique is not fully appropriate.

Study 3

A current controversy in education is mandated state testing for student achievement. One of the common concerns many express about standardized achievement tests is that teachers will simply "teach to the test" instead of making sure that their students have a more well-rounded educational experience. Vogler (2002) examines whether the publication of assessment results of state-mandated performance assessments influences how teachers teach. Below is an excerpt from his sample description and results.

On June 18, 1993, the Governor of Massachusetts signed the Massachusetts Educational Reform Act into law. The law addressed and mandated fundamental changes in the state's public education system. Among the areas affected by the legislation were school finance, school demonstration, teacher tenure and certification, and curriculum and assessment.

. . . New curriculum frameworks and learning standards were created in the academic areas of English language arts, mathematics, science, history and social science, and world languages. A high-stakes, state-mandated performance assessment called the Massachusetts Comprehensive Assessment System (MCAS) was designed to evaluate progress in meeting the state's new learning standards in the curriculum frameworks.

Beginning in 1998, every student in grades 4, 8, and 10 was required to take the MCAS examination. In November, 1998, the Massachusetts Department of Education reported the results of the initial MCAS examination to the public.

Narrowing the number of possible survey participant teachers down to only those teachers teaching at least one section of 10th grade English, mathematics, and science in a strictly academic high school still left thousands of potential participant teachers statewide. The researcher chose to further define the scope of this study by using geographic location. The Massachusetts Department of Education divides the state into six geographic regions: Greater Boston region; Northeast region; Central Massachusetts region; Southeast region; Greater Springfield region; and the Northwest region. The researcher chose to sample 10th grade English, mathematics, and science teachers teaching in a strictly academic high school located within the Northeast region of Massachusetts.

Four hundred thirteen (413) surveys were distributed to a stratified random sample of teachers who were teaching at least one section of 10th grade English, mathematics, and science in a strictly academic public high school located within the Northeast region of Massachusetts. Two hundred fifty-seven (257) surveys or 62% of the surveys were returned.

Table 2 is a comparison of the survey response sample and the Massachusetts teacher population in terms of teaching assignment and gender. [*Note:* Table is not shown but can be found on the Research Navigator website.]

As can be seen in Table 1, the percentage of 10th grade English, mathematics, and science teachers who responded to the survey is similar to the percent of English, mathematics, and science teachers who received the survey. The sample is a representative distribution of all 10th grade English, mathematics, and science teachers teaching in a strictly academic public high school within the Northeast region of Massachusetts. [*Note:* Table is not shown but can be found on the Research Navigator website.]

BOX 5.3 Evaluating Research: Samples, continued

The results of this study seem to indicate that the use of state-mandated student performance assessments and the highstakes attached to this type of testing program contributed to changes in teachers' instructional practices. The changes in teachers' instructional practices have included increases in the use of instructional practices deemed by educational researchers as the "best practices."

The implication for practice includes a possible expansion of the high-stakes testing program to involve the use of performance assessments in more subjects and in more than just the 4th, 8th, and 10th grades.

Source: Kenneth E. Volger, "The Impact of High-Stakes, State-Mandated Student Performance Assessment on Teachers' Instructional Practices," *Education, 123* (1) (Fall 2002): 39. **(AN 7717142).** Reprinted by permission.

Critical Thinking Discussion

1. This goal is description; therefore, it does lend itself to generalization. A probability sample would be the best choice and that is what the researcher uses.

2. Yes. The researcher states that he presents this information for both the population and the sample in Table 2. Table 2 is not specifically shown in this selection; however, students can easily find it on Research Navigator using the article search number.

3. Yes, the researcher says he used stratified random sampling; however, the stratification variable is unclear.

4. A person reading the research can probably find the number of teachers in the Northeast region of Massachusetts by contacting the Massachusetts Department of Education; however, without this information, it is difficult to assess whether the sample size is appropriate.

5. The relevant population for this study is 10th grade English, mathematics, and science teach-ers teaching in a strictly academic high school located within the Northeast region of Massachusetts. Even though the researcher talks about "teachers' instructional practices," he does not further qualify this. Since the researcher establishes in Table 1 (again, not shown) that this sample is representative of the broader population of teachers in Massachusetts, this broader generalization is acceptable.

6. Overall, the sampling is appropriate and the researcher correctly generalizes to the wider population.

Study 4

Although HIV and AIDS do not receive the public attention that they did in the 1980s when the disease first hit the national radar, the issue of HIV and AIDS remains an important one for many specific subgroups of both the American and global society. Simoni and Cooperman (2000) studied the experiences of HIV positive women in New York City.

Women are expected to account for more than half of the new HIV infections worldwide by the year 2000 (UNAIDS, 1998). In the USA, African-American and Latino women combined represent less than one-fourth of all women in the country yet account for more than three-fourths (76%) of all AIDS cases among women. . . .

. . . We recruited a sample of 373 women living with HIV/AIDS through convenience sampling at outpatient clinics and scatter site housing in New York City. We trained a diverse group of women, including members of the HIV community (see Simoni et al., 1999) to conduct face-to-face interviews with participants, who were paid $10 for their time. The sample comprised Hispanics (42%), African-Americans (44%) and women of other or mixed ethnic backgrounds (14%). Mean age was 39.61 years (SD = 7.22). In terms of current legal marital status, respondents indicated they were single—never legally married (52%), legally married

BOX 5.3   **Evaluating Research: Samples, continued**

(12%), separated (14%), divorced (11%) and widowed (11%). Fifty-three percent reported a steady male or female sexual partner, and 74% classified themselves as exclusively heterosexual. Forty-nine percent had at least a high school diploma/GED, and 7% were college graduates (mean years of education = 11.24). Only 15% were currently employed either full- or part-time. Most were poor, with 85% reporting less than $1,000 in monthly household income.

. . . Survey data from 373 HIV-positive women in New York City indicated significant stressors as well as notable strengths. For example, 59% had been sexually abused and 69% physically abused. In the past 30 days, 9% had injected drugs. However, the women also reported considerable strengths, including high levels of spirituality, mastery and HIV-related social support. Exploratory bivariate analyses indicated these resources were generally associated with less depressive symptomatology as well as better physical wellbeing . . . [Furthermore], social support was related to less depressive symptomatology as well as better physical wellbeing scores.

. . . The findings of the current study are subject to some methodological limitations. First, the sample was nonrandomly selected, with the majority of the women interviewed connected with services. Second, because all data were self-reported, their validity is subject to a social desirability bias. Third, the indicators of psychological adaptation were somewhat cursory. . . . [Third], the lack of a control group of HIV-negative women prevents us from determining whether the findings are unique to HIV-positive women or whether they are applicable to this demographic group in general.

. . . Despite these limitations, the results have important implications for HIV prevention and women living with HIV with respect to applications in counseling interventions. . . . Counseling that focuses on the trauma and works to build self-esteem may be more effective. . . . Data also suggest spirituality should be ex-

plored as part of a strategy of identifying and bolstering cultural strengths. Spiritual resources appear to be important psychologically and are readily and easily accessible—at no cost! Outreach by the religious and spiritual community could provide a valuable service to the HIV-positive population.

Source: J. M. Simoni and N. Cooperman, "Stressors and Strengths among Women Living with HIV/AIDS in New York City," *AIDS Care, 12* (3) (June 2000): 291. **(AN 3326751).** Reprinted by permission of Taylor & Francis Ltd., www.tandf.co.uk/journals.

Critical Thinking Discussion

1. The goals of this research are description and exploration. Even though a probability study is appropriate for description, because the researchers are studying a population for which it may be difficult to obtain a sampling frame (both because of the stigma of HIV that may prevent people from admitting they carry the virus as well as observation that many clinics may not make client lists available), a nonprobability sampling technique is acceptable.

2. Given the exploratory nature of the research, concrete description of the HIV/AIDS population may be difficult to obtain. However, the authors do present some population statistics in terms of gender and race, and they provide a detailed description of the sample.

3. The specific sampling technique is convenience sampling. As the authors imply here, this is a somewhat limited form of sampling; however, given the nature of the research question (exploration) and the difficulty in obtaining a sample from this population, this choice is valid.

4. Yes.

5. The researchers note the problems with their sample and, for the most part, they are cautious about their generalizations. However, in the last paragraph where they discuss some of their

BOX 5.3   Evaluating Research: Samples, continued

findings, they are lax in further noting the restrictions of generalizability and discuss the findings as if they apply to HIV/AIDS women in general. It may be that the authors felt that their previous statement of limitations adequately addressed the cautions and that anyone reading the rest of the study would know to keep these limitations in mind, regardless of how the findings are worded.

6. Overall, this method is very appropriate for the research topic. The researchers accurately acknowledge the limitations of their approach and interpret their findings accordingly.

Other Sources

U.S. Census Bureau: State and County QuickFacts. Data derived from Population Estimates, 2000 Census of Population and Housing, 1990 Census of Population and Housing, Small Area Income and Poverty Estimates, County Business Patterns, 1997 Economic Census, Minority- and Women-Owned Business, Building Permits, Consolidated Federal Funds Report, 1997 Census of Governments.

---

the researcher generalized to the appropriate population. Researchers who use nonprobability samples should not generalize their findings to wider populations. Because the people *not* in their sample did not have an equal probability of selection, we cannot be sure that the people who were selected and studied actually are representative of the wider population—even if they match the population on some key variables such as gender and race.

Furthermore, researchers may get lax and, even with a probability sample, generalize beyond their methodological capabilities. This is frequently done when, for example, people study college students. A researcher may use a simple random sample to select students from a particular college for a study, but then will use those specific students to generalize to "college students"—a much broader population (because it now includes students at other universities). Technically, unless that researcher establishes that the population of students at the particular college used in the study mirrors the population of college students in general, the only real population the research can generalize to is the population from that particular college. However, in reality, researchers frequently overstate their generalizing capabilities when using probability samples. To be precise, this is inaccurate; however, it is much less inaccurate than generalizing to "college students" as a broad group when one has done a nonprobability sample.

To summarize, the key issues one has to keep in mind when evaluating samples are:

1. Does the research goal lend itself to generalization? Is the broad sampling method appropriate for the research goal?
2. Does the researcher provide information regarding the sample?
3. Is the exact sampling method (e.g., simple random, purposive) specified? Remember, it is not sufficient for a researcher to simply state that a sample was selected "randomly."
4. Is the sample size sufficient, given the research goals, the degree of accuracy the researcher desires, and the nature of the population studied? Given the nature of the research, is the sample size is sufficient?

5. If the researcher uses a probability sample, does he or she generalize the findings to the appropriate population? If the researcher uses a nonprobability sample, does he or she refrain from generalizing to a wider population?
6. Overall, is the sampling appropriate?

Remember, these questions are just guidelines. In deciding how much weight to give a particular study for your interests, this is just one section that presents some considerations of many that readers like you need to later consider as a whole.

Key Terms

Accidental sampling (208)
Central limit theorem (185)
Cluster sample (202)
Confidence intervals (176)
Confidence levels (176)
Disproportionate stratified sample (197)
Elements (173)
Periodicity (195)
Population (173)

Population parameter (176)
Probability theory (186)
Proportionate stratified sample (197)
Purposive sampling (208)
Quota sampling (209)
Sampling error (176)
Sampling frame (174)
Sampling interval (194)
Sampling units (175)

Simple random sample (188)
Snowball sampling (210)
Standard deviation (187)
Standard error (181)
Statistic (175)
Stratification variable (196)
Stratified random sample (196)
Study population (174)
Systematic random sample (194)

Review Questions and Exercises

1. *Apply the sampling terms discussed to the material in the following articles.*

   a. Gijsberts, Merove, and Nieuwbeerta, Paul. (2000, December). Class cleavages in party preferences in the new democracies in Eastern Europe: A comparison with Western democracies. European Societies, 2 (4), 397. 34 pp. DOI: 10.1080/14616690020014343. (AN 3998502)

   b. Torkington, Claire, Lymbery, Mark, Willward, Andy, Murfin, Maureen, and Richell, Barbara. (2003, April). Shared practice learning: Social work and district nurse Students learning together. Social Work Education, 22 (2), 165. 11 pp. (AN 9330736)

   c. Nusbaumer, Michael R., and Reiling, Denise M. (2003, February). Where problems and policy intersect: Servers, problem encounters and targeted policy. Drugs: Education, Prevention & Policy, 10 (1), 21. 9 pp. (AN 9257378)

2. *Identify and evaluate the sampling techniques in the following articles.*

   a. Miller, Matthew, Hemenway, David, and Wechsler, Henry. (2002, September). Guns and gun threats at college. Journal of American College Health, 51 (2), 57. 9 pp. (AN 7530971)

   b. Schwartz, Chaya, and Armony-Sivan, Rinat. (2001, May). Students' attitudes to the inclusion of people with disabilities in the community. Disability & Society, 16 (3), 403. 11 pp. DOI: 10.1080/09687590120045978. (AN 4422653)

c. Chan, Kara. (2000, March). Critical thinking: Hong Kong children's understanding of television advertising. Journal of Marketing Communications, 6 (1), 37. 16 pp. DOI: 10. 1080/135272600345543. (AN 3960651)

d. Summers, Mike, Kruger, Colin, Childs, Ann, and Mant, Jenny. (2000, November). Primary school teachers' understanding of environmental issues: An interview study. Environmental Education Research, 6 (4), 293. 20 pp. DOI: 10. 1080/13504620050174561. (AN 3861532)

3. Evaluate the sampling design in the following articles.

a. Lee, Jo Ann, Havighurst, Lauren C., and Rassel, Gary. (2004, Spring). Factors related to court references to performance appraisal fairness and validity. Public Personnel Management, 33 (1), 61. 17 pp. (AN 12546970)

b. Hacker, Kenneth L., and Steiner, Robertt (2002, October-December). The digital divide for Hispanic Americans. Howard Journal of Communications, 13 (4), 267. 17 pp. (AN 8961948)

c. Niehaus, L., Myburgh, C. P. H., and Poggenpoel, M., (2003, Winter). Predictors of school and nursing service managers' coping ability. Education, 124 (2), 347. 17 pp. (AN 11979714)

Experimental Research

What do you think is the best approach for police to use when responding to a domestic violence call? Should they arrest the person they see being abused? Should they arrest the abuser? Well, what if both people were being abusive? What if both were abusive but one was abusive in self-defense? How would police know this when deciding about arrest? Should police simply separate the two individuals and wait for them to calm down? Responding to domestic violence calls are very tricky for police. They need to balance the desire to protect themselves from harm, they need to protect the victim (whoever that may be, although statistics suggest it is the wife) from current harm, and they need to protect the victim from future harm. Furthermore, police, social workers, and advocacy groups differ as to what response to domestic violence calls—arrest, mediation, or separation—is the most appropriate and beneficial to preventing future acts of abuse. In an attempt to resolve this controversy, the Police Foundation and the Minneapolis Police Department conducted a field experiment to test the three most common responses (arrest, separation, medication) to domestic violence calls (Sherman & Berk, 1984a).

For this experiment, police in Minneapolis agreed to either arrest, separate, or mediate (advise) when responding to domestic violence calls, depending on which response was written on a card that police randomly drew from an envelope that they took with them to the scene. In other words, the actions the officers would take depended on which of the three responses was written on the card they selected from the envelope. If the officers arrived at a scene, selected a card from the envelope that read "arrest," they would arrest the suspected abuser. If they selected a card that said "separate," they would remove the suspect from the scene for eight hours. The research goal was to see which of the three responses led to the lowest rate of recidivism (meaning which response was associated with a lower likelihood of getting another domestic violence call) in the following six months. In order to gather this informa-

In Sherman and Berk's study (1984), the Police Foundation and the Minneapolis Police Department conducted a field experiment to test the effectiveness of the three most common responses to domestic violence calls on minimizing future acts of domestic violence.

tion, researchers interviewed the victims every two weeks for the six-month period (Sherman & Berk 1984a).

Researchers found that arrest led to the lowest recidivism rates. Although 37 percent of the subjects who had mediation as their response and 33 percent of those who were separated from the scene for eight hours had committed another domestic violence offense during the six-month observation period, only 19 percent of those who were arrested at the scene recidivated (Sherman & Berk, 1984a). It appeared that arrest was the most useful response for handling domestic violence calls.

As the name of the study, the Minneapolis Domestic Violence *Experiment*, implies, this was a social experiment. Experiments are frequently used in both the traditional and social sciences; and the findings of this experiment are widely used in criminal justice practice—and the most widely debated. I will discuss the strengths and weaknesses of this study later in the chapter; however, for now I simply want to use it as a means of introducing the discussion of the first method of observation—experiments.

Appropriate Research Questions

People use the term *experiment* in their everyday language to mean seeing the difference in an outcome or behavior after they modify part of a situation. We talk about "experimenting" with lipstick shades, "experimenting" with recipes, "experimenting" with different game plays, and "experimenting" with different parenting tactics. In a sense, all of these are commonsense experiments. If a parent tries to prevent a child from touching an electrical outlet, that parent may say in a firm voice "NO!" Yet, sure enough, the child turns a sweet, angelic gaze toward the parent and immediately reaches for the electrical outlet again. This time, the parent may experiment with a different approach and, in addition to a loud "NO!" the parent may lightly swat the child's hand. The parent's swat of the child's hand is the experimental stimulus because it is the modification of the previous situation, which simply involved a stern "NO!" Now the parent waits to see if the child stays away from the outlet (a change in behavior) or tries to reach for the outlet again (the original behavior).

However, as I discussed in Chapter 1, the information social scientists gain from common sense is not as vigorous as the information they gain from well-designed scientific research. Even if a child stays away from the electrical outlet after his hand is lightly swatted, does that mean the swat "caused" him to realize that electrical outlets are dangerous, or did he just tire of the let's-touch-the-thing-with-the-holes game? What people think of as "experimenting" in their everyday lives is not the same as a scientific experiment, although we certainly can follow the same general logic.

The logic of these everyday nonscientific experiments is to manipulate a situation (cause) and see if it changes the outcome of a behavior (effect). This is the same logic researchers use in scientific experiments. In fact, scientific experiments (which I will now refer to simply as experiments) are the best research designs for establishing causality because they are the easiest to control the three criteria of causality: (1) establishing an association, (2) establishing a temporal order, and (3) ruling out rival causal factors. Hence, among the four purposes of research (exploration, description, explanation, and evaluation), experiments are particularly well suited for explanatory and evaluation research.

Hence, it is probably no surprise that the types of research questions that lead to hypotheses that are suitable for experiments are those that require some conscious manipulation of the independent variable (the cause in a causal relationship). For example, many parents, teachers, and criminal justice professionals are concerned that the types of music teenagers listen to will negatively affect their behavior. Essentially this is a hypothesis: Music, such as rap and heavy metal, will lead to aggressive behavior. This is also a topic in which researchers can manipulate or control the independent variable—the type of music someone hears. Gowensmith and Bloom (1997) studied 137 students in a psychology class where one group (the experimental group) listened to heavy metal music and another listened to country music (the control group). In this type of experiment, researchers can easily manipulate the independent variable: The researchers control which type of music the subjects hear and then see whether there are behavioral differences between the two groups after they listen to their respective musical selections.

Other general topics in which researchers can control or manipulate the independent variable are the following: Are juvenile delinquents who participate in a boot camp program less likely to break the law in a six-month span than juvenile delinquents who did not participate in boot camps? Are people who watch commercials featuring healthy food more likely to make healthy eating choices than those who watch commercials featuring junk food? Does a job-training program lead to increased employment among welfare recipients? Does a teacher's lecture style affect children's learning in primary school? Does police response to domestic violence influence the likelihood of future domestic violent episodes?

On the other hand, experiments are ill suited to study topics in which researchers cannot control or manipulate the independent variable. For example, experiments are *not* good design choices for questions such as, Do men do better in research methods courses than women? Does a college degree increase wages? Do college students favor abortion? Are girls from abusive homes more likely to be sexually permissive? Researchers cannot decide a person's gender, they cannot decide who will and who will not go to college, nor can they (or should they) decide who will grow up in an abusive home. Hence, these topics are inappropriate for experimental research.

Researchers may also decide to do experiments when they have relatively few variables of interest and when their concepts are well defined and easily observable. For example, in Gowensmith and Bloom's (1997) research, they were interested only in musical type. That is one independent variable. Furthermore, few teenagers (if any) would confuse country music with heavy metal music. Hence, the two types of music are easily defined and observed.

Finally, experiments are useful when researchers are studying relatively small groups. Researchers interested in the effects of music on teenage aggression have actually narrowed their focus to teenagers, as opposed to middle-aged adults and the elderly. This makes age less of an issue in research (and, incidentally one less variable to include in the design) and, even though teenagers are a huge group, in terms of research, they are a more focused group than people in general (which would encompass all ages). Hence, they are a group from which researchers can select a relatively small sample to study.

To summarize, experiments are an appropriate mode of observation when:

1. The hypothesis involves an independent (treatment) variable that a researcher can easily manipulate;
2. The researcher is interested in studying relatively few variables;
3. The independent and dependent variables have clearly defined and directly observable definitions; and
4. The researcher is able to study a relatively small group.

Remember, these are just loose guidelines, and some research questions can (and should) be studied in more than one way. In the following sections of the chapter I will present various forms of the experimental design. Before I do that, however, I will introduce the basic language of experimental research.

■ Language of Experimental Research

In the previous section, I already started to introduce some common terms researchers use in experimental research. These terms were *treatment*, *experimental group*, and *control group*. Other terms students need to understand are *dependent variable*, *pretest*, *posttest*, and *random assignment*. Let's discuss each of these, using an example for illustration.

Ventis, Higbee, and Murdock (2001) tested techniques that would help people overcome their fear of spiders. Here is a brief excerpt from their research:

> The participants were 40 undergraduate students (2 men and 38 women) from introductory psychology classes . . . [who] . . . replied to a mass testing questionnaire asking for ratings of a number of fears.
>
> . . . All participants were tested individually at pre- and posttest sessions with the [behavioral approach test] BAT and the paper-and-pencil measures. After pre-BAT scores were completed, participants were matched roughly on their pre-BAT scores . . . [each] was then randomly assigned to one of the three groups.
>
> . . . The 14 humor-desensitization participants . . . received a rationale, including mention of case study successes, the positive findings on systematic desensitization, and the therapeutic possibilities of either physical relief of anxiety associated with laughter or reduction of fear attributable to seeing a previously feared stimulus situation from a more humorous cognitive perspective. Participants next rated nonhumorous hierarchy items for fear on the 0 to 100 SUD scale, as the desensitization group had. They were then given a task to try to begin to elicit a humorous perspective on spiders. . . . [They] were then asked to list as many uses as they could think of in 5 minutes for an ominously realistic rubber tarantula (about 8 inches in diameter) that squeaked when squeezed. They

were then given a homework assignment of completing incomplete statements about spiders in a humorous way (e.g., "I would rather _____ than _____ a spider") in an exercise derived from Goodman (1983). The hierarchy presentation was then begun in which two thirds of the scenes were humorous versions of the scenes the systematic-desensitization group received and one third were nonhumorous. This was done to create an element of surprise as to whether the item was to be humorous or not. These participants also rated each item from 1 to 10 on the same humor scale immediately after it was completed. . . .

. . . *No-treatment controls.* After all participants had completed the *pretests* and the pre-BAT results were determined, the control-group participants were contacted by telephone. After being greeted and reminded of the study, they were given the following instruction: "For the group to which you are assigned, we will call you in approximately one month to assess any changes in fear, as a function of the behavioral exposure you have experienced and the ensuing passage of time. Your results will be of great importance to our study, and we look forward to seeing you again soon. Thank you for your participation thus far." The contact person then answered any questions that the participants had and assured them that their participation would meet their class research participation requirement in full. . . . Because this constituted a no-treatment control, the participants were given no activities or homework. . . . They were called again after 3½ weeks [sic], and a posttesting session was scheduled for the 5th week after their original testing. They were retested during the same interval when experimental participants were posttested, but on separate days to minimize contact between the groups.

As I alluded to earlier, the **experimental group** is the group that experiences the situation or stimulus that the researcher modified. What the researchers are manipulating is the **treatment,** which usually is a value of the independent variable. Here, the treatment is the humor desensitizing experience. Participants either participate in humor desensitizing or they do not. Those who do are part of the experimental group, since the researchers are interested in seeing if this particular tactic reduces people's fear of spiders. The **control group,** on the other hand, does not receive the stimulus and therefore serves as a comparison group to the treatment group. In Ventis, Higbee, and Murdock's (2001) study, the control group receives no treatment or spider counseling (if you will) and receives only the two paper-and-pencil behavior approach tests (BAT).

You may be thinking that the control group is not very important—after all, those in the control group miss all the excitement of the spider counseling. However, this isn't the case for a number of reasons. Remember, previously I said that experiments are good at establishing causality, and in Chapter 3 I said that the hardest criterion of causality to fulfill was the criterion of nonspuriousness, or making sure that any observed change was due to the treatment and not some outside factor. In many experiments, the control group is equal to the treatment group on all main variables of interest *except* the treatment. Therefore, researchers can attribute any changes in the experimental group as opposed to the control group to the treatment, thereby fulfilling the causality criteria of nonspuriousness.

Also, members of the control group frequently don't know that they are "missing" the treatment because they usually don't know that they *are* the control group, nor do they really know the purpose of the experiment (so they don't know they are missing out on anything). Wait a minute, you may be saying! You likely remember that in Chapter 2 I said that to ethically obtain informed consent, participants need to know any detail of the study that may influence their decision to participate. This is true; and what I'm saying now does not necessarily contradict that. Experimental researchers frequently use some level of deception in experiments. Researchers often tell participants *some* of the research goal, but not necessarily the hypothesis or a full description of a goal.

In Ventis, Higbee, and Murdock's (2001) study, the researchers told the members of the control group that they would be contacted in a month's time to see if there was any change in their level of fear. For all these people know, the researchers were studying whether people could overcome a fear of spiders on their own. They did not necessarily know that they were "missing out" on any treatment. Deception is important because it allows the researcher to control the conditions of an experiment. People who participate in experiments (or any study for that matter) already illustrate that they are helpful, and giving them too much information about a study may lead them to want to "help" the researcher "prove" what they think the researcher's hypothesis is. This will lead to the rival causal factor of reactivity, or the Hawthorne effect (which I discussed in Chapter 3). So, some level of deception is usually acceptable so long as participants know the *general* purpose of the study so they can decide whether or not to participate.

If the treatment, the humor desensitization, is the independent variable, then the dependent variable would be the outcome, or the behavior the researchers expect to change as a result of the experiment. In Ventis, Higbee and Murdock's (2001) study, the dependent variable is the fear of spiders. They intend to measure the fear of spiders among both the experimental and control groups. However, to show a change in the dependent variable, researchers usually need to measure the dependent variable before and after their treatment.

The first measure of the dependent variable is the pretest because it happens before (or "pre") experimental treatment. The **pretest** serves to establish the initial measure of the dependent variable. The **posttest** is a second measure of the dependent variable that occurs after (or "post") the experimental treatment. Both the experimental and control groups can receive the pre- and posttests. This is exactly what Ventis, Higbee, and Murdock (2001) did. They gave the BAT test to all participants initially. The researchers then gave a second BAT to the experimental group who received the humor therapy after they completed the program and to the control group 5 weeks after their pretest.

So far, I've given examples of what researchers mean by *treatment, dependent variable* (although you already encountered this in Chapter 3), *experimental group, control group, pretest,* and *posttest.* Only one other issue, random assignment, needs discussion before I move to an examination of the various types of experiments. I discussed what researchers mean by "random" in Chapter 5. If you recall, researchers do random samples to better ensure that their sample accurately represents the population. If people have an equal probability of selection into a sample, researchers are more confident that the people selected for a sample were not selected with any systematic bias and that the researcher can calculate the odds that any one person will be selected to be in a sample. To put this another way, researchers want to make sure that there is no real difference between their samples and the study population.

In experiments, researchers frequently use random assignment for similar purposes. Researchers want to do their best to make sure that there is no systematic bias that prevents the experimental and control groups from being similar. Essentially, like samples and populations, valid comparisons between treatment and control groups depend on the two groups being fundamentally alike. Ventis, Higbee, and Murdock (2001) state that they "randomly assigned" the people in their sample to one of three groups—the humor desensitization group, the systematic desensitization group (which I did not discuss in the excerpt but you can read on Research Navigator), and the control group.

That being said, this does not mean that random assignment will automatically lead to equal numbers of men to women, Whites to minorities, freshmen to sophomores, or values of any other group, in the experimental and control groups. The goal is for the groups to generally be alike. If everyone has an equal chance for being in either the experimental or control group, then generally, the two groups will be almost identical, even if the number of people in each group is slightly unequal.

The process for random assignment can be as simple or as complex as the researcher desires. It can be as simple as writing everyone's name on a piece of paper (provided the total sample size is small), putting those pieces in a hat, shaking the hat to shuffle the pieces, and then drawing them out individually. If I do this with a sample of 30 people, I may say that the first 15 I select are in the control group and the rest are in the experimental group (or vice versa). Or I might do a process similar to simple random sampling. I could assign a number to each person and use a table of random numbers to decide who is in each group (e.g., the first 15 numbers drawn from a table of random numbers are in the experimental group).

Some of you may be wondering why, if I am so interested in making sure that the two groups are alike, don't I just select one person to be in an experimental group and find someone with similar characteristics to be in the control group? For example, if Ventis, Higbee, and Murdock were truly interested in making sure that there were no real differences between the three groups, couldn't they just group three people with similar characteristics and then put one in each group? Researchers call this process *matching*. In theory, it is a wonderful technique; however, in reality, it poses some serious challenges.

How many characteristics do people have to have in common to be similar enough for a study's purposes? Could the students in Ventis, Higbee, and Murdock's study be matched on gender, race, and college year? What about the level of fear of spiders? What about whether a person is a full- or part-time student? What about this person's grades in the course? If we consider all of these, the researchers would have to find enough groups of three students who are the *same* for *six* different characteristics. That can be quite a challenge, especially if the university in which researchers are doing the study is relatively small, with only 30 to 40 students in a class.

Well, you might be saying, then just focus on matching students on characteristics *relevant* to the topic. Good idea—but how do researchers know what characteristics are "relevant"? If there are many, how do the researchers decide which are the most relevant and therefore should be used for the matching criteria? The answer is that researchers frequently don't know the response to these questions, and that is why matching is better in theory than in practice. However, this does not mean to say that researchers can't match on some variables and then randomly assign matched individuals to a treatment or control group. Some researchers do do this. In fact, this is what Ventis, Higbee, and Murdock. (2001) did. They loosely matched students based on BAT scores and then randomly assigned these students to one of the three groups. Figure 6.1 illustrates some examples of random selection, random assignment, and matching.

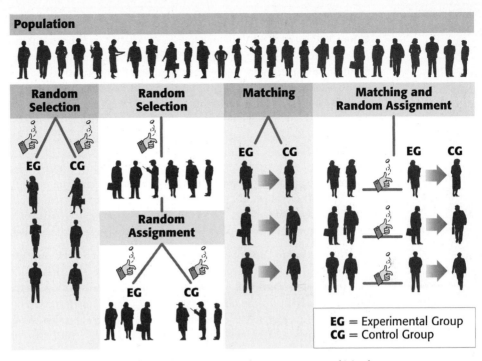

Figure 6.1 An Illustration of Random Selection, Random Assignment, and Matching

The point I am trying to make is that matching alone frequently is not enough for researchers to be confident that the control and experimental groups are equivalent. As we will see, though, there are some types of experiments for which matching is the only viable option, even with all its potential challenges. The issue with this research, as with sampling that does not involve random selection, is for researchers to be careful about how they interpret their findings.

Types of Experimental Design

There are three general types of experimental designs: true experiments, pre-experiments, and quasi-experiments. In this section I will focus on all three general categories and the specific types of experiments within each category. I will also discuss a common variation in these three designs called the factorial design.

■ True Experiments

True experiments have three general characteristics. First, and foremost, they involve random assignment. Random assignment is the main feature that distinguishes true experiments from the other two experimental types. Second, true experiments also have an experimental and a control group. Third, they commonly involve pre- and posttests. The three types of true experiments I will present are the classic experiment, the posttest-only control group design, and the Solomon four-group design.

Classic experiment

When most people think of an experiment, they generally are thinking of a classic experiment. Classic experiments involve all three of the characteristics of true experiments: randomization, experimental/control groups, and pre-/posttests.

Researchers frequently use notation to summarize an experimental design process, and the notation for a classic experiment is:

$$E \quad O_1 \quad X \quad O_2$$
$$E \quad O_1 \quad\quad O_2$$

where E = equivalence (established through random assignment)

O = observation

X = the treatment

1, 2 = time points (hence O_1 is the pretest because it appears before the treatment)

Notice that in the notation for a classic experiment, the only difference between the experimental and control group is the omission of the X, which denotes a treatment. Ventis, Higbee, and Murdock's (2001) study is an example of a classic experiment. They established equivalence by the random assignment of participants to one of three groups (humor desensitization, systematic desensitization, and control). Even though the excerpt I presented in this chapter didn't discuss the systematic desensitization program, their experimental design can be summarized as this:

$$E_H \quad O_1 \quad X_1 \quad O_2$$
$$E_S \quad O_1 \quad X_2 \quad O_2$$
$$E_C \quad O_1 \quad\quad O_2$$

where E = equivalence (established through random assignment)

H, S, and C subscripts = humor and systematic desensitization groups, respectively, and control

O_1 = the BAT pretest

X_1 = the systematic desensitization treatment

X_2 = the humor desensitization treatment

O_2 = the BAT posttest

Ventis, Higbee, and Murdock had two hypotheses. The first was that the humor desensitization treatment would reduce fear of spiders more than the systematic desensitization treatment. The second was that both the systematic and humor desensitization treatments would reduce fear of spiders more than no treatment at all. How could they test these hypotheses with an experiment? Well, the pre- and posttest establish any change in fear of spiders. For the first hypothesis to be supported, the change, or difference, between the pre- and posttest (O_1 and O_2) would have to be greater for the humor desensitization group (E_H) than the systematic desensitization group (E_S). According to Ventis, Higbee, and Murdock's data, this was not the case; therefore, the first hypothesis was not supported. For the second hypothesis to be supported, the change between the pre- and posttest for the two treatment groups (E_S and E_H) had to be greater than the pre- and posttest change for the control group (E_C). In this study, the data *did* support the second hypothesis; consequently, Ventis, Higbee, and Murdock found that both of the treatments were more effective in reducing people's fear of spiders than was doing nothing at all.

An important benefit of the classic experimental design is that the pretest allows researchers to see how equivalent the different experimental and control groups really are. This serves as a validity check. Another benefit is by having the control group do a pretest and posttest, researchers can estimate whether the rival causal factor of a testing effect is present. Without a control group taking both the pre- and posttest, researchers cannot be sure that any change in the dependent variable (such as fear of spiders) in the treatment group is not because the pretest sensitized them to the study issue, and therefore led to the change regardless of any influence of the treatment. If there is no pretest effect, the differences in the dependent variable (such as fear of spiders) should not be statistically different between the pre- and posttests for the control group. Consequently, if the pre- and posttest scores for the control group are statistically similar, but the posttest scores for the two groups are statistically different, because there are no real differences between the two groups themselves (due to random assignment), researchers can attribute any observed differences in the posttests to be a result of the treatment. This, too, improves the validity of a study.

Classic experiments also address some other validity issues. For example, in Chapter 3 I discussed the rival causal factor known as a *history effect*. To refresh your memory, a history effect occurs when an outside event (meaning not related to the study itself) occurs that may produce a change in the dependent variable that is independent, or is unrelated to, the treatment itself. However, if this is the case, once again because participants are randomly assigned to either the treatment or control groups and are therefore believed to be equal, any outside event should affect *both* the treatment and control groups. Therefore, the degree to which a treatment affects the dependent variable can be estimated based on the degree of change we notice in the control group (because if an outside event will affect participants' behaviors, it will affect the control group's pre- and posttest scores) relative to the change that occurs in the treatment group.

As you can probably tell, part of the reason classic experiments are so popular in science is because they are one of the best research designs for establishing causality. Remember, the three criteria for causality are (1) association, (2) time order relationship where the independent variable precedes the dependent variable in time, and (3) ruling out other rival causal factors. The criterion of association is easy to establish in classic experiments, like it is with many other research designs. If the change from the pretest to posttest is greater for the experimental group than for the control group, researchers have established an association. Classic experiments also address the time order relationship because researchers clearly administer the treatment (independent variable) to the experimental group before they do the posttest (which contains a measure of the dependent variable in it).

The third criterion, ruling out rival causal factors, is usually the most difficult of the criteria to satisfy. In fact, no one research design will fully satisfy this standard at all times, and the classic experiment is no exception. However, among the available research designs, it *is* the most effective approach to rival causal factors, even if it is not 100 percent foolproof. As I discussed, the classic experiment helps minimize the rival causal factors of selection bias (by random assignment), Hawthorne effect (after all, both groups are being observed and, thanks to randomization, there is no reason to believe that one group will react differently than another to being observed), and history effect.

Furthermore, even though pretests are necessary to establish whether the dependent variable changed as a result of a treatment, any time researchers do a pretest, they run the risk of a pretest effect clouding their findings. In a classic experiment, researchers can detect whether a pretest effect is present. However, with experiments come some other concerns. Although history may not be a problem, local history, which is when an outside event affects only one or some of the groups under study, is still a possibility. This is true also for diffusion of treatment if the control group learns of the treatment and tries to copy it.

The point remains: No research design is perfect or suitable in all conditions. However, among the various design options, the classic experiment is one of the best designs for establishing a causal relationship. A second type of true experiment is a *posttest-only control group design,* and, as its name implies, it differs from a classic experiment because it does not have a pretest.

Posttest-only control group design

When researchers are especially concerned that a pretest would bias their results, perhaps because the time between a pretest and posttest would be short or because the nature of the pretest itself may sensitize the subjects to the research goal, the researcher may decide to omit the pretest from the design and conduct a posttest-only control group design instead of a classic experiment. Other than the omission of the pretest, the posttest-only control group design has all the other elements of a true experiment. Researchers randomly assign participants to an experimental or control group; the experimental group experiences a treatment and both the experimental and control groups have a posttest.

This type of design was used by Dennis (2003, **AN 10282214**) in his study of how online versus tutorial groups helped problem-based learning among physical therapy students. Dennis hypothesized that students with computer-mediated problem-based learning would have different levels of academic achievement than those with more traditional face-to-face tutorial learning. The following is an except from Dennis's research:

> A post-test only control group design was used to investigate the effects of learning conditions on learning outcomes and processes. The experimental learning condition was defined as computer-mediated problem-based learning (CMPBL) and the control condition was traditional problem based learning [TPBL] in [face-to-face] FTF groups. The results for three dependent variables are reported: learning outcomes (measured by performance on course examination); time-on-task (the self-reported time spent in and out of class on learning activities related to the course); and generation of LIs (recorded by each group during the first tutorial. . . .
>
> . . . The sample of 34 was drawn from 54 second-year students. The sample size was a trade-off between availability of facilitators and ideal group size. Three faculty members were available as facilitators and the recommended group size for PBL is five to six students, with a maximum of seven (Barrows, 1992). Thus 17 students were randomly assigned to each of the learning conditions (17 to CMPBL and 17 to TPBL) with proportional representation of the remote campus students in each of the learning conditions. The three facilitators were each assigned a CMPBL and a TPBL group, and one worked exclusively with the Albany campus students. The principal investigator (PI) acted as "expert" for all students and as facilitator for the non-study groups. . . .

. . . The hypothesis that the CMPBL group would have a different level of academic achievement was not supported.

For this cohort of students, and this approach to PBL, computer-mediated communication resulted in significantly longer time-on-task for the same learning outcomes as the FTF group. The CMPBL group spent approximately 23% more time-on-task than the TPBL groups. It would have been appropriate had the finding been associated with superior outcomes. However, evidence that online students expended more time for outcomes similar to the FTF group is a matter for concern.

The notation for posttest only control group designs is:

$$
\begin{array}{ccc}
E & X & O \\
E & & O
\end{array}
$$

The symbols mean that same as they do for classic experiments, but notice that there is only one observation point (O), and since it appears after the treatment (X), it is the posttest. In Dennis's (2003) study, he randomly assigned the students to the treatment and control groups. His independent variable was the learning style. He considered the treatment group to be the students who experienced the newer form of learning (the computer-mediated problem-based learning), and the control group were those students who had the traditional problem-based learning in face-to-face groups. Dennis's dependent variables were the students' scores on examinations, the amount of time they spent in class on learning activities, and the amount of time they spent out of class on learning activities. According to Dennis, the students who had the newer form of computer-mediated learning, contrary to his hypothesis, did not perform any better on examinations than did the students in the control group who had the more traditional form of learning, although they did spend more time on their learning than the control group.

However, let's pretend that Dennis *did* notice a difference. Let's say that Dennis found that the students in his experimental group *did* do better on their exams than the students in the control group. Does this mean that the computer-mediated learning *caused* the students in the treatment group to do better? That certainly would have been the implication; however, this conclusion may be incorrect. Even though Dennis showed that his experimental and control groups were equivalent in terms of female/male ratio, GRE scores, Myers-Brigg scores for feeling/thinking and sensing/intuition, and knowledge of the computer and computer operating skills, without a pretest to establish base knowledge of material in this class beforehand, he would not be able to show concrete change in the dependent variable. If the students in the experimental group did do better, it may have been because they knew more about the topic prior to the class than did the control-group students, or it may be because of some other rival causal factor. Without a pretest, it is difficult to assess the amount a dependent variable changes and it is more difficult to rule out rival causal factors. Figure 6.2 shows the steps for doing an experiment.

Therefore, when researchers find differences in the posttest scores of treatment and control groups in a posttest-only control group design, they cannot really estimate how much of a change in the dependent variable the treatment caused, nor can they be sure that the differences in posttest scores really are due to the treatment the experimental

1. Choose a research topic that is appropriate for experimental research.

2. Review the literature to discover what is already known about that topic, where studies have produced conflicting findings, or where there are gaps/omissions in the research.

3. Formulate a hypothesis that can be tested with a laboratory or natural experiment (i.e., the researcher has some control over the manipulation of the independent variable).

4. Develop valid measures of the independent (treatment) and dependent variables.

5. Decide how to implement the treatment. Who will administer the treatment? What exactly will that person(s) do? What is needed to implement the treatment (e.g., props, space, etc.)?

6. Select an experimental design that can test your hypothesis, use your defined measures, and meet your practical restrictions (e.g., money, time, etc.).

7. Conduct a pretest of your experimental design (if relevant to the type of experiment you selected). Modify it as necessary based on administering it to a very small (it doesn't have to be random) sample of people whose only purpose on the study is to test the pretest (essentially to "pretest the pretest").

8. Obtain test subjects.

9. If using more than one group, decide how to assign subjects to different groups (random assignment? matching?).

10. Explain the experiment to the participants.

11. If using a pretest, administer it. Make sure to gather information that will illustrate whether the two groups are similar on relevant key variables.

12. Administer the treatment to the experimental group and monitor the conditions of all the groups involved (including the control group) if possible.

13. Administer the posttest or gather data for the posttest.

14. Debrief the subjects by informing them of the true purpose of the experiment, asking them if they have any questions or concerns, and thanking them for their participation. (This step is especially important if the researcher used deception at any point in the experiment.)

15. Analyze the data by making comparisons between the various groups.

Figure 6.2 Steps for Doing Experiments

group received. However, they can *infer* that the treatment led to the difference, but this is an inference, which is less grounded than a conclusion with a classic experiment. Nonetheless, as I stated previously, posttest-only control group designs are beneficial when the researcher is concerned about a pretest effect. If the researcher can establish that the experimental and control groups are similar on many factors, then any difference in posttest *is likely* to be from the treatment.

Solomon four-group design

The Solomon four-group design tries to address many of the strengths and weaknesses of both the classic experiment and the posttest-only control group design by combining them. As a result, the notation for a Solomon four-group design is:

$$
\begin{array}{llll}
E & O_1 & X & O_2 \\
E & O_1 & & O_2 \\
E & & X & O_2 \\
E & & & O_2
\end{array}
$$

Solomon four-group designs provide a method that more fully addresses a research question than either the classical or posttest-only control group designs do on their own. For example Probst (2003) used a Solomon four-group design to examine the effects of organizational restructuring on employees. Probst conducted her study in an area where five state government agencies that provide health and human services were being restructured and merged. The merger was going to affect some employees in these agencies more than others. Probst conducted a stratified random sample of employees from these agencies. Half of the people Probst selected for her sample were going to be affected by the reorganization ($n = 250$); half were not. The reorganization was her treatment. Her outcome of interest included measures of employee satisfaction, organizational satisfaction, perceived job security, physical health, and psychological health (among others).

Because Probst couldn't necessarily randomly assign people to either "be affected by the reorganization" or "not be affected by the reorganization," she randomly decided whether people were going to get the pretest or not. For those getting the pretest, she surveyed them immediately prior to them getting the announcement of the workplace reorganization. Everyone participated in the posttest that Probst conducted six months after the announcement of the merger. Due to variation in response rate and elimination of participants for other issues, Probst's final Solomon four-group design consisted of 64 people pretested and affected by the reorganization, 62 people pretested but not affected by the organization, 83 people affected by the reorganization but not pretested, and 104 people who were unaffected by the reorganization but also pretested (Probst, 2003).

Why go through all this trouble? Well, mainly because by testing the effect of the treatment in a variety of ways (here with a pretest and without), the generalizability of the findings increases, as does the finding validity. Furthermore, with Solomon four-group designs, researchers can assess the effects of any pretesting while still getting a premeasure of the dependent variable that they otherwise would not have in a posttest-only control group design. Last, researchers can test for interactions of effects. For sake of clarity, let me repeat the Solomon four-group design notation with the addition of some arrows showing the different possible comparisons:

$$
\begin{array}{lllll}
\text{Group 1:} & E & O_1 & X & O_2 \\
\text{Group 2:} & E & O_1 & & O_2 \\
\text{Group 3:} & E & & X & O_2 \\
\text{Group 4:} & E & & & O_2
\end{array}
$$

If organizational restructuring affects, say, job satisfaction, in Probst's study, she can expect four different findings:

1. *Comparison 1:* In the first experimental group (Group 1), the pretest score for job satisfaction should be different from the posttest scores for job satisfaction in this same group.
2. *Comparison 2:* The scores for job satisfaction should be different (and if one argues that restructuring will lower job satisfaction, then lower) in Group 1 than in Group 2.
3. *Comparison 3:* The Group 3 posttest scores should be different from the Group 2 scores. Again, if we are arguing that restructuring leads to less job satisfaction, then the posttest scores in Group 3 should be less than in Group 2.
4. *Comparison 4:* The Group 3 posttest should show less job satisfaction than the Group 4 posttest.

The third and fourth comparisons rule out any interaction between the testing and stimulus effects by systematically weeding out the effect of the pretest. But if your head is spinning by now, you're not alone. Solomon four-group designs are frequently expensive and difficult to implement, not to mention difficult to interpret. This discourages many from selecting this experimental design for their research purposes. Nevertheless, if you understand it and have the time, money, and expertise to conduct it, many researchers feel that it is the ultimate experiment to control for both internal and external threats to validity.

■ Pre-Experimental Designs

Designs that lack random assignment or that are shortcuts to gather information are frequently called *pre-experimental* designs. There are generally three types of pre-experimental designs: the one-shot case study (also known as the one-group ex-post facto design), the one-group pretest-posttest design (also known as the one-group before-after design), and the static group comparison (also known as the two-group ex-post facto design). For the most part, many researchers avoid using these design types except for the most exploratory research. Therefore, I am not presenting these designs as examples of good research options. Instead, I am presenting them more as examples of what *not* to do and why.

One-shot case study

This design has only one group, one treatment, and no pretest (only a posttest). An example of this type of study would be if I had children play violent video games for two hours and then measured the level of aggression in their non–video-playing behavior. Clearly, there is no way to conclude that the violent video games caused or led to any exhibited aggressive behavior because I do not know how aggressive these children were prior to their video game playing (there was no pretest), or how aggressive other children of this age are who do not play violent video games (there is no comparison group). Do not confuse the one-shot case study design with the posttest-only control group design. The notation for the one-shot case study design is:

$$X \quad O$$

But notice that this is different from the posttest-only control group design because in this instance, the group receiving the treatment is the *only* group. Therefore, the notation is only half of that for the posttest-only control group design. Furthermore, notice that the

E, present in the notation for true experiments, is now absent. It is absent because in the one-shot case study design, there is only one group; therefore, equivalence does not need to be established. However, even so, none of the pre-experimental designs has involved random assignment, therefore none of the notations will have an E present.

As you can probably tell, researchers cannot establish causality with the one-shot case study. Researchers also cannot really show an association between the treatment (independent variable) and outcome (dependent variable) because they don't have a measure of the dependent variable prior to the treatment. Furthermore, there is absolutely no control for rival causal factors. Consequently, many researchers discourage the use of the one-shot case study; it is appropriate only for the most exploratory research goals. Even then, there are other experimental design choices that will be more informative, even if they are not as vigorous as the true experimental designs.

One-group pretest-posttest design

This design improves on the one-shot case study design by at least adding a pretest to the design, but it still lacks a control group and random assignment. Using my previous hypothetical study of violent video games, if I gave all the participants a personality test that measured aggression before I let them start playing the video games (pretest) and then again after (posttest) their two hours of video game playing (treatment), then I would be doing a one-group pretest-posttest design. However, because I still lack a control group, I cannot discern whether the violence in video games led to any changes in student aggression or if another, unmeasured, variable did. The notation for this type of design is:

$$O_1 \quad X \quad O_2$$

Static group comparison

In this design, researchers take care of the problem of comparison by adding a control group, even though researchers do not use random assignment to decide who is in the experimental and control groups. However, they lose the benefit of a pretest. In the static group comparison type of design, I would let one group of students play violent video games for a couple of hours and I would have a second group of students play nonviolent video games. At the end of the two hours I would give both groups a personality test that measured their aggressive tendencies. A problem is that any differences in aggressiveness I notice between the two groups at the end of two hours may be due to differences between the two groups themselves. Why? Because the researchers do not randomly assign people to the experimental or control groups, *and* the researchers do not give a pretest to assess the similarity of the two groups prior to the treatment. Therefore, there is no way to assess whether or how much the two groups are equal prior to the experiment. As a result, researchers cannot be sure that any observed differences in the posttests are due to the treatment.

The notation for a static group comparison design is:

$$X \quad O$$
$$O$$

There are two groups, there is no equivalence (hence, no E), and, since the design is a "static" design, that means that the researcher has only one observation point. Therefore there is no pretest.

■ Quasi-Experimental Designs

There is a middle ground between the vigorous, often laboratory settings of true experiments and the more informal (but less informative) designs of pre-experiments. This middle ground is the quasi-experimental designs. Frequently, especially in the social sciences, the conditions that are necessary for true experiments are not feasible. True experiments may be too artificial if they require laboratory settings, they may take too long to implement, or it may not be ethically possible to randomly assign subjects to experimental or control groups.

For example, let's pretend I want to study the effects of job training on helping people find jobs. With this research goal, I may not be able ethically to randomly assign who will have job training and who will not because, on some level, most of these people will benefit from some type of training in general. Or if I want to compare the employment experiences of people near poverty who experience job training to their working-class counterparts, I cannot randomly decide who will be near poverty and who will be working class; therefore, again, I cannot really do a true experiment. Last, there may be political limitations on who can receive the job training. For example, local government officials may support my research only if the people who receive the job training have specific characteristics (e.g., are nearing the end of their five-year maximum welfare receipt, live in a certain political district, have specific family characteristics, etc.). Consequently, for ethical, practical, and political reasons, true random selection or assignment may not be possible.

When this is the case, quasi-experiments are a viable alternative to true experiments because quasi-experimental designs have many components of true experiments; they do not, however, involve random selection or assignment. Instead, in quasi-experimental designs, researchers frequently match the treatment and control groups on key variables to make sure that they are comparable in critical ways. Only a few pages ago I mentioned that matching treatment and control group members on special characteristics was less than ideal because researchers can't know what those "key" characteristics are, they don't know how many characteristics are necessary to establish that the groups are equivalent, and even if researchers could successfully address the first two issues, they *still* don't know if the groups are different in some other fundamental way that they aren't measuring! These issues are all true. However, sometimes, for the reasons I just described, researchers recognize that trying to match participants on *some* variables that researchers theoretically think are relevant is the best that they can do.

In quasi-experiments, researchers recognize these limitations and never claim to establish equivalence. Therefore, it is true that with quasi-experiments, researchers cannot be as confident of the inherent comparability of the experimental and control groups as they are in true experiments. However, that is a trade-off of doing work in the "real world" as opposed to a laboratory. Real-world research frequently does not involve the ideal conditions of observation that laboratory research provides. Consequently, in quasi-experiments, researchers realize that matching is the best they can do.

There are three types of quasi-experimental designs: the time-series design, the multiple time-series design, and the nonequivalent control group design.

Time-series design

Let's suppose I tell you that increasing the tax on alcoholic beverages reduces the incidences of drunk driving, as measured by the rates of arrest for drunk driving. To support my

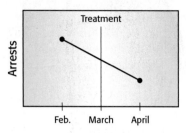

Figure 6.3 Hypothetical Rates of Arrest

claim I tell you that Missouri put this tax into effect in March and I noticed that the arrests for drunk driving were lower in April than in February. Figure 6.3 represents this simple relationship. The experimental notation for the time-series design is:

O X O

After consulting Figure 6.3, are you convinced that the tax reduced the incidences of drunk driving? Probably not. You may (correctly) argue that observing drunk driving rates at two time points (one before the change in taxes and one after) is not enough to conclude that the tax affected the drunk driving rates. You may also (correctly) ask how I know that there isn't some type of outside factor that affected drunk driving rates in this particular state. You might say that to have more confidence, I need to compare the rates in drunk driving with other states as well. Both of these are valid issues. If I extended the observations to more than two points, my data may look like one of the three graphs in Figure 6.4.

O O O X O O O

The notation and data in Figure 6.4 are for a time-series design, sometimes also called an *interrupted time-series design* (because the observations are "interrupted" by the treatment). This design involves multiple observation points both before and after the treatment, which may lead to a result pattern that looks somewhat like the ones presented in Figure 6.4.

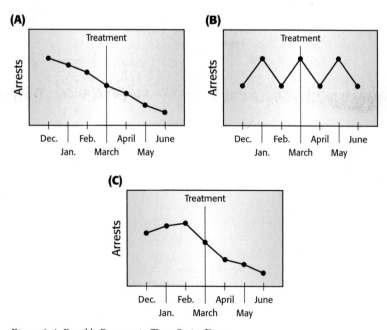

Figure 6.4 Possible Patterns in Time-Series Data

Would the first pattern (A) convince you that the alcohol tax decreases drunk driving? It shouldn't, because if you look at the graph closely, you will notice that the rates of drunk driving were already decreasing *prior* to the implementation of the tax. Therefore, it appears that some factor other than the tax is responsible for the decrease in drunk driving rates.

The second graph (B) also would not support my claim that the tax reduced drunk driving. The second graph suggests that drunk driving rates are cyclical. This means that they increase and decrease in somewhat predictable patterns. For example, the arrests for drunk driving may increase around the holidays (Christmas, New Year's, Valentine's Day, Memorial Day, etc.) because those are days that people have parties or picnics that may involve the consumption of alcohol. Once the occasion is over, the rates of drunk driving will also decrease.

The third graph (C), however, would suggest that the alcohol tax does successfully lower the arrests of drunk driving. Prior to the alcohol tax, the rate of arrest for drunk driving was fairly stable. When the tax went into effect, there is essentially a break in the line that begins decrease in arrest rates for drunk driving. This suggests that the alcohol tax reduced the incidence of drunk driving.

There are two additional points I want to mention. The first is that real-life, time-series graphs are not likely to look as neat as the patterns I have presented. In the real world, there are likely to be at least minor fluctuations in rates regardless of any implementation of a treatment. The patterns in Figure 6.4 are oversimplifications to illustrate a point. In real-world data, the lines before and after a treatment may not be as straight or as clearly zigzagged; however, the general pattern will be similar. In other words, even though there might be some fluctuation in the data, the overall pattern represented in these three graphs should be visible.

Second, because time-series designs are, by definition, quasi-experimental designs where the location or people are not randomly selected, some extraneous factor may still interfere with my treatment. For example, by coincidence Mothers Against Drunk Driving (MADD) may be doing public service announcements around the same time the alcohol tax was implemented. With the time-series design, I have no way of disentangling whether my alcohol treatment affected arrests for drunk driving or whether MADD's television campaign did. However, this design does still enable me to discern whether arrests for drunk driving changed due to some other factor that was already in effect prior to my treatment (Graph A) or whether arrests changed due to some regular fluctuation (Graph B).

Multiple time-series design

It may be obvious to you that one of the limitations of a time-series design is that it lacks a control group. Sometimes when doing natural experiments, this is necessary. For example, it may be difficult to identify a study group that is comparable to the experimental group on key characteristics. Many evaluations of drug treatment courts experience this. Judges and attorneys cannot necessarily randomly decide which drug offenders can participate in drug treatment court for ethical and political reasons. Furthermore, the people who do not participate in the program (either because they are not eligible or because they decline to participate) are usually fundamentally different from those who do take part in the program. Drug offenders who are ineligible for program participation or who decline participation may have more serious drug offenses (e.g., if the treatment court accepts only nonviolent drug offenders and someone commits a robbery while high), less serious drug offenses (e.g., someone convicted of marijuana possession may be out of jail in less time than it takes to complete the treatment court), or different degrees of other personal problems (e.g., mental health problems in addition to drug problems that may be beyond the scope of the program). Therefore, individuals who are denied participation or decline participation in the drug treatment court are not a reliable control group for evaluating these programs.

However, whenever possible, researchers can strengthen their confidence in quasi-experimental designs when they do use a control group. The only real difference between a time-series design and a multi–time-series design is that in the latter, researchers are examining multiple groups across time and one of these groups is likely to be a control group. The notation for this type of study would be:

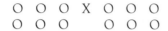

There is no E before the groups because I have not established equivalence. In the drug treatment court example, a control group might consist of people arrested for similar crimes, who have similar drug addictions, but who live in a nearby county that does not offer a drug treatment court. If I can match individuals on criminal offense, drug, treatment needs, gender, and race (for example), I may have a control group that is suitable for comparison in a quasi-experiment.

Wallen and associates (2003) used a multiple time-series design to test the effectiveness of a community alcohol prevention program on violence in Sweden. The authors noted that prior to their study, there was an increase in the number of licensed drinking establishments in Sweden, which they suspected were correlated to an increase in alcohol-related violence. Consequently, in a part of Stockholm, Sweden, called Central City, there was a 10-year-long communitywide alcohol prevention program created to train beverage service providers about responsible beverage service and to encourage police to more strictly enforce existing alcohol laws.

The community intervention program started in 1998 and was still in effect at the time of Wallen and associates' (2003) research; however, they wanted to test whether there were any early indicators of program effectiveness. Consequently, the authors gathered police-reported violence data between January 1994 (48 months prior to the program implementation) to September 2000 (33 months into program implementation). Since this program was operating only in a specific part of Stockholm (Central City), Wallen and colleagues used another part of the city, called Södermalm, as their control area. According to the researchers, Södermalm is a district similar to Central City in outlet density and reputation as an entertainment district. Hence, the recording of the annual rates of violence in these areas before and after the program implementation are the various observation points. Central City is the experimental group because it experienced the alcohol program, and Södermalm is the control group (that was matched on outlet density and entertainment reputation) that did not experience the program.

Wallen and colleagues (2003) found that the rates of violence in the Central City (treatment) area were reduced by 29 percent since the program's inception, and the rates of violence actually increased in the Södermalm (control) area, as well as in Sweden as a nation, during the same period. The authors conclude that, at least so far, the alcohol program seems to be effective in reducing rates of alcohol-related violence in that part of Sweden.

Both time-series designs and multiple time-series designs are good for studying the impact of new laws, taxes, and social programs, such as alcohol-reduction programs. The statistical techniques for analyzing time-series data is a little more sophisticated than that for analyzing other methods of observation. However, the basic idea remains to be able to analyze trends in data both prior to the treatment and after to see whether the treatment had any effect in altering the dependent variable.

Nonequivalent control group design

By now you have likely heard enough experimental terminology to have an idea about this type of design even without my explanation. By just reading the title, you probably already know that nonequivalent control group design (1) is a quasi- or pre-experiment (since it has the term *nonequivalent* in the title) and (2) it involves the comparison between at least two groups (at least one experimental group and one control group). The nonequivalent control group design is a quasi-experiment instead of a pre-experiment because it is lacking only one of the criteria, randomization, for a true experiment.

Culen and Volk (2000, **AN 2677827**) employed a nonequivalent control group design to examine whether using an extended case study involving evaluation and action skills training regarding wetland issues affected seventh- and eighth-grade students' environmental behavior, citizenship action skills, locus of control, and knowledge of ecological foundations. The goals of the wetlands instruction were fourfold and involved (1) an introduction to the topics of wetlands and wetland habitat loss, (2) an introduction to the problems and issues involving wetlands and to the importance of human beliefs and values in environmental issues, (3) the development of a plan and the conduction a wetlands habitat investigation, and (4) the compilation of a list of issues related to wetlands habitat loss along with suggestions for a solution and the evaluation of possible solutions.

As the first experimental group, Culen and Volk used four seventh-grade and two eighth-grade classes, and these classes experienced all four levels of wetland instructional goals. A second experimental group consisted of two seventh- and two eighth-grade classes, and these students experienced only the first two learning goals. A third group of two seventh- and three eighth-grade classes served as the control group, and received traditional science education. As a pretest, Culen and Volk gave various tests (not described here) to assess the knowledge of ecological foundations and environmental behavior. They found that there were no significant differences across the three groups (two experimental, one control). The various classes were not randomly selected or assigned to experimental and control groups; however, a pretest showed no real difference in two key variables: environmental behavior and knowledge of ecological foundation. This lack of difference helps the researchers establish that, at least with regard to these two key variables, the groups are comparable.

The researchers then administered the various modes of instruction and found that the first experimental group, which had all four learning goals, had significantly higher levels of environmental behavior than did the other two groups. They also found that the second experimental group, which had only the first two goals, also had suggestively (but slight) higher scores of environmental behavior than did the control group who received the traditional instruction. These tests were the posttests. The results regarding the other outcomes (citizenship action skills, locus of control, and knowledge of ecological foundations) were, however, inconclusive (Culen & Volk, 2000). The notation for Culen and Volk's research is:

Experimental Group 1	O	X_1	O
Experimental Group 2	O	X_2	O
Control Group	O		O

Again, the groups are not designated by E_1 or E_2, as they would be in a true experiment, because equivalence is not present. Therefore, writing out "experimental group 1" and so forth distinguishes between the two groups, as does the X_1 and X_2 because the subscripts by the treatment suggest different treatments.

■ Variation in Experimental Design: Factorial Design

All of the previous experimental design types I've mentioned so far address the single effect of a treatment, called the *main effect,* independent of other effects. In Culen and Volk's (2000) study of teaching about environmental issues, even though there were two treatments, each experimental group only received *one* treatment, therefore their design addressed only the main effects of a treatment. In fact, there really is no way their design really can be adjusted to a factorial design; I am only using it as an example to help you realize that main effect designs mean that the experimental group experiences only one treatment or independent variable, even if there were multiple experimental groups.

A *factorial design,* on the other hand, allows researchers to assess the impact of multiple treatment (or independent) variables on a specific group. For example, the Internet is indispensable as a tool for easily finding mass amounts of information. However, how do we know that the information we receive is accurate? You may have professors, for example, who tell you that you can cite only information from specific sources such as government agencies, or that the articles you read on-line have to be from peer-reviewed articles (which implies a bit of filtration from experts). Why? Because, as you well know, anyone can post information on the Internet, regardless of the accuracy of his or her statement. I could post a webpage with all kinds of scientific jargon stating that the sky is really a shade of purple, not blue, and back up my validity with the little "Ph.D." behind my name. I don't have to mention that my doctorate is in sociology and that I don't know diddly about the sky, atmosphere, or other weather issues. However, an uncritical reader may actually believe what I have to say simply because I sound intelligent and appear to have "expert" credentials. I discussed the danger of blindly believing the word of "experts" in Chapter 1; and, no where is this danger greater than the Internet. Figure 6.5 shows an example of a factorial design for Internet evaluation.

So how do people evaluate the merit of the information they find on the Web? Greer (2003, **AN 9542544**) used a factorial design to see how people use two cues, the source and the quality of advertising, to judge on-line information. Greer cites other studies that argue that if people see a source as providing information for information's sake, as opposed to trying to bias information or prove a purpose, they view the source as credible. Likewise, Greer also cites research that suggests that high corporate credibility and company trustworthiness enhance people's view of an advertisement. Taken together, Greer argues that some research has shown that when advertisement content matched the content of a site, people felt that that advertisement was credible.

Greer (2003) twists the previous research and instead of studying how source and credibility affect people's view of an advertisement, she studies how attitudes about advertisements affect the site content. Greer created four hypotheses about the relationship

Below is a table outlining the different possible patterns of source and advertisement credibility relationships used by Greer (2003) in her research on Internet site evaluation. The group letters correspond to the excerpt of Greer's research that appears in the text.

Level of Advertisement Credibility (Z)	Level of Source Credibility (X)	
	High	Low
High	Group A	Group B
Low	Group C	Group D

Group Letter	Design Notation		
A	X_1	Z_1	O
B	X_1	Z_2	O
C	X_2	Z_1	O
D	X_2	Z_2	O

Where X_1 = high advertisement credibility
X_2 = low advertisement credibility
Z_1 = high source credibility
Z_2 = low source credibility

Result Interpretation

The news story ratings are the dependent variable; therefore, "Group A" really means "Ratings for Group A."

Main Effects

(These are not actually in the study, but they are presented to give a complete picture of factorial design.)

Hypothetical Main H1: High source credibility benefits news story credibility more than low source credibility.
   Supportive results: Group A and Group C > Group B and Group D.

Hypothetical Main H2: High advertisement credibility benefits news story credibility more than low advertisement credibility.
   Supportive results: Group A and Group B > Group C and Group D.

Interactive Effects

(These are present in the study.)

Interaction H1: News stories that have high source *and* high advertisement credibility will receive higher ratings than news stories with low source *and* low advertisement credibility.
   Supportive results: Group A > Group D.

Figure 6.5 Example of Factorial Design for Internet Site Evaluation

Figure 6.5 Continued

between credibility, advertisements, and site evaluation. You can find all the hypotheses on Research Navigator, but I will just focus on two here:

> *Hypothesis 1:* Participants who see information surrounded by high-credibility source and advertising cues will rate a news story as more credible than participants who see the same news story surrounded by low-credibility source and advertising cues.

> *Hypothesis 2:* Participants' rating of the advertising will more significantly affect how they rate the story's credibility in the low source credibility conditions than in the high source credibility conditions.

Here is an excerpt of Greer's (2003) design:

> The researcher recruited 220 students from nine classes at a Western journalism school. . . .
>
> . . . Participants viewed one of five randomly assigned treatment pages: (a) a high-credibility source featuring high-credibility ads (n = 47); (b) a low-credibility source featuring high-credibility ads (n = 44); (c) a high-credibility source featuring low-credibility ads (n = 47); (d) a low-credibility source featuring low-credibility ads (n = 46); and (e) a control condition with no source cues or ads present (n = 36). After exposure to the treatment, participants' views of the credibility of the story, the site, and the advertising were measured.
>
> . . . All participants read the same short news story about choosing a nursing home. The story, taken from a Web site sponsored by a nursing home association, was assumed to be low in relevance to the participants. . . . The story was put on a mock Web page, which was printed out and included as the third page of the questionnaire. The page included mock headers and footers, making it appear as if it were printed from Netscape Communicator. . . . Everything except the source credibility and advertising credibility cues was identical on the five mock Web pages.

Manipulated Independent Variables

Source credibility. Source credibility was manipulated by using two extremes of the Web publishing continuum as source cues: nytimes.com, the Web site for The

New York Times [high credibility], or chrisbrown.com, a personal home page on the Web [low credibility].

 . . . To ensure that participants were attuned to the source manipulation, they were given five source prompts: in written instructions, in the URL contained in the page header, in a site logo at the top of the page, under the byline, and in a copyright notice at the bottom of the page.

Ad credibility. The researcher, through a pilot test of 15 real Internet ads rated by a group of 17 like participants, identified three high-credibility and three low-credibility Web ads. Those in the high-credibility ad conditions saw Flowers.com (rated in the pilot test as M = 5.3 on a 7-point scale), Neiman Marcus (M = 5.3), and Panasonic e-wear (M = 5.2). Those in the low-credibility ad conditions saw CDnudes.com (M = 1.2), Free psychic reading (M = 1.2), and Sleazy Money (M = 1.2). Those in the control condition saw no ads. In each experimental condition, one large banner ad spanned the top of the Web page, and two large banner ads appeared below a navigational bar at the bottom of the story. The ads constituted about one third of the total page content.

Greer's research is a factorial design because it involves the simultaneous analysis of two variables: source credibility and advertisement credibility. Because each of these variables has two values (high and low), Greer's design involves four experimental groups and one control group. How do I know this? Because the notation for a factorial design is the number of values in each treatment multiplied against each other. When the multiplication is actually done, the answer corresponds to the number of different patterns. Therefore, in Greer's study, the notation would be 2×2 or four patterns. This is in fact what Greer mentions in the second paragraph when she discusses treatment pages. The first four pages ("a" to "d") reflect the four different treatment patterns. The fifth is merely the control where neither treatment is present. Figure 6.5 illustrates the different treatment groups. (*Note:* there will be four treatment groups.)

Through this design, Greer can assess both the main effects of each variable as well as their interactive effects. If Greer was interested in arguing that people will find a news story to be more credible if the webpage has high-source credibility than if the webpage has low-source credibility (she is not; this is not one of her hypotheses), then she is interested in studying the main effect of source credibility, because that is the only variable of interest. This hypothesis does not even mention advertisement credibility. If her hypothesis is correct, then the ratings of news stories in groups A and C will be higher than in groups B and D because the first pair of groups have the high-source credibility values. Similarly, if she hypothesized a similar argument for advertisement source, we would expect the news ratings of groups A and B to be higher than those for groups C and D (see Figure 6.5).

However, with this design, Greer can (and does) examine specific interactive effects or how combinations of advertisement and source credibility affect ratings of news stories. For example, her first hypothesis argues that news stories that have high source *and* high advertisement credibility (group A using her definitions and Figure 6.2) will receive higher ratings than news stories with low source *and* low advertisement credibility (group D). This hypothesis looks at groups that are defined by *both* the source credibility and advertisement credibility. Greer's research found that this hypothesis was not supported; therefore, the news stories that had both high credibility sources and advertisements were not rated as more credible than news stories that had low credibility sources and advertisements.

BOX 6.1   **Practice Identifying Experimental Designs**

Below are excerpts from the design sections of two studies that use an experimental design. For each of the cases, (1) identify the general type of experiment (e.g., true experiment); (2) identify the specific experimental design within that type (e.g., classical experiment); and (3) identify all the components (e.g., what is the treatment, how do they pretest, etc.) for the experimental design you identify.

Case 1

> The imperative to address physician maldistribution has been directed in part at medical schools. . . . The Rural Health Scholars Program (RHSP) is an enrichment initiative that has been implemented at 2 medical schools to increase the number of students likely to practice primary care in rural, underserved areas. . . .
>
> . . . The effectiveness of the RHSP ultimately will be demonstrated by the extent to which scholars become primary care physician–leaders in rural, underserved areas in North Carolina. [In this design] postintervention comparisons are made between one group who participated in an intervention and one group who did not. From the matriculating classes of 1992–1995, 52 students were selected to participate in the RHSP (24 from ECU and 28 from UNC). Comparison groups were constructed at both schools and consisted of students who had expressed interest in practicing primary care during their 1st year of medical school and who were members of the same matriculating and graduating cohorts as the scholars, but who did not participate in the RHSP . . . .
>
> . . . Four outcomes were examined, the first of which was the proportion of scholars who matched into residency programs in family medicine, internal medicine, medicine and pediatrics, or pediatrics (hereafter denoted as primary care residencies). The second outcome examined was the proportion of scholars who matched into family medicine residency programs specifically because they would be very likely to practice primary care and unlikely to pursue subspecialty training. In addition, family

medicine physicians are more likely to practice in rural areas. . . . The third outcome [examined] scholars who matched in community hospitals. . . . The fourth outcome examined was the proportion of scholars who matched into residency programs located within North Carolina.

Source: Deirdre C. Lynch, Sari E. Teplin, Stephen E. Willis, Donald E. Pathman, Lars C. Larsen, Beat D. Steiner, and James D. Bernstein, "Interim Evaluation of the Rural Health Scholars Program," *Teaching & Learning in Medicine, 13* (1) (Winter 2001): 36. **(AN 4802852)**

  1. *Experimental Type:* Pre-experiment
  2. *Experimental Design:* Static group comparison
  3. *Components:* The treatment is the participation in the Rural Health Scholars Program. The experimental group is the 52 students who participated in this program. The control group is the other students in this cohort who did not participate in the program. Only two of the four outcome measures are in the above excerpt from the study. The first outcome, or dependent variable, is the proportion of scholars who matched into the various residency programs that the authors state; the second dependent variable is those who matched into their residency programs but who are unlikely to pursue specialty training. The third outcome is the percent of scholars who matched into community hospitals, and the fourth is the proportion of scholars who matched into residency programs within the same state that they went to medical school (North Carolina).

Case 2

> The development of pet facilitated psychotherapy, in which a pet is used as a co-therapist and becomes an integral part of the treatment process. . . . Pet-assisted therapy has been adapted by practitioners in social work, marriage and family counseling, psychology, and psychiatry. . . .
>
> . . . Among the benefits reported by therapists, we were especially interested in anxiety reduction. . . . [However, several] recent reviews

have raised serious criticisms of the abundance of descriptive studies and the paucity of adequate quantitative methodology in this area.

[Consequently, in this research], three questions were asked: (1) Is the effect on anxiety due to the object being a live animal? . . . (2) What types of pets are most effective? Are all pets equally effective, or is the potential effect specific to soft cuddly animals? (3) Is the effect of petting animals moderated by attitudes towards animals? . . .

. . . Non-clinical participants were exposed to a stressful situation in the laboratory, the presence of a Tarantula spider, which they were told they might be asked to hold. They were then randomly assigned to one of five groups: petting either a rabbit, a turtle, a toy rabbit, or a toy turtle, or to a control group that got neither an animal or a toy . . . .

. . . After administering the Companion Animal Semantic Differential and the STAI [State-Trait Anxiety Inventory] to participants individually, the stress manipulation was conducted. We used a spider as a stress-arousing stimulus because of its face validity in the context of the study, and its high fear arousing potential among non-clinical populations (Arrindell, 2000). The experimenter (a female graduate student) uncovered a glass jar containing a Tarantula spider, and said: "This is a spider. The experiment has two groups: one will watch the spider, and the other will be asked to hold it. You will be told your assignment shortly. Now, I have to ask you to wait a minute while I get something from the next room." The experimenter left the room for 2 minutes, returned and administered the STAI again. At this point the participant, who had been randomly assigned to one of the five groups, was handed one of the following: a rabbit (n = 13), a turtle (n = 11), a toy rabbit (n = 11), or a toy turtle (n = 12), which had been covered until then. The subject was instructed "to hold and pet it for a while." The control group (n = 11) was asked to wait a little while longer while the

experimenter left the room again. The uncovered glass jar containing the spider remained in the room the whole time. The petting/waiting period lasted for 2 minutes. The pet/toy was taken away by the experimenter, who administered the STAI for the third time. All participants were then told they would not have to hold the spider. At the end of the session a short interview was conducted on what they had done, felt and thought during the experiment. They were then debriefed and thanked.

Source: Shoshana Shiloh, Gal Sorek, and Joseph Terkel, "Reduction of State-Anxiety by Petting Animals in a Controlled Laboratory Experiment," *Anxiety, Stress & Coping, 16* (4) (December 2003): 387. **(AN 11281068)**

1. *Experimental Type:* True experiment (random assignment)

2. *Experimental Design:* Form of a classic experiment

3. *Components:* The pretests were the Companion Animal Semantic Differential and the State-Trait Anxiety Inventory. The first test assessed the participants' view of animals (and due to the random selection, there were no differences in this score among the different groups, but this information is not present in the excerpt). There were no initial differences in the State-Trait Anxiety Inventory score. Furthermore, in a sense, there is a second pretest, since the State-Trait Anxiety Inventory is administered after the subjects learn that they may have to hold a tarantula, but before they are given the real or toy animals to pet.

I say this is a *form* of a classic experiment because there is more than one treatment. This does not mean that there is more than one variable being studied; therefore, it is not a factorial design. There is one variable here, an object to pet; however, there are four different values for that variable (a live rabbit, a live turtle, a toy rabbit, and a toy turtle). Each value corresponds to a treatment.

The posttest is another administration of the State-Trait Anxiety Inventory.

Greer's second hypothesis was that advertising cues would be more closely tied to story credibility ratings on the personal homepage (low credibility source) than on nytimes.com (high-credibility source). The data also did not support this hypothesis (Greer, 2003).

Even though Greer's data did not support either hypothesis, her research methodology is sound and serves as a good example of how factorial experiments allow researchers to examine how more than one variable may interact in affecting a behavior or outcome. Factorial designs can be as relatively simple and straightforward as Greer's, or they can be very complicated. For example, a factorial design that is summarized as $2 \times 3 \times 3$ is one that involves three independent variables. One has two values and two have three values. If I wanted to study whether people contribute money to charity, for instance, I might want to see how gender (male, female), social class (upper-middle class, middle class, and working class), and family structure (never married, married, divorced) interact to influence people's charity. This type of design would produce 18 different possible independent variable combinations ($2 \times 3 \times 3 = 18$). Eighteen combinations are clearly much more than four, so you can see how a factorial analysis can become complicated very quickly.

Issues Involving Experiments

Earlier in the book I discussed general issues of research such as generalizability, validity, and ethics. You may also remember that I said that researchers must continually think about these issues, or, at the very least, keep them in the back of their minds as they continue with the various steps of the research process. In this section I am going to revisit those issues to further reinforce the importance of keeping them in mind when designing various modes of observation.

Internal Validity

You may remember that two types of validity are internal validity and external validity. To refresh your memory, *internal validity* is sometimes also called *causal validity* because it refers to our ability to fulfill the third criterion of causality—namely, to illustrate that the change in the dependent variable is indeed caused by the independent variable and not some other factor (technically this is showing that a relationship is nonspurious). *External validity* refers to a researcher's ability to generalize the results beyond the scope of the study itself. Because external validity is the foundation for generalizability, I will discuss this in the next section, and, for now, just focus on how experiments address issues of internal validity.

Selection bias

Selection bias occurs when the researcher examines nonequivalent groups. In experiments, this is an issue if the experimental and control groups are different in fundamental ways. For example, if I am interested in studying how an exercise program affects weight loss and my experimental group predominantly contains people who are at least 45 pounds overweight, whereas my control group primarily contains people who are only about 10 pounds overweight, I have a selection bias problem. If my experimental group shows greater weight loss than my control group, I will not be sure whether this weight loss is due to the treatment or simply because there was more room for weight loss in this group.

Clearly, random assignment, and therefore true experiments, are the best modes of observation to prevent this threat to validity. If researchers truly randomly assign subjects to a treatment or control group, then researchers are pretty confident that serious differences between the two groups are unlikely. A pretest will further increase their confidence if researchers use the results to empirically show that the control and experimental groups are not statistically different.

Quasi-experiments are less able to address selection bias because they do not have random assignment as part of their design. However, researchers can still minimize their concern (but not totally eliminate it) about selection bias if they match people in the experimental and control groups on predetermined characteristics. Once again, a pretest will help determine how similar the two groups are on the selected variables. If in a quasi-experiment a researcher can statistically establish that the experimental and control groups are essentially equal on the measures of interest, then the researcher has more confidence that the groups are alike and therefore comparable, in at least some theoretically important ways. Pre-experiments, on the other hand, do not make any real serious attempt to control for selection bias; therefore, selection bias is much more of an issue with these designs than with the other two.

History

History occurs when some outside event unrelated to the treatment happens during the experiment and consequently affects the dependent variable. Doing an experiment about ethnic attitudes and then having some members of that ethnic group commit a terrorist act that subjects learn about from the news would be a history effect. If feelings about that ethnic group are more negative in the posttest than in the pretest, it may be unclear whether this attitude change is from the treatment or whether it is a reaction to the newsworthy terrorist event.

Generally, in true experiments history should not be a problem because, once again, since the subjects are randomly assigned to treatment and control groups, any event that affects the subjects should equally affect the experimental and control groups. Therefore, if a history effect is present, researchers would notice a change in the dependent variable for *both* the experimental and control groups when the control group should not have shown a change in the dependent variable. Quasi-experiments and pre-experiments are less able to address history concerns because, even with matching, it is less clear if the experimental and control groups are truly equal.

However, *local history* is a threat to validity that no experimental design can adequately protect against. Local history occurs when the outside event happens to only one of the study groups—in other words, *only* to the experimental or *only* to the control group. When an outside event happens to one group, randomization does little to protect against this threat to validity, because although the two groups may have been equal prior to the study, they no longer are, after one group experiences some external event that was unplanned.

Maturation

Just as the term implies, maturation occurs when the change in the dependent variable is, at least partially, due to aging or a time process and not the treatment. This is really an issue only in experimental designs that continue over a long period. For example, I want to test the effectiveness of an antitruancy program for 13- to 14-year-olds, so I follow their school attendance records and the number of fights they had on school grounds until they were age 18. I notice that the number of fights decreased over time. I am not sure whether this is because of the treatment or because, as children grow up (or *mature*), they are less likely to get involved in fights.

The maturation effect is not limited to studies of children. If I did a study on happiness but found that over the course of the study people became less happy, I am not sure if the change in happiness is from my treatment or because people got tired and irritable over the course of the study. Hence, maturation may result from the aging (or maturation) process, from the experience the subjects may gain or lose, or from new knowledge the subjects may acquire over time.

None of the experimental designs, including the true experiment, protect against maturation effects. However, like with a history effect, a pretest will help researchers identify if a maturation effect is possible, because the results of the pretest for the control group should not change by the posttest. If the results do change, a history or maturation effect is present. How do you tell the difference? You use your own reasoning skills. If there was an event that received a lot of media attention that your subjects were likely to have seen or heard, then the validity threat is likely to be a history effect. If you reason that there was something about the length of the experiment that may have led to the results, the validity threat is likely to be a maturation effect. It doesn't sound scientific, does it? You're right; it isn't. Regardless of whether you identify the validity threat to be maturation or history, the end outcome is essentially the same. You are less sure that the results from your study are due to your treatment.

Experimental mortality

Although experimental mortality sounds kind of nasty, it simply refers to subjects' decreased participation in the study over time. The longer the experiment continues, the more likely subjects are to die or to stop participating. Decreased study participation is common in longitudinal studies, and experiments are no exception. Let's pretend I want to study the effects of an antismoking program on long-term (10 years or more) smokers. I have 60 long-term smokers in my experimental group and 50 long-term smokers in my control group. I study the smoking behavior of both groups every six months for the next two years. At the end of the two years I have 46 people in my experimental group and 30 people in my control group. Even though I did not lose many people in my experimental group (and remember, the risk of losing people is greater the longer the study), I lost 20 out of an original 50 people in my control group. In other words, only 60 percent of my control group remained in the study at the end of two years. The 20 people who left my control group could have differed from the 30 people who stayed, thereby possibly affecting overall reported smoking behavior of my control group.

As I said, people are likely to drop out of an experiment over time. Experimental mortality is a validity threat if (1) researchers lose a large proportion of one or more study groups or (2) the people who stop participating in the study share some similar characteristics that are different from those who remain. Therefore, if at the end of the second year, I have 51 people in my experimental group and 46 people in my control group, so long as the 9 people who left the experimental group and the 4 who left the control group are not significantly different from the remaining participants regarding key variables, then experimental mortality is *not* likely to be a problem.

Again, there is no specific type of experiment that prevents this. The only protection researchers have is to limit the length of the experiment. However, as I discussed earlier, sometimes we need to have a long span of time between the treatment and posttests to

How long after people attend an antismoking program would you test their behavior to see if they have stayed away from cigarettes?

ascertain the duration of treatment effect (for example, whether a change in alcohol laws have a longitudinal effect on people's drinking behavior). Therefore, it is important that researchers always record the number of subjects in all study groups (including control groups) at each stage of an experiment. The researcher, and others, can then determine whether experimental mortality is a validity threat in individual instances.

Testing

Even though, as I've just illustrated, a pretest can be a useful tool in identifying threats to validity, sometimes it can be a validity threat itself. A testing effect is possible if the pretest itself affects the outcome of the study because the pretest sensitizes subjects to the true nature of the experiment or leads them to further think about an issue by posttest time. For instance, I frequently make on-line practice tests available to my students prior to an exam. Initially I had no limitations on how many times students could take the practice test; however, some students would take the practice test as soon as it was available (pretest), focus their energy studying the questions they got wrong (treatment), then retake the practice test scoring much higher (posttest). They took their higher second scores as evidence that they understood the material, but were then confused as to why they still did not do as well as they would have liked on the exam (another form of a posttest).

After discussing the issue with students and realizing what they were doing, I realized that their second practice test scores were probably not a valid indicator of new learning because the students were now familiar with the questions after they first took the test (and read the correct answers that corresponded to each of their wrong answers). What students were probably testing was their memory skills more than their mastery of class material. As a result, I encourage my classes to take the practice tests only *after* they already study and I have also programmed the tests to be available only one time. Thus, students can no longer take the practice test multiple times, thereby avoiding the false sense of security that accompanied the pretest effect.

Although experimental designs that do not have a pretest clearly avoid this threat to validity, they do so at a rather high cost. The cost is that researchers cannot identify the presence of other rival causal factors such as selection bias, history, or maturation. The only design that really adequately addresses this issue is the Solomon four-group design.

Instrumentation

Suppose I wanted to study rape and I compared the Uniform Crime Report statistics for reported incidences of rape from 1950 to 2000 and I noticed that after the mid-1970s and again after the mid-1980s there seemed to be a noticeable increase in reported incidences of rape. Does that mean that more women are being raped since the mid-1980s? Not necessarily. During the mid-1970s, rape laws were broadened to include marital rape, and during the early 1980s, public consciousness about rape increased. If authorities broaden the definition of a crime, then they have changed how people measure that crime, and this change of measure may lead to the change in the outcome (reported incidences). In other words, if more behaviors are now included or identified as criminal, those new behaviors that were not criminal may still have occurred in the past but were not recorded because they were not included in the definition. Now that they are included, when they are reported, they are recorded as part of this crime.

Essentially this is a threat to validity known as an *instrumentation effect*. Changes in how a concept is measured during the course of a study may affect observations about the outcome or dependent variable. Another problem with concluding that the rates of rape have increased is that with increased public awareness, people are more likely to report a crime and authorities are more likely to act on those reports. This, too, affects instrumentation because these behaviors affect the measurement of reported rape. Hence, any change, such as in a definition, how data are gathered (e.g., the use of computers that facilitate record keeping of crimes), or public awareness (and therefore reports), may lead to an instrumentation effect that makes longitudinal comparisons of the dependent variable difficult.

Diffusion of treatment

Suppose I want to study the effectiveness of a neighborhood watch on people's fear of crime. I choose, as a control group, a nearby (but not adjacent) community that has similar demographics to the neighborhood watch community but does not practice neighborhood watch. Now further suppose that as a ploy for positive press, the head of this neighborhood watch group, who truly believes in the program, thinks that my research to empirically test the effectiveness of the program will confirm what he already knows to be true (that the program is effective in increasing sense of safety among residents) and contacts the press to give some exposure to it. The residents in the neighboring community, which serves as my control group, read the same local newspaper, hear of this "wonderful" program of neighborhood watch, and some people mobilize to create a neighborhood watch group of their own. Since my control group now experiences some form of neighborhood watch (or my treatment), the treatment has "diffused" or moved to the control group, thereby contaminating it and creating a validity threat. This is a form of study contamination that I discussed in Chapter 3.

General experimental designs themselves do not control for this threat to validity. The researcher has to do it. In other words, the presence of this threat to validity is, at least in part, my fault because I did not effectively isolate my two groups. The two main ways researchers protect against diffusion of treatment is to make sure they select experimental and control groups that would have no contact, directly or indirectly, with each other and to have subjects promise not to reveal anything about the study if isolation is not possible or practical. To the degree that the experiment occurs in a laboratory, that the members of the experimental and control group have no contact during the course of the experiment, and the length of the experiment is relatively brief, the threat of diffusion of treatment is negligible. However, the degree that these conditions are not met, the higher the threat to this type of validity. Unfortunately, experimenters frequently can detect this validity threat only by doing interviews with subjects at the end of the study, after the validity threat is already present.

Compensatory behavior

The control group does not have to adopt the treatment for a possible contamination threat to study validity. Even if the control group learns of the treatment but does not, or cannot, adopt it, you may have a threat to validity that researchers call *compensatory behavior*. If members of a control group learn that they are being denied some type of program or experience (the treatment), they may increase their efforts to compensate for not having this treatment.

For example, let's pretend I'm studying the effects of a school-sponsored tutoring program on high school students with low academic performance. If a control group of students with low grades learns that an experimental group of high school students with low grades received some special school-sponsored tutoring to help their grades, the control group may try to study extra hard (essentially they are compensating) so that their grades are no longer the only "low" ones. They do not have the special tutoring, therefore the treatment did not diffuse to them; however, their compensating behavior may alter the outcome of the study. On the other hand, if the students in the control group of low academic performers learn that they were left out of special tutoring, they may behave in the opposite extreme by becoming so demoralized that the school system as "given up" on them that they may, as a result, fall even further behind.

Hence, if members of a control group learn that they are being denied some type of program or treatment that they perceive as desirable, they may work to reduce the differences between them and the experimental group, they may develop a competitive rivalry with the experimental group, or they may be demoralized. Any of these can hinder a researcher's ability to conclude that the treatment led to the change in behavior (the dependent variable), and therefore is a threat to validity.

Like diffusion of treatment, no one experimental design protects against this. The degree that the experiment occurs in a laboratory, the degree of contact between the members of the experimental and control group during the course of the experiment, and the length of the experiment all influence the likelihood of this threat to validity. Furthermore, like diffusion of treatment, the only real way that researchers can accurately assess whether this is a validity threat is if they interview the subjects at the conclusion of the study.

Statistical regression

The students in the previous example may pose another threat to validity even if the experimental and control students never meet or interact. If I purposely select subjects, such as students, because they have extreme values in my dependent variable, such as academic performance, their behavior can really move in only one direction—in this instance, up (staying the same is not movement). For example, it is unlikely that my poor students in either the control group or the experimental group will have lower academic performance, simply because they *are* already poor students.

Statistical regression can occur in a second way. Perhaps I want to compare the effects of tutoring on academically poor students relative to tutoring on average students. Both the academically poor students and the average students experience tutoring for three hours a week for the course of the semester. I notice that the end of the semester the grades of the academically poor students are worse than at the beginning of the semester, whereas the grades of the average students did not change much. Because the academically poor students began at an extreme, it is unlikely that the tutoring made them *worse* students, therefore by random chance alone they appear to be worse students at the second measure.

Again, no experimental design compensates for this, but an examination of pretest and posttest scores can help detect whether it is an issue.

Experimenter effects

Even though one of the strengths of science is the efforts researchers take to be objective, sometimes they can influence the course of an experiment not because of any overt unethical behavior but because of some unconscious behavior. Researchers may very strongly believe their hypothesis to be true; as a result, they unwittingly exhibit subtle cues with their body language that either inform the subjects of the true hypothesis or lead to differential researcher treatment of subjects independent of the study treatment. This may especially be a concern in policy or program research if the staff are the ones administering the experiment because they have a vested interest in a positive evaluation or they may honestly believe that their program fulfills its intended goal.

For example, people running a self-esteem seminar may go out of their way to make those attending (the experimental group) feel welcome; therefore, these subjects feel important, which boosts their self-esteem. The same researchers, however, may not go to the same lengths to make the control group feel comfortable; consequently, these researchers conduct themselves in a more detached, scientific manner that they think is appropriate for an experiment. Thus, the control group's self-esteem may not be as high.

To protect against **experimenter effects,** researchers may use one of two methods. The first involves hiring research assistants, training them in experimental techniques, and giving them equivalent (through random selection and assignment) experimental and control groups, but telling the assistants that the subjects are different on a key variable (e.g., tell the assistants that one group has low self-esteem while the other group has high self-esteem). Essentially what you are telling the research assistant is the treatment. This does not have to necessarily be true (in other words, the people you tell the research assistant have low self-esteem may actually not), because essentially you are testing the observations of the research assistant. If the people with "low" self-esteem do better with the program than the people with "high" self-esteem, then experimenter expectancy is present.

Another way to protect against experiment expectancy is to do a **double blind study.** In this type of experiment, the people delivering the treatment do not know which subjects are getting the treatment and which are receiving a placebo (which looks like the treatment but is not). Hence, those administering the experiment directly to the subjects do not know which group is the experimental group and which is the control group. This type of experiment is frequently done in medical studies of drug effects. One group of people is given the drug the researchers are interested in testing and another group is given a similar-looking drug that is really not a drug at all, but a sugar pill instead. Only the researchers not directly interacting with the subjects may know which pill is truly the drug. Sometimes the researchers themselves do not know and some other individual, such as an administrator, does. Since the researchers or research assistants do not know what the real treatment is, they have no way of unconsciously altering their behavior in a way that will alter the study's outcome. Double blind studies can be done in the social sciences, but they are less common than other methods of observation.

■ External Validity and Generalizability

Even if an experiment produces accurate results, how can researchers be sure that those same results would occur in the "real world"? This is the main idea behind external validity. If a study lacks external validity, the findings cannot be generalized to people, settings, or times outside of the experiment itself. If you remember, I began this chapter with a description of the Minneapolis domestic violence experiment which found that, overall, arrest led to the lowest recidivism rates of domestic violence (Sherman & Berk, 1984a). Even though the original researchers were cautious about their findings, the national media quickly publicized these findings and, as a result, many police precincts nationwide quickly instituted a policy of arrest for domestic violence. This action, however, was premature.

Based on the success of the first study, the National Institute of Justice funded additional studies to replicate the findings of Sherman and Burke. These studies occurred in Omaha, Nebraska; Charlotte, North Carolina; Milwaukee, Wisconsin; Colorado Springs, Colorado; and Dade County, Florida. However, the findings from the first three cities did *not* replicate Sherman and Burke's initial findings; in fact, the rates of domestic violence *increased* after arrest (Sherman et al., 1992). However, in the last two areas, Colorado Springs and Dade County, Florida, the results were consistent with Sherman and Burke's original findings. The different results from the first three studies, however, question the generalizability of Sherman and Burke's initial findings because they did not hold in all of the different settings.

There are three threats to external validity that I will discuss here: testing effects, selection bias, and reactivity.

Testing effects

Pretesting may not only interfere with internal validity but it may also interfere with external validity. If the pretest sensitizes the subjects to the variables being studied, then their reaction to the treatment may not be the same as for people who were not pretested. By having the pretest, subjects are aware of the general issues that researchers are studying (even if they are not aware of how the researcher plans on using the treatment to affect those issues) and, during the course of the experiment, would have time to reflect and think about those issues. This reflection period may affect their behavior or answers in the posttest. However, if another person implemented a program in the "real world" based on experiments that had a pretest, this person may not notice the same effects or changes in the dependent variable as the researcher did, since the second person's subjects were not sensitized by a pretest.

Selection bias

This threat to external validity is fairly obvious; however, instead of just ensuring equivalence between the experimental and control groups, from the perspective of external validity, *selection bias* refers to the degree to which the experimental and control groups are representative of the wider population. If the study groups (both or either the experimental or control groups) are not representative of the wider study population, then researchers will not be able to generalize their results to that wider population.

Would you sing in the shower if you knew you were being observed? Like many people in everyday events, research subjects may behave differently if they know they are being watched. Researchers call this reactivity, *or the* Hawthorne effect.

This may sound like an issue of sampling to you; you're right, it is. In order to most effectively protect against selection bias as an external threat to validity, researchers need to do some form of probability sampling whenever possible. However, as I have discussed, sometimes is it not feasible for researchers to randomly select study subjects. Research, then, is a trade-off. Social scientists have the greatest confidence in the findings of samples that were randomly selected from the population, but when that is not possible, the researchers should try to use statistical means (like the comparison of various characteristics) to show that the study group and the study population are similar.

Reactivity

Have you ever behaved differently because you suspect someone is watching you? For example, perhaps you lower your voice when conversing with someone if you suspect another person is listening. Maybe you sing in the shower if you think you are alone, but not if you suspect someone else is present. Both of these, essentially, are examples of reactivity. *Reactivity* occurs when a respondent is aware that he or she is being studied and behaves atypically as a result. As I discussed in Chapter 3, the atypical behavior that people exhibit when they know they are being watched may be due to nervousness, a desire to show off, or, the opposite, a desire to downplay behavior.

Hence, when a reactivity effect, or Hawthorne effect, is present, it is unclear whether any change in the dependent variable led to the change in behavior or whether any change was simply due to being observed. Therefore, if people do behave atypically in a study, researchers cannot be sure whether they would receive similar results in the wider population where people do not think they are, and in fact are not, being studied.

■ Ethical Issues

Social science experiments frequently require some level of deception. Researchers have to be careful not to tell experimental subjects too much about the study hypotheses or purposes, because if subjects sense these, they may behave atypically (as we saw with the Hawthorne effect), and sometimes researchers themselves have to be deceived about parts of the research (as we saw with experimental expectations). Furthermore, sometimes experiments involve conditions that may cause discomfort among participants or that may lead to differential benefits that only one group (the experimental group) will experience. In this section I will briefly discuss three ethical issues that relate to these concerns: informed consent, the principle of nonmaleficence, and the principle of beneficence.

Informed consent

If you recall, in Chapter 2 I discussed the conditions for obtaining informed consent. One of those conditions was that the research participants had to know any information that might be relevant to their decision to participate in the study. This involves knowing at least the general research topic, but it does not necessarily involve knowing the actual research hypothesis because of reactivity concerns similar to what I just mentioned. Experiments frequently involve this type of deception in addition to other forms.

For example, in a previous chapter I discussed Solomon Asch's experiment on peer group conformity. Asch (1952) told his participants that the experiment was on visual judgments; however, he was really testing whether the one subject in a room of five or six "confederates" posing as fellow students would make a clearly wrong answer because everyone else in the room did.

Technically, Asch deceived the subjects, but he had no choice. If he told the subjects that he was trying to see whether they would conform to others, the subjects very likely would have not have selected the wrong line even if others did in order to show that they do not follow the group. However, notice that his deception was not completely unrelated to the study. For example, he did not tell participants that he was going to study their opinion of professors, their opinion of fellow students, a specific type of learning technique, or some other issue. He told a half-truth. Asch *did* study people's visual judgment; after all, the subject had to make a decision on which line visually matched the test line. Deceptions that are rooted in actual behaviors by the participants are more acceptable than random deceptions. What Asch told students they would be doing and what students did do was exactly the same; therefore, not knowing the real topic of study (conformity) was not necessary for informed consent because knowing the topic would not require any different behavior on the part of the subjects.

Understand that no social science field condones dishonesty just for dishonesty's sake. Although deception is tolerated, the amount of it and the nature of it is restricted. Neither the amount of deception nor the nature of deception should go beyond the parameters of deception in everyday life. In other words, the deception cause undue harm to respondents, nor should the results of the deception lead to any discomfort beyond what is present in everyday life. One of the best ways for researchers to overcome ethical issues involving deception is to keep the broad guideline of "everyday life" in mind and to **debrief** subjects at the end of the study. Debriefing involves telling the subjects the true nature of the experiment after their participation in it. This way, if respondents want to enact their right to privacy and withdraw from the study now that they truly have informed consent, they are able to do so.

Nonmaleficence

Sometimes experiments, like Stanley Milgram's prison experiment I discussed in Chapter 2, may lead to physical danger, anxiety, or embarrassment among participants. Purists argue that research that takes these risks should not be conducted at any cost. Others argue that if the chance of physical danger, anxiety, or embarrassment is present, but small, then the research may be feasible if the researcher closely monitors the course of the experiment and exercises rigid control over the experimental conditions.

Again, I think a good general rule of thumb here is to use the "everyday" yardstick that I discussed with informed consent. Research that might involve minor embarrassment that is similar to, or no more threatening than, potential embarrassment in daily life is unlikely to run the risk of nonmaleficence, especially if participants are debriefed. For example, if I want to study how people respond to flirting behavior from strangers, and I have experimental confederates (people who are part of the research team who are "playing along") whistle or make whooping sounds as people walk by and then record their reaction, this behavior may cause some people embarrassment or discomfort. However, if I have another confederate watching from the sidelines who can inform these people who are experiencing discomfort that this is an experiment and explain the nature of the experiment, the risk of nonmaleficence is small, especially since people may experience whistles and whooping in real life.

However, as in Milgram's experiment, if an experiment suddenly takes a turn in an unanticipated direction that may lead to undue distress, danger, or embarrassment, then the researchers have an ethical responsibility to stop that experiment, just like Milgram did. Unfortunately, sometimes researchers cannot detect maleficence until after the experiment. For example, Sherman and Berk's (1984a) study required that police officers randomly decide who to arrest for domestic violence (as opposed to the other two conditions of separate and mediate). Well, what about those individuals who were not arrested? Were the victims of the separation and mediation responses more likely to be beaten again because their abusers were not detained? After all, Sherman and Berk's dependent variable was recidivism—which essentially means whether a person committed another act of abuse. This means that someone (the victim) was vulnerable to physical danger and these people did not willingly participate in the study, therefore informed consent on behalf of the victims was not obtained (nor could it be, given the design of the research). Clearly, the issue of nonmaleficence is not necessarily as straightforward as initial consideration would imply. Therefore, researchers must be especially careful in contemplating these issues and designing their research.

Beneficence

Sometimes, especially in evaluation research, the distribution of benefits is not equivalent. Researchers may truly believe that a social program will benefit people; however, how can they then justify denying that program to the control group? In other words, if I truly think a drug treatment program will help a person overcome a drug addiction, am I being unethical in denying that treatment to those who are in the control group? This concern is compounded if I randomly assign people to the experimental and control groups. By nature of random assignment, there may be people with serious drug addictions who need help *now*, but I am denying them that help by randomly placing them in a control group. On the other hand, if I put all the people with serious drug addictions in the treatment group, now I have a potential selection bias problem that may interfere with the interpretation of my findings.

On a theoretical level, these are all valid concerns. In reality, however, people need to keep in mind that the purpose of research is to test whether a treatment (here, a policy or program) *does* actually benefit the participants. Assuming ahead of time that the experimental group is getting a special advantage over the control group is like stacking the deck. It presupposes that the treatment is already beneficial before the experimental results are available. Therefore, in a similar light, it is ethical to randomly assign individuals to treatment and control groups when the researchers really do not know whether a treatment is beneficial or not.

Furthermore, in the real world there rarely is sufficient funds for everyone to receive a treatment. Therefore, using random assignment to decide who will, in an experiment, is as fair a way as any. For researchers, however, to have to address public concern or political pressure, one way to minimize the ethical concern over the distribution of benefits is to offer the treatment to the control group after the conclusion of the experiment if the treatment, was indeed, beneficial.

Interpreting Experimental Results

Clearly, people do research because they want to explore a topic, describe a situation, explain a phenomenon, or evaluate a program or policy. These four goals imply that any information from research has to somehow be analyzed. Analysis usually involves comparisons, and experiments are no different. Researchers can compare the voting patterns of people who hear negative campaigns to those who do not hear negative campaigns. Researchers can compare peer conformity among teenagers who follow a counterculture and proclaim their individuality to those who are more mainstream. Or researchers can compare teenage smoking behavior between those teens who see antismoking commercials and those who do not.

Let's take the last example and create a hypothetical study. Pretend that I randomly selected 200 teenagers from three area high schools. I then randomly assigned 100 to be in my experimental group and I will show these teenagers three 30-minute documentaries about the effects of smoking on their health. I will show one documentary each week for three weeks. The other 100 teenagers are going to be in my control group and they will not see the documentaries. I will use a pretest to learn how many cigarettes they smoke in a day and how many days a week they have at least one cigarette. I will contact each of the teens by telephone one month after the experiment to measure their frequency of smoking again. What type of experiment have I done? If you answered a classical experiment, you're right and the notation would look like this:

$$E \quad O_1 (A) \quad X \quad O_2 \quad (B)$$
$$E \quad O_1 (C) \qquad \quad O_2 \quad (D)$$

Where the first observations are my pretest, the treatment (X) is the antismoking documentaries, and the second observations are my posttest. The A, B, C, and D after the observation points are not part of the traditional notation for classic experiments, but I added them to facilitate my discussion of comparisons. Based on a classic design, there are four general comparisons I can make.

The first comparison is between the experimental group and the control group's pretest (Comparison A–C, from above notation). Since this is a true experiment and we rely on random selection and assignment to ensure that the two groups are equal, you should not notice any statistically significant difference in the number of days the teenagers in these two groups smoke or in the number of cigarettes they smoke a day. Notice what I said here. I used the phrase *statistically significant difference*. The two groups are not likely to be exact. The experimental group may smoke an average of 6.7 cigarettes a day and the control group may smoke an average of 7.0 cigarettes each day. However, you will not be able to determine whether a 0.3 difference is different enough to mean that the two groups are not equal without doing a statistical test. I will briefly discuss some basic statistics in Chapter

12. For now, let's assume that when I say "difference," I mean statistically significant difference and that some type of statistical analysis has been done.

If you do find a difference in the pretest scores (comparison A–C) of the experimental and control group, you might have selection bias. Remember, random selection and assignment minimizes the risk of this, but they do not completely guarantee that selection bias will not occur simply by chance. A pretest, however, helps researchers determine whether this validity threat is present in their research.

The second comparison is in the posttests for the experimental and control group (B–D comparison). If the documentaries had an effect on the smoking behavior of the teens in the experimental group, the posttest scores for the experimental group should be noticeably different from those for the control group. However, researchers cannot conclude that the treatment, here the antismoking documentaries, successfully led to this difference without first considering two other comparisons.

A third comparison is between the pretest and posttest for the experimental group (comparison A–B). If the posttest *did not* change from the pretest, the smoking documentaries may be ineffective. If the posttest *did* change, then provided that the next comparison does show a difference, the documentaries may work.

The fourth comparison is between the pretest and posttest of the control group (comparison C–D). Because the control group did not experience a treatment, we should *not* see a difference between the pretest and posttest scores for the teenagers who did not see the antismoking documentaries. If we do see a change in the control group, there may be a history, maturation, or diffusion of treatment effect. If these are present, we can no longer conclude, based on the comparison in the previous paragraph (A–B), that the treatment had an effect. One of these threats to validity that produced the change in pre- and posttest scores for the control group may have done the same for the experimental group.

The A–B and C–D comparison should also involve sample sizes, and not just pre- and posttest scores. If the number of subjects in the control and/or experimental group change noticeably, experimental mortality may be a threat to validity. If the sample sizes have not changed much between the two testing points or in comparison to each other (experimental and control groups), then researchers can safely rule out this validity threat.

To summarize, looking only at the posttests for the experimental and control groups (B–D comparison) does not in itself justify whether an experimental treatment influences the dependent variable. Other comparisons help identify (and rule out) potential rival causal factors that could explain any posttest differences between the experimental and control groups and any change within the experimental group. That's one of the reasons why experiments, like the classic experiment, are so useful. They can be one of the most effective means for controlling for threats to internal validity.

Advantages and Disadvantages of Experiments

As I've just said, one of the biggest advantages of experiments is that they are one of the best research designs for controlling for factors that threaten internal validity. Experiments also can be useful in identifying whether internal validity threats exist. Therefore, not only do they give the researcher some level of control over these threats but they also help researchers assess how well they did in avoiding these threats.

If the researcher chooses, experiments can also be relatively easy and cheap. Asking people to identify which line is longer, even if you have a small group of people who you pay or otherwise convince to lie, is not complicated or inordinately expensive (compared to some other designs, like longitudinal surveys which I will discuss in the next chapter). Nor do experiments have to be very time intensive to be effective.

Furthermore, experiments can be manageable. If the experimenter designs an experiment in the laboratory, the researcher can control not only the treatment but also the environmental conditions surrounding that treatment. Of course, not all research topics lend themselves conveniently to controlled laboratory conditions. Experiments can address that, too. Researchers can do quasi-experiments. Sure, the researcher may have to trade some benefits of true experiments, such as random assignment, however, by simply using a pretest, the researcher can assess whether participants are similar on some key variables of interest. So, experiments lend themselves to manageable environments as well as natural ones.

Of course, not all experiments have these advantages or to the same degree. A researcher can make a very detailed complicated experiment just as readily as he or she can make a simple experiment. The point is that the various types of experiments provide researchers with a wide range of choices depending on their research topic and concerns. Worried about selection bias? No problem—minimize the risk by doing some type of true experiment. Not possible? Do a quasi-experiment with a pretest to assess the similarity between experimental and control groups. Worried about a pretest? Okay, don't do one. Unless you have random assignment, you may have some other methodological issues to address, but the point is that with experiments, researchers have a lot more options than they do with many other modes of observation.

Of course, these options can come with a cost. The manageability of laboratory experiments is offset with the artificial nature of them. Real life is not as controlled as a laboratory and can get quite messy. Therefore, generalizability may be an issue in some laboratory experiments. Likewise, as we saw, there are some ethical issues, such as informed consent, the role of deception, the ethics behind random assignment, and nonmaleficence. Finally, experimenters are people, too; and once you add more people to the method of observation, you may potentially add another dimension of validity threat. Experimenters can influence the course of a study simply by their presence, as I illustrated in the discussion of the Hawthorne effect and experimenter bias.

The moral of the story is that no method of observation is foolproof. They all come with benefits and trade-offs. By considering the research question, the validity criteria, the ethical concerns, and researcher resources (such as time, money, and skill), researchers can choose which method of observation suits their needs. Experiments are one option among many. In the next chapter, I will examine another option that social scientists frequently use: surveys.

Evaluating Written Research: Experiments

Because there are many different types of experiments, the guidelines for evaluating experiments are general. Some may apply to each study, some may not. Therefore, many of these evaluation questions have more than one question embedded within them to address the different experimental contexts.

1. *Can you identify a treatment variable that indicates that an experiment is the method of observation?*

The first step in evaluating experiments is to make sure that what you are reading is indeed an experiment! Students, and sometimes researchers who should know better, use the term *experiment* when they really mean a *study*, which is broader. To be an experiment, the study you are reading has to involve studying the effect of a specific treatment. In other words, the researcher, or someone else, has to consciously manipulate the independent variable so that is it a treatment where some people have it and some do not. Gender is not a treatment because it cannot be manipulated; researchers cannot specifically assign others to a particular gender.

2. *How many groups were studied? If there are two or more groups, did the researcher use random assignment? If the researcher did not use random assignment, did the researcher present evidence that the groups were similar regarding key variables at the beginning of the study?*

Once you are sure that the researcher really did do an experiment, and therefore the guidelines for experiments are relevant, then you need to see whether the researcher compares two or more groups. If the researcher does compare two or more groups, you need to be clear about how people were assigned to the different groups. Did the researcher use random assignment or not? It is important that you do not confuse *random selection* with *random assignment*.

Random selection deals with sampling issues (discussed in Chapter 5) and it affects the generalizability of the study findings to the population. Random assignment is a characteristic of true experiments that means that subjects had an equal probability of being selected for any one group. Random assignment facilitates the comparison between experimental groups. To put it another way, random selection affects the researcher's ability to generalize *outside* of the study, whereas random assignment affects the researcher's conclusions *within* the study. Ideally, experiments will involve both random selection *and* random assignment. However, as we've discussed, this is not always possible. Quasi-experiments do not have random assign, although they may have random selection; true experiments have random assignment, although they may not have random selection (but they can).

Like with random sampling, researchers will not always (in fact, they rarely do) explain how they randomly assign subjects; they will just state that they did so. The omission of the process of random assignment is less problematic than the omission of how subjects were randomly selected (if they were). So, for the most part, if a researcher states that she or he randomly assigned subjects to the experimental and control groups, readers can believe the researcher and assume that she or he did some type of true experiment.

However, if the researcher did not use random assignment, then you need to ask yourself whether he or she provided evidence that the various groups were equal in ways relevant to the research. Remember, there is no way of assessing whether the various groups are equal in *all* variables because we couldn't possibly identify all variables on which to match people.

Also, although I discussed the limitations of identifying "key" variables earlier in this chapter, sometimes attempting to do this is all we can do. Therefore, if researchers did not randomly assign subjects to the various groups of study, then the researcher needs to provide some discussion that establishes that *for the variables the researcher is interested in*, there are no real differences between the groups. This may involve a brief mention of statistical tests (ideal) or a simple comparison of percentages or means. Incidentally, sometimes researchers who do random assignment also provide statistics as further evidence that the groups of study are equal (and that chance differences do not exist); therefore, if you see statistical tests, don't automatically jump to the conclusion that the researcher did not do random assignment.

3. Is the treatment and any pre- or posttests described in sufficient detail that facilitates replication?

You want to make sure that the treatments were described in detail explicit enough that you could copy the treatment yourself. This means that the researcher should present what was done, to whom it was done, who did it, and the conditions surrounding the experiment. The researcher should also describe the measures used for any pre- or posttests. If these measures are complicated or too detailed for the limited space available (since many journals have a page limit for each study), then the researcher needs to provide citations where additional information can be found. Shiloh, Sorek, and Terkel's (2003) study about animal petting and stress that appears in Box 6.1 is a good example of a detailed treatment description.

4. Is deception necessary? If so, is the deception within the parameters of the research topic? Have the participants been debriefed so they know the true nature of the study (and can enact their right to privacy by declining to participate after the fact)?

As I said in the chapter, sometimes deception is necessary in an experiment; however, it must always be balanced with the ethical requirements of research. If deception occurs, it needs to be a "partial truth" if possible so as not to hinder informed consent. At the end of the study, participants should be debriefed so they can enact their right to privacy and withdraw their participation if they desire.

5. Based on the description of treatment and experimental procedure, do you see any red flags regarding ethical issues?

Even in studies that do not need deception, the other ethical issues we discussed still need to be addressed. Researchers will rarely directly state how their design addresses ethical concerns; however, as a reader, you can make some conclusions about this on your own based on the researchers' description of the treatment and experimental process.

6. Did the researcher use assistants? If so, did the researcher state that they were properly trained? If so, did the researcher specify any special measures to make sure that the assistants administered the treatment properly?

Sometimes researchers use graduate assistants, colleagues, or other individuals to help with the study. If this is the case, these people need to be properly trained in how to conduct an experiment and there should be some way for the researcher to double-check whether these people administered the treatment as the researcher designed. Neither of these issues needs to be elaborate nor described in great detail. Usually a few words that somehow mentions that the research assistants or helpers were trained or briefed about the experiment is sufficient. Researchers can usually check whether treatments were administered properly simply by watching parts of the experiment from afar or directly discussing the experiment with the assistants. In fact, since a researcher can explain assistant training and observation so briefly, people often miss it when reading a report, so be careful.

7. **Is the setting natural or artificial (in a laboratory)? If it's in a laboratory, does the researcher recognize that external validity may be weak? If it's in a natural setting, does the researcher recognize that there may be some differences in the environments of the various groups?**

The researcher should specify whether the experiment was done in a laboratory or a natural setting; then, as a critical reader, you need to make sure that the researcher's conclusions are appropriate for the type of setting. For example, research that is done in a laboratory is not a natural setting, and this may limit the external validity or generalizability of the researcher's findings. The researcher needs to recognize this somewhere (most likely in a discussion of conclusion section). Therefore, if the researcher states that the external validity or generalizability may be questionable, this is *not* a weakness, but instead is a knowledgeable recognition of the restrictions related to the study design. On the other hand, if a researcher conducts the study in a natural setting, the experimental and control conditions might not be exactly the same because the researcher has less control over the social environment of the study. Therefore, once again, if a researcher draws attention to the fact that the various sites of the study are similar, then, as critical readers, we cannot fault the researcher for not having complete environmental duplicates.

Now that you are halfway through the book, one point should be abundantly clear: No one particular piece of research is perfect. All of research is a trade-off. Where one aspect may be strong, another aspect may be weaker. Therefore, the skill in being a critical evaluator is in recognizing when those trade-offs are unavoidable, how they affect the research, and whether the researcher accurately interprets the findings relative to those trade-offs. A summary of the points I mentioned for evaluating experimental design in written research is as follows:

1. Can you identify a treatment variable that indicates that an experiment is the method of observation?

2. How many groups were studied?
   a. If there are two or more groups, did the researcher use random assignment?
   b. If the researcher did *not* use random assignment, did the researcher present evidence that the groups were similar regarding key variables at the beginning of the study?

3. Is the treatment and any pre- or posttests described in sufficient detail that facilitates replication?

4. Is deception necessary?
   a. If so, is the deception within the parameters of the research topic?
   b. Have the participants been debriefed so they know the true nature of the study (and can enact their right to privacy by declining to participate after the fact)?

5. Based on the description of treatment and experimental procedure, do you see any red flags regarding ethical issues?

6. Did the researcher use assistants?
   a. If so, did the researcher state that they were properly trained?
   b. If so, did the researcher specify any special measures to make sure that the assistants administered the treatment properly?

BOX 6.2   **Evaluating Written Research: Experiments**

In the following article, Kasprisin and colleagues assess the effectiveness of e-mentoring programs, which is a form of mentoring that involves electronic communication as opposed to more common forms of communication such as talking. Below is an excerpt from that study.

The goal of e-training in an e-mentoring programme is to increase involvement, satisfaction, and value. To accomplish this, it is necessary to take the lessons learned from face-to-face mentoring and investigate their application in the e-communication environment. [We hypothesize the following:]

. . . *Hypothesis 1.* Engaging in a required training tutorial will increase the number of students who stay involved with their e-mentors in a formalised [sic] e-mentoring programme.

. . . *Hypothesis 2.* Engaging in a required training tutorial will increase the overall satisfaction of students who participate in a formalised [sic] e-mentoring programme.

. . . *Hypothesis 3.* Engaging in a required training tutorial will increase the perceived value of participation for the students who stay involved with their e-mentors.

Method

In 2001–02, 3347 students applied for participation in the MentorNet cohort. Of these, 2557 were undergraduate students from four-year colleges and universities. A group of 400 students was randomly selected and assigned into one of two conditions. Half of this sub-sample was assigned to an intervention group where completion of the training tutorials was required and the other half of the sub-sample was assigned to a control group where participation was voluntary. A stratified random sample was used to ensure that the control and experimental groups were equally selected from upper and lower division baccalaureate . . . majors. There were no demographic differences between the control and experimental groups with respect to age, full-time status, and traditional/returning student status.

. . . Students were matched with mentors to form e-mentoring pairs. The names and contact information were provided by e-mail to students in the control group. For the experimental group, the students were told that their mentors would be identified after they had completed the tutorials. After each student completed the training, the mentor's name and contact information was made available. Students were requested to complete a comprehensive web-based questionnaire at the completion of the academic year. This questionnaire requested data that were used to evaluate the programme, to suggest modifications for programme development and to provide research data for analysis of the effectiveness of programme components.

Table I. Survey Items

Involvement

How often did you send e-mail to your mentor? _____ times a month

How often did you receive e-mail from your mentor? _____ times a month

Satisfaction

How comfortable have you been asking your mentor questions?

How comfortable have you been responding to questions from your mentor?

How satisfied have you been with your one-on-one mentoring experience?

How satisfied have you been with your MentorNet experience this year?

Please rate the "quality of the match" between your mentor and you.[*]

Value

Has your MentorNet experience affected your self-confidence about your ability to succeed in your field?

Has your MentorNet experience affected your belief that you would enjoy working in industry or a government lab or agency?

BOX 6.2   **Evaluating Written Research: Experiments, continued**

Has your MentorNet experience affected your desire to pursue a job in your field?

Note: Scale anchors are 1 (Not at all) and 5 (Very) for value and satisfaction.
*Scale anchors 1 (Poor) and 5 (Excellent).

Source: Christina Algiere Kasprisin, Peg Boyle Single, Richard M. Single, and Carol B. Muller, "Building a Better Bridge: Testing E-Training to Improve E-Mentoring Programmes in Higher Education," *Mentoring & Tutoring: Partnership in Learning, 11* (1) (April 2003): 67 (**AN 9756023**). Reprinted by permission of Taylor & Francis Ltd. www.tan

Critical Thinking Questions

1. Can you identify a treatment variable that indicates that an experiment is the method of observation?

2. How many groups were studied?

  a. If there are two or more groups, did the researcher use random assignment?

  b. If the researcher did *not* use random assignment, did the researcher present evidence that the groups were similar regarding key variables at the beginning of the study?

3. Is the treatment and any pre- or posttests described in sufficient detail that facilitates replication?

4. Is deception necessary?

  a. If so, is the deception within the parameters of the research topic?

  b. Have the participants been debriefed so they know the true nature of the study (and can enact their right to privacy by declining to participate after the fact)?

5. Based on the description of treatment and experimental procedure, do you see any red flags regarding ethical issues?

6. Did the researcher use assistants?

  a. If so, did the researcher state that they were properly trained?

  b. If so, did the researcher specify any special measures to make sure that the assistants administered the treatment properly?

7. Is the setting natural or artificial (in a laboratory)?

  a. If it's in a laboratory, does the researcher recognize that external validity may be weak?

  b. If it's in a natural setting, does the researcher recognize that there may be some differences in the environments of the various groups?

8. Overall, do you think the experimental design is sound?

Critical Thinking Discussion

1. Yes. The treatment variable is the training tutorial. All students are involved in web mentoring, therefore that is not the independent (or treatment) variable. The difference was that half of the students had to complete a tutorial (the experimental group) and the other half did not (the control group) before they found out who their mentors were.

2. Yes. The researchers stated that they used a stratified random sample both to select and assign students.

3. Yes. It appears as if there was not a pretest. However, the researchers present the questions for the posttest at the end of the article. Therefore, since we have the exact questions they used, replication of this is easy.

4. Deception is not really necessary. People in the experimental group were told that they had to complete the tutorial before they would receive the name of their mentor. There is no deception here.

BOX 6.2   **Evaluating Written Research: Experiments, continued**

5. Participation seems voluntary since the students applied to be part of the electronic mentor program; there was no deception since both the control and experimental groups did receive mentors. Likewise, there does not seem to be any foreseeable harm in participating in this study. However, the only issue is that the researchers do not comment on whether they guaranteed anonymity or confidentiality (if they guaranteed anything at all) regarding the surveys. This is a weakness, but it is less of one than we otherwise may think because the results (which are not shown, but which you can see on Research Navigator) are presented in such a way as no one reading the report can identify who individual respondents are.

   Therefore, from a reader's point of view (even if that reader is someone from the same universities as the students), anonymity is guaranteed. The lack of an anonymity/confidentiality specification is an issue from a purely methodological point of view, but it is not much of a problem in reality.

6. There is no evidence that the researcher used assistants.

7. The setting is natural; and, although environmental differences in the two groups are certainly possible, they are not likely to alter the results of the study. Why? Because subjects were randomly selected and randomly assigned to the groups and there is no real reason to believe that they are different. In other words, even if someone in the control group has a mentor who is not very active, there is no reason to believe that someone in the experimental group may also have an inactive mentor. The random nature makes environmental problems generally inherent in natural experiments less problematic.

8. Overall, this is a very good example of experimental design.

7. Is the setting natural or artificial (in a laboratory)?

   a. If it's in a laboratory, does the researcher recognize that external validity may be weak?

   b. If it's in a natural setting, does the researcher recognize that there may be some differences in the environments of the various groups?

8. Overall, do you think the experimental design is sound?

Key Terms

Control group (232)　　　Experimental group (232)　　　Pretest (233)
Debrief (264)　　　　　　Experimenter effects (261)　　　Treatment (232)
Double blind study (261)　Posttest (233)

Review Questions and Exercises

1. *Identify the type of experiment used in the following articles. Justify your conclusion. Apply the terms associated with experiments to each of the articles. If you do not think a term is relevant, provide an explanation as to why.*

a. Stanton, Neville A., Young, Mark S., Walker, Guy H., Turner, Hannah, and Randle Steve. (2001). Automating the driver's control tasks. International Journal of Cognitive Ergonomics, 5 (3), 221. 16 pp. (AN 6411673)

b. Mendelberg, Tali, and Oleske, John. (2000, April–June). Race and public deliberation. Communication, 17 (2), 159. 23 pp. DOI: 10.1080/105846000198468. (AN 3239361)

c. Baker, Roger, Baker, Emma, Allen, Helen, Golden Shirley, Thomas, Peter, Hol-Lingbery, tim, Newth, Jeffrey, and Gibson, Sarah. (2002, December). A Naturalistic longitudinal evaluation of counseling in primary care. Counseling Psychology Quarterly, 15 (4), 359. 15 pp. (AN 9215735)

d. Nagin, Daniel S., and Pogarsky, Greg. (2003, February). An experimental investigation of deterrence: Cheating, self-servicing bias, *and impulsivity.* Criminology, 41 (1), 167. 27 pp. (AN 12672866)

2. *Evaluate the experimental designs of the following articles.*

a. Beersma, Bianca, Harinck, Fieke, and Garts, Maria J. J., (2003). Bound in honor: How honor values and insults affect the experience and management of conflicts. International Journal of Conflict Management, 14 (2), 75. 20 pp. (AN 13276812)

b. Molfese, Victoria J., Molfese, Dennis L., and Modgline, Arlene A. (2001, November/December). Newborn and preschool predictors of second-grade reading Scores: An evaluation of categorical and continuous scores. Journal of Learning Disabilities, 34 (6), 545. 10 pp. (AN 6424799)

c. Dixon, John A., and Mahoney, Berenice. 2004, February). The effect of accent evaluation and evidence on a suspect' perceived guilt and criminality. Journal of Social Psychology, 144 (1), 63. 11 pp. (AN 11975612)

Survey Research

Although I know of no research confirming this (or denying it for that matter), survey research is the method of social research that students probably find the most familiar. Many of you have likely had to complete course evaluation forms, satisfaction surveys, warranty surveys, or other similar surveys at some point. You name it, there has probability been a survey of it. Part of that is because surveys *are* a very popular mode of observation in the social sciences.

Surveys are popular because, as I will show shortly, there are a variety of topics that surveys are good at addressing. For example, surveys can assess knowledge, attitudes, and characteristics (to name a few topics). Surveys are also pretty efficient. Researchers can survey a huge amount of people over a wide geographical area (like the entire United States) for relatively little cost. Also, because survey research fits so well with probability sampling, it is relatively easy for researchers to generalize findings from a sample to a wider population.

So, if I wanted to study college students' attitudes about the upcoming election (versatile topic), instead of having to ask all college students in the nation, I could draw a probability sample of college students in the nation (a manageable means of making conclusions about the population of college students), contact them via a telephone survey (relatively cheap), and have my assistants automatically input the answers in a computer while they are conducting the survey (what could be more efficient than that?).

In fact, you are probably so familiar with surveys that you may be wondering why I am devoting an entire chapter to how to do them. After all, they seem pretty straightforward: You write some questions, ask people those questions, and then get your results. Nothing could be simpler!

Yeah, right. You may *now* be saying to yourself, "Here she goes again, making something I thought was pretty simple more complicated!" Well, yes and no. Just like good magic seems simple until you try to do the trick yourself, survey writing is simple in theory but more difficult in application. Actually, it's not that writing surveys and gathering the data itself is hard; it's just that if you want to get valid and reliable *results* from your survey, you need to pay attention to some points that most people overlook unless they have been trained otherwise. You are about to become one of those trained individuals!

In this chapter I will discuss appropriate topics for survey research, some guidelines for constructing the various types of surveys, the ethical considerations of surveys, validity and reliability issues, and some advantages and disadvantages of survey research. Let me begin by discussing what topics are appropriate for survey research.

Appropriate Topics for Survey Research

Any of you who have ever had an e-mail account probably have experienced the joy of spam e-mail—those e-mail advertisements that appear to flood your mailbox and overrun your "real" e-mail messages. In fact, by some accounts, spam makes up 75 percent of all e-mail traffic! Annoying? Many seem to think so. The PEW Internet and American Life Project studies Internet issues and e-mail experiences. In a telephone survey of 2,204 American adults (1,371 were Internet users), researchers found that 86 percent of e-mail users reported experiencing some spam-related stress (with a margin of error of plus/minus 3 percentage points). In fact, according to the survey, 77 percent of respondents said that spam made the Internet an unpleasant experience. The survey also found that many of these people experience problems with spam even though the government has passed the CAN-SPAM Act, which is antispam legislation (Fontana, 2004).

The PEW Internet and American Life Project is a descriptive survey. Its research goal is to describe the respondents' experiences and views regarding spam e-mail. Survey research is also appropriate for the other three goals of research. Researchers can use surveys to explore an issue we know little about; they can use surveys as part of an evaluation of a program (for example, interview foster families to assess their views of the foster system); and researchers can use surveys to explain phenomena, because surveys allow researchers to measure many variables simultaneously (and usually multiple indicators of those variables as well), which they can later use to statistically address rival causal factors if they want to try to establish causality. Hence, surveys are a versatile tool for observing the world around us.

Opinion studies, such as the spam study above, are classic topics for surveys. In an earlier chapter, I discussed the Gallup Poll, which is a national survey aimed at assessing people's views about current social issues. Surveys that address people's opinions or beliefs ask questions such as: Do you think the president is doing a good job? Would you support a tax increase to fund educational reform? What is your view on the death penalty? As I said, opinions and attitudes are classic survey topics.

Surveys can also address people's self-reported behavior. Questions such as Did you vote in the last presidential election? Did you work for pay when your first-born child was an infant? How many times do you consume alcoholic beverages in a typical week? all address people's specific behaviors.

One caution about using survey research to address behavior: People are better at reporting recent behavior than past behavior. Researchers call questions that ask about behavior in the past **recollective questions.** Because human recall is questionable, these questions work best if the information asked is general and monumental. For example, peo-

How can surveys assess voting behavior and/or people's attitudes regarding political candidates and issues?

ple can easily remember if they voted in the last presidential election because this is a general and monumental event (it occurs only every four years and there is a lot of media hype about voting). Likewise, people are likely to remember if they worked for pay when their first child was an infant; however, they are not likely to remember how many hours a week they worked. Therefore, asking about the hours of work would be a poor choice. Surveys, then, are a great means of observing people's self-reported behavior; however, they work best when the behavior is current or if a past behavior is general and easily remembered.

Survey research is also appropriate for asking about people's specific characteristics. What year are you in college? What is your gender? What is you total household income? Do you belong to a church? This is why survey research is such a useful tool when the goal of research is to describe a population.

Survey questions can also assess people's expectations. Researchers can ask people what they think they will do regarding a specific situation and then conduct a second survey later to assess people's behaviors. Through this technique, researchers can examine how well expectations and behaviors actually match. Appropriate questions would be: Do you expect to vote in the upcoming election? If you are pregnant, do you expect to return to work before the baby is 1 year old?

However, I have to provide a caveat here as well. Researchers sometimes measure expectations for behavior and then mistakenly interpret those expectations as if they are the actual behavior itself. This is erroneous because many studies question the assumption that people actually *do* behave as they think they will. In fact, it is common knowledge in the social sciences that researchers cannot make this assumption because people often do *not* behave as they think they will. Therefore, if you are using a survey to assess people's expectations, you need to be clear that that is *all* you are assessing. You cannot make judgment about actual behaviors based on people's expectations of their behavior.

Surveys are also useful for self-classification. For example, I could ask someone, Do you think you drink a lot of alcohol? Do you think you are a lenient parent? You may think that this second question is about characteristics, and therefore not a unique category. To some degree, you are right; there is some overlap between characteristic questions and self-classification because, after all, in self-classification you are asking someone to use some type of adjective to describe himself or herself. However, the difference is that in self-classification questions, researchers are usually asking the respondents to place themselves along a continuum. Being a lenient or strict parent is a continuum of opposites, where one value is more or less than another. However, being Catholic, Jewish, or Baptist really isn't a continuum; it is simply a categorization. The distinction is subtle and the end result—that both are appropriate for survey research regardless of how you classify them—is the same.

Last, survey research is useful for assessing people's knowledge. Essentially, if you have ever taken a multiple-choice exam, you have, in a sense, completed a survey. True, surveys aren't graded; however, the format for a multiple-choice or short-answer exam and a survey that tests knowledge are very similar. Researchers can ask people: Who is the U.S. Attorney General? What percentage of your state's population is over age 65? How is the poverty line determined?

Of course, most surveys will include questions that fit a variety of these topics. For example, a general population survey about alcohol may test people's knowledge (What is your state's blood alcohol level to indicate intoxication?) as well as ask them their characteristics (What is your gender?), their behavior (How many drinks do you typically consume on a typical Saturday night?), their attitudes (Do you think the legal drinking age should be lowered from 21 to 18?), their expectations (Would you ever get into a car with someone who you think has had too much to drink?), and their self-classification (Would you consider yourself a light, moderate, or heavy drinker?). As I stated earlier, the versatility of appropriate survey topics are one of the reasons why surveys are such a popular mode of observation.

General Survey Construction

There are many types of surveys. The form people probably think of the most is the mailed survey, which is a survey you receive in the mail, complete, and then return via the mail. Phone surveys are also common; and, as the name implies, these are surveys that occur over the phone. In-person interviews are a third type of survey where a researcher or research assistant asks a respondent questions in person. Last, with the increasing popularity of the Internet, a newer form of survey is an electronic survey. In this section I will discuss each of these four survey types—mail, phone, interview, and electronic—in detail; however, before I do that, I want to discuss some general issues about survey construction. Figure 7.1 shows the steps for conducting survey research.

Question Wording

Writing surveys is more complicated than just jotting down some casual questions to ask people. Basically, jotting down questions is exactly what survey writing entails, but in order to produce valid and reliable results, there are some guidelines researchers keep in mind while they are writing survey questions. Why? Well, let me give you some hypothetical survey questions to illustrate the importance of not just using the "jotting down" method.

1. Have you used any drugs in the last month?

   a. Yes
   b. No

2. How frequently have you used these drugs?

   a. 1–3 times
   b. 3–5 times

1. Choose a research topic that is appropriate for survey research.
2. Review the literature to discover what is already known about that topic, where studies have produced conflicting findings, or where there are gaps/omissions in the research.
3. If doing explanatory or evaluative research, formulate a hypothesis that can be tested with a survey.
4. Develop valid measures of the concepts (especially any independent and dependent variables).
5. Select a survey type.
6. Construct a survey.
   a. Be conscious of question wording.
      (1) Be conscious of your audience. Tailor the language of question wording as appropriate.
      (2) Avoid vague/confusing wording.
         (a) Avoid unnecessarily lengthy questions.
         (b) Do not use language that is subjective.
         (c) State exactly what you mean; do not rely on the reader's interpretation.
         (d) Do not use double negatives in your wording.
      (3) Avoid biased questions.
         (a) Do not refer to the opinion of experts or other people in authority in your question.
         (b) Do not word questions in a way that any answer indicates agreement or disagreement.
         (c) Make sure there are the same number of positive as negative answer categories.
   (4) Avoid leading questions.
      (a) Avoid emotional language that may elicit a particular response.
      (b) Use both sides of an attitude continuum or a neutral way of asking an attitude.
      (c) Neutralize the action of deviant or illegal acts.
   (5) Avoid assuming prior knowledge on behalf of participants.
      (a) Do not ask factual information that is not common knowledge.
      (b) Do not ask respondents to recall information from the distant past.
      (c) Word questions in a way that makes sense to respondents.
   (6) Avoid double-barreled questions.
   (7) Make sure all answer categories are mutually exclusive.
   (8) Make sure all answer categories are exhaustive.
   (9) Avoid response set patterns.
   b. Be conscious of survey format/presentation.
      (1) Consider using both open- and closed-ended questions.
      (2) Make sure contingency questions are present if necessary and ensure that they correctly lead the respondent to relevant questions.
      (3) Put demographic questions toward the end of the survey.
      (4) Put threatening questions toward the end of the survey (after some demographics, but not necessarily all demographics).
7. Follow the steps for the specific survey format you decide to use.

Figure 7.1 Steps for Survey Research

c. 5–7 times

d. More than 7 times

3. Have your parents ever caught you using drugs and punished you for using drugs?

a. Yes

b. No

4. Do you think drugs should be illegal?

a. Strongly agree

b. Agree

c. Disagree

d. Strongly Disagree

5. What is your race?

a. White/Caucasian

b. African American

c. Latino

Suppose you were filling out this survey. Would you have any trouble with the first question? No? Think again. What if I had a headache and I took some headache medicine. Is this a drug? Technically, yes, but it may not be the type of drug that the researchers are trying to study. Even if, in a cover letter, the researchers said that they are interested in studying illegal drugs, this provides some clarification (if I read the cover letter carefully enough to pick up on this); however, what if I am a 20-year-old college student completing this survey? If I went to a party and had a beer, alcohol is an illegal drug for me at this age. Does this count? Or are the researchers interested in drugs such as marijuana, cocaine, and the like? This is unclear, and if respondents are not clear about a question, at best they will skip it and at worst they will just answer something (anything—the point is that they will just write or circle any answer), which will hurt the validity of the study (because this answer has no real meaning).

Let's assume that the "drugs" refer to marijuana, cocaine, crack, and heroin. A respondent will still have problems answering question 2. I may not have used any drugs. Therefore, where is there an answer for 0? There is none. Also, what if someone *did* use some of these drugs? It is unclear if the researchers are asking the respondent for a total frequency (e.g., a respondent smoked marijuana one time and tried heroin once, but never used the other drugs in the past month, therefore this person's answer would be "2"), or are the researchers asking the respondent about the frequency of each drug individually (in which, for my hypothetical respondent, there would be two answers of "1" but the opportunity to record only one answer). Let's assume the researchers clarified this question to read: "What is the total number of times you have used either marijuana, crack, cocaine, or heroin in the past month?" A respondent would *still* have trouble answering this question because if someone used these drugs a total of five times, for example, this person would have to circle answers "b" *and* "c" because both of those answer choices have the answer "5" in them.

The other three questions have problems as well. For question 3, what is a respondent supposed to answer if his or her parents caught the respondent using drugs but did not mete out a punishment? Or what if the parents *suspected* but did not actually catch the respondent using drugs, but still punished this person based on the suspicion? How would someone answer this question if the answer to one part of the question is yes but the answer to the other part of the question is no? Finally, the last two questions both have problems of omission. What if a person simply does not have an opinion about the legalization of drugs (question 4)? There is no answer category for this individual. Likewise, if this is a general survey, I am likely to have respondents who are of a different race than the ones I've specified, or people may identify with more than one race. How would these people respond?

Writing survey questions that have fundamental problems such as the hypothetical ones I have presented here seriously impede research. There is enough opportunity for error when researchers do everything in their control to construct well-designed studies. Having a method of observation that is clearly flawed or vague further complicates the interpretation and usefulness of any results. This is why I am about to extensively discuss some guidelines for survey construction that are common to most of the four survey types.

Be conscious of your audience

Researchers need to obtain valid and unbiased information, and respondents need to feel that their views are important to the researcher. Consequently, the language of the questions needs to fit the culture and expertise of the respondents. For example, if researchers are interviewing teenagers, they do not want to word their questions in an overly academic or lofty manner. This will only serve to alienate the respondents.

Avoid confusing or vague wording

Need an example of a confusing question? Look at the cartoon on the next page. You might think that this is an exaggeration for humor's sake, but the point is valid. Sometimes researchers, in their desire to make sure they are very explicit about what they mean so to avoid confusion on behalf of the participant, make a question so lengthy that the participants get lost reading it and end up being confused anyway. Although researchers are sometimes trying to test knowledge about complicated issues or are assessing attitudes about specific or detailed instances, researchers need to keep questions as short as possible to avoid "losing" the participant during the process. If a person has to read a question a number of times before understanding what the question means, the resulting data are likely to be suspect. Why? Because the odds are that many people *won't* reread the question, even if they need to; instead, they will just write the first response that comes to mind—even if it doesn't accurately reflect what they would have said if they did understand the question. If many people do this, it threatens the validity of the data.

Questions can also be vague or confusing based on the wording. For example, a question that asks, Do you regularly eat a sensible diet? is problematic for two ways. First, what is "regularly" to one person may not be the same to another. I may think that regularly is five days a week, you might think that it is at least three days a week, and your friend might think that it means at least one meal every day of the week. Similarly, what people consider to be "sensible" varies as well.

A recent controversy about a trail in Lake Ivanhoe in Orlando, Florida, illustrates another example of vague wording. City administrators surveyed residents about their views on expanding a sidewalk to a path. The question was worded as such: "Do you support the completion of the Lake Ivanhoe Path west of I-4?" followed by choices: "Yes," "No," and "Why?" This question seems straightforward, but because the path was a sidewalk, residents were confused as to whether this meant lengthening or widening the sidewalk or making it a path in the more conventional sense (Picket, 2004). This example illustrates the im-

"*Next question: I believe that life is a constant striving for balance, requiring frequent tradeoffs between morality and necessity, within a cyclic pattern of joy and sadness, forging a trail of bittersweet memories until one slips, inevitably, into the jaws of death. Agree or disagree?*"

portance of keeping your audience in mind when writing survey questions. To an outsider who would not be completing this survey, the question seems fine. However, to those for whom the survey is intended, and who are aware of the existing sidewalk, it is unclear.

Another example of vague is when researchers assume that participants know the specifics of a question. For example, if I ask, What is your income? do I mean total household income or just for the individual responding to the survey? Do I mean salary? Do I mean after taxes? If, as a researcher, you want to know the total before tax household income (e.g., the total salaries of any money earning people in the house before taxes are deducted), then simply and directly ask the respondent for this information: What was your family's total pre-tax household income last year?

Researchers also can unintentionally write vague questions when they use double negatives in the wording. For example: Do you disagree that we should not cut the defense budget? People reading this question will probably do a double-take because they will have difficulty identifying which response fits their view. Does "yes" mean that we should cut the defense budget or does "no" mean this?

To summarize, questions can be vague and confusing if (1) the questions are unnecessarily long or wordy; (2) researchers use terms that are highly subjective or indefinite, and can therefore have different meanings to different people (e.g., regularly, sometimes); (3) researchers do not take into account the characteristics of their respondents; and (4) researchers use double negatives in their question wording. Frequently, questions are vague or confusing not because the researcher is unskilled (although that certainly is a possibility) but more commonly because the researcher is so well versed with the topic that *he or she* knows what he or she is trying to convey and assumes that this meaning is clear to others as a result.

Avoid biased questions

Questions can be biased in a number of ways. They can be biased when no matter what the respondent answers, a specific behavior is implied anyway. For example, what if I had a question that asked, Do you still smoke cigarettes? A yes answer obviously means that the respondent is a smoker. However, if someone answers no, the implication is still that this person did smoke in the past and has now quit. Either way (yes or no), someone admits to smoking in the past, even if that person never smoked a single cigarette. There is no way that this question will address the possibility that someone has never smoked.

Another example is when researchers word questions in a way that elicits a specific response. For example: Do you think it's a man's God-given right to beat his wife so severely that she is on the brink of death? First, there's a lot of emotional words (e.g., *God-given* and *brink of death*) in this question which would lead people to react to the words instead of the issue. Second, in our current political climate, someone would have to be incredibly socially unaware to answer yes. Even if someone *does* believe that men have the right to beat their wives, given the wording of the question, they are unlikely to answer yes because they know that others are not likely to agree with them and they wouldn't want to appear to be politically incorrect. Bias doesn't have to be as obvious as the example I just mentioned. Rasinski (1989) found that even more subtle differences in question wording affects people's responses. For example, Raskinski found that if a question asked whether the government was paying too little for "assistance to big cities," only 17.7 percent of respondents agreed; however, if the question was worded as "solving the problems of big cities," then 48.2 percent of respondents felt that the government was spending too little (Rasinski, 1989). He found similar differences where people were more likely to support government assistance to "protecting Social Security," "improving conditions of blacks," "halting the rising crime rate," and "dealing with drug addiction," and were *less* likely to support the same causes if they were worded as "Social Security," "assistance to Blacks," "law enforcement," and "drug rehabilitation" (Rasinski, 1989).

Bias can also involve evoking prestige. For example, a question that reads, Experts feel that Americans use too much gasoline in their daily living. What is your opinion? may elicit a high agreement rate. Why? Average people may not want to contradict "experts" because perhaps they feel that experts have more knowledge about a topic, and if "experts" feel a particular way, then maybe the respondent should, too. Similarly, questions that refer to the opinions of doctors, sports figures, respected community members, and others may also produce misleading findings.

In addition, responses can be biased when response categories do not reflect the full range of possible meanings. For example, if a researcher words answer choices starting with "strongly agree," then that researcher needs to end the answer choices with "strongly disagree." There needs to be as many positive answer categories as there are negative.

Avoid leading questions

Sometimes researchers intentionally or unintentionally word questions so as to elicit a specific response. For example, compare the following questions: Should we pay even more taxes in order to assist the poor? and Should taxes be increased to assist the poor? The first is a leading question. By adding the word *even*, the implication is that respondents are already paying enough to help the poor and any additional taxes are unnecessary. The second question, however, is straightforward and there is no implication about how much people are currently paying. The first question, by its implication, leads a person to answer no. The second question does not lead the respondent to a specific response.

Leading questions can also occur when the researcher tries to get people to agree—for example: Should taxes be increased to assist poor families in giving better care to their children who are victims of their birth? Hopefully, no researcher would use such a blatantly leading question; however, it is an example of a leading question aimed at agreement. You might have noticed that one way of writing a leading question is to include emotional words (e.g., *victim* or *innocent*), which may also lead to the problem of biased wording. One survey question may have a multitude of faults.

One way to avoid leading questions is to prevent both sides of an opinion in a question. For example, instead of asking, Do you agree with the new health care plan?, researchers might word the question, Do you agree or disagree with the new health care plan? or perhaps, What is your opinion of the new health care plan? In both instances, the answer categories may range from strongly agree to strongly disagree with a neutral no opinion category in the middle.

A second tactic—one that is especially appropriate when studying deviant or illegal behavior—is to neutralize the action. For example, instead of asking, Have you ever used any illegal drugs? ask Have you ever used cocaine? or Which of the following drugs have you used? (and then list the drugs). Many respondents may find the word *illegal* to be disagreeable and may be hesitant to admit to these acts (most people do not shout or proclaim their deviant behavior from the rooftops).

Avoid assuming prior knowledge on behalf of participants

Unless one of your specific goals is to test knowledge (and if that is the case, then your questions need to actually test the respondents' knowledge before they can give an opinion), do not ask questions that may involve knowledge that the average person would not know. For example, do not ask a question such as, Do you think the government is spending too much money on the military? Do *you* actually know how much the government has budgeted for military spending? I don't—at least not without looking it up. Therefore, even though people may provide an answer to this question, the responses are likely to be meaningless. If a question such as this is important for your research, tell the people what the military spending is and put it in context before you ask the question: "The current military budget is $536 billion, which is 28 percent of government money brought in from the income tax. Human resources (education, health and human services, housing, and labor programs) together account for 33 percent of the income tax revenue ($633 billion). Do you think the government is spending too much money on the military?"

This question is an improvement over the previous because it not only gives a dollar amount but it also gives the proportion of the income tax revenue. Most people cannot really comprehend the real value of billions of dollars; therefore, the dollar amounts without any other reference material is not very enlightening. Once people have this knowledge, they are more equipped to answer the question.

Similarly, do not ask people information for which they will never be able to remember, such as, How old were you when you were toilet trained? Most people have no memory of this childhood event and anything they report, at best, would be a fuzzy memory of the stories they may have heard from relatives. Clearly, this is not an accurate piece of information.

Also, phrase questions in a way that makes sense to respondents. Few people know their total yearly work hours. Therefore, instead of asking, How many hours did you work for pay last year? ask How many hours do you work for pay in a typical work week? If, as the researcher, you truly are interested in yearly work hours, you can assume that most people have two weeks of vacation (either company recognized vacation or sick time) and multiply the reported work hours by 50 (52 weeks a year minus 2 weeks).

Avoid double-barreled questions

Simply put, double-barreled questions are single questions that actually ask two or more questions within them even though there is only one answer. This makes it impossible for a researcher to interpret someone's answer. Question 3 on page 281 is an example of a double-barreled question. Another example is, Do you think a person convicted of child molestation should be sent to prison and forced to undergo counseling once he or she is released? A respondent could believe that individuals convicted of child molestation should go to prison, but that once the prison sentence is complete, so is the convicted person's responsibility to society. Therefore, this person should not be forced to attend counseling once he or she is released. A better way of approaching questions like this is merely to separate the question into two distinct questions—for example: Do you think that a person convicted of child molestation should be sent to prison? and Do you think that people convicted and sentenced to prison for child molestation should be required to continue counseling once they are released from prison?

Every instance of the word *and* in a question does not necessarily indicate a double-barreled question. Sometimes researchers use *and* to set up a specific instance. The last sentence of the previous paragraph illustrates this point. In that question, the phrase *convicted and sentenced* establishes a specific instance—the instance in which a person is *both* convicted of a crime and sentenced for it. Another example is if I am describing a specific type of criminal as "a person who raped and murdered. . . ." In this instance, the *and* is still related to a single event—this specific type of criminal. Here, the use of *and* is appropriate. Therefore, when you see an *and* in a question, you need to ask yourself whether the researcher is referring to an entity that can be separated into more than one instance (and if this is the case, then the question is double-barreled and should be reworded to be separate questions), or if the researcher is establishing a specific condition for one instance.

Be sure answer categories are mutually exclusive

Mutually exclusive answer categories are categories for which respondents can select one and only one response unless directed otherwise. If you look back to an earlier example on page 279, you will see that the second question about the frequency of drug use violates this guideline. In this question, if a person has used drugs five times, then he or she needs to circle two response categories. I can improve this question by rewording the answer choices as such:

1. How frequently have you used cocaine in the past week?
   a. I did not use cocaine in the past week
   b. 1–2 times
   c. 3–4 times
   d. 5–6 times
   e. 7 or more times

I changed the answer choices so that there is only one response for everyone. Now a person who used cocaine five times would have only one appropriate answer choice.

However, sometimes a researcher may want participants to select more than one answer. For example, if I asked the question, Which of the following drugs have you used in the past week?, I might then add, "Circle all that apply" after the question. This way, when I list the various drugs, respondents who have used more than one of them know I want them to circle all the drugs that they have used in the past week. As I said earlier, it is okay for participants to have more than one response to circle *if* the researcher specifically directs them to do so. The assumption, however, is that there should only be one answer per question.

Be sure answer categories are exhaustive

Not only should respondents have only one answer choice to select (unless directed otherwise), but researchers must be sure that there *is* an answer choice for everyone. This is what researchers mean when they say that answer categories should be exhaustive.

Again, referring to my earlier example of a poor survey (page 281), the fourth and fifth questions violate this guideline. In question 4, if a person has no opinion about legalizing drugs, there is no answer choice to select. Likewise, in question 5, if a person does not identify his or her race as White, African American, or Latino, then there is no answer choice for him or her. One way to eliminate this problem is to add a "No opinion" category to question 4 and an "Other" category to question 5 so they look like this:

4. Do you think cocaine should be illegal?

    a. Strongly agree
    b. Agree
    c. No opinion
    d. Disagree
    e. Strongly Disagree

5. What is your primary race/ethnicity?

    a. White/Caucasian
    b. African American
    c. Latino
    d. Asian American
    e. Other (please specify _____)

How would you write a survey question that addresses people's race, but still ensures that the rules for question wording in this chapter are followed without making the answer categories exceptionally numerous?

Notice that with question 5, I added a fourth category: Asian American. This is because now the first four answer categories correspond to the four most represented races/ethnicities in the United States. I also reworded the question to read "primary race/ethnicity" in recognition that many people identify with more than one race. This is not a perfect solution to our multicultural society, but it's an improvement over the traditional, What is your race? wording.

The addition of the "please specify" comment in the "Other" category for question 5 is a means of capturing detailed information without having to list every conceivable ethnicity in the United

States. When respondents write in a race/ethnicity that is different from the first four, when the researcher codes the data, the researcher can look for patterns and create answer categories *after* the data are collected. For example, if I am the researcher and I notice that after I collect my surveys, 6 percent of my respondents write in that they are Middle Eastern, I can decide to add a fifth answer category "Middle Eastern" at this point. I will discuss the rules and guidelines for handling information in "Other" categories in more detail in Chapter 12.

Avoid response set patterns

Some of you may have half-heartedly completed a survey at some point where you just circled one answer (such as "strongly agree") right down the page for all questions. Wording questions in a way that facilitates responding the same way to all questions is a *response set*. What you probably understand now is that this answer practice may seriously threaten the validity of your findings. However, what if a person actually *does* feel the same way about each question? Well, in order to distinguish those respondents who honestly feel one way about all the dimensions of a concept as opposed to those who are not really paying attention to their survey responses, researchers need to word questions both positively and negatively. This does not mean using double negatives in the question (which I previously stated was a poor decision). It means wording questions so that a *positive* answer to one question supports the hypothesis and a *negative* answer to another question *also* supports the hypothesis. For example, suppose I am trying to learn more about student satisfaction with the university's dormitory situation. I might have the following questions on a survey.

1. I feel that the university dorms are comfortable.
2. I feel that the university dorms are well maintained.
3. I feel that the university dorms are not conveniently located to the classrooms.
4. I feel that the university dorms have enough closet space.
5. I feel that the beds in the university dorms are comfortable.
6. I feel that the university dorms are too small.

The answer choices to these questions may be a five-point continuum that ranges from strongly agree to strongly disagree with neutral being in the middle. If a respondent answers "strongly agree" to each of these questions, I know that that individual really was not paying attention to the survey, and I therefore might want to eliminate that person from my sample. How would I know this? Well, it's unlikely that someone who answers "strongly agree" to questions 1, 2, 4, and 5 will also answer "strongly agree" to questions 3 and 6, which are negatively worded. It is especially unlikely that someone who thinks dorms have adequate closet space (question 4) is going to turn around and also agree that the dorms are too small (question 6). This is an example of using reverse-worded questions.

Summary

To summarize, writing survey questions is not difficult, but it does involve more consideration than most people realize. In this section I described some of the more common guidelines for writing survey questions and responses. Once the questions and responses are worded to the researcher's satisfaction, the researcher turns his or her attention to the presentation of the survey, which also affects both respondent participation and the validity of the resulting data.

■ Survey Format and Presentation

How a survey looks and how questions are presented is also a bit of a science. Think about it; would you want to complete a survey that was cramped, hard to read, or confusing to follow, or how about a survey that opened with a question that asked you about your sex life? My guess is no. In this section I will address various tools for formatting your survey in a way that will encourage accurate and valid information as well as minimize the chance that a respondent will take one look at the survey and immediately throw it in the trash.

Some of these tools are more suited to specific types of surveys (e.g., a mailed survey) than others (e.g., a face-to-face interview); however, since the guidelines may apply to more than one survey technique, I am presenting them here as opposed to my discussion of each specific survey type.

Open- or closed-ended questions

Open-ended and closed-ended questions are pretty much what their names imply. Open-ended questions have no response options presented for the respondents to select; therefore, the respondents are "open" to write any answer they want. Closed-ended questions, on the other hand, do have specific answer categories for respondents to select. All of the examples I used in the previous section on question wording were closed-ended questions. Examples of open-ended questions would be What issues would you like to see your local representative present to the state legislature? If you could change two aspects about your local police, what would they be? Which sessions presented at this conference do you think were the best and why?

All of these questions allow respondents to freely express their views in their own words. A benefit of open-ended questions is that researchers frequently reach a deeper understanding of participant views because the participants express them in their own words. Hence, open-ended questions are an important component to qualitative research.

The level of detail that researchers can obtain from open-ended questions comes at a price, however. Coding and finding patterns among open-ended questions can be difficult because responses can be similar in content but worded so differently that, to an untrained researcher, the similarity is elusive. It is much easier to code and discern patterns from closed-ended questions because the researcher can simply assign a numerical code to each answer choice, enter that code in a computer, and have a computer program look for the patterns. (Some newer computer programs do, however, specifically help find patterns in qualitative data.)

Because of the complementary nature of closed- and open-ended questions, researchers are well advised to include both in their survey construction. Open-ended questions allow participants to more fully explain their views, but they are difficult to code. Closed-ended questions are easier to code (and therefore find patterns), but respondents may not be able to more fully explain their views. Where one form is weak, the other is strong.

Asking threatening questions

Because social scientists study people's lives and lives can be messy, social science research may involve asking respondents questions that the respondent finds to be sensitive, intrusive, or threatening. Even if people agree to participate in research, they frequently want to present a positive image of themselves to the researcher. A study by Bradburn and colleagues (1978) found that those who found a question topic threatening were also less

TABLE 7.1 Summary of Select Questions that Make People Uneasy

Topic	Percent Who Feel "Very Uneasy"
Masturbation	56
Sexual intercourse	42
Marijuana	42
Intoxication	29
Petting and kissing	20
Income	12
Gambling with friends	10
Drinking	10
General leisure	2
Sports activity	1

Source: Adapted from Norman M., Bradburn, Seymour Sudman, Ed Blair, and Carol Stocking, "Question Threat and Response Bias," *Public Opinion Quarterly*, 42(2) (1978): 221–234.

likely to admit to performing the action of that question. In Table 7.1, I present some of the questions that Bradburn and colleagues (1978) found made people uneasy. When respondents try to portray a positive image of themselves with regard to these behaviors, researchers call this a *social desirability bias*. Clearly, this bias can affect researchers' results by leading to the underreporting of behavior that respondents see as threatening or deviant and the overreporting of behavior that they see as socially acceptable and desirable (e.g., voting, reading, giving to charity, and having a happy marriage).

So how do researchers present threatening topics in nonthreatening ways? Barton (1958) proposed a comical response to this question by illustrating various ways to present the question "Did you kill your wife" in a nonthreatening manner. Some of his suggestions are:

1. *The Casual Approach:* "Do you happen to have murdered your wife?"
2. *The Numbered Card:* "Would you please read off the number on this card which corresponds to what became of your wife?" (Hand card to respondent.)
   a. Natural death
   b. I killed her
   c. Other (What?)
   (Get the card back from respondent before proceeding.)
3. *The Everybody Approach:* "As you know, many people have been killing their wives these days. Do you happened to have killed yours?"
4. *The Other People Approach:*
   a. Do you know any people who have murdered their wives?

b. How about yourself?
5. *The Kinsey Technique:* Stare firmly into respondent's eyes and ask in simple, clear-cut language, such as that to which the respondent is accustomed, and with an air of assuming everyone has done everything, "Did you ever kill your wife?" Put the question at the end of the interview. (Barton, 1958, p. 67)

Although this 50-year-old example is borderline politically incorrect today (but remember, the whole point was to ask questions that are socially undesirable in the first place), it does illustrate the difficulty researchers can have in asking threatening questions in a nonthreatening manner. Furthermore, some of the examples serve as the basis for the techniques researchers do use to ask questions like this.

Some suggestions for asking threatening questions are to use open and long questions with familiar wording. This way, respondents can write their responses in a way that makes them comfortable, and the researcher may be able to provide context to the question that will make it less threatening to the respondent. Another tactic is to use time frames. If you are interested in whether the respondent committed a deviant act in a very specific time frame (for example, the last six months), as opposed to any time in the past, and a respondent *did* do a deviant act at some point in his or her life, but not during this time frame, the respondent is less likely to feel threatened by the specific question.

Sensitive questions can also be embedded in less threatening questions or presented in vague terms. If the researchers embed sensitive questions in less sensitive ones, they may want to put those questions toward the end and make sure that other basic information (such as gender, race, and education) appear before the sensitive question. Why? Because sometimes when people feel particularly threatened by a question, they may decide that instead of simply skipping that particular question, they no longer want to participate in the study at all. When people stop participation, the researcher cannot force them to continue, and any information that would have been gained after the threatening questions would be lost for this respondent. Therefore, put these questions near the end of the survey (so the majority of information is already gathered in case the respondent decides not to participate) and embed them in less important material.

With regard to presenting threatening questions in vague terms, what this really means is starting with broad categories and getting increasingly narrow until the researcher has the level of information he or she is interested in obtaining or until the respondent declines to provide further information. For example, people may be hesitant to report their total household income. Therefore, instead of directly asking them how much they earn in a given year, the researcher can ask them whether they earn over or under a certain amount, such as $100,000. This is a broad classification and people may feel less threatened by it.

If someone answers, for example, "under $100,000," the researcher can then ask if that person earns over or under $50,000. The amount for comparison gets increasingly smaller until the researcher has the level of precision he or she desires or until the respondent declines to answer. Even if the respondent answered the first two questions ("under $100,000 and over $50,000"), but then decided not to answer any more questions about income, the researcher still has some valuable information. The researcher knows that this particular respondent earns between $50,000 and $100,000. This is more information than if respondents are directly asked about their income and decide that they didn't want to provide that specific figure. Other tactics involve using noninterview methods to preserve anonymity or using some other indirect means of gathering data, such as diaries or informants (although the latter is less than ideal because the researcher has to rely on reports of someone other than the subject).

Answer choice presentation

How researchers actually format the answer choices can affect the validity of the data gathered. For example, examine four possible ways of presenting answer choices:

| [ ] Yes | ( ) Yes | _____ Yes | 1. Yes |
| [ ] No | ( ) No | _____ No | 2. No |

According to Babbie (1995), of the four ways of presenting answer choices, the last way (having a number to circle by the response) is the most advantageous so long as the researcher provides clear instructions to circle and not cross out the appropriate answer. The numerical system shown in the last option gives the respondent's answer, but it also specifies the code number to be entered later, which facilitates the data entry stage of the research process (because researchers do not have to memorize or look up codes if they are part of the answer choice). Of the four, the third is the least acceptable, according to Babbie, because respondents frequently will enter large checkmarks or marks that may not be neatly on the line, making it difficult to interpret which answer is the one they specified.

Another way of presenting answer categories is a **matrix format.** Matrix questions are an efficient way of presenting several items that share the same answer choices. The answer choices are listed once across the top of a matrix and the questions sharing those choices are listed down the page. Then, instead of repeating the same answer choices for each question, the respondent just checks or circles a corresponding space or number for each choice that is lined up under the response categories listed at the top of the question set. Figure 7.2 is an example of a matrix question.

10. Now I'm going to read several more statements. As I read each one, please tell me whether you strongly agree, agree, disagree, or strongly disagree with it. For example, here is the statement:

	Strongly Agree	Agree	Disagree	Strongly Disagree	DON'T KNOW
A. A working mother can establish just as warm and secure a relationship with her children as a mother who does not work.	1	2	3	4	8
B. It is more important for a wife to help her husband's career than to have one herself.	1	2	3	4	8
C. A preschool child is likely to suffer if his or her mother works.	1	2	3	4	8
D. It is much better for everyone involved if the man is the achiever outside the home and the woman takes care of the home and family.	1	2	3	4	8

Source: *General Social Survey Codebook,* 1998 Questionnaire, The National Opinion Research Center. http://webapp.icpsr.umich.edu/gss/.

Figure 7.2 Example of a Matrix Question

As you see in Figure 7.2, each question has a five-point continuum that ranges from "strongly agree" to "strongly disagree" with a neutral "don't know" category. Instead of listing each of these answer choices separately and vertically for each question, the creators of the GSS have saved space by listing them horizontally. The GSS creators have also saved time—both for the respondent and the coder. Since the answer choices are all the same, the respondent does not need to reread each response. The respondent has to read the answer choices only once and then knows that the choices apply to each question. Coders save time because, since the answer choices are expressed as numbers for each question (e.g., strongly agree = 1, agree = 2), the coder knows exactly what number to enter into the computer for each response.

The GSS creators have left the "Don't know" category at the end. Some researchers are concerned that the inclusion of a "Don't know" category, although necessary to achieve exhaustiveness in response choices, increases the likelihood that people will select this response. One way to minimize this risk is to put that answer choice at the end of the selection (as opposed to the middle to complete the logical progression of the continuum), since respondents are likely to answer the first choice they see or hear that best approximates their view. By keeping the "Don't know" response at the end, this is the last response people will read, and if they have even a vague opinion, they are likely to have already circled it prior to arriving at this answer option. Notice, too, that the GSS includes reverse-worded questions. The first question is worded in a way that agreement with the statement suggests support for the nontraditional view of women working, whereas agreement with the other three questions suggest *lack* of support for women working.

Matrix questions have a number of advantages. First, they save space on a survey, allowing researchers to ask many questions without making the survey appear so long as to discourage people from participating. Second, participants find it easy to answer questions in this fashion because they do not have to read the answer choices directly for each question. Third, they are an excellent way for researchers to identify response set patterns to assess whether respondents are reading each question carefully. That is, matrix questions are a useful way of identifying response set patterns *if* the researcher makes sure to include both positively and negatively worded questions. If the researcher does not do this, then matrix questions are actually a liability because they may encourage someone to respond the same way to all questions. Including reverse-ordered questions are the only way the researcher can distinguish between those who quickly responded similarly to all questions without paying attention to question content and those who consistently answered in one direction.

Contingency questions

Most likely some questions you include on a survey will only apply to certain people. For example, if I am studying sexual behavior among high school students, it makes no sense to ask a high school student whether he or she uses birth control if that student is not having sex. Instead of continually including answer categories for "Not applicable" (in order to fulfill the guideline of having answer choices be exhaustive), I can simply ask a filter question that will separate those to whom the question applies from those to whom it does not. I can then direct those who do not possess a particular value of the filter variable to simply skip a set of questions and then have everyone resume participation at a specific point. For example:

20. Have you ever had sexual intercourse with another person?

[   ] Yes (please go to question 21)

[   ] No (please skip to question 25)

21. How long were you dating the first person you had sex with before you actually had sex?

[   ] 1 day to 1 month

[   ] 1 month and a day to 6 months

[   ] 6 months and a day to a year

[   ] Over one year

22. Did you use contraception the first time you had sex?

[   ] Yes (please go to question 23)

[   ] No (please go to question 24)

23. What type of contraception did you use? (check all that apply)

[   ] "The pill"

[   ] A condom

[   ] A diaphragm

[   ] A sponge

[   ] Other (please specify) _____

24. How long did you date this person *after* you had sex? Please specify _____

25. What is your current grade-point average (estimate)?

[   ] Under 1.0

[   ] 1.0–1.99

[   ] 2.0–2.99

[   ] 3.0 or above

This example is actually a moderately complex example of a contingency question, because it contains a contingency question within a contingency question. If a respondent has not had sex and therefore answers no to question 20, then that respondent does not answer questions 21 through 24 and resumes answering at question 25. However, if a respondent answers yes to question 20, that person proceeds to answer questions 21 and 22. This person continues to question 23 only *if* he or she used contraception (a yes response to question 22) and then that person continues to question 24. If this person did not use contraception, he or she proceeds directly to question 24, skipping question 23. Everyone, regardless of his or her answer to question 20, "meets" again and answers question 25.

Question 20 is called a **filter question** because it filters who will answer specific following questions. A "no" answer to that question establishes a **skip pattern,** because it directs the respondent to skip specific questions and proceed to a later question. Question 21 is the first **contingency question** in the set because whether someone answers it is "contingent" on his or her answer to the filter question.

Contingency questions make survey taking easier on the respondents because they do not have to answer questions that are not relevant to them. There are several formats for contingency questions. The one I presented is one format where the respondent knows which questions to skip or to answer, based on written directions after each response. This format is useful when contingency patterns will span a number of pages. It is easy for respondents to flip to relevant pages based on their answers to questions.

However, if the contingency patterns are short, another format option is to use arrows and boxed items to direct the respondent to contingency questions. In this format, the researcher isolates the contingency question from the other questions by placing it in a box and using an arrow to connect the filter response that leads to the contingency question to the question itself. For example:

20. Have you ever had sexual intercourse with another person?

[   ] Yes

[   ] No

> How long were you dating the first person you had sex with before you actually had sex?
>
> [   ] 1 day to 1 month
> [   ] 1 month and a day to 6 months
> [   ] 6 months and a day to a year
> [   ] Over one year

21. What is your current grade-point average (estimate)?

[   ] Under 1.0

[   ] 1.0–1.99

[   ] 2.0–2.99

[   ] 3.0 or above

However, notice that with this format, if I wanted to ask multiple questions within the contingency pattern like I did with the first example, my contingency pattern would get very confusing and cluttered quickly. Therefore, this pattern is really only suitable when there is one, maybe two, questions in the contingency pattern. Also, this format is not very conducive to having contingency patterns within a contingency pattern (like I did in the first example).

Order of questions

If you picked up a survey about intimate partner relations and the first question asked if you had cheated on your intimate partner in the last six months, would you continue with the survey? Probably not. The order in which questions appear on a survey not only influences how respondents will react to the survey (and whether they will continue with it) but also how they may answer some individual questions.

On the most basic level, many argue that survey questions should be organized into broad thematic categories. If you are surveying employees about their job experiences, you may want to group any questions about union membership together in one section, questions about workplace conditions in another, questions about workplace policy in a third area, and questions about their relationship with their boss and co-workers in a fourth section.

BOX 7.1   **Sample Questions from the General Social Survey**

The General (GSS) Social Survey is probably one of the oldest, most comprehensive and continual social surveys in existence. Started in 1972, the General Social Survey was conducted annually until 1985 when it began being conducted biannually. The GSS asks standard questions about demographics as well as questions about work, family, and views on social issues. Below are some sample questions from the 1998 GSS. Answer the critical thinking questions to assess how well you understand some of the issues surrounding question wording and format.

Section A

2. First I would like to talk with you about some things people think about today. We are faced with many problems in this country, none of which can be solved easily or inexpensively. I'm going to name some of these problems, and for each one I'd like you to tell me whether you think we're spending too much money on it, too little money, or about the right amount. First (READ ITEM A) . . . are we spending too much, too little, or about the right amount on (ITEM)? READ EACH ITEM: CODE ONE FOR EACH.

	Too Much	Too Little	About Right	DON'T KNOW
A. Space exploration	3	1	2	8
B. The environment	3	1	2	8
C. Health	3	1	2	8
D. Assistance to big cities	3	1	2	8
E. Law enforcement	3	1	2	8
F. Drug rehabilitation	3	1	2	8
G. Education	3	1	2	8
H. Assistance to Blacks	3	1	2	8
I. National defense	3	1	2	8
J. Assistance to other countries	3	1	2	8
K. Assistance to the poor	3	1	2	8
L. Highways and bridges	3	1	2	8
M. Social Security	3	1	2	8
N. Mass transportation	3	1	2	8
O. Parks and recreation	3	1	2	8

BOX 7.1   **Sample Questions from the General Social Survey, continued**

4. The United States Supreme Court has ruled that no state or local government may *require* the reading of the Lord's Prayer or Bible verses in public schools.

   What are your views on this—do you approve or disapprove of the court ruling?

Approve	1
Disapprove	2
NO OPINION	8

5. In general, do you think the courts in this area deal too harshly or not harshly enough with criminals?

Too harshly	1
Not harshly enough	2
ABOUT RIGHT	3
DON'T KNOW	8

14. Were you living with both your own mother and father around the time you were 16? (IF NO: With whom were you living around that time?) IF RESPONDENT MARRIED OR LEFT HOME BY AGE 16, PROBE FOR BEFORE THAT.

BOTH OWN MOTHER AND FATHER	(GO TO Q.15)	1
FATHER AND STEPMOTHER	(ASK A)	2
MOTHER AND STEPFATHER	(ASK A)	3
FATHER—NO MOTHER OR STEPMOTHER	(ASK A)	4
MOTHER—NO FATHER OR STEPFATHER	(ASK A)	5
SOME OTHER <u>MALE RELATIVE</u> (NO FEMALE HEAD) (SPECIFY AND ASK A)		6
SOME OTHER <u>FEMALE RELATIVE</u> (NO MALE HEAD) (SPECIFY AND ASK A)		7
OTHER ARRANGEMENT WITH <u>BOTH</u> MALE AND FEMALE <u>RELATIVES</u> (e.g., AUNT AND UNCLE, GRANDPARENTS)	(ASK A)	8
OTHER (SPECIFY AND ASK A)		0

   A. IF NOT LIVING WITH BOTH OWN MOTHER AND FATHER: What happened?

ONE OR BOTH PARENTS DIED	1
PARENTS DIVORCED OR SEPARATED	2
FATHER ABSENT IN ARMED FORCES	3
ONE OR BOTH PARENTS IN INSTITUTION	4
OTHER (SPECIFY)	5
DON'T KNOW	8

25. Last week were you working full time, part time, going to school, keeping house, or what?

    CIRCLE ONE CODE ONLY. IF MORE THAN ONE RESPONSE, GIVE PREFERENCE TO SMALLEST CODE NUMBER THAT APPLIES.

HAND CARD 3	Working full time	(ASK A) 1
	Working part time	(ASK A) 2
	With a job, but not at work because of temporary illness, vacation. strike	(ASK B) 3
	Unemployed, laid off, looking for work	(GO TO Q.26) 4
	Retired	(ASK C) 5
	In school	(ASK C) 6
	Keeping house	(ASK C) 7
	OTHER (SPECIFY AND ASK C)	8

    A. IF WORKING, FULL OR PART TIME: How many hours did you work last week, at all jobs?

    Hours: _____   NOW GO TO Q.26

    B. IF WITH A JOB, BUT NOT AT WORK: How many hours a week do you usually work, at all jobs?

    Hours: _____   NOW GO TO Q.26

    C. IF RETIRED, IN SCHOOL, KEEPING HOUSE, OR OTHER: Did you ever work for as long as one year?

    Yes   (ASK Q.26) 1

    No   (SKIP TO IQ-8 BEFORE Q.31) 2

26. A. What kind of work (do you/did you) normally do? That is, what (is/was) your job called?

    OCCUPATION: _____

    _____

    _____

Source: General Social Survey Codebook, 1998 Questionnaire, The National Opinion Research Center. http://webapp.icpsr.umich.edu.gss.

Critical Thinking Questions

1. Are there any examples of matrix or contingency questions among the sample GSS questions provided? Which questions are open-ended and which are closed-ended?

2. Are the questions worded accurately? Do they avoid biasing respondents? Do they avoid leading respondents?

3. What level of measurement is each question?

BOX 7.1   **Sample Questions from the General Social Survey, continued**

Critical Thinking Discussion

1. Question 2 is a matrix question. By listing the answer categories across the top of the page, the various statements down the page and a number (code) for each response (as opposed to repeating the answer categories), this is a matrix question. Notice that there are no reverse-worded questions, because the questions do not ask agreement about specific statement or scenarios; instead, the questions just list topics. There is no way to reverse-order a topic.

   Questions 14 and 25 are both contingency questions. For question 14, for example, if the respondent answers, "Both own mother and father," the respondent moves to question 15 (not shown). However, if the respondent answers, for example, "Both father and step-mother," then the respondent is directed to answer subsection A ("What happened?") before moving on to question 15. All of the questions, except for question 26, are closed ended, because there are answer choices for each question. Question 26 is open ended because the respondent gives his or her answer in his or her own words.

2. These questions are correctly worded, are unbiased, and are not leading. For example, look at questions 4 and 5. Both of these questions have answer choices, or both ends of the answer range, expressed in the question.

   Question 5 asks whether the respondent thinks that the area courts deal "too harshly or not harshly enough" with criminals. If the interviewer asked, on the other hand, "Do you think the area courts deal too harshly with criminals, yes or no?" *that* question would be leading, because the main text of the question presents only the term "too harshly." It doesn't present both ends of the range.

3. This is a review from Chapter 4 about level of measurement. The level of measurement for each question is:

   Question 2:   ordinal
   Question 4:   ordinal
   Question 5:   ordinal
   Question 24:   nominal
   Question 25:   nominal
   Question 25 A: interval
   Question 25 B: interval
   Question 25 C: nominal
   Question 26:   Open ended. No level of measurement is present, because open-ended questions are aimed at qualitative data, not quantifiable data.

Researchers also need to pay special attention to the first question (even the first few) of a survey. The first question lets the respondent know the topic of the survey and whether it will be interesting. Therefore, researchers do not want to begin a survey with basic demographic questions such as race or gender, because they are boring and may remind participants of generic forms. The first question should be topically relevant and interesting in order to get the respondents' attention and entice them to continue with the survey. Don't forget, however, that although the question should be topically interesting, it should not be threatening. Asking threatening questions right up front may certainly get the respondents' attention, but if the respondents feel uncomfortable in the very beginning of the survey, they are unlikely to continue with it or may rush through it.

Similarly, the first question should be answerable by everyone. This is not the time to establish a contingency question pattern, because the researcher does not want some respondents to feel excluded early in the survey. Consequently, according to Dillman (2000), the first question in a survey should be topically relevant, interesting, fairly easy to answer, and apply to all people.

Once the general broad topics are grouped and the first questions are written, then the researcher has to examine each additional question carefully to make sure that the question order will not lead to any **context effects,** where the wording of a question influences the participant's response to subsequent questions. For example, Bumpass (1997) found that when people were asked whether they believed abortion should be legal for any reason, 60 percent agreed if this question was the first in a series of questions that also asked whether the respondent favored abortion in specific instances. However, only 48 percent agreed that abortions should be legal when that question was posed at the end of the series.

Theoretically, grouping questions into broad topical patterns and worrying about contextual effects is supposed to facilitate the completion of the survey for respondents because (1) they do not have to switch their attention between different topics and (2) they can make sure their responses are consistent by looking at their previous responses to similar topics. In reality, however, some researchers question whether this practice actually works. Bishop and colleagues (1988) do not find that question order makes much difference in mailed surveys, although they do find some evidence of question order effects in interviews. On the other hand, a study by Ayidiya and McClendon (1990) finds that sometimes question order *does* affect participants' responses in mailed surveys on some topics.

There is some evidence that the importance of question order varies by the type of survey instrument and the characteristics of the respondents. Although researchers may not want to begin self-report surveys (such as mailed surveys) with demographic information, they may want to begin interviews by gathering demographic information about household members in order to "warm up" and develop rapport with the participant. Furthermore, there is also some evidence that question order has a different effects for different groups of people. Benton and Daly (1991) found that the order of questions influenced the responses of participants with less education than it did for participants with more education.

Consequently, it is very difficult to avoid the effect of the ordering of questions on participants' responses completely (since there are various factors that influence how or whether question order affects responses). The best strategy, then, is to be sensitive to the situation. If a researcher has theoretical reasons to believe that the order of questions might affect responses, that researcher may want to create more than one version of the survey, order the questions differently in each version, and randomly assign (in the real methodological sense) surveys to respondents. He or she can then compare the results of the different surveys and, if the surveys were truly randomly assigned, then characteristics of the sample groups should not create differences between question answers. If there are differences in responses to questions in the different surveys, the researcher can conclude that question order may have created those differences.

Because question order takes very little effort and its impact on how participants respond is up for debate, it is best to err on the side of caution and be sensitive to the general ordering of questions.

Survey appearance

The appearance of a survey can be important because if it is attractive, clearly presented, and easy to understand, respondents are more likely to complete it and interviewers are more likely to be able to follow it. These guidelines are basic and somewhat common sense, but because I find that students frequently try to fit as much as they can onto one page (so the survey appears short), they overlook many of these points.

First, it should be easy for the respondent to identify question and answer choices. This can usually be done by indenting or somehow setting apart the answer categories from the question. Second, there should be more space between different questions than between a particular question and its corresponding answer choices. Third, although response choice can be listed horizontally in a pinch, they look clearer if they are presented vertically (unless the researcher is using a matrix format) (Schutt, 2001). Fourth, questions and the corresponding answer choices should all appear on the same page. Do not put questions on one page and the answer choices on another, or, worse yet, the question and one or two answer choices on one page and the rest of the answer choices on another page. Computers with their easy margin, font, and lettering programs make it easier to keep question and answer choices together.

Pretest

When the researcher thinks that his or her survey instrument has all the questions and answer choices worded properly, has easy-to-follow question flow and organization, and is "ready" for study, it is time for the researcher to pretest the survey to make sure that it is as clear to respondents as it is to him or her. For a pretest, the researcher takes a small subsample of people from the study population and gives them the "finished" survey instrument. He or she then uses the information from the surveys to determine whether there are answers that do not make sense, questions that show little variation, or questions in which a noticeable amount of people either skipped the question or responded "Don't know." All these are subtle clues to the researcher that there is some problem with the survey itself. By pretesting the survey on only a small sample, the researcher does not waste the time and money of a full-scale research project only to learn that the resulting data are questionable due to problems with the survey design. Just remember that any person who is in the pretest sample is now *excluded* from the actual study so as to avoid a pretest effect.

The pretest is an integral step because researchers are very familiar with their research goals and probably think that their surveys are clear; however, to others who are not as familiar with the topic and material, this may not be the case. Think about it. You have probably written what you thought was "the best paper ever" for a class only to find that the professor did not agree. Perhaps you received comments that thoughts were not well developed or that the writing style was confusing. The same can happen on a survey. Researchers know what they *want* to ask and how, but that does not mean that *others* understand the procedure.

Summary

In sum, the formatting of survey and interview questions is fairly straightforward. Effective researchers will find a balance between open- and closed-ended questions, develop reverse-coded questions if they have multiple indicators of a concept, facilitate the use of reverse-ordered questions by presenting them in a matrix format if the answer choices are the same, clearly present contingency questions if they are applicable, and pay attention to the general ordering of questions. When early researchers are aware of these guidelines, they make sense and seem fairly obvious. However, without specifically identifying these guidelines, novice researchers often overlook them in their eagerness and concentration to put together a well-worded survey.

Types of Surveys

The guidelines and discussion I have presented so far address surveys in general. However, as I noted earlier, there are four main types of surveys and the degree to which the previous guidelines apply may vary a bit by the individual survey type. Therefore, in this next section I am going to discuss the four different types of surveys in more detail. I will explicitly discuss the format of these individual survey types, how researchers record information, issues involving the response rates, and the advantages and disadvantages of each type. Figure 7.3 suggests steps to follow for mailed surveys, face-to-face interviews, phone surveys, and electronic surveys.

Mailed Surveys

1. Follow the general steps from Figure 7.1 up to item number 7.

2. Write a cover letter to send with the survey:
   a. Include a personalized salutation.
   b. State the general research topic in an interesting manner that will encourage participation.
   c. Mention the importance of the participant's response.
   d. Mention how the results will be used.
   e. State the organization or affiliation of the researcher (lends credibility).
   f. State the sponsoring agency.
   g. Guarantee anonymity or confidentiality, whichever is appropriate.
   h. Provide any contact information that may be necessary (such as researcher contact information, counseling agency if applicable, etc.).
   i. Thank the respondent for his or her time.

3. Decide when to send the survey:
   a. Be conscious of seasonal issues (such as summer vacation).
   b. Be conscious of the time of the week (mailings that arrive early in the week may be better received).

4. Send the survey and begin a graph to track responses, marking this day as "Day 1."

5. Graph the number of surveys returned each day.

6. Conduct follow-up mailings using either a second survey, a reminder letter, a reminder postcard, or the like:
   a. *Option 1:* Send the first follow-up mailing when the graph in Step 4 shows a dip in survey return. This reminder may be a new survey or a letter/postcard reminder.
   b. *Option 2:* Send a postcard or letter reminder 3 to 4 days after the initial mailing.

7. Track returns in relation to the follow-up mailing:
   a. *Option 1:* If you sent new surveys in the previous step when you noticed the initial dip in responses, send a letter/postcard reminder when you notice this second dip in responses. If you sent a postcard/letter reminder only in the previous step, send a new survey this time.
   b. *Option 2:* Send a new survey 2 to 3 weeks after the initial mailing (the reminder/postcard from the last step was still sent prior to this).

8. Assign an identification number to each survey as it is returned.

9. Code and enter survey information into a computer.

10. Analyze the data.

Figure 7.3 Suggested Steps for Mailed Surveys, Face-to-Face Interviews, Phone Surveys, and Electronic Surveys

Face-to-Face Interviews

1. Follow the general steps from Figure 7.1 up to item number 7.
2. Select interviewers. Try to match to respondent characteristics if possible.
3. Train any individuals who are conducting the interviews.
   a. Familiarize the interviewer with the details and goals of the study.
   b. Familiarize the interviewer with the organization of the survey.
   c. Remind the interviewer to reinforce that the interview will be confidential.
   d. Teach the interviewer how to probe should the need arise.
4. Arrange the interview:
   a. Keep track of the times of your calls and vary timing of call-backs.
   b. If interviewing in a residence, do not schedule interview for before 10:00 A.M. or after 4:00 P.M.
5. Conduct the interview:
   a. Make sure you can identify the appropriate respondent.
   b. Establish a rapport with the respondent.
      (1) Dress appropriately for the context of the respondent, yet with an air of professionalism.
      (2) Use body language to illustrate that you are open and nonjudgmental.
      (3) Guarantee confidentiality.
   c. Start the interview with light conversation to "warm up" the respondent.
   d. Administer the survey:
      (1) Write responses verbatim.
      (2) Note body language of the respondent, questions respondent asks, background distractions, and so on.

      (3) Answer any questions the respondent has without adding any of your personal views.
      (4) Probe when necessary to obtain a specific level of information.
   e. Prepare for exit:
      (1) End with light conversation.
      (2) Ask any questions that were previously unanswered.
      (3) Ask the participant if he or she has any questions for you.
      (4) Thank the individual for his or her time.
   f. Go someplace quiet and record any other observations while they are still fresh in your mind.
6. Code and enter data.
7. Analyze data.

Telephone Surveys

1. Follow the general steps from Figure 7.1 up to item number 7.
2. Decide on a method of generating phone numbers.
3. Decide on whether support staff is needed.
   a. If yes:
      (1) Train them on telephone interviewing techniques.
      (2) Familiarize them with the questionnaire format and research goals.
      (3) Arrange them in one place where the researcher can monitor their interviewing.
   b. If no move directly to the next step.
4. Contact people, keeping track of call-backs and varying the days and times of contact attempts. Make sure you can identify the appropriate respondent to the best of your ability.

(continue to next page)

Figure 7.3 Continued

5. Decide whether computer-assisted telephone interviewing will be used.
   a. If yes administer the interview over the phone while simultaneously entering the data.
   b. If no:
      (1) Administer the interview over the phone.
      (2) Code and enter the data.
6. Analyze data.

Electronic Surveys

1. Follow the general steps from Figure 7.1 up to item number 7.
2. Decide whether to do an e-mail survey or a web survey.
   a. *E-mail survey:* Create survey to send via e-mail.
   b. *Web survey:*
      (1) Contact a specialist in posting web surveys or access a server on your own to post the survey.
      (2) Make sure there is a viable link to the survey that asks for a user ID and password from the respondent.
3. Post or send survey.
4. If doing an e-mail survey, code and enter the data. If doing a web survey, proceed directly to the next step.
5. Analyze the data.

Figure 7.3 Continued

■ Mailed Self-Report Surveys

The name for this type of survey pretty much says it all. *Mailed self-report,* or *self-administered, surveys* are surveys that respondents get in the mail, complete on their own, and then return to the researcher. This is probably one of the most common forms of survey research social scientists use.

Mailed surveys usually involve a **cover letter,** the survey instrument, and a stamped self-addressed envelope. Since the researcher never has any direct contact with the respondent, the cover letter is a key component for the mailed survey, for it includes all of the information necessary for the researcher to obtain informed consent. It also sets the tone for the entire survey. As we discussed in Chapter 3, a cover letter should contain the relevant information the respondent needs to know in order to make an informed decision about participating.

The cover letter needs to include a brief description about the general research topic (remember, no information about the specific hypotheses because this may bias results), information about the sponsor of the research and/or the researcher's credentials, why the study is being done, how the results will be used, an explanation of why you need that particular person to participate (essentially outlining the importance of the study results), any incentives to participate (if present), and relevant contact information (if necessary due to some potential for psychological distress).

Just like the survey questionnaire, how the researcher presents this information may make or break a participant's decision to participate. Therefore, the information in the cover letter should be personalized. This means that the researcher should address the letter to the respondent directly (as opposed to "To whom it may concern" or "Dear friend") and should personally sign the letter if possible (such as in blue ink which is less likely to be misinterpreted as a computer or photocopied signature).

The researcher should also present the research question in a way that is interesting and that will entice the respondent to participate in the study. For example, instead of stating the research topic as "This survey is about people's marital experiences," a researcher might say, "This survey examines the conflict-resolution patterns, cooperation strategies, communication patterns, and personal experiences of married couples." By providing a little more specific information, the topic of the survey may be more enticing to a respondent. It also, indirectly, provides even more information to ensure informed consent.

Last, the researcher needs to express concern about the well-being of the participant in the cover letter. Reassure the respondents that their comments will be anonymous or confidential. The researcher should also provide a contact number in case the respondent has any questions about the survey or would like a copy of the final report. Thank the respondent for completing the survey as well.

Response rate

How many of you have received surveys in the mail and immediately (or soon after opening them) tossed them into the trash? You're not alone. The main concern, and limitation, with mailed surveys is the response rate. Mailed surveys generally have very poor response rates relative to other methods of observation. People do not return mailed surveys for many reasons. Some feel that the survey is too much trouble to complete ("I don't have the time for this"), others think their response will not matter ("I'm only one person, it's not a big deal if I don't do this"), some consider it junk mail or a solicitation ("Ugh! Another one of *those!*"), and others are skeptical about sharing personal information ("I don't want strangers knowing too much about me").

Consequently, researchers take a lot of pains to encourage participants to complete and return the surveys. First, researchers try to make it easy for respondents to return the survey by including a stamped self-addressed envelope. The hope is that the subjects will realize that all they have to do once they complete the survey is slip it into the prepared envelope and drop the envelope in the mail. Simple.

Second, researchers should be conscious of when they mail surveys. For example, it could benefit researchers if their surveys reached businesses near the beginning of the week (Monday or Tuesday), when employees are fresh after the weekend and have not had a chance for a week's worth of work to pile up. Similarly, if the researcher is doing a general sample of the population or sampling families, he or she might not want to send the survey during the summer months, when families are likely to take their vacations.

Third, almost all researchers doing mailed surveys send follow-up mailings. One way to approach this is to monitor returns. The day the survey is mailed is Day 1 and the researcher marks this day on a graph. Each day after the initial mailing, the researcher marks on the graph how many surveys were returned. Once the returns start to decline, which will be visible by the graph markings, then the researcher can send out a follow-up postcard, thanking those who have participated and asking those who have not to please do so. Notice that in this example I have simultaneously thanked those who have participated and asked those who have not to please do so. This is a fast and cheap way of doing a follow-up mailing because it addresses both groups of people (those who have returned their survey and those who have not) in one postcard or letter.

Most social scientists agree, however, that researchers are going to get the best response rate if they mail two follow-up mailings, one of which includes another copy of the survey. Think about it. The reminder may encourage people who have not completed the survey to try to find it wherever they stashed it, but what if they threw out the survey intentionally or unintentionally? If respondents receive a second survey with a reminder to complete it, they are more likely to realize that the researcher is committed and are more likely to complete the survey.

Social scientists don't provide specific instructions as to when it is best to mail follow-up mailings. Graphing responses, as I suggested, is one way to decide when to send follow-up mailings. For this tactic, I would suggest graphing the initial survey mailing, sending a new survey when the survey return begins to drop, charting the return of *those* surveys, and then mailing a follow-up letter or postcard when the second return begins to wane. Others suggest that a two- to three-week space is appropriate between mailings (Babbie, 1995).

Fourth, researchers can include a small incentive to encourage people to participate. Coupons for a small amount off a purchase from a local retailer or a small cash amount (such as $1) may stimulate participation. Generally, when researchers include an incentive, they do so in the initial survey mailing and provide the incentive to everyone. The intent is that people who are rewarded ahead of time for doing the survey will more likely complete the survey because they feel obligated to do so since they were "paid" (even if that payment is a coupon they can use). Certainly some people will take the money and toss out the survey without completing it; however, researchers have found that response rates for surveys offering an incentive are higher than for surveys offering no incentive (Yammarino, Skinner, & Childers, 1991).

Alternately, researchers can monitor responses and send rewards only to those who actually returned the surveys. Doing this will involve a more detailed means of tracking responses; however, because each person in the sample would have to receive a unique identification number that is recorded on the survey. When the surveys are returned, someone matches the survey identification number to the sampling frame to identify the respondent and then mails that particular person the reward.

Incentives and identification numbers can lead to some ethical issues. If you remember when I discussed voluntary participation in Chapter 3, I said that some researchers believed that offering incentives to participate in research made voluntary participation unclear because different people may need, and therefore may be more attracted to, an incentive than others. However, so long as researchers make sure that any incentive is nominal, essentially just a token of appreciation, then most social scientists do not see offering incentives as a violation of voluntary participation.

Matching the survey to respondents' identities may also question the ethical responsibility of anonymity. After all, if a researcher can match survey responses to a specific person's identity, then that person's responses are not anonymous. Again, researchers can get around this. One option is to have someone other than the researcher track survey returns. In this method, the identification number may appear on the outside of the envelope. The person receiving the envelope records the identification number of who responded and forwards that number or envelope (but not the survey) to a second assistant who has the master list of participants. This second assistant matches the number to sample person, but since this assistant never has the survey, he or she cannot match responses to individual identities. The first assistant who received the envelope gives the survey (but not any identifying information) to the researcher. Since the researcher has no means of matching the survey to the master list, once again, anonymity is maintained.

An easier way to circumvent the anonymity issue is to guarantee confidentiality, not anonymity. Remember, confidentiality ensures respondents that the researcher will not match the individual's responses to his or her identity. This means that the researcher *can* match responses, but will not reveal the match in his or her discussion of the research.

Acceptable response rate

With all of this discussion about response rates, you may be wondering what an acceptable response rate for a mailed survey is. Good question. Researchers don't really agree on what an acceptable response rate is; they just agree that getting responses to mailed surveys is difficult. Most social scientists think that response rates of 30 percent or lower have too much bias and are too low to be useful. Some even argue that response rates need to be 70 percent or higher to produce meaningful statistics and accurate generalizations to the population (Dillman, 2000); others argue that the threshold should be 75 percent or higher (Neuman, 1997). However, public participation in surveys has declined since the 1950s and now response rates of 10 to 50 percent are common (Neuman, 1997). Therefore, a general rule of thumb is that response rates of 50 to 70 percent are acceptable so long as the researcher recognizes the potential limitations of this relatively low response in any written reports; response rates higher than 70 percent are considered good.

Matching surveys to computer data

It is important that the researcher assigns a case number to each survey and records that number on the survey when it is returned. The first survey returned is case 1, the second is case 2, and so forth. The researcher should then make sure that survey information is entered into a computer in the order that it was received. The first survey received (case 1) is the first entered into the computer, case 2 is the second survey entered, and so forth. This is important because if some information was mistakenly entered (errors become apparent in the data cleaning stage), the computer will identify which survey has the errors by the survey case number. The researcher can then simply find the survey with the matching number, look at the original answer for the question that has the mistake, and correct the mistake. If the survey information is not entered into the computer in the order of the case numbers, then it is important for the researcher to create an additional variable in the dataset that identifies each survey's case number so any mistakes of data entry can be corrected.

Assigning each survey a case number as it is returned is important also for assessing any potential history effects as a rival causal factor. For example, suppose I did a survey of workers in a major manufacturing plant in my city. After 20 percent of my sample completed their surveys and returned them, the workers learned that the company was moving production overseas and that 85 percent of the employees would be laid off. Consequently, the rest of my surveys were returned after this news. By comparing the responses of the surveys returned prior to the news of the layoff to the surveys returned after the news, I can see whether there is a history effect if the answers to particular questions changed noticeably. Therefore, keeping track of respondents helps the researcher correct data-entry mistakes and may facilitate the identification of rival causal factors beyond the researcher's control.

Advantages and disadvantages

The mailed survey is by far one of the cheapest and least cumbersome method of observation a researcher can use. The only cost in a mailed survey is the paper to print the surveys and the mailings themselves. Another benefit of a mailed survey is that researchers can survey a wide geographical area on their own. For example, if I want to survey Americans' views of the president, I can have access to the views of people who live in all 50 states, even though I am in Pennsylvania. Furthermore, respondents can complete the questionnaire when it is convenient to them. If they want to do it at 7:00 A.M. with their morning coffee or at 11:30 P.M. before they go to bed, that's fine. Since the researcher doesn't physically have to be present to administer the survey, when a participant completes the survey is not an issue.

Mailed surveys also offer anonymity. Even if a researcher wants to track responses, by using the process I outlined earlier (or a variation of it), the researcher can track responses without associating specific surveys to specific respondents. This anonymity makes it more likely that respondents will answer questions that they find to be threatening or sensitive and that they are more likely to give honest answers because they are less concerned with social desirability. Last, by eliminating any direct contact with the researcher, mailed surveys minimize the threat of interviewer bias. This, too, reduces respondents' tendency to answer in socially acceptable ways; it also reduces the possibility that the interviewer will interpret behaviors based on his or her own biases as well.

However, mailed surveys, like all forms of research, have their limitations. Probably the biggest limitation is the response rate. Compared to other survey techniques and other methods of observation, the response rate for mailed surveys is low. Mailed surveys can also take more time than the other survey techniques because the researcher has to take the time to do follow-up mailings in order to boost response rates.

Some other problems with mailed surveys involve limitations in the designs themselves. Because there is no interviewer, respondents cannot ask for clarification of questions they do not understand, which increases the percent of "Don't know" responses or skipped questions. Similarly, researchers cannot *probe*, or ask respondents follow-up questions in which the respondents clarify their initial answer. Also, if questions have special instructions or are presented in a contingency format, people may not accurately follow the directions or contingency pattern, which will lead to inaccurate results.

For example, I once did an informal survey for my department, which asked students to rank eight issues in increasing importance. I instructed students to give each issue a unique ranking between 1 and 8, where 1 was very important and 8 was not at all important. I received a number of responses where students gave two or three of the eight items the same rank, indicating that they did not understand my ranking instructions. These surveys had to be eliminated for the calculation of this question, and that was potentially important information that I lost.

The last disadvantage to surveys is that the researcher has to trust that the respondent is providing accurate information. The researcher really cannot validate respondents' information. For example, I can state that I am a young Asian American male when, in fact, I am a middle-aged White female. The researcher has no way of determining if I am lying. Furthermore, the researcher has no way of really telling whether I am the one completing the survey. If a person receives a mailed survey, anyone in the household could pretend to be the intended respondent and falsely complete and return the survey.

■ Face-to-Face Interviews

When you go to the doctor and answer the doctor's questions, you are essentially participating in a *face-to-face interview*. Likewise, employers interview prospective employees, universities interview prospective students, and police officers interview crime suspects. In all of these situations one person acts as the "researcher" and asks another person, the "participant," information about him or her that the interviewer/researcher will use to compare that person to others and to draw conclusions. Although there are similarities, social science interviews are different from job, medical, and criminal interviews because in social science interviews, the researcher is usually asking questions about an individual to find patterns in a larger classification of people.

Because the interviewer is such an integral component to this research strategy, let's discuss the steps for doing an interview.

Arranging the interview

In interviews, the construction of the survey instrument is only part of the design. Another part of the design involves training interviewers if the researcher is not going to be the only person conducting the interviews. Interviewer training entails familiarizing the interviewer with the details of the study, the organization of the survey, illustrations about how to effectively reinforce that the interview will be confidential, and how to probe should the need arise. Hence, interviewers need to be aware of the research topic and goals so that they are equipped to judge when respondents have given the level of information necessary for adequate analysis. This does not mean that the interviewer is looking for a specific response (e.g., an admission that someone smoked pot when he or she was a teenager)—it just means that the interviewer is looking for a specific *level* of information. This will allow the interviewer to determine whether a response needs clarification for the researcher's purposes.

After the interviewers are trained, the researcher needs to arrange for the interviews to be done. When interviewing people in their private residences, interviewers should not arrive prior to 10:00 A.M. or later than 8:00 P.M., unless specifically requested by the participant (Hagan, 1997). Within these parameters, the interviewer should primarily schedule the interview for when it is convenient for the participant.

In a world of dual-earner families, answering machines, and caller ID, contacting subjects may be challenging. There is little a researcher can do about people's habits of using answering machines or caller ID to screen calls. If an interviewer has trouble contacting a particular respondent, the interviewer should keep track of all call-backs in order to be able to vary the time he or she tries to reach a respondent. It may be that an interviewer cannot reach someone because that person is not home. For example, if I try to call a person at 5:30 P.M. on a Monday and do not get an answer, I would not try a second time at 5:30 P.M. on Tuesday. Instead, on Tuesday I would try a different time, perhaps 4:30 P.M. or 6:30 P.M. Keeping track of the times I call a person will help prevent me from not reaching that person simply because that person works until, for example, 6:00 P.M. and I keep trying to call her at 4:30 P.M.

Conducting the interview

Because interviews involve personal interaction, the demeanor of the interviewer is much more important than in other survey forms such as mailed surveys. As a result, the interviewer is in an interesting position. She or he must develop a rapport with the participant in order to make the participant comfortable enough to answer questions, but the interviewer also has to maintain a neutral and objective distance. In addition to these competing expectations, people usually have only a vague understanding of the norms regarding interviewing.

How you present yourself—for example, how you dress—is important when doing interviews. Subjects, such as prisoners, may react differently to you if you dress in a suit than if you wore more casual clothes.

All social interaction involves roles. Family interactions have the roles of mother, father, child, sibling, and so on. Work interactions have the roles of employer, employee, and co-worker. School interactions have the roles of professor, student, staff, teammate, classmate, and others. In each of these three instances, people have a pretty good idea of what the different roles entail. However, in interviews, people are less clear. Some see an interviewer as an intrusive individual who has to be dealt with as quickly as possible; others see interviewers as people to whom they can "tell their story"; and still others see interviewers as mouthpieces for organizations or bureaucracies. Because of the different perceptions and because most people are not interviewed (at least in the scientific sense) frequently, people are unclear as to how to treat and respond to an interviewer.

The truth is that many interviewers probably contain bits of all of these perceptions. Certainly, most interviewers are not conducting interviews to satisfy their own curiosity; therefore, there is likely to be some organization or bureau cry behind an interview (even if that organization is a university). Interviewers are also likely to ask some very personal questions that respondents may see as intrusive, whereas these same respondents may see other questions as an avenue to express their opinions or "tell their story." Therefore, how an interviewer presents himself or herself has important ramifications for how respondents will define the roles of interviewer and interviewee, and therefore how they will respond to the interview in general.

To some degree, the demeanor of the interviewer has to match the nature of the interview, which is why training interviewers in the nuances of the survey itself is so important. For example, if I am going to interview teenagers who play in a band, I don't think I'll arrive at the interview wearing a suit. Even though I was taught that wearing a suit is professional and I want to impress on these teens that this is serious business, a suit in this context may be alienating, thereby preventing me from establishing the rapport that is a hallmark of interviews. On the other hand, as a middle-aged woman, this does not imply that I should arrive at the interview in torn jeans and a T-shirt. This type of attire is likely to prevent the teens from taking me seriously as a researcher and it may hurt my credibility. It would be similar to parents' attempts to relate to their teenagers by adopting teen lingo and dress. Like the teenage children, my subjects would probably look at me, roll their eyes, and discount my presence.

Let's take a different example. Suppose I want to interview the elderly about their fear of crime. I would not necessarily want to send a police officer to do the interview because the respondents may not give honest answers, especially negative views, about the police *to* the police. The elderly respondents may feel dependent on the police for protection and they may fear that there could be negative repercussions if they criticize the police to the police. Nor am I going to send strapping, young men (even if they are clean-cut college students) to do the interviews because this type of person may be exactly who the elderly fear in the first place.

Therefore, part of overcoming the challenge of the demeanor of the interviewer is to try to match the interviewer with a respondent on race, age, or sex whenever possible. This match does not have to be exact. Researchers do not need to have 70-year-olds interviewing 80-year-olds, but having an adult interviewer (say someone older than age 40) may be beneficial.

Granted, researchers cannot always identify the demographic characteristics of the respondents. If all a researcher has is a name list, age and race/ethnicity may not be evident. However, sometimes the nature of the research question provides some information, as may the information gathered for the type of sampling. For instance, in my earlier example where I was interested in studying teenagers who participate in bands, clearly my subjects will all be teenagers, therefore I can select interviewers with this in mind. Or if, as a researcher, I know I am selecting a stratified sample, I may be able to use the information from the stratification variable to provide clues about my respondents. Therefore, this matching interviewers and subjects based on demographics is a suggestive guide whenever it is possible, but it by no means is a requirement.

There are also other ways that interviewers can make themselves more approachable to respondents, such as through their dress, the way they carry themselves, and their language. Even if, as a thirty-something-year-old college professor, I want to study teenagers, I clearly can't make myself look 16 again. I also may not have the resources to hire some of my students to do the interviewing for me. Therefore, I am going to have to alter my demeanor to fit the occasion. As I said before, if I were doing the interviews, I would not wear a formal suit. Perhaps I might just dress in casual pants and a decent (but not fancy) shirt. If my posture is erect, but not stiff, and I bring a clipboard, I am pretty much giving clues that I am there to ask and record information. The language I choose to use may also be more conversational than academic or business, meaning that I would speak as I do in conversation and not use unnecessarily long or complicated phrasing. Plus, I can use my body language to establish a casual, yet distinct, demeanor that would probably be appropriate in this instance.

On the other hand, if I was going to interview a group of trial lawyers regarding their opinions about tort reform, I would present myself differently. In this instance, I would definitely wear a suit—probably a conservative one at that. I would also alter my language to a more academic or educated phraseology. I would probably add a briefcase to my attire and I would address these individuals formally.

Appearance is only part of the demeanor of the interviewer. He or she can establish rapport by guaranteeing confidentiality, being friendly, being open, and being nonjudgmental. The last point is especially important if the interviewer is going to be asking rotationally uncomfortable personal questions. The more open a respondent sees the interviewer as being, the more willing that person will be to participate in the interview and to provide accurate answers. Casual conversation before the interview begins can facilitate this. This conversation can be about most anything: children, the weather, sports, appearance of the meeting place (whether it is a home or a public area), and so on.

The point I am illustrating is that the demeanor of the interviewer is important in establishing the balance between rapport and scientific identity. Although matching interviewers and respondents based on demographic characteristics may be helpful, it by no means is the only or even the main way to strike this balance in demeanor. Dress, verbal and body language, casual warm-up conversation, and interview conversation style all help the interviewer define the situation and help the respondent understand the norms of the interaction. The interviewer's goal is to appear interested, friendly, and diplomatic while also appearing scientific and subtly conveying the importance of the study and of the respondents' information.

When the interviewer and the respondent have established their relationship, it is time for the interviewer to administer the survey. Like other surveys, most interviews are likely to have both closed- and open-ended questions. The closed-ended questions are easy to administer, as the interviewer just reads the question and answer choices and records the respondent's answer choice. The benefit of having an interviewer administer closed-ended questions is that a real person who is familiar with the survey (since the interviewer presumably experienced some training prior to actually conducting the survey) can answer any questions or provide clarification if the respondent needs it.

Open-ended questions are particularly informative in interviews, but they are harder for the interviewer to report accurately because the interviewer has to record exactly what the respondent says verbatim. This means that the interviewer needs to be able to write fairly quickly, write legibly, resist correcting grammar in the subject's response, and avoid the temptation to summarize or paraphrase the respondent's answer. The last issue is particularly tricky because respondents' answers may be fairly long and detailed. For example, if a respondent says, "We are really worried about the chance my husband will lose his job. We have a lot of debt and very little savings. We don't want to go on welfare if we don't have to because my husband would just see that as a further sign of failure" and an interviewer writes, "Afraid of job loss due to debt," a lot of potentially useful information regarding the husband's view of welfare and how their savings relates to their current debt is lost.

On the other hand, sometimes respondents do not provide *enough* information for an open-ended question, which poses a different challenge. Part of training an interviewer involves educating that person about the level of information necessary as a response to a question. For example, if an interviewer asked someone if he or she smoked pot in the past and the interviewer knows that the researcher ultimately wants a rough estimate of the age a person first smoked pot, the interviewer would have to probe in order to get that level of information if the respondent wasn't forthcoming.

A **probe** is when an interviewer asks further questions that try to guide the respondent to a certain level of information. A probe does not mean that the interviewer is trying to get the respondent to say a specific answer. For instance, a probe does not mean that prior to an interview, a researcher predetermines a specific age, such as 13, that he or she wants a person to say. It only means that the interviewer is trying to direct the respondent to an age, or at least a general age range. Therefore, an example of a probe in which an interviewer might first establish whether someone ever smoked marijuana and then tried to get an estimate of the age that person had her or his first joint, might go something like this:

Interviewer: Have you ever smoked marijuana in the past?
Respondent: Yeah.

Interviewer: Roughly how old were you when you smoked the marijuana?

Respondent: Pretty young.

Interviewer probe: Were you a teenager? Young adult? . . .

Respondent: I was a teenager.

Interviewer probe: Were you in middle school or high school?

Respondent: I think it was high school.

Notice that in this example, the respondent still did not provide an *exact* age. This is an important point because there is a fine line between probing and badgering the participant. The first rule of probing is not to try to get more information than is necessary. Since I set up the scenario to say that the researcher was interested in general age, this loose age range (high school age) is acceptable.

The second rule of probing is to read the respondents' body language to see if that person is getting annoyed, frustrated, or exceptionally uncomfortable with the probe. Remember, all research participants have an ethical right to privacy, which means that they have a right to withhold information if they want. While probing, reinforcing the guarantee of confidentiality and reinforcing the importance of respondents' answers serve to minimize the amount of information a respondent decides to withhold. If the respondent looks as if the probe is causing undue discomfort or distress, even in light of these reminders, the interviewer has to back off and respect the person's right to privacy. The interviewer may delicately try to raise the question again later in the survey, but if the response is the same, the interviewer needs to cut his or her losses and move on.

There are also other types of probes that do not involve asking further questions. First, the interviewer may pause for a few seconds longer than the normal time one waits for a response. Probably the most common mistake made by new teachers, as well as other public speakers, is that they ask a question to a group of people, wait only a couple of seconds, and then proceed with the answer. Much like in a classroom, if an interviewer actually waits a few seconds past the natural pause after asking a question, respondents are very likely to elaborate their answers. A second type of probe is the nonverbal body language of the interviewer. A head tilt, raised eyebrows, or poised pen may also encourage participants to elaborate an answer. Therefore, there are multiple techniques an interviewer can use to probe a respondent for a deeper or more precise response. The interviewer just has to read the respondents' body language in order to know when to abandon the probe and when to continue the interview.

Once the interview is complete, the interviewer needs to prepare for his or her exit. Subjects frequently need a bit of a wind down at the end of the interview; in other words, the interviewer should not just simply say, "Okay, that's all I have. Thanks for your time" and then get up to leave. Signaling that the interview is over is a fine start, but then the interviewer should engage in a little more casual conversation to help the respondent wind down and to give the respondent an opportunity to add any additional comments that he or she might have been thinking about during the course of the interview. The interviewer might also ask respondents whether they have any questions for the interviewer. Then, after a little light conversation, the interviewer can then say "thank you" and leave.

BOX 7.2   **Example of an Interview: Student Social Movements in China**

Compared to the students of the 1960s and 1970s, current U.S. college students are frequently criticized for their political and social apathy and unwillingness to mobilize to enact social change. However, in the 1980s, Chinese college students who were dissatisfied with poverty and other social problems formed a pro-democracy social movement that culminated in the 1989 Tiananmen Square incident in Beijing. Zhao (1998) interviewed 70 college students whom he identified through a snowball sampling technique about the pro-democracy movement in Beijing. Below is an excerpt from his research methodology and findings.

A set of questions was prepared before the interview. These questions served as a guideline for further probing. In the interview, informants were asked slightly different questions and probed differently. Therefore, the sample size for statistics extracted from the interview is usually smaller than the number of informants interviewed. Before each interview, I explained the purposes of the study and the anonymity of their information, I also told them that they could refuse to answer a question if it made them uncomfortable for whatever reasons. In fact, very few informants refused to answer any questions, and the Beijing informants showed no more restraint than the Montreal informants.

The interviews were conducted between late 1992 and early 1993, while the movement occurred in 1989. So there is the possibility of forgetting and distorting as the result of their current state of mind. These problems cannot be totally eliminated, but I have tried to minimize their impact by avoiding questions that probe into personal views, impressions, or experiences of a short-term nature. After the interview, I cross-checked the precision of an informant's narrative by the other informants' descriptions of the same event. Sometimes, when an informant's description was part of a major event, the published accounts were also used to check reliability. Possibly because the period before and during the 1989 BSM was so dramatic in most informants' lives, the narratives of my informants showed a strong consistency.

The interviews were carried out in Chinese. All the quotes in this article are my translations. Each quote was labeled by a number to mark the source of information while maintaining anonymity.

One of Zhao's findings is that the close and dense living quarters of Chinese students facilitated the formation of the student movement, because even if an individual student did not want to participate in the movement, once movement involvement became associated with morality, that individual was continually pressured to join by those whom he frequently saw in his living quarters. As Zhao and some of his respondents say:

Students in the same or nearby dormitory rooms often checked each other's behavior. As one student commented: "All students joined the movement after several demonstrations. Students who did not go would feel isolated and hated. For example, when the government asked us to resume class, only one student went to class. As a result, that student was accused of being a renegade" (no. 4). . . .

Because of high student density in a dormitory building, coercion among students could sometimes go beyond a dormitory room. One student (no. 62) had given a vivid account of this:

During the whole process of the movement, one event left me with a very deep impression. In the law department, there were quite a few graduate students of the 1989 class who did not care about the movement at all and played mah-jongg in their dormitory rooms everyday. I knew this from a notice board in no. 46 building. It read: "Since the hunger strike, several scoundrels on the fifth floor have not cared about the movement at all and have lost all their consciousness. They have been locking themselves in their dorms and playing mah-jongg everyday. We belittle them very

very much. . . ." I also remembered a line in a big character post. It said: "Those red noses and black hearts are playing mah-jongg even when the other students are on a hunger strike. Beware of your dog noses!"

However, most pressure was more subtle. When a follow-up question was asked ("What did you think of those students who did not participate in the movement at all?"), the following was a rather typical response: "We did not care about those students. Because these people did not interact with classmates even at regular times, no one paid much attention to them" (no. 37).

Source: Dingxin Zhao, "Ecologies of Social Movements: Student Mobilization during the 1989 Prodemocracy Movement in Beijing," *The American Journal of Sociology, 103*(6) (1998): 1493–1529.

Critical Thinking Questions

1. Do you find the description of the interview process sufficient? Why or why not? If not, what would you like to see added?

2. Did Zhao fulfill his ethical responsibility to the subjects? Why or why not?

3. Are there any examples of probes in this excerpt? If so, can you identify it/them?

Critical Thinking Discussion

1. Zhao states when he did the interviews, acknowledges the potential issue of recollection error, and he says that the interviews were in Chinese. He does not state the interview questions but he doesn't have to. This information will become apparent when he discusses the results, since he presumably will progress through the information obtained from the various questions.

   He does, however, state that his questions also included some loose guides for probing, which is a plus, because that indicates that Zhao was aware of areas in which respondents might need probing prior to actually conducting the interviews.

   No information is given about interviewer training and he uses the pronoun *I* when discussing the interview, so the implication is that he did the interviews himself. If this is the case, he obviously doesn't need to train himself in terms of how he wants the interviews to be conducted, so this omission is appropriate.

   The only material that someone might question is that there is no information in this excerpt (or the source article) about how he worked to establish a rapport with the respondents other than the mention that the interviews were in Chinese.

2. Zhao claims that he protected anonymity and he implies that he protected privacy by letting respondents know that they didn't have to answer any questions that made them uncomfortable. He is correct in saying that he protected privacy; however, this is one of those examples where the researcher protected confidentiality even though he said he protected anonymity.

   It is true that those reading his research have no means of matching subject identity to response, but that should be the case in any research. Since Zhao did the interviews, *he* knew the identity of the people and protected it by referring to people he quoted as numbers. This is still confidentiality. In fact, for all interviews where the researcher is the one who actually conducted the interviews, the researcher can only guarantee confidentiality.

   However, since Zhao does not present any additional identifying information with each quote (e.g., gender, age, etc.), and refers to people only by numbers, this semantic issue is not a real limitation to the research.

3. No, there are no examples of probes here. It is not unusual for researchers to omit information about when or how they probed, because this information is likely to vary by the individual respondent.

Berg (1995, pp. 57–58) best summarizes the guidelines for good interviewing with his ten commandments of interviews. They are:

1. Never begin an interview cold.
2. Remember your purpose.
3. Present a natural front.
4. Demonstrate aware hearing.
5. Think about appearance.
6. Interview in a comfortable place.
7. Don't be satisfied with monosyllabic answers.
8. Be respectful.
9. Practice, practice, practice some more.
10. Be cordial and appreciative.

When the interviewer leaves, the very last step is for the interviewer to go somewhere where he or she can record any perceptions about the interview or comments he or she may have. This needs to be done soon after the interview, while the events and impressions are still fresh. This is also a good time for the interviewer to skim the interview for editing and other notes. For example, questions that were not applicable (perhaps because they were contingency questions that did not apply to a particular respondent) should be clearly marked with a "NA" for "Not applicable" (or some other notation that would distinguish from "No opinion" questions or questions the respondent declined to answer). If the interviewer jotted notes about participant demeanor or other observations during the interview, now is the time for the interviewer to clarify those notes or cross-reference them to other questions if appropriate.

Last, the interviewer might want to make notations near any questions in which the respondent asked for clarification. This would help validity tests later in the process. To summarize, then, at this final read through, the interviewer wants to make it as clear as possible to whoever is coding the interview what exactly occurred during the interview and how the respondent reacted to the questions.

Advantages and disadvantages

One of the strengths of interviews is their personal nature. If respondents relate to the interviewer, they are more likely to be willing to share personal information. If the respondent finds a question to be unclear or confusing, the interviewer can explain it, which will decrease the number of "Don't know" responses and increase the validity of the study. Furthermore, interviewers can act as observers. They can make note of their own impressions of the respondents, which may help the researcher get a better sense of who is participating in the study. Unlike mailed surveys, interviews are not hampered by literacy problems. Since the interviewer can read any questions, provided that the interviewer is fluent in the preferred language of the subject, whether the subject can read is not relevant. Therefore, the personal nature of interviews elicits a higher response rate and more accurate information than other survey techniques.

However, there are some drawbacks to interviews. Clearly, this personal touch comes at a price. Interviews can be expensive in terms of time and money. If the main researcher will conduct the interviews himself or herself, there is the cost of the researcher's forgone time as the researcher does the interviews; if the researcher elects to train others to actually conduct the interviews, then the researcher has to pay them for their time and invest the time in training them.

One of the main disadvantages is the concern over interviewer bias. There a lot of ways that interviews can unintentionally insert bias into the data gathered. The most obvious way is if an interviewer fails to maintain neutrality and keep his or her personal views out of the recorded information. For example, an interviewer may take a dislike to a respondent and that may affect how the interviewer interprets that respondent's demeanor. Therefore, a respondent who may be apprehensive or uncomfortable with the general interview process (a fairly benign or neutral description) is recorded as distrusting and uncooperative (a more ominous description). Interviewers may also insert bias into the data gathering by expressing shock or awe at something a respondent says, which may in turn affect how that respondent answers subsequent questions in the interview.

In essence, interviewers have to try to overcome any self-consciousness they may experience during the interview, avoid inserting their personality into the respondent's reporting of events, and resist providing a frame of reference for the respondent's answers (Gubrium & Holstein, 2002). The degree to which the interviewer can implement these guidelines influences the degree of bias present in the data.

■ Telephone Surveys

As the name implies, with *telephone surveys* an interviewer gives the survey to respondents over the phone. This is a very popular method of gathering data because most people in the United States have phones. In fact, it's very likely that you have been asked to participate in a phone survey at some point already.

The mechanics of doing a phone survey are not very different from doing an interview or a mailed survey. However, there are a couple of features that are unique. The first is the method of sampling. Researchers can obtain the sample for telephone surveys from telephone directories, lists, or a method called **random digit dialing.** In random digit dialing, the researcher can obtain a national list of area code exchange numbers and then a computer randomly fills in the remaining four numbers, thereby creating a probability sample. However, each of these sampling methods produce different levels of error. For example, 10 to 15 percent of directory listings will not be for valid households; more than 35 percent of U.S. households have phone numbers that are unlisted (and this can be as high as 60 percent in some communities); and, with regard to random digit dialing, many of

With computer-assisted telephone interviewing technology, researchers can monitor the data-gathering process of many assistants at one time.

those exchanges in a list may not be for residential units but rather for businesses or other establishments (Levy & Lemeshow, 1999).

Researchers can take random digit dialing one step further and do **computer-assisted telephone interviewing (CATI).** With CATI, the interviewer (or interviewer assistants) can sit directly in front of a computer while they either manually make telephone calls or have the computer do random digit dialing. With this method, the interviewer wears a headset and a microphone and directly reads the survey questions off the computer screen to the respondent. Then the interviewer can directly enter the respondents' answers into the computer, which saves the later step of data coding. Once the interviewer enters an answer, the computer shows the next question.

Yarosz and Barnett (2001, **AN 4485918**) used the National Household Education Survey to answer the question, "Who reads to young children?" They describe their dataset and sample as the following:

> Data for this study were obtained from the National Household Education Survey of 1995 (NHES:95; US Department of Education, 1995). The NHES:95 data set is based on a national telephone survey of households utilizing random digit dialing methods and computer-assisted telephone interviewing (CATI) technology. Interviews were conducted for the NHES:95 with the parents and guardians of a nationally representative sample of 14,064 children. This study focuses on the 7,566 under age six, who had not entered kindergarten. (p. 70)

Although random digit dialing and computer-assisted telephone interviewing can certainly facilitate the process of interviewing, there is a potential risk to validity in that it is difficult to make sure that the person completing the interview is actually the intended individual. To try to ensure this, interviewers have to ask many questions in order to establish the appropriateness of the person for the sample. For example, interviewers with the National Household Education Survey have to begin each interview with the questions presented in Figure 7.4. Even with these precautions, there is still no guarantee that the person answering the questions is the intended individual, but it is a better screening system than having no screening system at all.

Response rates

Telephone surveys generally have a high refusal rate, but not one as high as mailed surveys. The number of call-backs necessary in order to reach a respondent can also be high. With caller ID and answering machines, it is increasingly easier for people to screen calls and not answer the phone if they wish. With the increase in telemarketer calls, people conducting phone interviews have more challenges because respondents may regard a call for an interview to be the same as a telemarketer call, or people may be more used to saying no on the phone. This leads to a lower response rate than for face-to-face interviews.

Advantages and disadvantages

Telephone surveys are much cheaper to conduct than face-to-face interviews, yet, at the same time, the researcher benefits from some of the advantages of interviews. For example, the interviewer can explain any questions the respondents do not understand, they can read verbal clues about the respondent's views (e.g., a very long pause, or a drawn out "I . . . don't . . . know if I want to answer that"), and they can still use probes to get a more appropriate level of information.

S1. Hello, my name is (INTERVIEWER) and I'm calling for the U.S. Department of Education. We are conducting a voluntary and confidential study about the educational experiences of both adults and children. These first questions usually take about 5 minutes. Are you a member of this household and at least 15 years old?

YES . . . . *		(GO TO S5)
NO 2		(GO TO S2)
BUSINESS 3		(GO TO S5)
GO TO RESULT . . . . GT		
RETRY AUTODIALER . . . . RT		

S2. May I please speak with a household member who is at least 15 years old?

AVAILABLE 1		(GO TO S1)
NOT AVAILABLE 2		(GO TO RESULT CALLBACK APPT.)
THERE ARE NONE 3		(GO TO S3)
GO TO RESULT . . . . GT		

S3. May I please speak with the male or female head of this household?

PERSON ON PHONE 1		(GO TO S5)
OTHER PERSON, AVAILABLE 2		(GO TO S4)
OTHER PERSON, NOT AVAILABLE. 3		(GO TO RESULT CALLBACK APPT.)
GO TO RESULT . . . . GT		

S4. Hello, this is (INTERVIEWER) and I'm calling for the U.S. Department of Education. We are conducting a voluntary and confidential study about the educational experiences of both adults and children. This study will help the Department of Education plan educational programs in the U.S. These first questions usually take about 5 minutes. Are you a head of this household?

YES 1		(GO TO S5)
NO 2		(GO TO S3)
GO TO RESULT . . . . GT		

S5. I would like to confirm that this number is for home use rather than only used for business. (Is this a home phone?)

HOME USE 1		(CONTINUE)
HOME AND BUSINESS USE 2		(CONTINUE)
BUSINESS USE ONLY. 3		(GO TO THANK1)
GO TO RESULT . . . . GT		

Source: National Center for Education Statistics, NHES: 95 Basic Screener, *1995 National Household Education Survey Questionnaire* (February 1997). http://nces.ed.gov/nhes/pdf/quex/admited/ae_95.pdf.

Figure 7.4 Sample Script for Telephone Interview

Another benefit of phone surveys is that the main researcher can easily monitor the interviewers. For example, I can spend a minimal amount of time and money training seniors majoring in sociology who have had my research methods class on how to do computer-assisted telephone interviewing. I can then set up, say, 10 stations in one of the larger classrooms or a computer lab in my university each equipped with a computer, a phone, and a headset. My 10 students can then do the interviewing while I walk among them and eavesdrop on their end of the conversations to make sure they are following the interviewing script as designed, and I can look over their shoulders to see if they are correctly entering the data. This is both cost and time efficient, as well as design efficient in that I can spot and correct any errors as they occur.

However, phone interviews do have their limitations. Long distance calling can be expensive, although there may be discounted rates. Furthermore, the questions and answers on phone surveys also need to be relatively short. Since there is no way for the interviewer to use visual aids or for the respondent to reread a question a number of times (or read it slowly to absorb detail), long questions or answer choices will lead to invalid results. Also, the interviewer may have to deal with background interruptions in the interview as children get into fights, dogs bark, spouses ask questions, and doorbells ring. Because the respondent is at home during the interview and interviews do not occur at a prearranged time when the respondent can minimize outside distractions, disturbances that will take the respondent's attention away from the interview are likely. There is little interviewers can do about this; however, if interviewers pepper interesting questions throughout the interview, they may be able to keep the respondent interested enough to complete the interview despite the distractions.

This brings me to the last point. In interviews, when the respondent has decided that he or she has had enough or that a question is too personal or threatening, the response is likely to be to hang up. This poses a problem for the researcher because once a respondent hangs up, that person is not likely to appreciate a call-back to complete the interview. Therefore, interviewers lose any information about questions they still did not get to ask. To minimize this risk, keep the survey short. It is unrealistic for interviewers to think that a person will willingly spend 30 minutes or more on a phone. In fact, many people may not even be willing to spend 20 minutes on the phone with an interviewer. Also, make sure that threatening questions are toward the end of the interview with demographic questions sprinkled throughout. This way, if a person hangs up when an interviewer asks when the person last had sex, for example, or what the person's total household income is, if the survey is designed where demographic variables such gender, age, and education were earlier (as opposed to the end, where they frequently are), then the researcher at least has this key information.

■ Electronic Surveys

As of the year 2000, over half of all households had a computer (51 percent), compared to 42.1 percent just two years before in 1998. Furthermore, in 2000, 41.5 percent of all households had Internet access, an increase from 15.5 percent just two years earlier (U.S. Bureau of the Census, 2001). With the rapid increase in computers and Internet usage, it is not surprising that researchers have capitalized on this change to find a new avenue for conducting research: the *electronic survey*.

According to Dillman (2000) there are two ways researchers can use electronic surveys. The first way is for the researcher to structure an **e-mail survey.** In this type of survey, the survey is sent as an e-mail attachment to respondents who open the e-mail survey, complete it, and then send it back to the researcher. According to Dillman, these surveys are fairly easy for researchers to create themselves; however, they tend to be cumbersome if they are more than five pages long.

The second type of electronic survey is a **web survey.** These surveys appear on an Internet server and respondents are provided a link to the server and asked to visit the survey site and complete the survey. Clearly, this type of survey requires more programming skill than the e-mail surveys, but they do have the benefit of allowing for longer surveys. In fact, they can also be programmed so questions that do not pertain to an individual respondent (e.g., contingency questions) are not visible, so the researcher does not need to worry about whether respondents are skipping the questions that do not pertain to them.

Response rates

There are some issues of responses that plague electronic surveys. The first is that, compared to mail surveys, electronic surveys are more likely to suffer from undeliverable mail (Shannon & Bradshaw, 2002, **AN 6282924**). Furthermore, Shannon and Bradshaw found that the nonresponse rate for electronic surveys were higher than for mail surveys. Although 47 percent of the mailed surveys were returned, only 32 percent of the electronic surveys were returned (after adjusting for the number of nondeliverable surveys). A meta-analysis of research published by Cook and colleagues (2000) found a similarly low response rates for electronic surveys at 34.6 percent. Therefore, in order to obtain appropriate response rates, researchers are going to have to oversample. To avoid selection bias, electronic surveys are most suited for studies of populations that are already likely to have access to the Internet. Figure 7.5 shows an example of a Web survey.

Advantages and disadvantages

Electronic surveys are very flexible. The questionnaire itself can have graphics, long answer choices, multiple answer choices, and additional features such as word definition and instructions for answering questions. Plus, answers are directly recorded in the researcher's database so that data entry and coding are essentially eliminated. This helps prevent human errors in data entry and coding and helps improve the validity of the findings. Furthermore, the findings can be reported very quickly, since the data coding and entry steps were traditionally very time consuming.

However, the most noticeable drawback is the large percentage of people who still do not have Internet access. Although Internet access is definitely increasing, more than half of all households still do not have it. These households are likely to create a degree of selection bias in some electronic surveys because the people without Internet access are more likely to be poor, a racial minority, or elderly (U.S. Bureau of the Census, 2001). Researchers also need to be careful not to create surveys that have many graphics or are so long that the respondent's computer cannot read it. Researchers who want to do surveys electronically should use web surveys for longer, more elaborate surveys, where the user has to enter a user ID and password in order to access the survey. In fact, the user ID and password are a good characteristic of any web survey to better ensure that the person completing the

Survey.net is a server that offers a multitude of surveys and that allows people to post their own survey questions. Below is an example of a web survey that appeared on the Survey.net website about Internet spam.

A couple of points about this survey need to be made. First, in this web survey, the respondent would answer questions by clicking the blue box next to the answer box in order to get a drag down menu of response options and then highlight the particular response. I have done this for a number of questions; however, as with other forms of survey research, good web surveys will still offer "no answer" categories (or something similar) for respondents who do not wish to answer questions, like I did for questions 3, 10, 12, 13, and 14.

Second, anyone with Internet access can respond to the surveys, but because people are not explicitly solicited to participate (as they would be in most sampling instances), the sampling method here is accidental. Whether someone participates in the survey is accidental based on whether a person (1) finds the website on his or her own, (2) decides that a survey topic is interesting and clicks it, (3) actually completes the survey, and (4) submits his or her answers. Not all web surveys rely on accidental samples. For example, administrators at a university can electronically survey employees about morale by designing a web survey, drawing a sample of employees, and then e-mailing the link only to those employees selected as part of the sample.

Your source for information, opinions & demographics from the Net Community!

SUR☑EY.NET™

Internet SPAM Survey

SPAM is today's hot topic - not the meat product, but the practice of sending unsolicited information over the Internet. "Spam" used to refer to massive cross-posting of messages in usenet, but most people think of it as unsolicited, obnoxious commercial e-mail. How do YOU feel about Spam?

Remember, when you have a multiple-choice question, select the single best answer - even if you might agree with more than one of the options.

Let's get a little bit of background information on who is taking the poll - this will be for detailed analysis & reporting. NOTE that you are still completely anonymous.

1. What is your age?
   [No Answer]

2. Your Sex:
   [No Answer]

3. Who is your primary Internet provider?
   [No Answer]

4. Does your provider filter unsolicited commercial e-mail?
   [No Answer]

5. Select any of the items below which relate to your situation:
   ☐ Run a home-based business (full time)
   ☐ Run a home-based business (part time)
   ☐ Work for an Internet-related company
   ☐ Use E-Mail for marketing/solicitation
   ☐ Use Newsgroups for marketing/solicitation
   ☐ Work in the field of advertising/marketing
   ☐ Student
   ☐ Use the Internet to generate revenue
   ☐ I regularly send unsolicited commercial e-mail
   ☐ I regularly post usenet advertisements
   ☐ Manage/Administer an Internet server

6. Have you ever sent unsolicited e-mail?
   [No Answer]

7. How do you deal with spam/UCE?
   [No Answer]

8. Have you ever complained about unsolicited e-mail to: (check all that apply)
   ☐ My ISP
   ☐ The sender
   ☐ The company being advertised
   ☐ The agency doing the mass mailing
   ☐ An advertised 800 number
   ☐ An advertised phone number
   ☐ A domain administrative contact
   ☐ The ISP from which the spam originated
   ☐ A government agency (FCC,FTC,FBI,Attorney General,etc)
   ☐ Mail-bombed a spammer
   ☐ Other type of attack (ping, DOS)

Figure 7.5 Example of a Web Survey

survey is the person for whom the survey was intended. Also, like telephone directories, electronic surveys may suffer from inactive e-mail addresses, and, like mailed surveys, the response rates for electronic surveys are very low.

Therefore, the ease of conducting electronic surveys is hampered by low response rates and potential selection bias among respondents. On the other hand, if a researcher is focused on a very specific population that is likely to have access to the Internet (e.g., college students, corporate employees, middle-class people in a community) and oversamples to compensate somewhat for low response rates, electronic surveys can be an affordable and fast way to gather information.

■ When to Use What

As with many aspects of research, one of the challenges is deciding what method to use when. Even if a researcher decides to do a survey, the researcher *still* has to choose the type of design within the broader category. Once a researcher decides that a survey is appropriate for his or her specific research question, the next step of deciding which type of survey to do will involve the consideration of a number of factors. Table 7.2 summarizes the different characteristics of various survey techniques.

Three of the biggest factors in deciding which survey technique is the most suitable are the nature of the population studied, the desired response rate, and the resources available. Because mailed surveys and electronic surveys have the lowest response rates, generally they are the least preferred survey techniques. However, they are still very popular and can be highly effective when researchers have limited financial resources to train interviewers or when researchers need to read a very diverse population.

If a researcher has some financial resources, would like to study a diverse population, and does not have a very lengthy questionnaire, a telephone survey may be appropriate. The researcher can use either an established research firm to conduct the phone interviews or some well-trained students or volunteers.

On the other hand, if I had a lengthy survey with many complicated concepts within it, a face-to-face interview would most likely be preferable. In this instance, interviewers can clarify any questions respondents have and can encourage respondents to continue participation in person through the rapport they develop. However, with face-to-face interviews, there is the drawback of potential interviewer bias and an unwillingness to answer sensitive questions. If sensitive questions are a major component of the questionnaire, then a mailed survey may be your best bet.

Issues in Survey Research

■ Ethics

Survey research usually creates fewer ethical considerations than do experiments. The main ethical concerns in survey research are informed consent and confidentiality/anonymity. All survey forms should include either a cover letter or an introductory statement that tells the potential respondent the general topic of research, any sponsors, the purpose of the research, any potential benefits or harms, and a guarantee of anonymity or confidentiality. Once the respondents read or hear this, if they decide to participate, the researcher has fulfilled his or her ethical obligation of informed consent.

TABLE 7.2 Summary Points about Different Survey Techniques

	Mailed Survey	Face-to-Face Interview	Phone Interview	Electronic Survey
Administrative Issues				
Cost	Cheap	Expensive	Cheap to moderate	Cheap to costly
Ease of distribution	Easy	Moderate to hard	Easy	Easy to moderate
Speed	Slow	Slow to moderate	Fast	Fast
Geographical reach	Far	Limited	Far	Far
Design Issues				
Question clarification	No	Yes	Yes	Possible
Probe for additional information	No	Yes	Yes	No
Success with open-ended questions	Limited	High	Moderate	Moderate
Success with visual aids	Limited	High	Low	High
Success with special question directions	Limited	High	Moderate to high	Moderate to high
Success with threatening questions	Moderate	Moderate to high	Moderate	Moderate
Incidence of "Don't know" responses	High	Low	Moderate	Moderate
Sure responses from intended participant	No	Yes	No	No
Anonymity/Confidentiality	Either	Usually confidentiality	Either	Confidentiality
Response rate	Questionable	High	Moderate	Questionable
Any respondent limitations?	Literacy	Language barriers	Language	Internet access
Rival Causal Factors				
Interviewer bias	No	Possible	Possible	Unlikely
Identification of history effect	Possible	Possible	Difficult	Difficult
Social desirability	Limited	Moderate to high	Low to moderate	Low

Most survey techniques should guarantee confidentiality as opposed to anonymity because anonymity is a very difficult criterion to fulfill. Mailed surveys have the greatest potential for anonymity because, unless the researcher provides some type of identification number on the survey, the researcher has no real concept of who answered individual questionnaires. However, this anonymity comes at the price of efficient follow-ups. Remember, mailed surveys have notoriously low response rates; therefore, without some means of identifying individual questionnaires with specific respondents, the researcher will have to do mass mailings of all sample members in order to encourage people to return their surveys—even to those people who already did.

Sometimes, depending on the subject matter, surveys and interviews can cause some emotional distress among participants. If a researcher suspects that this is a possibility, he or she should include some contact numbers for resources that the respondent can use if need be in order to prevent the problem of nonmalefiscence, or harm to respondents.

Other than these considerations, there are few ethical issues for survey research, which is one of the many reasons why it is such a popular form of research among social scientists.

■ Validity and Reliability

Validity, as with any study, can be a bit difficult to establish. There are two main ways that errors can minimize the validity of surveys. First, researchers can have poorly operationalized concepts or poorly worded questions that prevent them from accurately measuring their research interests. If respondents do not understand a question on a questionnaire, they are likely either to skip it or to fill in the first answer that comes to mind—in other words, they will guess at what the researcher means and answer accordingly. Second, a poor sampling frame or other sampling errors (such as nonresponses) may produce bias that will hinder the validity of the findings.

However, the validity risk of both of these errors can be minimized. Researchers can minimize the problem of poorly operationalized concepts by extensively studying the literature and using preestablished and validated measures in their surveys. Likewise, they can pretest their surveys on a small sample of people from their main sampling frame to see if there are any questions people find confusing or if there are any questions in which people overwhelmingly respond the same. (The latter is a problem because if there is little variation in response, then a question will not be useful and will unnecessarily lengthen the survey.) Using a pretest is very important because then the researcher can correct any errors in questionnaire construction or presentation prior to investing the survey in a larger sample.

The only caveat is that the researcher has to remember to remove the people from the sampling frame who were part of the pretest so that these people are not selected to participate in the larger study. Otherwise, the researcher runs the risk of a pretest effect among these individuals. Last, there will always be some sampling error present in research. As I stated in Chapter 5, the key is to minimize this error, and this can usually effectively be done by following the steps for minimizing sample bias that I discuss in that chapter.

Provided the survey method is valid, establishing reliability is fairly easy. After all, once a researcher creates a survey instrument, it is fairly easy to share that instrument with other researchers who can then use it to study other populations, other geographical areas, or other time periods. Hence, survey research is very appealing to social scientists because it can be a fairly efficient means of collecting valid, reliable data about large and small populations.

Evaluating Written Research: Surveys

Evaluating survey, and other methods, of observation essentially revolves around assessing whether the research proceeded through the relevant steps and provided enough information to allow others to follow and evaluate what was done. However, as I have stated several times, it is important to keep in mind that many academic journals have a very fixed and limited page length. Therefore, researchers need to be selective about what details they present, especially since the bulk of any report is likely to be the presentation of research results.

The following guidelines will help you realistically assess what you are likely to read in a written research report. These guidelines will also indicate what type of information is and is not necessary for a researcher to present.

1. Is the research topic worded appropriately for survey research?

The topics appropriate for survey research are legion. Generally, appropriate survey topics focus on assessing people's knowledge, their behaviors, their attitudes, their expected behaviors, and their self-classification. Therefore, the real issue here is not necessarily whether the topic is appropriate but whether it is *worded* appropriately. In other words, is the topic sufficiently specific? Is it a topic that can be empirically testable? If you are unclear about some of these criteria, you can refer to Box 4.1 in Chapter 4, with the understanding that since survey research is appropriate for studying attitudes, questions such as Do Americans support campaign reform? is an appropriate topic, although Should we have campaign reform? is not. The first question assesses people's views or attitudes. The second tries to make a conclusion about what we should do, and research cannot do that. It can document only what is directly observable.

2. Did the researcher specifically state which type of survey method was used?

This may seem like a minor point, but different survey methods have different considerations. For example, if the researchers specifically state that they did computer-assisted telephone interviewing (CATI), then you can probably assume that there was some type of monitoring of the interviewing staff and that there is likely to be less error introduced from the coding and entering of data. Likewise, if the researchers state that they did random digit dialing, then even without any further information about what specific type of sampling method (e.g., simple random, systematic, etc.), you can be confident that the sample is a probability sample.

3. Do the survey questions adequately address the topic or hypothesis?

If my research hypothesis is "The more television a person watches, the more likely that person is to buy fast food," I should not have a survey question that asks, Are you more likely to buy fast food when you watch a lot of television? Why? First, because a hypothesis involves a dependent and an independent variable, and each variable has to have its own question. The question I posed contains *both* the independent and dependent variables within it. Second, you may consider watching more than 1 hour of television a day to be "a lot," but I may be a natural couch potato and think that watching more than 5 hours of television a day to be "a lot." Hence, the definition of "a lot" is vague and is a poor choice of words for a question because it can have different meanings to different people.

Better survey questions would be: Generally, how many hours of television do you watch in a day? and Generally, how many times a week do you eat fast food? In my operationalization section I can specify what *I* mean by "a lot" and by just asking for reported incidences from people, *their* definition of "a lot" is not necessary. Plus, I now have one question that pertains to my independent variable (amount of television viewing) and my dependent variable (amount of fast food consumed).

Due to limited publication space, researchers frequently will not provide their survey or interview questions in the body of the report. Sometimes the researcher will state that the survey or interview questions are available from the author upon request. Other times the reader can indirectly assess the appropriateness of the research questions based on any tables of results (which usually have a truncated version of the question in them) on quotes from participants, or on the researcher's written comments in the results section of the paper. Although not presenting the survey questions is acceptable, obviously is it much preferable when researchers do, because that makes it easier to evaluate the appropriateness of the question wording.

4. Are the survey questions constructed correctly?

Again, you may not be able to evaluate this because the researcher did not include the survey due to space limitations. However, if the survey or interview questions are present, you can evaluate whether the researcher constructed them with the guidelines I mention earlier in this chapter in mind. For example, does the researcher avoid double-barreled questions? Does the researcher avoid potentially biased wording of questions? Are answer choices exhaustive? Mutually exclusive?

5. Did the researcher provide any information about the response rate? Did the researcher provide any information about follow-up mailings or other ways of increasing response rate? What are the implications of the response rate?

Remember, many of the survey types do not have high response rates, which can affect the validity of the study. The researchers need to be clear about what their response rates were and what they did, if anything, to improve them. Did the researcher send follow-up mailings? How many times did he or she try to reach people by telephone?

Also inherent in this evaluation point is whether the researcher discussed the implications of the response rate. Does the researcher discuss how his or her response rate compares to the standards of the field? If the response rate was lower than the generally accepted standards of the field, did the researcher discuss how the response rate might affect the interpretations of the data? If the response rate is low, it is important for the researcher to recognize and to note that the resulting sample, and therefore the results, might be a bit biased. This bias in itself does not make the research completely useless; however, it may affect how much weight people give to the findings, especially if the findings of this research are different from those of other studies where response rate was not a problem.

6. Did the researcher explain how he or she guaranteed anonymity or confidentiality?

Technically, this is an ethical issue, but it is one of the main ethical issues for survey research; therefore, it is a relevant consideration when evaluating surveys. If a researcher does not successfully convey to a respondent about how that respondent's identity will be protected, then we need to be suspect of the comments that that respondent made.

BOX 7.3 **Evaluation of Written Research: Surveys**

Coulson, Riffe, Lacy, and St. Cyr (2001) surveyed 283 journalists (for a response rate of 67 percent) about station commitment to local government news. Some of the research questions that interested these researchers were how well the journalists felt that the stations were covering city government in their market, the journalists' views of how well the station covers city government varied by the size of the station, and how the journalists' perceptions of how well the station were covering city government differed by the journalists' level of experience. Below is a brief excerpt from their research, which can be found on Research Navigator.

Two of the three stations affiliated with ABC, NBC, or CBS were randomly selected from each of the 214 areas of dominant influence. . . . A researcher called each station's newsroom and asked the news director the name of a reporter likely to cover stories from city hall. Each of the 424 reporters was mailed a questionnaire, and 283 (67%) completions were obtained. The standard error for the entire sample is 2.9%, which gives a margin of error of +/− 5.8%).

The reporters reacted to eight statements using a 7-point scale (1 = strongly disagree, 4 = not sure, and 7 = strongly agree). Three statements asked about current city hall coverage (does the station give it adequate attention, prominence, and airtime), and two others asked how important the city hall beat is among reporters and news directors in the respondent's newsroom. . . .

Table 1: Percentage Agreement and Mean Scores of City Hall Television News Reporters ($n = 287$)

Statement	Agree (%)	Disagree (%)	Mean
Reporters at my station are given adequate time to cover city government stories.	41	54	3.71
City government news routinely is given prominent air time at my station.	59	36	4.45
My station routinely allows air time for thorough city government coverage.	53	43	4.18
Reporters in my newsroom think city government is the most important assignment at my station.	24	71	2.95
My news director thinks city government is the most important assignment at my station.	35	56	3.47

. . . In addition to the reporters' perceptions of coverage, demographic data were collected. Respondents were asked about their age, number of years in the broadcast news business, number of years and months at the current station, and if they had college degrees in journalism or broadcasting.

Source: David C. Coulson, Daniel Riffe, Stephen Lacy, and Charles R. St. Cyr, "Erosion of Television Coverage of City Hall? Perceptions of TV Reporters on the Beat," *Journalism & Mass Communication Quarterly*, 78 (1) (2001): 81–92. **(AN 4819483)**. Copyright by AEJMC. Used by permission.

BOX 7.3 | **Evaluation of Written Research: Surveys, continued**

Critical Thinking Questions

1. Is the research topic worded appropriately for survey research?

2. Did the researcher specifically state which type of survey method was used?

3. Do the survey questions adequately address the topic?

4. Are the survey questions constructed correctly?

5. Did the researcher provide any information about the response rate? Did the researcher provide any information about follow-up mailings or other ways of increasing response rate? What are the implications of the response rate?

6. Did the researcher explain how he or she guaranteed anonymity or confidentiality?

7. Overall, is the survey methodology effective and appropriate?

Critical Thinking Discussion

1. Yes. In the introduction, where I mention some of Coulson and colleagues' research questions, you should notice that they focus on words like *feel* and the journalists' *views*. Opinions are very appropriate for survey research.

2. Yes. Each reporter was "mailed a questionnaire," so they used a mail survey.

3. Yes. In addressing how well the journalists felt that their stations covered city government, the survey questions asked about issues such as the amount of air time and the placement of air time. Both of these can indicate the stations' treatment of city government.

4. Table 1 presents some of the survey questions under the "Statement" column. Technically, they are all worded correctly (e.g., there are no dou-

ble-barreled questions, they are relatively short and clear); however, given the seven-point scale and the similarity in response choices across questions, having a reverse-coded question may have been a useful validity check against someone simply checking the same response all the way down the matrix.

5. Yes. They noted that they had a 67 percent response rate. They did not mention anything about follow-up mailings or other actions to increase that response rate, but in this instance, that is probably okay.

Response rates between 50 and 70 percent for mailed surveys are generally acceptable, even though, of course, everyone does not agree about this. Therefore, with a 67 percent response rate, these researchers would have to balance the cost of a follow-up mailing (and the issues with successfully making sure they don't receive duplicates, meaning that someone responded to the initial mailing *and* the follow-up mailing) with the possible increase in response rate. These researchers are not likely to get a response rate that is much higher than 67 percent, so the lack of follow-up mailings and tactics are not too much of a problem here.

6. There is no mention of participant anonymity or confidentiality here, but since this was a mailed survey, anonymity is likely present. However, I am making an assumption here—one that may be false.

7. Overall, yes, the survey methodology is effective and appropriate. The biggest potential issue is the overreliance on positively worded statements without any reverse-coded ones. However, this alone does not negate the contribution of the findings or the overall quality of the methodology. The lack of any mention of anonymity or confidentiality may also be an issue, although, in my opinion, it is a rather minor point, since the respondents did mailed surveys, which are frequently anonymous in nature.

Furthermore, unlike experiments where researchers are interested in seeing how subjects react to a treatment (independent variable) of which they are not completely aware, surveys frequently rely on subjects' direct expressions of their attitudes or behaviors. This is why knowing that an identity will not be directly published with regard to a specific response is important. Even if researchers state how they protected anonymity or confidentiality, it does not mean that the subjects believed or trusted the researchers, but at least the reader can evaluate whether he or she thinks the researcher did enough for this ethical consideration.

You may be wondering why I did not mention informed consent as a specific criterion to look for when reading research. I omitted this because most researchers will probably not go into detail about how they obtained informed consent. They are likely to simply mention that they did, or they are likely to ignore the issue all together, perhaps under the assumption that achieving informed consent is such a basic requirement for research that it does not merit mention. Regardless, since researchers almost never discuss this issue, there is no way for a critical reader to assess it, and I do not want to imply that research is lacking if the researcher omits this in the report.

To summarize, here are the primary considerations to keep in mind when reading research that involves surveys:

1. Is the research topic worded appropriately for survey research?
2. Did the researcher specifically state which type of survey method was used?
3. Do the survey questions adequately address the topic or hypothesis?
4. Are the survey questions constructed correctly?
5. Did the researcher provide any information about the response rate? Did the researcher provide any information about follow-up mailings or other ways of increasing response rate? What are the implications of the response rate?
6. Did the researcher explain how he or she guaranteed anonymity or confidentiality?
7. Overall, is the survey methodology effective and appropriate?

Key Terms

Computer-assisted telephone interviewing (318)
Context effects (300)
Contingency question (294)
Cover letter (304)

E-mail survey (321)
Filter question (294)
Matrix format (292)
Open- and closed-ended questions (289)

Probe (312)
Random digit dialing (317)
Recollective questions (277)
Skip pattern (294)
Web survey (321)

Review Questions and Exercises

1. Are the survey questions in the following studies (1) appropriate for the research topic and (2) worded correctly (including answer choices)? Sometimes you may not have the exact question wording presented; however, tables may have the question topic and answer choices (with the corresponding data). In these cases, you are evaluating whether the question answer choices are correct. Sometimes the questions will appear at the end of the article in an appendix, other times the questions will be imbedded within the text. What is the level of measurement of each question?

a. Krysan, Maria. (2002, March). The residential preferences of Blacks: Do they explain persistent segregation? Social Forces, 80 (3), 937. 44 pp.

b. Menon, Maria Eliophotou. (2003, April). Views of teaching-focused and research-focused academics on the mission of higher education. Quality in Higher Education, 9 (1), 39, 16 pp. (AN 10282379)

c. Nociar, Alojz, and Miller, Patrick. (2002, August). Alcohol tolerance and illicit substance use among teenagers in Slovakia. Drugs: Education. Prevention & Policy, 9 (3), 247. 6 pp. DOI: 10.1080/09687630210130662. (AN 6933939)

d. Kakavoulis, Alexandros. (2001, June). Family and sex education: A survey of parental attitudes. Sex Education, 1 (2). (AN 4480158)

2. Evaluate the survey methodology in the following articles:

a. Kirby, Peter G., Biever, Joan L., Martinez, Isaac G., and Gomez, John P. (2004, January). Adults returning to school: The impact on family and work. Journal of Psychology, 138 (1), 65. 12 pp. (AN 13198752)

b. Shifren, Kim, and Kachorek, Lauren. (2003, July). Does early caregiving matter? The effects on young caregivers' adult mental health. International Journal of Behavioral Development, 27 (4), 338. 9 pp. (AN 10089083)

c. Gaarder, Emily, and Belknap, Joanne. (2002, August). Tenuous borders: Girls transferred to adult court. Criminology, 40 (3), 481. 37 pp. (AN 7248553)

d. Danforth, Marion M., and Glass, J. Conrad, Jr. (2001, September). Listen to my words, give meaning to my sorrow: A study in cognitive constructs in middle-age bereaved widows. Death Studies, 25 (6), 513. 17 pp. DOI: 10.1080/074811801316896098. (AN 5416857)

Field Research

Did you ever wonder what kind of person goes to strip clubs? It's not a practice parents encourage their children to do, nor is it a topic that is frequently or easily discussed in "polite" conversation. In most contexts, going to a strip club or even talking about a strip club are somewhat deviant. Sure, it may be acceptable for a bachelor or bachelorette party, but, for the most part, frequenting strip clubs is a non-normative behavior.

Consequently, if a researcher wanted to study who goes to these clubs, the forms of research that I have discussed so far would not be very appropriate. For starters, a question of who attends strip clubs does not involve any specific independent variable that a researcher could manipulate. Therefore, an experiment is not a good choice for this topic. Furthermore, it would be impossible to obtain an accurate sampling frame, and so it would be impossible to do a probability sample. A researcher may be able to attend a male strip club and interview the patrons, but then he or she would be studying *their* reported behavior instead of actually *reporting on* their behavior. To do the latter, report on their behavior, a researcher might decide to do participant observation research, much like Montemurro, Bloom, and Madell (2003, **AN 9780312**) did to study this very same topic. Montemurro and colleagues describe their research approach as such:

> In order to study patrons of male strip clubs we conducted participant observation at a club, to be known as the Hideaway, in a large northeastern city over a period of several months. We began observation in September 2001 and continued through February of 2002. We conducted our observation on a particular evening, Thursdays, as we learned that this was when regulars more often attended the club. . . . The majority of patrons at the Hideaway are White, although we estimate that approximately 25 percent of patrons were racial minorities. Mirroring the demographics of the city in which this club was located, most of

the minority women were African American, with fewer Asian and Hispanic women in attendance. Based on appearance (style of dress), tipping, cars in the parking lot, the large number of individual dances purchased, we estimate that the majority of patrons are middle or upper-middle class. The remainder, about 25%, were working class or lower class.

The data presented here are based on approximately 30 hours of observation. Field notes were taken after we left the research site, with the exception of a few inconspicuous jottings. In addition to observation we conducted an interview with one of the dancers. This interview lasted approximately one hour. While we requested interviews from four dancers, only one was willing to participate. Though not representative of the experiences of all dancers at the club, this interview is a useful supplement from a key informant as this dancer was able to provide insight that we could not have gained through observation.

. . . Prior to beginning research we obtained permission to conduct observations from one of the club owners. For the most part our presence was nonobtrusive. We were conscious of not disrupting the environment by soliciting interviews from patrons. We were very concerned with, as was the management, not making any of the patrons self-conscious about their behavior in the club. . . . We sat in the club and watched the show like other patrons. The club environment was characterized by a high degree of interaction between groups of patrons, thus we talked to women and dancers who approached us or asked us questions. However . . . we did not participate in the central activities of the club such as excessive tipping, purchasing stage dances, or interacting with any of the employees in the normative hypersexualized manner. . . . There was little physical distance between patrons and relatively no physical distance between different groups of women in the club. Thus, when women were nearby and the music was at a lower volume, we could easily hear conversations and observe interactions.

As you can see from the excerpt, Montemurro and colleagues studied patrons who attend strip clubs by actually *going* to the strip clubs themselves and observing the behavior. They did not create a fictional strip club to do an experiment and they did not disturb the patrons by interviewing them. They attended; they watched; and they took notes. This type of method of observation is called **participant observation** and it is a form of *field research*.

Field research is pretty much what the name implies: It is research that is done when researchers observe the behaviors of their subjects in a natural setting, as they happen—in other words, in the field. Contrary to an experiment that occurs in a laboratory, field research occurs in the "real world." Furthermore, contrary to a quasi-experiment, which also occurs in the real world, in field experiments, the researchers are generally not manipulating any aspect of the natural environment to see how it affects the subjects. The researcher may interact with the subjects to various degrees, but, for the most part, this interaction does not direct the subjects' actions. Therefore, field research is even more natural than the research in a quasi-experiment. Furthermore, since researchers are interacting with people in their normal environment, they avoid the artificial nature of the structured questions associated with survey research (Koegel, 1987). Other than this description, it is difficult to provide a specific definition of field research because field researchers may use various research techniques, which I will discuss later, to gather their information. As with the previous chapters, I would like to begin our examination of field research by discussing some topics that are appropriate for field research.

Appropriate Research Topics

Because field research occurs in a natural setting, it is a very useful method of observation for groups or circumstances that do not lend themselves to experimentation or surveys. Clearly, a survey of women who attend strip clubs is not the best means of discovering what type of women find this type of entertainment enjoyable. The nuances of how these women act in strip clubs and what their personalities are like would be lost in survey research.

Field research is also appropriate when the researcher wants to obtain a deeper understanding of a social setting, subculture, or social behavior either at one instance in time or longitudinally. The two key features that alert a researcher that field research may be appropriate is a desire for this deeper understanding and the recognition that that understanding is most likely to come from observation in a natural setting that involves little or no interference on behalf of the researcher.

John Lofland (1984, pp. 71–92) outlines nine general areas—what he calls "thinking units"—that benefit from field research:

1. *Meanings:* This includes the importance and interpretation of culture, norms, worldviews, and so forth.
2. *Practices:* This would be various kinds of social behavior.
3. *Episodes:* This generally refers to events such as divorce and crime.
4. *Encounters:* This is the interaction between two or more people who are in immediate proximity at the time of that interaction.
5. *Roles:* This is the positions people occupy and their behavior within those positions, such as son, gang member, inmate, and so on.
6. *Relationships:* This refers to the behavior that goes on between a pair of roles, such as mother–son, parent–gang member, inmate–warden, and so on.
7. *Groups:* Field researchers can study small groups that are comprised of many different roles, such as Little League baseball teams, gangs, cocktail waitresses, and the like.
8. *Organizations:* Field researchers can study formal organizations that are comprised of many small groups.
9. *Settlements:* Although very large groups are difficult to study with field research, smaller groups, such as neighborhoods, community organizations, or ghettos, provide interesting opportunities for field research.

In all of these instances, field research may reveal information what would not be possible to gather with other methods of observation. For example, Montemurro, Bloom, and Madell (2003, **AN 9780312**) state that the research on men who attend strip clubs shows that men are mainly drawn to the clubs for the show. However, these researchers found that this motivation does not apply to women. According to Montemurro and colleagues, women's primarily motivation to attend these clubs was to be with their friends and have "bonding" time. The enjoyment of the show was secondary to this desire for social interaction. Furthermore, the researchers found that although there was a small handful of patrons who regularly attended the shows, for the most part the women they observed were there for special occasions such as birthday or bachelorette parties, and many of the women on any given night were what Montemurro and colleagues call "virgins," meaning that it was their first time at a strip club.

Furthermore, Montemurro and colleagues (2003, **AN 9780312**) found that 73 percent of those attending the strip club were what they called "girlfriends" because their behavior at the club signified that the "girlfriends" used their club visit as a bonding experience that they could reminisce about later with their friends who also attended. According to the researchers, this was evidenced a couple of ways:

> First, many of the women in the Girlfriends category took pictures while in the club. . . . What women seemed to be capturing in these photographs was the fun that they were having together. . . . Another way Girlfriends demonstrated that the show was an opportunity to bond with one another were their reactions following close contact with a dancer. . . . While a patron was having an individual dance on stage, "She kept looking out at her friends and making, 'oh my god' faces. Her friends in the crowd were just laughing and pointing at her." (p. 343)

As you can see from this excerpt, most of the women were not at a strip club for some type of sexual release or fantasy. They were there to have a good time with their friends and they seemed to treat the sexual nature of the entertainment as a secondary joke. This nuance of behavior that fits five of Lofland's thinking units: meaning (the meaning the women attributed to this experience—having fun with their friends), practices (dancing, taking pictures), episodes (the episode of visiting a strip club), encounters (people's reactions to the dancers), and relationships (with their friends who also attended). Montemurro and colleagues' research produced richly descriptive data that would not be available in a survey or experiment.

■ How Field Research Differs from Experiments and Surveys

There are a number of ways that field research differs from experiments and surveys. The most obvious way is that experiments and surveys tend to be deductive and quantitative research techniques, whereas field research is frequently inductive and qualitative. If you remember, inductive research begins with observation then moves to form a theory, whereas deductive research begins with a theory and then uses observation to support that theory. Experiments and surveys are frequently deductive forms of research because the researcher selects a general research topic, does an extensive literature review to learn about the topic, applies a theory to explain some aspect of the topic, and then tests that theory with observations from the experiment or survey. Field research and inductive research, however, do not involve hypotheses to formally test theories. Some researchers might do literature reviews to see what is already known about a topic, but these literature reviews frequently do not shed much light on an issue, and even if they do provide some direction, field researchers do not use them to create hypotheses. The literature reviews, if they are used, just give the researcher enough background information to figure out how to enter the field and to get a general sense of how to present oneself in the field.

The deductive/inductive differences relate to the quantitative/qualitative differences between these three types of research. Experiments and surveys are usually quantitative in that the researcher is comparing the percent of people who do X as opposed to Y, or statistically comparing the behavior of two groups, or trying to mathematically determine a likelihood of a certain event. Qualitative research, on the other hand, is not very concerned with the percent of people who behave a certain way or the statistical likelihood of an outcome. Qualitative research, in fact, is generally not very interested in numbers at all, at least not beyond the most rudimentary statistics that might describe a sample (e.g., 80 percent of the people who live in this community are Latino). Qualitative research, in general, and field research, in particular, are interested in observing the natural behavior of people in a natural setting in order to obtain a deeper understanding and empathy for what people experience, as well as a fuller understanding of the social context in which people live.

A third difference between field research and experiments or surveys is that experiments and surveys are designed so that there is little subjectivity in the study instrument. If you recall, in Chapter 4 when I discussed the conceptualization–operationalization process, I said that researchers generally have to ask themselves "What do I mean?" continually until they arrive at an answer that has the same meaning to everyone. The goal of surveys and experiments, therefore, is to create measures that are *not* subjective to interpretation. Field research, on the other hand, is more concerned with the meaning that people themselves give to events—not the meaning that researchers have imposed and ask respondents whether they agree. Therefore, field research wants to understand the meaning the people give to their social experiences and how people's different meanings may differ. Hence, field research is predominantly based on the subjective responses of subjects instead of their objectively checked boxes on a form.

Not only are the participants subjective in field research but the researchers are as well. Field research differs from surveys and experiments because the researcher's role in field experiments is likely to be more subjective than is the researcher's role in experiments or surveys. Field experiments, by definition, involve the researcher entering an environment and interacting with subjects on their turf. It involves a cultivation of interpersonal relationships that provide the researcher with a closer look into the lives of his or her subjects. This also means that the researcher is interpreting the events; therefore, the researcher's own personality, views, and experiences are likely to act as a filter for how he or she interprets the interactions observed.

On the contrary, when the researcher is manipulating a laboratory environment or is a faceless entity sending out a survey, subjectivity on the researcher's behalf is less likely. True, there may be some subjectivity in the interviewing process, but even here, researchers try to minimize it by having more than one person coding subject responses. That is not the case in field research. There are no inter-rater checks for consistency in field research. Nor is the researcher a faceless entity. In field research, the researcher is, in many cases, interacting directly with the subjects. Hence, in addition to focusing on the subjectivity of the respondents, field research is likely, more so than surveys and experiments, to reflect the subjectivity of the researcher as well.

Last, once an experimental stimulus or survey questions are created, they are generally fixed. The researcher may pretest them to see if they are working to the researcher's satisfaction, and then the researcher may tinker with them as a result, but when the "real" study begins, the experimental stimulus and survey questions are set. The researcher is not likely to decide half-way through an experiment or a survey to change the research approach. In fact, doing so would introduce the rival casual factor of instrumentation and threaten the validity of experimental and survey findings. However, field research, by its inductive nature, is not concerned with instrumentation, since it does not try to establish causality in a statistical manner. Because field research occurs "on the fly" to some degree, meaning that since the researcher is studying natural settings, the researcher has no control over instances that may arise during the course of the research, the design of field research has to be flexible. For example, Montemurro and colleagues (2003, **AN 9780312**) originally planned just to observe the types of women who attended male strip clubs. However, during the course of their study, they adapted their design a bit to include an interview with one of the male dancers in order to obtain a fuller understanding of the male strip club scene.

To summarize, field research is different from experiments and surveys because field research focuses on:

1. Inductive rather than deductive processes
2. Qualitative instead of quantitative reasoning
3. A focus on the meaning that people give to their social environment—on subjectivity rather than objectivity
4. Sensitivity to researcher subjectivity in addition to participant subjectivity
5. A design that is fluid, changing, and developing as the research progresses

The degree to which the field research encompasses these characteristics depends on the role of the researcher/observer.

■ Roles of the Researcher during Observation

The steps for conducting field research are more flexible than those for experiments or surveys, and part of that stems from the continuum of roles a researcher can assume in field research. Gold (1958) identifies four points on the continuum that range from complete participant to complete observer.

According to Gold (1958), **complete participant** observation occurs when the researcher not only observes and interacts with the participants but also actively seeks to manipulate the participants' activities. In many instances, to avoid the threat of reactivity, a researcher will hide her or his identity as a researcher when doing this type of research and, instead, pose as a member of the group. Because the researcher is not really a group member, some social scientists call complete participation research *covert participation* research. A classical example of covert or complete participation research is Laud Humphrey's study, *Tearoom Trade* (1970). Humphrey pretended to be a "watchqueen" (voyeur) who served as a lookout and a hidden observer of secret male homosexual behavior in public restrooms. In order to obtain some background information on these people, Humphrey copied the license plate numbers of the people he observed and then showed up at their homes pretending to be a mental health researcher (he changed his appearance so he wouldn't be recognized) who wanted them to participate in a study.

Undeniably, Humphrey obtained some very valuable information from a very stigmatized and hard to identify group: male homosexuals who engage in impersonal sexual liaisons in public places. However, there are a number of problems with this type of research. First, of course, is the ethical issue of studying people when they do not know they are being studied. If people do not know they are being studied, they have no opportunity to provide informed consent, they cannot enact their right to privacy (the withholding of desired information), and their participation is not voluntary.

Second, there are other practical methodological issues as well. Covert participants cannot ask any questions that may arouse suspicion of their membership, even if these questions are important for the research. Plus, it is difficult to know how a member of a group would act at all times. For example, for obvious reasons, there is not a lot of research about satanic cults. Randall Alfred (1976) pretended to be in such a cult in order to study the cult's members. However, how would he know how members of these groups act if (1) he isn't one in real life and (2) there is little research describing them?

If the group a researcher covertly joined is not friendly to outsiders, this type of deception can be problematic for a researcher if her or his identity becomes known. Alfred was lucky. When he was finished with his research and revealed his true identity to the group leader, the leader informed him that he was not surprised, since he and other members of the group thought that Alfred was "strange." In retrospect, Alfred was probably lucky that this was the only reaction; it illustrates that he, like other researchers, did not disguise his identity as well as he thought. The group members did not know Alfred was a researcher, but they did know that he didn't act like they did and was therefore "strange."

Consequently, complete participation research is rarely the observational method of choice. It is only really appropriate in studying very marginalized groups or people who participate in marginalized and stigmatized behavior who may not otherwise be willing to participate in a study. However, even in these instances, some argue that it may be unethical to deceive people in the hope that they will confide in you as a person when they otherwise would not if they knew that you were a researcher. There is no clear answer to this.

The **participant as observer** is the second point on the continuum and it is the method of observation that people most commonly associate with field research. In fact, many researchers use *participation observation* synonymously with the term *field research*. In participant observation research, researchers participate fully with the people being studied, but they make their identity as researchers known. Darden and Worden (1996) examined the world of cockfighting to see how such illegal and deviant activities are marketed. Because, as the authors state, cockfighting is a predominately male sport, Worden did most of the observation and data gathering (since Darden is a White middle-class woman). To complete the research, Worden observed formal and informal cockfights in various settings and had informal conversations (as well as some interviews) with the people attending. Through these interviews and conversations, Darden and Worden found that those who breed birds for

This photograph depicts a cult ritual. How would you update Randall Alfred's (1976) study of cults?

cockfighting see themselves as participating in a time-honored tradition that was supported by Abraham Lincoln and George Washington.

The researchers also found that although their subjects see themselves as upstanding citizens, they only marginally trust other "cockers" (which they call themselves) because their birds may end up fighting each other. In these exchanges, word of mouth is an important means of advertising, since the activity is illegal. Hence, Darden and Worden found that those interested in the sport market it as a respectable and historical pursuit that values honesty, even though there is, in reality, little trust among those who sell the birds. Why is this participant observation? Because by attending the matches, Worden was able to see the sellers, owners, and other "cockers" in their natural environment, but these people also knew that Worden was a researcher, since he was asking them research questions during their informal conversations.

This is one of the benefits of participant observation research. The researcher can observe subjects in their natural setting, but the researcher does not have to participate in any unethical or dangerous behavior because the participants recognize that the researcher is an outsider. Furthermore, the participants, since they know they are being studied, have the ability to decline to participate in the study all together or to withhold information they prefer the researcher not know (thereby enacting their right to privacy).

The third point on the continuum is the **observer as participant** research. In this instance, the researcher makes his or her identity as a researcher known but only marginally interacts with the participant. In other words, the researchers do not partake in whatever activity they are observing with the participant. One example of observer as participant research is the one-visit interview. In this instance, researchers interact with the participants by asking the participants the interview questions; the researchers are not answering questions themselves (as one would in a conversation), therefore the level of give-and-take interaction is less here than in participant observation research.

The last point on the continuum, as you can probably guess, is the **complete observer.** In this type of research, the researcher observes social behavior without becoming involved in any way. Sitting on a bench at a playground observing the dynamics of children's play would be an example. Clearly, in this type of research, the participants may not know that they are participating in research. If this is the case, then the ethical issues of complete observation are similar to many of those in complete participation.

In reality, field research generally does not fall neatly into just one of these continuums. In Darden and Worden's study of cockfighting, for example, Worden not only attended cockfights, thereby participating in the activity with his subjects to some degree, but he also did interviews, which are a type of observer as participant research, as I just mentioned. I will focus on the steps for how to do participant observation research, since that is the most common form of field research. I already discussed how to do observer as participant research in Chapter 7 in survey research; and, little research falls into the complete observer or complete participant categories.

Steps for Doing Field Research

Field research is generally inductive research. Researchers observe behavior, form hypotheses from that behavior, and relate those hypotheses to a theory. Frequently, researchers do not even start with clearly defined research questions. Any research question is likely to be broad and ambiguous. Once researchers have a general topic, such as studying the women who attend strip clubs, they may use any of the following guidelines for gaining access to the field and conducting their research.

■ Preparation

To some degree, we are all field researchers. If you have ever sat on a bench and watched people pass by or sat in a courtroom and observed a trial, chances are that when you were watching these interactions, you were taking mental notes of the actions around you, such as who was doing what, who looked bored, who appeared middle class, who was a racial or ethnic minority, and so on. You may even have interacted with some of the people you observed by having short conversations or exchanging pleasantries. The skills that you may have developed as a "people watcher" are an important foundation for participant observation; however, they need honing to be ready for serious scientific research.

If you think you want to do field research, begin by sharpening your observation, listening, and short-term memory skills. If you remember, in Chapter 1, I had you look at a photograph for a few seconds and then I asked you questions about what you recalled from that photo. Perhaps you were able to answer all of the questions accurately, perhaps not. The point is that most of us need to consciously work on refining our observational skills if we want to do scientific research—especially field research.

You also need to develop a way that will allow you to take quick, but unobtrusive, field notes. Learn shorthand or develop a personal shorthand of your own. Learn how to write key words that will jog your memory of events. Also practice writing descriptions in detail. Although quick field notes are essential in field research, each night you need to look at those quick field notes and write more detailed and nonabbreviated descriptions that will serve as your data for later analysis. This takes practice and you can begin by writing observations of the world around you.

If you're sitting on a park bench watching children play, how many children are there? How many boys? How many girls? What different racial or ethnic groups are present? Who is playing alone? Who are in groups? What are the characteristics of the children who appear to be leaders in the groups? What are they wearing? Where are their parents? Which parents are watching and which are not? How are children's behaviors different based on whether their parents are or are not watching them? Which piece of playground equipment has the longest line? You get the idea. If you have successfully developed your short-term memory skills, you can jot quick notes that will stimulate your memory yet allow you to draw attention away from participants' recognition that they are being observed.

Also, learn the art of "defocusing." This involves emptying your mind of preconceived ideas and allowing your mind to witness a broad range of situations and the people in them before deciding what to include and exclude in your notes. To some degree, try to take notice of everything that is going on around you. You may not know what is important or relevant until days or weeks later; therefore, you have to develop the ability to observe a wide range of phenomena and the skill to be able to recall the details of those phenomena. This is more difficult than most people think because, as I've stated before, we are somewhat passive observers of our social world and undoing that passivity takes practice. Figure 8.1 shows the steps for conducting field research.

1. Select a topic of study appropriate for field research.
2. Review the literature to assess what is already known about the topic and to direct some general lines of inquiry.
3. Prepare by practicing observation and note-taking skills.
4. Select a site (preferably one in which you are unfamiliar).
5. Identify and address gatekeepers.
6. Develop field relations.
   a. Establish your presentation of self.
   b. Build rapport with subjects.
      (1) Appear open and interested.
      (2) Participate in small favors.
      (3) Try to remain neutral in conflict.
      (4) Identify a few "key" people to help you navigate the cultural contexts.
      (5) Consider your role in the field research experience and how you will manage your own emotions.
7. Observe information and take field notes.
   a. Observe people's characteristics, people's attitudes, physical surroundings, people's behaviors, the language people use, and the context in which they interact. In a nutshell, observe and take note of everything (this is why early preparation and practice is necessary—to refine this skill).
   b. Take various levels of notes.
      (1) Jotted notes.
      (2) Direct notes.
      (3) Researcher interpretation notes.
      (4) Analytic notes.
      (5) Personal notes.
   c. Follow tips for note taking.
      (1) Record notes as soon as possible, even if the notes are just jotted pieces that will trigger your memory.
      (2) Begin each field note by recording the date and time of the observation.
      (3) When you are jotting or writing field notes, write quickly to get down your observations, feelings, and ideas.
      (4) Find a few *private* moments frequently throughout the day to jot down some notes.
      (5) Take notes frequently; rely on memory as little as possible.
      (6) When you do have to rely on memory, the use of mnemonics may be useful.
      (7) Make notes specific.
      (8) Record *everything*. What seems insignificant at one point may be very important at a later date.
      (9) At least daily, if not more frequently, transcribe your field notes and jottings into more comprehensive and detailed notes.
      (10) Whenever possible, include diagrams, drawings, or pictures of the places you frequent during your research, of the people you are with (if they are willing to be photographed, that is), and of the social dynamics of the groups you are observing.
      (11) Reread notes periodically, jotting down comments or remembered bits in the margin (to distinguish that they were added at a later date).
      (12) Keep multiple copies of your field notes.
8. Exit the field.
   a. Decide on process of leaving—quick or gradual exit.
   b. If gradual exit try to
      (1) Announce intent to leave in advance.
      (2) Fulfill any obligations to subjects.
      (3) Ask any remaining unanswered questions.
9. Organize and analyze data (see Chapter 11).
10. Write the report.

Figure 8.1 Steps for Conducting Field Research

■ Selecting a Site and Gaining Access

Before researchers can embark on a field research project, they have to decide *where* to do the research. The selection of a "site" may be a somewhat misleading term because field research may not occur in only one setting like it did in Montemurro and colleagues' research (2003, **AN 9780312**) on strip clubs. These researchers did their participant observation research in one club only, but other research frequently occurs in a variety of settings in a somewhat localized geographical area. For example, Mark Hamm (1993) did field research on skinheads where he "started the investigation by visiting various U.S. cities where I tracked down skinheads in their natural habitat (street corners, bars, coffee shops, record stores, survivalist outlets, rock concerts and motorcycle shops)" (p. 100). Hence, Hamm did not use one "site"; he used many sites (cities) and many different areas within these broad sites (stores, bars, etc.).

According to Lofland and Lofland (1995), there are three important considerations for selecting a site. These considerations are the richness of the data, the unfamiliarity of the site, and the suitability of the site. Sites that provide a lot of opportunity for social interaction in a variety of activities over time are likely to provide rich data because the researcher can observe how individuals act in a variety of different situations and with a variety of different people. Likewise, research is a little easier in unfamiliar settings. Why? Because unfamiliarity lends itself to more comprehensive observation. This isn't a hard concept to grasp. If you have ever been on vacation or visited somewhere outside your normal environment, you may remember the sheer awe you experienced as you looked around you and tried to "soak it all in." Good field research involves a similar amount of observation (without the jaw-dropping whispers of "Wow!" that frequently accompany other forms of this new observation), and it is easiest to get started with this if the site is not familiar to you.

Furthermore, if you are unfamiliar with the site, you are more likely to be able to defocus and enter the site without preconceived ideas of the people or environment. Likewise, these same people are not likely to know you. Therefore, any baggage that may accompany you from your "real life" (e.g., "Participant A" knows who you are because you dated someone she knows and the relationship, at least based on what she was told, ended badly and you are really scum) will be left behind. Last, clearly the suitability of a site is important as well. If you want to study how poor African American women get by with little money, like Carol Stack did in *All Our Kin* (1974), you may not want to choose a site that has a small, socially isolated community of poor African American women, because this may limit the nature of your observations.

A researcher's ascribed status may influence the selection of a site. In fact, it might also influence the selection of the research question. *Ascribed statuses* are the statuses that people are born with, such as race and gender, which are very difficult to change. Because of this, if a researcher's ascribed statuses block his or her access to sites or to studying a research question, the researcher needs to think of other ways around the problem. For example, in Darden and Worden's research (1996) on cockfighting, since cockfighting is generally a male sport, Darden recognized that she would not be welcome at most sites because she is a middle-class female. Therefore, her male colleague, Steven Worden, is the one who actually entered the site and gathered the data. If Darden couldn't find a male colleague to collect the field research, she probably would not have been able to study this particular research question.

Even if the researcher can both match the ascribed statuses of the people he or she is interested in studying *and* identify a site that fulfills the criteria I just discussed, that does not mean that the researcher can immediately enter the site, walk up to the first person he or she sees, and say "Hi! I'm a researcher and I'd like to follow you around for a while so I can observe your life. Is that OK with you?" Such an approach is likely, at the very least, to earn the researcher a weird look as the intended "subject" walks away. In his study *Street Corner Society* (1955), William Foote Whyte tried to enter the community of "Cornerville" so he could study male gangs. He was having trouble getting any of the men to participate in his study, so he entered a hotel bar to see if he could find some women who might be willing to talk to him. Whyte describes the encounter:

> I looked around me again and now noticed a threesome: one man and two women. It occurred to me that here was a maldistribution of females which I might be able to rectify. I approached the group and opened with something like this: "Pardon me. Would you mind if I joined you?" There was a moment of silence while the man stared at me. He then offered to throw me downstairs. I assured him that this would not be necessary and demonstrated as much by walking right out of there without any assistance. (p. 289)

Instead of barging into a situation on one's own, and running the risk of being thrown out, or worse, researchers should use **gatekeepers** to help them gain entry into a site. Gatekeepers are people who can help an outsider, such as a researcher, gain access to a setting by vouching for the researcher's presence. Gatekeepers can be formal or informal. Formal gatekeepers are those who are associated with formal organizations and have to provide permission for a study to occur. Informal gatekeepers are not associated with a formal organization, but they justify a researcher's presence by taking this person under their wing and vouching for him. In *Street Corner Society*, Whyte finally solved his problem of access by going to a social worker at the local settlement house (a community organization that is run by community members for community members in order to best address the needs of that particular community) and explaining his research to that person. The social worker then introduced Whyte to "Doc," the leader of the Norton Street Gang, who made Whyte's access to the people in Cornerville possible by vouching that Whyte was his "friend." "Doc" told Whyte:

> Well, any nights you want to see anything, I'll take you around. I can take you to the joints—gambling joints—I can take you around to the street corners. Just remember that you're my friend. That's all they need to know [so they won't bother you]. (Whyte, 1955, p. 291)

Even if the researcher identifies a gatekeeper, the researcher may have to negotiate with this person or may encounter more than one gatekeeper in the process of gaining entry. The more bureaucratic and complex the organization one is trying to enter, the more gatekeepers one is likely to encounter. Plus, the researcher has to make it clear to the gatekeeper that this person's role is to help the researcher gain access to the subjects, not to have a say in data collection or analysis. Consequently, researchers have to be clear up front about what they need from the gatekeeper and what they expect the gatekeeper's role to be.

A gatekeeper's main interest in the research usually stems from whether the findings are going to lead to criticism or negative outcomes for this person directly. For example, in Montemurro, Bloom, and Madell's (2003, **AN 9780312**) research that I discussed in the beginning of the chapter, the club owners are formal gatekeepers. Without their support and approval, these researchers would not be able to enter this site to do their research. Furthermore, the researchers imply that the management was not interested in the researcher's study per se. They were interested in making sure that the researchers would not make any of the patrons feel self-conscious about their behavior in the club. In other words, the managers were interested in making sure that allowing the research would not hurt their interests by making patrons feel uncomfortable and, consequently, leading to decreased profits or a bad reputation for the club.

Also, in the course of field research, one may find the need for *both* formal and informal gatekeepers. For example, if I want to study prison inmates, I would first have to get the approval of the prison warden (a formal gatekeeper) and I would likely need to use one of the counselors or guards to direct me to a prisoner who will vouch for my presence among the other inmates. This prisoner would be my informal gatekeeper.

The process of gaining entry into a site can take a very long time—even months. Some people may turn you down; other times you will have to wait for the slow bureaucratic cogs of formal organizations to move. Either way, whenever a researcher approaches a gatekeeper, the researcher needs to be prepared with a general description of the study (meaning a general description of the research question), a rationale for the study (Why is this study important? Why should these people help you?), and some sense of potential benefits the participants may experience. Gaining entry is a "sale," where the researcher has to sell the research idea to the gatekeepers so they will be willing to help him or her enter the field.

Researchers may need to cultivate gatekeepers at more than one stage. Each time the researcher enters a new area, it is likely that there are new gatekeepers—especially informal ones—with whom the researcher should establish a relationship.

Therefore, having basic social skills is beneficial to any researcher dealing with human subjects, but social skills are especially important in field research. The right social connection between a gatekeeper and researcher can lead to a wealth of information. Getting "off on the wrong foot," however, can seriously impede the research process. Furthermore, this is not a once-and-done issue. Relations with gatekeepers, and subjects for that matter, are continually negotiated throughout the course of the study. Unlike in an interview where the researcher and subject have, perhaps, a 45-minute relationship, in field research, the researcher, subjects, and/or gatekeepers may have relationships that span months. Consequently, each time a new person enters the study, the researcher has to be continually prepared to explain his or her purpose, presence, and the general benefits to the participants.

■ Sampling

Since field research is a qualitative form of research, field researchers are not worried about methodologically representative samples, therefore they do not need to do probability sampling. In fact, in many cases, they probably couldn't do probably sampling even if they wanted to, because field research is often exploratory analysis and involves subjects for which comprehensive listings are unavailable. Therefore, field research frequently involves nonprobability samples.

Since field researchers try to observe everything around them, one could argue that they don't really sample at all. By studying everyone they see, they are studying the population of their immediate vicinity. However, most researchers recognize that field researchers do not study *everyone* they see, and they certainly do not obtain the same level of information about everyone. Therefore, most researchers recognize that field research involves *some* type of sampling, and the most frequent type of sampling is a snowball sample.

Field researchers may also do a purposive sample in which they try to make close connections with individuals whom, based on the researcher's expertise, the researcher thinks adequately represents the research phenomena. The general point about sampling in field research is that the sampling form is likely to be nonprobability and it is likely to be flexible. Since field researchers are not interested in generalizing findings to a wider population or in calculating complex statistics, they have a lot of leeway in how they identify subjects.

■ Developing Field Relations

Just as with the gatekeepers, developing relations in the field is a continual social negotiation. Clearly, the researcher and subjects negotiate in the same manner as I just described for gatekeepers; however, researchers also must manage their field relations in a way that allows them to balance the need for a social relationship with the need for scientific objectivity. Leaning too much in the direction of the social relationship threatens the perspective of the researcher if he or she begins to identify too closely with the group of study. Remaining too scientifically detached, however, may lead to a more pronounced Hawthorne effect, where participants never truly get comfortable with the researcher, and consequently behave atypically. Hence, the development of field relations is akin to an intricate social dance between the researcher and who the researcher is studying that deserves closer discussion.

Self-Presentation

As in any interaction, how researchers present themselves is likely to dictate whether subjects will relate to them and therefore how honest the relationship is. Here, the field researcher can learn some basic techniques from the interviewer. Like an interviewer, field researchers should dress in the manner of their subjects. If a field researcher is studying corporate culture and observing CEOs and other high-ranking corporate officials, a suit or business attire would be appropriate if that is what these individuals generally wear. On the other hand, if a researcher is studying the dynamics of women who attend strip clubs, then business attire would clearly be inappropriate. However, as I said in the previous chapter, copying the dress of the subjects is also not always appropriate. For example, if a middle-aged professor is studying teenage cliques, the attire of 16- or 17-year-old girls is generally not appropriate for a 40-year-old professional. Therefore, as in interviews, manner of dress in field research is somewhat of a commonsense issue. The researcher should not dress to offend, but dressing completely like participants may also be counterproductive.

Self-presentation also involves the demeanor we portray to others. Although researchers may have impressive educational credentials, they are not likely to win many informants if they continually "show off" their expertise. On the other hand, being open, nonjudgmental, and approachable can overcome some seemingly serious problems with self-presentation. For example, it will probably be easier for an African American to study a poor African American community. The amount of work for self-presentation this researcher would have to do may be minimal, since the researcher's physical appearance already matches that of the subjects.

If you were going to do field research of the process for how a proposed bill is approached in the Senate, how would you present yourself?

However, Carol Stack in her study *All Our Kin* (1989) was a White researcher who managed to gain access and develop relations in a low-income African American community. How did she do it? She performed small favors for the participants, such as driving people around and visiting sick children, and she was willing to share personal feelings and information about herself. In time, the African Americans of this community treated Stack as "kin," even though she clearly was not one of them. They even created an endearing nickname for her: "White Caroline" (to distinguish her from an African American Caroline in the community). Stack's experience illustrates that although dress, speech, and physical appearance may help the presentation of self, researchers do not have to fake social similarity to their subjects. In fact, faking social similarity can create more problems than solve. Researchers can use their personality as a means of presenting a front that subjects will see as open, personable, and interested. The more personable subjects find researchers, the more willing they may be to allow the researcher to temporarily become a part of their lives and to observe their actions.

Developing rapport

How a researcher presents himself or herself is an initial key component to developing rapport with field subjects. Ultimately, the goal of field research is to move beyond mere observation to the development of empathy—seeing events from the subjects' perspective. To accomplish this, the subjects have to take the researcher into their confidence.

Sometimes this is easier said than done. For example, if a researcher is studying deviant behavior, the participants may see the researcher as an "open" expert who will be able to justify their behavior to others, hence they may be very open with him or her. However, subjects may be afraid that the research, especially if any parts are published in the popular press such as newspapers, may hurt their personal status. Consequently, developing rapport may involve some tests on behalf of the research subjects.

Martin Sanchez Jankowski (1991) studied gangs in Boston, New York, and Los Angeles between 1978 and 1989. In most of the gangs, Jankowski's acceptance involved two tests. For one test, Jankowski had to prove that he was not a police informant by refraining from turning in gang members when they committed illegal acts. The second test usually involved some type of initiation right that involved violence—namely, some level of a fight. In the "beat downs," as these initiation rights were frequently called, Jankowski had to prove how tough he was by fighting some of the gang members. Luckily for Jankowski, he had training in karate and was able to hold his own in most instances. In fact, he was seriously injured only two times during the 10 years of his research. Once Jankowski passed these tests, gang members were willing research participants and, as a result of Kankowski's work, social scientists learned some useful information about gangs. Clearly, Jankowski may have gone through more vigorous testing by participants than most field researchers would experience, but given the deviant nature of much of the gang activity, it is easy to see how the gang members would have a lot to lose if they did not trust Jankowski. Therefore, some type of test is not surprising.

Part of developing rapport may also involve disclosing some personal information about oneself. However, at times, this can directly work against the research goals, as Van Maanen (1982) discovered when he had a debate with a police officer, who was a subject in Van Maanen's field research, about residential desegregation. Van Maanen explains:

> My more or less liberal leanings on the matter [of residential desegregation] were bothersome to this officer, who later reported my disturbing thoughts to his friends in the squad. Before long, I was an anathema to this friendship clique and labeled by them as undesirable. Members of this group refused to work with me again. (Van Mannen, 1982, p. 110)

Unfortunately, there are not a lot of concrete directions for developing rapport; however, some commonsense advice is worthwhile. In many (but not all) instances, being friendly, showing a genuine interest in others, and sharing a little bit about yourself will help researchers gain the trust of participants. Likewise, as Stack did, becoming an active member of the social network may also facilitate the development of rapport. However, this is a tenuous balance and may not be applicable in all instances. Stack was able to participate in relatively minor social exchanges, such as visiting sick children or driving people to the welfare office, which endeared her to her participants. On the other hand, behaviors such as giving and receiving money or gifts are generally believed to be forms of assistance that are inappropriate and lead to social obligations that are beyond the researcher role (Wolcott, 1995). Consequently, to develop rapport, researchers need to follow the ethical rules of reciprocity, but make sure that their reciprocal interactions are relatively small and do not obligate the researcher or put the researcher in other unethical positions (e.g., silence about a crime).

Clearly, developing rapport is going to take time. Relationships, at least the kind that lead to meaningful scientific field data, do not spontaneously occur. First, like the researcher, respondents are going to have an interest in *their* presentation of self. They will act in a way that they think will give the researcher a positive view of them. Clearly, there may be a mismatch between how respondents want to appear to the researcher and what they are really like in a nonresearch setting. Part of the reason field research is time consuming is that the researcher has to be in the field for a sufficient amount of time so that the participants focus less on the researcher's scientific role and more on continuing with their normal interactions. It is difficult to manage your presentation of self for an extended period, and researchers bank on respondents' inability to do so.

A second issue in developing rapport (and in maintaining field relations) is how to handle conflict if it arises between groups or individuals a researcher is studying. Ideally, the researcher needs to remain neutral. Choosing sides is likely to result in the loss of balanced information, as the side not chosen freezes out the researcher; therefore, the researcher will not be able to develop the empathy necessary to provide an objective analysis. However, this is easier said than done, and, in reality, many recognize that it is almost impossible to remain completely neutral in issues of conflict (Wolcott, 1995).

Obtaining key informants

Cultivating a couple of **key informants** may be useful to the field researcher. Key informants are members of the study group who serve as knowledgeable insiders for the researcher. Key informants help the researcher understand the cultural context of the group or environment. Like an informal gatekeeper, key informants can also help the researcher gain access to groups that the researcher otherwise would have trouble entering. They also give the researcher insights on interpretations of group actions.

According to Neuman (1997), there are four characteristics of a good key informant. First, a good key informant is someone who is completely immersed in the culture the researcher is studying. Key informants can participate in the culture so completely that they are not even thinking about what they are doing. Second, the key informant should be currently involved with the culture that the researcher is studying. For example, if a researcher manages to get access to an Amish community, a good key member would be someone who is currently an active participant in that community, not someone who once was but has since been excommunicated or has left the community. Third, good key informants should be available to the researcher. They should have time to spend with the researcher, educating the researcher about the culture, helping the researcher gain access to groups and events, and just generally being around to answer the researcher's questions. Last, according to Neuman, good key informants are not analytical. This means that the informant should not explain the setting in preformed categories but instead should be able to explain events from the perspective of one of those who is currently living in that culture.

Key informants can be an important resource for the field researcher, but researchers still have to critically evaluate what the key informants tell them. Does the key informer's view mesh with what the researcher observes? If not, why? Therefore, key informants can be important components of field research, but researchers should not just blindly accept their information or interpretations.

One last point must be made. So far, I've been focusing on the researcher's actions toward the participants as an effort to get the participants to relate to the researcher. I have not mentioned that, as a social being, the researcher is likely to develop feelings and connections that will lead her or him to relate to the participants as well. In other words, the social dynamics of field research are a give and take. Both the researcher and the participants are likely to develop emotional connections during the context of the study. To the degree that researchers are more active in the lives of those they study, the stronger the personal and emotional connections the researcher is likely to feel. Some of this personal connection is instrumental to field research and helps the researcher move beyond understanding to empathy. On the other hand, too much of a personal connection can result in the researcher "going native," meaning that the researcher has developed *too much* empathy and has lost his or her ability to critically examine the group under study.

Clearly, there are no hard and fast rules for developing relations and managing personal emotions (including the researcher's emotions). Some of field research is more art than science and depends on the natural personality of the researcher. However, Whyte (1955, pp. 300–317) does provide some general guidelines that may be helpful to people considering field research:

1. Take the time to consider how you want to relate to your potential subjects as people.
2. Speculate about what personal problems might arise and how you will respond to them.

Bounty hunters are an interesting example of where private contractors meet the criminal justice system. According to Johnson and Warchol (2003, *not* available in Research Navigator), researchers know little about the real experiences of bounty hunters. Instead, they argue that popular understanding about this group is fueled more by myth than by fact. Therefore, Johnson and Warchol argue that field research is an appropriate means of gathering concrete information about the roles and relationships of bail agents and bounty hunters. Below is an excerpt from their research where they discuss their field tactics.

Gaining Access

One of the authors has previous private and public law enforcement experience. Prior to the commencement of this study, the researcher worked with an experienced bounty hunter for two months and participated in several fugitive apprehensions to familiarize himself with the nature of the job. This experience facilitated the researcher's understanding of the nature of the business, allowed him to learn the jargon of the profession, and helped assess the effectiveness of various sampling strategies, data collection techniques, and observation methods for the study. After becoming acquainted with the nature of the industry, a bail/bond company in Michigan hired the researcher as a bounty hunter. Gaining entry was a surprisingly simple task because there are no state licensing or certification requirements for bounty hunters. The researcher's university education and previous law enforcement experience were sufficient to ensure his acceptance.

The researcher assumed the role of a covert observer where his true identity was not revealed to the subjects being studied. This approach was taken to ensure that the subjects did not alter their behavior due to the presence of a researcher in their midst. Anonymity of the researcher's true identity and purpose was maintained with clients and members of the criminal justice system.

The Study Group

The next task was to design a sampling strategy. Purposive or judgmental sampling was selected is the most appropriate method. . . . The data were collected from October 1998 to January 2000.

The researcher worked with bail agents and bounty hunters employed for a large bail company in Michigan during this period. This company was selected because it covers the entire state and contracts with 35 bail agents who service the 83 counties in Michigan. This company also uses four bounty hunters to apprehend fugitives throughout the state. Over the course of 14 months, the researcher participated in 23 successful or attempted apprehensions of "skips."

Data Collection

Data collection was accomplished by taking structured field notes that detailed the operations of the bail/bond business, the nature of each case, and any meaningful interactions. To protect the identities of the subjects, field notes were constructed without reference to the names of the suspects, bail agents, bounty hunters, and other members of the criminal justice system. A system of numeric codes was employed to identify each subject.

The researcher recorded field notes after every encounter or contact with bail agents fellow bounty hunters, police officers, jailers, prosecutors, and suspects arrested for violations of the bail contract. These notes were reviewed and transcribed each night. Occasionally, the researcher would find it necessary to fill in gaps by re-interviewing subjects to clarify responses and adding needed details. . . . In addition to the bounty-hunting activities, additional information was collected from direct observation of bail agents and through unstructured interviews. Specific information included the nature or rationale for the apprehension; the demeanor,

BOX 8.1   **Studying Bail Bondsmen, continued**

reactions, and comments made by police who assisted in the apprehension, if applicable; and the attitudes of law enforcement, corrections, and court personnel toward bounty hunters.

Source: Brian R. Johnson and Greg L. Warchol, "Bail Agents and Bounty Hunters: Adversaries or Allies of the Justice System?" *American Journal of Criminal Justice: AJCJ, 27* (2) (Spring 2003): 145.

Critical Thinking Questions

1. Did the researchers do any preparation before they entered the field? If so, what?

2. How did the researchers select their site?

3. How did the researchers gain entry to the lives of bail bondsmen?

4. How did the researchers develop field relations?

5. Did the researchers employ any special skills for taking field notes?

6. What kind of information were the researchers looking for (recording)?

7. Are there any ethical challenges that you can think of in this research design? Are they avoidable? If so, how? If not, why not?

Critical Thinking Discussion

1. One of the researchers worked with a bounty hunter. This gave him experience with the nature of the job (which he would later use to gain entry into a research site) and the jargon used in the business. This experience also gave one of the researchers insight into some methodological issues, such as observation techniques, that would be relevant to studying this subgroup of people.

2. The researchers' site selection depended on who hired the researcher who prepared for the field. As it turns out, the researcher was hired by

a site that served many of the counties in Michigan and that uses both bail agents and bounty hunters.

3. One of the researchers had law enforcement experience, which provided him with the background to work with a bounty hunter. Once the researcher had some bounty hunting experience, he was able to apply and obtain a job working for a bail company. In fact, the researchers recognize that the process of gaining entry into the bail company was surprisingly simple due to the relatively unstructured guidelines for employment.

   However, the researchers did covert field research, which means that the people they were studying were not necessarily aware that they *were* being studied. If the researchers identified themselves as researchers, they may have experienced more trouble gaining entry because of the nature of bail work.

4. There is not a lot of information on how the researchers actually developed their field relations. We know what the researcher who actually did the field research did prepare for the field, but since he was a covert observer, the subjects did not necessarily know that they were being studied. Therefore, he didn't really cultivate any relations with them beyond the professional relations of being a fellow bail collector.

5. The researchers document that notes were taken frequently (after every encounter) and transcribed later that night. This is all good, and standard, practice.

6. The researchers note that they were looking for information about the actual activities of the bail bondsmen, of the bondsmen's justifications for apprehension and the relations with police or other criminal justice personnel during the apprehensions and toward the bounty hunters.

7. The biggest ethical challenge is informed consent. By being covert participant observation

BOX 8.1   **Studying Bail Bondsmen, continued**

research, subjects do not know that they are being studied; therefore, subjects cannot give informed consent indicating voluntary participation (since participation really isn't voluntary) and they can't utilize their right to privacy. The researchers say that they are guaranteeing anonymity, but it is more likely that they are guaranteeing confidentiality by identifying individual participants by number instead of by name.

The researchers claim that they needed to do their research covertly because they didn't want to alter people's behavior. However, it is unclear (both in the excerpt and the full report) how covert the research really was, because at

times the researchers state that they used unstructured interviews to "fill in the gaps" that became evident after the transcribing of notes.

We have no information (in the excerpt or in the full report) as to the degree that the researchers obtained informed consent from the people they interviewed or whether these interviews were so conversational and unstructured as to be what most people would consider directed conversations (even though the researchers are correct in methodologically identifying them as unstructured interviews). Consequently, there are a lot of unanswered questions regarding the ethical issues surrounding this study.

3. Keep in touch with other researchers and personal friends outside the research setting.
4. Maintain standards of conduct that make you comfortable as a person and that respect the integrity of your subjects.

Thinking about the parameter of interaction with the subjects prior to the study and how you might handle some possible conflicts can mentally prepare you for the social and emotional issues involved in field research. Keeping in touch with members of your social network who are not involved in the research and remembering the standards of conduct in your field will help prevent you from "going native" and keep your research perspective.

■ Observing Information and Taking Field Notes

Contrary to most areas in which experts do their work, experts in field research are not in the field to share their expertise but instead to observe and learn from others. In fact, field researchers have to actually exhibit a bit of naiveté. They need to convey some understanding of their environment, but at the same time they have to appear nonthreatening and in need of some local education (Lofland & Lofland, 1995). This naiveté allows the researcher to act and be accepted as an observer.

And field researchers have to observe *a lot!* Unlike a survey in which the researcher knows what is important to the research topic (since the researcher, after all, created the survey questions or accepts the survey questions of others), field researchers are not completely sure of what observations are important until later in their field experience or when they are reviewing the notes they have previously collected. Thus, field researchers have to try to observe *everything* in order not to miss information they discover, two weeks after the fact, was actually important.

Therefore, field researchers frequently take notes on the environment (Where did people meet? Was the building new or old? In good repair or poor? What was the lighting like? How was the room organized?); on people's physical appearances (How did people dress? Who looked clean shaven; who did not? What were the hairstyles like? What types of jewelry did people wear? What types of body art did people have? Was someone tall or short, heavy or thin, muscular or spindly?); on social interactions (Who was getting along? Who was not? Who was the leader? Was there more than one leader? What made a person a leader? Who dominated the conversation? How was this person able to do this? Who spoke loudly? Softly?); and on views (Who supported a tax increase? Who felt that the local service agencies were inadequate? Who wanted the be more active in getting rid of local crack houses?)—just to name a few general issues.

Furthermore, field researchers take notes not only on what they directly observe but also on what they *think* is happening. The field researcher pays attention to how subjects say things, what their body language portrays as they say things, and the nature of the shared language (which is frequently called *argot*) among these people. It's easy to understand how this is important, because *how* people say something is sometimes more informative than *what* they say. We all know someone, for example, who can make very cutting and mean-spirited remarks with the most pleasant tone and facial expressions. This mismatch in messages (mean or critical message packaged in a polite or nice façade) can be very socially informative.

In other words, field researchers take notes on their interpretations as well as their direct observations. These interpretive notes may remind them of issues they want to discuss with key informants, they may alert the researcher to behaviors or nuances in behavior in the future, and/or they may trigger points for later analysis.

Field researchers sometimes have to ask very direct questions of subjects. In fact, a lot of field research may involve interviewing subjects. These interviews are mostly unstructured, meaning that the researcher has some general questions that he or she wants to ask a subject, but they are open ended and the researcher is willing to give the subject some leeway in terms of additional information the subject presents. For example, let's assume that I am talking to "Daisy," who is a prostitute that I have been observing in the field for four weeks. I am at the point in my research where I am ready to start asking Daisy some specific questions about how she got into prostitution, because I have been interacting with her for a while and we have developed a rapport between us. Our conversation may go something like this:

ME: You didn't look very content working last night.

DAISY: Would you be if you had to do what I do for a living?

ME: You've expressed to me a number of times in passing that you wish you could find some other type of employment that paid as well. How did you get involved with hooking in the first place?

DAISY: I was young, I didn't know any better. I thought it would just be temporary until something else came a long.

ME: How young were you?

DAISY: I was just 14.

ME: What led you onto the streets at 14?

DAISY: My Mom married a guy I didn't like. We fought a lot so I left home. I didn't know how to waitress or nothing, and a man I met said that I could make some money hooking and that he would protect me. He became my pimp. I was 14 and I didn't know any better.

There are a couple of important points from this interview. First, as I said, I was interested in finding out what led Daisy to a life as a prostitute. I didn't just jump into that question; rather, I led into it after some warm-up conversation. Second, even though I wanted to know what led Daisy to do what she did for a living, she wasn't prepared to answer that right away. She answered my question by providing her age when she started hooking. Instead of just forging on with my intent, I temporarily abandoned the goal of my interview and let her follow her line of thought until I could bring the focus of the interview back to my original purpose. The second time, I received the level of information I was seeking. This is an unstructured interview. I had some general idea of what I wanted to learn (why Daisy became a hooker), but when the interview turned to a new direction (Daisy's age when she started prostitution), I did not adhere to a specific interview script and I let her lead the direction for a bit.

Therefore, field researchers have to balance a need to gather a variety of information both indirectly (through observation) and directly (through conversation or unstructured interviews). This sounds like a lot to remember, doesn't it? It is. Spending two months in the field and then, at the end of that two-month period, recording what you remember is not going to be a very systematical or scientific way of conducting research. Nor is it necessarily appropriate for a researcher to walk around like a reporter with a handy-dandy notebook, taking notes every minute.

Note taking in plain view obviously may work against the researcher–subject rapport because the subjects will continually be reminded that they are being observed and are therefore likely to act atypically longer. In other words, the researcher's role as researcher will continually be spotlighted, which may hurt the researcher's ability to form the types of relationships with the subjects that are instrumental to overcoming any potential reactivity effect. To be fair, sometimes note taking in plain sight is possible. For example, Thorne (1993) studied school children's behavior on the playground to see how they defined gender-appropriate behavior. Because the children knew that Thorne was observing them, she was able to openly take notes. As she describes it:

I went through the school days with a small spiral notebook in hand, jotting descriptions that I later expanded into field notes. When I was at the margins of a scene, I took notes on the spot. When I was more fully involved, sitting and talking with kids at a cafeteria table [for example] . . . I held observations in my memory and recorded them later. (p. 17)

Examples like Thorne's, however, are not very common. In many instances, the field researcher is going to have to take notes more surreptitiously. Brewster (2003, **AN 9473623**) examined the tipping behaviors of men who attend strip clubs. Like in Montemurro and colleagues' study of strip clubs, Brewster recognized the stigma associated with attending these establishments and realized that taking notes in plain sight would probably make patrons uncomfortable and possibly lead to a loss of business on behalf of the establishment. Therefore, in order to take field notes, Brewster periodically went to the restroom to jot down notes regarding various aspects of the setting and patrons present. For the purpose of analysis, these jotted field notes were extended into full field notes or a detailed description of events the morning after each observation period. (p. 228)

The issue of note taking is compounded by the fact that there are various levels of notes field researchers need to keep. Let's discuss each of these briefly.

Types of field notes

The most basic type of field note is **jottings.** Taking detailed field notes while in the field is essentially impossible. It would be way too time consuming. While a researcher is busy writing detailed notes, he or she would be missing more of the interaction, which is the foundation of the research. Jotted notes are just what the name implies; they are notes that are short and temporary and that are designed to trigger the researcher's memory when he or she has the time to write more detailed notes. Researchers can take jotted notes on a little notebook that can conveniently be stashed into a pocket, but other more informal pieces of paper, such as napkins and receipts, will also do (provided the researcher doesn't lose them).

After the researcher leaves the field for the day, he or she needs to take the jotted notes and transcribe them into more detailed **direct notes.** These notes should be detailed but not summarized. For example, instead of writing, "John introduced me to Herb," the researcher would write something like, "John introduced me to Herb, a tall, sandy-haired man of about 35 who is surprisingly soft spoken for his robust frame." Furthermore, whenever possible, the direct notes should include exact quotes of people. It is much more informative to record John telling Rodriquez, "If you don't like the way I do business, then take your business elsewhere. I don't need no troublemaker causin' problems wit' my men. Got it? Just take your friends and get outta here. I don't wanna see you back unless ya got a change of attitude" than to record "John told Rodriquez to leave and to not come back until he was willing to do business John's way."

Why is the first option preferred? Because by quoting exactly what John says, the researcher can analyze *how* John told Rodriquez to leave, John's own justification, and whether there are any subtly hidden meanings in the words John used, all based on John's own words. In the second quote, the researcher's interpretation of the events was given (doing "business John's way"), which is blending into the next type of notes. If the researcher's impression or interpretation is off in his or her summary notes, the researcher loses the ability to go back and reanalyze that interpretation because the raw data (the actual quote) are missing. Remembering exact quotes is a skill that researchers develop with practice, which is why I suggest some memory preparation before embarking on field research. To distinguish quotes from paraphrased conversations, researcher might distinguish exact quotes with double quotations marks and paraphrased comments with single quotations marks.

The material I used as an example of the wrong way to record detailed notes—the researcher's interpretation of the conditions under which Rodriquez can return to John— is an example of the next level of notes: **researcher interpretation.** The researcher in the hypothetical example interpreted John's comments to mean that John didn't want to see Rodriquez unless Rodriquez was willing to play by John's rules. This interpretation may be correct; it may not. Most likely, later observations will help decide this. It is *because* inter-pretations may not be correct that they should be kept as separate notes and should not be incorporated into the direct notes the researcher keeps. Researchers might mistakenly interpret a situation, the meaning of the situation could be ambiguous, or the subjects may be purposefully deceiving each other or the researcher. In John's quote, he mentions not wanting someone making trouble with his men. Does he mean giving his men ideas that would lead them, in turn, to further question John and maybe rebel against him? Does he mean trouble that may lead his men to behave in a way that will get them in trouble, per-haps with the authorities? The meaning of John's comment, as it stands alone, is unclear. As a researcher I need to try to make conclusions about what John meant, but I have to be open to changing my conclusions if they turn out to be incorrect.

Field researching isn't just about observing and interpreting human behavior. Because it is, above all else, *research*, there needs to be some type of analysis as well. With **analytic notes,** researchers try to give meaning to what they observe. Researchers also, however, record different methodological issues that arise and how they handle them. For example, Montemurro and colleagues decided to add unstructured interviews with dancers to their field research. Although they only had one dancer willing to talk with them, they note that this one person still provides useful insight that strengthens the validity of the research, even if what he says cannot necessarily be generalized to other male exotic dancers. Let's look at another example. If a conflict arises between two people being stud-ied and the researcher is asked to take sides, how the researcher responds to this situation would be important information to include in these notes, because the researcher's response may affect her or his later interaction with the subjects.

Last, researchers should keep detailed **personal notes.** As I discussed earlier, researchers are not doing field research in a vacuum. They are likely to form relationships with the sub-jects and their personal views are more likely to color their interpretations of what they observe than if they were doing a survey where people were just checking answer choices. Likewise, the researcher may have an "off" day, a day where he or she is collecting infor-mation but his or her heart just isn't into it. All of these issues can color the nature of the interpretations; therefore, it is important for the researcher to keep notes (that are dated) about any personal feelings on various days. Then, as the researcher analyzes the data, he or she can look back to see how he or she was feeling on particular days and can assess whether those feelings may have colored any interpretation of events. Since the researcher also kept direct notes, he or she can compare personal notes, inference notes, and analytic notes to the direct notes to see if any detectable personal bias may have appeared. If biases have appeared, the researcher still has the direct notes and can reexamine them and per-haps alter any conclusions.

Consequently, there are various levels of note taking involved in field research (see Figure 8.2). They each serve a different purpose and they help the researcher detect any biases present, sequence events, and draw general conclusions. The degree of success in field research has a lot to do with the nature of the field notes. However, as you can prob-ably tell, taking field notes is a lengthy, time-consuming process. In fact, field researchers likely spend more time transcribing, writing, and organizing field notes than they actually do making observations. How field notes are collected is almost as important as what researchers do with them once they are collected. So let's discuss some strategies for col-lecting field notes.

Jotted Notes

Bill and Jessica have an argument
about Sally in the car

Researcher Interpretation Notes

Saturday, July 28, 7:30 p.m. Bill and Jessica seem to
have an ongoing disagreement about Jessica's
relationship with her sister. I think it is interfering with
their relationship.

Detailed Notes:

Saturday, July 28, 7:30 p.m. Bill and Jessica are sitting in
Bill's car with the windows down. I can hear Bill's voice
loudly through the window as he says, "Sally is taking
advantage of ya." He slams his hand on the steering
wheel. "She always asks you to watch her kids, but she
never is there when ya need her. I'm sick and tired
of seeing ya bend over backward for that woman."
Jessica looks out her window, not facing Bill, so I can't
hear her response as clearly. It's something like, "Because
she's my sister. You knew what my family was like when
you married me. I'm tired of arguing with you about her."

Personal Notes

B and J's problem about family
involvement is similar to that my sister
has with her husband. I am
concerned that this will affect how I
view any discussions B and J have. I
feel like stepping in with advice on
how to set boundaries.

Analytic Notes

Family interference may threaten marriages, even if the unhappy
person in the marriage knew the family dynamics prior to the
marriage. Perhaps the person thought that he or she could change the
situation once married. Try to conduct an unstructured interview with
Bill to assess the degree he and Jessica discussed the role of
extended family prior to their marriage.

Figure 8.2 Levels of Field Notes

How to collect field notes

There is a lot of flexibility in how people can take field notes, and what you do will largely depend on the nature of the group you are studying. If you are studying deviant behavior, taking field notes in the open is probably not wise, as it may make the subjects uncomfortable. If you are studying more mainstream behavior and are in the field for awhile, some open note taking may be possible.

Even though there is no one right way to take field notes, here are some suggestions to help you get started. First, record notes as soon as possible, even if the notes are just jotted pieces that will trigger your memory. Waiting too long to record notes may lead to forgotten information, misperceived situations (since with time people start to filter and interpret what they experience), or misquoted comments.

Second, begin each field note by recording the date and time of the observation. This will help you piece information together and sequence events later. Your main goal at the time you write notes is to get the details of your observations and feelings. Analysis comes later. Therefore, when you are jotting or writing field notes, write quickly to get down your observations, feelings, and ideas. This is not the time to worry about grammar or spelling.

Third, even if you can take some notes in front of the subjects, but especially if you cannot, find a few private moments frequently throughout the day to jot down some notes. These brief periods can be bathroom breaks, solo trips to the store, or running an errand for people in the group. These bits of privacy give you the opportunity to recall what you've seen without outside distraction; they also minimize the amount of note taking in front of subjects, which may lengthen the reactivity effect inherent in most field research. To help with this, take notes frequently. Rely on memory as little as possible.

However, when you do have to rely on memory, the use of mnemonics may be useful. Mnemonics are little ditties that help us remember things. For example, in grade school you probably learned the mnemonic "ROY-G-BIV" for the colors of the rainbow (Red, Orange, Yellow, Green, Blue, Indigo, Violet), or you may have a little song that helps you to remember some things. Little tricks such as mnemonics may be helpful if they are used sparingly.

Fifth, make notes specific. Remember to use the convention of distinguishing direct quotes from paraphrased comments. Also, instead of using general descriptions such as, "The room was run-down," be as specific as possible. For example, write, "The room was painted white but had begun to yellow with age. Some of the windows were broken and the window sills were peeling paint. In addition to broken windows, some of the chairs that people were using were broken or about to break." The second example clearly does a better job at setting the scene for the interaction. Remember, environments may have important implications for understanding behavior, and the point of field research is to obtain that fuller and more in-depth understanding of a subject.

I've said this before, but I'll say it again. In order to obtain that level of detail, record *everything*. What seems insignificant at one point may be very important at a later date, and you simply will have no way of telling this ahead of time. But clearly recording everything means that you cannot always provide deep descriptions—after all, bathroom breaks can only be so long! This is where the note-taking technique of jotting becomes very important. However, since these notes are not comprehensive, it is important that field researchers, at least daily if not more frequently, transcribe their field notes and jottings into more comprehensive and detailed notes.

Seventh, whenever possible, include diagrams, drawings, or pictures of the places you frequent during your research, of the people you are with (if they are willing to be photographed, that is), and/or of the social dynamics of the groups you are observing.

Eighth, reread notes periodically, jotting down comments or remembered bits in the margin (to distinguish that they were added at a later date). As the research progresses, later events may shed some light on previous events that field researchers would forget about if they didn't read over their notes frequently. Rereading notes helps remind the researcher what has occurred and helps to put current behaviors and experiences into context.

Last, keep multiple copies of your data. This is *very* important. Computers make all but the initial field notes scribbled on scraps of paper easy to read, easy to copy, and easy to store. However, one computer virus can easily wipe out months of work that cannot be reclaimed if there are no backup copies. Therefore, keep your notes in various locations. Download them onto disks or CD-ROMs and keep *those* in different locations. This way, in the unlikely but disastrous event of a fire or robbery, your data are safe, even if your computer or hard copy of notes are stolen or destroyed.

■ Leaving the Field

As with all research projects, field research has to come to an end at some point. Sure, researchers can exit by just disappearing into the night. There one day, gone the next. However, in most instances, the researcher is likely to withdraw more gradually by reducing involvement over a span of time. How one decides to end the research depends on the nature of the setting. Clearly, if events take a turn against the researcher, the here-today-gone-tomorrow approach may work best. However, if the researcher has formed relationships with her or his subjects and remains on good terms with them by the end of the study, the gradual approach may be better.

If the researcher intends to gradually leave the field, he or she needs to let members know ahead of time that interaction with them is coming to an end. This gives the subjects and the researcher a chance to emotionally prepare for the researcher's exit—which may be an issue if the researcher and subjects have formed relationships with each other. From a more pragmatic view, giving subjects notice of the researcher's intent to leave also gives the researcher the opportunity to tie up loose ends. The researcher can fulfill any commitments he or she may have made to the participants and can ask participants more directed questions that may have arisen from the review of his or her written notes (remember, a researcher should be reviewing his or her notes continually throughout the process).

Even with a gradual withdrawal, there are likely to be emotional issues the researcher needs to address as he or she leaves the field. Subjects may become distant toward the researcher—essentially freezing him or her out—as the primary status of researcher begins to overshadow the temporary status as honorary group member. Hence, the researcher becomes an outsider after being, at least for awhile, an insider. Or the opposite may occur. The subjects may try to draw the researcher back into a more enduring relationship—essentially, continuing the field research without the actual research. Whether researchers want to maintain any relationships with members of the field is their call; however, from a scientific point of view, it is beneficial for researchers to maintain at least some distance in order to minimize the chance of "going native."

■ Data Organization and Analysis

Since field research is qualitative research, the process for analyzing data and writing reports is different from that of experiments and surveys. I will address qualitative data analysis in detail in Chapter 11; however, a few brief comments are worth mentioning here.

The first step in writing the research report is to make sure that your various types of notes are organized. The most common way to organize them is by date. This way, you can piece together a chronological progression of events, impressions, and people. This should serve as your master note file and should not be cut, scribbled on, or otherwise altered. In many instances, if you've done this on a computer, the date is easy to record and organize.

Second, make or print multiple copies of your field notes, not for safe keeping, but for analysis. Clearly, there are many ways that you can organize field notes in order to find patterns among your observations. In Chapter 11 I'll discuss how to do this in more detail. What I'll say for now is that, as you have many types of notes, you are likely to have many types of data analysis files. You may not use all of the files (some may be dead-ends), but many will eventually help form an analytic picture of your field experience that will help you move to the creation of a theory.

Computers have greatly aided the analysis of field research, especially the cutting and pasting option, which allows you to reorganize your notes easily. Having your files on computer can also help you with the actual analysis, which I will discuss in Chapter 11. However, if you still find computers daunting, many researchers have successfully conducted field research the old-fashioned way—with paper, tape, and scissors. Computers make creating field notes easier, but they are by no means a mandatory piece of equipment.

Advantages and Disadvantages of Field Research

By now you probably understand that field research is very useful in obtaining an in-depth understanding of a research topic in a natural setting from a subject's viewpoint. This is probably the strongest advantage of field research. Furthermore, compared to surveys and experiments, field research can be relatively cheap. It does not require survey or questionnaire printings, mailings, complex apparatus, or the hiring of assistants. In its most basic form, field research can be done by one researcher with a notebook and pencil. True, computers make field research easier, but they aren't necessary.

Another advantage of field research is its flexibility. To some degree, researchers decide when to enter and exit the field and they are not wedded to a specific research design. In other words, the researcher is not committed to specific survey questions or experimental techniques; he or she can quietly observe, subtly discuss, or more directly interview as the need and opportunity presents itself. In addition, field research avoids the artificiality of surveys and experiments by studying people in their natural surroundings. The focus on natural surroundings can also make the research less disturbing to participants because they are less likely to feel like "lab rats" and they do not have to take time out of their day to complete a potentially lengthy questionnaire.

On the other hand, there are many disadvantages to field research. First, because it is qualitative rather than quantitative, the findings usually cannot be generalized to larger populations and are viewed as subjective instead of definitive. This means that the findings from field research alone would not fuel policy and any causal explanations are limited to the particular group studied. Nevertheless, the information learned from field research *can* fuel more quantitative studies that will fulfill these research goals.

Another weakness has to do with the amount of time it takes to conduct field research. Many field research studies take several months—sometimes even years—to conduct. In order for the field research to be comprehensive, the researcher needs to be in the field long enough for any reactivity or Hawthorne effect among subjects to dissipate, for adequate observation of the group in a variety of circumstances, and for enough observation to truly get a sense of the main subjects of interest. This does not even include the amount of time necessary to write, transcribe, organize, and analyze field notes.

Third, researchers conducting field research have little control over action. Most people's lives are not so continually interesting that an observer would gather useful information every day—or even every weak. Therefore, in field research, the researcher spends a lot of time waiting for things to happen. This is not to say that this time is not productive—that the researcher can't use it to learn more about the people or the environment—it just means that there is only so much observation of personal characteristics alone, without the context of interaction or outside events, that someone can do.

Another problem that researchers may face is **"going native,"** which I mentioned earlier. Since field researchers spend so much time with their subjects, there is a very real risk that they will start to empathize with their subjects to a degree that may color their ability to effectively and objectively analyze their observations. The opposite may also occur. The field researcher may develop such a disdain for the subjects that this too can affect his or her analysis.

Last, there are a host of ethical dilemmas that threaten the field researcher more so than experiments or surveys. I will discuss these ethical dilemmas in the next section.

Issues in Field Research

■ Ethics

The balance between the scientific nature of field research and the personal relationships that result creates a minefield for potential ethical problems. Let's discuss some of the main ethical issues field researchers have to address.

Voluntary participation

In surveys and experiments, voluntary participation of subjects is much more straightforward than it is in field research. In surveys or experiments, the subject either reads or listens to a brief blurb that outlines the research goals, the potential harms and benefits, the guarantees that participation is voluntary, and the guarantees of confidentiality or anonymity. If the subject does not like the terms of the research, he or she can decline to participate.

In field research, obtaining voluntary participation clearly isn't as easy. If field researchers recited a litany of goals, potential harms/benefits, promises of confidentiality, and finished with a comment about voluntary participation to *everyone* they encountered as a possible participant, then researchers would spend the bulk of their time in the field obtaining voluntary participation. Furthermore, they would so effectively reinforce their role as researcher that respondents would be unlikely to relax enough around them to behave naturally, thereby creating a Hawthorne or reactivity effect that would muddy the validity of any findings.

We may decide that field researchers only need to obtain voluntary participation from the people they will interact with frequently. Well, this is problematic, too. Voluntary participation needs to be obtained at the beginning of the research. How can a field researcher identify those who will be frequent participants in the research? Field research is fluid. Some subjects may be more involved in the beginning of the research; others may be tangentially present in the beginning of the research but become more involved as the study progresses. Identifying who will be main participants can be difficult.

Last, participants may have different views. A leader of a gang may be willing to participate, but some of his gang members (especially if they are currently at odds with or questioning their leader) may be ambivalent. Furthermore, members of any opposing gangs you encounter may be dead-set against participation. So how do you handle the different levels of voluntary?

Clearly, obtaining everyone's voluntary participation would limit field research to extremely small settings of only a few people with similar levels of involvement and/or settings in which there are no real conflicts of interest. Consequently, obtaining informed consent in field research is tricky, and there is no clear rules for how to do this. The level and manner of informed consent largely depends on the nature of the research question.

Confidentiality

The most obvious way to protect confidentiality is for the field researcher to use pseudonyms for subjects. However, pseudonyms alone are not sufficient if the researcher also provides so much description of the person or includes information that is unique to an individual that others can recognize the person regardless of the pseudonym. Hence, confidentiality is a balance between providing description that allows the reader to create a mental image of a person and that person's role in the environment and the need to protect a respondent's identity.

Principle of nonmaleficence/Protection from harm

Even though many events in field research cannot be preconceived, field researchers have to give some thought to how to prevent harm to participants prior to their studies. Certainly, they are not likely to avoid all forms of harm. Subjects may get upset with a researcher if he or she does not side with them in a conflict, they may feel betrayed or insecure when a researcher exits the field, or they may be unhappy with how the researcher portrays them in the written report. However, these instances of discontent may stem from any research—or even from everyday interaction. Therefore, most researchers do not consider them to be a violation of protection from harm.

However, like other researchers, field researchers do have the ethical responsibility to protect their subjects from direct harm. For example, if police can identify a gang member based on a researcher's report and can then link that gang member to a crime and arrest the gang member, the researcher violated the ethical responsibly of nonmalefiscence, because it was his or her report that led to the arrest of the gang member. The best way to protect against many forms of direct harm is to be careful about confidentiality.

Making sure one's actions do not create conflict among the subjects is another way to protect from harm. For example, Whyte (1955) regretted inviting a specific politician to speak at the social club because the politician's speech led to some serious disagreements in the club. Furthermore, this action strained Whyte's relationship with some of his subjects. The conflict among subjects that resulted from Whyte's invitation of the politician is an example of this type of ethical violation. It is also a good example of how protecting subjects from harm is more complicated than simply making sure they do not get physically or legally hurt by your research. In hindsight, Whyte probably should not have been so involved with his subjects that he was taking an active role, like bringing in guest speakers, for their activities. Or at the very least, he should have spoken with the politician ahead of time to try to ascertain the nature of his speech and whether it would be appropriate for his subjects. However, it is obviously easier to identify this trouble in hindsight.

Deception

Some level of deception in field research may be necessary in order for the research to occur. Some researchers vehemently argue against any form of deception on its own basis (it's unethical) and because of the other ethical problems, like voluntary participation, informed consent, and privacy, that usually follow (Elms, 1994; Erikson, 1970). Others support its limited use in very specific instances (Homan, 1991; Douglas, 1976). For example, it may be extremely difficult, if not impossible, to study deviant groups without some measure of deception. Lauder (2003, **AN 9756052**) tried to study an anti-Semitic group without much deception; and although he was granted access to the group, he found that the subjects censored their anti-Semitic feelings or omitted them from discussion altogether. In order to get around this clear Hawthorne effect, he had to recast himself as a convert in order to get people to discuss their views more openly.

■ Validity

I already noted that common criticisms of experiments and surveys is that they are artificial. People's behavior in a laboratory setting may not really reflect their behavior in the real world and responses people provide on written or verbal surveys only address their opinions or what they *think* they would do (or how well they remember what they claim to have done). Furthermore, conceptual definitions in experiments and surveys are limited to the researcher's definition. True, researchers spend a lot of time and energy trying to create conceptual definitions that the researcher thinks genuinely captures the behavior or attitude of interest. However, what about those instances where the researcher is off the mark? I'm talking about those times when the researcher's definition of a situation is not the same as the definition of the research subjects. Or what about instances where the researcher's definition is more limited than the respondents think is appropriate? Field research provides an opportunity for researchers to involve subjects in the definition of concepts and quantitative research that builds on qualitative work and are more likely to involve conceptual definitions that are consistent with the respondents' definitions.

For example, how would you define a "good sports fan"? Is it someone who sticks with a team through good and bad? Is it someone who not only sticks with a team but also advertises that support with various sports paraphernalia like T-shirts, banners on houses, and little flags in their yard? On my way to work, I pass a house that is essentially a tribute to the race car driver Dale Erhnheart, Jr. This particular house has a mini-license plate with Dale Earnhardt's name on it, sports shirts hanging in some windows, a big racing flag on a fence, and various other forms of memorabilia. Would race car enthusiasts think that this person a "better fan" that someone who does not display all the visible paraphernalia? Surely people know that by having all the sports memorabilia, they are no more likely to meet any of their favorite athletes or be better sports players themselves. So why are people spending so much money on these items?

The best way to answer this question is to ask self-described sports fans themselves. Derbaix, Decrop, and Cabossart (2002) did just that when they asked similar questions about sports fans in Belgium, where soccer is just as popular there as football, basketball, and baseball are here. These researchers were not interested in why manufacturers were producing so much soccer merchandise (they suspected it was because there was a market for it) but why people were buying so much of the stuff. In other words, *why* was there such a market for sports paraphernalia?

To study this, Derbaix, Decrop, and Cabossart did intensive interviews of some soccer fans and they observed 20 matches of the Belgium championship. They found that for fans who are local people, who support their home team, and who attend all the games, support for a specific team serves a social function of establishing group membership, much in the same way that school colors may help students show their group membership. These researchers found that the same dynamic also holds for fans who are not local, but who travel long distances to catch at least some of the games. Hence, according to the people Derbaix, Decrop, and Cabossart studied, the degree of paraphernalia and how it is used sends messages to others as to the degree one is a fan, where the goal is to establish oneself as a "good fan."

The creation of a "good fan" identity creates a sense of unity among people who otherwise are unlikely to interact due to other social characteristics such as socioeconomic status. In other words, possessing team paraphernalia, and the degree to which one exhibits it, provides an opportunity for people to make social connections between (1) players (producers) and fans (consumers) and (2) between fans who now can interact based on shared sports interests when, otherwise, they may not have anything in common. Hence, the paraphernalia becomes a symbol of group membership that takes on an almost religious connotation during the actual sporting events. As people in Derbaix, Decrop, and Cabossart's study note:

> This is someone who encourages his team whatever the results or the quality of the game and who comes every time. He comes for fun. He supports his team even more enthusiastically when they are losing than when they are winning.
>
> We exhibit our color and try to attract attention with that color. We are the "mauves" and the others are dressed in another color. It enables us to recognize each other.
>
> Round the stadium everyone wears something mauve. If you do not have anything mauve, people stare at you strangely. (2002, pp. 513–514)

Hearing the subjects' answers in their own words helps the researcher piece together what *they* mean by concepts. Although as a researcher, I might define group identity as someone who wears team colors, I would miss the richer meaning that the first respondent gave, because I would be excluding the notion that these people wear their colors in support of their teams, even when the teams are losing, and I would miss the fun nature of the group identity. The passion that these people describe in their team identification comes through much more clearly in their own words than if I simply presented a statistic of the percentage of people wearing team colors at a sporting event, or the percentage of people who identify with their team even if that team is experiencing a losing streak.

Let's look at another example. The social movement promoting social and legal rights for people with disabilities is gaining momentum here in the United States as it is in other countries. Baker and Donelly (2001, **AN 4052844**) examined how the social environment affects children with disabilities in Sydney, Australia. Their research involved participant observation of four children with fragile X syndrome, which leads to intellectual disabilities, and their families. Baker and Donelly's observation took place in these students' school. One father notes the following about the role of principals in the school:

> There's a really good acceptance [of children with disability]. It's driven strongly by the headmistress. . . . She had really set the culture for this school. . . . Last year the headmistress had a year off and there was another headmaster from another school for a year. His brief was really to maintain the status quo. . . . He came from a Special Ed. background many years ago. . . . Not an inclusion background but a background I now believe that was really into segregation. It was interesting to see the change in the culture, in the students, and probably a little bit in some of the teachers. . . . But certainly in the students. We noticed, last year, more discrimination against children with disability. . . . Craig has been at that school since Kindy . . . and in all that time I can't think of any major act of discrimination against any of them. . . . And last year, our youngest daughter had a sleepover party at our place, and one of her friends is someone who's in the special needs program there. And one of her friends called this girl at the sleepover . . . a "cry-baby retard." . . . And in that same year one of the boys did call Craig a "retard." Now it's never happened before. It's because of the attitude that this headmaster had. . . . He looked down on the kids in the Special Ed. program and I think that that culture then permeated through the school. . . . It doesn't take much for that culture to start to change if the person at the top's giving those sort of messages.

Again, notice the rich understanding of a parent's perception of the influence of the principal (headmistress or headmaster in Australia) on the socioenvironment of a child with a disability. A survey would just have been able to ask a closed-ended question as to whether the parent felt that the principal could shape the environmental experience of a disabled child in school, or whether the parent noticed any discrimination a child experienced at school and *thought* that the principal could control it. However, a researcher is unlikely to get the same degree of personal information with a survey as a researcher is with field research. The entire example of the girl's sleepover experience is likely to be lost in a survey question—even an open-ended one—because the question would deal with the researcher's view of discrimination in schools. The researcher is not likely to have thought of a spillover effect into something as common as sleepovers and the parent is also not likely to relate this type of information simply based on a written question.

Hence, field research provides comprehensive, in-depth understanding of a topic. Because of that, by definition, these studies are generally highly valid. Since people are describing their own experiences, in their own words, under natural circumstances, which are collaborated by the researcher's own observations in the field, we can be pretty sure that the researchers are really observing and measuring what they think they are—which is, essentially, the issue behind validity.

■ Reliability

Field research is generally very high on validity, but the same cannot necessarily be said for reliability. Have you ever been with a friend who said something that others took the wrong way? *You* might have known what that friend really meant (high validity), but others interpreted the same information or actions differently (low reliability). Another related example is if you have a friend who is dating someone who you do not think is right for her. You may raise all kinds of issues to your friend, but your friend is likely to respond that you do not know her significant other the way she does. This may be true; in essence, this example illustrates how different people may have different interpretations of similar events or circumstances.

Field research falls prey to the exact same problem. Different people may have different interpretations of field observations. One researcher can interpret an action, such as a change in leadership of the group being studied, as potentially threatening to the group. Another researcher can interpret that same change of leadership as a promise of growth for the group. One way to minimize this mismatch of interpretations is for field researchers not to make subjective conclusions in isolation. In other words, instead of saying that person A is conservative—a conclusion that is likely based on the researcher's own definition of what conservative is, a researcher could say that person A is more conservative than person B. The subjectivity is still present (after all, the definition of conservative is still the researcher's), but by establishing a comparison, you still get an idea of *relative* rankings on a trait, such as conservatism.

This is why it is important for field researchers to provide a lot of description of what the people studied are like. This way, you, as a reader, can better form your own opinion as to whether you agree with the researcher's conclusion (thereby the conclusion being reliable) or not (hence the conclusion is less reliable). However, researchers are limited to some degree about the amount of description they can provide. As I stated with the confidentiality issue, the researcher needs to strike a balance between providing enough information for an outside reader to evaluate the researcher's conclusion, but this cannot come at the cost of "insiders" being able to identify the people in the study. If something has to be sacrificed, it is the detail of description, since the need to protect confidentiality is paramount in this instance.

■ Generalizability

Related to the problem of reliability are some concerns for the generalizability of field research. The personal involvement of the researcher is, to some degree, going to influence the quality of data that that researcher obtains. Other researchers with different personalities or different approaches will not completely replicate the relationship with respondents that the initial researcher experienced. Therefore, their findings may be different. These differences carry over to differences in other contexts with other people. Even if the same researcher tried to replicate a study in a different setting, that new setting will involve different people, and the researcher will not have the exact same relationship with these new people as with the people in the original study. Because the research circumstances cannot be copied with other researchers in the same site or with the same (or different) researchers in different sites, the generalizability of any findings is questionable.

Also, as I stated earlier, field research does not involve probability samples. Even if a site is chosen by a probability sampling technique, the people who are in that site are not randomly selected. Therefore, what people attending strip clubs in rural areas say is not necessarily representative of what people attending strip clubs in urban areas may say. However, the material you learn from studying strip clubs in one location will serve as an excellent *foundation* for what to look for or ask in another location.

Hence, field research is not very generalizable. In summary, field research is generally very high on validity. The in-depth information researchers get of a specific group serves to reinforce that the researchers are truly studying what they think they are; thus, validity is high. However, the high validity comes at the price of reliability and generalizability. In fact, you probably have noticed that field research is a fair complement to the more quantitative methods of observation, experiments, and surveys. Unlike field research, experiments and surveys are generally lower on validity (but not necessarily *invalid*) and higher on reliability and generalizability. When people answer pre-created surveys, researchers can use the same surveys in a variety of geographical areas, with a variety of people, which facilitates reliability. Hence, in an effort to create as methodologically accurate research as possible, some researchers utilize *both* qualitative and quantitative methods in their research. Where one method of observation is low, the second method of observation is generally high, and vice versa. Let's take a look at a study that blends both qualitative and quantitative research.

Covering the Bases: Blending Qualitative and Quantitative Research

In an attempt to create studies that have an in-depth understanding of a phenomenon, as well as involve measures that can be replicated in other areas, some researchers blend quantitative and qualitative methodologies in their research or do research with multiple forms of qualitative analysis. For example, Ayoke, Härtel, and Callan (2002, **AN 8780049**) blend various qualitative approaches in their study of interpersonal conflict people experience in diverse work groups. The researchers wanted to see how communication behaviors either created or dissolved conflict in heterogeneous work groups. In order to do this, Ayoke and colleagues did two studies. The first study's goal was to explore the characteristics of conflict in heterogeneous work groups and see what strategies people employed in order to resolve the conflict. This part of the study involved three methodological approaches: complete observer field research, participant observation field research, and semi-structured interviews. Ayoke, Härtel, and Callan describe their methodology for the first study in this excerpt:

Observation

Group meetings with a total of six culturally diverse workgroups from two large organizations were observed and recorded for a minimum of two hours twice a week over a period of twelve weeks. Each group was observed at various times throughout the workday. . . . During the *observation* period, the researcher did not interfere with the day-to-day functioning of the workgroup and attempted to remain unobtrusive by sitting apart from the group and working on other non-organizational tasks while taking notes. . . .

. . . Data were collected on the types, intensity, frequencies and amount of conflict in these workgroups. . . .

Participant Observation

One workgroup was selected (based on accessibility) for a *participant observation* study. . . . [The] first author was a participant observer for a period of six months, assisting with group tasks and recording observable verbal and nonverbal reactions to conflict. Observation of this group commenced before the interviews and other observational studies so that information gleaned from this study informed the design of the interviews and observational measures.

Semi-Structured Interviews

Semi-structured interviews were conducted with the six managers of the six culturally heterogeneous workgroups to provide information about the participant organizations and workgroups. In addition, a total of 30 interviews with 25 members from these six workgroups were conducted. The length of the interviews ranged from one to four hours depending upon the time it took to build the rapport and trust necessary for informants to disclose details about conflict experiences in their workgroup. All interviews were carried out in private at the workplace and were audiotaped.

During the interview sessions, the interviewer (first author) did not use the word "conflict." Instead, interviewees were asked, "Do you encounter any difficulties or problems as you work daily in your work unit?" This question would be followed by the question, "Can you tell me if these difficulties or problems concern your duties or were related to interactions between you and other people at work?" . . . Next, informants were asked to recount the conflict episodes in their unit (their triggers, development, and resolution). Specific questions included, "Can you describe how you felt during this particular problem or difference or difficulty?," "Can you describe to me the processes by which the difference was resolved?," "Please describe how you communicate with each other as employees especially during conflict," "How would you describe how the manager communicates to the staff in the group?" and "What role do you think language plays in the difficulty you previously described?" The aim of this line of questioning was to determine the communicative strategies for conflict and its management in culturally heterogeneous workgroups. At the conclusion of each interview session, interviewees were debriefed and particular attention was given to those who revealed a particularly sensitive conflict or displayed angst about the experience. (pp. 172–173)

As you can see, Ayoke, Härtel, and Callan have a very comprehensive research method-ology. The observation part of the first study largely serves as their initial warm-up. Through the observation stage, the researchers began to familiarize themselves with the dynamics and conflicts of the various workgroups. This served to prepare Ayoke for his role in the second part of the study, the participant observation. By learning about the group's dynamics, he was able to take the information that pertained to one of the groups and immerse himself in the workings of that business for six months. Last, he supplemented his observations with information from semi-structured interviews. If you recall, semi-structured interviews are interviews in which the researcher enters the study with some predetermined research questions (or measures, so to speak), but these questions are frequently open ended and the researcher is free to follow up on any pieces of information participants

Have you ever had to work in groups while in college? What are the dynamics of those groups? How does conflict arise and how do group members address it?

present in their answers. Hence, the researcher has a guideline for the study (the predetermined questions), but has to "wing it" at parts if the respondent provides unanticipated, but relevant, information.

The second part of the study used the information from the first study to test communication accommodation theory strategies in creating and managing both productive and destructive conflict. In this study, however, instead of using business work groups, the researchers used two different sets of undergraduate students enrolled in a business class at a large university for six weeks. The first group of students participated in heterogeneous work groups to complete a major project required as part of the course. The researchers observed the students in their work groups and the students completed a survey that measured the students' perceptions about the achievement of their goals, their difficulties, the conflicts that arose as a group, and how conflict was resolved. The second group of students were also in a business course, but one offered by a different campus of the same university. In this second group, participants worked for the entire semester as part of the course requirement in Self Autonomous Learning Teams (SALTs), where they used a problem-based learning approach in completing assigned tasks. Ayoke observed both groups. The group members kept self-report journals of their experiences and also completed a survey at the end of the semester.

As you can probably tell, Ayoke, Härtel, and Callan's study is a very complex one. The first stage of the study involved two forms of field research and one form of survey (semistructured interviews) in business work groups. The second stage involved one form of field research (observation), one form of surveys (a self-report survey), and a form of nonreactive research (the student journals), which we have not discussed yet (but which I will address in Chapter 9). However, through this very in-depth qualitative analysis, using multiple forms of qualitative and quantitative methods of observation, Ayoke, Härtel, and Callan were able to learn that in a culturally heterogeneous work group, group members who were observably different experienced more exclusive communication.

Specifically, the researchers found that people were less receptive to the use of languages other than English and that the misuse of English often led to misunderstandings, which could in turn provoke conflict. However, they also found that communication exclusion was really only evident in the initial stages of group work. They also found that domineering behaviors, verbal aggression, and criticism were communicative strategies and behaviors associated with destructive conflict that impeded the fulfillment of the group's goals. Talking about differences and empathizing were key communicative strategies for productive conflict, which led to a more or less shared consensus and airing out of different issues.

Wight and Buston (2003, **AN 11714960**) used quantitative and qualitative methods to evaluate whether teacher training for a sex education program aimed at 13- to 15-year-olds is effective. The sex education program Wight and Buston evaluated was called SHARE: Sexual Health and Relationships—Safe, Happy and Responsible, which teaches adolescents about the quality of sexual relationships, how to practice safe sex, and how to reduce unwanted pregnancies. SHARE tries to accomplish this by developing pupils' understanding and skills to negotiate relationships, to delay sexual intercourse, and to use condoms effectively. The program consists of 20 taught sessions to the 13- to 15-year-olds and a five-day training course for those delivering the program. Wight and Buston conducted their study using a cluster randomized sample. They selected 25 schools and then randomly allocated them either to deliver the SHARE pack to two successive year groups (e.g., a group aged 13 to 14 and a group aged 14 to 15) or to keep existing sex education. The teachers in the treatment (SHARE) group and control group did not vary significantly in sex, age, years of experience in teaching sex education, subject specialization, and seniority.

Like Ayoke, Härtel, and Callan's study, Wight and Buston's research involved an initial observation period where the researchers observed the first morning and last day of the teacher training course. According to the researchers, this approach allowed them to gain an initial idea of the relationships between participants and to later observe what problems or issues the teachers raised at the conclusion of the training. The researchers also did semi-structured interviews with at least one teacher in each of the 13 schools that received the SHARE training.

However, unlike Ayoke, Härtel, and Callan, who used various forms of participant observation and semi-structured interviews, Wight and Buston also used self-report surveys immediately before the start of the training course, at the end of the first module (one year later), and then a year later just prior to the final day of training. The survey involved 7-point Likert scale questions on the teacher's experiences and confidence in administering the sex education training to students. This was supplemented by field observation from the researchers. Wight and Buston describe their fourth mode of observation and analysis strategies as such:

> In each school in both arms of the trial the two teachers who delivered sex education to most classes were asked if one or two of their sex education lessons could be observed. Of those approached 20 out of 25 SHARE-trained teachers, and 21 out of 26 control teachers, agreed to have their lessons observed. The researchers arranged to observe skills-based lessons in intervention schools and in control schools lessons that might have involved skills development (e.g., covering negotiation and/or contraception). Following the lesson the researchers completed a schedule detailing the teacher's performance, her or his interaction with pupils and the pupils' responses to the lesson, plus detailed ethnographic notes. It is primarily the data on teachers' performance that are presented here.
>
> In order to summarize the observation data and facilitate comparisons, scores were given for 12 aspects of teachers' delivery that the training aimed to affect. The two authors independently derived scores from the observation notes according to standardized criteria agreed with the trainer, using a simple scale of 1—very good, 2—OK, and 3—poor. Where the researchers' scores differed the data were discussed until a consensus was reached. (pp. 527–528)

One of the goals of the SHARE program, according to Wight and Buston, is to increase teachers' comfort for talking about this socially and personally sensitive issue. By blending both qualitative and quantitative research methods, Wight and Buston can compile a comprehensive picture of teachers' reactions to the program. For example, Table 8.1 presents some of the information Wight and Buston found based on the answers to the self-report survey.

These figures in Table 8.1 are very useful for a quick summary of what participating teachers felt about the training. For example, you can tell that organizing role-plays to resist unwanted sexual behavior was the issue in which teachers showed the greatest increase in confidence after the training because the increase between the baseline and posttest training score was 1.4 (column 3), which is higher than for any other item. You can also see that the increase in confidence wanes after a while, but is still present, for all issues of sex education since the numbers in column 3 are lower than in column 2 but are still positive (as implied since the researchers do not present any negative signs before the numbers).

However, these numbers lack the personal element that would enable a reader to really get an idea of the issues that concern teachers. Wight and Buston address this by also including comments from their field observation or semi-structured interviews, such as the one by "DI" from School 3:

> You're in your room and you're left to teach your own subject the way you think right, in many cases, and I always found sex education quite a difficult one. I wasn't sure if I was delivering it properly and how much I should be delivering. There's always the question of . . . how far you go with it. . . . But I think having been on the programme and having heard what other people were doing in schools, how they were delivering it, I felt much more confident that this was probably how far I should go with it. (DI, Sch.3) (Wight & Buston, 2003, p. 531)

TABLE 8.1 Excerpt of Findings from Wight and Buston's Sex Education Study

Teaching Issue	Pretraining Mean Score	Increase from Baseline	
		Posttraining	After 1 Year
Organizing role plays to resist unwanted sexual behavior	4.5	1.4	0.7
Discussing sexual pleasures/orgasms	4.7	1.1	0.6
Demonstrating condom use with model phallus	4.0	1.1	0.5
Educating about STDs	5.5	0.9	0.4
Remaining true to own personal values	5.6	0.5	0.4

Scores range from 1 (low) to 7 (high)

Source: Adapted from Daniel Wight and Katie Buston, "Meeting Needs But Not Changing Goals: Evaluation of In-Service Teacher Training for Sex Education," *Oxford Review of Education, 29* (4) (2003).

In this quote from DI, you really get a sense of the discomfort some feel in teaching sex education—a level of understanding that simply is not present in the table of survey results. Wight and Buston's research has the strengths of both qualitative and quantitative research. By including comments from the teachers themselves and by observing the trainings, Wight and Buston achieve the in-depth level of information that improves study validity. This validity is reinforced by the cross-coding done by both researchers to make sure they were in agreement about what they witnessed. The quantitative information from the tables and the randomized nature of the study also contribute to the study's validity, but also improve its generalizability and reliability.

It is probably obvious that these two studies were very time intensive. Combining research techniques can be time intensive from a field perspective (the researchers in these studies made field commitments between six months and two years) and from a data coding, cleaning, and analysis perspective (the double coding by researchers, the discussion of disagreements, the coding of semi-structured interviews or open-ended questions). Therefore, most researchers use only one technique—quantitative *or* qualitative research. However, the benefits of combining both, whenever possible, should be clear. By using both quantitative and qualitative research together, researchers can obtain a fuller understanding of their research question at the time of their study. Therefore, whenever possible, the extra time and effort of combining both forms of research is desirable.

Evaluating Written Research: Field Research

Since field research is a very flexible form of observation, guidelines for its evaluation, by necessity, need to be vague and flexible. Therefore, not all of these guidelines may apply in all instances.

1. *Does the research describe the selected site? Does the research provide some explanation as to how that site was chosen?*

An important component for evaluating field research is understanding the site the researcher selected. Was it a neighborhood? If so, what are the geographical, economic, and demographic characteristics of that neighborhood? Was the site a strip club? Does the strip club predominantly cater to male or female clients? How large is it? In what general geographical area (e.g., northeastern United States, western United States) is it located? The characteristics of the field site help give the reader insight about the environment that the people being observed experience.

2. *Did the researchers explain how they addressed gatekeepers?*

Remember, even qualitative research needs to have enough information to facilitate replication. Therefore, it is important for researchers to explain who the gatekeepers were in the study and what (if anything) special steps the researcher took to have the gatekeepers grant them access to the site. Even if a researcher did *not* use gatekeepers—for example, if he or she studied a group that was easily accessible—then the researcher needs to state that as well.

3. *Did the researcher describe how he or she defined the researcher role in the setting?*

Was the researcher a complete participant? A complete observer? Or was the researcher a participant observer? Knowing the researcher's role in the study is an important piece of information because it affects the evaluation of the validity of the study. If a researcher was a complete observer, there is little worry of him or her "going native." On the other hand, if the researcher was a complete participant, this is a very real concern, and a person reading the research has to be on the lookout for biased evaluation that may result from this loss of objectivity.

4. Did the researcher address how he or she developed field relations? If conflict arose, did the researcher make any comment about how personal or research problems in the field were addressed?

What did the researcher do to relate to the subjects? How much time did he or she spend with them? What types of activities did the researcher do with the participants? Did the researcher do any special preparation, such as learning special jargon, prior to entering the field in order to facilitate field relations? If there was any conflict among subjects, did the researcher explain how he or she reacted to the conflict? Did the researcher take sides? Did the researcher try to mediate conflicting parties? Did he or she stay completely on the sidelines and just observe? What about any research concerns? Did the researcher comment on any ethical issues pondered during the course of the study?

All of these questions may not be relevant to each research report, but if a researcher describes some conflict between subjects as part of the analysis, for example, then the researcher also should at least comment about his or her role in the conflict. Likewise, if the researcher is studying deviant behavior, clearly there are some ethical concerns that should come to mind, such as protection from harm and confidentiality. Did the researcher acknowledge these challenges and describe how he or she addressed them?

5. Did the researcher adequately protect the identity of the respondents? Did the researcher address other ethical considerations?

Related to the previous point, commenting about ethical considerations alone is not enough. Since the analysis of qualitative research frequently involves quotes from individuals as supporting evidence, the researcher needs to be especially careful about protecting his respondents' identities. Some researchers use pseudonyms, others use initials, and still others use even less personal identifiers such as numbers. All of these are a step in the right direction, provided that the researcher does not include so much description about individuals, or even special traits that will help others identify individuals, that even without the use of real names, some readers can identify specific subjects. There is a delicate balance between the need for detail and the ethical obligation to protect identity.

As I said before, qualitative research deals with many ethical issues. Principle of nonmalefiscence (do no harm), reciprocity, and privacy are three common concerns, although there certainly can be more. If, as a reader, you become concerned about how the researcher addressed a particular ethical concern that he or she fails to mention, then the researcher may not have done an adequate job addressing that ethical issue.

6. Did the researcher describe, at least in passing, his or her method of note taking? Does the method seem adequate?

Since most of use want to create favorable impressions among others, few people will act "normal" when they are aware that they are being recorded—at least, that is, unless they are being observed for an extended period. Remember, part of the reason field researchers spend so much time in their field setting is so their subjects become desensitized to being observed. People can be on "good" behavior only for so long.

However, if a researcher is continually walking around with a notebook or tape recorder in hand and thrusting it in people's faces at every turn, people are not likely to become desensitized to the notion of being "watched" and may continue to act atypically for an extended period of time. Hence, whether a researcher generally takes notes unobtrusively or not may influence the quality of her or his data, and therefore the validity of her or his findings.

7. In the analysis, does the researcher present general patterns of behavior and support those patterns with data such as quoted comments? Does the researcher use quotes selectively?

As readers, we are not likely to be privy to the various forms of field notes, such as background files and analytical files. We are only going to see a researcher's end result—his or her analysis. Therefore, evaluating the validity of the researcher's conclusions is difficult. The best we can do is read the selected excerpts that the researcher included as evidence of his or her claims and see if we agree with the researcher's conclusions. Therefore, the researcher should include some information, such as quotes—even though it is clearly going to be selective—to illustrate or support his or her claims.

This means of evaluating conclusions may seem "wishy washy," but remember that field research does not have the same goals as a survey or experiment, for example. Field research is interested in discovering the nuances behind behavior that are not necessarily generalizable to wider populations. Therefore, what a researcher observes in a gang from Los Angeles may also apply to a gang in Philadelphia, but it may not, and this difference does not invalidate either study. Because the goal of field research is different from the goals of other, more qualitative, methods of observation, the criteria for evaluating the findings are different as well.

Also, since field research is focused on a more personal, in-depth understanding of subjects, quotes are a more appropriate means of data presentation than are more quantitative issues such as the number of times a researcher spoke with an individual or the number of times an individual behaved a certain way. Researchers may include quantitative information if it is relevant; however, it will not, and should not, be the focus of the data presented.

Furthermore, field researchers need to selectively present their evidence. Quoting every person a researcher examines who fits a pattern is not necessary. In fact, many strings of quotations can be confusing. The researcher should present only a few short quotes or one longer quote (as in a conversation) to support any individual point.

8. Does the researcher make any mention of issues of validity and/or reliability?

As noted in the chapter, field research is generally high on validity and low on reliability. Does the researcher spend any time discussing the validity of his or her findings? You can evaluate the validity based on your answers to the previous questions, but it is a bonus if the researcher also recognizes validity issues in his or her study. Since reliability is likely to be weak, if a researcher mentions this at all (and if they do not, the omission alone should not lead you to question the merits of the study), the researcher is only likely to recognize the study's limitations regarding this issue. Calling attention to the reliability limitation is *not* a problem, because this limitation is inherent in almost all field research. So

BOX 8.2   **Evaluating Written Research: Field Research**

Below are two examples of field research. One involves the decline of a religious social movement; the other involves an exploration of a new method of teaching science to upper-primary and middle school students. Read the excerpts below and evaluate the research using the guidelines from the Evaluating Research section of the chapter.

Example 1

Social movements come and go. In fact, the majority of social movements fail to produce any real social change. Therefore, it is scientifically and practically useful to study a social movement that has begun to decline in order to establish some reasons why social movements fail to achieve their intended goals. With this information, organizers of other social movements may be able to avoid some of the pitfalls that have led to the demise of their earlier cousins.

Bates uses field research to examine the social dynamics and structural issues that have led to the demise of the Oregon's Citizen Alliance (OCA), a Christian right lobbying group. An excerpt from his research follows:

> Since this is a continuing evaluation of the OCA, the promises of anonymity and the agreement of informed consent still obtain. In the summer of 1997, the Director of the OCA reiterated to his staff and followers that I would be continuing my study. I reinterviewed the Director twice, the Political Director several times, and selected OCA members and staff that had been interviewed for the previous paper, to gain some insight into their perceptions of the changes in the OCA. . . . These interviews were both in-person and telephone interviews.
> . . . Pseudonyms, with the exception of public figures, are used throughout this paper to protect the privacy of participants. All interviews were tape recorded and transcribed to enhance accuracy. Interviews with OCA leaders were on-site, thus allowing for continued observation of the state of the OCA headquar-

ters. This proved to be useful for drawing some conclusions about their financial and organizational decline. Other interviews were also in the field, in homes, offices and restaurants, rather than in my office or home. . . . Movement literature review and analysis, medial analysis, and a review of State of Oregon records on registered political action committees were also employed. Coding and classification schemes were devised by this author and based on schemes appropriated from a variety of qualitative methodology handbooks. . . .

Results

. . . The OCA has always faced competition for choice signature gathering sites, but the competition for these choice sites increased dramatically when a variety of interest groups began to pay signature gatherers a specific amount of money for each signature.

> I think most of the initiatives were using volunteer efforts to quality even through the early 1990s, but the trend has accelerated very quickly to the point in 1996 when every one of the 16 initiatives and the one referendum that made it to the ballot used paid signature gatherers to get them on the ballot. We did an analysis that came out this Spring that estimated that about 2.5 million dollars was spent just on paid signature gathering. Some people reported making $1,000.00 per day for the work that they did. (Secretary of State Kiesling, interview, August 4, 1997)

> The OCA did not and does not have the money to pay its signature gatherers. The OCA Director indicates that this has negatively impacted their ability to be successful.

> The competition is stiff for signatures. In the last election there were no volunteer-based initiatives that made it to the ballot. We know this was coming so we file earlier than ever but we were hit pretty hard. The paid signature gatherers push very hard and

BOX 8.2   Evaluating Written Research: Field Research, continued

get the best spots. We will not pay for signatures. We want people committed to our cause gathering those signatures. I would rather adjust to paid petitioners than to restrict them. (Lon Mabon, interview, May 28, 1997)

Source: Vernon L. Bates, "The Decline of a New Christian Right Social Movement Organization: Opportunities and Constraints," *Review of Religious Research, 42* (1) (September 2000): 19. (**AN 10812277**)

Critical Thinking Questions

1. Does the research describe the selected site? Does the research provide some explanation as to how that site was chosen?

2. Did the researchers explain how they addressed gatekeepers?

3. Did the researcher describe how he defined the researcher role in the setting?

4. Did the researcher address how he developed field relations? If conflict arose, did the researcher make any comment about how personal or research problems in the field were addressed?

5. Did the researcher adequately protect the identity of the respondents? Did the researcher address other ethical considerations?

6. Did the researcher describe, at least in passing, his method of note taking? Does the method seem adequate?

7. In the analysis, does the researcher present general patterns of behavior and support those patterns with data such as quoted comments? Does the researcher use quotes selectively?

8. Does the researcher make any mention of issues of validity and/or reliability?

9. Overall, is the research adequate?

Critical Thinking Discussion

1. The researcher does not provide any of this information. The site was probably chosen based on convenience, meaning that the researcher somehow already had access to this organization; or, the researcher may have explained the site selection in his previously published study. However, in this publication, we do not know.

2. Directly, no. However, the director of the OCA is a formal gatekeeper, since he is the one who explained the researcher's presence to the staff.

3. He describes some of his work as participant observation, since he attended some meetings; however, the majority of it appears to be complete observation, since Bates does not give any indication of how he actually participated in the meetings and most of his data is from interviews and his observations.

4. There is no mention of this; however, if he truly was a complete observer (contrary to his statement of participant observation), this is not necessary beyond the introduction he received from the director.

5. He used pseudonyms for those participants who were not public figures. Presumably we can detect pseudonyms from real names because he includes the titles of people who are public figures and just names and interview dates for others. When Bates does not present a title, we can assume that the names of the people in interviews are pseudonyms.

    There really are no other ethical considerations that are present, other than informed consent, and Bates mentioned that he obtained that in the earlier phase of the research. The participants know Bates is a researcher, therefore deception is not an issue.

    No one can really be harmed by this research; therefore, principle of nonmaleficence is not an issue. Furthermore, since he is not really interacting with participants in their daily routines, reciprocity is not an issue either.

6. Bates describes his method of note taking clearly. He recorded conversations and then transcribed them. This is all the detail researchers are likely to provide. Granted, the tape recorder is likely to make people realize that they were being interviewed, versus observed in their natural role of the organization, but, given Bates's focus on observation field research, this is acceptable.

7. Only a short except of the results are presented, but you can find the complete article on Research Navigator and see that, yes, generally he does selectively present quotes as support for his patterns of observations.

8. There is no clear mention of either validity or reliability issues in the excerpt or in the original.

9. That is hard to evaluate. Certainly, it is a useful research topic and it produces some clear findings. However, there are some important omissions, such as how the site was selected and how the researcher approached gatekeepers. Perhaps the researchers explained this in the earlier research that the author cites.

    For observer as participant research (the form of research where the researcher is primarily an observer but does participate marginally), his method of taking notes is appropriate. He explains his analysis and there are not many ethical concerns that he needs to address. Therefore, this study is probably a fairly adequate, but not stellar, form of field research, as it is described in this article.

Example 2

In order to get late-primary and middle school students interested in science, some schools have adapted an approach to teaching science that involves trying to replicate (in a watered-down fashion) the work of active scientists. This approach, called the Voyage of the Mimi, uses computers, videos, and other print material to teach an integration of math, science, social science, and language arts. Huberman and Middle-brooks (2000) conduct field research to explore the use of this new teaching paradigm.

[Method]

After some initial, often unavoidable, difficulties (e.g., access to records), the publishing staff (WINGS) randomly chose 54 sites, focusing on cases on the Eastern seaboard of the U.S. . . .

    From a total of 11 exploratory site visits, 6 were selected for the study. . . . As we were well aware that six sites are not representative of the hundreds using the Voyage of the Mimi, an initial criterion was to look for diversity of use and variation of local conditions.

    During the school year, the six schools were visited at least three times, 1 to 3 days at a time, making a total of 45 days on site. . . . [An] estimated 100+ hours of formal interviews with 17 teachers, 66 students, 11 principals and other support staff were carried out, along with 135 hours of observations.

    . . . Like much case study research . . . [s]uccessive waves of site visits brought on revisions in research questions, instruments, and codes. . . . Note that during these visits, researchers tried simply to melt into the school setting. . . . Also, we had worked out the conventional arrangement with each informant, promising confidentiality, anonymity, and a full debriefing at the end of the year. . . .

[Analysis]

We worked with 17 functional coding categories, regrouping 32 thematic codes and a larger set of general codes. An illustrative sample of thematic codes is shown in Appendix 3.

    In the end, the thematic material was subjected to an analysis using templates devised by Miles & Huberman (1994). In particular, checklist matrices, event listings, time- and role-order matrices displayed similarly plotted data on one chart. . . . Comparisons then allowed for clustering cases, for establishing variations and, from there, to the identification of potentially systematic patterns.

BOX 8.2   **Evaluating Written Research: Field Research, continued**

[Results]

The "faithful" user [is] the teacher who follows closely Mimi's Overview guide. Typically, the showing of an episode or expedition is preceded by preview questions and followed by selected follow-up questions.

. . . The two third-grade classes, 40 pupils, gather on the rug in HP's room at Site 1; the adults . . . sit or stand around the edge of the group. The children face KC as she asks questions suggested in Mimi's Overview guide for Expedition 5 related to animal adaptation, and gives a brief summary.

. . . After the show—and more humming—KC asks more questions from the Guide and then goes over several vocabulary words, including "chemo-receptor."

. . . Toward the end of the period, KC asks the group for their "thoughts and feelings" regarding the removal of animals from their habitats for the purpose of research and experimentation.

. . . Children's responses are diverse; many seem eager to voice an opinion:

I wouldn't want to experiment on an animal.

I wouldn't want to be that animal experimented on.

If we don't do it, we don't find out things that are helpful to us.

Even if the animal returned to its habitat, I don't think it will find its family again.

KC then wraps up: "We get information from experimenting on animals and that helps us, and we shouldn't take more than is necessary."

Source: Michael Huberman and Sally Middlebrooks, "The Dilution of Inquiry: A Qualitative Study," *International Journal of Qualitative Studies in Education (QSE), 13* (3) (June 2000): 281. DOI: 10.1080/09518390050019686. (*AN 3334896*)

Critical Thinking Questions

Same as in Example 1

Critical Thinking Discussion

1. There is information about site selection. The researchers imply that they first based selection on school records (which they initially had trouble obtaining) and then randomly selected 54 possible sites from these school records. Then they visited 11 sites and selected 6 to be in their study. They describe the 6 as all being on the eastern seaboard of the United States. When they discuss the actual sites (2 appear in the article and 1 in the excerpt I've selected), they also describe the classroom setting in detail.

2. The excerpt does not, but the original articles says that they contacted teachers, who are the formal gatekeepers, and asked permission to observe their classrooms.

3. Yes. They said that they were there primarily to "melt into the school setting." This means that they were generally observers, although in the complete article they do state that they temporarily would take over the classroom; thus, their role was not exactly a complete observer.

4. There is no mention about how the researchers specifically developed field relations. However, since they were primarily observers there for short periods, this was probably not highly necessary.

5. Yes, the identities were generally protected. The researcher just used initials; however, given the detailed description of the classrooms, those familiar with the participants might be able to identify them. Therefore, it is unclear how *well* they did this, even though they did make an attempt.

   The researchers also imply that they had voluntary participation since they discussed with participants their guarantee of their protection of anonymity, confidentiality (even though they couldn't technically guarantee both simultaneously), and a debriefing at the end of the study. Their ethical obligations are generally fulfilled.

BOX 8.2 **Evaluating Written Research: Field Research, continued**

6. Somewhat. They do not specifically state how they took notes, but they do note that they did formal interviews and that their research questions and goals were revised after each meeting. In fact, they provide a very detailed description of their method of analysis.

7. Yes. In the excerpt presented here, the researcher classifies one pattern of teacher behavior, what they call the "faithful user" who teaches from the study guide, and they provide some notes and quotes from a classroom expe-

rience to support this claim. In this part of the excerpt, the researcher does use the quotes sparingly and effectively.

8. They do not mention validity in the excerpt, but they do recognize the limitations for reliability, even though they used random selection in an early stage.

9. Overall, yes, this is a fairly good example of field research.

---

do not discount the study simply because the researcher is well aware of the limitations of his or her work and wants to make sure that the readers are as well.

To summarize, these are the general questions readers need to keep in mind when reading published reports of field research:

1. Does the research describe the selected site? Does the research provide some explanation as to how that site was chosen?
2. Did the researchers explain how they addressed gatekeepers?
3. Did the researcher describe how he or she defined the researcher role in the setting?
4. Did the researcher address how he or she developed field relations? If conflict arose, did the researcher make any comment about how personal or research problems in the field were addressed?
5. Did the researcher adequately protect the identity of the respondents? Did the researcher address other ethical considerations?
6. Did the researcher describe, at least in passing, his or her method of note taking? Does the method seem adequate?
7. In the analysis, does the researcher present general patterns of behavior and support those patterns with data such as quoted comments? Does the researcher use quotes selectively?
8. Does the researcher make any mention of issues of validity and/or reliability?
9. Overall, is the research adequate?

These questions may not be relevant to all field studies, since there is a lot of variation in research questions, settings, and subjects. However, they should get you started in effectively reading written reports of field research.

Key Terms

Analytic notes (355)
Complete observer (339)
Complete participant (337)
Direct notes (354)
Gatekeeper (343)

"Going native" (360)
Jottings (354)
Key informants (348)
Observer as participant (339)
Participant observation (333)

Participant as observer (338)
Personal notes (355)
Researcher interpretation notes
 (354)

Review Questions and Exercises

1. Evaluate the field research techniques in the following articles:

 a. Baccaro, Lucio. (2000, April). Negotiating the Italian pension reform with the unions: Lessons for corporatist theory. Industrial & Labor Relations Review, *55 (3), 413. 19 pp. (AN 6535589)*

 b. Barker, Bernard. (2001, February). Do leaders matter? Educational Review, *53 (1), 65. 12 pp. (AN 4230092)*

 c. Derbaix, Christian, Decrop, Alain, and Cabossart, Olivier. (2002). Colors and scarves: The symbolic consumption of material possessions by soccer fans. Advances in Consumer Research, *29 (1), 511. 8 pp. (AN 7705818)*

 d. Baker, Kristan, and Donelly, Michelle. (2001, January). The social experiences of children with disability and the influence of environment: A framework for intervention.

Disability & Society, *15 (1), 71. 15 pp. DOI: 10.1080/09687590020020877. (AN 4052844)*

 e. Wight, Daniel, and Buston, Katie. (2003, December). Meeting needs but not changing goals: Evaluation of in-service teacher training for sex education. Oxford Review of Education, *29 (4), 521. 23 pp. (AN 11714960)*

2. In the following article, Lauder makes an argument for the need for deception when researching nonnormative behavior. Do you agree with his argument? Why or why not? Can you think of any other ways Lauder may have been able to approach the research that would involve less deception?

 Lauder, Mathew A. (2003, May). Covert participant observation of a deviant community: Justifying the use of deception. Journal of Contemporary Religion, *18 (2), 185. 12 pp. (AN 9756052)*

Unobtrusive Research Methods

The link between the media and people's behavior, especially children's behavior, is a widely studied one. Earlier in this book, I talked about research that tries to make a causal connection between viewing violent video games and violent behavior among children. Other researchers have examined how television shows lead to violence (Felson, 1996; Orange & Amiso, 2000). However, violence is not the only concern people have about the media's effect on those watching. Other concerns are about the media's portrayal of gender roles (Patton, 2001), even in politics (Kahn, 1994), and racial stereotypes (Ford, 1997). Furthermore, some researchers (Davis, 2003, **AN 10719904)** argue that other, often overlooked, forms of media, such as commercials, can also give people, especially children, messages about their social world. To explore this, Davis studied 467 characters that appeared in the commercials between children's cartoons. She found that even though there are fewer sex-typed behaviors in the real world and in the cartoons than earlier researchers found, the commercials that appear between children's cartoons persist in depicting sex-role stereotypes.

Davis's conclusions were based on a form of observation known as *content analysis*. Content analysis is a type of unobtrusive research because it is nonreactive, meaning that it is a form of data collection in which the researcher has no contact, directly or indirectly (e.g., as in writing a survey and collecting responses) with the people studied. It also includes research in which the researcher studies the results of social behavior and not the person directly doing the behavior. Clearly, cartoons are inanimate; therefore, they cannot be aware or unaware of being studied. They are the results of someone's imagination (hence, the product of behavior, not the individual doing the behavior). If you remember from Chapter 3, social artifacts are objects or evidence created by people that can be studied. People made the commercials that Davis studied. She did not interview the people who made the commercial, she did not survey children who watched commercials, and she did not experiment with commercials to see if different ones had different effects on children's views. All three of these approaches are **reactive research** forms of data gathering because they involve interaction with people. However, content analysis is **nonreactive research** because it does not involve any *direct* interaction with people; it examines the results of their behavior—namely, the commercials they created.

Scientists can be very creative about developing nonreactive measures. For example, instead of interviewing or surveying people in a town that was supposedly "dry" (meaning it outlawed the sale of liquor) about their drinking habits, Sawyer (1961) simply went around counting empty whisky bottles in people's trash cans. This form of research, called **physical trace analysis,** involves studying deposits or accretion of matter left by human behavior. When you stop to think about it, Sawyer's approach was a very smart way of studying a topic that had a social bias to preconceived answers. In a town that is dry, it is unlikely that many people will admit to consuming alcohol. On the other hand, few people will bother to deposit their empty liquor bottles in a neighboring city that is not dry— it is simply too much hassle.

Another example of physical trace analysis is studying graffiti. Klofas and Cutshall (1985) studied graffiti in an abandoned juvenile correction facility in the United States, and Gyasi Obeng (2000, **AN 3424355**) studied graffiti in men's lavoratories in dormitories and academic departments at Ghana University to assess like or dislike for certain ethnic groups. An excerpt from Gyasi Obeng's research illustrates how telling a simple act of bathroom graffiti can be:

> The negative attitude expressed about the Ewe language is "couched" in its
> homograph with the English word for a female sheep, ewe. Note that T stands for
> turn and T1 refers to turn one.
>
> (1)
>
> (T1) A: If we don't stop these No. 9 guys they will desecrate this holy place
>   with their language.
>
> (T2) B: Bush boy; But God speaks our language.
>
> (T3) C: How can God speak a female sheep's language? Is God a sheep?
>
> (T4) D: At least God doesn't say Kolet. He can say rrrrr.

In excerpt (1), A refers to the Ewe people as "No. 9" and to the Ewe language in a derogatory way as a language that can violate the sanctity of a holy place. In Ghana, the expression "No. 9" is often used to refer to people of Volta Region descent, because the Volta Region was the ninth political region to be created in Ghana. Through semantic extension, "No. 9" has been used to refer to speakers of the Ewe language. Although other languages besides Ewe are spoken in the Volta Region (e.g., languages from the Togo Remnant group), and speakers of these languages are sometimes called "No. 9," this expression is primarily used for the Ewe and their language. In addition, A manipulated pronouns such as the exclusive third-person plural pronoun *they* and the third-person plural possessive pronoun *their*. These pronoun choices indicate distancing and imply that the graffiti author does not belong to the group he is writing about (Chilton, 1985; Cross, 1989).

In T2, B responds to A's comment. The initial phrase in B's response, "Bush boy," is a "disagreement flag" (Moonwomon, 1995), thus showing that B disagrees with the proposition expressed in A's text. Among Legon students, insults and especially expressions relating to being uncouth (such as "bush boy") may be used to preface an utterance indicating difference of opinion. From the functional and logic-semantic point of view (Dillon, 1990; Hargie, Saunders, & Dickson, 1987), the conjunction *but* may also signal difference in opinion, suggesting that the expression about to be presented refutes the previous proposition. In the string "God speaks our language," B is challenging the suggestion that Ewe is unholy. The word *God* anaphorically refers to the expression "holy place" in T1. Moreover, the first-person plural possessive pronoun *our,* an inclusive form, shows that the graffiti author identifies with Ewe and the Ewe people. Use of such inclusive pronouns helps to gain other interactants' allegiance because they suggest shared interests or group identity (Chilton, 1985).

The young men who left this graffiti discourse are not directly part of the research. In fact, it is likely that Gyasi Obeng does not even know who they are. Therefore, this form of research is clearly nonreactive, yet fairly sophisticated in its analysis of the nuances of language.

There are other common forms of nonreactive, or unobtrusive, data strategies. Three of the most frequently used are content analysis, secondary analysis, and analysis of existing statistics or agency data. In this chapter I will focus on each of these three individually. In fact, because these three are all unique forms of data gathering, this chapter is actually organized as three "mini"-chapters in that for each of these research designs, I will follow the general format that I have used in the previous chapters. However, I will postpone the discussion of how to evaluate each of these forms of study until the end of the chapter.

Content Analysis

When researchers first recognized the usefulness of content analysis is unclear. According to some, content analysis was first used to study newspapers and Nazi propaganda broadcasts in World War II (Schutt, 2001). According to others, Max Weber first suggested using content analysis to study newspapers at the first German Sociological Society meeting in 1910 (Neuman, 1997). Regardless of its historical content, content analysis can be done with any medium that can be transcribed or visually observed. Hence researchers can do content analysis of newspaper articles, political speeches, rock songs, photographs, and television shows, just to name a few examples.

Content analysis can be either quantitative or qualitative. For a *quantitative* approach, researchers can simply count the appearances of predetermined themes or words. For a *qualitative* approach, researchers can give subjective meanings or interpretations to the content. As with other methods of observation, purely quantitative or purely qualitative methods are limited in specific ways, whereas a combination of the two will produce a more comprehensive, valid, and reliable analysis. So, before I go too much further into a general discussion of content analysis, let's start by looking at some appropriate topics for content analysis research.

Appropriate Topics

As with surveys, the possible topics for content analysis are almost endless. The only real requirement is that the data be able to be transcribed and/or visually observed. Even songs and speeches are fair game for content analysis because their words can be audiotaped and transcribed. Therefore, content analysis is good for studying who says what, how people communicate, the subtle messages behind words, and what effect communication can possibly have on others. However, keep in mind that content analysis is limited to the cultural meaning of a social artifact. It cannot determine the truthfulness of communication (e.g., people may lie about their personal feelings in a speech in order to appeal to the majority so they can gain their support) or the aesthetic quality of work (e.g., the words transcribed from a country song will not affect whether someone does or does not like country music). Content analysis can only say what the message may be, not how others may interpret the message.

Within the broad topics just mentioned, content analysis is also appropriate for topics in which there is a large amount of text. Having a large amount of text available means that the researcher can use probability sampling techniques to select specific elements for study. The use of probability techniques improves the generalizability of the study.

Content analysis is also appropriate for topics in which direct observation is not possible. For example, obtaining and studying the news stories shown on television in a country hostile to the United States may shed some light on the views people may have toward Americans (if we want to argue that people's perceptions are influenced by what they see on the news). Making a trip to a hostile country is certainly not advisable or even feasible. However, if we get a sense of the type of information those citizens are receiving about the United States, we may have a better idea as to how they will react to Americans and why.

Finally, like Davis's (2003) study that I cited at the beginning of this chapter, content analysis may be useful in ascertaining subtle messages that the messengers may not even be aware they are submitting. The people who write children's cartoons are increasingly sensitive about how their characters portray gender roles. With cartoons such as *Dora the Explorer* and *Kim Possible*, cartoon creators are consciously trying to depict girls in untraditional, take-charge, adventurous roles. However, there is less emphasis or visibility regarding the messages of commercials. Therefore, any gender bias in commercial characters may be a subconscious reflection of the gender views of those who create the commercials. Even subconscious messages on the part of the transmitter may affect the formation of subconscious views on behalf of the receiver.

Perhaps you are feeling a little adrift regarding the appropriate topics for content analysis. This is because, as with surveys and experiments, the possible topics are endless. The main idea is to be sure that the data can be transcribed or visually observed.

General Procedures

After you select your research topic and decide that content analysis is an appropriate method of observation, your next step is to identify the population of text or other visual documents to observe. For example, Billings, Halone, and Denham (2002, **AN 7195816**) studied the gender differences in broadcaster commentary for the 2000 Men's and Women's National Collegiate Athletic Association Final Four tournament games. Their population, technically, was championship basketball games.

Pritchard (1986) studied a more indirect population when he wanted to see whether newspaper coverage of individual criminal cases affects prosecutors' decisions to go to trial or to plea bargain. To do this study, Pritchard analyzed police and court records for all the people arrested for homicide in an 18-month span in Milwaukee County, Wisconsin, in order to determine whether prosecutors pleaded a case or took it to trial. He also analyzed all of the newspaper coverage for those cases. His population was the prosecutors' decisions. Since he did content analysis, an unobserved means of gathering data, he did not directly survey or interview his population. He obtained information about this population more indirectly by observing their behaviors as indicated in the police and court records.

The next step in content analysis is deciding what the units of analysis will be.

Units of analysis and units of observation

Broadly, the units of analysis in content analysis are social abstracts. However, sometimes (but not always) these social abstracts need to be broken into more manageable pieces. For example, let's suppose I wanted to study how social problems textbooks addressed the issue of spousal abuse. My units of analysis would be the textbooks themselves. However, most textbooks will not be solely devoted to studying spousal abuse. At most, they are likely to have a chapter on this topic. Therefore, my units of observation may be the chapter. Or some books in my sample may have only a passage or subsection devoted to this topic.

To maintain consistency in analysis between those textbooks that devote a substantial amount of space to this problem (e.g., an entire chapter) and those that do not (e.g., a subsection within a chapter), I may decide to study a sample of pages within textbooks, whether they are selected from an entire chapter or from a subsection within a chapter. These pages are what I am actually observing *within* the textbook, and so they are my units of observation. It is important for researchers to be clear in determining what their units of observation and units of analysis are if the two are different, because it alerts readers to the scope of the data collected. Studying chapters is a much broader scope than just studying select pages within a chapter.

Sampling

As with surveys, content analysis can involve entire populations or it can involve samples—either probability or nonprobability, although probability samples are preferred. Any type of probability sample is possible. Let's stick with my textbook example. If I wanted to study how sociology textbooks addressed husband abuse, I could do a simple random sample of all the textbooks available in a given year and analyze the entire sections on husband abuse within them. Depending on the number of textbooks available, I might even decide to do a systematic sample, or perhaps I'll do a stratified sample. I might stratify my textbooks by large or small publishing firms. I could then draw a sample of textbooks from the large publishing firms and a sample from the small firms (both of which I would have to define). I could even do a cluster sample. I could first select textbooks (perhaps using simple random sampling), then within the textbooks I've selected I could do another simple random sample of the paragraphs on spouse abuse to select the paragraphs to study.

Sampling may not end when researchers reach the units of analysis. If I am studying the content of popular rock songs, I may first select a sample of rock artists. I could then select a sample of songs from that artist that have reached the top 20. I could then do a subsample of verses within the songs and then analyze the content of the sample lyrics to the songs themselves. In this sample design, my sampling units were (in order) rock artists, songs, and lyrics. My units of analysis were the songs, the middle step, but, as you can see, I did not stop sampling at my units of analysis. I continued one step further to a sample of the lyrics, which were my units of observation, and used that sample to make conclusions about the songs.

The Billings, Halone, and Denham study (2002), as well as the Pritchard study (1986), examined populations. Billings, Halone, and Denham studied *all* the commentary of the sports broadcasters for the 2000 NCAA Final Four basketball games from the beginning to end (pregame to postgame commentary). This resulted in 272 transcribed pages of broadcast commentary. There was a total of 185 transcribed pages of broadcast commentary from the men's games and a total of 87 transcribed pages of broadcast commentary from the female games. In Pritchard's study, the real data he used for the content analysis were the newspapers. There were 90 homicide defendants who had newspaper stories written about them between January of 1981 and June of 1982 in the Milwaukee newspapers. These newspapers included the morning paper (*The Sentinel*) and the evening paper (*The Journal*). In these papers there was a total of 744 staff-written items that included articles, editorials, and staff opinion pieces. All of these articles were included in Pritchard's analysis.

Coding

Content analysis really gets interesting in the coding procedures. So far, everything I have mentioned is fairly straightforward, even if some unusual decisions need to be made about sampling and units of analysis. However, the heart of content analysis is in the coding, since, after all, that's what will be analyzed. However, before embarking on a discussion of coding, as with other forms of quantitative research, researchers first have to decide what they will be measuring. Essentially, researchers need to operationalize their concepts.

According to Neumann (1997), there are four different types of coding schemes commonly used in content analysis: frequency, direction, intensity, and space. As the term implies, *frequency* refers to a count of how often something, such as a word, phrase, or picture, occurs. For example, how many times does the term *husband abuse* appear in the textbook? What percentage of references are to husband abuse, as opposed to wife abuse? Billings, Halone, and Denham (2002) developed 16 categories to measure different dimensions of broadcaster commentary. According to Billings, Halone, and Denham:

> Broadcast commentary accounts were initially categorized, and subsequently analyzed, according to (a) physicality and athleticism (e.g., can physically dominate the lane), (b) intelligence and mental skill (e.g., can read defenses easily), (c) hard work and effort (e.g., going the extra mile tonight), (d) determination and motivation (e.g., he simply won't let them lose), (e) speed (e.g., blows past everyone), (f) positive consonance (e.g., he's feeling it), (g) negative consonance (e.g., her entire game is completely off), (h) leadership (e.g., everyone follows from her example), (i) versatility (e.g., he does it all out there), (j) team orientation (e.g., always does what is best for the team), (k) physical power (e.g., knocks him over on the way to the hoop), (l) mental power (her smarts are the top reason she dominates), (m) personality (e.g., if you've ever met her, you'd know she's a good kid), (n) looks and appearance (e.g., sleek body), (o) background (e.g., grew up in Compton), and (p) other (e.g., she does not always get the credit she deserves). (pp. 304–305)

These researchers and their coders then counted the frequency that each of these categories appeared in the commentary of men and of women's basketball.

The second type of coding is *direction*. Measures that address positive/negative, support/not support, or common/rare are all examples of continuums and therefore measures of direction. I could measure whether an author looks favorably or unfavorably on the issue of husband abuse as a social problem. I can measure whether popular songs about current social conditions support or do not support a war that a country is fighting. Direction refers to a general continuum of view.

Researchers can also measure *intensity*, which is somewhat similar to direction, but goes one step further and refers to the strength or power of a direction. My earlier example where I said that a researcher could measure the treatment of husband abuse as (1) a serious social problem in its own right, (2) a social problem but one that is not as serious as wife abuse, or (3) an issue that is not a social problem in its own right is an example of direction. The way of measuring how the textbook deals with husband abuse is along a continuum that ranges from a serious problem to not a problem. Seriousness is a type of intensity.

In Pritchard's (1986) study of newspaper stories' effects on prosecutors' behavior, he measured the news stories' intensity with a measure of the "routineness" of the news piece. If the content was based on routine police or judicial sources, Pritchard categorized a news piece as "routine." If the piece involved information that required more effort to obtain on the reporters' behalf, information such as witness testimony, interviews with friends or relatives of the suspect, or additional comments by law enforcement offices, Pritchard categorized that news piece as "nonroutine." He then used this information to calculate the proportion of nonroutine stories in the newspaper.

Last, according to Babbie (1995), researchers doing content analysis can measure *space*. How many lines does a textbook author devote to the discussion of husband abuse compared to wife abuse? How much space on a page is devoted to different pictures in a book? How many minutes are devoted to discussing a particular news story? Space can be the measure of words, lines, paragraphs, pages, space (e.g., the proportion of page), or time allocated. In Pritchard's (1986) study, he also measured the length of newspaper stories and the nature of the article, editorial, or commentary content. To measure the length of newspaper stories, Pritchard divided the total number of paragraphs about a case by the total number of stories about that case. This is an example of measuring the space devoted to a topic.

Any one study can include all of these measures or just one of them. Billings, Halone, and Denham's (2002) study involves various frequency calculations; however, the calculations are all of the same type—frequencies. Pritchard's (1986) analysis involves examining the spacing of events as well as the intensity of the treatment of event.

Aside from these four characteristics of coding, exactly *what* a researcher codes falls into two categories: the coding of manifest or latent content. **Manifest content** involves coding the visible surface content of communication. An example of manifest content is counting the number of times a specific word or phrase appears in a text or when a specific action or characteristic appears in visual communication.

To do manifest coding, researchers begin with a list of words, phrases, actions, or characteristics that they will specifically look for when analyzing the content of the data. Clearly, no matter how hard researchers try, they may not be able to create a comprehensive list at the beginning of the study. Therefore, every time the researcher encounters a word that is not on that list, but may be an appropriate indicator, the researcher makes a decision whether to add that word to the list or not. It is important that researchers makes this decision *the first time* they encounter a new possible word. If the researcher decides to add that word to the list, he or she does so (by physically documenting it as part of the list) and then continues to include any inference to that word later encountered in the count. However, if the researcher decides *not* to include that word, he or she should make note of the omitted word on a separate list so that if the researcher has to take a break from the research and comes back to it at a later date (even a day later), the researcher does not have to rely on remembering what words he or she decided not to include in the count. The same applies to analyzing other forms of communication such as pictures, movies, or commercials. Instead of noting words, researchers could note specific actions (e.g., kisses, hugs, groupings as a sign of attraction) and decide on specific actions to include or not include (e.g., handshakes) in the counts.

When researchers are analyzing text, computers can greatly facilitate the collection of manifest content. Most word-processing programs have a "Find" tool that researchers can use to quickly and easily count the frequency of usage of specific words or phrases Furthermore, if properly used, the "Thesaurus" function can aid in the compilation of the master list of words included. However, the use of computers does not preclude the researcher from at least doing a quick manual scan of the text for related words or phrases that may not be direct synonyms, but may still have a similar meaning.

However, manifest content does not take into account the various meanings of words or phrases. Suppose I included the word *bang* as one of the words in my coding of manifest content. Take this hypothetical recollection of a man who was a victim of husband abuse:

> I don't know, she was really skittery-like. Every little **bang** she heard would set her off, make her nervous, ya know? Those days, the kids and I just tiptoed around the house. The kids looked at me like "What's her problem? Why don't you do something?" I would give them one of those "You don't quite understand the situation" looks. I mean, how could I explain to them that the bruise on my cheek was from when she **banged** me with the frying pan in one of her rages? They don't understand that. They wouldn't understand how a man could be hit by a woman— after all, I'm taller and stronger. But I was raised that no matter what, "Boys don't hit girls!" Plus, afterwards, she'd be all sorry and stuff and the make-up lovin' would be great. I mean, after she'd act all sorry and stuff, we'd just **bang** all night long. I know she didn't mean to **bang** on me; she just gets frustrated some times.

Based on manifest content, there would be a count of 4 for the frequency that the word *bang* occurs. However, if you read the context of the references, only two actually refer to husband abuse. The first instance of the word *bang* refers to a loud noise. The third instance is a slang for sex. Therefore, there are only two instances where the word *bang* really refers to an act of abuse.

Latent content is the complement to manifest content and refers to coding the underlying meaning behind words. Instead of just counting the words used to indicate abuse, I could code latent content by reading a paragraph of text and making an overall assessment about that author's view of husband abuse based on the context in which he or she presents the information. When I spoke about coding the treatment of the issue of husband abuse as a serious problem in its own right, a problem but not one as serious as wife abuse, or as not a problem at all, I was essentially referring to latent content. I would not be able to make that decision simply by looking at individual words. I would have to read entire passages in order to classify a paragraph or page into one of my three categories. As you can probably tell, latent coding is somewhat subjective. Different people may interpret the context differently. One way to minimize this is to use more than one coder and then do statistical reliability tests to assess the degree of agreement. The higher the agreement, the higher the reliability. If agreement is low, reoperationalize concepts until the inter-coder reliability is within an acceptable range.

However, even with statistical tests, where manifest content is strong, latent content is weak, and vice versa. Manifest content is generally very reliable. Given a list of words I used, it's likely that an outside person will reach the same count as me. However, the validity of this form of coding is weak because, as I illustrated with the word *bang* I may not be measuring what I think I am. On the other hand, for latent coding, reliability is generally weak. You may read the same passage and think that the textbook author presents husband abuse as a problem, but not one that is as serious as wife abuse, whereas I may think that, in the same passage, the author does not even treat husband abuse as a problem at all and instead brushes it off. Hence, reliability in latent coding can be suspect. On the other hand, validity is generally high, since there is little confusion as to whether the words in a passage address husband abuse or not. I can read the entire passage and determine that. This is why, as I said, manifest and latent content are complements.

Therefore, it behooves researchers to combine both forms of coding whenever both can be theoretically related to the research topic. Billings, Halone, and Denham (2002) did this when they ascertained how much of the discourse involved commentary about athletic performance. They found that within the 2,367 spoken lines, a total of 1,118 accounts of athletic performance were identified. They note that the majority of the lines contained no descriptors accounting for athletic performance; however, 549 (23.2 percent) lines contained one descriptor, 177 (7.5 percent) lines contained two descriptors, 51 (2.1 percent) lines contained three, and 16 (0.7 percent) lines contained four descriptors accounting for athletic performance in a single broadcast commentary line. These are simple counts and are therefore examples of manifest coding. However, the classification of commentary into one of the 16 categories is an example of latent coding. The researchers had to read and interpret the meaning

What types of manifest and latent codes do you think would be appropriate for studying the content of political campaign speeches?

of the comments in order to classify them into one of the categories. To ensure reliability between coders, Billings and colleagues assessed inter-relater reliability with statistical comparisons. They report their level of success in the following excerpt:

> Descriptor codes collectively achieved an overall reliability of .79. Individual reliabilities for each descriptor code were (a) physicality and athleticism (.84), (b) intelligence and mental skill (.82), (c) hard work and effort (.79), (d) determination and motivation (.77), (e) speed (.83), (f) physical power (.72), (g) mental power (.70), (h) positive consonance (.80), (i) negative consonance (.77), (j) leadership (.81), (k) versatility (.79), (l) team orientation (.82), (m) personality (.79), (n) looks and appearance (.84), and (o) background (.82). (p. 305)

The coefficients presented all have generally high ratings (the lowest is 0.77), which illustrates general, but not complete, agreement. However, this was not initially the case. Billings and colleagues found that some of their sub-categories did *not* have sufficiently high inter-coder reliability:

> Due to inconsistent coding practices among the 4 coders, the categories for (a) physical power and (b) mental power were subsequently collapsed with (a) physicality and athleticism and (b) intelligence and mental skill, respectively, establishing new reliabilities of .85 for (a) physicality and athleticism and .83 for (b) intelligence and mental skill. Two members of the coding team subsequently continued to independently code the remaining lines of broadcast commentary (pp. 305–306)

Their collapse of some categories into new categories that had more acceptable levels of inter-coder reliability was an effective way to address this problem.

Record keeping

Although content analysis may have some characteristics of qualitative data analysis, most researchers do quantitative analysis, so a couple of key points need to be mentioned. First, this means that the end product of the coding must be numerical. For manifest content, this is straightforward; the researcher just counts the number of occurrences for a particular word, phrase, picture, or whatever. However, for latent content, this means that each meaning has to have a corresponding numerical code. For example, in my hypothetical study of how textbooks address husband abuse, if the author makes no mention of husband abuse at all or if the author does mention it but only in passing and does not treat it as a social problem, those excerpts may get a code of 0. Likewise, "treats as a social problem, but not one as serious as wife abuse" could be coded as 1 and "treats as a social problem in its own right" as 2.

Second, researchers need to make sure that their records distinguish between units of analysis and units of observation, if the two are different. If my units of analysis are the textbooks, but my units of observation are the paragraphs within the family violence chapters, I need to be clear about that. In some instances, I may be able to combine various units of observation to make conclusions about my units of analysis. For example, if I want to study rock artists (units of analysis), but I observe their songs (units of observation), and if they have more than one song I am observing, I may combine the information from all of their songs to make conclusions about that particular recording artist.

Third, if I was doing content analysis, I would also want to record the base number of observations. For example, if I am interested in evaluating war sentiment in popular songs, how many times the word *war* appears is not relevant if I cannot put it into context regarding the number of words in that song. A song that mentions *war* 15 times out of a total of 200 words may have a different degree of war sentiment than a song that mentions the word *war* 15 times out of a total of 100 words. In the first song, *war* accounts for 7.5 percent of all words in the song, whereas in the second example it accounts for 15 percent—twice as much.

Last, a code sheet should also include basic identifying information. What is the identification number assigned to each piece of work analyzed so it can easily matched to the results if there is a question? What is the identification number indicating who coded the content in case there is a disagreement? What other identifying information can be presented for each piece of information? These are all questions that a researcher should be able to answer simply by looking at the record, or code, sheet. Table 9.1 has a hypothetical record sheet that could correspond to the type of data that Pritchard gathered for his study on newspaper coverage and prosecutor behavior in murder cases.

Analysis

Since, ultimately, researchers frequently take a quantitative approach to content analysis, their findings are generally going to be numerical. This can be a simple description of percent differences, as Billings, Halone, and Denham (2002) did. For example, Table 9.2 is an excerpt of Table 2 from their research, which provides the evidence for their claims. As you can see, only 0.5 percent of the commentators' descriptions of men referred to male players' personalities, whereas 3.5 percent of the descriptions of female players referred to their personalities. Also, 61.1 percent of the commentators' remarks about male players were about those players' physical abilities/athleticism, but only 21.8 percent of their remarks about female players were the same. The ability to compare percents like this is a classic example of quantitative analysis. In fact, Billings, Halone, and Denham also did statistical tests for significant differences called *chi-square* tests (which I will discuss briefly in Chapter 12) and the table footnotes let the reader know the chi-square critical value, degrees of freedom, and statistical significance (probability of error) for those differences that were large enough to be statistically significant.

Pritchard (1986) did even more sophisticated statistical analyses to test his hypothesis. He did discriminate analysis to determine what was the strongest predictor regarding whether a prosecutor would take a case to trial or initiate a plea bargain. Table 9.3 shows results for Pritchard's discriminate analysis. It shows that, of the discriminant variables Pritchard measured, the length of the news story was the strongest predictor of whether a prosecutor tried to plea bargain or not. The other variables present, such as whether the suspect knew the victim and prior record, were control variables.

If you remember, in Chapter 4, I discussed topical rival causal factors—factors that may be related to the dependent variable and produce a change in it regardless of the presence of the independent variable. I also said that researchers can statistically "control" for these factors by including them in their analysis. This is what Pritchard did, and he found that even when considering issues such as prior record and whether the suspect knew the victim, the length of news story *still* had a statistically significant effect on whether the prosecutor plea bargained or not. In fact, he found that this variable, the information from which came from his content analysis, was a *stronger* predictor of whether a prosecutor plea

TABLE 9.1 Hypothetical Example of a Partial Record Sheet for Pritchard's Study of Newspapers

Newspaper	Issue	Morning, Evening, Sunday	Classification	Page Numbers	Homicide Victim/Alleged Perpetrator	Number of Paragraphs	Source	Coder
Sentinel	January 11, 1986	Morning	News story	1–2, 5	Smith/Carclione	20	Routine	Jones, Carson
Sentinel	January 13, 1986	Morning	Editorial	36	Smith/Carclione	2	Not applicable	Jones, Carson
Sentinel	February 3, 1986	Morning	News story	2–3, 7	Hamm/Higgens	14	Routine	Jones, Carson
Sentinel	February 4, 1986	Morning	News story	2	Hamm/Higgens	14	Routine	Schnell, Nguyen
Sentinel	February 5, 1986	Morning	Editorial	35	Hamm/Higgens	3	Not applicable	Schnell, Nguyen
Journal	January 11, 1986	Evening	News story	1	Smith/Carclione	16	Nonroutine	Rodriquez, Martin
Journal	January 12, 1986	Sunday	News story	2	Smith/Carclione	10	Routine	Rodriquez, Martin
Journal	February 3, 1986	Evening	News story	2–3, 7	Hamm/Higgens	14	Routine	Rodriquez, Martin
Journal	February 4, 1986	Evening	Commentary	10	Hamm/Higgens	6	Not applicable	Schnell, Nguyen

TABLE 9.2 Excerpt of Table 2 from Billings and Colleagues' Basketball Study

Table 2: Accounts of Athletic Performance by Gender of Athlete

Descriptor	Man	%	Woman	%	Total	%
Physicality/athleticism	526[a]	61.1	56[a]	21.8	582	52.1
Intelligence/mental skill	92	10.7	13	5.1	105	9.4
Hard work/effort	15	1.7	2	0.7	17	1.5
Determination/motivation	28	3.3	11	4.3	39	3.5
Speed	27	3.1	15	5.8	42	3.8
Positive consonance	13[b]	1.5	28[b]	10.9	41	3.7
Negative consonance	19	2.2	5	1.9	24	2.1
Leadership	20	2.3	8	3.1	28	2.5
Versatility	16	1.8	4	1.5	20	1.8
Team orientation	8	0.9	4	1.5	12	1.1
Personality	5[c]	0.5	9[c]	3.5	14	1.3
Looks/appearance	2[d]	0.2	22[d]	8.5	24	2.1
Background	49[e]	5.7	32[e]	12.5	81	7.2
Other	41	4.8	48	18.7	89	7.9
Total	861		257		1,118	

[a] $X^2(1) = 27.05$, $p < .001$. [b] $X^2(1) = 21.85$, $p < .001$. [c] $X^2(1) = 6.20$, $p < .02$. [d] $X^2(1) = 29.39$, $p < .001$. [e] $X^2(1) = 5.73$, $p < .03$.

Source: Andrew C. Billings, Kelby K. Halone, and Bryan E. Denham, " 'Man, That was a Pretty Shot': An Analysis of Gendered Broadcast Commentary Surrounding the 2000 Men's and Women's NCAA Final Four Baskeball Championships," *Mass Communication & Society, 5* (3) (2002): 309. Reprinted by permission.

TABLE 9.3 Results of Discriminant Analysis in Pritchard's Research

Table 1: Results of Discriminant Analysis, with Whether the Prosecution Negotiated as the Dependent Variable

Canonical correlation squared	.238
Improvement in ability to predict	53.3%
Relative contribution of significant discriminating variables:	
Average story length	34.8%
Suspect knew victim	26.9%
Prior record	19.5%
Initial charge	12.4%
Multiple charges	6.5%

Source: David Pritchard, "Homocide and Bargained Justice: The Agenda-Setting Effect of Crime News on Prosecutors," *The Public Opinion Quarterly, 50* (2) (Summer, 1986): 143–159. Reprinted by permission of Oxford University Press.

bargained than were the control variables. However, Pritchard also found that whether the news story was routine or not did not have a statistically significant effect on the prosecutor's decision. This is why that variable does not appear in the table.

So, as you can see, content analysis is the process of taking some type of text or picture, transforming it into a quantifiable measure (in many instances) that can address both quantitative and qualitative issues, and statistically analyzing any patterns. However, throughout the entire process, researchers do not directly contact individuals in order to measure their behavior, therefore it is a nonreactive, unobtrusive form of measurement.

■ Validity, Reliability, and Generalizability

As I mentioned previously, manifest and latent coding are complementary and address the issues of validity and reliability differently. Manifest content is very reliable because it involves a simple counting of the surface content, such as the occurrence of specific words. However, manifest coding does not consider the content of the words, as I illustrated in my example with the word *bang*. Because manifest coding does not account for the context, there are times when a mere recording of the word will not address the researcher's concept and therefore will not measure what the researcher thinks he or she is measuring. Consequently, manifest coding is weak on validity.

Latent coding is the opposite. Because latent coding addresses the underlying meaning of a text, it is much more likely to truly measure the concept of interest than is manifest coding. Therefore, latent coding is usually valid. However, because different coders may interpret the meaning of text in various ways, they may both agree that a text addresses husband abuse, for example, but they may disagree as to *how* it addresses that topic. One coder may think that it downplays the issue, and another coder may disagree. Therefore, latent coding is valid in that it is likely to correctly identify an issue (e.g., an instance of abuse as opposed to a loud noise), but it is less reliable than manifest coding because it is difficult to consistently identify themes.

Content analysis may involve the analysis of a large amount of written text; therefore, researchers may employ more than one coder to analyze the data. Frequently a researcher will develop a coding system that addresses manifest and latent content prior to actually beginning the research, and then the researcher will train coders about how to use the coding system. Researchers need to make sure that coders understand the research topic, the variables, and the coding system. If coders have questions about additional examples of manifest coding or how to interpret latent coding, during the training is the time to raise these issues so that the group members can reach a consensus for when they actually begin the study. Even so, if any new decisions need to be made during the course of the study, coders need to note these decisions so that they can be consistent. In order to test for reliability, researchers can give coders some texts that are the same and then check the consistency of the coding among the various coders for these same texts. Since two people are unlikely to agree *exactly*, the researcher can then use statistical tests to see if the degree of consistency among coders is within an acceptable range. Another possible way of assessing reliability is to have coders recode a text that they have previously coded at a later date without looking at their earlier codes. Again, the degree of agreement can be statistically tested, and if the agreement is within an acceptable range, then the researcher has confidence that the codes are reliable.

1. Choose a research topic.
2. Identify a population of pictures, photographs, documents, or other forms of communication that can be transcribed into written form.
3. Determine the units of analysis.
4. Decide whether to study the population of units or to select a sample of units.
   a. If selecting a sample of units, some form of probability sampling is preferred.
5. Coding
   a. Decide what characteristic of text content you will measure.
      (1) Frequency
      (2) Direction
      (3) Intensity
      (4) Space
   b. Decide what level of content you will code and record on a code sheet.
      (1) Manifest content
         (a) Create an exact list of words, phrases, actions, or characteristics you will count as an indicator of a concept.
         (b) As new words, phrases, actions or characteristics appear, decide whether to add those to your master list or not the first time you encounter them. For those added, directly add them to the list and now include that specific entry as you analyze the rest of your material. For those not added, keep track of them so if you resume coding at a different time (e.g., a week later), you are aware of the words you decided not to include and will know to ignore them the next time they appear.
      (2) Latent content
         (a) Read the passages you have selected as your final unit of analysis.
         (b) Code the underlying meaning of each, based on predecided characteristics (which should be documented in Step 5).
         (c) Use more than one coder and statistically test the similarity between their responses in order to boost confidence in reliability. If tests reveal low inter-coder reliability, reoperationalize codes until higher reliability is achieved.
6. Pretest with coders to identify any problems with operationalization of codes and/or coder training.
7. Record keeping
   a. Identifying information of unit of analysis and unit of observation analyzed
   b. Coder information
   c. Manifest codes (if applicable)
   d. Latent codes (if applicable)
8. Analysis

Figure 9.1 Steps for Doing Content Analysis

Content analysis can be designed in such a way that the findings can be generalized to a wider population. If the topic of content analysis is sufficiently specific, such as an analysis of how a local paper presents two candidates during an election year, a researcher may be able to study the entire population of elements within a specific span of time. On the other hand, some forms of text are extremely large in number and can more feasibly be studied with a probability sample. For example, let's pretend I was interested in studying the nightly news to see the proportion of negative (e.g., crime, war, and political conflict), neutral (e.g., general health pieces, economic pieces), or positive (e.g., hero stories, stories of remarkable accomplishment) stories. Even if I focused my study to one calendar year, across the major networks there are thousands of news stories I'd have to include in my analyses. In order to make this task more manageable, I may decide to do a stratified random sample from the main networks (based on some criteria I would have to establish that would define "main"), then randomly select a sample of days and include all of the news stories from the selected networks on these days in my analysis. By doing a probability sample, I do not necessarily need to study each individual day and each individual news story covered in a day across the span of a year, but I can still generalize my findings to what the major networks consider to be "news." Thus, my ability to generalize to a wider population is based on the same issues of how I draw my sample, as we discussed in Chapter 5.

Therefore, through a combination of using manifest and latent coding, a researcher can generally produce valid and reliable results, if that researcher uses some means of assessing reliability, such as recodes across time or tests of inter-coder reliability. Since content analysis may involve the analysis of mass amounts of data, probability sampling will allow me to study a small sample of that data and make generalizations to the wider population within a statistically established range.

■ Advantages and Disadvantages of Content Analysis

One of the clear advantages of content analysis is that it is relatively affordable both in terms of money and time. Since there is no need for stamps or mass mailings, the financial cost of content analysis can be reasonable. Furthermore, because a large research staff is unnecessary, a single college student can do content analysis even within the course of a semester. Other forms of research such as surveys, interviews, or field research may not be so feasible for a single college student to accomplish in a limited amount of time. Even the training required for content analysis, if a researcher is using coding assistants, is relatively financially cheaper and less time intensive than is training an individual on how to do interviews.

Another benefit of content analysis is that the data in their original form are continually present for validity and reliability checks. If any questions arise about the wording of a phrase or the inclusion of a word, researchers can go back to the original data and add to their analysis at will. This is not the case for other observational methods. For example, in an interview, it is difficult to contact respondents after the conclusion of the interview to ask them for clarification. If there is a question in content analysis, on the other hand, the researcher just has to go back to the text in question and reexamine it. The same principle makes it easier to correct mistakes in content analysis than in other forms of research. If a researcher makes a mistake in field research, for example, by antagonizing and alienating the people being studied, by misinterpreting information, or by forgetting to get some answers to key questions, correcting these mistakes may be impossible. However, if someone makes a mistake in content analysis, provided that person has kept an accurate code sheet that identifies each piece of data, then that person can go back to the data and correct the mistake relatively easily.

Because content analysis is unobtrusive, there is nothing that the "respondent" can forget to say or misunderstand. In fact, since content analysis is unobtrusive, the very nature of observing the data will not have any effect on that data. The book has already been written, the song already sung, the movie already aired, and the painting already painted. The involvement of an individual person is already over by the time the researcher examines what a person has done, therefore that person can no longer react to being studied.

A final advantage of content analysis is that it is relatively safe. In field research, a researcher may be working in a dangerous neighborhood or may be studying a potentially threatening group. In interviews, a researcher may have to travel to an unfamiliar or unsafe part of town. Both of these present some risk to the researcher. However, since content analysis is the analysis of social artifacts, this personal risk to the researcher is essentially absent.

Clearly, content analysis is not without disadvantages, however. For instance, content analysis is limited to recorded information. That information may be a picture, a movie, a transcribed song, or a transcribed speech, but, in all instances, it must be recorded. Unrecorded thoughts, attitudes, or the like cannot be studied with content analysis.

However, perhaps the largest disadvantage of content analysis is the risk of making an incorrect inference. Content analysis describes what is present in a text; it cannot, however, tell how the presence of specific themes affect individuals. For example, content analysis shows that the representation of racial minorities in prime-time television shows is usually limited to comic roles or roles that mimic negative stereotypes of minorities (Baptist, 1986; Hammer, 1992). However, content analysis *cannot* argue that the stereotypical television portrayal of minorities affects those minorities' view of themselves or their place in society. Nor can content analysis argue that this portrayal of minorities affects the behavior of either members of the minority group in question or members of other groups. Other forms of research need to relate the conclusions of content analysis to the effects of media messages on behavior. Using content analysis to argue that television shows present minorities in a negative manner, which, in turn, affects their self-concept and behavior is inaccurate. Only the beginning of that statement—that the media portrays minorities in a negative manner—can comfortably be made by content analysis.

Secondary Data Analysis and Agency Data

In previous chapters I have mentioned the General Social Survey, called the GSS for short. To refresh your memory, the GSS is a large national probability survey that began in 1972 and has been collected 24 times since. For the most recent surveys (since 1994), 3,000 people participated in interviews that lasted about 90 minutes. Clearly, this is quite an undertaking—one that is not really feasible for most individual researchers to do on their own. First, collecting this amount of information takes hundreds of hours; and, since the survey is done every other year, by the time you and a few assistants finished a round of interviewing, it would almost be time again to start the next wave of the survey.

Second, coding and entering the information for this amount of data would also require a huge number of hours, and therefore would not be feasible for most individual researchers, even if they do work with a small research team (when most individual researchers work with assistants, they comprise a small team at best). Even for an individual doing a smaller study, of say 500 people, it is not unusual for that person to devote several months or even a year to conceptualizing the data, writing the survey, pretesting the survey, selecting a sample, and then actually distributing the survey and entering the data.

However, thanks to computers, it is now possible for ordinary individual researchers to have access to massive amounts of data without having to go through the time and expense of collecting that data themselves. This type of data analysis is called **secondary data analysis** because, for most people, the researchers using the data are not the ones who collected that data. You may be wondering how a survey, which clearly involves some level of interaction with people, can be an unobtrusive method of research. A survey, designed by a researcher and used by that same researcher, is *not* a form of unobtrusive research. However, when a survey is collected by a government agency (for example, the U.S. Bureau of the Census) or by a "think tank" whose main job is to collect data (such as the National Opinion Research Council, which is responsible for the GSS) and used by someone *other* than those who collected the data, that "someone" using the previously collected data is a secondary researcher. The label of "secondary" is used because this person is not responsible for the collection of the data, but can nonetheless reassemble the data in its raw form to conduct analyses. Since this second person did not collect the data, then the researcher did not have any interaction with the respondents, and therefore he or she could not influence the respondents to answer questions one way or the other regarding *this particular* research question. Therefore, for *this researcher's purposes*, the data are unobtrusive because *this researcher* had no contact with the research respondents.

■ Topics Appropriate for Secondary Data Analysis

Because researchers doing secondary analysis are reorganizing data that may have been collected for one purpose to use for a different purpose, specifying appropriate topics is difficult. Any topic suitable for the primary data-collection method is fair game for the secondary data use also, provided that the relevant variables are present in the dataset. Secondary analysis is perhaps best suited to topics that have been studied by public or private organizations, such as the National Opinion Research Council, whose entire job is to systematically gather various types of information. These organizations gather information on a broad array of topics as a public service or to fuel policy decisions. Since the data these sources gather are broad, researchers usually have some flexibility in examining social issues in new ways, for they can conceivably consider how a wide array of variables interact to influence a specific behavior or attitude. Secondary data analysis is especially suited for topics that a researcher wants to study over a long span of time, because the core variables in these datasets are generally relatively stable and because these data agencies frequently gather the data over multiple time points.

My own research (Wolfer, 1998; Wolfer & Moen, 1996) about the effects of maternal employment on adolescent daughters' life transitions is an example of how these broad datasets can be used to study a variety of issues over a long period. I conducted this research using the Panel Study of Income Dynamics, a longitudinal study of over 8,000 families that began in 1968. At the conclusion of the 2003 data collection, the PSID had collected information about the economic and demographic experiences of more than 65,000 individuals spanning as much as 36 years of their lives. From 1968 to 1996, the PSID interviewed and reinterviewed individuals from families every year, whether or not they were living in the same dwelling or with the same people. The PSID has followed adults as they have grown older, and children have been observed as they have advanced through childhood and into adulthood, forming family units of their own.

Because the PSID is broad, it also contains some variables on the social and psychological experiences of these people. For my research, I was able to focus on women who gave birth to daughters between the years of 1968 and 1972. I was able to follow the yearly employment experiences of these mothers from the first year of their daughters' lives through the daughters' adolescence. This allowed me to see if there was any long-term relationship between maternal work characteristics and whether daughters left school, got married, entered employment, or had a child by their early twenties—an age considered to be relatively young by today's standards. In other words, I had complete employment information on the mothers for *every* year from 1968 to 1996 (the year I stopped using the data) as well as information about the daughters' own behaviors up to 1996. The social and psychological variables in the PSID are somewhat secondary to the economic and demographic variables; however, my research illustrates a way that variables can be reorganized to address different research topics. Because I never had contact with the people in the PSID sample and because I did not organize or collect these data on my own, from my perspective, this research is a form of secondary analysis because I am a person secondary to the original researchers and I am analyzing the data in a way specific to my own research question.

■ Where to Access Secondary Data Sources

Many sources of data are available to the average researcher. Some are free and some require various degrees of payment. Secondary data sources can be in the form of raw data, such as I discussed with the PSID, or they can be in the form of tabulated statistics that researchers can use, such as the *Statistical Abstracts of the United States*.

If you are interested in doing secondary data analysis of survey data, such as I presented with the General Social Survey and Panel Study of Income Dynamics, you may need to have a preconceived idea of what dataset to use or you may need to contact a reference librarian. Although you may be able to identify organizations responsible for broad collections of data with an Internet search, without some idea of the dataset ahead of time, you are likely to spend a lot of time using a "hit-or-miss" approach. A conversation with a reference librarian may speed the search or at least give you a direction in which to head. However, keep in mind that the quality of a researcher's analysis when using secondary data is only as good as the quality of that dataset in its primary form. Therefore, it is important to use data gathered by reputable sources and to examine the data-collection methods closely.

Another useful source to find secondary data in its raw form is the Inter-University Consortium for Political and Social Research (ICPSR), which is located at the University of Michigan. It is one of the major collections of social science data in the world and it houses over 17,000 datasets that researchers can access rather cheaply (especially when compared to the cost in time and money for collecting this type of data by oneself). Therefore, if a researcher wants to use data gathered by someone else, ICPSR is an excellent place to start the search.

If you do not want to use raw data and instead want to examine already tabulated data, the *Statistical Abstracts of the United States* may be a good place to start. The *Statistical Abstracts of the United States* has generally been published annually since 1878 and is available in almost all libraries and can even be easily accessed on-line. It contains statistical tables compiled by various U.S. government agencies. The 2003 version contains information on 27 different broad topics, including population, education, law enforcement, banking, and entertainment. Within the 27 different topics are a total of 1,279 different tables of statistical information. There are also statistical tables on foreign commerce and aid, Puerto Rico and outlaying areas, congressional district profiles, and comparative international statistics. These tables are very detailed and the type of information is very broad.

For example, I can learn that in 2001, there were 7,958 applications for firearms in the United States (*Statistical Abstracts of the United States, 2003*, Table 332). I can also learn that in the fourth quarter of 2003, 81.5% of arrivals at Chicago O'Hare airport were on time while 89.6% of arrivals at Denver International airport were on time (Statistical Abstract of the United States, 2003, Table 1,066). Figure 9.2 contains a very annotated list of what type of information is found in the *Statistical Abstracts of the United States*.

■ Using Secondary Data

When using secondary data, it is important for researchers to understand the dataset as if it was one that they created themselves. As I said earlier, the quality of secondary analysis is only as good as the quality of the data during its primary collection. Therefore,

Population projections	Information on individual income tax returns
Illegal immigration	Federal budget outlay for defense
U.S. population by gender, race, and age	Information on military reserve personnel
Information on teenager birthrates	Information on charity contributions
Death rates by race and sex	Labor force participation characteristics
The amount people paid for health care via insurance, physician costs	Productivity and related measures
Prescription drugs and nursing homes	Labor union membership
Nursing home characteristics and cost	Disposable personal income per capita
School enrollment by race and age	Children and families in poverty
Characteristics of public charter schools	Cost of living index
Characteristics of higher education	Racial minority-owned and women-owned businesses
Crime rates	Patents by state
Delinquency rates	Characteristics of U.S. multinational companies
Prison inmates by sex and race	Space vehicle systems—sales and backlogs
Information on oil spills in U.S. waters	Farming information
Threatened and endangered wildlife	Oil, lumber, and mineral availability—usage and other characteristics
Women holding state public offices	Utility use and cost
Expenditures of state and local governments	Consumer purchase of sporting goods by characteristics of consumers
Salary differences in state and local government by various characteristics	Arts and entertainment in public schools
Department of Homeland Security budget	

Figure 9.2 Selected Topics from the Statistical Abstracts of the United States

researchers must be aware of how the sample was obtained, what concepts are addressed within the data, and how those concepts are measured, as indicated by the wording of the question. This information is important in helping the researchers determine whether that method of research design and collection is suitable to his or her research needs.

One of the issues someone using secondary data is likely to encounter is a mismatch between how he or she would ideally define a concept and how the researchers who created the primary dataset defined a concept. If a researcher follows the traditional form of research that I've outlined earlier in the book, the researcher may spend a lot of time defining complex variables to his or her liking only to learn that there is no dataset available that uses the same or similar definitions. If a secondary researcher operationalizes concepts in a different manner than those who first designed the research instrument (e.g., the survey), then the survey the researcher hopes to use will not have questions that directly correspond to this secondary researcher's definitions. In other words, a secondary researcher will have spent a lot of time defining concepts only to realize that there are no measures available in the preexisting data for those definitions he or she created. Therefore, in practice, people who do secondary research frequently *begin* to operationalize their concepts but have flexible definitions until they find a dataset that employs questions that are *close* to what the researchers would have written if they were creating the questions from scratch themselves.

This flexibility of definition allows different researchers to use the same variables but for different research purposes. For example, let's look at three studies each using the National Longitudinal Survey of Youth (NLSY) as secondary data. First is an excerpt from an article by Kodrzycki (2001, **AN 4436679**), who uses the National Longitudinal Survey of Youth to study the migration patterns of people after they graduate college. Kodrzycki was interested in examining the geographical mobility of young adults in relation to the demands of the labor market. Here, Kodrzycki describes the National Longitudinal Survey of Youth and the variables she will use from it:

> To track migration patterns, this study uses the National Longitudinal Survey of Youth (NLSY), a project of the U.S. Bureau of Labor Statistics. The NLSY is based on a nationally representative sample of about 6,000 persons who were 14 to 22 years old in 1979. . . . These youths and young adults were reinterviewed once a year until 1994 and once every other year thereafter. The final year of data available for this study is 1996, when the interviewees were 31 to 39 years old.
>
> Given that the NLSY is a general-purpose survey intended to be representative of an entire cohort, the experiences of sample members varied widely. For example, some members of the sample did not complete even high school, while others completed not only high school but various levels of higher education. Some individuals in the NLSY remained in the same state throughout their lives, while others showed considerable geographic mobility.
>
> The NLSY pertains to fewer individuals than some other data sets containing migration information, so the data from the sample may reflect actual national figures with a greater margin of error. However, in contrast to other surveys, the NLSY has the advantage of tracking residential location over a long time interval. . . . The NLSY indicates the state in which respondents were residing at birth, at age 14, and in each year of the survey. (p. 14)

In this excerpt, Kodrzycki identifies her variables as well as the pros and cons of using the NLSY over other data sources in order to study migration.

In the second study, Antecol and Bedard (2002, **AN 7482454**) use the same dataset to examine the earnings of African American, Latina, and White women. Like Kodrzycki, Antecol and Bedard use the respondents who were ages 14 to 22 in 1979, and they are interested in an aspect of these people's employment history—but their specific employment focus is different. Antecol and Bedard are interested in the earning differences of a specific subset of this sample—African American, Latina, and White women. Instead of just comparing rates of employment found in the U.S. Census, for example, Antecol and Bedard justify their use of the NLSY as such:

> We use the National Longitudinal Survey of Youth (NLSY), which contains longitudinal data from 1979 to 1998 for a sample of men and women aged 14–22 in 1979. Several features of these data are crucial for our purposes. First, the NLSY contains information that allows us to construct actual (rather than potential) work experience. This is particularly important when studying women. Second, these data include detailed information regarding marital and childbirth patterns. Finally, the NLSY allows us to identify non-immigrants and to separate individuals into racial/ethnic origin groups. . . . The NLSY contains 2,350 non-immigrant Mexican, black, and white women who were employed. (p. 123)

Antecol and Bedard (2002) also use the existing variables to create new variables. For example:

> Given our interest in the number of children present in 1993–94, we construct all child variables using the number of children ever born. The lone exception is children born during 1993. Since the number of children ever born was not reported in 1993, we use retrospective day, month, and year of birth reports from 1994 to 1998 and the month and day of the interview date in 1993 to calculate the number of children born in 1993. We then add the number of children born in 1993 to the number of children reported in 1992.
>
> We use two measures of work experience: Mincer experience and actual experience. Mincer experience is calculated as age minus years of education minus six. Actual experience is years of employment for individuals greater than 18 years of age reported between 1976 and 1994 and is based on weeks worked since the last NLSY interview. We convert the weekly experience into annual experience by dividing total weekly experience by 52. (p. 124)

Hence, Antecol and Bedard create *new* child variables based on information about the number of children that is present in the dataset and they create *new* employment variables: the Mincer experience variable and the actual years of experience.

On the other hand, Ven and Cullen (2004) use the same dataset to study whether maternal employment affects crime among young people, along with some other NLSY data. Here is a description of what NLSY data they use and how:

> In 1986, the NLSY began supplementing the youth data by giving a variety of developmental assessments that measure cognitive ability, motor and social development, behavior problems, and home environment to the children born to NLSY mothers. By 1994, 980 of the children born to NLSY mothers were

identified to report on their home environment, family relations, and school and occupational experiences in addition to reporting on their involvement in crime over the past year. Known as the Young Adults of the NLSY, these 14- to 23-year-old children are the offspring of female respondents originally interviewed in 1979. Because the mothers have been interviewed annually since 1979, data on maternal work and welfare experiences are available for the 15 years leading up to 1994. To investigate the relationship between maternal work and youth crime, we conduct our analysis on a sample of the 702 adolescents and young adults who were between the ages of 15 and 19 in 1994 and who completed the self report survey on criminal involvement. To study the cumulative effects of maternal employment on crime, we follow this sample from 1994 back to 1986 when study children were between the ages of 7 and 11 years old. We trace work experiences back to 1986 because it was the first year that NLSY researchers collected extensive data on the original sample of mothers and their children. The first time the behavior and temperament of study children were assessed, for example, was 1986. Furthermore, because the sample mothers were between the ages of 14 and 21 in 1979, a large fraction of them were not employed prior to 1986 because of their youth. Fewer than 50% of sample mothers, in fact, were regularly employed prior to 1983. And the number of working mothers in the sample does not approximate the national average until 1985. Therefore, we selected 1986 as our starting point. (p. 279)

. . . To measure serious criminal involvement, we created an index by summing 11 highly correlated items that measure a variety of criminal acts involving theft and property crimes (e.g., stealing from a store, vehicle theft, breaking and entering for the purpose of theft), vandalism, and violent crime (e.g., assault, fighting, the threat of violence). Respondents were asked to report on their involvement in these crimes over the last 12 months (i.e., the 12 months preceding the 1994 survey). If respondents reported that they had no involvement in any given act, that variable received a score of 0. If the respondent had been involved in that activity over the past year, the variable received a score of 1; thus, the index range is 0 to 11 acts. (p. 281)

Ven and Cullen use the NLSY for information about the members of the NLSY sample who are *mothers* of children who are ages 15 to 19 by 1994. For the children, Ven and Cullen used information the NLSY began to add to the original survey that assessed the cognitive and social development of children. The NLSY provides a unique opportunity, as Ven and Cullen state, to follow the mothers' employment experiences (the independent variable) for *each* year of the children's lives. The majority of datasets do not include information for individual years across a long span of time. With this type of information, Ven and Cullen can create a comprehensive picture of the employment experiences of these mothers during these children's *entire* childhoods. Furthermore, like Antecol and Bedard (2002), Ven and Cullen also created their own unique variables based on a compilation of variables that are present in the NLSY.

There are a number of points that these three studies illustrate. First, they are a small illustration of the wide range of topics one can study with a large, broad dataset. The topics here range from the geographical mobility of college graduates, to how earnings vary by race, to the longitudinal effects of maternal employment on children's deviant behavior. Therefore, if you are wondering how useful a dataset like this can be for studying a variety of topics, the answer is that they are potentially very useful—provided that the dataset covers a broad range of topics. Face it, if some funding agency is going to invest the money and time to study people every year or every other year for an extensive period of time, it makes sense to design the measurement tool to cover a broad array of topics so that researchers with a variety of interests can use it.

Second, although researchers are limited to the variables included in the dataset, they still have some degree of freedom to manipulate those variables into *new* variables. They can summarize yearly variables into counts (for example, a researcher can combine monthly employment information into a new variable that addresses yearly employment information) or they can combine variables to create indexes or scales. Creating new variables is one way to expand the usefulness of a dataset.

Third, researchers can select subsamples of the original samples to analyze. In each of these three studies, the researchers restrict who will be included in *their* individual analyses. Kodrzycki (2001) does not imply any real restrictions in who she includes in her study. Antecol and Bedard (2002) limit their analysis to 2,350 nonimmigrant Mexican, Black, and White women who were employed. And Ven and Cullen (2004) limit their analysis to 702 adolescents and young adults ages 15 to 19 in 1994 who completed the self-report survey on criminal involvement. Three different samples: One is broad, one contains employed women of specific races, and another contains children, all drawn from the same dataset. So secondary analysis of primary data, like survey data, can be an affordable means of studying a large variety of topics in a multitude of different ways.

■ Considerations When Using Secondary Data

When using or selecting a secondary data source, researchers have to pay special attention to their units of analysis and the nature of the existing variables in the dataset. Units of analysis can be a special concern when a researcher wants to study individual behavior, but the data are only available in a more aggregate form, such as groups. For example, if a researcher sampled drug abuse clinics from all 50 states to study their characteristics, the unit of analysis is a group (the clinics). In this dataset, there may be variables about the percentage of people in each clinic with specific drug addictions (for example, heroin or cocaine), the percentage of people who have family members also addicted to drugs, and the percentage of people who have a criminal history.

Let's suppose I am interested in studying how drug addiction affects people's criminal activity, and let's assume that the variables in this dataset are valid for this topic. Even if this is the case, this dataset is not appropriate for my study. Why? Because the dataset contains information about *the clinics* and I am interested in information about *individual* drug addicts. Incorrectly linking these two statistics is an example of the **ecological fallacy** that occurs when researchers use aggregate data (such as counts within a clinic) to make conclusions about individual behavior (whether a person hooked on drugs has committed a crime). The risk of committing the ecological fallacy is somewhat less when the secondary data are from a survey that was collected by other researchers, as opposed to agency data, which I will discuss next, because these surveys frequently are collected using individuals as the units of analysis. However, as I just illustrated, secondary analysis of primary data is not without this risk; therefore, the units of analysis for the data source remain an important consideration.

Furthermore, a researcher needs to pay particular attention to how the primary researchers define the attributes of their variables to see if a particular dataset is appropriate for the secondary researcher's needs. For example, if I want to study the effects of divorce on teenagers' likelihood of becoming parents and the dataset measures family status as "Never married," "Married," "Divorced/Separated," "Widowed," and "Other," that dataset may not be appropriate for my needs because the information about who is divorced is lumped with the information on who is separated. I may have very real theoretical reasons for believing that having parents who are divorced has different effects on young people's behavior than does having parents who are separated. However, since I have no means of identifying which respondents have parents who are separated and which have parents who are divorced, this dataset is not appropriate for me.

To aid in your decision as to whether to use a specific secondary dataset, ask yourself the following questions adapted from Riedel (2000):

1. Why did the agency collect the data?
2. What qualifications, such as years of experience and training, did those responsible for gathering the data have?
3. What year was the information collected?
4. Is there an available codebook that details the questions asked, the answer choice format (open- or closed-ended questions), answer choice possibilities (for closed-answer questions), coding practices (for open-ended questions), and code values (e.g., a. Never Married = 1, b. Married = 2, etc.)?
5. What method of data collection was used? Surveys? Interviews? Is the method of collection available to those who are considering using the data? If not, the researcher cannot really know important information such as question order and what the contingency questions were. Without this information, a researcher should be hesitant to use this dataset.
6. Can the researcher identify different respondents? Are there identification numbers that link respondents to their individual answers?
7. In what form are the data available? Internet download? Mainframe? CD-ROM? This is important to know because if a researcher does not have access to a mainframe computer, but that is the only format for the dataset, then the researcher needs to choose a different dataset.
8. Is there documentation that describes the research process, such as the treatment of missing data, the response rate, and the sampling methods, available to the researcher? Without this information, the researcher cannot evaluate the quality of the primary data and therefore should be hesitant to use that specific data source.

Answering these questions helps researchers to fully understand the dataset they are using as if it was their own primary data. This understanding helps researchers identify the strengths and weaknesses particular to specific datasets. These strengths and weaknesses may influence not only the decision to use a specific dataset but also the nature of statistical analyses and conclusions a researcher can make.

■ Validity, Reliability, and Generalizability

Secondary data analysis allows researchers to use data that may be sophisticated in terms of sample size, longitudinal design, and breadth of variables without the expense and challenge of collecting that type of data on one's own. This may allow researchers to better establish content validity if the dataset has multiple measures for concepts. If the dataset is a large probability survey, then the researcher is more likely to be able to gather data that are generalizable to a broader population. Furthermore, many of these datasets have been pretested and/or have been collected at more than one time, which allows researchers to check the reliability of findings across time. Therefore, on the surface, secondary datasets may appear to have all three components of methodological quality.

However, validity may be an issue, even with very well designed secondary datasets, because the variables may not address a researcher's particular concepts exactly how the researcher would like them to. For example, if I want to measure a person's economic well-being, based on my literature review and interests, I may define economic well-being to be a calculated measure of a ratio between a person's income and the cost of his or her needs, which I may further define as the cost of items such as housing, food, clothing, and miscellaneous expenses necessary for daily living. However, a particular dataset may have great measures for my independent and control variables, but only limited means of measuring my dependent variable, as I've defined it. For example, the dataset may have information pertaining only to a respondent's direct income. There may be no information about the respondent's estimated costs for the issues I just mentioned. Therefore, if I want to use this dataset, I am going to have to reconceptualize "economic well-being" to reflect only income, as opposed to a ratio of income to needs.

However, as I've stated before, and I will continue to state because the point is an especially important one, analysis with secondary data is only as valid, reliable, and generalizable as the original dataset. Not all datasets have multiple measures of concepts, or are longitudinal in design, or involve probability samples. Datasets without these characteristics are not necessarily poor, but any methodological limitations present in the original dataset will be present in the secondary data analysis as well. Therefore, researchers have to be aware of both the strengths and weaknesses of a dataset in order to determine whether those data suit the validity, reliability, and generalizability needs of their particular study.

■ Advantages and Disadvantages

The advantages and disadvantages of using secondary data have already been raised to some degree in the previous sections, so I will only restate them briefly here. First, the clear advantage of using secondary data is that it frequently is an affordable means of obtaining data, especially of obtaining data that address broad topics and use large probability samples. Second, depending on who did the survey, a researcher may benefit from the work of others who are more skilled in gathering data than the researcher himself or herself may be.

However, as with all forms of observation, analysis of secondary data has some disadvantages as well. The main disadvantage is a potential limitation on validity. If the secondary researcher did not operationalize a concept the same way the primary researchers did, then the secondary researcher has to decide whether he or she is willing to make a trade-off between the ability to use a specific dataset and the ability to use any specific hypotheses or operational definitions. Data quality is also a concern, even if the data are gathered by a government agency. Data can be distorted by changes in measurement across time points, by incorrect answers given by respondents, or by inadequate coverage of specific subpopulations (Rives & Serow, 1988). These concerns are present even if researchers design and institute their own survey. The point I am making is that just because a dataset is from a government agency or is conducted on a large scale by a team of researchers does not necessarily mean that a particular dataset is without fault.

Agency Data

Agency data are sometimes treated as a form of secondary data analysis because, in this case, some official agency, such as a government agency, has collected the information, which it then makes available to others to analyze. However, when I discussed secondary data, I generally referred to secondary analysis of primary data, meaning that a secondary researcher studied raw data gathered by another researcher. In agency data, the researcher frequently does not have access to raw data and, instead, studies the statistics, or aggregate data, that another agency has already compiled. Data from the U.S. Bureau of the Census and the Uniform Crime Reports are good examples of agency data.

■ Appropriate Topics for Analysis with Agency Data

Analysis of agency data is a useful methodological approach when researchers want information on the aggregate level that is too expensive and time consuming to gather on one's own. For example, Barnett, Mencken, and Carson (2002, **AN 7709390**) used the Uniform Crime Reports to study violent and property crime rates in nonmetropolitan, or rural, areas:

> This research explores violent and property crime rates in nonmetropolitan counties. It is argued that crime rates are lower in these counties because of higher levels of social integration. We test the hypothesis that predictors of crime from social disorganization theory exert different effects on violent and property crimes at different levels of population change in nonmetropolitan counties. We . . . predict the 1989–1991 average violent and property crime rates for these counties, taken from the Uniform Crime Reports (UCR). . . . In the analysis we . . . estimate both violent and property crime rates in nonmetropolitan counties in the 48 contiguous states. The dependent variables are FBI violent crime and property crime rates, averaged for each county in the contiguous 48 states between 1989 and 1991. We use the mean of the years 1989–1991 to control for variations in reporting from year to year. Although criticisms of the UCR data are well documented . . . the data are considered for the most part to be representative of crime reported to law enforcement agencies in a particular area. We calculated the dependent variables in this study using the county-level files available from the National Archive of Criminal Justice Data at the Inter-University Consortium for Political and Social Research. We calculated the violent crime rate (murder and nonnegligent manslaughter, forcible rape, robbery, and aggravated assault) and the property crime rate (burglary, larceny-theft, motor vehicle theft) using the populations of counties reporting six months or more of crime data. Missing data occur when the crime data reported cover more than six months but less than the full year. Table 1 shows the number of nonmetropolitan counties for which the property and violent crime rates required imputation.

Obviously, is it too costly and time intensive for Barnett and colleagues to have contacted each individual county in the nation on their own and to record that county's property and crime rate. It's much easier for the authors to use the data gathered by the government and reported in the Uniform Crime Reports. Since Barnett, Mencken, and Carson are studying counties, they are looking at aggregate information. They are not concerned with the behaviors of the individual criminals in these counties. They are only interested in comparing the statistics that tally the total numbers of reported property and violent crime across the different counties. Therefore, agency data are a perfect match for Barnett, Mencken, and Carson's research needs.

Let's look at another example. Have you ever wondered what the deadliest job in America is? Hershbein (2003, **AN 12350740**) did, so he used data from the Bureau of Labor Statistics to study workplace fatalities. He found:

> The U.S. Bureau of Labor Statistics reported 5,524 fatalities in civilian workplaces in 2002. . . . By number of deaths, commercial truck driving is the deadliest occupation. 808 truck drivers (out of 3.2 million total) were killed on the job last year—80 percent of them on the road. Many other common occupations also experience a large number of deaths: for example, farm workers, construction laborers, police and detectives, and electricians.
>
> Which occupation had the highest fatality rate? The fatality rate, calculated as deaths per 100,000 people, accounts for the fact that some occupations are much more common than others. For example, 162 store owners and managers were killed on the job in 2002, making it the fifth most deadly occupation as measured by number of deaths. But since nearly 5 million people work as sales supervisors, only 3.4 store supervisors per 100,000 died on the job—a rate better than the national average.
>
> Fatality rates are preferable when trying to compare the risk of death across occupations. By this measure, truck driving and construction are still deadly, but they no longer top the list. Instead, timber cutters lead the index, with a fatality rate more than 30 times the national average. Last year about one out of every 750 lumberjacks died on the job, a staggering figure. Many of the occupations that people think of as hazardous have lower rates. Construction workers are eleventh on the list (28 deaths per 100,000 workers), firefighters are thirteenth (20 per 100,000), and police are eighteenth (12 per 100,000). But the jobs with the highest fatality rates account for a very small fraction of workers nationwide. . . .
>
> On the flip side, what is the safest occupation? It is difficult to say, but a major contender is: economist. None has died on the job since the government started keeping records.

This example illustrates that federal statistics can be used for interesting research questions involving relatively simple statistics, such as the calculation of a rate of incidence. Of course, as Barnett, Mencken, and Carson (2002) illustrated, the analysis can also be more sophisticated and involve the comparison of rates for different groups as well. The key is that all descriptions or comparisons need to be of *groups*.

■ Locating Agency Data for Analysis

Agency data are usually gathered from national or international governments. However, as you can imagine, the number of possibilities for identifying agency data are multitude. For example, in the United States alone, researchers can use data from the Bureau of Justice Statistics, the Bureau of Labor Statistics, the National Center for Health Statistics, the Bureau of Economic Analysis, the Environmental Protection Agency, the National Center for Education Statistics, and the National Agricultural Statistics Service—just to name a few.

In the past, because the possibilities were so numerous, it was difficult to conduct agency data without the help of a reference librarian who could get a researcher started in the right direction. For example, a researcher using agency data needs to ask, Which agencies collect the type of data I need? Which ones have information available? How can I obtain that information? These questions, and others, are ones that reference librarians are well equipped to answer, making them a useful resource today.

However, with the advent of the Internet, many federal statistics are easily accessible on-line and require only a brief examination to determine whether they are appropriate for one's research needs. For example, for federal agency data in the United States, an on-line resource called Fed Stats (www.fedstats.gov/) has access to statistics from over 100 federal agencies alone. One can search for federal agency statistics by topic, by geographical location, by agency, and by other published statistical sources, such as *The Statistical Abstracts of the United States*. Most of these data can be accessed on-line and most of it is free. Similar federal information is available for Australia, Canada, Denmark, France, Germany, Ireland, Russia, South Africa, and Britain (under "United Kingdom"). In fact, the U.S. Bureau of Labor Statistics has a webpage of Internet links to international statistical agencies accessible on the Internet (www.bls.gov/bls/other.htm) for 59 other countries and some international organizations.

In fact, contrary to in the past when people needed a reference librarian because they may not have had enough information as to where to start looking for agency data, now researchers may need a reference librarian to help them navigate the enormous amount of information readily available at their fingertips!

■ Considerations When Using Agency Data

The main consideration for agency data analysis, as in the secondary analysis of primary data, is awareness of the units of analysis used in the agency data. For example, if a researcher wants to study whether family structure affects birthrates among teenage women, a table in a government document, such as one by the U.S. Bureau of the Census, may have information about both the divorce rate and the teenage birthrate for a specific area, say Pennsylvania. However, comparing these figures does not address the research question about the effects of family structure on teenage births. Why? Because the research question is on the individual level: Is a teenager whose parents are divorced more likely to have a child than a teenager whose parents are married? To answer this question, researchers need to match the marital status of *that teen's* parents to *that teen's* own status as a parent (being one or not). The marriage and divorce rates, however, are aggregate pieces of data that summarize a group (the people in Pennsylvania) and cannot be linked to an individual teen who has had a child. Similarly, the birthrate for teen mothers is also an aggregate measure that is a count for the entire state of Pennsylvania and cannot be reduced to the individual level of teens.

■ Validity, Reliability, and Generalizability

The issues for validity, reliability, and generalizability for analysis of agency data are the same as that for the secondary analysis of primary data. Concerns over study and measurement validity may be present if the agency collecting the data does not use the same definition for a concept that a researcher ideally would. Furthermore, there may be concerns that the validity, reliability, and generalizability of agency data may all be less than ideal because (1) specific subpopulations may be under- or overrepresented relative to the population, (2) some people may not have responded truthfully to the research questions asked, and (3) definitions or questions may change across time and/or be incorrectly weighted relative to the population the sample is trying to estimate.

In the earlier excerpt from Barnett, Mencken, and Carson's (2002) research, they note that some researchers criticize the information available in the Uniform Crime Report. The authors do not specifically state these limitations; instead, they direct the reader to another article that does—a practice that you now know is completely appropriate. However, one of the criticisms of the Uniform Crime Reports is the changing definitions of crime, which make longitudinal comparisons suspect.

For example, in 1993, marital rape, which occurs when a husband forces his wife to have sex with him, became a crime in all 50 states. This change broadened the definition of rape, meaning that now another action is legally defined as rape, and may have been related to an observed increase in reported incidents of rape after the law. In other words, after this definition of rape was broadened, it is impossible to determine how much of any increase in the subsequent number of reported rapes was due to an increased incidence of rape itself, to increased reporting of rape, or to the new definition of rape that now included behaviors previously overlooked (marital rape) as rape.

Other problems with the Uniform Crime Reports are the fact that they document only crimes for which people have been arrested and only by the policing agencies that actually submit their crime rates to the government. (Even though all agencies are supposed to submit this information, in reality many of them do not.) In other words, not all police agencies consistently provide the government with this crime information, and, even when they do, the information reflects only crimes reported to the police. It does not necessarily reflect the *incidence* of crime, since many crimes (based on, for example, comparisons to the National Crime Victimization Survey, in which people report their victimization experiences) go unreported to police.

The bottom line with agency data is the same as I've mentioned before. Researchers need to know the who, what, where, when, and how of data collection in order to determine whether the agency data are both appropriate for their research needs and valid and reliable enough to effectively produce generalizable data.

■ Advantages and Disadvantages

As Barnett, Mencken, and Carson's (2002) research indicates, agency data are an efficient means of collecting information on a large number of groups, possibly even over a span of time. Furthermore, since agency data are produced and available from many different countries, depending on the consistency of measurement, international comparisons of aggregate information is relatively feasible—at least more so than if an individual tried to embark on collecting this information on his or her own.

However, differences in measurement across time or across agencies can make comparisons difficult, even impossible, depending on the degree of disagreement. Furthermore, researchers frequently have to alter their original hypotheses or definitions of concepts in order to fit the information available. If too much alteration is necessary, a particular agency dataset may no longer be useful to an individual researcher.

Ethical Considerations for Unobtrusive Research

Because all of the forms of unobtrusive research mentioned here—content analysis, secondary analysis of primary data, and analysis of agency data—do not directly involve interaction between the researcher and the respondents, ethical issues are not as relevant as they are with other forms of observation, such as surveys and experiments. Content analysis is the study of social artifacts, so people per se are not really involved in the research at all. Agency data frequently involve the tabulation of statistics from smaller agencies, like police precincts or hospitals. Again, the people who lead these counts are frequently not directly interacting with the researcher.

Even the secondary analysis of primary data is unobtrusive from the perspective of the *secondary* researcher. This may seem somewhat contradictory to you—after all, how can survey data, which presumably had to be completed by individuals, who therefore have some contact with the research instrument, be unobtrusive? The answer is that it is *not* unobtrusive from the perspective of the primary researcher who is gathering the data. Therefore, from the perspective of the researchers who conduct the General Social Survey, the GSS data are not unobtrusive. However, if I use the GSS data that these other researchers have collected, I have not had any contact with the respondents and the respondents have not had any direct contact with the survey as it relates to *my* research issues. Therefore, from *my* perspective, it is an unobtrusive measure, since my personality, skills, and biases had no effect on the nature of the data I will be using.

Even with saying all of this, the primary ethical concern with unobtrusive research is the issue of confidentiality. Secondary researchers have to extend the primary researchers' guarantee of confidentiality if it was given (e.g., if the primary researcher can match responses to a person's identity, but promises to not do this, so must the secondary researcher). Issues of anonymity are not an issue, because if the primary researcher could not match responses to respondents, the secondary researcher is even less likely to be able to do so, so if anonymity was present in the primary research, it is easy to preserve in the secondary research.

Ethically, researchers cannot overstate the implications of their research because, perhaps even more so than with survey data or experiments, research such as agency research frequently is a product of the political climate at the time the data were gathered. There may be political reasons why data were gathered only about a particular topic or about how a measure was defined. For example, due to limited social and economic resources as well as social and political stereotypes about who are "logical" victims, agency data may document instances of wife abuse but ignore the issue of husband abuse. Or, as I illustrated with the example of marital rape, as new behaviors become defined as social issues, early definitions may be broadened or restricted in response to political and social pressure. Therefore, unobtrusive research methods frequently do not require the same degree of ethical considerations as other, more interactive, means of gathering data.

Evaluating Written Research: Content Analysis and Agency Data

I discussed three forms of unobtrusive research in this chapter: content analysis, secondary analysis of primary data, and analysis of agency records. Research that uses secondary analysis of primary data is only as good as the original dataset. Therefore, to evaluate written research using this method of observation, researchers must apply the Evaluating Written Research guidelines for the particular sampling technique and method of observation of the original, primary dataset. For example, if I am evaluating a research article that uses the General Social Survey (GSS), to assess the methodology of this study, I need to understand how the primary researchers obtained their GSS sample and the details of the GSS survey. Because I already discussed issues to consider when evaluating samples in Chapter 5 and issues for evaluating surveys in Chapter 7, I would just use those guidelines to evaluate the research in my particular (hypothetical) article. The same would apply for any other secondary analysis of primary data. The reader needs to use the Evaluating Written Research guidelines from other chapters where relevant. Since research involving secondary analysis of primary data can feasibly involve *any* sampling design and *any* method of observation, there is no utility for providing guidelines here. They are simply too varied and are repeated elsewhere.

Therefore, this section will focus on evaluating research that involves content analysis and, separately and to a lesser extent, evaluating research involving agency data.

Content Analysis

One of the general evaluation principles is not only whether the data were collected accurately but also whether there is enough information available for someone else to replicate the study. Therefore, the evaluation questions involving content analysis revolve around whether the researchers makes their sample, units of analysis, definitions, and manifest and latent coding techniques clear.

1. *What is the researcher's research purpose or hypothesis? Is content analysis an appropriate method of observation?*

   As you know, there are many possible ways people can do content analysis. However, the key unifying theme is that the material has to be visually observed, such as with a painting, a transcribed speech, or a newspaper article. This point simply involves making sure that the researcher's units of analysis are appropriate for content analysis.

2. *What are the researcher's units of analysis? What are the units of observation (if they are different from the units of analysis)?*

   What are the researchers studying? Are they studying books? Pictures? Newspaper articles? What are their units of observation? If researchers are studying books, are they looking at the books in their entirety (possible, but unlikely) or are they studying select pages (which would be their unit of observation)? To answer this question, the researchers first have to identify clearly their units of analysis and their units of observation (if they are different). Also, the researchers have to appropriately discuss the data and findings with these units in mind.

3. *Is the researcher studying a population or a sample of these units? If the researcher is studying a sample, is it a probability sample? If so, was it correctly drawn? If the researcher is not studying a population or a probability sample, is he or she appropriately cautious about the nature of any conclusions?*

   This is really an issue of sampling. The skills in evaluating samples that you learned in Chapter 5 apply here, so I won't repeat them. The point is to remember that even though content analysis does not involve a selection of individuals per se, it does involve a selection of *something*. Therefore, it is important for researchers to explain how material was selected (e.g., a random sample of songs in the top 10 over a period of two months) if they did not study an entire population (e.g., all the songs by a particular musical group).

4. Does the researcher identify the characteristics and level of content being analyzed? Does the researcher explain how material is coded, especially for issues of latent content?

What is the researcher studying? Is the researcher looking at the frequency of occurrence or the amount of space information occupies? Quantifiable observations such as these are examples of manifest content. Is the researcher examining the direction (e.g., positive or negative) or meaning behind the content? If so, this is a form of latent content. Does the researcher do both types of content coding, or just one?

It is unrealistic to expect researchers who have limited space available in a journal to list all of the words or each special measurement that they counted under manifest content. Likewise, it is also unrealistic to expect researchers to include a code sheet documenting all their individual codes for issues of latent content. However, it *is* feasible to expect researchers to broadly describe what kinds of words or phrases they are counting for manifest content. It is also feasible to expect researchers to describe their general coding themes for latent content. Without even a general description, readers are ill-equipped to evaluate content analysis findings; therefore, it is better to error on the side of caution and be suspect of the quality of the research printed if this information is missing.

5. Did the researcher do any type of pretest with other coders to test for reliability? Were there any tests for validity?

Since the decision about what types of words, phrases, expressions, or other visual content to count in manifest status is subjective, even if the actual counting of the decided criteria is not, having another coder help decide or interpret whether a word or some other unit is appropriate to include in the analysis is important for validity. A second coder helping to identify what units should be counted for manifest content helps to better ensure that a fuller range of meanings is included in the analysis, which also boosts content validity. Also, having a second coder work on the latent coding helps improve reliability because the degree of agreement between the two coders can be statistically assessed, and where there is significant *disagreement*, the reason for the disagreement can be discussed until a mutual agreement is reached. Once the two (or more) coders agree, then reliability is more likely.

6. Are the conclusions consistent with the units of analysis?

Remember, units of analysis and units of observation are not necessarily the same. If a researcher is studying particular word phrases (units of analysis) within selected chapters of a book (units of observation), then the units of analysis and units of observation are different. It is important for the researchers to make sure their conclusions are consistent with the distinctions between these two that they make.

7. Are the results clearly presented and the conclusions appropriate?

This section is self-explanatory. It does not matter how well-organized and executed a study is if the reader cannot make sense of the results that the researcher presents. Therefore, the first part of this point addresses whether the written results are easily understandable. The second point serves as a double-check to the researcher. The temptation may be to overstate the importance of one's findings, but researchers need to make sure that their conclusions do not move beyond the capabilities of their data. For example, if the researcher sampled from a specific population, then the conclusions can be only about that specific population, not a more general one.

To summarize, some guidelines for evaluating content analysis are:

1. What is the researcher's research purpose or hypothesis? Is content analysis an appropriate method of observation?
2. What are the researcher's units of analysis? What are the units of observation (if they are different from the units of analysis)?
3. Is the researcher studying a population or a sample of these units? If the researcher is studying a sample, is it a probability sample? If so, was it correctly drawn? If the researcher is not studying a population or a probability sample, is he or she appropriately cautious about the nature of any conclusions?
4. Does the researcher identify the characteristics and level of content being analyzed? Does the researcher explain how material is coded, especially for issues of latent content?
5. Did the researcher do any type of pretest with other coders to test for reliability? Were there any tests for validity?
6. Are the conclusions consistent with the units of analysis?
7. Are the results clearly presented and the conclusions appropriate?
8. Generally, is the method of observation done appropriately?

The articles in Box 9.1 illustrate how to apply these guidelines.

◼ Agency Data

Evaluating research using agency data primarily involves two issues. First, readers assess whether they think a researcher was truly familiar with the dataset the researcher decided to use. Within this assessment, the reader is then deciding whether the researcher is also using the agency data appropriately. The second issue is whether the agency collected the data with the best techniques possible, given real-world constraints. Beyond these two issues, like secondary data, the evaluation of agency data may involve a revisit to one of the earlier chapters in this book, depending on how the agency collected that data initially. Let's look at some guidelines in more detail:

1. *What is the researcher's research question or hypothesis? Are agency data an appropriate method of observation to study this stated question or hypothesis?*

If I am interested in comparing the property crime rates of states based on the region of the country, the Uniform Crime Reports may be an appropriate source of agency data because the UCR organizes reported crime rates by region of the country, state, rural/urban location, and even city (at least cities that have at least 10,000 residents). However, if I want to find information about property crime rates in different parts *within* the same city, the Uniform Crime Reports may not be a viable data source because the data are not reported in units that are that small. A researcher needs to explain, at least briefly, to the reader *why* he or she believed a particular dataset was appropriate for the selected topic.

| BOX 9.1 | Evaluation of Written Research: Content Analysis |

Researchers can do content analysis on any form of communication that can be transcribed or any object that is a social artifact, but content analysis is frequently done to study some aspect of the media. The two research examples here are no exception. The first article examines whether women's advertisements predominantly have information-based content or emotional content, depending on whether the magazine is aimed at women in Hong Kong or women in Australia.

The second article looks at how newspapers in Dallas, Texas, present news related to local gang activity. Let's take a look at excerpts of both of these articles in more detail in order to evaluate key points of their methodology. As always, you can find the articles in their entirety on Research Navigator.

Article 1

You are probably well versed in the global nature of our economy. Advertisers who are trying to capture a global market are increasingly banking on the assumption that cultural distinctions are weakening. Therefore, they are trying to save money by developing uniform brand images for their advertising campaigns.

However, Man So (2004, **AN 13929818**) argues that this cultural hedogamy overlooks differences in cultural expressions and perceptions of information that would damage advertising effectiveness. For example, Man So argues that women in Hong Kong are culturally more likely to pick up on advertising cues that involve sensitivity and nonverbal signals, what she calls *process-oriented advertisements*.

On the other hand, she argues that Australian women are more likely to respond to *outcome-oriented advertisements*, which have targeted messages. She argues that this difference in interpretation of advertisements stems from cultural differences in communication patterns between people in Hong Kong and in Australia.

To study Man So's hypothesis, she examined the print advertisements from two Hong Kong and two Australian women's magazines. Here is a description of her methodology:

The magazines sampled are in the top 5 best sellers in their countries, they have similar readership profiles so that they are comparable with each other, and they are locally published, reflecting the advertising styles and cultures of their places. . . . The magazines were chosen from the time period October 1998 through December 1998.

. . . For each magazine, judges were asked to evaluate all advertisements in the magazines, including advertisements on the cover, the content pages and also the ones being loosely attached. This study considered at least quarter page advertisements or larger, such as full-page or double-paged advertisements, because of their dominant use in women's magazines. . . .

. . . Two independent raters, MBA students with trained advertising background, were responsible to evaluate the two sets (Hong Kong and Australia) of sample advertisements by using an evaluation form. This form was set to evaluate advertisements based on their (1) presentation styles, (2) information content, and (3) level of emotional appeal. The two raters coded all the observations in the study using the criteria in Table 1 and Table 2. . . . A pilot test on 20 advertisements was conducted to check the clarity and appropriateness of the rating criteria. . . . Since the two raters might have different opinion towards the same advertisement, whenever disagreement arose, that particular advertisement was discussed and examined in depth to determine the cause of discrepancy until consensus was reached. . . . [The] average interjudge agreement was greater than 93% for both emotional content (92%) and informational content (93%).

Table 1 [excerpt] Criteria for Classification as Informative or Non-Informative

1. Price
   - What does the product cost? What is its value-retention capability?
   - What is the need-satisfaction capability/dollars?

BOX 9.1   **Evaluation of Written Research: Content Analysis, continued**

2. Quality
   - What are the product characteristics that distinguish it from competing product based on an objective evaluation of workmanship, engineering, durability, excellence of materials, structural superiority, superiority of personnel, attention to detail or special services?
3. Performance
   - What does the product do and how well does it do? What it is designed to do in comparison to alternative purchases?

Table 2 [excerpt] Definition of Moods for Emotional Appeal

1. Happy/Pleasant/Delicious
   - Feeling or showing pleasure, contentment, impressed, humor and/or warmth
   - Feeling or showing highly enjoyable, including taste and/or smell
   - Pleasing in mind, feelings or senses
2. Sexy
   - Feeling or showing sexually attractive, stimulating or aroused by all means, including text, posture and/or dressing
3. Sensational/Mysterious
   - Feeling or showing dazzling, wonderful, elegant, personal, touching and/or romance
   - Feeling or showing secrecy, hidden, obscurity, inexplicable, amazing and/or puzzling

Source: Stella Lai Man So, "A Comparative Content Analysis of Women's Magazine Advertisements from Hong Kong and Australia on Advertising Expressions," *Journal of Current Issues & Research in Advertising, 26* (1) (Spring 2004): 47. (**AN 13929818**)

Man So then compared the proportion of print advertisements that had information content and the proportion that had emotional content. The Table 5 excerpt addresses the proportion of print advertisements in the Hong Kong and Australian magazines that had information content.

Table 5: Proportion of Information Cues in Print Advertisements in Women's Magazines in Hong Kong and Australia

Number of Cues per Ad	Australia (n = 640)	Hong Kong (n = 585)
At least 1	99.3%	100%
At least 2	90.6%	96.4%
At least 3	70.6%	82.2%
At least 4	42.0%	51.8%
At least 5	16.7%	24.0%
At least 6	6.8%	7.4%
At least 7	1.5%	2.4%
At least 8	0.1%	0.4%

$x^2 = 25.16$, $df = 8$, $p < 0.01$; $F = 16.01$, $df = 1964$, $p < 0.01$

As Table 5 shows, Man So's hypothesis was not supported. The proportion of advertisements regarding information content were not statistically significantly different for the Australian women's magazines compared to the Hong Kong women's magazines. There was also no difference in the proportion of emotion content advertisements (findings not shown but available on Research Navigator).

Critical Thinking Questions

1. What is the researcher's research purpose or hypothesis? Is content analysis an appropriate method of observation?

2. What are the researcher's units of analysis? What are the units of observation (if they are different than the units of analysis)?

3. Is the researcher studying a population or a sample of these units? If the researcher is studying a sample, is it a probability sample? If so, was it correctly drawn? If the researcher is not studying a population or a probability sample, is he or she appropriately cautious about the nature of any conclusions?

4. Does the researcher identify the characteristics and level of content being analyzed? Does the researcher explain how material is coded, especially for issues of latent content?

5. Did the researcher do any type of pretest with other coders to test for reliability? Were there any tests for validity?

6. Are the conclusions consistent with the units of analysis?

7. Are the results clearly presented and the conclusions appropriate?

8. Generally, is the method of observation done appropriately?

Critical Thinking Discussion

1. As I stated in the narrative, Man So was studying advertising tactics, here the cultural messages given in magazines targeted to Australian and Hong Kong women. Since she is interested in advertising messages, and since that can be visually observed, content analysis is an appropriate method of observation.

2. Man So's units of analysis and units of observation are the same. In both cases, it is the print advertisement in its entirety.

3. Man So is studying a sample of magazines. She does *not* do a probability sample because she does not provide any information as to how she *randomly* selected the magazines. However, she does establish (and cite the supporting information) that the magazines are all in the top five of their readership and she claims that they share similar characteristics; she just does not mention how she selected the two magazines from the list of five for each country. Therefore, it appears that she selected the magazines based on her professional evaluation of criteria that she felt was important.

The lack of probability sampling, in and of itself, is not a weakness, although probability sampling is generally a more desirable sampling technique, especially in this instance, since we don't know *why* Man So selected these particular magazines from each country. Since Man So did a purposive sample (if you remember, a form of nonprobability sampling), then she cannot generalize her findings to print advertisements, but instead must limit her discussion to print advertisements in two of the top five magazines published in each country.

4. Man So describes the characteristics of the content that she is analyzing in two tables that appear in the full article. One table describes the readership of the five main magazines in each country, and the other table presents information regarding the percent distribution of the different types of advertisements in the magazines. However, this information is not presented in this excerpt.

Based on the material in this excerpt, Man So's analysis is primarily an analysis of latent content, or the message behind advertisements. In Tables 1 and 2, for which there are excerpts, Man So defines what types of depictions she considers to be information content and emotion content. For example, price, quality, and performance are three of the issues that Man So considers to provide information content.

If the advertisement contains information about what a product does relative to other similar products, Man So considers that to be an example of performance information. Her coding criteria seem straightforward and clearly expressed. Furthermore, it appears that she had a code sheet that would facilitate any coders in following her coding definitions (although that code sheet is not included in the publication, and its omission is standard, therefore, not a weakness).

5. Even though, in the previous question, I said that Man So's coding seemed clear, that does not mean that the codes themselves are easily applied to the actual advertisements. It also does not mean that you and I might agree about how to interpret a facial expression for a code of emotional content.

BOX 9.1   **Evaluation of Written Research: Content Analysis, continued**

Man So rightly recognizes this as well and, therefore, uses two coders and tests their agreement with a pilot study.

She conducts statistical tests for reliability (which produce results indicating high reliability) and she notes that whenever there is a disagreement about an article, the researchers discuss the article until an agreement is reached, which boosts validity.

Also, Man So borrows her coding practice from other researchers, which she cites (citations in full article, not in excerpt), which further aids in establishing the reliability and validity of her research *if* the methods described by these other researchers were appropriate. Remember, researchers can avoid lengthy summaries of what they borrow from other researchers simply by citing where that information can be found. This is a common, and proper, practice. Therefore, all of these tactics are very appropriate and very well done in this article.

6. As Table 5 illustrates, Man So's analysis is based on the percent of cues in each individual advertisement (any individual advertisement may have more than one cue in it). This is completely in line with her units of analysis, which are, in fact, the advertisements.

7. The results are quantitative and are clearly presented in a table that compares the percent of advertisements that had different numbers of cues. For example, 90.6 percent of the advertisements in the Australian women's magazines had at least two information cues, and 96.4 percent of the advertisements in the Hong Kong women's magazines had the same proportion of information cues.

Based on an entire reading of the table, the conclusion that there were no statistically significant differences between the proportion of information cues in the advertisements of these women's magazines is accurate. Plus, Man So writes her results in a way that implies that she is only comparing these four magazines, which is appropriate, given her somewhat limited method of sampling.

8. Although the sampling technique is somewhat limited, overall, Man So's method of content analysis seems to be appropriate.

Article 2

We read the newspapers or listen to the news to hear about world events. People tend to think of the news media as an unbiased reporting system aimed at informing the general public about local, state, national, and international events. However, does *how* the media present this information affect *our* view of a situation?

For example, we know that although the elderly (those age 65 and over) have some of the lowest crime victimization rates, they tend to be the age group that is the most fearful of becoming a victim of crime. Some of this fear may stem from a perceived vulnerability that is associated with the aging process, but some researchers argue that this fear also comes from the nature of the news. The nightly news frequently has stories of crime, elderly people tend to watch a lot of television, therefore they interpret crime rates, and by analogy their own risk of victimization, as high (Wolfer, 2001).

Does a similar process work with the depiction of gangs in the media? In other words, do we read much more about gang problems as opposed to solutions to those problems, and, as a result, see gang activity as particularly troublesome and difficult to address? Thompson, Young, and Burns (2000, **AN 3679037**) were interested in some of these questions. These researchers studied 4,445 newspaper articles from the *Dallas Morning News* between 1991 and 1996 to study the images that newspapers portray of gangs and the social responses to them. Here is an excerpt of their methodology and findings:

> We selected all articles that included the words *gang* or *gangs* from the years 1991 through 1996. A content analysis of the articles was performed with the intention of identifying major discourse themes. . . . We analyzed the data through a detailed reading of each article. Initial coding categories were derived by comparing

BOX 9.1   **Evaluation of Written Research: Content Analysis, continued**

each article with all preceding articles. As coding progressed and no new categories emerged, emphasis shifted to a comparison of each article with previously derived categories. Through this procedure, we identified major themes and used them to code articles for all years. As expected, some articles included multiple themes and were more difficult to categorize. In such cases, we listed and kept track of the co themes, but each article was eventually classified according to the theme that appeared most prominently, by virtue of its position within the article, the number of lines devoted to it, and/or its mention in the headline. We participated in the data coding. We discussed ambiguous cases and reached a consensus before the final coding of such cases.

. . . Through content analysis, we identified eight major themes. . . . The first theme, gang crime, which constituted approximately 19 percent of all articles, refers to articles that focused on the criminal activities of gangs. . . . [The] articles we analyzed tended to emphasize serious high-profile crimes such as shootings, stabbings, or robberies.

"It was a gang-related shooting," he said. "It was a holdover from an argument they had several weeks ago. The guy just pulls a gun out of his pocket and kills him." ("Sixteen-year-old Ft. Worth Boy" 1993: 38A)

. . . Articles presenting the themes gang busting, gang resisting, and gang accounts shared the characteristic of focusing on community responses to gangs. As shown in Table 2, when combined, these community response articles actually outnumbered gang crime articles over the 6-year period (30 percent vs. 19 percent).

. . . Far from galvanizing public opinion, however, such talk often takes a divisive turn. For example, . . . [o]ne topic on which such discourse centers is the social control of youth. As numerous gang account articles have shown, the specter of gang crime is a prominent tool used by adults, such as school officials, in their efforts to exert control over various groups of young people.

Table 1: Typology of Newspaper Articles Dealing with Gangs [partial]

Type	Description
Gang crime	Reports of all criminal gang and gang-related activity
Gang busting	Articles about gang arrests, trials, convictions, and sentences; also includes articles on gang-busting efforts of the police and governmental agencies
Gang accounts	References to gangs and gang activities in order to justify or oppose the creation or suspension of rules/norms not directly or exclusively aimed at gangs or gang activity
Gang resisting	Reports of efforts of and activities sponsored by police, schools, civic organizations, and parents designed to provide kids with alternatives to gangs and efforts to discourage gang activity

Table 2: Gang Article Types, 1991–1996 (N = 4,445) [partial]

Gang Article Type	Number of Articles	
Crime	830	18.7%
Busting	538	12.1%
Accounts	223	5.0%
Resisting	578	13.0%

Source: Carol Y. Thompson, Robert L. Young, and Ronald Burns, "Representing Gangs in the News: Media Constructions of Criminal Gangs," *Sociological Spectrum, 20* (4) (October–December 2000): 409. Copyright 2000. Reproduced by permission of Taylor & Francis Group, LLC, www.taylorandfrancis.com. DOI: 10.1080/02732170050122620. (**AN 3679037**)

Critical Thinking Questions

Please see those stated for Article 1.

Critical Thinking Discussion

1. The researchers are interested in the depiction of gangs in newspaper stories. Newspapers are a classic forum for content analysis, and analyzing how newspaper articles treat issues of gang behavior is very appropriate.

2. The unit of analysis and observation both appear to be the articles themselves.

3. It depends on how you look at it. The researchers are studying the population of articles that appear in the *Dallas Morning News* between 1991 and 1996. In other words, they are studying *all* of the articles that contain the word *gang* or *gangs* that appear in this newspaper between 1991 and 1996.

   However, clearly they are studying only a *sample* of editions of the *Dallas Morning News*. Presumably the *Dallas Morning News* has been in circulation before 1991 and after 1996. Therefore, the best way to summarize the researchers' technique is to say that they take a sample of newspaper editions by focusing on those between 1991 and 1996, but that they study the population of articles within those newspapers.

4. The researchers do not describe the characteristics of the newspapers in this excerpt or in the full text. They also do not describe the characteristics of the articles, because, to some degree, that is the purpose of their research and more appropriate in a discussion of results.

   However, they do provide some guidelines for how they coded the gang material in the articles. In Table 1, the researchers provide information as to what type of information they coded into each of the eight themes (four of which are presented in the excerpt) that they found after a preliminary reading of the articles.

The material in Table 1 is an example of latent coding. However, indirectly, the researchers use manifest coding as well. Counting all of the articles with the word *gang* or *gangs* is a form of manifest coding.

5. The authors note that they all participated in the coding and discussed disagreements; however, we have little information as to how they proceeded with the coding. Were there code sheets that each person did independently and then used to statistically compare ratings, like Man So did? Were all articles coded by each researcher, for a total of three coders providing information that had to be verified and agreed on? Or did each coder participate by dividing the 4,445 articles between them so they all coded articles, but no articles were coded by more than one person unless an individual was unsure about what coding to use (and then the article was discussed)? This is unclear and, in my opinion, a potentially important omission because now we have no concrete measures of validity or reliability between coders or in the information itself.

   Two people may interpret an article in two different ways, but if they did not both read the article, we do not know if that would have happened, therefore we do not know if a coding is valid or reliable. Furthermore, the researchers state that there were some articles with mixed themes and that they used some type of criteria based on the theme's position within the article and the number of words to convey it, but again, without any more information, we cannot assess whether we agree with their method.

6. Yes. The units of analysis are the articles and the conclusions are about the number of articles that exhibit a certain theme.

7. Yes. The conclusions are quantitative comparisons of the percent representation of each theme in the articles. This is consistent with the units of analysis and is easy to understand.

BOX 9.1   **Evaluation of Written Research: Content Analysis, continued**

8. I have some concerns that we have no information on the real reliability and validity of the coding of the latent content, which is the focus of the data-gathering strategy. However, all else looks fine. Therefore, I would pay attention to these results, but with caution.

If other similar articles find results that are not very different from these, I would be more confident about the information in this particular study. However, if the findings of this study differ noticeably from the findings of other similar studies, I would look at all of the studies and pay the most attention to those that have the strongest methodological design. I am not sure whether this particular study would be one of those.

---

2. *Are the researcher's units of analysis consistent with the units of analysis for the agency data?*

The Uniform Crime Reports report crime rates for groups—states, cities, regions, for example. However, if I am interested in studying whether men are more likely to commit murder than women, because they are socialized to be more physically aggressive, then the Uniform Crime Reports is not appropriate. Why? Because in order to assess motivation for crime, my units of analysis have to be the same as those present in the agency data. The Uniform Crime Reports deals with group data, whereas my unit of analysis for the research question I just posed is the individual (individual motivation for crime). Research using agency data is particularly vulnerable to the ecological fallacy because agency statistics are usually presented in the aggregate (or group), and the temptation to make individual conclusions from those data is very strong. As an informed reader, one has to make sure that the researcher does not commit this mistake.

3. *What is the quality of agency data collected? What are its strengths? What are its weaknesses? How do those weaknesses affect interpretation of the data?*

As I mentioned, researchers frequently use the Uniform Crime Reports to study crime in our nation. However, definitions of crime may vary by state, and the data are gathered by individual agencies submitting their reports. Clearly, due to administrative restrictions in time and personnel, not all law enforcement agencies are going to submit crime statistics to the Federal Bureau of Investigation. Other times, computer problems or changes in record management systems may make reporting impossible. Therefore, even the FBI recognizes that the data that comprise the Uniform Crime Reports is likely to be incomplete. To address the first issue of differences in crime definitions, the FBI sends a handbook to each agency that explains how the FBI would like them to define crimes for reporting purposes in an attempt to have some uniformity (hence the name *Uniform* Crime Reports) in national statistics. Again, even with a handbook, the accuracy of any individual agency's report is based on the reporting person's level of understanding of the handbook and that person's attention to the detail of the differences between his or her definitions and the FBI's preferred definitions. The FBI recognizes that most agencies probably do their best in terms of reporting, but the possibility of error is undeniable.

Furthermore, the Uniform Crime Reports reflect only *reported* crime. However, other data (most notably the Crime Victimization Survey compiled by the U.S. Department of Justice) suggest that the majority of crimes committed do not even get reported. Therefore, there clearly is another omission here.

So, there are a lot of weaknesses in the Uniform Crime Reports. However, considering that over 17,000 agencies contribute data, even with these limitations, the Uniform Crime Reports can be a very informative tool in understanding crime in our nation—that is, so long as the researcher recognizes the methodological limitations I just described in any written report so that the readers can make their own conclusions.

4. If the study is longitudinal, is it clear to the reader that any definitions of concepts or techniques for measurement have been consistent within the time span studied?

Laws change legal definitions, new politicians change public policy characteristics, and standards of operations can change over time. Any change that can affect the way a concept is defined and measured is a potential threat to causal validity known as instrumentation, which I discussed in Chapter 3. For example, if someone decided to study the characteristics of the people on welfare over the past 20 years, this person would have a hard time doing so. Why? Because in 1996, President Bill Clinton ended the traditional welfare policy known as Aid to Families with Dependent Children (AFDC) which, among other features, had no limits on how long one could accept government assistance or welfare. In its place, he enacted Temporary Assistance for Needy Families (TANF), which *does* restrict welfare receipt to two years at a spell and five years as a lifetime maximum. From the year 2000 on, reports of the percent of the population on welfare (based on agency data of welfare recipients) has suggested that the percentage of the population on welfare has gone down. However, does this mean that fewer people are in economic distress and need welfare (the implication is that our economy is better) or that some people have now reached their lifetime limit and no longer qualify for welfare even if they need it (the implication is that our economy has not necessarily improved, just that welfare has gone down due to a change in eligibility definition)? This question is almost impossible to answer; in fact, it would make such a longitudinal comparison essentially meaningless. Readers of research need to be cautious of changes in definition.

To summarize, the main points to consider when analyzing agency data are:

1. What is the researcher's research question or hypothesis? Are agency data an appropriate method of observation to study this stated question or hypothesis?
2. Are the researcher's units of analysis consistent with the units of analysis for the agency data?
3. What is the quality of agency data collected? What are its strengths? What are its weaknesses? How do those weaknesses affect interpretation of the data?
4. If the study is longitudinal, is it clear to the reader that any definitions of concepts or techniques for measurement have been consistent within the time span studied?
5. Overall, is the report well researched and/or well written?

| BOX 9.2 | Evaluation of Written Research: Agency Data |

When researchers and other people read reports based on agency data, the reports can be analysis oriented, like the example in the chapter with the Uniform Crime Reports, or they can be short blurbs that disseminate the results of an agency study. However, even in the latter case, or sometimes *especially* in the latter case, when people read statistics that are compiled by a government agency, they assume that those statistics are accurately gathered and accurately interpreted *just because* the reporting agency is associated with the government, which in all likelihood would have the resources to conduct a methodologically sound study. However, this assumption can overlook the key fact that first, no research is perfect; and, second, even if the data that are collected are good, that does not mean that the person reporting or using the data is doing so accurately.

Below is an excerpt from an article that uses data from the National Center for Education Statistics to examine the effectiveness of financial aid systems in encouraging people to attend college—what is otherwise known as *secondary education.*

> The National Center for Education Statistics recently published "College Access and Affordability," which examined the extent to which financial aid systems promote access to postsecondary education by equalizing income differences. It was found that sophomores in high school are twice as likely to be advised to go to college as their counterparts in 1980. In fact, immediately after high school, 65% continued their education in higher education institutions. Graduates from lower income families are less likely to enroll in college than those from higher income families. Those whose parents had less than a high school education were less likely to enroll than those whose parents had a bachelor's degree. However, if low-income graduates take the steps necessary for admission, they are as likely as middle-income graduates to enroll in a four-year institution. Unfortunately, the price of a college education has increased faster than family income. Families cope with these rising costs by using savings, income, borrowing, and work. At least 79% of undergraduates work. While some work experience may improve employment prospects after graduation, full-time work appears to have some negative consequences such as reducing the choice of classes and limiting their class schedule and the number of courses taken. To increase a student's chance of completing a degree, students should work no more than 15 hours per week.

Source: "Access to Postsecondary Education," *Gifted Child Today Magazine, 22* (4) (July/August 1999): 8.

Critical Thinking Questions

1. What is the researcher's research question or hypothesis? Are agency data an appropriate method of observation to study this stated question or hypothesis?

2. Are the researcher's units of analysis consistent with the units of analysis for the agency data?

3. What is the quality of agency data collected? What are its strengths? What are its weaknesses? How do those weaknesses affect interpretation of the data?

4. If the study is longitudinal, is it clear to the reader that any definitions of concepts or techniques for measurement have been consistent within the time span studied?

5. Overall, is this study well done or well reported?

Critical Thinking Discussion

1. The researcher's research purpose is somewhat unclear. The writer implies in the beginning of the excerpt that he will discuss the "extent to which financial aid systems promote access to postsecondary education by equalizing income differences." The title of the article suggests that

BOX 9.2   Evaluation of Written Research: Agency Data, continued

the topic is just about access to postsecondary schooling.

To answer whether the agency data are appropriate for either of these topics, one needs to look at how that agency data were collected. This means that a reader should know about how the data for the National Center for Education Statistics were gathered. Probably the easiest way to do this is to go to this agency's website at http://nces.ed.gov/ and look up the report from which the data were selected.

The report is entitled "College Access and Affordability." You can find this by using the National Center for Education's Statistics search function on their website. This report is available in PDF format and when you open it, you find that *this* report comes from a variety of different data sources, such as the U.S. Bureau of the Census and various other reports from the National Center for Education Statistics. This makes the evaluation harder because technically one needs to look at the sources of *those* data to see whether the data apply.

Admittedly, this sounds daunting, and many people will not do it, including other researchers. However, not doing so runs the risk of misinterpreted statistics, much like the fabled and inaccurate 50 percent divorce rate that I discussed earlier in the book. When agencies or researchers use data from a variety of different sources as data in different reports, the risk for errors in interpretation heightened.

But to get back to the original question as to whether the agency data are appropriate for this research topic, that's difficult to answer. What is now taken as "agency data" were gathered from a variety of different surveys. On the surface, the data from the variety of sources cited within the report "College Access and Affordability" seem appropriate, and they seem to address the issue in the title of the article—namely, access to secondary education. But remember, we are not clear if that is the *main* research question because the author is not clear.

If financial aid systems, as implied early in the article, is a goal, you may notice that the arti-

cle doesn't really discuss any financial aid issues concretely. The article discusses the financial condition of students and the effects this has on entering and performing in school, but there is nothing about *aid,* such as scholarships or student loans (at least not any concrete information). Therefore, from the writer's actions (not necessarily the research content itself), the purpose is somewhat unclear and *may not* match with the information in the article all that well, although it does discuss access to higher education, as the title implies.

2. The researcher's units of analysis are the experiences of the students, hence individuals. Most of the surveys and census information is also about individuals, so the units of analysis seem appropriate.

3. This question is impossible to answer unless one looks up *each* of the studies that produce the specific information in the article. This is possible and, in a perfect world, should be done. But, as I stated, in reality most people will not do so. They will simply accept the data as high quality because they was gathered by a government agency. If the data were indeed gathered by a *federal* agency, this assumption is probably safe, since the federal government has a lot of resources to make sure their data are the highest quality possible.

However, if the agency data are from a local or private agency, this assumption is more problematic, as these agencies may not have the necessary resources to make sure the data are highest quality. State agencies are likely to produce quality data like federal agencies, but they are a grey area because they may be more prone to "farm out" their data collection to smaller research units than the federal government may do. Since all the data here were collected by federal agencies, and ones with good research reputations at that, even though there is no such thing as perfect data, I will make the assumption that the quality of these data are the best that it *can be.*

BOX 9.2 **Evaluation of Written Research: Agency Data, continued**

4. The information presented here is not longitudinal.

5. Because people may just be reporting on agency data here, as opposed to using data to answer specific research questions, the overall evaluation is one of research *or* reporting. In this circumstance, it is difficult to answer because the research or article purpose is unclear, and this lack of clarity in itself is a problem.

If the purpose of the article is to provide general reports on *access* to secondary education, then the article is well done and, aside from the vague purpose, well written. If the purpose is to look at *aid* to secondary education (which is the main purpose of the report, which the data are drawn from and which is stated in the beginning of the article), then, overall, this report is *not* well written because that purpose is not addressed even though the agency data used are likely to be quality data.

Key Terms

Ecological fallacy (403)
Latent content (387)
Manifest content (386)

Nonreactive research (381)
Physical trace analysis (381)

Reactive research (381)
Secondary data analysis (397)

Review Questions and Exercises

1. *If popular culture is a reflection of the interests of today's youth, according to songs in the top 10 countdown, what issues do today's young people find important? Select a random sample of 30 songs that appeared in a top 10 weekly musical list over the past year. Conduct a content analysis to determine what themes are popularly expressed in these songs and which themes are the most prevalent (e.g., order them by frequency).*

2. *Using agency data, track the murder or robbery rate for your home state over the past 20 years. What do you find? What are some explanations? What are some potential limitations that you encountered?*

3. *Evaluate the following published research for its methodology:*

   a. McCullick, Bryan, Belcher, Don, Hardin, Brent, and Hardin, Marie. (2003, March). *Butches, Bullies and Buffoons: Images of Physi-*cal Education Teachers in the Movies. Sport, Education & Society, 8 (1), 3. 14 pp. (AN 9428442)

   b. Higgins, Daryl J. (2004, July). *The importance of degree versus type of maltreatment: A cluster analysis of child abuse types. Journal of Psychology, 136 (4), 303. 22 pp. (AN 14702958)*

   c. Kline, Kimberly Nicole, and Mattson, Marifran. (2000). *Breast self-examination pamphlets: A content analysis grounded in fear appeal research. Health Communication, 12 (1), 1. 1 p. (AN 3344066)*

   d. Riebschleger, Joanne. (2004, Summer). *Good days and bad days: The experiences of children of a parent with a psychiatric disability. Psychiatric Rehabilitation Journal, 28 (1), 25. 7 pp. (AN 14406368)*

Evaluation Research

With the seemingly frequent news stories about school violence, gangs, and teenage crime, the common perception is that the rates of juvenile delinquency are on the rise. The cost of incarcerating juveniles is also increasing and juvenile detention centers are becoming overcrowded. To address this issue, various states began to experiment with alternatives to imprisonment for juveniles. One such tactic is juvenile boot camps. According to the Office of Justice Programs, as the name implies, a juvenile boot camp is a program modeled after military boot camps that include physical training, education (along with job training and placement), community service, substance abuse counseling and treatment, health and mental health care, continuous individualized case management, and intensive aftercare services that are fully integrated with the boot camp program (National Institute of Justice, 1997).

Even though boot camps vary in design across the country, they are generally supposed to address these seven components. The philosophy behind these programs is that juvenile delinquents need a highly disciplined environment to learn new social, technical, and personal skills. Once juveniles learn these skills, the hope is that they will be able to use the skills in socially normative manners and, consequently, avoid behaviors that may lead to trouble with the law. Therefore, the ultimate goal of juvenile boot camps is to reduce recidivism among juvenile delinquents.

On the surface, the program sounds good. After all, many researchers, practitioners, and academics theorize that juveniles commit crimes because they lack the structure, discipline, and nurturing environment to develop the social and technical skills that will encourage them to be productive, law-abiding citizens. Perhaps these kids come from an abused home, perhaps they are from low-income families where the parent or parents are spending significant hours away from home working just to make ends meet, or perhaps their parents are drug addicts who do not have the energy to actively parent their kids—the reasons are endless. But the hope is that by providing a comprehensive program that will teach discipline, respect for authority, and life skills, while also addressing issues such as drug addiction and mental well-being, these juveniles will turn their lives around and stay away from crime.

The philosophy seems logical, but the ultimate question many ask in evaluation research is: Does it work? Although that question seems simple enough, a better question may be: Does it work better than other available programs? Kempinen and Kurlychek (2003) addressed this question by studying the State Motivational Boot Camp Program that was established in Pennsylvania in 1996. This program had two primary goals: to reduce prison overcrowding and to reduce recidivism. The program was a six-month alternative to a prison program that involved 16-hour days that blended a military-like physical regimen with a rehabilitative focus that addressed education, life skills training, and cognitive behavioral therapy to help these juveniles deal with drug addiction and antisocial behavioral issues. In their research, Kempinen and Kurlychek primarily focused on the goal of reducing recidivism. They wanted to see whether offenders who graduated this boot camp program were less likely to recidivate than offenders who were released from traditional prison programs. To answer this question, Kempinen and Kurlychek did a quasi-experiment, which they describe below:

> This study employs a quasi-experimental design, as the offenders were not randomly selected for boot camp or prison. The sample for the current study included offenders who graduated from Pennsylvania's Motivational Boot Camp Program during 1996 and 1997 ($n = 508$), along with a comparison group of offenders who were released from state prison during those 2 years ($n = 532$). Thus, the entire sample consists of 1,040 offenders. The comparison group consists of those offenders who met the statutory eligibility criteria for boot camp but did not attend because they were not recommended by the judge, were not accepted by the Department of Corrections, or did not volunteer for the program. In an effort to control for some of the resulting sample differences and for additional variables found to relate to recidivism . . . we obtained information from the Department of Corrections on the following: race, county, current conviction offense, and sentence length. Also, to test our interaction hypotheses, information was collected from the Department of Corrections on age at release, and criminal history information, collected by the state police, was provided via the Pennsylvania Commission on Crime and Delinquency. Because conviction information was missing in more than one third of the cases, we used prior arrests as a measure of prior criminal record. We also received recidivism information, along with the offender's employment status, from the Pennsylvania Board of Probation and Parole (PBPP). The information from PBPP allowed us to distinguish whether the offender had been arrested for a technical violation or convicted of a new crime, though not necessarily reincarcerated, as two different measures of recidivism. We received recidivism information on the offenders in our sample through May 2000, which allowed for a minimum of a 2-year tracking period for offenders released in 1997 and of 3 years for offenders released in 1996. From this information, we defined those offenders who had either completed their maximum sentence on parole or were still on parole but had no violations as being successful. (pp. 589–590)

Our bivariate analysis in Table 2 reveals that the boot camp group is more likely than the prison group to recidivate (44% vs. 39%), although the type of recidivism is different for the two groups. [We also] find that the boot camp group is more likely than the prison group to fail on parole as a result of a technical violation (32% vs. 24%) rather than for a new crime conviction (12% vs. 15%). . . . [We] expected that Pennsylvania's rehabilitative model would result in less recidivism among its graduates. However our findings did not support that expectation. Although we found evidence that boot camp graduates are more likely than offenders released from prison to commit technical violations and less likely to commit new crimes, this finding was not significant after controlling for other variables. (pp. 592–593)

Kempinen and Kurlychek's (2003) research found no direct benefits of boot camps on recidivism (although, in further analysis, they did find a slight benefit in reducing recidivism for repeat offenders, which I did not include in the above excerpt). The findings of no benefit are not very different from the findings of other programs. Zaehringer (1998) and more recently a report by the U.S. Department of Justice National Institution of Justice (Parent, 2003) both reviewed and summarized the findings of many other evaluations of boot camps and all came to the same conclusion: Essentially, boot camps do not reduce recidivism in the long term among juvenile delinquents.

So, why do these programs continue? The answer to that question is complex and probably varies for each individual program; however, there are some common reasons that are instrumental to understanding the nature of evaluation research. In addition, there are some points from Kempinen and Kurlychek (2003) that are also relevant to our discussion. First, even more so than research that is primarily to educate about a specific topic (for example, what are some contributing factors to homelessness? Are the children of teenage mothers more likely to become teenage parents themselves?), evaluation research does not occur within a vacuum. Social, political, and economic factors affect the nature of the research, the design of the research, and how the research findings will be used. If you remember, reducing recidivism is only one goal of boot camps. Another major goal is to reduce prison overcrowding, and with regard to that issue, many agree that boot camps are generally effective. Since boot camps generally reduce prison overcrowding, they are politically popular. Boot camps also are socially popular because people like the idea of teaching juveniles discipline. In light of general political and social support, statistical findings questioning the effectiveness of these programs become less relevant to the public. I'll discuss outside factors such as political and social support and their relationship to evaluation research more in a bit.

Second, seemingly ineffective programs such as boot camps continue because social policy or programs are not static. They vary over time (e.g., changes can be made within a program, perhaps in response to earlier evaluation research) and across space (programs can differ in different areas). Therefore, just because research suggests that *some* programs do not work, it does not mean that the *idea* of the program does not work. The negative findings may just mean that the program needs to be altered to better reach its goals.

Third, *people* vary; therefore, even though the people any program or policy addresses may share some common elements (e.g., these juveniles were all arrested for a crime), their social backgrounds, personalities, and aptitudes may differ. This may affect for whom a program is successful. For example, Kempinen and Kurlychek (2003) found that the boot camp program, in general, did not reduce recidivism compared to incarceration; however, they also found that this was *not* the case for juveniles who were repeat offenders. Therefore, the program did work for people with a very specific characteristic (repeat offenders), even though it did not work for the juveniles as a whole.

Last, you may have noticed that Kempinen and Kurlychek used a quasi-experimental design, which we already discussed in Chapter 6. What is different about evaluation research that warrants its own chapter when I've already discussed the method of observation previously? It is not the method of observation, necessarily, that distinguishes evaluation research from other forms of research like quasi-experiments and surveys, but it is the *context* of the research itself that distinguishes this type of research and warrants a closer look.

So, let's begin addressing some of these issues by starting with a general discussion of how to use social research to address solutions to social problems. The chapter will then address appropriate topics for evaluation research and the different types of evaluation research you may encounter. I will then discuss some steps in conducting evaluation research and the social context of evaluation research, which I briefly mentioned previously. The chapter will end with a short discussion of the ethics involved in evaluation research and with some guidelines for evaluating written research that itself evaluates a social policy or program.

Using Social Research to Find Solutions to Social Problems

As you can probably guess with the example of the boot camps, evaluation research is an applied part of social research that works to guide public policy. Contrary to the traditional purpose of social research, which is to learn about the social world and derive theory that will explain social processes, evaluation research stems from technology (as opposed to science) (Hagan, 1997). Just as technological tools are designed to accomplish a specific goal (e.g., vacuum cleaners suck up dust and dirt) and are tested for product service (e.g., will the vacuum cleaner break after a few uses?), so too is evaluation research. Evaluation research empirically and scientifically tests whether a social policy reaches its goal (e.g., reduces recidivism) and whether that policy has a successful delivery (e.g., long-term or short-term effects).

Evaluation policy frequently also addresses whether a specific program is cost efficient relative to other programs that already exist. For example, even if recidivism is not necessarily reduced by a person's participation in a boot camp, is it cheaper to send someone to boot camp or to send the person to jail? In fact, evaluation research is now such an accepted component of policy and programs that few government or private funding agencies will grant money to organizations that want to try a new program, unless that organization has a detailed plan regarding how to evaluate the program it wants to implement.

■ Appropriate Topics and Programs

In the most general sense, evaluation research is appropriate whenever a person or an agency is planning an intervention that will alter the course of social events. For example, evaluation research can apply to the changes of laws, such as how no-fault divorce affects divorce rates. Rodgers, Nakonezny, Shell (1999) compared the divorce rates in 32 states that enacted no-fault divorce early, between 1965 and 1974, to 15 states that enacted the statute relatively late, after 1974. They found that although the institution of no-fault divorce increased the divorce rate significantly (based on statistical tests) for 25 of the 32 states that instituted the new stature early (before 1974), there was *no* corresponding increase in divorce rates among the 15 states that instituted no-fault divorce later. They concluded that initially, no-fault divorce led to an increase in the divorce rate that would not have occurred had the law not been changed, but that later, the effect dwindled.

Evaluation research can also address whether a public policy or program is working, which is what Kempinen and Kurlychek's (2003) research did. But whether a public program is reaching its desired goals is only one issue of studying public policy. Whether a public program is working as intended is another possible topic for evaluation research. For example, under the current form of welfare, Temporary Assistance to Needy Families (TANF), welfare recipients are expected to find work quickly. In fact, they can accept government assistance for only two years at a spell and five years total in their lifetimes.

Pavetti, Derr, Anderson, Trippe, and Paschal (2001, **AN 5329193**) examined how welfare offices address the component of the program that helps welfare recipients locate jobs. They found that in many instances, welfare offices used intermediary agencies to help TANF recipients locate work. They also found that some communities have made more progress in finding a creative cooperation between their welfare office and job placement agencies than others. The authors argue that understanding how welfare agencies work to successfully link their recipients to jobs will have important ramifications for understanding what makes a stable work-based assistance program, and ultimately, whether TANF will be successful.

But evaluation research does not have to be on programs that reach very large audiences, such as laws or federal/state programs. Evaluation research can involve local programs, such as parenthood education programs aimed at helping unwed teenage fathers be involved in their children's lives. For example, evaluation research can be done to assess whether teenage dads who attend the program spend more time with their children three months, six months, or even longer, after they complete the program than teenage dads who do not participate in the program. Evaluation research can also assess the nature of that interaction.

Frequently, evaluation research is fueled by grant money that local agencies receive. As I stated earlier, government and private funding agencies are increasingly requiring a well-thought out evaluation component as part of the grant proposal. As an example of policy evaluation on the local level, a colleague and I were contacted by a local police department in Pennsylvania to help them assess their policing practices, create a policy for improvement, and evaluate that policy. This research involved two types of evaluation research: needs assessment and outcome evaluation. I will discuss this research in more detail later in the chapter when I cover the different types of evaluation research. I mention it here only as an example of how evaluation research can also occur on a more localized and specific population—here, the residents of a rather small Pennsylvania town.

Although the topic possibilities may appear endless, not all programs lend themselves to evaluation. According to the Office of Juvenile Justice and Delinquency Prevention (1978), three questions need to be answered when considering whether evaluation research is appropriate:

1. Will the findings be used?
2. Is the project evaluable?
3. Who can do the work?

Although the publication of these guidelines is somewhat dated, they are brief and still appropriate enough to suit our purposes. Let's discuss each of these briefly.

Will the findings be used?

The agency associated with the program being studied obviously will have a vested interest in illustrating that the program is working as desired. People usually do not take the time to implement a program unless they honestly believe that on some level it will be beneficial to those it aims to address. However, people also have a vested interest in protecting their jobs, their status in the agency, and/or the perception of the agency to the public. Therefore, the people involved in a program frequently hope for a specific outcome with the research. Sometimes, however, they *more* than hope for their desired outcome. To the degree that key players are less interested in the objective scientific quality of the research and are more interested in having the research tell them what they want to hear, the higher the likelihood that the findings either will not be used (if they do not give the message administrators seek) or that the research methodology will be weakened in such a way as to taint the credibility and interpretation of the findings. Unless the agencies involved in the research make a conscious and sincere commitment to the production of unbiased or objective research (which means they may not hear what they want to hear), any evaluation research may be nothing more than a charade.

Is the project evaluable?

This broad question involves a consideration of the agency's objectives, the agency's design, and the resources available. For example, if a goal of the program is to "increase well-being," unless the agency has a concrete means of operationalizing "well-being" or the agency does not keep any information about program participants' feelings that can be measured, then researchers can save themselves some hassle and just avoid evaluating such a program *until* the agency has a clearer sense of its goals. Simply saying "to do good" or "to better an individual" without providing any concrete and observable definitions of what these phrases mean, makes evaluation essentially impossible. Of course researchers can, and frequently do, help agencies clarify their goals. The point I am making here is that the evaluation itself should not begin until those goals are clearly defined—regardless of whether the agency was able to reach measurable definitions on their own or whether a researcher helped the agency in this process.

Similarly, if doing an evaluation will require the cooperation of people from other agencies, and these people or agencies are *not* willing to cooperate, then an evaluation also may not be possible. For example, if I am asked to evaluate a court-mandated antitruancy program, and one of the goals is to see if the antitruancy program improves the grades of the students involved, if the school that some program participants attend refuses to release individual grades to me, then this aspect of the program cannot be evaluated.

Specifically, the following questions, some of which are borrowed from Wholey (1983), will help guide you in determining whether a program can be evaluated.

1. Can the program and the interrelationships of program activities be modeled?
2. Can the program activities and objectives be defined in a way that is observable?
3. Are data regarding the program's activities, objectives, and assumptions available?

You need to be able to answer yes to all of these questions in order to consider conducting an evaluation.

Who can do this work?

This question basically involves whether the evaluation will be done by people within the agency (or "in-house," as it is frequently called) or whether an outside evaluator will be conducting the evaluation. If the evaluation is in-house, then the agency has to make sure that it has people skilled enough in research methods to be able to do a scientifically sound and objective evaluation; also, the agency has to provide the time and resources (e.g., data, computers, etc.) for these people to do this job.

Frequently, people use outside evaluators. Outside evaluators lend an air of objectivity to the evaluation, plus sometimes people associated with an agency do not possess the research skills to be able to conduct the research. Furthermore, people "in-house" may be too close to the program. Their job may depend on the outcome of the program (an impossible situation from a scientific viewpoint, since programs rarely work *exactly* as planned and any negative findings may jeopardize a person's job) or they may be vulnerable to other social or political influences. Outside evaluators, however, range from formal research firms to local university professors with skill or expertise in the relevant project topic. If outside evaluators are going to be used, then they need access to agency information and data, and they will very likely need to be paid. Even if in-house people are used, if doing research is not a specific requirement of their job, then resources have to be available to either pay these people extra or to hire supplemental help who will assume some of the in-house people's duties while they are conducting the research.

Qualitative and Quantitative Approaches to Evaluation Research

Throughout the book so far, I have outlined both qualitative and quantitative methods of gathering information. Both of these general methodological approaches can be used for informative and effective evaluation analysis. Here, I will briefly discuss two approaches to evaluation analysis. The first, action research, is frequently associated with qualitative research methodologies (Berg, 2004); the second, a systems model of evaluation research, is more commonly associated with quantitative analysis. However, I want to make it clear that, depending on how a problem is defined, quantitative research methods may have a place in action research and qualitative methods may have a place in systems model research. In other words, these two categories are not necessarily completely distinct; they are just more commonly associated with one type of general approach over another.

■ Action Research

Sometimes agencies suspect that they need some type of evaluation to assess if their program is working as planned or being effective, but they do not really know where to begin. For example, a neighborhood organization is interested in evaluating its youth after-school programs. The members of this agency may have only a vague sense of what the problems with this program may be, what groups they are failing to target, or how the program can be improved. According to Berg (2004), action research would be appropriate here because it is a collaborative approach to evaluation that uses a population's culture, interactive activities, and social context to work to identify and resolve specific problems.

In its most general terms, the action research approach follows some basic guidelines that are similar to the overall research approach I've discussed so far. Action research involves (1) identifying the research question, (2) gathering data that will answer that question, (3) analyzing and interpreting that data, and (4) sharing the results with the participants involved (Berg, 2004).

In identifying the research question, researchers involve those who are vested in the program, called *stakeholders*, to make sure that the interests studied are their interests and not just the interests of the researcher. One effective way of identifying and defining the issues important to stakeholders is to hold focus groups, departmental meetings, and community group meets and then to qualitatively analyze the resulting information (Berg, 2004). The identified issues will guide the particular methodological approach and be suited to more intensely study the identified problems. Some problems may lend themselves to quantitative analysis (hence, the reason why these two approaches to evaluation research we're discussing are not necessarily completely opposite of each other); others may lend themselves to more qualitative analyses, such as unstructured or semi-structured interviews, descriptive accounts, or observational research.

As the data collection (stage 2) relies on the problem formation (stage 1), so too does data analysis (stage 3) rely on the information gathered in the previous stage (data collection). The method of data collection will decide the most appropriate method of data analysis. Observational data may be analyzed somewhat differently than data collected in unstructured interviews. I will discuss both qualitative and quantitative data analysis more in Chapters 11 and 12, respectively. The last step, sharing the results with participants, is where researchers present the conclusions of their research to the stakeholders in ways that provide opportunity to inform and help those who are involved with the studied program to produce some valuable change.

One of the keys to the action approach to evaluation research is the ongoing interaction between the researchers and the stakeholders in a way that ensures that the stakeholders' voices are reflected in the data analysis and gathering procedures. This is frequently done with qualitative research approaches, although, as I stated, it is not limited to these methodologies. Nor is the action research approach diametrically different from the next approach, the systems model of evaluation research. Some commonalities do exist.

■ Systems Model of Evaluation Research

Although the qualitative approach to evaluation research is becoming increasingly popular, quantitative approaches still dominate. A general guideline to evaluation research that is frequently, but not always, associated with quantitative research methods is the systems model. Much evaluation research is expressed in systems model terms, so I will spend a bit more time discussing this approach to evaluation research than I did the action approach.

In the systems model, which is summarized in Figure 10.1, a researcher recognizes that all parts of a policy or program, which I will just call "program" from now on for brevity, are interrelated; therefore, they all need to be examined in an evaluation if one is going to obtain a comprehensive view of the strengths and weaknesses of a program. So a systems model of evaluation essentially begins at the beginning by examining what resources, guidelines, and operating procedures go into the program. These basic issues are called **inputs** in systems model language. Clients entering the program are also inputs because without them, there would be no program. When examining a drug treatment program, the inputs would be the grant money that will pay for the start-up of the program, the number of drug treatment providers (and their names), the agencies that will provide additional services such as job counseling or family counseling (aside from that received in treatment), and the general guidelines of the program (for example, the stages clients will progress through as they work toward graduation). Essentially anything that contributes to the start-up of the program is an input.

Once all of the inputs are arranged, a program is likely to provide one or more specific services. These services are **activities** in systems model language. More specifically, an activity is what people do with the inputs. In a sense, it is the *process* of the program, and consequently some people use the term **program process** to mean the same as activities. So, regardless of what we call it, activities or program processes, the next step in the model is a description of exactly what the program is going to do. To continue with my drug treatment program example, the activities could be 30 days of in-patient drug treatment to

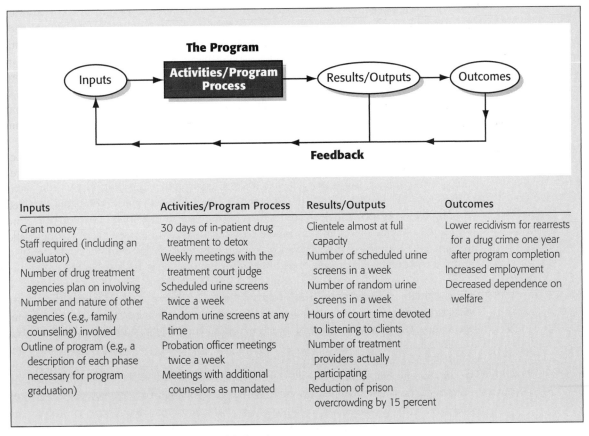

Inputs	Activities/Program Process	Results/Outputs	Outcomes
Grant money	30 days of in-patient drug treatment to detox	Clientele almost at full capacity	Lower recidivism for rearrests for a drug crime one year after program completion
Staff required (including an evaluator)	Weekly meetings with the treatment court judge	Number of scheduled urine screens in a week	Increased employment
Number of drug treatment agencies plan on involving	Scheduled urine screens twice a week	Number of random urine screens in a week	Decreased dependence on welfare
Number and nature of other agencies (e.g., family counseling) involved	Random urine screens at any time	Hours of court time devoted to listening to clients	
Outline of program (e.g., a description of each phase necessary for program graduation)	Probation officer meetings twice a week	Number of treatment providers actually participating	
	Meetings with additional counselors as mandated	Reduction of prison overcrowding by 15 percent	

Figure 10.1 *General Example of a Systems Model of Evaluation*

detox, weekly meetings with the treatment court judge, scheduled urine screens twice a week, random urine screens at any time, meeting with a probation officer twice a week, and meeting with any additional counselors as directed by the treatment court team. These activities do not need to be the same the entire length of the program. For example, in each phase of the program, let's say there are four phases, the number of activities will gradually decrease as clients progress through the phases and near graduation, since after graduation the clients are supposed to be equipped to live and work on their own, drug free. Regardless, each activity has to be able to be directly observed and measured—if not the quality of the activity (e.g., it's difficult to objectively evaluate the quality of individual counseling sessions), at least the quantifiable nature of the activities (e.g., how many counseling sessions each client attends).

Now that you have information about what each activity or program process is, you are in a position to evaluate how effectively the services are delivered. These are a direct result of the program delivery; some people refer to them as **results,** whereas others call them **outputs.** Results/outputs or outputs/results—the two are the same. So regardless of what you call them, and I'll just use "results," they are descriptions of program process or delivery. For example, results may be that the program is operating at near-full capacity. In other words, it has the resources to serve 100 clients and is currently serving 84 clients. Or the results may be the opposite—the program is over-capacity—serving 110 clients when it was only designed to serve 100. Results may also be the amount of scheduled or random urine screens conducted each week, the hours of court time devoted to hearing client reports, or the number of in-patient treatment providers participating in the program and the nature of the services they are giving. Sometimes a result may be a desirable goal in itself. For example, if a program goal is to reduce prison overcrowding, a result that prison overcrowding is reduced by 15 percent both describes the service delivered *and* answers how the service addresses one of the goals of the program.

Finally, a researcher is ready to see whether the program has fulfilled its intended goals toward the clients. **Outcomes** refer to both the direct results of the specific accomplishments (and failures) of the program regarding client experience and it also refers to the success (or failure) in reaching broader societal goals. For example, lower likelihoods of getting arrested for a drug crime one year after graduation for drug court clients compared to those who do not experience the program, increased employment (compared to when entering the program), and decreased welfare receipt are all examples of outcomes.

However, since programs continue long after initial evaluations may be completed, and since evaluations partially hope to provide information that will help improve programs, if the evaluation process ended here, that improvement is unlikely. Instead, information from the results and the outcomes provide feedback that may get recycled into the inputs, thereby creating a continual loop of adjusting resources and guidelines. This feedback may, in turn, lead to changes in activities or program processes, and *that*, in turn, will lead to new results and outcomes. These new outcomes will also provide feedback, and so the process continues. Hence, unlike other forms of research, such as descriptive surveys or experiments, evaluation research is designed to be ongoing. As the nature of any part of the program process changes, so too may the results and outcomes. This change may be internal to the evaluation process, such as change resulting from evaluation feedback, or it may be external, such as the reduction of available funding.

The goal of evaluation research is to provide credible analysis of program operations and outcomes. Using a systems model is one step in producing credible results, because this model involves all aspects of the program from the initial program organization to the end results, and these components are tied together in a systematic way. There is one consideration regarding this model, which isn't really a part in and of itself (hence, it is not included in the figure), but it may be an external influence all the same. This external, but related, part is that of **stakeholders.**

Stakeholders are the individuals or groups who have some specific interest in the program and concern for its outcomes. Stakeholders can be managers for the agency that houses the program, they may be service providers within the program, they may be local politicians who have endorsed the program, or they may be the clients themselves. Some stakeholders may fund the program (and/or evaluation), some may provide services within the program, or some may receive the services offered by the program. The point is that each stakeholder has a different interest and specific goal for the program. Most stakeholders want the program to "succeed," but their definitions of success may vary. Stakeholders who provide financial resources want the program to show that it is cost effective, meaning that the program saves money relative to alternative programs available. Those who provide services may want their role in the program justified so they can rely on having a job. Clients may simply want the program to work for them individually and have little care for "overall" effects of the program.

Why is this discussion of stakeholders included in this chapter? Because program stakeholders have an active role in setting the agenda of the program and an indirect, but potentially influential, role in the nature of the evaluation research. As a result, stakeholders frequently set the agenda within which the researcher works. Therefore, a researcher may not be able to use the most advanced scientific standards for designing the research because the stakeholders, not just the researcher, may decide, for example, what goals are most important from an evaluative point of view. Stakeholders may also decide whether there will be a control group (and if so, what that control group will look like). For research purposes, a researcher may find that improving family relations and that the client has created a social support network that will help him or her stay away from drugs are important goals for continued program success. However, stakeholders may want more quantifiable information and therefore may not provide the resources for the researcher to pursue evaluation of these other issues. Whenever possible, researchers should, at the beginning of the process, try to negotiate for inclusion of any outcomes or results that they find important to the study. Frequently, stakeholders will allow researchers freedom in following their own research interests within the framework of the stakeholders' interests, at least if doing so will not cost the stakeholders any additional resources. However, if the stakeholders deny this request and the researchers agree to do the research anyway, then the researchers are obligated to put the stakeholders' needs or requests first. Hence, a stakeholder can have some influence in the nature of the study.

Types of Evaluation Research

Sometimes a researcher is not called on to do a complete evaluation as I described in the systems model. Aside from providing a general framework from which to proceed with an evaluation study, the systems model also serves to acquaint you with the general terminology, such as inputs and activities, used in evaluation research. But evaluation research itself can take many forms. In this section I will discuss four different forms of evaluation research, summarized in Figure 10.2. A study can entail just one form, or it may entail several.

Figure 10.2 Summary of Different Types of Evaluation Research

■ Needs Assessment

Just because a few people feel that a program is necessary or is in need of serious alteration does not mean that they should automatically create a new program or tinker with an existing one. After all, what one person or a small group of people believe may be necessary is frequently based only on their experience with their specific cog in the social or political wheel. Political advocates may think that one aspect of a social problem needs to be addressed, whereas politicians may believe that another is important, and moral advocates, such as religious leaders, may feel that a third component is the issue that needs addressing. Through no fault of their own, these people may not be aware of other avenues that could address this perceived need or perhaps they have a very narrow view of the need based only on their own experiences or perspectives. In other words, these people can all be stakeholders, but they may be focused on a narrow aspect of the social problem and therefore have different views of the problem and different ideas for solutions.

The change of investing resources in potentially redundant programs or designing a program that does not adequately address the existing need can be minimized simply by doing a **needs assessment.** Needs assessment research is a scientifically reliable means of obtaining more objective descriptions of a social issue and the corresponding program need. Needs assessment addresses questions such as, How prevalent is a problem in a community? How many people need help addressing this problem? What other resources to address this problem are available? What gaps in delivery exist among these programs? What is the demographic composition of the community in need? Is the proposed program appropriate to fill in the gaps of delivery? Questions such as these are important because their answers can help avoid the waste of resources on improperly targeted or repetitive programs.

■ Program Monitoring

Once a program is up and running, a researcher may first be asked to do a **program monitoring** evaluation in which the researcher examines whether the program is operating as planned. Determining whether a program is running as designed is an important step prior to evaluating if a program is having its intended effect on people. Part of program monitoring involves determining whether a program is reaching its target audience, whether the program is operating as expected, and what resources are being used (including the "all important" money!).

For three years I conducted the program monitoring of a local drug treatment court program and I found three major issues with program implementation in those early years. First, in this particular program, the clients must progress through four stages. The initial stage was designed to last 60 days during which clients had a 30-day in-patient stay to detox the drugs out of their system. Among other requirements, clients had to be drug free (as assessed by urine tests) for the entire 60 days. The second phase of treatment was originally designed to last 120 days. Through the program monitoring, I learned that almost three-quarters of clients were staying in Phase 1 much longer than the designed time frame and that frequently no one was able to progress through the second phase in the designed amount of time (Wolfer, 2001a, 2001b).

It appeared (based on reviews of sanctioning behavior) that the combined length of the phases and the required number of consecutive drug-free days were too much for the early stages of drug treatment. The clients inevitably failed during this phase and had to start over—which contributed to their exceptionally long time in this phase. As a result, the treatment court team altered the design of the phases so clients would feel progression early, which would (theoretically) encourage them to continue on their drug-free course. Consequently, the length of time in the second phase and the length of consecutive days drug free in each phase were shortened a bit.

Second, during these very early months of operation, I also found a mismatch in program acceptance rates based on gender. Even though men represented the overwhelming bulk of drug offenders in this particular location, women, even when accounting for issues such as criminal offense and level of addiction, were disproportionately accepted into the program, given their representation in the drug offending population. More pointedly, women *with children* were disproportionately accepted into the program. After indicating this subconscious bias toward women with children, the treatment court team worked to allow more men into the program. After a couple of years of operation, this county's treatment court was a smoothly running program in which clients generally no longer spent exceptionally long periods in early phases and in which the representation of men and women in the program more closely approximated the gender representation of the offending population.

Last, even though the inputs specified scheduled (usually during probation officer meetings) and random drug tests, random drug tests were essentially absent during the early program implementation. Hence, theoretically it would have been easy for program clients to use drugs yet appear "clean" during their drug tests, since they knew when they were meeting with the probation officer each week well in advance. Since most drugs stay in the system 24 to 48 hours, if one was meeting the probation officer twice a week and wanted to use drugs, all a person had to do was wait until *after* a specific probation officer meeting, then use drugs and by the next meeting, the drugs would no longer be detectable in that person's system. When the team realized the erratic and almost nonexistent nature of random drug tests, which were a required component of their program, they immediately worked to create a systematic method of random testing (not necessarily "systematic" on the clients' end because the team obviously did not want the clients to recognize any patterns).

As I've illustrated here, program monitoring can involve an evaluation of whether the program is actually working as intended—for example, whether a program is doing everything it said that it will, as in the random drug screens. It can also involve evaluating whether the activities are working as designed. For example, I illustrated the mismatch between the guidelines for phase length and the reality of how long most clients were spending in phases. Program monitoring can also involve assessing whether the program is adequately reaching the relevant population. In this instance, the relative population was overwhelmingly male, but females were being disproportionably accepted into the program at the expense of overlooking men who were the primary offenders.

Program evaluations are very important because if the program is not working as designed or is not effectively capturing the target audience, a researcher has no means of determining if the desired outcomes are related to the program operation itself. For example, suppose I did not do a process evaluation. What would I be able to conclude if I did an outcome evaluation at the end of the program for the treatment court and I found that clients in the treatment court program were just as likely to be caught using drugs six months after graduating from the program as were people with similar addictions who did not attend the program and went to prison instead? After I write my report I find that random drug screens were never done and that instead of being in the program for 12 to 18 months, as designed, most people were in the program for 18 to 24 months. Well, if the program did not operate as planned, there is obviously no point in asking whether it had the intended outcomes. The outcomes are directly tied to the activities and guidelines. If the activities do not meet the guidelines, then it is not a logical leap to think that the outcomes will not meet the goals either. Remember, as I showed in Figure 10.1, all the parts of a program evaluation are related; change one component and you've essentially changed the shape of the program and outcome. However, since the treatment court *did* have a program monitoring research piece, we were able to make the necessary changes in program delivery and then later assess whether the program goals were fulfilled.

■ Outcome and Impact Evaluation

If a researcher can establish that a program progressed as intended, the next step would be to see whether it achieved the desired goals or outcomes. Since this is really the nuts and bolts of most evaluation programs, when you hear the term *evaluation research* this is probably the type of research you automatically consider. Outcome evaluation essentially asks, Did the program have the intended consequences? What were the positive changes resulting from the program? What were the negative changes? and What did not change at all? The goal of outcome evaluation is essentially to make a causal connection between the program and the desired results.

I've already discussed some of the relevant research questions for evaluation research in other chapters. For example, Does arrest decrease incidence of repeat calls for domestic violence cases compared to other responses such as mediation and separation? Do boot camps reduce recidivism among juvenile delinquents compared to more traditional juvenile detention settings? Are people who experience a drug treatment court program less likely to be rearrested for a drug-related crime than drug addicts who are sent to prison or traditional drug counseling?

Meyer, Roberto, and Atikin (2003) studied whether radio public service announcements aimed at educating people about gun safety actually made people more aware of how to safely handle guns. This educational goal was part of a broader program aimed at decreasing gun-related deaths in a mid-Michigan county. The public service announcements were one of the activities in this broader program that had its own goal of increasing knowledge about gun safety. The program coordinators believed that in order to reduce gun-related deaths, people first had to be educated about gun safety, hence the public service announcements were the activity to teach about gun safety. Therefore, the effectiveness of the public service announcements had to be evaluated, because if people did not learn about gun safety from the announcements, then their potentially lethal behavior around guns was not going to change and the overall program to reduce gun deaths would not be achieved. In order to conduct the outcome evaluation of the gun safety public service announcements, Meyer, Roberto, and Atikin's studied two counties in Michigan. One county served as the experimental group, where residents received both a coupon with gun safety facts by mail and were exposed to public service announcements on three local radio stations. The other group was a control group that did not experience either of these treatments. The authors describe their program activities (the mail coupons and public service announcements) and some of their findings:

> A direct mail coupon was designed primarily to increase individuals' knowledge of 10 gun-safety practices. These gun-safety practices were selected because they were most commonly cited and agreed on by gun-safety experts and the gun-safety literature. The direct mail coupon was sent to 70,000 households in the experimental county. The front of this coupon advertised and provided general details about the promotion including participating stations, the purpose of the promotion, and prize identification. . . . The back of the coupon contained the list of 10 gun-safety practices. Recipients were instructed to indicate the *three* gun-safety practices they thought were most effective . . . and to mail the coupon to any participating station to be entered in the drawing to win one of three free trips to Las Vegas. The back of the coupon also encouraged readers to listen to participating radio stations for additional methods of entry. . . .

. . . Three 60-sec radio PSAs . . . were designed to increase listeners' knowledge of 10 gun-safety practices. The three PSAs contained the same semi-humorous game show theme to capture and maintain the listeners' attention and interest. In the first two PSAs, a male or female contestant was asked to list five important gun-safety practices in 30 sec. In the third, the male and female contestants from the first two PSAs "competed" to see who would be the first to answer three gun-safety questions correctly. This PSA ended in a tie as both contestants blurted out the answer to the final question simultaneously. The PSAs concluded by noting when and how listeners could win a free trip to Las Vegas and an identification of program sponsors. All PSAs followed the same script, but were independently produced by each station using a disk jockey and voices with which their target audience could identify. . . .

. . . The effects of this intervention can be measured both by the number of respondents who indicate they learned something new from the messages, and most importantly, from differences associated with knowledge of gun-safety practices between exposed and unexposed individuals.

. . . Individuals exposed to the PSA in the treatment county mentioned almost two gun-safety practices related to locking and storing practices, whereas those in the control county and those unexposed in the treatment county mentioned significantly less, 1.24 and 1.32, respectively. Further, a significant difference was found when all gun-safety practices were included in the analysis, with those exposed to the PSA identifying a mean number of 2.5 gun-safety practices, those in the control county 1.6 gun-safety practices, and those unexposed in the treatment county 1.39 gun-safety practices. (Meyer, Roberto, & Atikin, 2003, pp. 306–310)

How would you approach evaluating a campaign to promote gun safety?

The full context of this study includes a process evaluation in addition to the outcome evaluation; however, I focused only on the outcome evaluation. The goal of Meyer, Roberto, and Atikin's study was to show that the joint venture of the coupon and the public service announcements increased people's knowledge of gun safety, and their findings suggest that the program succeeded in doing this. Note that the goal of the mail coupon and public service announcements were *not* to decrease gun-related deaths, but instead were one part of a larger program to do just that. Therefore, to evaluate their part of the program, their goal was not the reduction of gun-related deaths, but instead the increased knowledge of gun safety. Programs can have multiple goals embedded within a broad societal goal. When evaluations are done to see if the more manageable goals, such as increasing gun safety knowledge, are accomplished, that is an example of outcome evaluation. When the evaluation is to see whether there is an effect on a broader societal goal, such as to reduce gun-related deaths, that would be an impact evaluation. Sometimes researchers use the two interchangeably (Bachman & Schutt, 2001) and what is an impact in one program may be an outcome in another. The point is that the distinction itself is not necessarily important or necessary. However, when there are multiple levels of goals, the distinction *can* be useful in separating smaller immediate goals with broader, longer-term goals.

■ Cost-Benefit Analysis and Cost-Effective Analysis

Social policies exist in the real world; therefore, not only is research more likely to be influenced by real-world issues, such as political ambition and restricted funds, but so are the policies themselves. Although the bottom line may be Does the policy work?, a very close follow-up question is, Is it efficient?—in other words, Can we afford it? or Will it save us money relative to other already existing programs? If the sky was the limit in terms of funding, agencies probably could design programs that would successfully address many social issues. After all, social problems are not simple, therefore the policies aimed at improving them cannot be simple either. However, complex, comprehensive policies cost money—a lot of it—and the sky is *not* the limit when it comes to social programs. So, a very real concern when doing evaluation research is to determine the relationship between the costs of the program and the benefits the program produces. People generally call this type of evaluation research **cost-benefit analysis.**

In cost-benefit analysis, the program costs, such as staff wages and material costs, are compared to the evaluation outcomes measured in monetary terms. In my treatment court comparison, some costs would be the costs of in-patient treatment, out-patient counseling, probation officer salaries, urine drug tests, and analysis of drug tests. The benefits could be a comparison between these costs and the money saved by *not* sending a person to jail. In other words, the cost can be estimated for a client who is in the program for one year and compared to the cost of housing that person in jail for one year. If the treatment court costs are lower, that's a monetary cost that is a benefit, but if the cost is higher, that is an unfavorable cost-benefit analysis that may suggest that this program is too expensive.

Cost-benefit analysis comes from the field of business, where it is rather straightforward to estimate the cost of a product in terms of materials, labor, and distribution that go into a program, and the benefits of that product—namely, the profit that it generates. However, in social research, frequently the benefits are not as easily quantifiable. Sure, a researcher can compare the cost of being in the program to the cost of being in jail for the same amount of time, but what about other benefits that may evolve from being in the treatment court that are not as easily quantifiable? For example, how can we quantify the benefits of a person who goes on to provide counseling for other drug addicts, or who gets his or her children back from social services because he or she is no longer drug dependent? Although these behaviors may be quantifiable in one sense (e.g., the money one earns from being a counselor as opposed to being in a lower-paid job or perhaps on welfare), quantifying these behaviors is less clear cut. What about the psychological and social benefits of having more counselors available to help others, or the social benefits children may experience by being able to live with Mommy or Daddy again? Because social benefits are not as easily quantifiable, an alternative to cost-benefit analysis is **cost-effective analysis.** In cost-effective analysis, inputs are estimated in monetary terms (like with cost-benefit analysis), but outcomes are estimated in actual impacts, such as the number of families that are reunited.

Although cost-effective analysis better addresses the social benefits, the importance of financial benefits in a world of limited financial resources cannot be denied. Therefore, a safe approach is to use *both* cost-benefit and cost-effective analysis whenever trying to estimate program efficiency. Pritchard and Williams (2001) do this in their analysis of the integration of school-based child and family social services to the academic setting. The purpose of the program was to see whether having a child and family social worker actually on site at the schools, available both in the classroom and outside of it, would reduce truancy and delinquency while also improving academic performance three years after the program was initially instituted. To test this school-based social services program, Pritchard and Williams (2001) studied four schools, all of which attracted students from the most socially disadvantaged areas. The primary schools they called "Atlee" (the experimental school) and "Churchill" (control comparison). The secondary schools were "Bevan" (experimental) and "Disraeli" (control). The researchers found that the children in the experimental group had lower rates of drug use, less truancy, and better academic experiences (both in terms of reported attitudes of liking school and in academic performance) than the students in the control schools. However, as Pritchard and Williams recognize, the issue of the cost of such a program cannot be ignored. Here is an excerpt of their cost-benefit analysis with regard to school budgeting and criminal activity:

> Educational budget "savings" are based upon comparing numbers of children "excluded" versus "transfer-in" to the four schools and then looking at the cost of special educational provision, either home tuition or an admission to an Educational Behavioural Disturbed Unit [EBDU]. Table 4 shows the numbers of children excluded and transferred-in children from the four schools over the period.

Table 4 "Savings" from Project v. Comparative Exclusions v. New Entrants (Transfers-IN) (all numbers in 3 years in £1,000s)

School: Numbers Children	Enter	Exclude	Gains +/–	Likely Savings £1,000s
'Atlee': Savings +	28	0	28	+ £230.3
'Churchill': Costs =	3	10	−7	−£51.7
'Bevan': Savings	37	9	28	+ £217.7
'Disraeli': Savings	14	8	6	+ £49.2

Project v. Control schools exclusions and transfers by each year X2 = 13.20575 d/f Yates Correction applied $P < 0.05$. All exclusions and transfers Project v. Control X2 = 19.66 1 d/f $P < 0.0001$.

[A]ssuming that most adolescent theft does not cost the same as "adult" crime, we compare only those most at risk of a criminal career, i.e. those from disadvantaged backgrounds such as ex-"Atlee" with ex-"Beta." In the event of theft, rates were 22 per cent and 53 per cent respectively. The differential in terms of numbers of offenders suggests a "saving" of 14 offenders, who, at the Cooper-Lybrand rate, yields a notional saving of £37,800. However, based upon a . . . separate study of 16–17-year-old offenders in the county, who are only a "year-on" from our 14–16-year-olds, these 183 older adolescent offenders cost £854,000, an average of £4,600 each for the year (Pritchard and Cox, 1997), and figures close to the Audit Commission's estimates (1996). Moreover, there is evidence to show that 50 per cent of inmates of Young Offenders Institutions had at some time been excluded from school (HM Chief Inspector of Prisons, 1997; Lyon et al., 2000), reinforcing the point that our estimates of cost are cautious and conservative. Consequently, the claimed £37,800 "delinquency" savings for the ex-"Atlee" is a very modest estimate indeed. Continuing on the side of caution, and including only the minimal savings to criminal justice of £37,800, and the £87,200 education "savings," after deducting the annual cost of the project, we are looking at an estimated gross saving in excess of £65,700, or a 111 per cent return on the "investment."

This does not seem an excessive claim, especially when remembering the potential inter-generational implications, and the savings to Social Service and Health budgets, which are excluded from the estimate. Exclusion however, carries not only a cost to education, but also to the criminal justice system. In a separate study which analysed police records of a 5-year cohort [1990–95] of former excluded-from-school adolescents, now aged 16–23 (n = 227), it was found that 63 per cent had post-discharge convictions. This cost the Criminal Justice system a *minimum* of £4.2 million pounds, i.e. £30,000 per pupil (Pritchard and Cox, 1998). Consequently if we projected forward, the reduced delinquency and exclusions from the project schools, instead of the 111 per cent return on the preventative investment, it might still cautiously be claimed to be more than 250 per cent. (Pritchard & Williams, 2001, pp. 37–39)

Pritchard and Williams (2001) first identify the benefits as the difference in number of offenders with the program to without the program, which according to them is about 14 people. Estimating the number of children in the program who avoided becoming offenders is an example of a cost-effective analysis. However, they go further and do a cost-benefit analysis by putting a dollar tag on the amount of money those 14 people would save the government. They estimate that the savings from *not* having to deal with these 14 people was £37,800, which converts to about $67,715 in U.S. dollars (www.oanda.com/convert/classic). They also estimate educational costs, such as the costs of having to provide special education to students, and compare it to the costs of having students excluded from school. This savings comes to £87,200, or $156,210 in U.S. currency. This means a total "benefit" of $223,925 (in U.S. dollars). However, in order to truly put this "benefit" in context, it has to be compared with the costs of the program—the "cost" half of a cost-benefit analysis.

The researchers do not specifically state the cost of the program, but they do state the net savings (the result of the comparison) to be more than £65,700. If one does the math, this means that the cost of the program was about £59,300 (total benefit of £37,800 + £87,200 = £125,000 minus the "net benefit" of £65,700). To explain this in U.S. dollars, the program cost about $106,230, led to a total benefit of $223,925, and when you compare the numbers by subtracting the cost from the benefit, the program came out "ahead" for a final savings of $117,695. The program Pritchard and Williams studied would be considered a financial "success" because the financial benefits clearly outweigh the costs.

■ Summary

If it appears to you that there are not necessarily clear distinctions between the types of evaluation research or that a "good" evaluation would include more than one of these types, you are not mistaken. Each of the four evaluation types—needs assessment, program monitoring, outcome/impact assessment, and cost-benefit analysis/cost-effective analysis—complement each other. Needs assessment generally occurs before any program is actually implemented (and in some cases even designed). Program monitoring is done to ensure that the program, once designed and implemented, is functioning as intended. Hence, it would make sense that program monitoring occurs *after* needs assessment and *before* any evaluation that assesses whether the program is "successful."

Success can be defined in many ways, however. I discussed two. One way is to determine whether the program has accomplished its goals—what most people consider when they talk about whether a program is "working." This would be an outcome/impact evaluation. The second way is to determine whether that program is working *better* or *more cost efficiently* than if that program was not present (in other words, if people did nothing) or whether it is cheaper and more effective than other available programs. This would be a cost-benefit or cost-effective evaluation. The latter frequently involves some analysis of whether the program is "working," but it takes that form of evaluation one step further and tries to estimate the program's efficiency as well.

Steps in Conducting Evaluation Research

Evaluation research is not exactly a distinct form of research from the other methods we examined in previous chapters. In other words, doing evaluation research frequently entails using one of the methods of observation that I have already discussed. For example, Pritchard and Williams (2001) did a quasi-experiment, as did Kempinen and Kurlychek (2003)'s study of boot camps that I presented in the beginning of the chapter. In fact, evaluation research frequently involves quasi-experiments because laboratory settings are not generally appropriate for studies in which researchers *want* to observe people in their natural environment and people frequently cannot be randomly assigned to program participation in the real world. We discussed quasi-experiments in Chapter 6, and the issues in this type of research apply in evaluation research as well. Furthermore, the gathering of data in quasi-experiments may involve surveys. For example, in the treatment court evaluation that I did, in order to assess clients' characteristics at entry into the program, each applicant (including those who were later denied participation in the program) completed a background survey that asked about the person's family, employment, educational, drug, and previous treatment experiences.

So why an entire chapter on evaluation research? What distinguishes evaluation research from the other forms of research, and hence warrants a chapter devoted to this method of observation is twofold. First it is the relative unimportance of social theory. As I stated earlier, evaluation research is not research designed to test whether a theory is accurate. Although theories are often a part of evaluation research, their involvement is "extra" and not required. Second, the independent and dependent variables in evaluation research have to be more clearly quantifiable than in other forms of research. This is because the findings of evaluation research are more likely to be utilized than other forms of research, therefore they need to be more concrete, as opposed to abstract. In this section, we will examine the steps of evaluation research, which are summarized in Figure 10.3, in more detail. Some sections will be short, since the procedure may be very similar to other forms of research I have already discussed; others may require a bit more explanation. So let's get started!

■ Problem Formation

On the surface, doing an evaluation seems to be rather clear cut. After all, there's a program or policy and people want to see whether it "works." What can be so difficult about that? You probably already have the idea from the earlier part of this chapter that this simplified view of evaluation research is misleading and obscures the most difficult phase of the process, which is problem formation. Yet, this is a frequent view, especially of people who are in the "real world" and trying to evaluate the effectiveness of their programs.

1. Formulate the evaluation problem.

  a. What are the program goals?

  b. Can they be measured? (If not, then continue to define the goals until they are. Otherwise, evaluation research is not advisable.)

2. Design the instruments.

  a. Do a thorough reading of the existing literature (in other words, a literature review) to identify the various definitions other researchers use and the context in which they use them.

  b. Based on your literature review and the particulars of your program:

    (1) Identify clearly observable program goals (replicate the literature whenever possible)

    (2) Identify all observable interventions and create measures for each intervention

    (3) Identify and measure possible experimental contexts:

      (a) Environmental contexts external to the program operation

      (b) Personal contexts that may affect individuals' experiences within the program

3. Select a research method.

  a. Any research method is technically possible, although experiments are most commonly used. In deciding what type of experiment, consider:

    (1) The issue of random assignment:

      (a) Is random assignment possible? If so, try to do a true experiment.

      (b) If random assignment is not possible, a quasi-experiment may be more appropriate.

  b. Design the actual research method based on the material presented in the relevant chapter corresponding to your method of choice.

Figure 10.3 Steps in Evaluation Research

For example, the university in which I work offers a week-long intensive training for people who are in the field of victim services. Perhaps unsurprisingly to you, during this event, I am responsible for teaching the research and evaluation component. Many of the people attending this training have already been given the responsibility from their agencies for creating an evaluation instrument, but they frequently discuss with me that they have trouble "getting started." So, in conversation with them and in wider discussions during my presentations, I begin by asking these people what the goals of their program are. Invariably, people give me responses such as, "To help people get over their victimization experience" or "To help make people feel 'whole' again" or "To help them to live independent, happy lives." Good! These are all worthy goals, but it is no wonder that people are having trouble deciding actually how to measure these goals. After all, how do we measure "getting over a victimization experience"? What exactly does that mean? Frequently these people, when pushed, will say that their program hopes to benefit people in ways that are not directly measurable.

And that's the inherent problem.

If we cannot concretely recognize what is supposed to change from the implementation of a program, we cannot possibly evaluate that program. Evaluation research is the process of discerning whether a behavior changed or did not change, whether a condition is or is not there. In order to do that, we need to clearly identify, operationalize, and observe what is under study. Therefore, if your program goal is to help people live independent lives, you need to be able to measure that. If your goal is to help crime victims receive restitution, you need to measure that. With the people in the week-long training, I keep pushing them with the question, "What do you mean?" (much like I did in Chapter 4 with you), until the rest of the people in the class agree that there is no further answer needed. When the rest of the class is satisfied that they are clear as to what a definition means, then that definition is very likely measurable, which means that the particular individual from an agency has a measurable goal or outcome.

For example, Fergusson (2002, **AN 8815191**) wanted to study a program in Britain aimed at helping youth who are on welfare find jobs. This program is closely borrowed from a U.S. model of youth employment and is called the New Deal Youth Project. As Fergusson explains, the program is directed toward 18- to 24-year-olds who have been on Job Seeker's Allowance (a form of government aid for the young unemployed). The project's goals are to help these young people "find work and improve their prospects of remaining in sustained employment" (Fergusson, 2002, p. 177). In order to assess these goals, Fergusson's problem formulation is pretty clear. He would need to be able to measure what he means by "find work" and "improve . . . prospects of sustaining employment." The most direct ways to assess these goals would be whether a young person found work that was unsubsidized by the government and how long that person remained in that job. In fact, variations of these two measures was how Fergusson did observe these program goals. However, the point is that the goals of the New Deal Youth Project were quantifiable, and this is a key issue in formulating a problem for evaluation.

■ Instrument Design

On the surface, instrument design seems like a pretty basic step—one that would flow directly from Chapter 4 and our discussion of operationalization and measurement. However, challenges in instrumentation arise from confusion as to *what* to measure and differences in *how* to measure concepts. Let's begin by discussing what to measure.

As you have learned, when one does evaluation research, that person wants to measure whether the program "succeeded." Researchers measure the outcome or impact of the program and these impacts or outcomes have to be able to be directly and quantifiably observed. But researchers also have to design measures for the interventions themselves and for the experimental contexts. To measure the intervention, this may mean measuring what specific services within the programs people experience, how often or how long they receive these services, and what resources they use during these services.

For example, earlier I mentioned the drug treatment court program I was involved in evaluating. Some examples of the intervention issues I had to measure were (1) the inpatient program an individual attended (to see if some programs were more effective than others); (2) how long that person remained in that program; (3) who provided out-patient counseling for an individual; (4) how many hours of outpatient counseling that person received; (5) any additional programs a person experienced (e.g., job training) and for how long; and (6) how many random and scheduled drug tests (and the results) that person received. Furthermore, clearly with any program, some people get personally invested in the program; others simply go through the motions. Therefore, I included measures of client behavior while in the program, which included ratings of the client's compliance and responsiveness by both the probation officers and the nurse clinician, both of whom meet with the clients regularly.

Why bother with all of these measures about the characteristics of the program itself? I will discuss this later in the chapter, but, in a nutshell, the reason is because not all individual aspects of a program are likely to work effectively, or even at all. When deciding how to change a program, it is important for those administering the program to know the strengths and weaknesses of individual program components so that when altering a program, they have a sense of what to keep as is, what to change, and what to abolish.

Measuring experimental contexts is a little more abstract. Experimental contexts are variables that are external to the experiment itself but may affect either the implementation of the program, or an individual's experiences within the program (and ultimately the success or failure of that program for the individual). For instance, if one of the goals of the treatment court, in addition to having individuals live drug-free lives, is to help people obtain stable employment, if the area in which the treatment court is operating is currently experiencing an economic downturn, this may affect the achievement of job stability, *regardless* of the treatment court program itself. In other words, superficially, it may appear that the treatment court has not succeeded in helping clients obtain stable employment; however, if a researcher included measures of experimental context, the researcher may realize that employment prospects are low for *everyone*, not just those participating in the program.

Now, here's a quick test: Can you remember from Chapter 4 what rival causal factor may be muddying the causal connection between participating in the treatment court and obtaining stable employment? If you said a history effect, you'd be correct! Measuring experimental contexts essentially means identifying and keeping an eye out for factors, like history effects, that may affect the evaluation of the program.

An example of an experimental context that may affect an individual's success or failure in the treatment court program may be whether or not the individual has family members who use drugs. Even if a person participates in the best drug treatment program in the world, it may be difficult for that person to remain drug free if members of his or her immediate family are still using drugs, and essentially tempting this person to do the same. Because variables such as this—or other demographic factors such as race, age, or gender—may not be directly relevant to the program evaluation itself, but may affect individuals' experiences within the program (and if they affect enough individuals, then it may be a program issue), these variables are frequently called **control variables.** Control variables are variables extraneous to the program implementation itself, but they need to be addressed (or "controlled" if you will, methodologically speaking) because they can affect how individuals or groups of individuals experience the program.

The second issue with the design of instruments in evaluation research has to do with the disagreement in definitions among researchers. Differences in operational definitions may lead to differences in study findings and perspectives as they relate to theory. In traditional research, these differences ultimately confound the overall meaning or interpretation of an issue, but at the end of the day, this disagreement or muddiness is abstract. It affects our understanding of an issue, yes; but it has less direct and concrete consequences as to whether a specific application of that theory (e.g., a program) will or will not continue. That is not the case with evaluation research, whose *whole* purpose is real-world application, and therefore results may directly lead to the continuation or cutting of a program and of jobs that go with that program. Consequently, disagreement about definitions that involve evaluation research, very literally, can affect the continuation of a program because these disagreements may impact how a program is studied (by the instrumentation) and ultimately the evaluation of the program and the utilization of findings.

For example, many social programs aim to improve "quality of life." But what does this mean? Brown (1999) discusses what "quality of life" may mean for those researching people with disabilities:

> Although the term *quality of life* is used often today in many fields, its meaning sometimes still seems obscure. At the semantic level, the word *quality* means excellence or superiority. Thus, it stands to reason that a *quality life* must refer to an excellent or superior life. It is the ultimate, the best of life. It is life at its ideal, a golden vision towards which we strive. . . . When we speak of quality "of" life, however, we do not refer to the ultimate, the best, or the ideal. Instead, we refer to the parts or portions of one's life that are good, to those things in one's *life* that are ideal and that represent the best of our lives. Or, we refer to the degree to which our lives as a whole are good, the degree to which they approach our ideal of what life should be like.
>
> . . . [F]ocusing on the quality of life can simply mean, if we are not careful, that we explain and understand all the ways in which the lives of people with intellectual disability are not ideal, and may never be as good, as the lives of the rest of us. Such a focus would be tragic, for it brings with it the strong possibility that people with intellectual disability will be marginalised even more than they already are. The danger is that such a focus will identify that people with intellectual disability do indeed have poor quality of life, and this knowledge will infer that people with intellectual disability comprise a group who are inferior because their lives are inferior. At a time when most developed and many

developing countries are striving to integrate and include people with intellectual disability, such an inference is not helpful.

Still, to be realistic, the term that is widely used today is *quality of life*, not a *quality life*. Thus, for the term *quality of life* to be helpful, we need to combine the meanings of the two terms. When we use the term *quality of life*, we must imply that we are focusing on how good life is at the present time, with a view to making life better, and closer to the ideal, in the future. This surely is helpful, and it is in this sense that the term *quality of life* is used in this paper.

How do we make life better, closer to the ideal? We do so by paying attention to maintaining and improving quality of life for individuals. We do so by seeking out what is essentially important to individuals in their lives, the things that can make their lives fulfilling for them. The quality of life of people with intellectual disability can be maintained and improved by focusing our attention and action on the those things that really matter most to people as individuals.

Does this make the definition of "quality of life" any clearer? Probably not. In fact, Cummins (1995) recognized that, by the mid-1990s there were over 100 definitions of *quality of life* in the academic literature, and researchers within a discipline do not even agree on the definitions. For example, Zekovic and Renwick (2003) also studied quality of life among individuals with disabilities and they define the concept as "health-related quality of life" and "holistic related quality of life." According to Zekovic and Renwick, health-related quality of life refers to the following issues:

> There are two general types of health-related quality of life measures: generic and disease specific (Spieth & Harris, 1996). Generic measures are designed for broad use with many groups of individual and many types of conditions and treatment cross the core health-related quality of life domains. Consequently, generic measures are considered particularly useful in studies comparing patients with different diagnoses or with different treatment interventions. However, comprehensiveness makes these instruments insensitive to small changes in patients' conditions, or may not tap some clinically relevant aspects (Levi & Drotar, 1998). Therefore, disease-specific measures that lack generalisability [sic] across different populations, but which are highly responsive to symptoms of a particular condition or to effects of a particular treatment are widely used. Because of the strengths and weaknesses of both types of measures, many authors suggest their combined use (Bowling, 1991, 1995; Spieth & Harris, 1996). One example is the Pediatric Quality of Life Inventory (PedsQL) (Varni *et al.*, 1999). The PedsQL measures health-related quality of life for healthy children and adolescents and for those with acute and chronic health conditions by integrating both generic core scales and disease-specific modules into one measurement system. (pp. 21–22)

On the other hand, here is what Zekovic and Renwick (2003) have to say about holistic measures of quality of life:

> While health-related quality of life is traditionally used to evaluate different treatments and provide the basis for allocating resources (Lantos, 1998), holistic approaches have frequently been related to social policy with the aim of bringing

about social changes and reforms (Raphael, 1996a). 'Holistic approaches' is a broad term that attempts to include a variety of different theoretical and methodological approaches to quality of life. Therefore, it is difficult to identify a set of characteristics that encompasses every model. However, there are certain characteristics common to most holistic models. Specifically, quality of life is usually viewed as a multidimensional phenomenon that results from complex person-environment interaction (Brown *et al.*, 1996; Felce & Perry, 1996b; Schalock, 1996), although these interactions are seldom explicitly discussed. Different holistic approaches incorporate different dimensions of quality of life, but there is a growing consensus on core dimensions of quality of life (Borthwick-Duffy, 1990). Schalock (1996) reviewed the literature and distilled the following core dimensions typically included in holistic frameworks: emotional well-being, interpersonal relations, material well-being, personal developments, physical well-being, self-determination, social inclusion and individual rights. (p. 22)

Confused? This is not surprising. As I've said, differences in the design of instruments or measures is very problematic for evaluation research because it can lead to differences in both how programs are designed and, consequently, how they are evaluated. This, in turn, leads to conflicting findings about programs, which makes improvement within a specific program challenging, makes comparisons across programs challenging, and makes the design of new programs by others challenging (since others reading these various studies may be unsure as to what to include or not in their *own* program designs).

So what do you do? In this case, the best answer is also the most obvious—you can replicate the measures found in other research. Doing an extensive review of the existing literature will give you an idea as to what measures are the most frequently used and what measures are used by those who would be operating similar programs or programs in similar sociopolitical environments as yours. Once you identify some possible measures, simply borrow them (citing those who you borrowed them from, of course). Not only does this reduce the plethora of definitions likely to be available but it also aids in establishing reliability across studies and findings. The inconsistency in already existing studies will give you choices from which to select your measures. Your decision to select from existing measures helps contribute to consistency across studies.

■ Research Design

Evaluation research can be qualitative or quantitative. As I discussed earlier in this chapter, action research is very qualitative in focus. Qualitative approaches—such as focus groups, case studies, structured interviews, or unstructured interviews—can provide contextual and environmental information about a program that may otherwise be missing in more traditional quantitative approaches (Marvasti, 2004; Berg, 2004). However, as I have also mentioned, although qualitative approaches are becoming more popular, the bulk of evaluation research is still quantitative, so I will focus on quantitative methods here.

We have already encountered a number of quantitative studies aimed at evaluation research. In Chapter 6, I discussed the Minneapolis Domestic Violence experiment where police officers randomly selected, among sealed envelopes, responses to domestic violence calls in order to see which response was most successful in preventing a repeat domestic violence call. Essentially, this was a type of program evaluation because it was designed to see which intervention was the most successful in a real-life application. It also was a true experiment because it involved a treatment group (those receiving arrest, which was the main response of interest), control groups (those receiving the other, more traditional means of responding to these calls), and randomization. Although the Minneapolis experiment was not without its flaws, it is an example of how a true experiment can be conducted in the field (i.e., in real-life situations).

Frequently, however, it is impossible to randomly assign treatment to groups. Those involved in the actual implementation of the program or who are other stakeholders may resist randomization of subjects to treatment and control groups, and instead argue that program receipt needs to be based on need or merit. For example, a district attorney may argue that individuals with the strongest drug addictions, and therefore the most difficult to treat by conventional methods (hence, the most likely to recidivate and contribute to high crime rates), should receive priority over other treatment court applicants because they "need" some innovative form of drug treatment more so than other people. Randomization may also not be accurately done, based on missing information, for example, which would lead to nonequivalent experimental and control groups. Or, a third possible barrier to random assignment may be a reactivity effect. This is especially a concern if the new program is publicized and people who are in the control group desire the program and alter their behavior accordingly in order to be allowed to receive the experimental treatment (essentially, they want to change from the control to the experimental group) (Cook, Cook, & Mark, 1977). In a review of the development of evaluation research, Rossi and Wright (1984) summarize this dilemma:

> The realization quickly emerged, however, that randomized, controlled experiments could only be done correctly under very limited circumstances and that the demand for evaluation covered many programs that simply could not be assessed in this way. Not only were there frequent ethical and legal limitations to randomization, but many existing programs that had full (or almost full) coverage of their intended beneficiary populations could not be assessed using controlled experiments because there was no way to create appropriate control groups. It also turned out that field experiments took a long time—3 to 5 years. (p. 335)

Because of the difficulties with random assignment, quasi-experiments are the usual method of data gathering in evaluation research.

In this chapter I presented a couple quasi-experimental studies; one addressed boot camps (Kempinen & Kurlychek, 2003) and another addressed welfare-to-work programs (Fergusson, 2002, **AN 8815191**). These studies were quasi-experimental because they did not involve random assignment to the experimental or control groups. In fact, Fergusson's study did not even have a concrete experimental group. Instead, he compared the rates of behavior of his subjects to the rates for the rest of that population who did not experience the program.

Let's look at an in-depth example of a quasi-experiment for evaluation purposes. Briggs, Sundt, and Castellano (2003, **AN 13435825**) studied a specific type of prison called a "supermax" prison (i.e., supermaximum security prison). These prisons are designed to house the most serious and violent offenders, yet provide a safe place to work for those who are in charge of controlling these types of prisoners. In order to achieve the goals of safety for staff and other inmates, in supermax prisons, inmates spend about 23 hours in their cells, are isolated from other inmates, and have very limited contact with the staff (even going so far as having food delivered through a slot in the doors without any contact between the inmate and the person delivering the food). The rare times prisoners *do* move about the prison, they do so in shackles and handcuffs. If these steps sound extreme, remember that these supermaximum prisons are reserved for prisoners dubbed "the worst of the worst" because they have shown that they are violent and threatening in other prison settings The ideology behind these tactics is that if the prison limits the opportunity for violence (presumably by limiting the contact of inmates with other people), the incidence of violence will decrease.

Briggs, Sundt, and Castellano note that there is a lot of public support for these types of prisons, but that there is no vigorous scientific evaluation to see whether these prisons actually do protect inmates from each other and the staff from the inmates. Although Briggs and colleagues were able to identify 34 states that had supermax prisons, they could study only 4 due to issues of prison size and availability of longitudinal data on inmate–inmate assaults and inmate–staff assaults. Hence, to evaluate this program, the researchers conducted a time-series design using three experimental prisons (Arizona, Illinois, and Minnesota) and one control prison (Utah), the latter of which was designed to help identify (hence, control) any local history effects. Because, obviously, a researcher cannot randomly decide what states will and will not have supermax prisons and because the criteria for inclusion in Briggs and colleagues' study eliminated many of the 34 state programs present, random selection and assignment was not possible; thus, this study is a quasi-experiment.

Briggs and colleagues conducted a longitudinal study where they obtained statistics from each of the four prisons regarding inmate–inmate assaults, inmate injury, and inmate–staff assaults for a number of years prior to the construction and use of a supermax prison and a few years after the advent of these prisons. For example, Figure 10.4 charts, with some statistical adjustment (see the original article for details, if interested), the three measures for the Illinois supermax prison.

Looking at Figure 10.4 you may notice that Briggs and colleagues were able to gather information regarding the inmate–inmate assault rate (called *inmate assault rate* on the graph, the light line) and the inmate–staff assault rate (called *staff assault rate* on the graph, the bold line) for 9.5 years prior to the opening of the supermax prison. The Illinois supermax prison is called "Tamms" and its opening is indicated by the vertical line on the graph. These researchers also have data on these assault rates for 2.5 years after the opening of the supermax prison.

There are a couple of important points I want to make about this graph that are relevant to evaluation research. First, as you may see in Figure 10.4 and recognize from Chapter 6, this quasi-experimental design is a time-series design. In time-series designs, researchers observer multiple time points *before* the advent of a program (in experimental language, the treatment) and *after* the program advent. In this graph, as in many good time-series graphs, the indication of when the treatment occurred is depicted by a vertical line through the relevant time point. This allows researchers to more clearly decide if they see a pattern or change occur before or after the treatment.

Second, during the course of the study, the Illinois prison changed the way in which they defined "assault." If you think back to Chapter 3, you may remember that when the definition of a concept changes during a study, researchers call that an *instrumentation effect*. In quasi-experiments, the researchers rarely have any say in how agency records are going to be maintained and how actions will be defined. Therefore, the best that they can

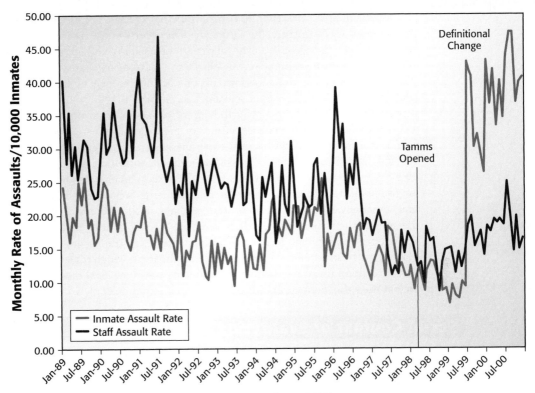

Figure 10.4 Illinois DOC Inmate and Staff Assault Rates (1989–2000)

Source: Chad S. Briggs, Jody L. Sundt, and Thomas C. Castellano, "The Effect of Supermaximum Security Prisons on Aggregate Levels of Institutional Violence," *Criminology, 41* (4) (2003): 1363. Reprinted by permission from the American Society of Criminology.

do if a change *does* take place during the course of the study is to mention it in the report. This is what Briggs, Sundt, and Castellano do in this graph where they note the "definitional change." Without noting this on the graph, it would appear to someone reading the graph that the incidence of inmate assaults actually *increased* after the implementation of the supermax prison, but this may not be the case because, as noted, the Illinois prison broadened their definition of assault. This means that after this definition change, more behaviors were defined as assault, hence the rate appears to increase. Could some of the increase have resulted from the creation of a supermax prison? Sure, but a researcher (and the rest of us) will never know. We have to err on the side of caution and assume that the increase is due to the change in definition, not necessarily the program itself.

Last, if you examine the graph, you will see that the advent of the supermax program did not seem to affect the staff assault rates (we won't consider the change in inmate assaults, which is impossible to interpret due to the instrumentation effect). True, the rate of staff assaults are down compared to when the researchers first started collecting the rates in 1989, but these rates have been down for awhile. In fact, just looking at the graph alone suggests that the addition of the supermax prison served to increase staff assaults because the graph line is generally higher after the supermax prison opened (it increases to the right of the vertical line). However, statistical tests that the researchers conducted reveal that this increase is not statistically significant—in other words, the increase may be due to changes in other issues or in a cyclical pattern of assaults that have nothing or little to do with the supermax prison system itself. Hence, it appears that at least with regard to staff–inmate assaults, the supermax prison did not reduce violence, contrary to the researchers', and the anecdotal, evidence suggesting that it would. Briggs, Sundt, and Castellano found similar results for the other two supermax prisons as well.

Any type of research method technically may be feasible for evaluation research. However, experiments, especially quasi-experiments, are frequently the method of choice because they are the best methodological means of controlling for extraneous factors (or at least being able to identify their presence). Quasi-experiments also lend themselves well to longitudinal analysis, which helps determine whether a program truly produced a change or whether any change just reflects other, perhaps, cyclical factors that are independent of the actual program or policy itself. Researchers frequently use quasi-experiments because evaluation research tries to observe social processes in the natural, social environment. Consequently, sociopolitical forces affect the climate in which researchers are able to conduct evaluation research—frequently producing less-than-ideal research conditions. Let's look at the social context of evaluation research in more detail.

Social Context of Evaluation Research

In academic research, as opposed to program evaluation or other forms of applied research, the researcher usually has the majority of control over the research question as well as the research process. Because of this, researchers have more immediate methodological control, which allows them to design research that has clearly operationalized concepts, well-selected samples, and minimal rival causal factors—at least in theory. In other words, in nonevaluation research, most (but not all) methodological limitations or problems are more likely to be the result of restrictions that the researcher imposed on herself or himself or mistakes that the researcher made.

The involvement of second parties is usually tangential and, at the very most, in the form of research assistants. This is not the case with evaluation research. As I stated earlier in the chapter, in evaluation research, the researcher is really an instrument (to some degree) of the stakeholders involved with the policy. A researcher's ability to effectively evaluate any program can be influenced by those who do *not* want to see the program succeed. People with special interests contrary to the goals of the program or who feel that the money spent on a program could be better spent elsewhere can create barriers that will impede a researcher's ability to get reliable information. The point is, unlike in other forms of research, evaluation research is more vulnerable to the support, or lack of it, from non-researchers. This doesn't mean that research *can't* be done, but it may mean that *good, reliable, accurate* research cannot be done. Let's look at some of the obstacles in evaluation research a little more closely.

■ Administrative Issues

Administrative issues abound in evaluation research. As I've said, program administrators are the ones frequently in charge of defining the research problem. They are the ones who are likely to commission a researcher to evaluate their program, therefore they tell the researcher what the research goals are, since these administrators are the ones most familiar with the program itself.

The first problem with administrative issues in evaluation research is that the program administrators frequently are not very clear as to the program goals they want evaluated. David (2002, **AN 5893585**) notes that it is important to be clear as to what administrators want the research to ultimately show. Are the goals of the research those of the coordinators, meaning should the research show whether the coordinators are doing their job well? Are the research goals those of the program developers who want to show that they produced a well-developed and effective program (and how do we measure such)? Are the goals those of specific agencies involved with the program who have a vested interest in showing that their particular agencies are busy (in order to better insulate them from financial cutbacks) and contributing to society? Or are the goals those of the clients, so that the research should show how those who use the program are somehow better off than those who did not? (David, 2002). Usually, the program administrators themselves are not clear as to the goals; and, until they are, designing effective evaluation is impossible.

Other times administrators want to evaluate *all* of these factors, which is feasible but ultimately creates a complicated research design that current resources may not be able to adequately support. Therefore, "throwing it all into the hat," so to speak, is not a viable response to the question of program goals, unless the resources to effectively evaluate all of these interests are present. Furthermore, the program coordinators may not be able to adequately define the program goals, at least in a measurable manner, because those goals themselves were written very vaguely in order to allow specific agencies the freedom to act as they see fit and to satisfy competing political interests present in the formation of the program (Wholey, Scanlon, Duffy, Fukumoto, & Vogt, 1970).

A second administrative concern is administrative intervention that may affect the nature of the research. For example, suppose that you are evaluating a work-release program for a local prison and you randomly assigned prisoners who had similar criminal offenses and criminal histories to either the work-release program or to remain housed in the prison their entire term. One of the convicts on work release rapes a co-worker after hours. Due to the ensuing public pressure, the warden decides to stop the work-release program all together. Now you have no evaluation. Another possibility is that the warden does not decide to stop the program, but instead demands to examine all of your sample members so that he or she can identify those who are more "at risk" for negative behavior and insist that these individuals are not released in the public, even for limited work experiences. Now you have lost random assignment and your experimental and control groups are no longer comparable. A third possible scenario is that the work-release program becomes even stricter. Perhaps prisoners can only get certain types of jobs or work certain hours. Now your experimental stimulus has changed, creating an instrumentation effect, and likely altering the observed outcomes before and after this change. Table 10.1 summarizes many of these obstacles in evaluation research and offers some solutions as well.

■ Population Definition

Population definition involves deciding who the target audience will be for the program—essentially being clear as to the units of analysis. There are two potential issues with this. The first is that sometimes target populations are so explicitly defined—for example, "people who have had a clinically defined addiction to alcohol for more than two years and who have already tried unsuccessfully to receive treatment in the past year"—that the program will reach only a small, specific target population that is not comparable to other broader populations. This makes any program intervention very specific and piecemeal—meaning that the program itself is going to address only a small minority of individuals and

TABLE 10.1 Obstacles to Evaluation Research and Some Possible Solutions

Obstacles	Possible Solutions
Administrative Issues	
• Unclear research goals. What is a researcher evaluating? Are the goals those of the coordinator, the specific agencies involved, clients? Different administrative parties may have different outcomes of interest for the same program.	• Meet with key figures prior to starting of research in order to agree on goals. If goals continue to be unidentifiable, then decline to do the evaluation, because a program without clear goals cannot be evaluated.
• Actions on behalf of participants that lead to administrative intervention (e.g., program changes).	• Note the date and circumstances of any program changes and conduct before/after comparisons. If the change is severe, the evaluation may have to be aborted.
Population Issues	
• Target population is so specifically defined that comparison to other programs is not beneficial because results can be interpreted in such a way as to benefit the program, regardless of evaluation. In other words, positive comparisons are due to the program, negative comparisons are not applicable because the "target populations differ"—thereby creating a win-win for the agency.	• Try to have target population be comparable to those served by other programs unless the entire purpose of the program is to serve a very select target population (and then understand the evaluation limitations with this framework).
• No target population is identified. Hence, the program can, technically, apply to "anyone," which limits comparison to other programs and limits the establishment of findings reliability.	• Either identify the target population or decline to conduct the evaluation.
Ethical Issues	
• Ethical debates about randomization to treatment and control groups.	• If no previous programs are available, the debate may be less viable. If other programs are available, try to have them serve as your comparison group.
• Ethical responsibility of objectivity.	
• Be aware and recognize in all reports any potential personal bias.	

TABLE 10.1 Continued

Obstacles	Possible Solutions
Political Issues	
• Specific parties feel that their clients should experience the program over other clients. Denial of program participation may lead to loss of cooperation to various forms of program undermining.	• One of three tactics may work: (1) promise the control group first access to the program if evaluation shows that the program is beneficial; (2) do staged innovations where some people are admitted early in the evaluation and some later (with random assignment within); (3) do a basic random assignment for all people at all stages (preferred when resources are limited).
Use of Research Results	
• Those commissioning the evaluation do not always use the researcher's findings. Three common reasons are:	• To address these issues (in order):
—Findings contradict firmly held beliefs.	—Cite as much external evidence as possible in favor of your findings (essentially, establish reliability).
—Findings contrast with the values of those with vested interests in either defining the problem (needs evaluation) or defining program success (outcome evaluation or cost-benefit analysis).	—Unfortunately, here there is little a researcher can do. It is very difficult to undo someone's belief system.
—The researcher presented the findings in a way that nonresearchers do not understand.	—Write two reports—one for other researchers, which is very technical, and one for those who commissioned the study, which focuses on the practical ramifications of the findings. (But have the answers to detailed questions ready in case someone asks.)

will likely exist in a vacuum relative to other programs available. This makes the evaluation of program efficiency difficult.

If the nature of the target population of Program A is very specific, it is almost impossible to compare the viability of Program A to Program B and to Program C, which may already exist because anyone involved in Program A can dispute the comparisons to the other programs with the airy, "Well, they deal with a different population than we do." Essentially, those involved with Program A can focus only on positive findings by stating that all other comparisons or negative findings deal with a different target population. This loads the dice in the favor of the specific agency, which essentially negates the role of evaluation, since these program organizers can interpret findings in a way to benefit them, regardless of what research may or may not say.

The second issue is that sometimes evaluators are not clear as to who the target population even is. Sometimes administrators are unclear ("The target population is anyone who needs the service"), sometimes program creators are unclear. In either case, not knowing the target population, and just administering the program to "whomever," also prevents comparative analysis and reduces the ability to replicate the findings (Breedlove, 1972).

■ Ethical Restrictions

In previous chapters, I discussed ethical issues that corresponded to the various methods of observations as their own subheadings. However, in evaluation research, the discussion of ethics really fits in with our discussion of the social context of evaluation research. After all, evaluation research is of programs that directly deal with the quality and nature of people's *lives,* therefore the ethical considerations inherent in this type of research can easily affect the scientific quality of the research.

Probably the biggest ethical issue in evaluation research is random assignment. In true experiments, which would be the method of choice for evaluation research in a perfect world, participants would be randomly assigned to either receive the program of interest (the treatment) or not. People create programs because they ultimately think that those programs will benefit the people who receive them. Therefore, the ethical concern lies in randomly *denying* someone participation in a program that may benefit him or her. However, there are some counterarguments to this point. First, if the program is new, and therefore one that is not available to the target population previously, then having a comparison group that does not receive the program is not a change from the status quo. In other words, under previous circumstances (those prior to the implementation of the new program), people did not have access to the program (treatment) because it did not exist. Therefore, their lack of access after it initially exists does not alter their circumstance of not experiencing the program. As a result, there is no breech of ethics.

Second, the argument that people are being "denied" a benefit of the program is based on the *assumption* that the program is beneficial in the first place. Just because a program is instated does not mean that that program produces the desired outcomes. In fact, research has illustrated that many intervention programs are either ineffective or actually have unintended negative consequences (Boruch, 1975).

The third counterargument is that being in a control group does not necessarily mean that someone experiences *no* treatment. Being in a control group may just mean that people in this group do not experience the program being evaluated. They may still be receiving some other program. In evaluation research, people can have varying degrees of program treatment. For example, if researchers are evaluating a family planning program, they can compare a district that is utilizing a new family planning program (the treatment group) with one that is operating under the old program (the control group). In this instance, no one is denied family planning education; what varies is the method of that educational delivery (Bauman, Viadro, & Tsui, 1994).

Random selection or assignment is not always possible, however. For political and community support for a program, researchers may not be able to randomize. The point I am making here is that, according to some, *ethically* randomization is possible.

The second ethical issue that may arise is the responsibility for the researcher to be objective or impartial. Not all programs are social intervention in the classic sense, and, as I've just alluded to earlier, no evaluation research goes on in a vacuum. All evaluation research, to varying degrees, is influenced by the social, political, economic, and /or moral climate in which the program is operating. Consequently, it is very difficult for the researcher to study a program without becoming involved in, or at least aware of, the different views.

For example, suppose that you are studying the effectiveness of mandatory standardized tests on students' learning. You randomly decide which students (or if you are doing this study on a larger scale, which schools) will experience mandatory standardized tests to assess student learning and which will not. Currently, mandatory standardized testing is a social, political, and ethical issue in itself. What if some of the students who are randomly selected to experience standardized tests (or their parents) are fundamentally *against* such testing? When students and parents become angered that they have to experience testing, you are the one responsible. It will be impossible for you to explain the necessity of the randomized testing and the program evaluation without becoming embroiled in the debate surrounding mandatory standardized tests yourself. In the course of your involvement, you are likely to develop firm views of the situation on your own, and making sure that these views do not color the research is challenging.

■ Political Involvement

Few programs exist outside of political influences. Here, "political" can mean the support (or lack thereof) of local officials, or it can mean the various sides and perspectives of the different stakeholders involved. Either way, politics undoubtedly plays a role in any policy implementation, and therefore evaluation. For example, different groups may feel that those they serve may be more "entitled" to a program, and therefore exert pressure to have their clients in the treatment group at the threat of losing this group's cooperation. Clearly, giving into pressures such as these are going to threaten the validity of the evaluation. Programs are frequently hard to implement on their own without the added interference of spurned feelings of unfair treatment, negative word-of-mouth exposure by unsatisfied individuals to others, or other means of thwarting program success. Furthermore, if a researcher or program organizers submit to one group's political pressure, they are likely to experience additional pressure from other groups who feel that their clients should experience the treatment.

Campbell (1969) describes three strategies for reducing political pressure. The first is to present the program as a pilot project which, if found effective, will be made available to those in the control group before it is made available to others. This approach both recognizes that not all programs are successful (and essentially uses this uncertainty to the researcher's advantage with the implication that the researcher would not want to unduly harm the control group) and satisfies the desire of particular interest groups to have their clients experience any program benefits. This guarantee also facilitates the use of random assignment, since in the end everyone will be eligible for the program if it is a success.

The second approach is called *staged innovation*, which recognizes that people are chosen more haphazardly in the beginning of program implementation than in later phases. Consequently, researchers can have two phases of study—early and late—and randomly select treatment and control groups for each. Third, when there are limited resources for program implementation, and consequently only a relatively small group or target audience will be able to receive the program, random assignment may actually be the best way to ensure fairness. After all, in random assignment everyone has an *equal* probability of being selected, and essentially it is "fate" as opposed to political manipulations that will decide whether someone receives the treatment or not.

■ Use of Research Results

Even though the goal of evaluation research may be to see whether a program is working or not, this does not mean that the evaluator's findings will be directly used, even if the research is the best-designed study available. Ultimately, people have a vested interest in an evaluation providing results that either support their role in the program or fit with what they "know" to be true. In other words, most people use evaluation results to confirm what they "know" or "feel" to be correct. To the degree that it does, the research is likely to be used as a "strong" example of how "scientific research" supports the goals or views of those behind the program. The research is likely to be held as an example of valid and reliable confirmation of what is already happening—even if the quality of the research is not that great. In other words, it's not the quality of the content that's important, it's the end result.

On the other hand, if the end result does *not* say what those involved in the program were hoping it would, then those involved are likely to denounce the research as biased, or uninformed, or otherwise incorrect—even if the methodology is the most advanced, sophisticated, and valid available. For example, in 1985 sociologists Murray Straus and Richard Gelles conducted the National Family Violence Survey of 6,000 adults that was funded by the National Institutes of Mental Health. In their study, Straus and Gelles (1986) found that women were almost as likely to initiate violence against their male partners as men were against their female partners. In other words, according to Straus and Gelles, husband abuse is just as common as wife abuse. However, Strauss and Gelles's findings run *counter* to our current notions of domestic violence; consequently, there has been little push for programs aimed at helping men (essentially we can view Straus and Gelles's study as a "needs assessment"). Instead, in fact, a great deal of energy has been directed at contradicting these findings—energy that ranges from questioning Straus and Gelles's research methodology to recognizing that a problem may be present, but claiming that men are less serious victims than women. Interestingly, there is little push for new research that would resolve some of these disputes. Therefore, the (potential) social problem of husband abuse and the ensuing lack of program implementation is an indirect example that illustrates some key reasons that evaluation research findings may not be followed—partially or at all.

The first reason that evaluation findings may not be used is because the findings may contradict deeply held beliefs. For example, ever since domestic violence has been defined as a "social problem," domestic violence has been synonymous with wife abuse. Women as social victims, especially as victims of domestic violence, make sense to us because there is a long history of men denying women equal treatment. For a long time, men controlled the legal system, denied women the right to vote, were legally allowed to beat their wives so long as the switch was "not bigger than the width of his thumb" (hence the phrase "rule of thumb"), and received higher pay relative to women regardless of their education or years of employment. Furthermore, most women are physically weaker than most men. Hence, women as "victims" makes sense; men as "victims" does not. These beliefs remain even today.

The second reason that evaluation findings may not be used is that people involved in the program obviously have a vested interest in that program. Advocates for abused women frequently look at the report rates for spousal abuse in the Uniform Crime Reports (UCR) and continually note that the rates of abuse for men are lower than that for women.

But these advocates and researchers frequently gloss over the content of the UCR and discuss rates of *incidences* of abuse as if they were the same as *reported* rates of abuse, the latter of which is actually what the UCR publishes. However, it should not be a mental leap to see how the two—rates of incidence of abuse and reported rates of abuse—may tell different stories. Clearly, the idea of a man being beaten by his wife may initially seem somewhat ludicrous due to our deeply held beliefs about gender relations. Suppose *you* were a man being abused by your wife. Would *you* report your abuse to the police—who primarily consist of men who are in positions of strength and power, who embody, at least stereotypically, everything that is meant to be "manly"? Furthermore, most men learn as boys not to hit women, *no matter what,* and some abused men report *not* retaliating because they are afraid of what they would do to their wives if they did so. Also, McLeod (1984) studied UCR reports and found that women, recognizing their strength vulnerability, are more likely to use weapons when attacking a man.

I am not trying to downplay the important problem of wife abuse. Obviously, no one deserves to be physically or emotionally battered. The point I am making is that from an academic and scientific point of view, it is difficult to even study the less socially popular concept of husband abuse *because of* the social and political climate surrounding this issue. Strauss and Gelles's study is just one of a small number of conducted studies on husband abuse that questions our current stereotypes of domestic violence. Yet, these studies get little attention and are hotly contested because of the political ramifications of the findings. There are limited resources for helping victims of domestic violence, and women fit the profile of a victim more so than men, they traditionally have fewer economic resources than men, and they traditionally have less social power than men. Therefore, there is political and social support for focusing solely on women as victims of domestic violence, regardless of whether statistics may suggest that the story is more complicated than popular conception. The issue of domestic violence illustrates that there are vested interests in deciding *how* research findings are going to be used. This is common in many forms of evaluation research.

Similarly, what if research shows that a program does not have its intended effect? It's human nature to want to deny involvement in anything that produces negative effects or appears to waste money. "Passing the buck," so to speak, is common when outcomes are less than favorable, and blaming the research is a convenient scapegoat. The stakeholders can blame the researcher's design, and the researcher, in turn, can blame the financial, social, or political ramifications. Either way, blaming the research is a way for everyone to avoid full accountability for the failure of a program.

The last reason evaluation findings may not be put to use is if the researcher presents findings in ways that nonresearchers cannot understand. Essentially, researchers have to write for two audiences. One audience is that of other researchers, and this refers to the type of information that would be included in a research report written for publication in an academic journal. In this case, the intended audience is other researchers, therefore issues such as operationalization, sampling technique, experimental design, and statistical tests are important. However, most program administrators could not care less about whether a researcher conducted a Cronbach's alpha to test for bias in treatment and control groups; whether the researcher did a chi-square test or a t-test to test for statistical significance; or whether the findings had a probability of error value less than .05 or less than .01. Presenting results and implications in this language is likely to leave average nonresearchers confused or asleep. Their concern is the bottom line: what works, what didn't, and what do you suggest to change what did not work? The detail about how you made those conclusions is not important to them. Therefore, administrators and practioners frequently do not have the time to educate themselves about research matters, so they trust their evaluator to have done everything "right"—at least if the findings are favorable.

■ Summary

I did not include the practical limitations inherent in many evaluation projects to discourage you from doing evaluations. In fact, unless most of you reading this book intend to go to graduate school in one of the social science fields, any encounter you have with research once you graduate is likely to be applied research such as program evaluation. Rather, I included this section in order to acquaint you with the reasons why the academic and practical evaluation of research evaluating programs (sounds confusing, I know) has to be less stringent than the evaluation of studies whose primary purpose is academic—the gaining of knowledge for knowledge's sake.

Because evaluation research takes place in the context of people's daily lives, the researcher does not have as much control over the events of the study as may be the case in other types of research. Hence, although random selection and assignment are clearly the methodological choices of sampling and assignment to treatment/control groups, in evaluation research that may not be feasible because of political issues, resources, or the nature of the target population. Therefore, just because an evaluation study does not use random assignment, that does not mean that the study itself has no merit and should be discounted.

I will touch on realistic assessment of written evaluation research in the Evaluation Written Research section of this chapter; however, I cannot reiterate enough that the standard rules of the game, so to speak, may not apply in evaluation research. Even so, that qualification does not absolve the researcher from designing the best possible study for the political, economic, and social context of the program *or* from abandoning an evaluation when too many insurmountable barriers are present.

Grants and Proposal Writing

Since most people who conduct research are not independently wealthy, they frequently obtain grants that will pay for the financial costs of research. In order to obtain a grant, any grant, people first have to write a **proposal,** which is essentially a written plan for what the applicant intends to do with any money awarded. This plan is reviewed by a panel of people who decide whether to give (or *grant*) the applicant the requested money. People write grants for lots of reasons, and researchers are only one type of person who apply for such funding. For example, community leaders may write for grants to implement new programs (e.g., to build a new recreation center for young people). People who head agencies may also write for grants to help fund their services (such as a family planning clinic or a domestic violence shelter). Researchers who are not doing evaluation of a program may also apply for grant money that will cover the cost, for example, of printing and mailing a national survey. So, any time someone wants money to help add something to a community, to begin or test a program, or to do academic research, they may apply for a grant by writing a proposal.

Therefore, my discussion of grants could technically be in any chapter (or a chapter of its own). I am including it in the evaluation chapter because my goal is to provide you with a basic idea about the grant process (as opposed to a detailed, step-by-step guide for writing proposals, which could entail an entire book on its own) and because, unless you decide to get a job in a college, most of you who will ever encounter the need to write a grant will do so in order to either implement or evaluate some type of program. So in this chapter I will discuss the concept of *grantsmanship* and some basic elements of a grant proposal.

■ Grantsmanship

Although anyone may write a proposal and apply for a grant, it does not mean that anyone who applies for a grant will actually get it. In fact, most grants are competitive, meaning that a lot of people apply for a limited amount of available funding. If I wanted to write a grant to supplement my income while I did a study, or if I wanted to write a grant because obtaining one would add to my prestige, I would very likely be turned down flat by those who are reviewing the proposal. In fact, given the competitive nature of grant applications, according to MacKenzie and McCarthy (1990) grantsmanship is "an art form, which requires faculty members to combine hard work and creativity in their efforts to define and communicate their researcher objectives and strategy" (p. 1). (MacKenzie and McCarthy refer to "faculty" but the same applies to any one writing a grant.)

MacKenzie and McCarthy (1990) see grantsmanship as a means to obtain the necessary resources to study "salient" and "tractable" problems (p. 1). Here, *salient* refers to problems that are important and worthwhile. Therefore, proposals for grant money to fund an innovative means of fighting drug use, such as a drug treatment court, would be salient (at least they were before many other counties started such programs) because drug use is an important social concern and, at least initially, drug treatment courts were an innovative idea to combat drug recidivism. However, a proposal to survey college students about the day they prefer to take classes may be less salient. To some (such as college administrators) it may be interesting, but that topic itself does not suggest either why it is important (since the days college students want to take classes may not have as wide a social significance as, for example, drug use) and there is nothing to imply why grant money would be needed to conduct this survey.

On the other hand, reviewers are also likely to reject a grant proposal to "erase poverty from our nation's experience." Why? Ending poverty certainly is a salient topic—with about 12 percent of our population in poverty, and many of those people being children, ending poverty would definitely seem to be socially important. However, the topic, as presented, lacks the second characteristic of good grantsmanship. It is not *tractable*. According to MacKenzie and McCarthy (1990), tractable problems are those that are feasible to address. "Erasing poverty" is not feasible. Perhaps a person can create an innovative program to *reduce* poverty in a specific location, which may better fulfill the requirement of tractability, but for a proposal to argue that (1) it wants to "erase" poverty and (2) it wants to do so "nationwide" is far too much of an undertaking for one research project or program to do.

So, you think you have a salient and tractable research problem. Now what do you do? There are two more issues that a person writing a proposal needs to address, and to some degree they may go hand in hand. The first is to find an appropriate funding agency; the second is to write a proposal to submit to that funding agency.

■ Funding Agencies

There are many funding sources available, but they do not fund the same type of projects. Most universities and some organizations have offices that are responsible for helping with the grant-writing process, and these offices will frequently publish announcements regarding funding opportunities as they arise. Furthermore, the *Guide for Federal Funding for Social Scientists* lists U.S. government agencies that frequently offer funding for social science projects. Some of these agencies are, and this is by no means a comprehensive list, the National Institute of Justice, the National Science Foundation, and the National Institute of Health. The *Foundation Directory* lists private foundations and some of them may have funding opportunities. Finally, many professional organizations, such as the American Political Science Association, the American Sociological Association, the Academy of Criminal Justice Sciences, the National Education Association Higher Education, and the American Psychological Society, have information on various grants available in their respective fields.

Even if you start by looking at the websites for the national organizations associated with your field, you still are likely to have to carefully select from a fairly long list of possible funding sources. Therefore, here are some questions to consider when deciding which funding agency may be most appropriate (and therefore most likely to give you money) for your topic.

1. What types of projects does the funding agency fund?
2. What are the deadlines?
3. How large are most grants?
4. Are there any aspects of a project not funded?
5. What are the details of the proposal requested by the funding agency?

Let me briefly discuss some of these in more detail. First, some agencies fund only specific projects or topics. Some fund only applied research, as opposed to basic or academic research. Some fund only projects that relate to certain topics. For example, it would not make much sense to submit a topic about a new approach to mainstreaming children with disabilities in elementary school classrooms to the National Institute of Justice. Clearly, this example is pretty obvious. The topic deals with education, whereas the funding agency is interested in issues relating to the criminal justice system (although if you could make an argument linking mainstreaming with delinquency, the National Institute of Justice may be fair game). A real mismatch between topic and funding agency may not be as evident as the basic example I gave. Therefore, an applicant has to carefully read the description of the types of programs that individual funding agencies are willing to consider.

The second point is pretty obvious. Many funding agencies have consistent deadlines for proposals. Some of these deadlines are on a fairly regular basis (e.g., the agency always has three deadlines—one in April, one in August, and one in December). If the funding deadlines are regular, and you learn of an appropriate agency in mid-November whose deadline is the first of December, it is better to wait until that agency's next deadline than to submit a hastily thrown-together proposal.

Third, some agencies will set a grant limit. For example, an agency may advertise that it has grant money available to fund three grants where each does not exceed a request for $15,000. Other agencies may leave the amount open. In the latter case, it behooves an applicant to research the general grant awards given in the past. If the applicant finds that the agency does not generally provide grants over $10,000 and the applicant needs an award of at least $50,000 to adequately put together and/or evaluate a program, then that funding agency is not appropriate for the applicant's needs and he or she should continue looking elsewhere. This alludes to an important point in grantsmanship. An applicant cannot have a "sky is the limit" attitude about the request for funds—in other words, an applicant should not unnecessarily inflate the request for funds. On the other hand, applicants also should not apply to funding agencies that they know cannot accommodate the financial requests they are making. The idea of "every little bit helps" generally does not work with grant writing because one is unlikely to find a multitude of funding agencies each willing to pay a little part of the program or evaluation. Furthermore, trying to make do with an amount of money that seriously falls short of that necessary to run the program or do the evaluation is only asking for disaster, since limited funds frequently lead to cutbacks and those cutbacks frequently affect the overall nature of the program. Hence, the grant money (if it is even awarded) ends up being used for a program that differs in reality from that outlined in the proposal.

Funding agencies also sometimes limit the items for which they are willing to pay. For example, a person may be able to obtain a grant from the State Department to hire additional police officers to institute a community-oriented form of policing, but that same grant money may not apply to training those officers in community-oriented policing tactics. The funding agency may stipulate that the applicant hire officers already familiar with that type of policing.

Last, a researcher needs to know the details the funding agency requires to be in the proposal. Each funding agency's proposal requirements are likely to be different (sometimes only slightly different, sometimes very different), and the researcher needs to make sure that any proposal is in the format requested by the funding agency. Otherwise, the agency is likely to disregard the proposal before anyone even reads the abstract. I will discuss some general components to a proposal in more detail in the next section.

The questions suggested in this chapter are just guidelines to help you decide which funding agency is most appropriate for your proposal submission. The websites of professional organizations frequently include links to funding agencies or opportunities. Librarians can also be a good source to find or help make sense of funding opportunities. The point is, finding an appropriate funding source for your research can take some research itself.

■ Grant Proposals

As mentioned, many funding agencies have their own requirements for the format of their proposals. However, some agencies do not, and many general aspects of the proposals are similar. Therefore, in this section, I will discuss some *basic and common* elements of a grant proposal. Although many of these components are basic, I've borrowed from Don Thackrey's *Proposal Writer's Guide* listed at the University of Michigan's Research website (www.research.umich.edu/proposals/) and S. Joseph Levine's *Guide for Writing a Funding Proposal* (www.learnerassociates.net/proposal/) to synthesize the basic elements of a research grant and a program grant. To help organize my discussion, I have briefly listed the individual components in Figure 10.5. There are some minor differences in general proposal format based on whether one is proposing a project (which will later be evaluated) or whether one is proposing a research project (which may be an evaluation of an already

Research Grants: Grants for funding independent research projects (which may include general academic research, the evaluation of the need for a program, or the evaluation of an existing program)

1. Title Page
2. Abstract
3. Table of Contents
4. Background Information
5. Description of Proposed Research
   a. Short-term research goals
   b. Long-term research goals
   c. Clearly stated assumptions or hypotheses
   d. Outline schedule of the proposed work
   e. Clear explanation of research method
6. Description of Resources
   a. Available and needed resources
      i. Personnel
      ii. Facilities
      iii. Equipment/Supplies/Communication
7. Budget
8. List of References
9. Appendices

Project Grants: Grants for implementing new programs or policies

1. Title Page
2. Project Overview
3. Background Information/Statement of Problem
4. Project Detail
   a. Goals and objectives
   b. Clientele
   c. Activities
   d. Staff/Administration
5. Description of Resources
   a. Available resources
   b. Needed resources
      i. Personnel
      ii. Facilities
      iii. Equipment/Supplies/Communication
      iv. Budget
6. Evaluation Plan
7. Appendices

Figure 10.5 Basic Components of Grant Proposals

existing program). Let's look at each of the components in more detail. Whenever appropriate, I will comment on how the two grant formats differ in the follow sub-sections.

Title page

Generally, the title page contains information regarding the name, the department, and the signature of the key people involved in the program. For example, in a project proposal for a drug treatment court, the title page might include the names and signatures of the district attorney, the chief of police, the judge who will preside over the program, the head of probation and parole, and the project coordinator.

Abstract/Project overview

On a research report, the abstract, if you remember from Chapter 2, is a short, usually 150- to 200-word summary of the research. Since no research has been done at the proposal phase, when writing a grant proposal for research, the abstract would contain a quick overview of the major objectives of the research and some general (proposed) method to address those objectives. The abstract should also include a very brief comment about the importance of the research. In fact, even though the abstract appears first in the proposal (after the title page), researchers generally should not write the abstract until *after* they are done with the rest of the proposal. This is because the abstract can arguably be the most important component of the entire proposal. It is what most people will read first, and based on the merit of the abstract, it will directly determine whether anyone will read further. Therefore, researchers need to make sure that the abstract touches on each of the important and unique features of the proposal that will be developed further in the heart of the proposal itself. It is easiest to do this when the researcher has the entire completed proposal to serve as a guide.

Project overviews are a little different from abstracts and are present in proposals aimed at funding specific projects. Like an abstract, a project overview should, as its name implies, overview the entire project. Think of it as an executive summary. The program overview should give a brief but comprehensive picture of what the project will be, how it fits into the schema of the funding organization to which the researcher is applying for money, and the role of other agencies that may be involved in any collaboration. Like an abstract, the project overview is the first piece of information someone will read, and the quality of it will determine whether a second (and third, and fourth, and so on, until you either receive funding or a brief letter of rejection) person sees your proposal. Consequently, it also should be written after the main body of the proposal, and it should stress why the problem is important, how the proposed idea is original or different from current programs, that the outcomes are clear and observable, and that the project is manageable.

Table of contents

A table of contents for a proposal is no different from that in any other type of work, therefore it does not merit real discussion with the exception of the comment that it is usually present in a research proposal only if an individual funding agency specifically requires one.

Background information/Statement of problem

Essentially this is the same as a literature review that I discussed in Chapter 4. However, for a grant *or* project proposal, it is important that the literature review is selective. People do not want to spend their time wading through pages and pages of research conducted by other people. The literature review that appears in this section should establish the research that is similar to what the researcher is proposing in order to illustrate to the funding agency that he or she is familiar with other studies or programs that already exist. It should also contain a critical evaluation of this literature. Remember, "critical" does not mean that the review mentions only the weak points of the previous research. "Critical" means that the researcher should add analysis that makes it clear to those reading the review how the *proposed* research will complement, build on, or clarify current knowledge or programs. In this section the researcher should subtly reinforce why the study or program being proposed is important and necessary. The researcher can most effectively do this by weaving in the strengths of the project as a response to the evaluation of the existing research or project.

If there are any special reasons why the researcher or his or her organization is especially well situated to embark on this study or project, this is the place to convey those special reasons. For example, does the researcher live in a geographical location that is unique to the phenomenon, or, conversely, illustrates a strong need for research or a program? In fact, if the researcher has done a needs assessment, even a rudimentary one, inclusion of those findings here would help strengthen his or her argument while simultaneously illustrating his or her dedication to the topic for which the researcher is requesting money.

Therefore, essentially this section serves to (1) establish the research problem or need, (2) establish the researcher's knowledge in this area, (3) discretely educate others who may not be quite as knowledgeable regarding this specific topic, and (4) justify the need for the research or project relative to what is already known or available. Researchers should not write this section in overly technical terms; therefore, they should avoid using unnecessary jargon or abbreviations, they should write more formally (as opposed to conversationally, which should apply to the *entire* proposal), and they should be especially clear in relating their research or project to current knowledge or practices.

Description of proposed research (if doing a research proposal)

This is where the researcher gets more technical, for the researcher is now writing for people who have expertise in this particular area, and it is essentially the heart of the proposal. This section should begin with clearly defined and observable goals. If the research project has long-term goals, the researcher should state these separately from more immediate, short-term goals. Why? This is usually important because funding agencies require periodic (usually yearly) reports regarding the progress of the project for which they grant funding. As the name implies, long-term goals may take years to be achieved. By identifying short-term goals, the researcher can show progress by illustrating that the short-term goals were accomplished. Furthermore, although it is essential for researchers to periodically state why their research is important, they need to resist the temptation to *overstate* the goals of the research. For example, if a researcher is requesting money to determine whether educational children's programs such as *Sesame Street* or *Blues Clues* foster intellectual development, the researcher may write the following goals in this section of the proposal:

1. To identify a sample of children, ages 3 to 6, who will be allowed to watch one of three shows (*Sesame Street*, *Blues Clues*, or *Dora the Explorer*) for at least 30 minutes a day for three months
2. To design a pre- and postmeasurement of intellectual development, which includes (but is not limited to) the Peabody Picture Vocabulary Test and Peabody Individual Achievement Test Math Assessment
3. To statistically compare the posttest scores of the children who did and who did not watch these three television shows (and see if there is any variation in development by the frequency each show was watched)
4. To use this information to help children's programming develop more effective means of using television to educate children

The first three goals are appropriate. The first two are relatively short term and the third is longer term. However, the fourth goal is not really relevant. First, there is no indication that the people responsible for these three shows *want* this research. If they do not even want it, there is no way the researcher will help create change. Second, even if they did want it, the researcher cannot assume that the shows' creative teams will actually *use* the researcher's information. Therefore, the fourth goal completely overstates the utility of this research; and, more important, someone reading the proposal and deciding whether to grant funding for it will realize that as well. Remember, those giving grants want to give the money to projects that they think are feasible, and stating goals that are not likely to be achieved defeats that purpose.

If researchers have any specific hypotheses to test or assumptions underlying the design of the research, they should state these early in the Description of Proposed Research. Such statements are important components of the grant that will affect how reviewers evaluate the salience and tractability of the proposal.

Also, some research will occur in phases. If this is the case, it is important for the researcher to clearly define what each phase is, what the goals for each phase are, what the approximate time line to accomplish those goals is, and how the phases relate to the over-all research objective. A clear and direct breakdown of phases makes it easy for those who are reviewing the proposal to see how the project will unfold, and it makes it easier for the researcher (if the researcher includes a clear list of goals for each phase) to illustrate progress throughout the research process.

Last, a detailed description of the actual research methodology is necessary. This essentially means a clear description of all the information presented so far in this book. Once again, the researcher will identify key hypotheses or purposes (albeit briefly so as not to appear too repetitive), operationalization of terms for clearly observable points, a description of the sampling process, a description of the selected method of observation, and an explanation of any ethical considerations that may arise given the method just described. Because this subsection is likely to be very detailed in its own right, the use of subheadings to help the reviewers follow the researcher's train of thought may be especially useful.

Project detail (if doing a project proposal)

Like the research proposal, the detail section of a project proposal begins with a clear statement of the project goals. Essentially, the goals are the same as the outcomes that I mentioned earlier. What does the project hope to accomplish? Remember, the key here is that these outcomes need to be measurable. Just like I discussed in the earlier part of the chapter, if the outcomes are not measurable, then an evaluation cannot occur. The same applies to proposal writing. If the outcomes are not measurable, and therefore directly observable, then the proposal will not receive funding.

Unlike research proposals, however, project proposals are often designed to create some type of program that will affect the life experience of individuals. Consequently, it is very important for the proposal to be clear about who the target audience is for the program and how the researcher plans on identifying them to offer them the services of the proposed program. This is a good way for applicants to illustrate a cooperation of efforts. Recognizing that no one agency or program is likely to be able to create real change in and of itself, funding agencies particularly like proposals that involve collaboration. Discussing how various agencies that directly deal with the target population intend to cooperate in the operation of this program would be a strong addition to the proposal.

In some instances, the clients themselves may have input on the design and implementation of the program. For example, if a school board is considering a new educational change, the board may invite the parents of some children who attend the school to participate in planning meetings. Other times, clearly the involvement of clients themselves may not be feasible or desirable, such as a proposal to start a work-release program. It would not be surprising if prisoners were generally in favor of such a program (think about it—a chance to be out of prison for part of the day!), and prisoners may argue for even more leniency in such a program than other planners are able or willing to provide. In either case, establishing support from collaborating agencies is an important point to make in this section if possible.

However, just stating collaboration without some concrete means of illustrating support is not very useful. Therefore, this section should *concretely* state the role of each agency and that agency's contribution to the project. Additionally, letters of support from people in key positions in these agencies in order to further illustrate the agency's commitment to cooperation and to reiterate the agency's role should be included in an appendix of the grant application.

The third component of this section is a thorough and detailed explanation of the activities that the grant money, if provided, will fund. There should be a very clear link between these activities and the goals/outcomes discussed earlier in this section. The funding agency will be especially interested in seeing what is unique or creative about the activities the researcher proposes. The specific role of any collaborating agency should be described here as well, if the researcher elects not to do it in the previous subsection.

Last, the researcher needs to describe the roles of each person involved in the program and the importance of those roles. Essentially, each role has to be justified and linked to at least some of the activities and some of the goals. The clearer and more pervasive this link, the more likely a proposal is going to be granted funding. Also, the researcher needs to make it clear *why* each of the people were selected to be involved in the project. Therefore, the researcher can also include a brief explanation of why each person is instrumental to the project—not just in terms of the role the person serves, but *how* the individual serves that role as well. The researcher wants to convince the funding agency that well-qualified and experienced people are involved in the project and are dedicated to carrying out the project as it is designed.

As the heart of the proposal, this section is probably second in importance only to the Project Overview. Therefore, it is essential that the applicant make sure that all subsections of this part reinforce each other and flow well. It is also important to make sure that any collaborative efforts are well described, well justified, and clearly documented (with letters of support or commitment). After all, this section will outline what will be done with the grant money and it will lead to the next section, which is the resources necessary to accomplish the proposed project.

Description of resources

It is generally good to begin this section with the resources that a person already has available, because doing so shows a funding agency that the person (or team) writing the grant has already explored what is on hand and is not automatically looking to the funding agency to provide *everything*. Therefore, some suggestions of available resources from a university perspective (if one is involved) is an explanation of the expertise that individuals involved with the project have to offer, the supportive services at the university that may help the project, and/or any resource facilities (such as space or equipment) that the university already has accessible that will benefit the project.

Collaborative projects are especially popular with funding agencies, therefore regardless of whether or not a university is involved in the project, a discussion of available resources should also include any mention of local resources that will benefit the project. Some examples of local resources are volunteers who are willing to donate time with the project, any businesses that are willing to donate or discount goods that will facilitate the project, or any members of agencies who are willing to contribute expertise, time, or resources. As I've stated previously, including letters of support from the people who will provide these resources in an appendix strengthens the applicant's claim to collaboration.

However, people apply for grants because they do not have *enough* resources to conduct or evaluate a project completely on their own. So after a discussion of the resources available (and how they will contribute to the project), an applicant *finally* gets to the meat of the funding request—which is exactly what the researcher hopes the funding agency will contribute to the project. For funding requests for personnel, a general approach is to provide a short description of the role these people will be playing in the project and why they are the best people available to be involved in the project. Essentially, the researcher is trying to convince the funding agency that these people are worth the salary you are requesting for them. As part of this justification, you may want to include a vitae or resume for these people in an appendix that clearly outlines their qualifications for the proposed position. If relevant, the personnel request should also include a percentage that will cover staff benefits; however, not all funding agencies will allow this, so whether it is included depends on the services that the funding agency is willing to pay. Last, it is important that the people the researcher claims are going to be involved in the program give their approval for their inclusion in the grant *prior* to submission of the grant. It would be very embarrassing (and possibly result in a loss of funding) if an applicant claims that certain people will be involved in the project and they later decline to do so.

The facilities section would explain why certain spaces would need to be rented (if this is the case) and a comparison of costs for different spaces, if possible. However, this is not always necessary. Depending on the project or research, facilities may not be relevant. For example, if a researcher is writing a research grant, there may be no need for facilities because the researcher is evaluating an already existing program. The only need for *his or her* facilities is office space, which the researcher may already have, especially if he or she is affiliated with a university (and presumably has a university-provided office for those duties, which can also serve as an office for the research duties).

The last example of a needed resource is equipment. Equipment is a resource in which funding agencies may be more restrictive regarding what they will and will not cover. Equipment that a funding agency is more likely to consider relevant includes tape recorders, video equipment, computers (for general program support), office furniture if office space is necessary (e.g., lamps, tables, chairs), photocopy machines, telephone/Internet lines, office supplies (letterhead, photocopy paper, pens, etc.), and mailing costs. Any special equipment such as urine tests for drugs or the membership in a listserve may also be appropriate. Not all of this equipment will be necessary for all programs. For example, if, as a university employee, I am applying for funding to evaluate a local family planning program, I am not going to include office furniture or computer equipment in my grant proposal because I already have an office and a computer available at my university. For all equipment requests, as with the earlier requests for personnel and facilities, each item needs to be justified. Therefore, it is not good practice to "throw everything into the hat," and plan on using the "extra" money for other expenses. Grants, however, generally will not fund expenses such as beverages, cups, snacks, or other purchases for "breaks" or refreshments at workshops. Those expenses are generally considered to be more "personal" and optional.

Budget (if doing a research proposal)

Once you have outlined all of these costs, you are ready to summarize them into a budget. Again, it is important to be realistic about your budgetary requests. People at funding agencies see *many* proposals; therefore, they are generally skilled at identifying proposals that are too cheap to be true (their translation is likely to be that the writer did not do enough budgetary research to put together an accurate proposal) as well as those that are unrealistically expensive.

In addition to the personnel, facilities, and equipment costs I described previously, budgets may also include costs for travel (e.g., to conferences for training or to present/share information). Indirect costs may also be relevant. These are usually a fixed percentage that is based on the total budget up until that point and then added to that budget. These costs can be established by the funding agency and/or any agencies indirectly involved in the project. For example, universities frequently tack on a percentage to a grant, which essentially is their "payoff" for allowing one of their employees (usually the researcher) to direct some of his or her attention away from the university per se and toward the proposed research project. The point of indirect costs, and their calculation, is because, unlike the other issues in a budget, they are hard to estimate. Therefore, they are not directly presented, but instead are *loosely estimated* by the fixed percentage of all other budget items.

A sample budget for a hypothetical drug treatment program appears in Figure 10.6. Notice the middle column, "CC," which loosely stands for "Collaboration Costs." This column illustrates the parts of the operating costs that *other* agencies will cover, and they would be explained regarding who was paying for what in the Available Resources section of the grant. Including this column (or one similar) is a good idea because it (1) reinforces the collaborative nature of the project; (2) pictorially shows what the funding agency, as opposed to other resources, will finance; and (3) reinforces to the funding agency that they are paying only a *portion* of the costs for the program or project. Even if an applicant is requesting a funding agency to pay the *bulk* of the costs, reminding the agency that outside resources will be provided is good because it illustrates that an applicant is not totally dependent on that agency. Therefore, for example, Figure 10.6, under the section "Personnel" is the item reflecting the costs for "in-patient treatment." Under the middle column, "CC," for "in-patient treatment" is the cost of $40,000. This means that the agencies collaborating in this project will contribute $40,000 to the costs of in-patient treatment.

Evaluation plan (if doing a project proposal)

Funding agencies want some type of verification as to whether their investment is a wise one. Therefore, they will want to see that anyone receiving money has at least a general idea for evaluating the proposed project. This is where at least a basic understanding in research methods is beneficial to anyone who will be working in the public sector. This section does not need to be a full-blown explanation of an evaluation study. However, it *should* include at least a brief description of both a process evaluation and an outcome evaluation.

It is easier to do a process evaluation if the earlier part of the proposal has concretely outlined clear steps and goals for each phase of program development. If this is the case, then all an applicant has to do to illustrate a plan for process evaluation is to write a brief summary about what will be observed, and how, at different time points in order to illustrate that the program is moving along as planned. This may involve a relatively simple

Twelve-Month Budget

Personnel	Sponsor	CC	Total
Project coordinator	$30,000	$0	$30,000
Probation officer (50% salary)	$12,00		$12,000
Public defender (50% salary)	$20,000	$0	$20,000
Clerk/Typist, 50%	$7,000	$0	$7,000
In-patient treatment		$40,000	$40,000
Out-patient treatment		$15,000	$15,000
Subtotal	**$69,000**	**$55,000**	**$124,000**
Evaluator			
University professor, 25% salary	$10,000	$0	$10,000
Materials and Supplies			
Drug tests (order and analysis)	$2,000	$3,0000	$5,000
Phase graduation materials		$500	$500
Subtotal	**$2,000**	**$3,500**	**$5,500**
Travel			
Registration for training seminar in New York City for coordinator, public defender, probation officer, judge, and evaluator (2 days @ $200/person)	$1,000		$1,000
Air fare @ $400 × 5	$2,000	$0	$2,000
Lodging @ $150/day (× 2 days × 5 people)	$1,500	$0	$1,500
Food @ $40/day	$400	$0	$400
Subtotal	**$3,900**	**$0**	**$3,900**
Total Direct Costs	**$74,900**	**$58,500**	**$133,400**
Indirect Costs (30% of modified total direct costs)	$22,470	$17,550	$40,020
Grand Total	**$97,370**	**$76,050**	**$173,420**

Figure 10.6 Sample Twelve-Month Budget for a Project Proposal

count of services offered, clients using the program, and so on. The point is, the researcher needs to tell the funding agency how he or she will *generally* measure program progress.

The outcome evaluation can also be fairly simple—at least, that is, if the applicant included clearly defined goals earlier in the proposal. In this instance, the applicant may want to describe, briefly, whether program participants will be compared to a control group (and if so, who the specific control group is and why this group is appropriate) and the nature of observation (for example, a survey).

Last, including a plan for how the program will be sustained after the grant money ends is also a useful piece of information to include in the evaluation section. For example, an applicant may want to speculate as to how the program will be funded once the grant money is gone or the applicant may want to explain how other agencies will increase their support once the program is smoothly running. This forecasting improves a grant proposal because it lets the funding agency know that, if it grants the funding request, it is helping a long-term program "get its start," and that the program has the cooperation and commitment of other agencies that share the desire for the program's success.

Evaluating Written Research: Evaluation Research

Unlike in previous chapters where I discussed one specific aspect of the research method (e.g., abstracts, sampling, survey methodology), this chapter on evaluation research is not exactly presenting an entirely unique skill relative to the other chapters. Therefore, evaluation research has to be, well, *evaluated* in its whole context. That means we have to look at the reason for the research (for example, needs assessment or outcome evaluation?), the feasibility of evaluating the program, and the unavoidable fact that evaluation research occurs in the context of *real life* more so than other forms of research. Hence, those conducting the research may have more restrictions affecting the quality of the research (and thus need more evaluative leeway from our perspective) than others who are doing more academic research. We have to consider these issues *in addition* to the other evaluation points I raised with each step of the research process that I have described in other chapters. Therefore, from an assessment point of view, our approach to considering an example of evaluation research involves the following acknowledgments or guidelines.

1. What is the purpose of the evaluation presented?

If the article you are reading describes a program evaluation that focuses on sharing the experiences of starting or operating a specific project with others, then criticizing the article because it does not provide any scientific test of the *effectiveness* of the program is inappropriate. Although that may be interesting and relevant on one level, it is not the purpose of that particular piece of written research, therefore it is not relevant to the evaluation of the quality of that piece of research.

2. Is the nature of the program described in detail?

In order for someone to evaluate whether the research methodology is appropriate for evaluation research, he or she needs to know *what* a researcher is evaluating. A researcher evaluating a program aimed at helping the homeless, a group that is difficult to study, may have different restrictions (and therefore different considerations when others are assessing the merit is this evaluation) than does a researcher who is assessing the effectiveness of an after-school program for middle school children. The more detail the researcher provides about the program being evaluated, the more information an outsider has to assess the merits of the researcher's research.

3. Are the program goals presented and can the goals that the author presents be evaluated?

Presumably, someone would not evaluate a program that did not have clearly observable goals. However, sometimes this *does* happen, or what one person thinks of as observable goals really are not. Making sure that the goals are documented and observable is an important step in evaluating the quality of a piece of research.

4. What type of observation method is used? Is it appropriate, given the real-life restrictions of evaluation research?

As we've discussed in this chapter and in Chapter 6, true experiments, methodologically, are the most effective means for evaluating the effect of a specific treatment, such as a public program. However, *realistically,* that is not always possible. People may not be able to be randomly assigned to treatment and control groups for political and ethical reasons; researchers may not even be able to *have* a control group due to population, political, and economic constraints. Therefore, the method of observation needs to be evaluated in the context of the environment in which that program operates.

In some instances, researchers will publicize the restrictions that affect their research. In this case, it is the reader's responsibility to assess whether he or she accepts the researcher's response to those restrictions or not. Other times, the researcher may not directly state these restrictions. In this case, it is the reader's responsibility to assess whether the researcher's decisions are appropriate given the topic and any other indirect information about program climate that the researcher may provide. Remember, it is unfair to expect a researcher doing evaluation research to be able to accomplish things that you, if you were in the researcher's shoes, could not. It is also unrealistic to hold an evaluation researcher to the same rigid standards that we may otherwise employ for people doing academic research.

That being said, however, it does not mean that the evaluation researcher can do anything he or she wants. The researcher should justify any deviation from a "best practices" approach to research methods. This means that the researcher *should* state or explain why he or she selected the specific method presented. Even if this does not involve a full-blown explanation of environmental limitations, some justification should be provided. A sign of strong research is when the researcher tries to take steps to minimize any weakness and, correspondingly, explains those steps to the reader.

5. *Is a control group used? If so, how has the researcher tried to show that it is equivalent to the experimental group? If not, does the researcher adequately explain its omission?*

If the goal of the research is a needs assessment or a program assessment, no control group is necessary because both of these types of research focus on the needs and processes of an individual program. However, an outcome evaluation needs to somehow establish that a program is more effective than other programs or the current status quo. To show that the program of interest is more effective than another program, that "other" program has to serve as a control group because comparisons need to be made in order to claim "better than." On the one hand, if the evaluated program is to show that it is an improvement over the status quo (e.g., no program or whatever the previously operating program was), then a researcher *could* use a control group. On the other hand, if the researcher elects not to use a control group, the researcher may imply effectiveness by showing a change within the experimental group across time (before the new program and after).

If, however, a researcher uses a control group, then he or she has to explain or try to show that that control group is similar to the experimental group. If the researcher uses random assignment, we are fairly confident that the two groups will be equal; therefore, any further illustration (e.g., a statistical comparison of relevant characteristics between the groups) is not necessary. Of course, if a person uses random assignment *and* a statistical comparison, then we have even more faith in the comparability of the two groups.

As I've said, though, random selection or assignment may not be possible. When this is the case, the researcher especially has an obligation to statistically compare the experimental and control groups in order to ascertain whether they are similar. If the two groups differ in fundamental ways (e.g., one group has a more serious drug addiction than another, one group is more violent than another), any differences in outcome measures may be due to differences that were present *prior* to the research, and this weakens the evaluation of the program.

Control groups, then, are not necessary in all situations, but when they are necessary, the researcher needs to show that they are similar on key variables (whatever those may be for a given topic).

6. How are people selected for program participation? Does this affect the interpretation of findings, and, if so, does the researcher discuss this?

In evaluation research, as I've stated previously, random selection or assignment is not always possible. The detail regarding the program (item 2) will help readers assess whether random selection or assignment was *feasibly* possible (as opposed to the researcher just taking the "easy way out"). When researchers *can* and *do* use random assignment, that is generally a plus in their favor. When researchers *cannot* use random assignment, for whatever reason, they need to state those reasons and at least briefly discuss the implications either in the sampling section or later in a discussion of research limitations (which is sometimes just hidden in the "Discussion" section of a report). Remember, no study is perfect, and evaluation research is frequently less perfect (but the best form of available assessment) than more academic research, so the issue is not a researcher stating limitations (which is a good practice) but instead whether the researcher is trying to sneak the limitations past a reader (which is not a good practice).

7. Are the results clearly explained?

Perhaps in evaluation research, even more so than in other forms of scientific research, the clarity of results are important. After all, the results of an evaluation study may directly affect whether another agency will copy, or at least borrow, elements of a program for its own use. Therefore, the results of an evaluation have to be clearly stated with their implications for use also mentioned, at least briefly.

8. Do the researchers describe who funded the research? Does this affect the interpretation of findings at all?

A reader might be more skeptical about highly positive evaluation results when the agency who conducted or sponsors the program is also conducting or providing the funding for the evaluation of that program. Clearly, in these instances there may be an incentive to present findings or to conduct the evaluation in a specific way. Generally, we have more confidence in the objectivity of findings when the funding agency is not directly affiliated with the program (e.g., the funding comes from a government grant) and when those conducting the research are third party to the program (e.g., professional research firms or academics). This does not mean to imply that people who are closer to a program are incapable of producing objective, scientifically sound evaluation studies. Nevertheless, who is funding and conducting the evaluation *may* affect how a reader evaluates the merit of the findings.

In addition to these eight guidelines are the guidelines for evaluating the specific segments of research that I discussed in previous chapters. Therefore, even though I mentioned a consideration for sampling here, for example, that does not mean that the points

Many argue that if childhood aggression is not addressed early, it can lead to problematic adult behavior when the child is older. Frey, Hirschstein, and Guzzo (2000, **AN 3183611**) use data gathered by Grossman (1997) to assess the effectiveness of Second Step, a program aimed at preventing childhood aggression by promoting social competence.

The Second Step program utilizes observation, self-reflection, performance, and reinforcement to develop socioemotional skills that will help children deal with situations that may create aggressive feelings and tendencies. Specifically, the program tries to teach empathy, social problem solving, and impulse control, in addition to specific behavioral skills. To accomplish this, teachers help students apply perspective-taking, problem-solving, and anger management strategies to help children decide what to do in frustrating situations. Then, to foster behavioral skills, the program trains the children to learn and to rehearse specific steps for how to actually enact these strategies.

Frey, Hirschstein, and Guzzo studied the effectiveness of this program on two levels: a preschool/elementary school level and a middle school/high school level. Below is an excerpt from their research regarding the preschool/elementary school level.

The Lessons

Program lessons are typically taught twice a week by regular classroom teachers or counselors trained in the use of the curriculum. . . . [Lessons] are structured around large black-and-white photo cards depicting children in various social-emotional situations. On the reverse side of the card, teachers are provided with key concepts, objectives, and a suggested lesson script. . . .

Second Step also provides video-based lessons, skill-step posters to display in classrooms and throughout the school, and a Family Overview Video to engage parent support. Lessons are accompanied by notes to teachers about child development, transfer-of-training

ideas, and extension activities, such as children's literature that illustrates Second Step concepts. . . .

Teacher Training

The Second Step training model consists of a 1-day teacher workshop. . . . The training for teachers focuses on two critical aspects of the program: conducting lessons for student skill development and improving the environmental context in which those skills are expected to be used. . . .

Outcome Evaluation

Grossman and his colleagues examined the impact of Second Step on aggression and positive social behaviors of second- and third-grade students in 49 classrooms (n = 790). Twelve schools from urban and suburban areas of western Washington state were paired on the basis of (a) school district, (b) proportion of students receiving free or reduced-cost school lunch, and (c) proportion of minority school enrollment. One school from each matched pair was randomly assigned to receive the Second Step intervention. Teachers in the control group were given their choice of implementing classroom materials in areas that did not include the social-emotional skills addressed by Second Step (e.g., self-esteem).

Classroom teachers taught Second Step lessons twice a week during a 4- to 5-month period. Data were collected three times: (a) in the fall of 1993, prior to the start of Second Step lessons in intervention schools; (b) in the spring of 1994, 2 weeks after completion of the curriculum; and (c) in the fall of 1994, 6 months after completion of the curriculum. Outcome data included teacher ratings, parent ratings, and direct behavioral observations by trained observers blind to condition. Twelve students from each participating classroom (n = 588) were selected at random to be observed in classroom, lunchroom, and playground settings. Using the Social Interaction Observation System (Neckerman, Asher, & Pavlidis, 1994), observers recorded physical and verbal aggression and prosocial and neutral behaviors.

Behavioral observations revealed that physical aggression decreased from autumn to spring among students in the Second Step program, but not in the control group (see Figure 1). Reductions were greatest in the least structured settings—the playground and lunchroom—where aggression most frequently occurs. A similar but nonsignificant trend was found for hostile and aggressive comments (e.g., name-calling). . . .

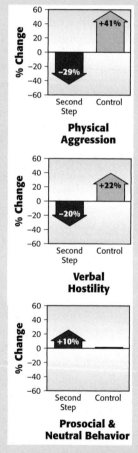

Figure 1. Changes, from Autumn to Spring, in Children's Social Behaviors in Playground and Lunchroom Settings

Note: Based on Grossman, Neckerman, Koepsell, Ping-Yu, Asher, Beland, & Rivara (1997).

[However] . . . ratings of student behavior provided by teachers and parents did not show any differences between intervention and control groups in the study. Neither the improvements observed in the Second Step students nor the problems observed in the control schools were reflected in ratings of individual students. . . .

. . . The discrepancy between teacher reports of student behavior and observations by trained personnel identifies a potential problem for educators: benefits are not always obvious. . . . Teachers who are presenting a program . . . will not know what their students would be like if the program were not taught. This poses an important challenge because teachers need to know that their time and effort are paying off if they are to persist.

[Well-] designed programs alone are not sufficient to produce these changes, however. Districts or schools that fail to allocate sufficient time or resources to implementing a social skills curriculum will likely fall short of desired results.

Source: Karin S. Frey, Miriam K. Hirschstein, and Barbara A. Guzzo, "Second Step: Preventing Aggression by Promoting Social Competence," *Journal of Emotional & Behavioral Disorders, 8* (2) (Summer 2000): 102. Copyright 2000 by PRO-ED, Inc. Reprinted with permission. **(AN 3183611)**

Critical Thinking Questions

1. What is the purpose of the evaluation presented?

2. Is the nature of the program described in detail?

3. Are the goals presented and can the goals that the author presents be evaluated?

4. What type of observation method is used? Is it appropriate, given the real-life restrictions of evaluation research?

5. Is a control group used? If so, how has the researcher tried to show that it is equivalent

to the experimental group? If not, does the researcher adequately explain its omission?

6. How are people selected for program participation? Does this affect the interpretation of findings, and, if so, does the researcher discuss this?

7. Are the results clearly explained?

8. How does the article address the other areas of evaluation discussed in earlier chapters?

Critical Thinking Discussion

1. Frey, Hirschstein, and Guzzo (2000) discuss the research of Grossman and colleagues (1997). However, Frey and colleagues do so in enough detail to essentially evaluate Grossman and colleagues' study, even though Grossman and colleagues' study is not directly available on Research Navigator. Consequently, to answer this first question, as the third subheading in the excerpt indicates, they are focusing on an outcome evaluation.

2. Yes. The first two subheadings "The Lessons" and "Teacher Training" explain how the preschool/early childhood program is implemented. Even more detail is present in the original article; however, what is in the excerpt is sufficient to get an idea as to how the program is implemented.

3. The goals are stated in the introduction (before the excerpt). Ultimately, the goal is to reduce childhood aggression. Specifically, the researchers hope to do this by promoting empathy, social problem solving, and impulse control. However, it is the general goal of reducing aggression that is the focus of the outcome evaluation. Whether the students were learning empathy, social problem solving, and impulse control could be included, but they are not necessary since they are not the overall goal, stated in my introductory comments (which are paraphrased from the article) and the first sentence of the outcome evaluation subsection within the boxed excerpt.

The researchers in this article do not specifically state *how* aggression is measured; however, they cite the original study. Remember, people can save time by not describing all of the nitty-gritty details of other research so long as they cite where that original research can be found. Therefore, this omission is not a problem.

4. Grossman and colleagues essentially did a classic experiment. They paired 12 schools from urban and suburban areas of western Washington state and randomly assigned one of each pair to the treatment or control group. I say "essentially" because there is no evidence that these 12 schools were randomly selected, but the matching process is fairly detailed, and they did use random assignment. Therefore, their technique is probably acceptable from a practical point of view (see the next question). Their experiment can be summarized with the following notation:

$$E_e \quad O_1 \quad X \quad O_2 \quad O_3$$
$$E_c \quad O_1 \quad \quad O_2 \quad O_3$$

Where O_1 = the pretest and the first observation period of aggression prior to the Second Step program.

X = the Second Step program experience

O_2 and O_3 = the two posttest observations—one two weeks after the program completion and the other 6 months after completion

This is a very appropriate design because it addresses not only before/after comparisons, or changes within a group (with the three observation points, one of which is a pretest) but it also addresses changes *across groups,* with the experimental and control group. Since both avenues of outcome possibility (improvement within a group and differences across groups) are present, this is a very appropriate design.

5. They achieved equality by random assignment after matching for three criteria: (1) school district, (2) economic well-being as indicated by the proportion getting free or reduced-cost school lunch, and (3) proportion of minority school enrollment.

Because the districts were first matched and *then* randomly assigned, Grossman and colleagues can be relatively (although not completely, but this *is* a real-life study) confident that the experimental and control groups are similar. Because of their matching and random assignment technique, no further statistical tests are really necessary.

6. There is no mention of how Grossman and colleagues selected these school districts in *this* article; however, that information is likely to be in the original published work.

7. The results are clearly explained. Grossman and colleagues provide an easily read graph that summarizes the long term (six-months, from autumn to spring) differences in aggressive behavior.

8. To fully assess the other components of research that we have previously discussed, one would need to read Grossman and colleagues' original research. This is not available on Research Navigator, but for those of you interested in finding it in an alternate source, the citation is: Grossman, D. C., Neckerman, H. J., Koepsell, T. D., Liu, P. Y., Asher, K. N., Beland, K., Frey, K., & Rivara, F. P. (1997). Effectiveness of a violence prevention curriculum among children in elementary school: A randomized controlled trial. *Journal of the American Medical Association, 277,* 1605–1611.

I raised in Chapter 5 on sampling are not relevant. Many of them may be. These points mean that a reader of evaluation research needs to consider the points I raise in specific chapters in light of the considerations that I present here. To summarize, the considerations for evaluation research are:

1. What is the purpose of the evaluation presented?
2. Is the nature of the program described in detail?
3. Are the goals presented and can the goals that the author presents be evaluated?
4. What type of observation method is used? Is it appropriate, given the real-life restrictions of evaluation research?
5. Is a control group used? If so, how has the researcher tried to show that it is equivalent to the experimental group? If not, does the researcher adequately explain its omission?
6. How are people selected for program participation? Does this affect the interpretation of findings, and, if so, does the researcher discuss this?
7. Are the results clearly explained?
8. Do the researchers describe who funded the research? Does this affect the interpretation of findings at all?
9. Overall, is the evaluation methodology adequate?

Key Terms

Activities (433)
Control variables (448)
Cost-benefit analysis (441)
Cost-effective analysis (442)
Inputs (433)

Needs assessment (437)
Outcome (434)
Output (434)
Program monitoring (437)
Program process (433)

Project overviews (467)
Proposal (462)
Result (434)
Stakeholders (435)

Review Questions and Exercises

1. *Choose a social program of interest to you and find articles evaluating it. Overall, is your program of interest effective or not? What evidence, from research, do you have to support your conclusion?*

2. *Evaluate the following published research for its methodology:*

   a. Marcoux, Marie-France, Sallis, James F., Mckenzie, Thomas L., Marshall, Simon, Arm- *strong, Colin A., and Goggin, Kathleen J. (1999). Process Evaluation of a Physical Activity Self-Management Program for Children: Spark. Psychology & Health, 14 (4), 659–678. (AN 3963416)*

   b. Johnson, Lewis R. (2000). Inservice Training to Facilitate Inclusion: An Outcomes Evaluation. Reading & Writing Quarterly, 16 (3), 281–288. (AN 3357026)

Chapter 11

Qualitative Research Analysis

The previous eleven chapters have focused on how to actually *do* research: how to decide, select, and refine a research topic; how to decide who to study; and how to create a method of observing those you want to study. The next two chapters, on the other hand, focus on what to do with all that collected information, or what we call *data*, that results from these efforts. In other words, now that you have all these data, what do you actually do with it? How do you use it to answer research questions or test hypotheses? Basically, this is the fun part of research methods. I know, you're probably thinking, "Fun? Yeah right!", but really, it *is* fun because here is where you see the fruits of your labor. Here, you actually can get some *answers!*

As you probably remember, there are two general types of research: quantitative and qualitative. I'm going to begin our discussion of analysis by focusing on qualitative data analysis because it usually does not involve as much numerical comparison (although some may be present) as quantitative research, therefore many people are more comfortable with it. For example, when people think of studies involving qualitative research, they probably think of snippets of quotations from participants, which essentially create a "story" about the research question. Qualitative research frequently does involve a presentation of quotations and anecdotal evidence, but it is much more.

For example, Maidment and Cooper (2002, **AN 6998092**) studied how field educators tried to teach diversity issues to students of social work. Social workers frequently deal with clients who are from different cultures than their own, and the cultures of social workers' clients are often those that are the object of discrimination in the wider society. The goal of field educator supervisors is to teach students how to interact with people of cultures that are different from that of the dominant group in a respectful, nondiscriminatory way. Maidment and Cooper studied seven student–field educator dyads to see how the field educators taught social work students to address "differences" in clients. One tactic that these researchers found that field educators used was what they called "unmasking subtle themes of oppression," and they provide the following example of a student–teacher interaction where the teacher tried to get the student to acknowledge a subtle theme:

Scenario: the student is working on a hospital ward with elderly people. The discussion is focused on how working with older people is different from working with other client groups.

Dialogue

Field educator: So what are the things you've noticed about working with elderly clients?

Student: Speak very clearly.

Field educator: Yes. Because . . . ?

Student: Because their hearing is not as good as a younger person. Being quite clear about what you are doing and also just in general interaction with them, being quite clear.

Field educator: Uh huh. And what's that based on?

Student: I guess trying not to confuse them.

Field educator: Are you saying that your experience of older clients is that they are confused?

Student: No, most of them have been alert.

Field educator: So does this confusion picture fit? I'm intrigued.

Student: Not sure.

Field educator: On the one hand you're saying that older people you've met have been alert, and on the other hand you're saying you need to be very clear about what you're doing because they'll get confused easily.

Student: I guess its more where I come from. The way I do things, that come across . . . yeah, I guess its more me than them. I like to be clear for me.

Field educator: So you like to be clear for you. (p. 403)

As Maidment and Cooper (2002) explain regarding this passage:

This scenario shows two features. First, the educator challenges the student's stereotypical view of older people. Second, the educator helps the student to gain self-awareness about why he chooses to communicate with the clients in a particular way. (p. 403)

This example may imply that qualitative analysis is "easy" because is it not statistical. After all, Maidment and Cooper (2002) supported their conclusions with excerpts from training sessions like the one presented here. However, such a view would be misleading because, by some accounts, qualitative analysis can be even *harder* than quantitative analysis, because with quantitative studies, a computer is likely to examine all of the individual pieces of data, apply them to a statistical formula that you choose, and then tell you whether there is any statistical relationship between all the bits and pieces (provided that the researcher knows what to look for). However, in qualitative data analysis, researchers have to sift through each piece of information, each comment, each context, and find patterns all on their own. There are some computer programs that now help with this process, but depending on your comfort with using them, they can be just as hard as the more statistical programs associated with quantitative analysis, at least until a researcher learns to use them (which is the same for those quantitative programs, so the "ease" really becomes a "draw").

In this chapter, I'm going to discuss some basic steps in analyzing qualitative data. These steps would be useful for reaching conclusions based on field research (Chapter 8), nonstructured interviews (Chapter 7), and some aspects of content analysis (Chapter 9). This information would also be helpful when researchers use qualitative techniques to do evaluation research (Chapter 10). To some degree I began this process in Chapter 8, when I discussed the various forms of field notes researchers take when doing field research. I'm going to build on those notes now after a brief reintroduction to catch us all up to speed (after all, it's been a while since we've discussed field research!). However, before I do that, I want to summarize some differences between qualitative and quantitative research, which will be instrumental in understanding this chapter and the next.

Qualitative versus Quantitative Research

At the beginning of this chapter, I mentioned how quantitative research is more focused on statistical tests than qualitative research. That is a very simplistic comparison, but one that generally captures a notable essence of the difference between these two research strategies. However, because it is simplistic and because this is a research methods text-book, it is appropriate for me to expect you to develop a more advanced understanding of the differences between the two.

First, as shown in Table 11.1, quantitative and qualitative research generally follow different logical pathways. Quantitative research presumes that the researcher is the expert in a given area. This "expertise" may come from personal experience, from a formal education, or from a thorough review of the literature, which will lead someone to be "informally" educated. Because of the researcher's expertise, in quantitative research, the research usually begins with the researcher creating a hypothesis to test against a theory. On the other hand, in qualitative research, although the researcher may be an "expert," this expert knowledge is not the focus; instead, the people being studied are the true "experts." Therefore, the qualitative researcher enters the field wanting to "learn" from the participants. Only later, after thorough interaction, will the researcher resume his or her expert role and try to find patterns in what he or she has learned from the participants. Hence, qualitative researchers generally do *not* enter the field with hypotheses specifically to test theories, but instead they enter with basic research questions to explore and form theories *after* they collect the data.

Methodologically, quantitative research is also usually more rigidly organized. It tries to follow the scientific process of topic selection, literature review, hypothesis formation, conceptualization/operationalization, sampling, and research design. Because one of the goals of quantitative research is to produce reliable findings, this organized and systematic approach is essential. It allows other researchers to see exactly how a study was conducted so that they can work to replicate it.

Qualitative research, however, is not interested in replication. In fact, some critics of qualitative research argue that the findings are only relevant to the population studied (since no attempt at random selection is present) at that one point in time. Qualitative

TABLE 11.1 Differences in Qualitative and Quantitative Research

Quantitative Research	Qualitative Research
• Researcher is expert.	• Participant is expert.
• Research is hypothesis and theory driven.	• Research is driven by broad research questions.
• Concepts are clearly defined (to the point where they are easily understood by all).	• No focus on concept definition until *after* the research is in the form of the identification of themes.
• Systematic steps for research facilitate replication.	• No systematic research steps. Replication is not a strong goal.
• Data are primarily in the form of numbers.	• Data are primarily in the form of participant explanations, hence quoted or pharaphrased conversations.
• Analysis involves statistical tests, usually for significance and association.	• Analysis is in the form of general patterns or trends. Any numerical analysis is descriptive with no detailed statistical tests for significance or association.

researchers are not daunted by this. They respond that the goal of their research is to show the intrinsic meaning of their data. They focus on trying to understand the subjective nature of human views, interactions, and social experiences. As Geertz (1988) explains by what he calls "thick descriptions," data from field notes try to show the context and meaning of a scene or interaction by drawing connections between other contexts and scenes that occur. Therefore, by definition, qualitative researchers are not focused on having others produce the same results in different settings; they are interested in explaining the subjective interpretations of a group of people in one specific setting and how that interpretation is affected by the holistic nature of the environment, interactions, and context within that setting.

Because of this, qualitative researchers let the social context of their research dictate the flow of the research. They are not concerned with hypotheses (as I've just said) or concrete, observable concept definition, or random sampling. Therefore, they do not follow a systematic, orderly gathering of information, contrary to those doing quantitative research (or at least not to the same degree as quantitative researchers do). For example, an anonymous survey already has specific questions in a specific order that everyone generally reads. Qualitative researchers, on the other hand, frequently have broader questions and the researchers probe and create follow-up questions on the spot, depending on the nature of individual response. This "on the spot" or impromptu elaboration is often absent in quantitative research. This more flexible methodology does not mean to imply that qualitative researchers do not involve following general methodological "rules" or guidelines. The previous chapters I just mentioned outlined the methodological guidelines for doing different types of qualitative research. The only point I am making is that the rules of qualitative research are more flexible than they generally are for quantitative research because the research goals for these two forms differ.

Last, how data are presented and analyzed is a major difference between the two forms of research. Quantitative data are largely numerical, with statistical tests for significance and/or strengths of association between variables. Hence, most data are presented in graphs or tables that summarize the findings of these statistical tests. However, for qualitative research, data are usually presented as the organization of various themes, frequently with quotes or paraphrased comments as supporting evidence. There are usually no tests of statistical significance associated with the presentation of these findings.

However, that being said, you can probably tell that the strongest research is that which tries to combine some elements of both quantitative and qualitative analysis, provided that this combination is done well. For example, quantitative researchers doing surveys might include some open-ended questions. The researchers might try to take these open-ended comments and quantify them (e.g., "50 percent of respondents had positive comments about the program"), but they rarely conduct statistical tests on these comments (although it is possible) and frequently support their basic calculations with sample quoted comments. Similarly, qualitative researchers may try to give a simple tally of their findings, as well (e.g., "Of the 35 women interviewed, 12 of them said they had trouble forming relationships"). Alternatively, qualitative researchers might provide a table or written description summarizing the demographic characteristics of their sample—also a form of quantification.

There are other differences between quantitative and qualitative research. I have highlighted only some of the more obvious differences from a practical methodological point of view. In other words, I focused on the differences that might help you better understand *how* qualitative and quantitative research is done, and therefore how to present the results of the different types of studies. Because of these differences, if you hold qualitative researchers to the same rules as quantitative researchers, you are setting yourself up for disappointment. Studies that are generally quantitative are unlikely to have lengthy discussions of subjective meanings, therefore they may seem to "gloss over" some points. They are also unlikely to have personal snippets or quotations that make qualitative research so appealing to read for many. Qualitative research, on the other hand, is likely to be highly specific to the group being studied; therefore, others reading the research may get frustrated in trying to figure out how that research pertains to them and their specific needs.

In this chapter, I will focus only on how to make sense of data obtained through qualitative means. We will tackle quantitative data in the next chapter.

Getting Started

If you recall, in Figure 8.2 I showed the different types of field notes researchers may take. To briefly recap, these notes are jotted notes (the short notes you take while in the field), detailed notes (the notes to add to the jotted notes later the same day), researcher interpretation notes (your understanding of the situation, interaction, etc.), analytical notes (relating your notes to theory or other research), and personal notes (any personal feedback, reflections, etc.). If you also think back to Chapter 8, I said that you essentially need to try to write anything and everything. According to Gubrium and Holstein (1997), you will see that the notes you take are likely to fall along three dimensions—the who, the what, and the why of a situation—which they describe as such:

Typically at the forefront are the *what* questions. The commanding focus on much of qualitative research is on questions such as *what* is happening, *what* are people doing, and *what* does it mean to be them? The questions address the content of meaning, as articulated through social interaction and as mediated by culture. . . .

At the same time, a sensitivity to the ways people participate in the construction of their lives and social worlds has led qualitative inquiry toward equally compelling *how* questions. While not ignoring *what* concerns, those pursuing how questions typically emphasize the production of meaning. Research orients to the everyday practices through which the meaningful realities of everyday life are constituted and sustained. The guiding question is *how* are the realities of everyday life accomplished?

. . . There are, of course, other questions, most notably those dealing with *why* things are as they are, *why* people act in particular ways, and the like. Such questions, while not uncommon in qualitative researcher, are typically deferred until the *what* and *how* questions are deal with. (Gubrium & Holstein, 1997, pp. 14–15; emphasis in original)

To relate this to the various types of field notes I discussed in Chapter 8, the jotted and detailed notes are likely to be largely (but not necessarily solely) focused on the *what*. What are people doing? What are the feelings and explanations they give about their actions? Your research interpretation notes may focus more on the *how* and some preliminary

This photograph shows an antiwar rally. What types of field observations would you make if you were studying this political protest?

why as you use your expertise and reflection to put the "what" into context. The analytical notes would focus more on the *why*. In unstructured or semi-structured interviews, the *what, how,* and *why* might be more evident because, unlike in field research where the researcher tries to blend into the surroundings, researchers doing interviews are usually more obvious in their researcher role and can therefore take more action in probing respondents for particular levels of information.

But the point that Gubrium and Holstein are making is that if the researcher keeps in mind the *what* and the *how* (because the *why*, as they state, can't be addressed until after the first two components) during the research process, the researcher will already have some sense of direction regarding what to do with the analysis of data during the next research phase. In other words, if researchers are sensitive to observing the *what* and the *how*, then as they are observing, they will also very likely make mental notes and comparisons (that may be reflected in the researcher interpretation notes or personal notes) during the study that will direct them to conclusions after the study. Researchers will be better able to spot the emerging patterns as they are actually doing the research. So, on some level, analysis is ongoing. It informally begins during the data-collection phase.

The Method of Analysis

Whenever researchers refer to *data analysis*, they are essentially talking about the process of trying to find patterns, or recurring themes, in the data. Therefore, all data analysis involves examining, categorizing, recategorizing, comparing, and evaluating the information collected from a specific method of observation. Just as with quantitative data analysis, which can involve descriptive statistics, statistical tests of hypotheses, or statistical tests of association between variables, there are a variety of approaches to analyzing qualitative data as well. Here, I will briefly discuss some common specific methods of qualitative analysis. I will also discuss a fourth method of analysis, *successive approximation,* in more detail because it is a method commonly employed in qualitative analysis.

■ A Selection of Specific Approaches to Qualitative Analysis

Regardless of the specific analytic approach you select, all forms of qualitative analysis will require some form of data reduction. Data reduction is necessary because qualitative research is likely to generate much more data than you will ever be able to use in a final report. Data reduction makes analysis much more manageable, and, according to Marvasti (2004), this process begins as soon as the research question is posed. By selecting a specific topic (e.g., keeping kids occupied after school), by further defining that problem (examining the nature and use of a local after-school program), by specifying a specific population (focusing on teenagers who use that after-school program), and by locating a specific location to study that population (a program in a specific city), a researcher is already beginning to reduce the quantity of data gathered.

Nevertheless, even with early reduction, a qualitative researcher is *still* likely to gather many more pages of notes than he or she will ever analyze in any one report. These specific approaches to qualitative data analysis that I will discuss will help give you further ideas as to *how* to reduce those pages and pages of notes to more meaningful patterns that, in turn, will lead to your conclusions.

Illustrative method

The first type of qualitative analysis method I will briefly discuss is the **illustrative method.** This method of data analysis, contrary to some of the other forms, is very theory driven. Researchers using this method of analysis apply a theory to a concrete historical situation, social setting, or experience. Essentially, the theory is a guideline and the researchers assesses whether qualitative observations support or refute the theory in a specific instance (remember, qualitative research is generally not very generalizable).

For example, Gratch (2002, **AN 9529329**) studied 15 classroom teachers who participated in a graduate-level foundations course called Schools in Modern Society. This class was designed to teach people who were studying to be teachers themselves about how their individual social experiences affect their views of the academic environment in which they teach. The course trained teachers to critically evaluate school practices and to recognize the role their personal assumptions played in their evaluations. The intent was that this evaluation of self, along with a recognition of how the self affects teachers' views of educational practices, would better empower teachers to advocate for social change when necessary. Gratch's article focuses on how private theory is the basis for understanding one's experiences (in and out of classroom settings) and she uses the case study of "Ellen," a first-year teacher to illustrate how this theory works.

Essentially, according to Gratch (2002), private theory argues that teachers need to recognize their assumed beliefs about teaching and their self as a teacher in order to understand and analyze the context of school experiences, practices, and relations of power. To accomplish this, the teachers used stories told by other teachers, students, administrators, and parents at the school in which they worked to construct a description of the school. The teachers then analyzed this qualitative information in order to identify themes and to form the problem or practice, such as issues of discipline or textbook selection, intended for deeper study. Once these teachers selected a problem, they examined the practice in their school, relating to this problem more deeply by using document analysis, interviews, and observation. However, they did so by linking these experiences in school to their personal experiences in order to try to disentangle how their (the teachers') pasts affected their views of the current problem in their school that they were studying.

Gratch (2002) provides the following information for one of the students, "Ellen," who works in a Christian school in Georgia that has been open since 1958. According to Ellen, she decided to work in this school because she felt that it mirrored the Christian beliefs that were central to her concept of self. In the following excerpt, Ellen describes her experiences. This description is interspersed with comments from Gratch, who puts the excerpts into context for the reader (which appears in italics).

A few students in [my 11th-grade] class were set on giving me a hard time as a new teacher and testing my limits. . . . I was unsure of how to handle their disrespect and disobedience. . . . I had taken the advice of several veteran teachers and started the year off being stricter in my classroom management. . . . This was difficult for me because I genuinely wanted to build caring relationships with students, but I was told that I needed their respect first.

Ellen expresses her concern that the discipline practices encouraged by her colleagues conflicted with both the school's stated mission and her own goals to create a caring community of learners.

[Additionally] I heard rumors that my class was more difficult than the 11th-grade honors class, so I began to wonder if I was being too hard on them academically. My gut told me that they were very capable of the work I was giving them. . . . Helen [the 11th-grade honors teacher] came to me upset because some of her students . . . complained that her class was too easy. She was astonished that students would gripe about such a thing. She indicated that the English Department head and guidance counselor, Gloria Conners, told her to step it up a notch. Gloria later told me that Helen got angry and "assigned tons of homework" instead of following the format . . . for an honors class. . . .

    . . . The administration felt that the best solution to the problem was for us to switch classes.

    . . . When I announced the switch to my classes they did not seem disappointed but rather excited to be getting the "easy teacher." But according to Helen, after the move took place the regular students "resented the fact that they had not been asked" or made a part of the decision. . . . I got a general sense that the regular students felt like they did not have a voice in the school. Orders came from the top down without meaningful dialogue or discussion of the issues.

    As Ellen examined the decision by the administration to switch classes, she became increasingly concerned that neither teachers nor students were able to participate in the decision. . . . Ellen finds that the practices are in conflict with her beliefs and values. . . . The following statements reflect the degree to which her critical examination of self and school practices has helped her make explicit the impact of accepted school practices as well as motivating her to become more engaged in the discourse of school change:

- In light of this information, I have wondered if our school has created a caring, supportive environment where all students feel that their opinions are important and that they are a vital and valuable part of our school.
- Does the administration and faculty favor certain groups over others?
- . . . Based on my findings, I would like to explore ways to work toward more effective communication and a more caring environment where students have a voice and feel valued. (June 27, 2000, pp. 429–432)

Gratch's presentation of Ellen's case illustrates the various components of personal theory. The first component is understanding personal description of experiences, which Gratch presents in the first three paragraphs of Ellen's account. These paragraphs set the scene for Ellen's Christian beliefs and her teaching experiences. The second aspect is how those experiences fit with an individual's personal beliefs. In Ellen's case, this is clear at the end of Ellen's first paragraph account, where she talks about the clash between her teaching goals (based on her beliefs) and her teaching realities (the discipline problem in the classroom). Gratch also supports this point with the first bulleted point at the end of the article where Ellen questions whether the school, which she purposely selected because she thought that it fit her beliefs, actually does practice what it claims. The last goal of the theory is to understand if and how someone can advocate for social change. Gratch uses Ellen's claim to want to explore ways to facilitate communication and caring in her school as an illustration of this (the last bulleted point). Gratch concludes the article by stating that personal stories and self-reflection enable teachers to better place themselves within the school context, and therefore recognize where educational practices might conflict with people's personal, ethical, or moral beliefs. Gratch directly states that recognizing this conflict is the first step for teachers to realize whether change is necessary and what their role in presenting that change may be.

In other words, Gratch uses Ellen's story to illustrate the viability of personal theory and then she links this theory to the role of enacting social change. Hence, Ellen's account *illustrates* what Gratch means by the theory and how the theory can be used. Notice that in this excerpt, or the entire text for that matter (which you can see on-line in Research Navigator), Gratch does not present statistical tests or tables of numerical results or even graphs. The entire article essentially reads as a story, with the snippets from Ellen's experience illustrating Gratch's general theme. Qualitative analysis is frequently like this, which makes reading it very appealing to others.

Analytic comparison

Another type of qualitative analysis **analytic comparison.** In this type of analysis, the researcher does not begin with a theory, but instead develops ideas about regularities from preexisting theories and contrasts them with other explanations within a specific social context. In other words, for illustrative analysis, the researcher is essentially, as the name implies, using qualitative data to illustrate the theory. There is no real comparison or analysis involved in that illustration. In analytic comparison, on the other hand, the qualitative observations are used to compare (not just describe) a theory to other existing explanations.

Analytic comparisons can focus on either a method of agreement or a method of disagreement. In a *method of agreement,* the researcher finds cases that have a common outcome, such as teen suicide, and then tries to find common causes between the cases, even if the details differ. For example, one may be studying the family and school experiences of teenagers who have committed suicide by doing unstructured interviews with members of the suicide victim's immediate family and teachers. What all the cases have in common is the nonaccidental death of a young person, even if some of these teenagers hung themselves, overdosed on drugs, or used more violent means of ending their lives. Through the unstructured interviews, a researcher doing agreement analysis would try to see if there are common patterns behind *why* these individuals might have killed themselves, even though we clearly will never *truly* be able to know the cause for certain since we obviously cannot ask the teenager in question. Perhaps many parents and teachers reveal that the teenager in question was having trouble fitting in at school, or perhaps the person was being picked on by other students. Or perhaps a researcher will learn that many of these teens were perfectionists, who expressed to family and teachers extreme negative self-concepts if they did not excel at every task.

On the other hand, a *method of disagreement* analytical comparison would focus on the opposite, or a combination of both agreement and disagreement. Like the previous example, the researcher identifies cases that have a common outcome, such as teen suicide. But instead of just focusing on the similarities in cause, the researcher would also (or instead) focus on how cases that have the same end result (a prematurely dead teenager) differ. For example, a researcher might find that teens from highly successful families were more likely to be perfectionists, who perhaps were afraid that they could not live up to their family's example. A researcher may find that the perfectionist theme was less present among teens who killed themselves from working-class backgrounds. This would be an example of a method of disagreement analysis.

Network analysis

Qualitative research can be very adept at disentangling the various social relationships people possess and how these relationships affect individuals' behavior. Qualitative researchers can "map" the social relationships, frequently called *social networks* or simply *networks*, between people to discover and analyze sets or relations (hence, the term **network analysis**). These "maps" are frequently called *sociograms* because they are pictures of social connections between people or groups.

For example, Abel, Plumridge, and Graham (2002, **AN 7584462**) studied 44 adolescents between the ages of 10 and 13 to try to disentangle how social networks affect smoking behavior among adolescents. These 44 students participated in a three-year study that included focus groups, surveys, and intensive interviews. However, the research that Abel, Plumridge, and Graham discuss in this article focuses on examining the social networks of the entire academic class of these 44 study adolescents. The researchers argue that most of the studies of peers and adolescent smoking are cross-sectional; therefore, it is difficult to disentangle whether peers affect smoking (e.g., people become friends and then begin smoking) or if people who are inclined to smoke select other smokers as their friends.

Abel, Plumridge, and Graham (2002) hoped that by studying the social networks among these 44 adolescents in relation to the social networks of their entire classmates, they would be better able to disentangle the peer–smoking relationship. They argue that until researchers better understand the social relationships of the adolescent target audience, any antismoking strategy is likely to be met with resistance and to result in failure. To facilitate their analysis of social networks, the researchers use a special computer software program called Negopy, which according to them worked this way:

> Each student in year 10 was given a code and, when named by another, the relevant code was inserted as a friendship link. This was recognized by Negopy when analysis was carried out. Pupils were also asked to indicate which category of smoking best described them. The categories were "never tried smoking," "tried smoking a few times," "smoked one cigarette in the last 4 weeks," "smoke one or more times per week," and "smoke at least once a day." Correlations were then made between group membership and other network positions, and smoking behaviour. (p. 329)

The sociogram shown in Figure 11.1 illustrates a group and the lines illustrate how the various groups are (or, in the absence of a line, are not) connected to each other. Seem confusing? It can be, and this is mainly because, as Abel, Plumridge, and Graham note, this basic sociogram identifies and addresses the general relationships among groups. It does not note whether any one individual is a core member of that group, what they call a "node," who, if absent, would lead to the demise of the group. In other words, this sociogram does not account for the individuals who are particularly influential in a group (and if absent would lead to the group's demise) and between groups (as a strong link), who may exert more than their share of influence on the behavior of others. However, software programs such as Negopy do not necessarily address these nuances of nodes, therefore they should be a complement to other forms of data gathering, like the focus groups and interviews that Abel, Plumridge, and Graham did. In fact, as these researchers state:

> If an individual is a focus for an aggregation of a number of people, that aggregation will therefore not qualify as a group. Arguably, this is the social

dynamic of "popularity," often suggested to be a crucial determinant of peer influence. Yet "popularity," in the sense of being widely and mutually considered a friend, is not only missed in Negopy definitions, but at odds with its focus on "group membership." Negopy definitions may therefore render invisible much of the social dynamics that "group formations" are assumed to illuminate.

That was the case in this study. One girl among this group of densely networked "liaisons" was especially popular, with 12 reciprocated friendship links. When she was treated as a critical node and a further sociogram drawn removing her and her links, the result was radically different [Figure 11.2]. This set of "liaisons" was then seen as three different "groups" with one "direct liaison" connecting two of the "groups." Under these conditions with the highly popular "critical node" removed, three groups fitted Negopy definitions. There was one link between group A and group B, and one link between group B and group C, and no link between group A and group C. The critical node had held the entire set together, having five links to group A, five links to group B and two links to group C. The critical node would have been accepted by Negopy as a member in any *one* of these groups, but the fact that she had so many links with people across groups rather than solely within any one particular group meant that she broke the Negopy definitions. (pp. 332–333)

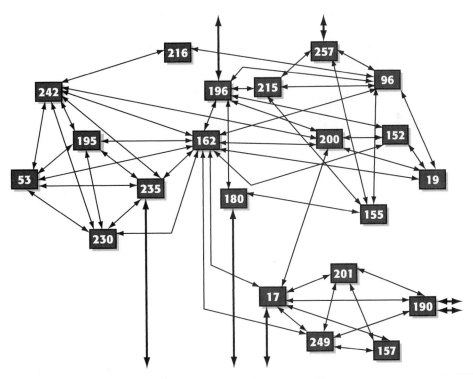

Figure 11.1 Section of the Network Depicting Some Negopy-Defined Liaisons

Source: Gillian Abel, Libby Plumridge, and Patrick Graham, "Peers, Networks or Relationships: Strategies for Understanding Social Dynamics as Determinants of Smoking Behaviour," *Drugs: Education, Prevention & Policy, 9* (4) (2002): 332. Reprinted by permission of Taylor & Francis Ltd. www.tandf.co.uk/journals.

Consequently, based on what these researchers learned from their other qualitative information, they redirected the computer to search for links *after* omitting this particular girl. After doing so, the Negopy software created the altered sociogram shown in Figure 11.2.

As Abel, Plumridge, and Graham stated in the excerpt, now it is clear that there are three main social groups, with group B (the middle one) being the one that links the other two (A [the left-most one] and C [the bottom one]). Therefore, they learned that there was one girl who served as a "node" and exerted a lot of influence over the other peer groups due to her popularity and various social relations, and that when her influence was removed, the depiction of the dynamics of the adolescent peer groups changed. Not being able to understand the nuances of how these groups interact (e.g., groups A and C do not interact with each other directly) may provide crucial information in learning how adolescent peer groups affect behavior—however, that information may be missed if only one type of data strategy is employed (e.g., the use of computers alone without other qualifying information).

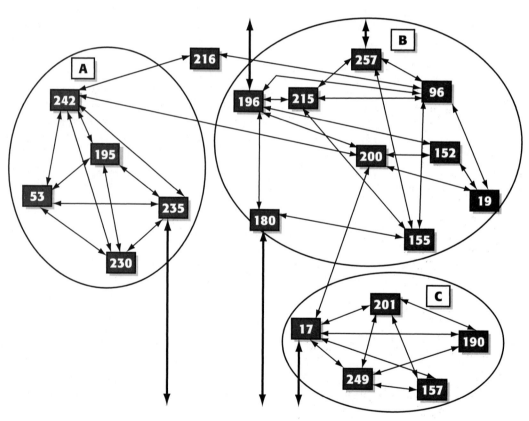

Figure 11.2 Section of the Network After Removal of the Critical Mode

Source: Gillian Abel, Libby Plumridge, and Patrick Graham, "Peers, Networks or Relationships: Strategies for Understanding Social Dynamics as Determinants of Smoking Behaviour," *Drugs: Education, Prevention & Policy, 9* (4) (2002): 333. Reprinted by permission of Taylor & Francis Ltd. www.tandf.co.uk/journals.

Successive approximation

The fourth and last analysis method involves repeated iterations, usually in the form of repeated readings of notes, which move toward a final analysis. Since this process is, in some ways, more detailed than the other three, I will discuss it in more depth. In **successive approximation,** the researcher progresses through various readings of the field notes, identifying patterns or concepts which, after repeated read-throughs, will allow broader generalizations to be made. In various passes through the data, the researcher focuses on different coding issues or techniques, which I will describe here.

The first step of successive approximation is to become *very*, almost intimately, familiar with your data. This means that before you begin to formally analyze it, you need to read and reread your notes a number of times. And don't be fooled—this can be a lengthy process. For example, Chaudry (2004) conducted field interviews with 42 low-income mothers who were trying to combine work and family responsibilities under the "new" welfare reform called the "Personal Responsibility and Work Opportunity Reconciliation Act." Chaudry notes that for the 42 mothers she interviewed, she amassed over 320 hours of taped interviews and over 3,900 pages of transcription. That's *a lot* of field notes!

Even though this process may be long and somewhat tedious, by rereading your data you are likely to notice different points or observations. Conversations with colleagues, information you read, some television shows—any of these may trigger something that causes some specific, previously unconsidered point in your data to become evident. Because this process is so open to external influences, it is sometimes called **open coding.**

During open coding, researchers need to be open-minded about what they see in their notes so that they do not miss something. As researchers engage in open coding, they look for critical terms that participants repeatedly use, key events they describe, or different themes that emerge more than once. When researchers see a piece of data as part of a theme, concept, or the like, then they might want to make note of that theme on the data itself—either in an colored-inked heading (to later recapture the researcher's attention and help reorganize many sheets of paper if using paper notes) or in a separate file (if using a computer). Essentially, when open coding, the researcher is making preliminary decisions about what is important or interesting in the data. Sometimes, especially with researchers new to qualitative research, *everything* seems important at this stage. Unfortunately, that perspective does not help the researcher with the overall research goal, which is to make some conclusions. If you find yourself having difficulty in deciding what to code during this stage, ask yourself, What is the *most* compelling aspect about my data? Is there something unusual about my setting or the people I am studying? What surprised me the most? What experience stood out to me the most? Why? Use these questions as your starting point, and as you become comfortable with them and the themes that emerge, other themes are likely to become evident as well.

After researchers think that they are done with the open coding, then they go back and make a list of these themes. However, notice that I said *after* they done with the coding. Many qualitative researchers argue that the list of concepts should not be done simultaneously to the open-coding process itself. In other words, if I am reading my notes from interviews with teenage runaways and the first theme that I notice is one of despair, I would not immediately whip out a second sheet of paper, head it with the title "Open Coding Themes" and write "1. Despair" and then go back to my notes looking for theme number 2. Instead, I would read all of my notes and do the coding on its own. Then when I am done, I would go back and look at the highlighted color headers identifying the theme or go through my various file names that I have for open codes. This way, when I go back over these notes I made from my open coding, seeing my code notes may refresh my memory regarding the nature of the excerpt I coded and make me see other open-coded themes. Alternately, if I try to compile my list as I do the first coding run-through, I may unintentionally focus on finding evidence of the themes I have already identified, as opposed to being "open" to new themes that emerge. So why bother with the list? Well, the list helps the researchers see at a glance the themes they've identified. Also, the list will help the researchers organize any of these subthemes into wider ones that may be important for the overall message.

The second stage of the coding process is the **axial coding.** During this phase of coding, the researcher begins to organize the codes, which is why an open-code list may be useful. The axial coding requires at least one additional review of the data, but this time the researcher is focusing on reading and comparing the content within coded themes, as opposed to the data as a mass itself. During this phase, the researcher now keeps the original open codes in mind and rereads to see if there are any other codes to add, whether new ideas or codes emerge and how the codes may relate to each other. For example, can some codes be lumped together into a broader category? Are there any codes that are complements of each other and therefore illustrate opposites? Are there any codes that are too broad and can be subdivided, based on a reading of the material within them, to smaller codes? Can the codes be sequenced? Based on the answers to these questions, some themes may be dropped or new ones made.

Remember, coding in qualitative research is a process—one that is refined and adapted based on many readings of the data. For example, in my hypothetical study of teenage runaways, I may find that my codes relating to "despair" focus on despair regarding work opportunities, despair regarding romantic relationships, and despair regarding family relationships. I may mark all the notes that deal with despair in family relationships and relate them to subthemes of relationships with the same-sex parent, with the opposite-sex parent, and with siblings. I may relate these subthemes to themes about despair in romantic relationships—how runaways who express the greatest trouble with their opposite-sex parent (as opposed to their same-sex parent) are more likely to express feelings of despair in forming romantic relationships. I may also relate this to other themes such as gender differences in runaway experience to see whether male or female runaways perceive these dimensions of despair differently.

The last step of data coding is **selective coding.** By now the researchers have identified the major themes of their research. Now is the time to be selective about which codes they will develop as main themes and which will be ancillary or supporting themes.

■ An Illustration of Qualitative Coding and Analysis

Sometimes the process of coding will make the connections clearer, such as in network analysis, but this is not always the case. In fact, frequently, researchers (especially those new to qualitative research) end up with a pile of notes and files with various links, diagrams, and comments, but little clue as to how to combine them, summarize them, and make conclusions. In fact, the essence of data analysis is to summarize tons of information into a somewhat neatly packaged conclusion that someone who did not see all of your data (and, quite honestly isn't very likely to want to anyway) can understand. Dammer (1992) studied 55 inmates in two maximum security prisons in Pennsylvania to explore the meaning of religion in a prison setting. A detailed examination of his analytic strategies serves as an illustration of one possible way to approach qualitative data analysis.

As I stated, the purpose of Dammer's research was to study the function and meaning of religion in prisons, including from the perspectives of inmates, and how this meaning relates to imprisonment. Dammer conducted both participant observation research and intensive interviews to gather his data. In the following excerpt, he explains how he analyzed the data using a successive approximation method:

> Following these ideas, the participant observation data in this research were analyzed constantly during the first three months of the study. Field notes were checked weekly for theoretical propositions or puzzlements. The field notes were then labeled and separated into categories or files. Headings for the files were mundane, methodological, and analytic. The first analytic stage produced tentative propositions to be tested and specific questions to be asked during the intensive interview.
>
> . . . The second analytic stage of analysis served to being a final order to analytic concepts that surfaced during the participant observation period and intensive interviews. This stage occurred after the data were collected. Because the processes were quite involved, a detailed explanation is necessary.
>
> As mentioned, the first step of coding by methodological, analytical, and mundane categories was completed during the weekly review periods. After the data collection, each line or paragraph of coded data was cut from the field notes and placed in a large folder labeled mundane, methodological or analytic. Over 2,000 separate "pieces" of data resulted from this process. Each folder was then analyzed separately by listing each concept alphabetically, placing similar concepts in like groups. If a line or paragraph of analytic data stated "religious inmates feeling discriminated against," any piece of data that reflected that concept was coded within the greater analytic category.
>
> After completing this task, an alphabetized list of concepts emerged for each of the three major categories. The mundane list included 42 concepts, methodological 108, and analytic 126. Next, concepts which seemed to be similar in context were collapsed. The concepts, for example, expressing "ecumenical participation" were combined with "relationships of different religious groups." This step was essential because of the large volume of date collected.
>
> Two bodies of information resulted from these procedures: 1. an outline for the ethnographic account of the religious programs at both research sites; 2. common themes were later used to augment the results extracted from the intensive interview data.
>
> . . . The final and most important step in the analytic process was the application of the constant comparison method. The purposes of the constant comparison method, as explained by Glaser and Straus (1967), are:
>
> 1. generate conceptual categories and use evidence (data) to illustrate,
> 2. provide empirical generalizations to have generality and explanatory power,
> 3. specify a concept for a one-case study,
> 4. verify theory already developed,

5. generate theory by accounting for much (not all) of the relevant behavior. (Pg. 101)

Constant comparison in this research was used to list the responses to each question for each group interviewed (e.g., Muslim, Catholic, etc.), to compare and contrast them with other denominational groups and with non-religious inmates and correctional officers, both between and among the prison sites.

The use of the constant comparison method was integral to this research because it served four major purposes. First, it provided a mini-analysis of each question. Second, the constant comparison provided the evidence for what questions were significant enough to be developed into themes. Third, constant comparison develops substantive theory that can be applied to the field—a result which will be helpful for prison Chaplains and administrators. And fourth, the constant comparison method, provided a procedure to "grounding" the findings back to the relevant literature (Glaser and Straus, 1967).

Because of the need to explore the number of possible concepts, categories, and questions, it was essential to work the large volume of information into some manageable and readable form. The development of appropriate themes provided this structure. It is important to mention, however, that the themes selected do not precisely reflect the individual questions in the interview guide. The various questions were integrated into a theme only if their responses were found to be common, interesting, theoretically significant to the research, and supported by the constant comparison method (Glaser and Straus, 1967).

The significant themes which developed arose from the analysis were: (1) the *process* of becoming a religious inmate; (2) the *reasons* why inmates attend religious services, and (3) the *lifestyle* of the religious inmate, (4) the *relationships* that are impacted by the practice of religion in prison, and (5) the ways in which religious inmates act out their religious behavior. This last theme is entitled *Religious Response Styles*. (pp. 72–74, 76–78)

Presenting Qualitative Findings

There are many approaches to the actual presentation of qualitative findings, but most of these approaches take on an essay form as opposed to an essay form mixed with tables and graphs of quantitative data (although some basic representation of quantitative data may be present). However, even within this format, the researcher has a couple of decisions to make.

First, researchers need to decide on the perspective they will take in the writing process. Whose voice will be the center of the narrative? Will the researcher take his or her own perspective and cast himself or herself as the center actor, detailing the conclusions as they fit the researcher's experiences, or will the researcher put respondents at the center of attention? For example, Carol Stack (1974), in her classic work *All Our Kin* writes about her experiences living among African American women. Given the limited economic resources and the discrimination that African Americans, especially African American women, experienced at the time of her study, Stack was interested in how low-income African Americans survive and what their family life was like.

An example of Stack's description of her first meeting with the Waters family and a discussion with Ruby illustrates the concept of narrative unfolding.

I first came by the Waters' home in the summer of 1968. Magnolia, her sixty-year-old "husband" Calvin (father of six of Magnolia's children), Magnolia's oldest son Lenny, and five of the younger children . . . were methodically folding several piles of newspapers for Lenny's five evening paper routes, a daily family routine. . . . After a lesson from a seven-year-old on how to make the fold, I joined in on the rhythmic activity that absorbed everyone's concentration. It was an hour and a half before all of the newspapers were ready for delivery. Magnolia joked about my hands, black with newsprint. I told them I would like to begin a study of family life in the Flats. Magnolia and Calvin told her to come by again and to bring my baby.

Several months later Magnolia told me that she had been surprised that I sat with them that first day to fold papers, and then came back to help again. "White folks," she told me, "don't have the time, they's always in such a rush, and they don't sit on the black folk's furniture, at least no Whites that come into The Flats." (p. 10)

. . . Ruby and I enjoyed comparing our attitudes and approaches toward everything. . . . For example, she insisted that I ask my friends to take care of Kevin or to loan me money. She was in fact teaching me how to get along. Ruby and I also enjoyed comparing our culturally acquired tests in the furniture and dress. With no intention of buying, we loved to go to the local used furniture store to mock one another's preferences. Ruby admired new, vinyl and Masonite, tough, fake wood modern furniture. I was only interested in finding old turn-off-the-century oak furniture. She laughed at my love for old, used furniture, often warped with age. To her, aged and worn stood for poverty. (pp. 14–15)

In this excerpt, Stack is the center of the narrative. She is describing her experiences in the field. In the first instance, she is describing her initial encounter with the Waters family, and in the second instance, she describes how her discussion with Ruby, a resident of the Flats, helps Stack to see different cultural perspectives on social issues. Essentially, in this presentation style, Stack "invites" the reader to see what she sees and share her experiences with the additional benefit of having the researcher share her interpretations with the reader. It's essentially like taking a guided tour of a social issue.

On the other hand, Patterson, Collins, and Abbott (2004, **AN 12670768**) illustrate the second approach to representation, a placement of the individuals studied at the center of the action. They researched 16 teachers who worked in urban settings, but who, contrary to the common expectations, also were able to create classrooms in which their students scored equal to or higher than state averages on standardized tests of reading and math. Because this degree of achievement is less expected in urban than suburban schools, these researchers were interested in what made these teachers different. They used the term *resilient*. Their research was based on two general questions: What drove these successful teachers to stay in challenged, urban schools, and what strategies did these teachers use to cope with the adversity common in urban schools? They found that these resilient teachers generally shared nine characteristics, one of which is presented in the excerpt below:

[Theme 4]. Resilient teachers take charge and solve problems.

Resilient teachers and teacher leaders were willing to ask for help when they needed it, even if it meant pursuing a non-traditional path. One example came from a seven-year veteran in an elementary school, Ms. Aguirre. She'd worked hard for three months trying to get Emilio, a fifth grader, to do his work. He was inattentive and had no interest in school beyond being with his friends. She reported, "Emilio really got to me, to my heart. I knew he had something so amazing to share; he just had fear written all over his face." She went to the school administrator for help and was connected with a community liaison. The liaison got to know him in a positive way. But, he still wasn't doing his classwork or homework. He did not care about school. Finally, the principal came to Ms. Aguirre and told her he was moving the child to another class because he felt the boy needed a "fresh start." Ms. Aguirre refused and explained that if the child were moved, he would think she had given up on him. She committed to finding a way to reach Emilio even if she couldn't do it by herself, even if she had to go outside the school district.

Ms. Aguiree talked with many people in the community and learned of a partnership with the U.S. Navy; she contacted the officer in charge and was assigned a mentor for Emilio. She described what happened next:

I explained the problems with Emilio and told Lt. Romero, frankly, that I was out of ideas but that I would not give up on the boy. He and I established a close relationship because of Emilio. He would come in about once a week and sit with Emilio in the classroom for a couple of hours. Then, after a month or two, he started to take Emilio out on the weekends. They had activities that they would do together, like hiking. Romero set a purpose, and he would say, "The purpose of today is . . . ." He became a mentor for Emilio, helped him with his schoolwork and convinced Emilio how important it was to do his work, to get decent grades. By the end of the year, he was doing most of his work on time and was able to be promoted. If it weren't for Romero, I don't think I would've been able to reach Emilio.

Resilient teachers are not victims. They solve problems that are barriers to student learning, including creative solutions to school district bureaucracy. (pp. 8–9)

This type of presentation of results is an example of placing the individuals at the center. The role of the researcher is only in an analytical capacity. The "real" information comes from the perspective of the respondent, Ms. Aguirre, in her own words. There is no indication of the researcher's experiences, feelings, or thoughts during the course of the research.

Researchers have to decide how they want to arrange the presentation of the data. Three common approaches are typologies, continuums, and story-driven models (Richardson, 1990; Marvasti, 2004). A *typology* classifies the data into categories and then uses excerpts or quotations to illustrate each category. The example I just used from Patterson, Collins, and Abbott (2004) is a typology. They found nine themes, of which I presented one (the fourth), and then they provided the experience of Ms. Aguirre as the evidence to support the identification of that theme. This identification of categories and supporting or illustrating quotes is characteristic of the typology approach.

On the other hand, a *continuum* arranges the data along some type of imaginary line that is linked together. The third type of presentation, a *story-driven model*, is pretty much what the name implies. Some qualitative researchers see the presentation of the data as a presentation of a story where they emphasize descriptions of characters, settings, the au-

Patterson, Collins, and Abbott (2004) studied successful teachers in low-income schools to learn about how they coped with limited resources.

thor's actions, and the author's thoughts (Marvasti, 2004). Whyte's *Street Corner Society,* which we discussed in Chapter 8 on field research, is an example of the story-driven model.

The last consideration for the presentation of results is how many examples you find to be sufficient to illustrate your point. There is disagreement regarding this point. Students frequently like concrete information such as numbers, even in qualitative research. They frequently want to know "how much" or "exactly what do I do?" Researchers who subscribe to this same desire for concrete and direct guidelines suggest three as the magic number (Berg, 2004). According to these researchers, for every point or theme a researcher wants to present, there should be at least three examples that illustrate that theme, but that a researcher should not present so many that the reader becomes bored or distracted by the quotes. On the other hand, Esterberg (2002) disagrees and states that there are no "magic numbers" and that the criteria for whether there is enough evidence should be, like qualitative research, more subjective.

She argues that a researcher should include enough examples so that the reader finds the point or analysis "believable." In other words, there should be enough examples to convey to the reader that the researcher's point is not an outlier (e.g., only expressed by one person), but that this can sometimes be accomplished with few quotes and other times more may be needed.

I realize that by presenting both views, I have not given you concrete directions in this matter. This may be a good topic to discuss with your professor and to debate as a class. My personal opinion is that, in recognition of limited available space in publications (most publishers impose a page limit), I would go with the "believable" criteria, but space permitting, try to include at least three quotes when possible. Your professor, however, may have a different view, as this point is far from resolved.

Assessing Data and Analysis Quality

For quantitative researchers, quality data are data that are both valid and reliable. With quality quantitative data, researchers will assume that they have precise and consistent measures that provide the same kind of "truth" to different researchers in different settings. To some degree, researchers can statistically assess this. However, for qualitative researchers, data quality is less concrete, largely because unlike quantitative researchers, qualitative researchers do not necessarily believe that there is one "true" condition that should be measurable by concise and precise measures. In fact, the main purpose of qualitative research is to observe the *subjective* meanings (or measures) of phenomena of the people experiencing the phenomena. So, for example, a quantitative researcher may want to know how test scores vary among students before and after they attend a study group; a qualitative researcher, however, is interested in the students' own perceptions of both what they learned from the study group and what they thought of the study group itself. The two goals are fundamentally different; therefore, the two means of assessing data quality need to be different as well. In this section, I'm going to discuss how the benchmarks of data quality— validity, reliability, and generalizability—apply to instances of qualitative research.

Validity

Remember, validity is when a researcher is truly measuring or observing what the researcher thinks he or she is. In more technical terms, validity is the closeness between what the people really did, what their relationships and experiences really are, and what outside occurrences really happened to what the researcher concluded about these things. But how do you know that what you saw is really what happened and not what you *wanted* to think happen? Warren and Karner (2005) make the following three suggestions for assessing the validity of your interpretations.

1. Evaluate your data in the context of your methodological and analytic choices.
2. Reframe your analysis and test its "goodness of fit" with the data.
3. Obtain external verification from respondents, from other researchers, or by triangulation.

The first point involves being clear about what your original research questions and goals are. For example, if you are interested in studying why teenagers run away from home, the study should be composed of interviews or conversations with teenage runaways, not interviews with members of social services agencies that try to help these teenagers. Although these latter data may be interesting, they should be secondary; your main conclusions should stem from the teenage runaways themselves. So essentially, this is an issue of whether the data are the right kind; however, it is also an issue as to if there is enough data to make the claims you hope. For example, one of my last interviews with a teenage runaway may reveal some type of street slang that I did not pay attention to previously. If this is the case, then my data are incomplete and I don't have enough information to put this slang in context with the other respondents. I may need to schedule some follow-up interviews to assess the importance of this slang usage.

In quantitative analysis, goodness-of-fit tests are statistical in nature. In qualitative analysis, goodness of fit is not statistical but is still possible. With this, researchers essentially play devil's advocate and propose alternative explanations for their conclusions and then see if they can find evidence to support these alternative explanations.

According to Denzin (1989), one way of accomplishing this is **negative case testing,** where the researcher looks at the lists of themes and supporting points compiled earlier in the research process and reexamines the data to see if there is evidence of data and themes that are counter to those that the researcher already found. For example, earlier I mentioned that among teenage runaways a theme might be despair. If I decided to do negative case testing, I might reexamine the data to see if I can find any evidence of the opposite of despair, or hope. If I find enough evidence to suggest a new theme of hope, or some other theme counter to despair, then I need to rethink my analysis to account for this new theme as well. In this case, I am essentially my own worst critic with regard to evaluating my conclusions, and this backward and forward motion of theme testing will, theoretically, improve the validity of the conclusions I finally achieve.

Third, Warren and Karner (2005) suggest that the researcher use external sources, such as other researchers or respondents, to assess the validity of findings. The third suggestion they make within this point, triangulation, is usually treated as support for reliability, so I will cover that in the next section. External validation by other researchers or participants simply involves researchers taking their interpretations back to the subjects and essentially asking them if the researchers' conclusions fit what the subjects know of the circumstances. When researchers present their conclusions to the study participants, this form of validity is sometimes called **member validation.** A project, then, is valid if the subjects involved recognize and understand the researcher's description of their experiences and views.

Likewise, instead of personally asking other researchers to review your field notes (which is entirely possible and acceptable, just not always feasible), researchers can obtain external validation by other researchers by reviewing the published work of other researchers and seeing how it fits with their observations in this instance. For example, in her study of low-wage working mothers, Chaudry (2004) includes comments about other research that validates hers in notes that correspond to each chapter. This boosts the validity of her findings.

So what are other types of validity in qualitative research? Do they differ from the types of validity presented in Chapter 4? Many of the forms of validity I discussed in Chapter 4 are harder to establish in qualitative research due to the subjective focus of this research style. Some forms of validity, not generally discussed in Chapter 4, that do apply, however, are ecological validity, natural history validity, and competent insider performance. **Ecological validity** is the degree to which the social relationships and experiences that the researcher describes actually matches those of the participants. It is basically a thought game where the researchers ask themselves whether the events observed would occur even without their presence. The goal is for that answer to be yes, but it cannot empirically or concretely be tested, which is why I describe it as a "thought game."

Natural history validity is the researcher's full explanation about how his or her study was conducted. It is the researcher's documentation of the methodological procedures, his or her actions during the experience, and the assumptions that the researcher had during all phases of the experience (meaning before, during, and after). If others reading the research agree with the researcher's actions, then natural history validity is achieved. Essentially, this is where the researcher makes the case for the chosen methods and describes the methods, experiences, and decision-making process in detail so that others can evaluate it.

Last, there is **competent insider performance.** This is when the researcher determines if he or she has been able to interact effectively with the subjects to the point where the "researcher" identity is no longer the main identity from the participants' views and they, theoretically, begin acting more "typical" in the researcher's presence. Therefore, this form of validity refers to the degree to which the researcher is accepted among the participants and whether the researcher provides enough information about the field to give outsiders a sense of the social context in which the study occurred. The more competent the researcher is in fitting in with the participants, the more valid the findings will be because the participants will act "naturally" as opposed to how they think they *should* act when being observed.

■ Reliability

Parts of the third question that Warren and Karner (2005) present for a validity check are usually treated as an issue of reliability by others. Warren and Karner suggest that researchers try to establish external verification, which, in a sense, is really an issue of reliability.

Reliability in quantitative analysis addresses the question, Would the researcher make the same conclusions if the research was gathered at a different time or place? Since qualitative researchers know that the answer to this question is likely to be no for them, because of the inherent focus on subjectivity in qualitative research, this question does not apply to them. Reliability in qualitative research, on the other hand, addresses the question, Are a researcher's observations about a specific incident or person in the field internally or externally consistent? In quantitative research, the questions pertain to a comparison of a particular study to other studies or data *outside* of the particular study in question. In qualitative research, this is the opposite. The comparison is between notes and information gathered at other points *during* the study.

Internal consistency refers to whether the information makes sense, given all that the researcher knows about a person or setting. Do the researcher's notes create a coherent picture of people and events? Do the notes about a person depict that person consistently? In other words, do the researcher's notes show that a person is generally kind and courteous? Are there any notes with anomalies? Are there any notes where this person emotionally lashed out or "snapped" at someone? If there *are* notes of contradictory behavior, is there some additional piece of information that explains the odd behavior? For example, were there any notes that indicated that this person was under a lot of stress at the time of this anomalous behavior? Was there a death in the family? Was the person laid off from work? If there are no notes putting the unusual behavior in context, and if this behavior as noted *was* unusual, then the researcher may not have accurately observed it. In other words, at least in this instance, this information may not have internal validity.

External consistency, on the other hand, refers to when outside sources, such as other people, verify a researcher's observations. For example, if I ask people about their perception of "Ann" and they describe her as caring, thoughtful, and considerate, then that pretty much verifies my conclusions that she is a kind and courteous person. The exact descriptions of others does not have to agree with mine verbatim, but if the general sentiment is the same, then I have external consistency.

Obstacles to reliability

Although *establishing* reliability seems to be fairly straightforward—one looks for consistency in one's notes and in discussions with others—that does not necessarily mean that *obtaining* reliable data is straightforward. For example, even my external consistency is only as good as the credibility of those to whom I am using as comparison. If I talk to "Jane" about her perception of "Ann," and Jane and Ann, who normally get along just fine, had a fight the previous evening, Jane may not give me a very credible account of Ann. She may say something like, "Well, I used to think that Ann was a caring person, but recently she's been very short-tempered, and I find her difficult to be around." This one comment actually seems to support the "odd" note that I said I found in my discussion of internal consistency. However, without knowing about the fight—and more importantly, without trying to probe a little deeper and understand Jane's view of Ann (remember, after all, I thought they got along just fine)—I may make an unreliable conclusion about Ann's personality. (I might conclude that she has a "hot" and "cold" personality, which may not be the case.)

Other obstacles include *misinformation* by the respondents, which is unintentional falsehoods. For instance, a person may misinterpret a policy or relationship and pass it on to the researcher as "fact," even though the information is incorrect. The reverse of misinformation is *lies*, which are intentional untruths that people may tell in order to protect themselves, give favorable impressions in some instances, or give negative impressions in others. For example, a gang member might claim that he never participated in a drive-by shooting even though he has. He may lie about this because he does not want the researcher to view him negatively. Or a politician's aide might lie about poll statistics supporting the politician to make that politician seem more popular than he is. Both of these are intentional untruths, and therefore lies.

Respondents can also be *evasive*. They might change the subject or embark on detailed, tangential explanations that never really address the question at hand. If the researcher is not careful and observant, he or she may discover the evasive tactic too late and not be able to take another shot at getting at the real story. Last, people may present *fronts*. In other words, people may not present themselves as they really are. A teenage runaway who wants to appear street smart and tough may continually act tough, disdainful, and disengaged from others when actually she is a scared and lonely child. Places can be fronts as well. A neighborhood bar, by all outside appearances may be just that, but more careful investigation reveals that it is an establishment that launders money.

The point of these cautions is that researchers must continually be aware of their surroundings, try to obtain insight as to the relationships around them, and question their observations. By not taking things at face value, by digging deeper into what the researcher sees and thinks he or she sees, a researcher is better equipped to gather data that are internally and externally consistent, and therefore reliable.

Triangulation

One tactic for obtaining reliability is triangulation. *Triangulation* involves using different forms of data observation to obtain a more complete and complimentary view of a social phenomenon. For example, earlier I discussed the research of Abel, Plumridge, and Graham (2002), who studied adolescents to examine the effect that peer groups had on smoking behavior. I presented a figure they compiled based on computer analysis of survey results about adolescents' friends. But, if you remember, these researchers noted that this first figure (Figure 11.1) would have been misleading if it had been used as the only piece of information, because it ignored the extensive influence of adolescents that these researchers called "nodes." How did they know about the influence of "nodes"? Through other methods of observation—namely, interviews and focus groups. By using interviews, focus groups, and surveys, Abel, Plumridge, and Graham were able to adapt their initial figure into the second one (Figure 11.2) I presented to achieve a more accurate, hence *valid*, view of adolescent peer groups. This blending of different methodologies is an example of triangulation.

■ Generalizability

Quantitative researchers generally try to establish generalizable knowledge—knowledge that can be applied to a population based on observations in a sample randomly drawn from that population. Qualitative researchers, on the other hand, are not concerned with generalizability at all. They know that their conclusions apply only to the specific group they are studying and, most likely, to the specific time that the group was observed. So, generalizability, as a benchmark of data quality, is not even relevant to the qualitative researcher. In the view of qualitative research, the potential high validity and detailed understanding of a specific subgroup compensates for the lack of generalizability. Therefore, since generalizability is not even a goal of qualitative research, its absence is not a limitation in its data quality—provided that others using the research understand the goal of qualitative research and do not try to inappropriately use any conclusions.

■ Summary

There are no set standards for evaluating the validity of conclusions, and, to some degree, doing so is more challenging in qualitative research than it is for quantitative research because of the focus and importance of the respondents' subjectivity. In my opinion, the safest course of action is to try to address as many aspects of validity and reliability as possible and to be clear as to why some are inappropriate, given the observational method. Few researchers can address all individual components in their work, but being clear in why specific validity and reliability techniques are not used in and of themselves lends credence to the researcher, because it illustrates that the researcher is at least aware of their presence, even if they are not applied in a particular instance.

Evaluating Written Research: Qualitative Findings

Because the rules of the game are a bit different for qualitative research than for quantitative research, people who read this type of research cannot necessarily use the same criteria for evaluation as they would for quantitative research. For example, in quantitative research, I will discuss the importance of appropriate statistics and accurate statistical interpretation. However, in qualitative research, statistical tests rarely, if ever, are present.

This does not mean that qualitative research cannot be effectively evaluated. The quality of the evidence still has to be critically examined. It's just that readers need to use somewhat different criteria for doing so. Shown here are some suggestions to keep in mind when assessing the quality of the findings and conclusions of qualitative research. Some of these guidelines are for the evaluation of results in general, and therefore are repeated in the quantitative section, but others are specific just to qualitative research. Let's take a look at the individual points more closely.

1. *Is the results section a cohesive essay?*

The results section should not just be a presentation of quotations or statistics. Instead, the results section should flow like an essay. The researcher should make a point, and then use the data to illustrate or support that point. For example, researchers might state different themes that evolved from the data, and then, in essay format, they should elaborate on these themes by presenting evidence, analysis, and discussion for each. Even if researchers present a table of findings, such as a basic table of descriptive statistics in *either* qualitative or quantitative research (although such a table is more likely to be found in quantitative research), the main points of that table need to be discussed in essay format as well. The researcher cannot just present a table of information and be done with it. The researcher has to make sure that the reader understands what the researcher considers to be the key points of information in that table, and the researcher needs to do so by discussing those points in essay form.

2. *Does the researcher connect the results to any general research questions or goals?*

The results section is where the research *finally* is supposed to come together. This is where the research questions, posed in the introduction, are supposed to be answered. However, the researcher should not expect readers to connect the dots on their own. It is the researcher's responsibility to illustrate to the reader how the material presented in the results section addresses the questions posed in the introduction.

3. *Is the perspective of the results presentation appropriate? Does it match the research technique?*

This is more of a technical question. If the researcher did field research and decided to present the results as a discussion of his or her experiences in the field, that is appropriate. This is because, by the very nature of field research, the researcher *is* a component of the field and develops a relationship with the participants that may give the researcher particular insight into the research questions. On the other hand, if researchers do intensive interviews or focus groups, their interaction with the participants are minimal and likely to be just within their role as researcher. They are not likely to develop more personal relationships with the respondents, and so it is not really appropriate to discuss results from the researcher's perspective since the researcher's role is minimal. Therefore, the presentation of results from the participants' view is more appropriate.

On the other hand, field researchers *could* still present their results from the view of the participants instead of the researcher's personal view, if he or she so chooses. So, essentially, the point is that field researchers have a choice regarding how they want to present the results—from their view/experiences or from the view/experiences of the participants. However, other forms of qualitative research should probably be presented from the view of the participants as opposed to the researchers' view.

4. *Has the writer presented enough examples to support the conclusions? Do the examples make the readers "believe" the researcher's points?*

As I said before, I favor the "believable" criteria but appreciate when a few illustrative quotes are present. Due to space limitations, researchers may not be able to present many examples to illustrate their key findings, yet they need to make sure that they present enough to get their point across. More complex themes may require three to five illustrations; simpler themes may need only one or two examples. In my opinion, the real issue here is twofold: (1) Does the evidence make the reader believe that the researcher's point is accurate? and (2) Has the researcher avoided presenting *too many* illustrations of the point? If you are reading an article and find yourself getting bored or distracted by the sheer number of quotes the researcher presents to illustrate the point, then he or she probably has presented more than necessary.

5. *Do you have reason to believe that the presence of the researcher influenced the actions or statements of other group members? If this is possible, has the researcher addressed it in the research?*

Reactivity is always a concern in qualitative research. In field research, where participants are likely to know the researcher's identity, researchers may try to counteract this by staying in the field for extended periods of time so that the subjects get "used to" them and their research identity becomes secondary to who the researcher is as a person. In intensive interviews or focus groups, this desensitizing, so to speak, is less likely. Regardless, in any of these situations, if researchers compare what they observe with what their subjects say in their own words, and what the researcher learns happens when they are not present (e.g., through a key informant or through one-way glass in more formal interviewing sessions), then researchers may be able to assess the extent of any reactivity to some degree. Either way, researchers should discuss the steps they take to minimize reactivity and/or the steps they take to assess the degree of reactivity because reactivity is such a common characteristic of qualitative research.

6. *Especially in field research (although this may be an issue to a lesser degree in other forms of qualitative data gathering), does the researcher discuss how he or she interacted with subjects in the field, what problems arose, and how the researcher addressed them?*

The more honest and open researchers are about their account of their experiences in the field or dealing with subjects, the more confidence a reader can have in the quality of the researchers' observations. Regardless of the amount of preparation one undergoes prior to entering the field, the researcher is *not* the expert of that particular area, community, setting, or situation. In fact, that is what the researcher turns to the participants to explain. Therefore, it is natural for researchers to have concerns, come across situations they are not sure how to handle, have unforeseen problems arise, and have to make spur-of-the-moment judgment calls about how to act or react. These little "kinks" or quick decisions can influence how the researcher interprets a situation, and therefore how the researcher presents that interpretation to others.

To revisit Stack's (1974) field research of family life among low-income African Americans in "the Flats," Stack recounts some warnings she received from colleagues about how to approach her study and the course of action she ultimately followed.

Some of my colleagues strongly advised me to enter the black community through the older black establishment; they cited various reasons: contacts were available;

the research setting, they argued, was physically dangerous to a white person and I might need the sponsorship and protection that such contacts could provide; and tradition dictated such a procedure. I decided instead to find my own means of entrée.

Through my own efforts and good luck I came to know a young woman who had grown up on welfare in The Flats and had since come to my university. She agreed to introduce me to some families she had known as she was growing up there. She would introduce me to two unrelated families and from then on I would be on my own. (p. xi)

Accounts like this help others understand the complexities of the research and the decisions that researchers make. This information is useful in evaluating the quality and findings of qualitative research. Researchers who recognizes this, and present that recognition to others, illustrate that they are both skilled and aware of the subjective nature of the research. It also illustrates that the researcher is fairly confident in his or her conclusions because *he or she* has considered how these situations may have affected the data interpretation. Therefore, when researchers discuss problems that arose in the research, and how they addressed them, do not consider this a weakness. On the contrary, it is a sign that the researcher tried to be as objective as possible in his or her interpretations and wants the reader to know that.

To summarize, the key points to consider when evaluating the findings or results of qualitative research are:

1. Is the results section a cohesive essay?
2. Does the researcher connect the results to any general research questions or goals?
3. Is the perspective of the results presentation appropriate? Does it match the research technique?
4. Has the writer presented enough examples to support the conclusions? Do the examples make the readers "believe" the researcher's points?
5. Do you have reason to believe that the presence of the researcher influenced the actions or statements of other group members? If this is possible, has the researcher addressed it in the research?
6. Especially in field research (although this may be an issue to a lesser degree in other forms of qualitative data gathering), does the researcher discuss how he or she interacted with subjects in the field, what problems arose, and how the researcher addressed them?
7. Overall, do you think that the researchers adequately presented the results of the study?

Hunt, Joe-Laidler, and MacKenzie (2000) were interested in the role alcohol played among female gang members. They argued that much of the current research focused on male gang members and the drug activity among them. They felt that female gang members, especially their drug (in this case, alcohol) use, were essentially ignored in the research.

To conduct this research, the authors did qualitative interviews of 97 female gang members in San Francisco, California. These 97 women were part of a larger study on gangs conducted by the same researchers, and this larger study consisted of interviews with over 500 gang members (male and female) between 1997 and 1999.

The researchers used in-depth interviews that involved both a quantitative survey and a more qualitative semi-structured taped interview where respondents discussed their gang experiences. Those who conducted the interviews were generally of the same racial or ethnic background of the gang members, were familiar with the specific communities where gang members lived, and had experience in dealing with "hard to reach" populations.

All of these factors, in the researchers' view, helped the interviewers establish a rapport with the respondents, which helped the respondents feel comfortable with the interviewers and that facilitated the gathering of valid information. Here is an excerpt from Hunt, Joe-Laidler, and MacKenzie's findings from their interviews with female gang members:

Table 4 Beverage of Choice (*n* = 95)

Alcohol Used Most Often	No. of Responses	%
None	14	14.8
Beer	31	32.6
Wine	8	8.4
Hard liquor	42	44.2

Of those who did drink, hard liquor was the beverage chosen by most of the respondents. . . . Hennessey brandy was a favorite among the African American women, Presidente brandy was the brand chosen by Latinas. Almost a third of the respondents, the majority of them Latinas, were beer drinkers, and often the gang girls got together with each other and/or with their homeboys . . . on the streets or at the park to share some "40s," 40 ounce bottles of beer, usually malt liquor.

Although the girl gang members were not specifically asked about the effects of alcohol, most young women we interviewed were well aware of its effects, recognizing that both their own and others' behavior could change significantly. For example, Susan, who had come to normalize drinking and violence as part of Korean culture, found herself becoming not only a very heavy drinker in her early teens, but also acutely aware of the transformations that took place when drinking:

"Well, its like for me, personally when I drink, I get either very depressed or usually I get violent. And then just start talking shit, and it just kinda blows up from there. . . . It intensifies whatever mood I'm in. If I'm hella sad, I drink up. Then you know, I be like talkin about my sadness whatever. And if I'm hella hyped up and a jug I drink, I'll get hyper. If I'm angry, I get violent." (HG018)

In addition to realizing both the pleasures of drinking and the fact that alcohol could alter their behavior, the respondents reported using alcohol for a number of reasons including the following:

. . . *Improving self-esteem.* Some of the respondents noted the way that alcohol improved their sense of themselves. For example, by giving them more confidence as in the following quote:

"Well for me, I did it to fit in. . . . And, then, after a while, I guess it's just kind of a way to relaxed to forget about things. You know, just get a cool buzz on—act crazy. Cuz, you know, like when you drink, you get kinda . . . you get more confidence. You're not that fearful of stuff." (HG018)

Alcohol also helped to alter their feelings about themselves: "Alcohol boosts your mentality. Like right now I can be fat but if I go to the store and get a tall can, I would forget all about being fat. It just takes away how you are feeling for the moment." (HG027)

Finally, in addition to the positive effects of alcohol, some respondents noted the way in which alcohol operated as a two-edged sword. Although drinking initially led to positive developments, such as being more open, this could, in turn, potentially lead to conflict 'You argue more cuz you get more personal when you drink. And when you're not drinking, you could just hide it and put it aside. But when you drink you put everything out and say it and start arguing." (HG015)

Source: Geoffrey Hunt, Karen Joe-Laidler, and Kathleen MacKenzie, "'Chillin', Being Dogged and Getting Buzzed: Alcohol in the Lives of Female Gang Members," *Drugs: Education, Prevention & Policy, 7*(4) (November 2000): 339–340. Reprinted by permission of Taylor & Francis Ltd. www.tandf.co.uk/journals. DOI: 10.1080/ 09687630050178226. (***AN 4139735***)

Critical Thinking Questions

(*Note:* Some of the evaluation material relates to other methodological issues, such as research problems. Any relevant information was presented in my discussion of the article, so in applying the critical thinking discussions, consider both my commentary and the excerpt presented.)

1. Is the results section a cohesive essay?

2. Does the researcher connect the results to any general research questions or goals?

3. Is the perspective of the results presentation appropriate? Does it match the research technique?

4. Has the writer presented enough examples to support the conclusions? Do the examples make the readers "believe" the researcher's points?

5. Do you have reason to believe that the presence of the researcher influenced the actions or statements of other group members? If this is possible, has the researcher addressed it in the research?

6. Especially in field research (although this may be an issue to a lesser degree in other forms of qualitative data gathering), does the researcher discuss how he or she interacted with subjects in the field, what problems arose, and how the researcher addressed them?

7. Overall, do you think that the researchers adequately presented the results of the study?

Critical Thinking Discussion

1. Yes. Hunt, Joe-Laidler, and MacKenzie combine quantitative information with qualitative information. Table 4 is quantitative, but they discuss the findings in essay format after the table. In fact, they use their qualitative information to supplement the material in the table by discussing what type of hard alcohol is popular among gang members of different ethnicities. Their qualitative information is also presented in essay format.

2. In my commentary, I stated that the researchers' purpose was to explore the alcoholic drinking practices among female gang members. The material in the excerpt does that. There is a table about the types of preferred alcohol, a discussion of ethnic variations in this, and a discussion of the reasons why these young women consume alcohol. So yes, the researchers do connect the results to the research question.

3. The researchers use the perspective of the subjects. They do not describe their experiences

while interviewing these women; rather, their contribution is purely analytical. The words and experiences presented are strictly those of the subjects. Considering that the researchers did semi-structured interviews, this is appropriate.

4. In the example, Hunt, Joe-Laidler, and MacKenzie seem to follow the "three-rule." They present three pieces of evidence to support their claim that one reason these women used alcohol was to improve their self-esteem. At other places in the research (information not shown, but can be found on Research Navigator), they used fewer than three examples, but in those instances the examples they did present were more detailed and longer.

   I think that in both instances (what I included here and what is in the original article), their evidence passes the "believability" criteria, which I use as my main criterion. I consider instances where there are at least three quotes to be a "bonus."

5. Perhaps, since with interviews some reactivity is always possible, but not too much. In my commentary I discuss the steps Hunt, Joe-Laidler,

and MacKenzie took to get as valid data as possible. They used interviewers who were both the same ethnicity as the girls interviewed and from the same community. Therefore, the risk of the girls overstating their exploits is unlikely, since the girls knew that the researchers were familiar with the girls' community.

   Plus, the researchers state that the interviewers had experience dealing with difficult populations. I took this to mean that the interviewers were experienced in trying to get people who are not accustomed to opening up to outsiders to do just that. Therefore, again, I think that some reactivity may be possible, but I do not think that it is a serious threat to validity in this instance.

6. This is not mentioned, and, since the method of observation was not field research, it's probably less of an issue. The method of observation was semi-structured interviews. These are somewhat planned in advance and do not occur in spontaneous field situations; therefore, problems of the nature addressed in this question are less likely. Hence, the researcher cannot be faulted for not mentioning any.

Key Terms

Analytic comparison (491)
Axial coding (496)
Competent insider
  performance (504)
Ecological validity (503)

Illustrative method (489)
Member validation (503)
Natural history validity (503)
Negative case testing (503)
Network analysis (492)

Open coding (495)
Selective coding (496)
Successive approximation
  (495)

Review Question and Exercise

1. In Chapter 8, you evaluated the methodology of field research in the following articles. Now go back to these articles and evaluate their presentation of results.

a. Baccaro, Lucio. (2000, April). Negotiating the Italian pension reform with the unions: Lessons for corporatist theory. Industrial & Labor Relations Review, 55 (3), 413. 19 pp. (AN 6535589)

b. Barker, Bernard. (2001, February). Do leaders matter? Educational Review, 53 (1), 65. 12 pp. (AN 4230092)

c. Derbaix, Christian, Decrop, Alain, and Cabossart, Olivier. (2002). Colors and scarves: The symbolic consumption of material posses-sions by soccer fans. Advances in Consumer Research, 29 (1), 511. 8 pp. (AN 7705818)

d. Baker, Kristan, and Donelly, Michelle. (2001, January). The social experiences of children with disability and the influence of environment: A framework for intervention. Disability & Society, 15 (1), 71. 15 pp. DOI: 10.1080/09687590020020877. (AN 4052844)

e. Wight, Daniel, and Buston, Katie. (2003, December). Meeting needs but not changing goals: Evaluation of in-service teacher training for sex education. Oxford Review of Education, 29 (4), 521. 23 pp. (AN 11714960)

Quantitative Research Analysis

P erhaps one of the most widely studied early education intervention programs is Head Start. The federal government initiated Head Start in the 1960s to help children from low-income families, and their parents, via early educational intervention for the children and social support services for the parents (that cooperate with the children's early education). The specific characteristics of individual Head Start programs vary by community, because the programs are supposed to be tailored to meet individual community needs; however, even so, there are some broad federal standards to address needs in child development, family development, community development, and staff development, which the government requires of all Head Start facilities.

One branch of the Head Start program is Early Head Start, which has the same philosophy and general goals as the broader program but is tailored to helping younger low-income children—sometimes starting when a mother is pregnant and not ending until that child is 3 years old. Recognizing that low-income children may be at a higher risk for developmental disabilities, the Education for All Handicapped Children Act was passed in 1986. As part of tailoring needs to individuals within the community, Early Head Start programs work with other social services agencies to include components that address children with disabilities. This component is "Part C programs."

To analyze the effectiveness of Early Head Start programs, the Early Head Start Research and Evaluation project drew a random sample of 3,100 families who the researchers randomly assigned either to experience the Early Head Start treatment or to be in a control group. Children with disabilities were included in this random selection; therefore, they were just as likely to be in either the experimental or control group. Although this study had many research goals, the one I will focus on here is the effectiveness of Part C programs in developing basic life skills among low-income children with disabilities, relative to their developmentally challenged peers who do not receive the Early Head Start program. Peterson and colleagues (2004) used Table 12.1 to describe the identification of children who were in need of Part C services, meaning that these children had either diagnosed or suspected developmental disabilities.

The table is one example of quantitative data analysis. It is called a **univariate** or *descriptive table* (or statistics) because it describes the sample a single (or "uni") variable at a time. Remember, I said that Peterson and colleagues studied 3,100 people. However, unlike in qualitative research, where the perspective of one person or a few people can be very important to a researcher, in quantitative analysis, the goal of the research is really to summarize what many people experience. Consequently, both the researchers and us, as readers, do not want to know what 3,100 people said individually. We want some type of number that *summarizes* what many people said. This is why quantitative analysis frequently involves tables such as Table 12.1. It provides counts, such as 99 or 1,421 of people who respond a particular way. To get back to the specifics of this table, Peterson and colleagues (2004) explain:

> The incidence of disability indicators among the low income children participating in this study was alarmingly high, despite the very small number of families (99) who actually received Part C services. Altogether, more than 87% of the children [calculation not shown] who participated in the Project were identified as having at least one disability indicator. . . . Clearly, many children were identified as having multiple disability indicators, but having an indicator was not necessarily associated strongly with receipt of Part C services. (pp. 81–82)

This excerpt illustrates a basic practice of research—one that we also saw in a somewhat different form in qualitative analysis. Any time researchers make conclusions, they need to present some material that they think supports those conclusions and helps the reader understand the basis for the conclusions. In qualitative research, the researcher presents a conclusion and then supports it with selective quotations from field or interview

TABLE 12.2 Excerpt from Peterson and Colleagues (2004) Results: Children Receiving Part C Services, by Disability Indicator Category

Disability Indicator Category	Total Sample		EHS Program Group		Comparison Group		X^2
	n	(%)	n	(%)	n	(%)	
All children	2093	4.7	62	5.7	37	3.7	4.97*
Children who had diagnosed conditions	250	39.6	62	43.4	37	34.6	1.97
Children who had suspected delays	995	8.3	54	10.8	29	5.9	7.94**
Children who had biological risks	1163	6.8	49	7.9	30	5.5	2.64

*$p < .05$.

**$p < .01$.

Source: From "Early Head Start: Identifying and Serving Children with Disabilities" by C. A. Peterson, S. Wall, H. A. Raikes, E. E. Kisker, M. E. Swanson, J. Jerald, J. B. Atwater, and W. Qiao, 2004, *Topics in Early Childhood Special Education, 24,* pp. 76–88. Copyright 2004 by PRO-ED, Inc. Reprinted with permission.

notes. In quantitative research, the researcher commonly presents the information as a table or graph.

Technically, findings like the ones I just presented can be done in qualitative research, and frequently are. After all, descriptive statistics are essentially just a count, transformed into a percentage, of what the researcher saw. However, most quantitative studies involve analysis beyond individual variables in isolation, in order to see how two or more variables relate to each other. Let me illustrate this with another excerpt from Peterson and colleagues' (2004) research. If you remember, one of Peterson and colleagues' goals was to see whether Early Head Start programs were effective in helping to identify those children who were likely to have learning disabilities. They present their findings regarding this in Table 12.2.

Explaining the table, Peterson and associates state:

First, children enrolled in EHS [Early Head Start] were significantly more likely to receive Part C services than were children in the control group (Administration, 2002b). Approximately 5.7% of families enrolled in EHS reported receiving Part C services and having Individualized Family Service Plans (IFSPs), which contrasts with 3.7% for the control group. Higher rates of identification are attributed to program screening and support of parents through referral, eligibility, and IFSP development, as well as to coordination with Part C service providers (Administration, 2002b). Table 6 presents comparisons among rates of Part C service receipt for all children participating in the Project and for the children within each disability indicator category. (pp. 84–85)

Contrary to the first example, this is a **bivariate table or statistics** in that it examines the effects of two ("bi") variables simultaneously. To put it another way, it presents the effect that one variable has on another variable. Here, the one variable is group membership, with the values being "the Early Head Start (EHS) group" or "the comparison group." Remember, variables, by definition, have to have more than one value—and what you see presented in Table 12.2 are the two values I just stated. The second variable is the disability indicator category, and its values are "all children," "children who had diagnosed conditions," and so on. The purpose of the text that follows the table (which is quoted here) is to help the reader know how the table should be read and to indicate what the researcher feels are the most important findings.

For example, Peterson and colleagues note that families in the EHS program are more likely to receive Part C services than are families in the comparison group. How do I know this? They state the comparison: 5.7 percent of families in the EHS program have Part C services, whereas only 3.1 percent of those in the comparison group did, which suggests that the Early Head Start program was more successful in identifying children with potential learning disabilities than were the more traditional, non–Early Head Start avenues.

Also notice at the bottom of Table 12.2 that there are some notations, such as "* $p <$ .05." Statistical significance is a characteristic of quantitative data analysis that distinguishes it from qualitative data analysis. The notation at the bottom of Table 12.2 is a shorthand used by the researchers to let the reader know when differences are believed to be statistically significant and not due to random chance. Think about it. Just by looking at the numbers 5.7 percent and 3.1 percent, how do you know if that difference of 2.6 percent is meaningful? After all, 2.6 percent seems like a small difference.

By "eyeballing" the percents, so to speak, we may be tempted to think that there really is *no* difference between the EHS program's abilities to spot learning disabilities and other traditional avenues of identification. In other words, we might be tempted to conclude that the difference of 2.6 percent just occurred by chance. After all, it is unlikely that two groups are going to have *exactly* the same percentage of people with disabilities, and this little difference we notice may not mean much. However, statistical tests that the researchers conducted suggest that our initial interpretation is incorrect. In fact, the statistical tests suggest that the researchers are 95 percent confident that the difference is *not* due to chance and that the numbers really do illustrate a "real" difference between the two groups. That is what the note at the bottom of Table 12.2 tells the reader.

The "*p*" stands for the **probability of error,** which loosely translates into the probability that the two variables really are unrelated. The ".05" is the **alpha level,** or the actual error probability, and means "5 percent." Taken together, the "$p < .05$" means that there is a less than 5 percent likelihood that this difference between the two groups occurred by chance. Interpreted another way, you can be 95 percent sure that these differences are *not* due to chance (since 95 percent confidence and 5 percent error = 100 percent of your ability to predict in this instance), and that instead, there is a *real* difference between these two groups' ability to spot learning difficulties.

I don't want to go into too much detail about tests for statistically significant differences or comparisons between univariate and bivariate results now. I presented this somewhat lengthy introductory example to illustrate some of the ways in which quantitative analysis is different from qualitative analysis. In this chapter, I will discuss some common, but selective, statistics in quantitative research. I will also discuss the various ways in which these findings are presented. However, before I do all of that, we need to start at the beginning—or at the beginning of data analysis, that is. This means that we first need to discuss how to code, enter, and clean quantitative data.

Dealing with Data

One characteristic that qualitative and quantitative analysis both have in common is the need to code the data in order to facilitate the researcher's ability to find patterns among the participants' responses. Quantitative researchers usually code the data by assigning numerical values to responses and entering those values into a computer so that the computer can perform statistical tests on the data. In this section, I'll discuss some basic issues in data coding and data entry into a computer. I will also present a brief discussion on how to construct a scale or index, which is one way a researcher can manipulate the data to reach a higher level of measurement.

■ Data Coding

As I stated, most quantitative analyses are done with a computer. Computer programs, including those for PCs, can do complex statistical tests on thousands of cases involving many variables in a matter of seconds. However, computers only recognize numbers. They can't read the word *male* and compare it to the word *female* but they can compare all cases identified as a *1* to all cases identified as a *2*. Here lies a fundamental problem in that people, like you and me, are much more comfortable in reading words such as *male* and *female* than *1* and *2*. Furthermore, since quantitative instruments, such as surveys, frequently have many questions, we may very feasibly have to remember what *1* and *2* mean in 50, 100, or even more different questions, depending on how many questions appear on a survey. This would very quickly boggle our minds. **Coding** in quantitative research bridges this gap between our personal preference for words and the computer's preference for numbers by assigning numerical responses to the words, or, methodologically speaking, *values* to a question. For example, take a look at the following survey excerpt:

12. Approximately how many hours of television do you watch a week? _____
13. What is your favorite type of television program?
    a. Situation comedy
    b. Drama
    c. Sports
    d. News programs
    e. Reality TV
    f. Other _____

    For the following questions please circle the number that best approximates your feeling. The numbers are: 1 = strongly agree, 2 = agree, 3 = neutral, 4 = disagree, 5 = strongly disagree.

14. I feel safe walking home alone in the dark.   1   2   3   4   5
15. The world is an unsafe place.   1   2   3   4   5
16. I believe that television gives an accurate
    portrayal of real-world violence.   1   2   3   4   5

For a computer to recognize answers to specific questions, I would need to write an abbreviated name for that question, what is called a *variable name*, and give each noninterval/ratio level of measurement a numerical value that would be the code. I would keep this all together in a codebook that might look something like what is presented in Table 12.3. Notice that the sample codebook has columns marked for the question number, the variable name, the question wording, the column location, and the codes that correspond to the possible answer choices (values of the variables).

A couple of points about this codebook are important. First, notice that I have a specific column where I identify the variable name. For the most part, this name, without a codebook, may not be immediately evident as to what that name refers. This is common. Many computer programs allow only 8 to 10 characters for a variable name; therefore, variable names sometimes seem more like a jumble of letters than anything meaningful. That's just the reality of computer limitations.

Take, for example, the variable name "safedrk." What does this mean? Does it mean whether someone feels safe in the dark? Does it mean whether someone feels safe in the dark in a specific instance, such as after watching a scary movie? The meaning of "safedrk" is unclear even if someone can piece together that that combination of letters has *something* to do with feeling safe and the dark. Without more information, we do not know exactly *what* that variable means, even if we have a general idea. However, the other column entitled "Item/Question Wording" *does* let you know what that variable name indicates. That column lets me program the computer so that I, and others, know that the variable "safedrk" means whether someone feels safe walking alone in the dark. It lets me know the specific context of safety and darkness. This is another reason why codebooks are an important part of coding. Not only do they remind the researcher which numerical codes correspond to which answer choices but they also remind the researcher which questions correspond to each variable name.

Second, you might also notice that the first two variable names in the codebook, "case" and "coderid," do not have specific question numbers or question wording that corresponds to them. This is because these two pieces of information are not questions. The first variable, "case," assigns a number to each survey so that I can match a string of data to the original survey if I later notice a coding problem, such as a mistake, when I "clean" the data. I haven't discussed cleaning data yet, and I will do so shortly, but the point I am making is that sometimes data involve keeping track of information that is not directly in the survey or other instrument of observation. Sometimes data also include more bookkeeping identifiers such as case number, the ID of a coder if more than one person is entering data, or the study/wave data if the data are longitudinal (an example of this would be a variable called "year" that notes the year the particular survey information was collected). A codebook may have all, some, or none of these identifiers, depending on the nature of observation, although having at least a case number somewhere in the data file is usually advisable.

The third point I want to make about this codebook is the column that is entitled "Column Number." In some programs, such as a PC format of the Statistical Package for the Social Sciences (SPSS), which is commonly used in social sciences research, this column may be unnecessary and therefore be omitted. However, if you are dealing with data on a mainframe computer system, the raw data may be expressed simply as a string of numbers. In this case, knowing how many columns correspond to each question will help the

TABLE 12.3 Excerpt of Sample Codebook

Question No.	Variable Name	Item/Question Wording	Column No.	Code
	case	Case number	1–3	Assigned
	coderid	Coder identification	4	Assigned
. . . 12	hrstv	Approximately how many hours of television do you watch a week?	16–17	As entered 99 = missing
13	favtv	What is your favorite type of television program?	18	1 = situation comedy 2 = drama 3 = sports 4 = news program 5 = reality TV 6 = other 9 = missing
14	safedrk	I feel safe walking home alone in the dark.	19	1 = strongly agree 2 = agree 3 = neutral 4 = disagree 5 = strongly disagree 9 = missing
15	worldsaf	The world is an unsafe place.	20	1 = strongly agree 2 = agree 3 = neutral 4 = disagree 5 = strongly disagree 9 = missing
16	tvacc	I believe that television gives an accurate portrayal of real-world violence.	21	1 = strongly agree 2 = agree 3 = neutral 4 = disagree 5 = strongly disagree 9 = missing

researcher identify specific pieces of data when necessary. For example, a computer data string or a code sheet may read:

1	2	3	4
0	0	5	1

16	17	18	19	20	21
0	9	4	2	2	4

As illustrated in Table 12.3, the code sheet is partial. It has the identifying information that addresses the case number and coder ID (that is, columns 1–4) and then I only present information from questions 12–16 (columns 16–21). The information for questions 1–11 are not shown in Table 12.3 and therefore the corresponding columns of information (columns 5–15) are missing. But what does this string of data mean? Without the codebook, nothing. However, *with* the codebook, I know that this particular string of information is for case number 5 and that this information was entered by coder number 1.

How do I know this? The first three columns, based on what the codebook from Table 12.3 tells me, contain the subject's case number. The numbers in columns 1–3 are 005, which means that these data refer to respondent number 5. If the numbers in the first three columns were 102, that would mean that the data refer to case number 102. If I only had 50 people in my sample, I would have only two columns referring to case number, because 50 has two digits and each column essentially refers to a digit. The fourth column, based on the codebook, lets me know that coder number 1 entered these data, because the number in that column is 1. Therefore, if there is a problem with the data entry in this string of data, I know I may want to contact coder number 1, because this person is the one who entered the data.

Columns 16 and 17 tell me that respondent number 5 watches about 9 hours of television in a given week, and column 18 tells me that this person generally watches news programs, which are presented in column 18 and which, according to the codebook, correspond to a value of 4.

Why might I want to be able to read this data string? Because, as I mentioned, when I check the data for data entry errors—a process called *data cleaning*—there may be errors in how a number was entered. For example, a coder may enter an "8" in column 18 and I know (based on the codebook) that the number in that column should range only from 1 to 6, with a possible 9 for someone who skipped that question. Therefore, the 8 is a mistake. The other information in the data string will help me identify (1) who coded the data so I can pay particular attention to other errors and (2) what case or survey was miscoded so I can go back to the original and see what the answer *should* be.

The fourth and fifth points I want to make address the coding of specific values for a variable. Notice in Table 12.3 that all of the variables have a code for missing information. In single-column questions, this code is 9, and in double-column questions, this code is 99. Sometimes people just do not answer questions. Sometimes questions are in a contingency format, which, based on an answer to a previous question, a person is directed to skip. And sometimes people just don't feel like answering a question, don't understand a question, or simply overlook it. Regardless, the end result is the same: There is no information for a specific question. In order to distinguish between questions in which respondents did not provide an answer from questions in which a coder, the person entering the information into a computer, *forgot* to submit a code, coding missing information is useful. Hence, the code, which can be anything a researcher wants so long as it is not confused with legitimate responses to a question, for missing information should be included in the codebook and entered as such.

The last point is this: You might notice for question 12, the variable "hrstv," which asks the respondent how many hours of television that person watches per week, there is no code other than the missing code. This is because hours of television viewing is an interval/ratio level of measurement and, in these cases, the numbers themselves have intrinsic meaning.

For example, if someone answers "13," I know that that person watches about 13 hours of television a week, which is 2 more hours than someone who answers "11" and 7 hours less than someone who answers "20." This number 13 has "real" meaning, and therefore doesn't need a code because both the computer and I understand it. On the other hand, if I ask the computer what the favorite type of television is for respondent number 120 and the computer answers "2," that has no meaning to me. I need the codebook to translate that the "2" the computer understands corresponds to the word *drama*, which I understand. Therefore, variables measured at the interval/ratio levels of measurement do not need codes to be entered into the computer. Both the computer and I can understand the resulting number.

Remember, though, not all computer programs will require all of the material presented in this sample codebook, nor will all codebooks looks alike. There is no "cookie cutter" codebook because what your codebook looks like depends on whether you are working on a PC or a mainframe, what type of computer program you are using for statistical analysis, and what your particular instrument of observation (survey, interview, etc.) looks like. This example served only as a guideline as to what a codebook *might* look like, what type of information is useful, and how you may be able to use that information.

■ Handling Qualitative and "Other" Information

I discussed how to code qualitative data in the previous chapter, so why am I mentioning it here? Mainly because studies that are generally quantitative in nature, and therefore largely consist of closed-ended questions, which are easily coded, may also include some qualitative measures in order to minimize some of the limitations in purely quantitative data that I discussed previously. However, although inclusion of these data is likely to improve the overall quality of the data obtained, it means that the researcher has to follow the same steps outlined in Chapter 11 regarding how to find patterns among the written responses. Because I discussed how to do this in Chapter 11, I will not repeat myself here. I will, however, discuss what to do with information that participants may specify in the "Other" category.

Coding "Other" information is a bridge between the purely quantitative nature of closed-ended questions and the purely qualitative nature of open-ended questions. "Other" categories in which respondents write in responses other than those the researcher already included in a closed-ended question are not as difficult to code as are purely open-ended questions, primarily because the responses that people usually write are short. The process for coding these categories, however, is somewhat similar to coding qualitative responses.

Probably the easiest way to code "Other" categories is for the researcher to read through the data and note the different responses people make. Every time a unique response (one that no one else has noted) occurs, the researcher writes it down. Every time a respondent writes a question that has already been expressed by a previous respondent, the researcher makes a "check" or other notation to keep count of how often that particular response is specified. New responses that have a sufficient number of "checks" can then become their own unique answer choice, which will be coded in addition to the previously specified choices in the closed-ended question. Categories that do not have a sufficient amount of checks on their own may be able to be grouped with other categories to create a new category as well. The remaining categories, those that have only a few isolated responses, would then be grouped into a true "Other" category. The general rule of thumb is that codes require revision when 10 percent or more of the responses are classified as "Other" or do not fit any of the existing categories. Take the following hypothetical example:

1. What type of music do you generally prefer?

   a. Rock
   b. Folk
   c. Classical
   d. Jazz
   e. Blues
   f. Other (please specify _____)

Let's pretend that I distributed this survey to 200 people and 35 of them circled the "Other" category and of those 35, 25 actually specified some other type of music. Based on the rule of thumb, I want to have no more than 10 percent of my 200 people classified as an "Other" category. This means that I need to make sure that a maximum of 20 of those 35 people (10 percent of 200 is 20 and I have 35 people who responded "Other") can be in an "Other" category. The 10 people who did not specify any specific musical preference (and this is likely to happen—not everyone will take the time to write a specific answer) are already in any revised "Other" category. They did not provide information, so I have no information to try to recode. That means I have 25 responses (35 "Other" selections, minus the 10 who did not specify further) I need to code, and no more than 10 of them (20 total minus the 10 that I have no choice but to leave as "Other") can be in some miscellaneous "other category." Let's say that I read through all of the remaining 25 surveys where "Other" was selected and some qualitative information was written. These are the categories I came up with based on what people wrote:

Rap	12 people
Reggae	2 people
Techno pop	3 people
Easy music	4 people
"Muzak"	3 people
Punk	1 person

Based on these categories, it's pretty clear that "rap" can be an additional category. That leaves me with 13 other people I need to code (25 − 12 = 13), which is more than the 10 maximum I can have. If I look at the categories, I may be able to say that "easy music" and "muzak" are similar. To me, they both are styles of music that are supposed to be for easier listening or quiet. Therefore, I decide to combine those categories. I can call this new category anything I want, so long as it's descriptive enough and accurate enough to convey to people generally what type of music to which I am referring. So I decide to take the easy way out and call the new category "easy music/musak." That leaves me with six other people (those who like reggae, techno pop, and punk) who are not part of revised codes. Six is under my 10 limit and when I combine those 6 with the 10 who never provided additional information, my total observations in a revised "Other" category would be 16. This is under 20, so I can safely consider myself to be done coding the "Other" information for this question.

Now my answer choices, with corresponding numerical codes in bold, would look something like this:

46. What type of music do you generally prefer?

a. Rock	**1**
b. Folk	**2**
c. Classical	**3**
d. Jazz	**4**
e. Blues	**5**
f. Rap	**6**
g. Easy music/Muzak	**7**
h. Other	**8**

I went from a question that had five distinct answer categories (not counting "Other") to one that has seven. That means I teased out two more categories of "useful" information. Why did I use the word *useful* just now? Because, from a statistical point of view, "Other" is not a very meaningful category. When a participant's information is coded as "Other," it means only that that participant's views are not captured by the previously existing options, but it does not give the computer, or anyone else who does not have the individual surveys, any idea as to what those views are. Even in my revised question, for the eight people who have "Other" listed, both the computer and anyone else using the data are not going to have any idea that the music specified by those people were reggae, techno pop, or punk. That information will essentially be "lost."

You may be asking yourself why I wouldn't just code each unique response even if only a few people actually selected that particular category. In other words, why use the 10 percent cut-off? The answer is simple. Statistically, I need sufficient variation in each cell in order for the calculations the computer will do (which is called *statistics*) to be accurate. The more sophisticated the calculations/statistics, the more observations I need in each answer category. Having only a few answers in a category may result in misleading statistics, since there will not be enough meaningful variation in the sample for the calculations to work as effectively as they should.

Another question you might be asking is, What is "sufficient"? I can't give a direct answer to that. As I said, more sophisticated statistical calculations require more observations in the different categories being compared. To some degree, this decision is based on the research question for a particular study and the nature of the statistics the researcher intends to use. Using the rule of thumb is one step in trying to make sure that there are enough meaningful observations in the different response options.

Data Entry

This is a fairly straightforward, somewhat monotonous task that simply involves typing the codes and information from each survey into the computer. In most computer programs, a row corresponds to a case, or respondent. In computer terms, each row of information is a *data record*. This simply means that it is the record of data for a specific individual. The individual variables read down columns so that the variables columns and case rows create a grid, much like the SPSS excerpt you see in Figure 12.1.

There are four common ways in which coders can enter data from individual surveys to create the grid you see in Figure 12.1. The first method is **code sheet entering.** In this instance, the data-entry person reads a code sheet, much like I presented in the previous section about what you may see if coding a mainframe computer. The data-entry person would have a hard copy of a code sheet, like the one shown earlier, and would then just type the corresponding numbers that appear. This method has a little more room for error than some of the other methods because the respondents' answers are handled twice by people other than the respondent. The answers from the surveys are first coded onto a code sheet (first handling of data) and then the numbers on the code sheet are entered into the computer (second handling of data). The more times the data are handled by people, the more opportunity for someone to make a mistake.

If, in the data-cleaning process, a mistake is made from code sheet entering, the researcher first has to look at the code sheet to see if the error appears there. If the code on the code sheet is a viable code for that particular variable, but the code on the computer is not, then it means that the person typing the code into the computer made a mistake. The researcher simply changes the computer entry. If, however, the code on the code sheet

	sub	race	sex	age	welfcur	welfpast
1	crack	white	male	37.00	no	no
2	heroin	white	male	22.00		
3	heroin	white	male	22.00	no	no
4	crack	white	female	20.00	no	no
5	alcohol	white	male	25.00	no	no
6	alcohol	white	male	20.00	no	no
7	heroin	white	female	33.00	no	yes
8	prescription	white	female	42.00	no	no
9	heroin	white	male	22.00	yes	yes
10	heroin	white	male	41.00	no	yes
11	heroin	white	female	29.00	no	no
12	heroin	white	male	33.00	no	no
13	alcohol	white	male	46.00	no	no
14	heroin	white	female	22.00	no	no
15	heroin	white	male	19.00	no	no
16	heroin	white	male	42.00	no	no
17	heroin	white	male	20.00	no	no
18	prescription	white	male	38.00	no	no
19	heroin	white	male	23.00	no	yes

Figure 12.1 SPSS Data Box

is wrong or invalid, then the researcher has a second step of finding the original survey that was coded onto that code sheet and recording the correct response instead. This involves potentially two steps to correct errors.

The second way to enter data is called **direct-entry method** and is what happens when a coder sits at a computer with the individual surveys and directly enters the information on the survey to the computer. To do this, a computer is already programmed to recognize the variable names and which codes correspond to which answers. The coder simply types in the number that corresponds to a particular answer or selects the written response from a drag-down menu (which the computer has already been programmed to relate to a number) that is already in the computer. Hence, coders look from the survey, to the computer and back, entering the codes as they go. Contrary to the code sheet entry method, with the direct-entry method, the data are handled only one time. It is read directly from the survey and entered into the computer (one and only one handling of data). Hence, there is only one avenue for faulty data—a misentered code into the computer.

A third option is an **optical scan sheet.** In this method, the survey itself is on an optical scan sheet. You probably know what these look like. The answer choices (values of a variable) are represented with little bubbles that the respondent colors in to indicate his or her answer. With this process, special scanners read the information on the sheet directly into a computer and no human coding is involved. Since this involves no human coding, it is probably the most accurate of all from a data-entry viewpoint.

The last method of data entry I mentioned in passing in Chapter 7 on surveys. It is the **computer-assisted telephone interviewing (CATI)** method. As the name suggests, this method can be used only with telephone interviews. The person conducting the interview automatically enters a person's response into the computer while the interview is actually taking place. Since the time between response and coding is almost immediate, there are generally few errors with this approach as well. However, as I said, it is limited to telephone interviews.

Even though the last two methods, the optical scan sheet and the CATI method, may produce the least error in data entry, they are only good for data that already have clear codes for the initial response. They are not useful at addressing open-ended questions, which may be part of a more quantitative survey, nor are they helpful at coding information that respondents specify when they answer "Other" to a question. The first two methods of data entry, code sheet entry and direct-entry method, on the other hand, can account for some qualitative response. This is because people serve as a coding intermediary and can therefore examine the data and find possible patterns in qualitative responses that will lead to additional quantitative codes.

■ Data Cleaning

After the data are entered into the computer, researchers need to check the entered data for errors. This process is called *data cleaning,* and no matter how careful someone is when entering data, some errors are always going to be present. In order to obtain accurate analysis, these errors need to be identified and corrected.

One of the most common ways of identifying errors is to run a **frequency distribution** to make sure that no invalid codes have been entered. For example, the variable gender is likely to have two possible codes: *1* for *male* and *2* for *female* (or something like that). If a researcher runs a frequency distribution and notices that the code of 5 appears, then there's an error, because 5 is not a valid code the researcher designated for gender. The researcher would then find the case, usually by the identification number assigned to each person, in which the invalid code appeared, match that case number to the information from which the data were obtained (e.g., the survey for that person), find the relevant question on that information sheet, and then enter the appropriate corresponding answer. For example, let's assume that I mistakenly input a 5 for someone's gender. Looking at the data screen, I'd find the variable that corresponds to a respondent's ID. Let's say that the invalid code of 5 for gender occurred in respondent 346's data. I then find the original survey for person 346 (I probably wrote the ID number on top of the survey for each respondent), look at the question about gender, and see that this person circled "female," and therefore the appropriate code for gender would be 2. I then change the 5 to a 2.

Another problem with data coding is when people answer questions that are not relevant to them; for example, they answer a contingency question that they were directed to ignore. Identifying these errors is a bit more time consuming because they involve some type of contingency comparison, such as cross-tabulations in which there should not be any information recorded for categories of people directed not to address a question. For instance, if a question asks people whether they are registered to vote and someone answers no, then there should not be information in a later question about who this person voted for in the last election. If a person is not registered to vote, then he or she *can't* vote and the information in the second question is not valid. Perhaps the person misunderstood the question and read it as who he or she *would* vote for, but regardless, this person cannot and did not vote, so information presented in the second question would be ignored. Therefore, the researcher would have to delete the corresponding code for a candidate entered and should instead enter the code corresponding to "not applicable" or "missing."

Some computer programs already help with the data-cleaning process. For example, they might beep when an invalid code is entered. However, not all programs do this; therefore, knowing the basic errors to identify and how to correct them is a useful skill in data analysis.

Data Manipulation

After the data are coded, entered, and cleaned, researchers can do analysis with it as it appears or they can further manipulate the data as needed. There are two forms of data manipulation I will discuss here. They are the issues of collapsing categories and how to use scales or indexes to create more robust measures that may also be a higher level of measurement than the existing individual measures.

Collapsing Categories

Sometimes the number of observations for a particular value of a variable will be too small to be able to contribute to meaningful statistical analysis. For example, let's assume I surveyed 100 people, asking them about their view of an increase in local taxes to help local low-income programs, and got the following data as illustrated by the frequency distribution:

> What percent increase in your taxes would you be willing to pay in order to provide better social services for local low-income individuals?

	f
a. No percent increase	53
b. 1–2% increase	32
c. 3–5% increase	12
d. 6% or more increase	3

The last two answer options, "3–5%" and "6% or more increase" have very low response rates, especially the last answer category. I will not be able to get any statistically meaningful trends from three people. One answer to this dilemma is to try to collapse, or combine, answer categories. I might decide to combine the last two categories into "3% or more increase." If I do so, my frequency distribution would now look like:

What percent increase in your taxes would you be willing to pay in order to provide better social services for local low-income individuals?

	f
a. No percent increase	53
b. 1–2% increase	32
c. 3% or more increase	15

Granted, I lose some precision between the different answer choices, but at least now I might be able to do some statistical analyses. If the third, new, answer category *still* does not have enough answer choices, I may have to alter the answer choices even more to "support a tax increase" and "not support a tax increase." This loses even more precision, however, and should be done only if (1) I *absolutely* want to include this variable, in some form, in my analyses, and (2) I find I cannot conduct accurate statistical tests with the first attempt at collapsing categories.

To the best of my knowledge, all statistical computer programs have a means to collapse answer choices or categories, even though the steps they use to do so may vary. There are a couple of points to keep in mind, however, whenever you find yourself having to resort to this tactic. First, whenever you combine categories, make sure you specify that you did so in any written reports using the variables whose answer categories you combined. This may be done in the body of the text or in a footnote—so long as it is mentioned *somewhere*. Second, as a general rule of thumb, whenever altering a variable in a data file, instead of recoding the original variable, create a new variable that you can label and identify as a recode of the original to make any changes. Once a computer accepts changes in variables, it is almost impossible to revert to the original data that were entered. Doing any data alterations as a new variable preserves the original variable in its unaltered form (for example, you may want to recode the same original variable a different way for different analyses). It also gives the researcher access to the information for that variable in a new form.

■ Index and Scales

In Chapter 4 I discussed that one type of validity is content validity, which is determining whether a measure addresses the various dimensions of a concept. It can be difficult for one measure or one survey question to accomplish this. However, that does not mean that a researcher cannot *create a new measure* from existing ones that is comprehensive and that addresses many dimensions of a concept. Researchers frequently use indexes and scales both to create more integrated measures of a concept and to boost the level of measurement of individual variables from nominal to at least ordinal. Scales also have the benefit of not relying on just one indicator to get a feel for respondents' views on a topic. Any one indicator may be erroneous or a poor measure, and therefore basing a study completely or predominantly on that indicator may lead to erroneous conclusions. However, using more than one indicator to measure a concept and doing so in an integrated manner, such as a scale, decreases the importance of any one specific indicator to the overall conclusions the researcher makes.

In fact, scales and indexes are frequently used in the social sciences, and the terms *scale* and *index* are also often used interchangeably, although technically some differences between the two exist. The main distinction is that indexes frequently address multiple dimensions of an concept, whereas scales usually only focus on one attribute (Hagan, 1997). However, since most people use the two terms interchangeably, I will do so as well. For clarity, I will simply use the term *scale* in the rest of this section.

I will briefly discuss how to create two types of scales: attitude scales and prediction scales. There are many other types of scales, and some researchers have devoted entire books to scale construction. However, social scientists frequently want to describe people's attitudes or predict their future behavior, hence, for the sake of brevity, I decided to focus on these two broad types of scale. Before I discuss how to create scales, I want to stress the importance of using already available scales if possible. First, doing so helps with replication, which is a key factor in the quality of any measure. If a researcher uses a scale previously used by others for a similar topic and gets similar results in terms of that topic, then that's one additional piece of evidence that supports that scale's replicability. Second, previously constructed scales may also have been tested for various forms of validity, and by using them, the researcher can assume a certain degree of validity as well.

If a preexisting scale that suits your needs is not available, then here are some basic guidelines to create your own attitude or predication scales. However, like the previously used scales, if you are creating a new scale, then you need to conduct tests to assess that scale's validity at the very least, and if you can, you should also test its reliability (e.g., through a spilt half method, for example). I will discuss this more a bit later.

■ Attitude Scales

Just as there are different types of scales, so, too, are there different types of attitude scales. I will discuss two. The first type of scale is a Likert scale, which is very similar in nature to the opinion questions I discussed in Chapter 7. In fact, the opinion questions that have two favorable responses, a neutral middle category, and two negative responses are typically called Likert questions, and they are the basis for the first type of scale. The second type of scale I will address is the Guttman scale, which provides a different type of information than does the Likert scale.

Likert scale

Sometimes people refer to questions expressed as "strongly agree," "agree," "neutral," "disagree," and "strongly disagree" as Likert scales, although this is incorrect. An individual question cannot be a scale, although true Likert scales *are* based on these Likert-type questions. The attractiveness of the Likert scale is that it allows researchers to assess the relative intensity of different items. You have probably seen Likert scales before—especially if you have filled out course evaluations at some point in school. For example, Sheehan and DuPrey (1999, **AN 2283958**) did a study on course evaluations and the following is an excerpt from 5 of 27 Likert-type questions used for a Likert scale common in these evaluations:

1. The assigned reading material (text, papers, etc.)
   was appropriate for the course.   SD   D   N   A   SA
2. If used, the films used by the instructor were
   incorporated into the course.   SD   D   N   A   SA
3. When used, in-class exercises and labs helped me
   understand the material.   SD   D   N   A   SA
4. Grading procedures were fair.   SD   D   N   A   SA
5. Assessment procedures (papers, tests, presentations,
   etc.) allowed me to demonstrate what I had learned.   SD   D   N   A   SA

Notice a couple of points about this example. Likert questions are frequently presented in a matrix format. If you recall, this format is beneficial for two reasons: (1) it is space efficient and (2) it allows the researcher to assess, at a glance, whether there are any response set patterns if the researcher had the forethought to include reverse-coded questions (where a "strongly disagree" response, for example, was actually a positive response).

To calculate a Likert scale, a researcher would first create a series of related Likert questions to include in the measure instrument, such as a survey. Typically, it is a 5- to 9-point scale, with 5 points (such as in the preceding example) being the most common. However, not all individual questions may be useful in a scale, so researchers typically include more questions than they anticipate using. The second step is to trim down the number of items to keep in the scale by determining which items would be the most informative (and therefore useful) in assessing relative degrees of difference among respondents. To do this, researchers analyze individual items *after* the survey is conducted in order to determine which are the most discriminating. *Discriminating* items are those that add something to the final scale measurement by distinguishing between high and low scores. Items that fail to do this—in other words, items that have little variation in the high to low scores—are not useful to the overall analysis and can therefore be eliminated.

To be discriminating in Likert scales, there are two criteria. First, there has to be sufficient variation between the highest scores (those at the top 25 percent of respondents) and the lowest (those at the bottom 25 percent). Second, there cannot be a preponderance of "don't know" responses. So how do I determine this? The first step to do this is to assign numerical values, or codes, to the specific answer choices. It is customary that responses that show a favorable view, either in general or in relation to the researcher's hypothesis or purpose, have high scores and those that do not have low scores. Let me illustrate this by substituting the codes for the five items borrowed from Sheehan and DuPrey's (1999) research with an added hypothetical sixth item to illustrate reverse-coded questions. I also bolded answers that a hypothetical respondent selected.

1. The assigned reading material (text, papers, etc.)
   was appropriate for the course.   1   2   3   **4**   5
2. If used, the films used by the instructor were
   incorporated into the course.   1   2   3   4   **5**

3. When used, in-class exercises and labs helped me understand the material.	1	2	3	4	5
4. Grading procedures were fair.	1	2	3	4	5
5. Assessment procedures (papers, tests, presentations, etc.) allowed me to demonstrate what I had learned.	1	2	3	4	5
6. The instructor did not illustrate a strong understanding of the subject matter.	5	4	3	2	1

What you see here took the worded responses "strongly agree," "agree," and so on, and substituted the numerical codes that corresponded to those responses. The first five questions all are positively worded, in that responding "strongly agree" or "agree" shows a favorable view of the class, and therefore these responses get high codes in this instance. However, the last question is negatively worded, or reverse coded, so that saying "strongly agree" or "agree" actually depicts a negative view, and hence gets a low value when someone selects it. In many instances, this coding process should be taken care of in the earlier stages of data coding and cleaning. I just reiterate it here to illustrate the purpose.

Once the codes are established and people have completed the survey, a researcher can instruct the computer to find the average response for the upper and lower quartiles. To do this, a computer (or, in the instance of small datasets, researchers can do this on their own, although a computer is faster) will order the data into a frequency distribution, which means it will list all of the responses of "1" for an item together, and then all of the responses for "2," and so on. The computer will then divide the total sample size into quarters, or quartiles, and then average the responses of the lowest quarter (quartile) and the highest quarter. Although a computer will do this task, I find that students understand the process better if I actually illustrate it by hand. So here goes. In Sheehan and DuPrey's (1999) research there were 3,632 observations, or different course evaluations included in the analysis. Suppose a hypothetical frequency distribution for Item 1 is such:

Item 1:	Assigned reading material was appropriate.	
	Strongly agree	698
	Agree	1873
	Neutral	301
	Disagree	503
	Strongly disagree	257

If you add the observations, we see that there are 3,632 total observations. Now, by dividing that number in quarters (by 4), there are 908 observations in each quarter or quartile. There are 698 observations in the highest answer category and we need to account for 908 for the first quartile. That means that the first quartile of responses addresses all 698 answer choices in the "strongly agree" category and 210 (908 − 698 = 210) categories in the "agree" category. To find the average score of the first quartile, we take 698 × 5 (since the value for the "strongly agree" category is "5") and add it to 210 × 4 to get a total of 4330. To get the average score for the first quartile, we next take this resulting number and divide it by the number of people in the first quartile, which is 908. Therefore, the average score of the highest quartile is 4330 ÷ 908, or 4.77.

We follow the same procedure for the lowest quartile of scores. We have 257 people in the lowest category ("strongly disagree") and 503 in the next lowest category ("disagree"). Taken together, they equal 760 observations. We need 908, so we need to further dip into the "neutral" category for the remaining 148 people. To calculate the average score of the low quartile we take:

$$[(257 \times 1) + (503 \times 2) + (148 \times 3)] / 908 = 1707 / 908 = 1.88$$

Now, let's suppose I, or a computer, calculated the average score of the top and low quartiles for all six of these items. The resulting comparison (and the numbers are all hypothetical, since Sheehan and DuPrey did not present this information and since I made up the sixth category) is shown in Table 12.4.

Looking at Table 12.4, Item 2 appears to be nondiscriminating, as there is not a lot of variation between the average top and low quartiles (3.77 and 3.26, respectively). Therefore, I would eliminate that item from my final scale. You may also be wondering about Item 5, since the top and low quartiles are 4.67 and 3.29, respectively. This is trickier. There are no hard and fast rules as to what difference is discriminating and what is not. To some degree in the "gray" areas, like Item 5, it is up to the researcher. I advise the following two considerations when making decisions based on "gray" items. First, if the item is theoretically important, I'd leave it in. On the other hand, if its theoretical relevance is weak or mediocre or if there are other, clearly more discriminating items that address a similar issue, I'd omit it in favor of the more discriminating item. Second, I may have some predetermined loose idea of how many final items I want in my scale. For example, there are 27 different items in Sheehan and DuPrey's research. I may decide that I want to limit the scale to the 15 items that have the greatest discriminatory characteristics. If that is the case, then I take the 15 items for which the difference in top and low quartiles are the greatest—once again, making sure that I am not omitting any theoretically important items that should be included if they are at least somewhat discriminatory.

Once I decide on the items to include in my scale, I calculate the total score by summing all of an individual's scores for each of the included items, making sure that I appropriately reverse the codes of negative items. The respondents' answers to the items I did *not* select for my scale are not relevant here, so I ignore them. For example, suppose my scale for professor ratings ended up with 13 items in it and the hypothetical person I noted earlier

TABLE 12.4 Hypothetical Item Analysis

Item	Average Score of Top Quartile	Average Score of Low Quartile
1	4.77	1.88
2	3.77	3.26
3	4.10	2.01
4	3.92	1.23
5	4.67	3.29
6	3.90	1.10

had the following scores for the 13 items I selected for the scale: 4, 3, 4, 4, 2, 5, 5, 2, 3, 4, 1, 2, 5. This person's score would be 44. The highest possible score would be 65 (13 items $\times$ 5 points as the high score) and the lowest score would be 13 (13 times $\times$ 1 point for the lowest score). Therefore, this person has a score of 44 on a scale of 13 to 65.

The strength of the Likert scale is that it uses the respondents' own answers to decide whether an item is discriminating, and appropriate for the scale, or not. Therefore, questions that may have been unclear to respondents or showed little variation in response, even though the researcher thought that they would (which is the presumption since the question was included in the survey in the first place), can be identified and omitted. However, a disadvantage is that the researcher, or anyone reading the results of the study, will not be able to identify the exact answers to any of the scale items simply based on the scale score. For example, for someone who has a score of 39, it is impossible to determine, with any likelihood, what that person said for Item 4 without actually looking at that person's survey—which defeats the purpose of data analysis. Similarly, we won't be able to predict what that person said for Item 13. We would have no idea what that person said for *any* of the individual items included in the scale. The second attitude scale I'm going to discuss, the Guttman scale, on the other hand, addresses this limitation.

Guttman scale

Louis Guttman (1944) developed a scale during World War II in which items that are progressively more difficult to answer or more likely to elicit a negative response are included in the scale. By doing this, it is possible to determine, with a certain degree of likelihood, what a person answered to individual items based on that person's total score. Remember, as with all data analysis, people do not want to look at the individual answers of everybody included in a study. The purpose of statistics (and here, scales) is to create one measure that summarizes people's views. However, sometimes we want to know what a *group* of people said. We can do this statistically by comparing groups. We can, similarly, do this with Guttman scales by saying that people who have a score of "2" responded _____ (where we fill in the material relevant to a particular scale). We don't need to look at each individual survey to see what people with a score of "2" said. We can conclude that, based on the nature of how this scale is constructed.

The premise behind a Guttman scale is that anyone who gives a strong indicator of a concept, or who answers the question that is the least likely to get a yes response, will also give positive (yes) responses to weaker indicators. For example, Ross (2000) used the 1995 Community Crime and Health Survey in Illinois to assess the relationship between neighborhood disadvantage and depression for 2,482 respondents. In this study, she includes measures of individual socioeconomic disadvantage, and one of these measures addresses a person's criminal activity. Ross created a Guttman scale to measure criminality, which she describes here:

> Criminal activity in the last year was measured by summing "yes" responses to four questions: "In the past twelve months, have you done anything that would have gotten you in trouble if the police had been around?"; "In the past 12 months, have you been caught in a minor violation of the law?"; "In the past 12 months, have you been arrested?"; and "In the past 12 months, have you been in jail for more than 24 hours?" These activities form a Guttman scale of increasing trouble with the law. On a scale scored from 0 to 4, the mean is .156.

In Ross's scale, the question least likely to get a yes response is whether someone has been arrested, so this is the "strongest" indicator in her scale. She presumes that if someone said yes to this indicator, that person will also have said yes to the previous three indicators. Based on this assumption, we can create a Guttman scale, test it's scalability, or trustworthiness, and use the scale to predict the exact responses of individuals. I will use hypothetical data from Ross's scale to illustrate how to construct such a scale. Incidentally, with both the Likert scale example and this scale example, you may notice that I continually illustrate the scaling process with hypothetical data. That's because the scales I'm using are from published research, and researchers do not present individual data in their publications. Therefore, I have to "make it up" to illustrate the point. So if you were looking at the original articles and wondering where these data come from, look no further. It comes from my own imagination and is simply presented to show how one *could* use data to obtain these conclusions.

Frequently, but not always, Guttman scales are based on items with simple yes/no responses. They can involve items that have Likert-type questions, but those are more complicated to construct and beyond the general intent of this book. Therefore, I will focus only on illustrating this scale type with yes/no responses. Guttman scales also are *unidimensional*, which means that they focus on one dimension of a concept at a time. In Ross's example, her dimension was criminal behavior. The first step in a Guttman scale is to select items that, based on face validity, are unidimensional and appear to measure a concept. Ross selected four items: Did the person do anything wrong to get into trouble? Did the person get caught doing something minor? Did the person get arrested for this action? and Was the person sent to jail for this action?

The next step is to construct a type of grid that lists the items from left to right, from the weakest indicator (most likely to get an affirmative response) to the strongest indicator (least likely to get an affirmative response). Each row of the grid would correspond to a listing of the possible response patterns. I have constructed a grid that uses Ross's identification in Table 12.5.

The left-most column identifies a possible pattern of responses by a number. For example, one pattern of responses (here called #1) is that a respondent says yes to all four questions. A yes response is indicated by a + sign and a no response is indicated by a − sign. How do you know the number of possible patterns in which people could respond? If you have two answer choices, your pattern number is two raised to the number of questions. Ross had two answer choices (yes/no) and four questions; therefore, there are 2^4 patterns, or 16 patterns.

The next four columns correspond to the four questions of criminal behavior Ross included in her scale. The item that asks whether someone did anything that would have gotten him or her in trouble if the police had noticed the behavior appears on the left of the other items because it is the item of the four that is likely to get the most yes responses. Therefore, it is the *weakest* indicator of criminal behavior, since the highest percent of people is likely to respond to it. The item about going to jail is the right-most item on the grid because it is the one the *least* amount of people will experience, and therefore respond yes, so it is the *strongest* indicator of criminality. So essentially, Ross expects the most people to say yes to doing something wrong but not getting in trouble (if they did anything at all), fewer people to say that they were caught for doing something minor, even fewer for saying that they were arrested, and fewest of all saying that they were sent to jail.

TABLE 12.5 Hypothetical Grid Based on Ross's Identifications

Pattern #	Item: Did Anything to Get in Trouble	Item: Caught for Doing Something Minor	Item: Arrested	Item: Sent to Jail	Number of Cases (hypoth.)
1	+	+	+	+	65
2	+	+	+	−	187
3	+	+	−	+	2
4	+	+	−	−	435
5	+	−	+	+	10
6	+	−	+	−	3
7	+	−	−	+	8
8	+	−	−	−	752
9	−	+	+	+	16
10	−	+	+	−	2
11	−	+	−	+	18
12	−	+	−	−	6
13	−	−	+	+	0
14	−	−	+	−	11
15	−	−	−	+	2
16	−	−	−	−	965

How can Ross determine this order? A couple of ways: First, she can base the order on theoretical degrees of strength based on material she finds in a literature review. Or second, she can run a frequency distribution on the variables of interest and empirically see which item gets the fewest yes responses, the most yes responses, and all shades in between.

The last column of numbers, and here they're hypothetical because this type of information is not typically included in research reports, is the number of cases or respondents who answered according to each possible pattern. Therefore, 65 people answered yes to all four items, 187 answered yes to the first three but "no" to the last item, and so on.

The body of the grid is the relationship between different answers as indicated by "+" for "yes" and "−" for "no" that I stated earlier. To fill in the pluses and minuses, one could use logic and try to come up with all the unique patterns by just going through mental reiterations of combinations, but this approach is cumbersome and prone to error. It is much easier simply to follow a standardized approach where in the far left item column (here, the item "Did you do anything to get into trouble?") the first half of the cells are "+" and the second half are "−." For example, there are 16 rows, corresponding to 16 patterns of responses. The first 8 receive pluses and the second 8 receive minuses. Moving left to right, in each additional column, the ratio is divided in half. So the ratio of the first column is 8:8. In the second item column, the ratio is 4:4, or alternating four pluses and four minuses until you get to the bottom of the grid. In the third column, the ratio is 2:2, and in the last item column, the ratio is 1:1, or alternating pluses and minuses all the way down. Now your grid is complete.

However, before we use this scale to its fullest extent, we need to assess whether we have any confidence in it. In other words, we need to assess whether it accurately measures that concept that we think it is measuring. To do this, we first need to assess which response patterns are errors, based on the logic of the relationships between items that are assumed in a Guttman scale. In other words, to assume that a Guttman scale is accurate, we need to illustrate that, for the preponderance of subjects, their responses mirror the assumptions of weak and strong indicators that we presumed in establishing the order of the items. I can actually give you a concrete statistic we can calculate to assess the strength of this scale. This statistic is called the *coefficient of reproducibility*, and is calculated as such:

Coefficient of reproducibility = 1 − (number or error responses/number of responses)

But wait—how do I know what an "error response" is? Easy. It's the number of people (or responses) who responded in ways (patterns) that did not follow the assumed relationship between items. Looking at pattern 1, does it make sense, given our order of most likely to say yes to least likely to say yes, that someone can say yes to all four items? Of course, so that pattern is not an "error." Likewise, pattern 2 makes sense as well. It is perfectly feasible, given our assumptions of severity, that someone could have done something that would have gotten him or her in trouble, could have been caught for doing something minor, and could have been arrested, but did *not* go to jail. Hence, we see the three pluses in the first three columns and the one minus in the last column. So pattern 2 is not an error. However, it does *not* follow, or make sense given our assumptions, that someone would have done something that would have gotten him or her in trouble, would have been caught for doing something minor, would *not* have been arrested, but *did* go to jail. If you are not arrested, you cannot go to jail, therefore, pattern 3 *is* an error response. Following the same logic, the following patterns are "error" patterns because the pattern of responses that they illustrate do *not* follow the assumptions of severity, and therefore do not "make sense" as we've constructed the scale:

Error patterns: 3, 5, 6, 7, 9, 10, 11, 12, 13, 14, 15
Nonerror patterns: 1, 2, 4, 8, 16

Be careful. All I've done so far is to identify the patterns that are errors. I haven't identified the number of error responses quite yet. To do so, I need to look in the last column of information to see how many total people answered patterns 3, 5, 7, and so on. By adding the numbers in the last column for these people, I see that I have 78 people who responded in a way that violates the assumptions I made in my scaling procedure. Therefore, to calculate the coefficient of reproducibility, I fill in the following numbers:

Coefficient of reproducibility = 1 − (78 / 2482) = .97

According to Guttman, a 90 percent coefficient of reproducibility (or a proportion of 0.9 or better) establishes the minimum threshold of accuracy. Anything higher than 90 percent or higher than a probability of .90 suggests that the scale is accurate. If my hypothetical data were really Ross's data, then she would have a coefficient of reproducibility of 97 percent, and could therefore assume that her scale was accurate. She does not produce such a measure in her article, which is a notable omission.

I'd like to point out that at least for 78 of my hypothetical respondents, the scale did not behave the way I anticipated. Seventy-eight respondents did not follow the assumptions about severity of trouble with the law that I presumed. Having some people respond contrary to the assumed order is not unusual. Some people may misunderstand a question or may have different interpretations of seriousness than a researcher does. That is why the coefficient of reproducibility is important. It tells a researcher whether too many people did not share his or her ordering of items, and if this is the case, then a scale is not accurate and should not be used. However, so long as the coefficient of reproducibility is greater than 90 percent or .90, some disagreement between the researcher and the respondents is not problematic.

This illustrates a second important point. When I discuss scaling with my students, they frequently want to take a shortcut and identify the patterns with low responses (as indicated by the last column) as the errors without going through the logical analysis of each individual pattern. This is problematic because it makes the assumption that those patterns with a higher number of responses are valid. Essentially, this makes the test for the coefficient of reproducibility useless and assumes a scale is accurate when it may not be. Don't be tempted to take shortcuts here. It takes little time to read through the patterns if you keep the underlying assumptions in mind.

So, after all of this calculation, how do we actually use this scale? As Ross did, every yes response gets a value of 1 and every no response gets a value of 0. Therefore, Ross's scale of trouble with the law can range from 0 (no yes responses at all) to 4 (all yes responses). If we can assume reproducibility, then we are at least 90 percent sure that a person who had a score of 2, for example, did something that would have gotten him or her in trouble if it was observed and was caught for doing something minor, but this person was *not* arrested and did *not* go to jail. How do I know this? If I have a coefficient of reproducibility of .9 or better, then there are only five valid responses (shown in Table 12.6).

TABLE 12.6 Valid Response Patterns for Ross's Hypothetical Grid

Pattern #	Item: Did Anything to Get in Trouble	Item: Caught for Doing Something Minor	Item: Arrested	Item: Sent to Jail	Score
1	+	+	+	+	4
2	+	+	+	−	3
4	+	+	−	−	2
8	+	−	−	−	1
16	−	−	−	−	0

As you can see in Table 12.6, if someone has a score of 2 and the scale is accurate, then the only valid pattern with a score of 2 is the fourth one—a respondent who said yes to the first two items and no to the second two. Likewise, we are at least 90 percent sure (based on the coefficient of reproducibility) that a person with a score of 1 said yes to the first item but no to the other three. The Guttman scale is an improvement over the Likert scale in that with a Guttman scale, a person's score gives you insight into which items they were likely to answer in the affirmative. I use the word *likely* because remember, not necessarily everyone with a score of 2 responded this way, but we are 90 percent sure that the majority did even without looking at the grid ourselves. A summary of the steps for creating Likert Scales, as well as Guttman Scales, appears in Figure 12.2.

Likert Scales

1. Select possible items for scale inclusion based on face validity.
2. Create a series of related Likert questions to include in a survey. Create more questions than you anticipate being in the final scale.
3. Identify which items are discriminating.
   a. By computer
      (1) Ask the computer to calculate the mean score for high and low quartiles of the distribution.
      (2) Omit mean high and low scores that are too close.
   b. By hand
      (1) Run a frequency distribution of all the scores for an item.
      (2) Take the sample size and divide it into quarters (by four). This resulting number tells you how many observations are in each quarter.
      (3) Look at the distribution of scores. Find the number of highest scores that correspond to a quarter of your population. Calculate the mean of these scores.
      (4) Look at the distribution of scores. Find the number of lowest scores that correspond to a quarter of your population. Calculate the mean of these scores.
      (5) Compare the mean of the highest and lowest scores.
      (6) Omit mean high and low scores that are too close.
4. Calculate an individual's score by adding the scores for all of the items included in the scale. This scale will be a new variable added to the data set and an individual's score will be the data entered for that variable.

Guttman Scales

1. Select possible items for scale inclusion based on face validity.
2. Use a frequency distribution and/or theoretical justification to establish a continuum of the degrees of relations from most likely to say "yes" (weak indicator of concept) to least likely to say "yes" (strong indicator of concept).

Figure 12.2 Steps in the Construction of Likert and Guttman Scales

3. Create a grid with the selected scale items across the top, the number of patterns in rows, the number of respondents fitting each pattern as the last column, and a series of pluses and minuses illustrating yes/no response combinations within the grid.

   a. If answer choices are yes/no, the number of possible response patterns is 2 raised to the number of items in the scale (e.g., if there are four scale items, the number of possible response patterns are 2^4 or 16).

   b. Fill in pluses/minuses starting at the first item and dividing the number of response patterns in half to create a 50-50 ratio. Each subsequent column ratio is also divided in half until the last item column is a series of individual alternating pluses and minuses (e.g., in a 16-pattern grid, the ratios across the four items are 8:8, 4:4, 2:2, 1:1).

4. Identify the response patterns that are "errors" based on the assumption of the progression of item severity.

5. Calculate the coefficient of reproducibility to determine accuracy of scale. Coefficient of reproducibility of 90 percent (or .9) or higher assumes accuracy.

6. Calculate a scale score by assigning a "1" to each "yes" response and a "0" to each "no" response (in the case of yes/no responses) and summing the scores.

7. Create a new variable in the dataset that corresponds to the newly created scale variable and whose data are an individual's scale score.

8. If the scale is accurate, use the scale score to predict the exact nature of responses someone is likely to say.

Figure 12.2   Continued

Basic Data Analysis

When researchers have all of their measures and codes in line, then they are *finally* ready to begin analysis of the data! As you can see, it takes quite a while to proceed from a general research idea to actually being able to analyze the data when researchers use well-designed and well-thought methods. Doing research is not something than can be done well in an afternoon or two. But now, at last, we are ready for the payoff—we can finally see whether our research purposes are met and our hypotheses are supported.

I will discuss some basic issues of data analysis. This is not a statistics textbook, and, believe me, there are many textbooks devoted solely to the discussion of statistics, so this discussion is in no way complete. My intent is to give you an understanding of basic statistical concepts and how to use some statistical techniques common in the social sciences.

Before I start discussing specific statistical techniques, I want to make a few points. First, the purpose of statistics is to use one, or a few, numbers to tell us what participants think about various topics. Without statistics, the only way for me to make any conclusions about people I study is for me to describe literally what each and every respondent said about each and every question. Now imagine, even with a relatively small sample of, say, 200 people, how tedious (and meaningless) that would be. In other words, without statistics, I'd have to say something like: Respondent 1 is male, age 24, a Democrat, and believes that workplaces need more family-friendly policies, and so on, until I reach the end of the study instrument. Then I'd have to say: Respondent 2 is female, age 23, a Democrat, and believes that workplaces need more family-friendly policies, and so on. Respondent 3 is a male, age 24, and so on, for *each* individual. Not only are you likely to tune me out after, say, 4 or 5 people (and remember, I'd have to do this for 200 people) but by reporting findings this way, I'd have almost no way of seeing whether there are any patterns in responses. By the time I reach respondent number 200—heck, even by the time I reach respondent number 10—I'm likely to have already forgotten what earlier respondents said, not to mention that I won't be able to start making connections in similarities and differences in what these folks said. Statistics make this tedious and unproductive process unnecessary. Statistics summarize what *everyone* says in relatively few numbers. So, by reducing the responses of 200, 5,000, or even 10,000 people to a couple of summary numbers, I am much more able to see patterns within and across responses from which I can then derive some kind of meaning.

Second, there are three general categories of statistics, each of which serves a different purpose. These categories are descriptive, analytical, and predictive. Within the analytical category, statistics can either analyze the statistical significance of data, which means determining whether any relationship we notice between two variables is real or is just observed by chance, or the substantive significance, which means determining how strongly two variables are related if there is a statistical significance. To put this another way, descriptive statistics tell us what our sample said and looks like. Descriptive statistics tell us the demographic characteristics of our sample (e.g., what percent are male or female, what the average age of a respondent is, how much variation in age there is) and what our sample, as a whole, said with regard to each question (e.g., the percent of our sample who are Democrats or Republicans, the percent who agree that companies should have more generous family leave policies, and the percent who do not agree with this issue).

Tests for statistical significance help test research hypotheses by telling the researcher if any patterns noticed in the data really do indicate a relationship between two (or more) variables or if this pattern is likely to have occurred by chance. Tests for substantive significance tell the researcher how strongly variables are related. The effect one variable has on another may be statistically significant, meaning that the observed relationship is not likely to be due to chance. But the degree of association between the two (or more) variables can be very weak, which means that even though the two variables may be related, they really don't have a strong effect on each other, so in reality are unrelated anyway (they lack substantive significance). The third type of statistic is predictive. Just as the name implies, researchers doing predictive statistics use information from their sample to try to predict what *others* in the population are likely to do.

In this section, I'll briefly explain some statistics that relate to descriptive analysis, inferential analysis (hypothesis testing or tests for statistical significance), and measures of association (substantive significance). I will not address predictive statistics, as these are generally more complex than the other types and are therefore better suited to be explained in a statistics textbook.

◼ Descriptive or Univariate Statistics

Distributions

The term **distribution** refers to all of the responses to a particular question. For example, if I studied 50 lawyers and I wanted to tell the reader their ages, I could simply list all 50 ages. This list of 50 ages is the distribution of ages among my respondents. However, reading a list of 50 ages isn't very informative, and if I list 50 responses for all of the variables I'm studying, it becomes quite cumbersome very quickly. Therefore, people generally *summarize* the distribution of responses. They commonly do so in one of two ways. First, they can just list all of the ages and tell the reader how many people are of each age. Researchers refer to the number of people in each answer category, such as age, as the *frequency* because it is how *frequently* each answer is represented. This frequency is usually a raw number, but it can be expressed as a percent as well. Such a distribution could look like this:

Lawyer Ages	Frequency	Percent
31	2	4
32	5	10
34	8	16
36	4	8
40	1	2
41	5	10
46	7	14
51	4	8
53	5	10
55	2	4
56	7	14

Notice that there is no age 33 or 35. That's because if no one in the sample is a particular age, then it does not appear on the distribution. However, listing all of these ages can be cumbersome as well, especially when you have some categories with very few people in them, such as we do for age 40. A second way of presenting the distribution is to give a frequency count and/or percent, but instead of using individual scores, a researcher may group them, such as this:

Lawyer Ages	Frequency	Percent
30–39	19	38
40–49	13	26
50–59	18	36

Which way is better? It depends on your research needs and the best way of presenting the information so others can understand and evaluate your research. Both formats are technically correct. However, in both formats, it may still be difficult for the reader to get a sense of what the typical response is and how the scores vary in relation to each other because there simply are so many numbers to examine and consider. Two univariate statistics help summarize frequencies even further into a single number (or when used together, into a maximum of two numbers). These statistics are measures of central tendency and dispersion.

Measures of central tendency

As I said earlier, statistics that tell the reader the typical, or *central*, response are called **measures of central tendency.** There are three measures of central tendency: the mode, the median, and the mean. Which one is appropriate depends on two considerations: the level of measurement and the distribution of the data.

The **mode** is simply the most frequent response in the distribution. In my example of lawyer age, the mode is age 34 because it is the age with the most responses; eight people are this age. This is the simplest measure of central tendency and can be used with all levels of measurement (nominal, ordinal, interval, or ratio); however, it is the *only* statistic appropriate for nominal measures. What if there were two different ages with eight people in them—say, age 34 and 46? Well, then we have two modes. In other words, it is perfectly fine to have more than one mode.

The **median** is the middle value. It is the value in the distribution that divides the distribution exactly in half. Half of the scores will be higher than the median, half will be lower. The median can be used with all levels of measurement except nominal (i.e., the median can be used with ordinal, interval, and ratio measures). If your sample is small enough, you can sometimes identify the median just by eyeballing it. For example, the following distribution shows the number of times in the past ten years that people have made political contributions:

3   3   5   3   6   1   4   5   2

If we reorder the list from low to high, we have:

1   2   3   3   **3**   4   5   5   6

We can just look at it and see that the bolded 3 is the middle value. Half the scores (1, 2, 3, 3) lie below it and half the scores (4, 5, 5, 6) lie above it.

But what about when you can't eyeball the middle or the middle doesn't fall neatly in the distribution like it did in the example? There is a simple formula that helps you identify the middle position and from there you can find the median. This formula is

$$\text{Median position} = (n + 1) \div 2$$

where *n* is the total sample size. To use our example of lawyers' ages, the median position would be $(50 + 1) / 2$, or 25.5. Wait! I don't have a whole number here! No problem. That happens when there is an even number of people in the sample. All the decimal means is that the median position is going to lie between the 25th and 26th person (when the ages are listed in order). If I keep counting the frequency of responses I have in the lawyer age example, I see that the 25th person is 41 years old (the frequencies, starting with age 31 are: $2 + 5 + 8 + 4 + 1 + 5 = 25$). The 26th person is 46, which is the next age. When the median lies between two positions (the 25th and 26th position in the distribution), we take the average of the two values and that is our median value. The average of 41 and 46 is 43.5. Therefore, the median age is 43.5. Notice, on the original table of ages, no one reports being age 43.5. That's fine. The median does not have to be an actual number in the distribution, since the number that divides the distribution in half may not have been the response of anyone in the sample.

The last measure of central tendency is the **mean,** or what many people call the *average*. This is the most widely used statistic, but it is only accurate for interval/ratio level data. Many of you already probably know how to calculate averages, so the mean is no different. You add up all the individual scores, and then divide that answer by the total number of scores (observations). To begin getting you acquainted with some statistical formulas, here's the formula for the mean:

$$\bar{X} = \Sigma X / N$$

where $\bar{X}$ is the symbol for the mean, and we read it as "X bar," the Greek symbol Σ means "the sum of" so that tells people that they will be adding something, the X stands for the individual values of the variable of interest, and the N stands for the sample size. In our lawyer example, the mean age of the lawyers in this sample is 43.52. How did I get that number? If you look back at the frequency table, two people were 31 so I begin by adding 31 + 31, five people were 32, so to the previous number I add 32 five times, and so forth. So the first part of the equation will be (31 + 31 + 32 + 32 + 32 + 32 + 32 + etc.). There are 50 people, so I take the sum of my scores (which is 2,176) and divide it by 50 to get the mean of 43.52. The mean, or average, age of the lawyers in my sample is 43.52 years.

Since all three measures of central tendency—the mode, the median, and the mean—can be calculated for interval/ratio levels of measurement, researchers sometimes have to decide which of the three measures is the most appropriate. Even though the mean is the more sophisticated measure and can be used only for interval/ratio levels of measurement, it is not always the *best* statistic to use. This is because the mean can be strongly affected by extreme high or low values. For example, suppose that in our lawyer age distribution, instead of having seven people who are age 56, we had three people age 56 and four people being 76. Our mean age would then be 45.12, which is different from 43.52, even though we changed the ages of only four people. When there are extreme values that could distort the value of the mean, researchers say that the distribution is *skewed*. When a distribution is skewed, the mode, median, and mean will be very different from each other, and therefore the mean is not a good statistic in these instances.

Hence, the second criteria in deciding what measure of central tendency to use is based on whether the distribution is skewed or not. When the mean is less than the median and the mode, the data are negatively skewed, as shown in Figure 12.3, because the bulk of scores are *more* than the mean. When the mean is greater than the median and the mode, the data are positively skewed. When the three measures are almost equal, the data are normally distributed, or not skewed.

When a distribution is skewed, the median is the best statistic to use because it is less influenced by extreme values (as opposed to the mean) and it is more informative than the mode (since the median can still tell you what score 50 percent of the sample is above and below). In our example of lawyers' ages, the mode is 34, the median is 43.5, and the mean is 43.52. The low mode suggests a slight positive skew; therefore, to be safe, the median would be the most appropriate statistic to use.

Measures of dispersion or variation

Measures of central tendency are useful because they tell the researcher and others the typical or central response to a question. However, they do not provide any information regarding the variation between scores. Two questions can have the same median and/or mean but still be distributed very differently. For example, we may have five people waiting in line at a candy store and their ages are 10, 25, 35, 40, 50. The median and mean age are both 35. Now I may have another group of people who are standing in line at a bar and their ages are 25, 30, 35, 40, 45. The median and mean age of these folks at the bar is also 35, but their ages are much more closely clustered together. When you line up the ages in chronological order, there is only a 5-year difference between any age and the one before or after it; but when you line up the first set of numbers in chronological order, there can be as much as a 15-year difference between ages (e.g., between the person who is 10 and the person who is 25). Hence, the ages in the candy store are more variable—they are more

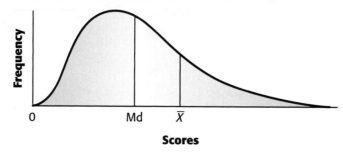

A. A POSITIVELY SKEWED DISTRIBUTION
(The mean is greater in value than the median.)

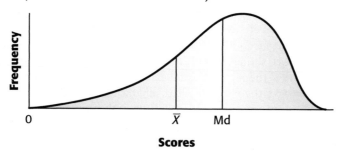

B. A NEGATIVELY SKEWED DISTRIBUTION
(The mean is less than the median.)

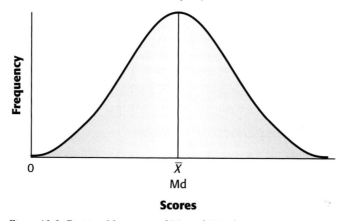

C. AN UNSKEWED, SYMMETRICAL DISTRIBUTION
(The mean and median are equal.)

Figure 12.3 Positive, Negative, and Normal Distributions

spread out than are the ages in the bar. But the mean and median alone would not inform anyone of this. A **measure of dispersion,** on the other hand, would.

As with measures of central tendency, not all measures of dispersion are suitable for all levels of measurement. Three measures that I will discuss are ranges, percentiles, and standard deviations. Ranges and percentiles can be used with ordinal-, interval-, or ratio-level data. The standard deviation, however, should be used only for interval or ratio levels of measurement. Although there are statistical calculations for measures of dispersion for nominal levels of data, they are infrequently used because they are generally not very intuitively interpreted; therefore, you are not likely to see them in published research. So I will not discuss them here.

A *range* is probably the easiest measure of dispersion to calculate because it simply compares the true value of the largest and smallest scores. What do I mean by the *true value*? The true value simply increases the highest score by 0.5 and decreases the lowest score by 0.5 to make sure that all possible scores in the range of scores are accounted. For example, the age range for my line of people in the bar is 45.5 − 24.5, or 21. Notice how I added 0.5 points to the high age (45) and subtracted 0.5 points from the lowest age (25). Why do you think I did this? Well, if I just subtracted 25 from 45, my range would be 20. But that's one shorter than the possible range because if I listed all of the possible ages between 25 and 45 in a row and counted them, I'd see that there are 21 possible ages between 25 and 45. Alternately I could also simply state that my subjects in line at the bar had a mean age of 35 with the ages ranging from 25 to 45. That range of 25 to 45 adds some information for the reader, but it still is not the most informative measure of dispersion.

Percentiles are another option. Percentiles are a little different than the calculation of distribution percents that we discussed earlier in that percentiles usually refer to the score in which a certain percent of the sample (or distribution) falls below. You already learned the 50th percentile—that's simply the median, since it is the score that divides a distribution of answers exactly in half. Other common percentiles are the 25th percentile (which tells the researcher the score at which 25 percent of the respondents fall below) and the 75th percentile (the score at which 75 percent of the responses fall below). However, even this has its limitations. People can compare the 25th, 50th and 75th percentiles for variation, but that requires a lot of work and some numerical savvy on behalf of the reader. Ranges and percentiles are appropriate for ordinal, interval, or ratio levels of measurement. The *standard deviation*, on the other hand, is more suited for interval or ratio levels of measurement and is more difficult to calculate than the range and percentile. However, it is the most comprehensive of the three and it is also the most widely used.

You are not likely to calculate a standard deviation by hand in most instances (because calculators and computers can do it very quickly), but it is still useful to know how to do the calculation by hand so that you understand both the formula and the meaning of the statistic. Plus, if you do not have a fancy scientific calculator (and in some instances they are harder to program than just doing a quick calculation by hand) or you have a small distribution, sometimes it is just faster to do the calculation by hand. To start our discussion of the standard deviation, let's look at the basic formula first:

$$s = \sqrt{\Sigma\left(X - \bar{X}\right)^2 / N}$$

where:
  s = the symbol for the standard deviation
  Σ = the symbol for the "sum of"
  $\bar{X}$ = an individual value for the variable under consideration
  X = an individual value for the variable under consideration
  N = the sample size

The purpose of the standard deviation is to tell the researcher how the individual scores on a question vary in relation to a common, central number (here, the mean) in a standardized manner that makes the unit of analysis (year, drinks, children, etc.) irrelevant. So breaking down this formula, we see that the standard deviation is going to compare each score to the mean (the $X - \bar{X}$ part of the equation). So let's start with that. Look at Figure 12.4 to follow this calculation.

As you can see in Figure 12.4, if I need to compare each score to the mean, then the first step in calculating the standard deviation would be to calculate the mean. In the figure, the mean number of years the respondents are in prison for robbery is 1.74. Once I calculate the mean, then I can proceed to the second step, which is to subtract each score from the mean (Step 2, Figure 12.4). I said before that the standard deviation (and all descriptive statistics) are summary statistics, which would imply that you add them. Since the standard deviation examines how each score deviates from the mean, you might be

Steps for Standard Deviation

1. Calculate the mean.
2. Subtract the mean from each score.
3. Square the resulting difference for each score. These are the squared deviations.
4. Add the squared deviations. (Now you have the numerator of the formula.)
5. Divide the squared deviations by the sample size. This is called the variance.
6. Take the square root of the variance. This is the standard deviation.

Example of Calculation

X = years in prison for robbery

Number of Years in Prison For Robbery (X)	Step 2: $(X - \bar{X})$	Step 3: $(X - \bar{X})^2$
2	$2 - 3.63 = -1.63$	2.66
2	-1.63	2.66
3	$3 - 3.63 = -0.63$	0.40
3	-0.63	0.40
4	$4 - 3.63 = +0.37$	0.14
4	$+0.37$	0.14
5	$+1.37$	1.88
6	$+2.37$	5.62
	Check: $\Sigma(X - \bar{X}) = 0$	Step 4: $\Sigma(X - \bar{X})^2 = 13.9$

Step 5: $\Sigma(X - \bar{X})^2/N = 13.9/8 = 1.74$

Step 6: $s = \sqrt{\Sigma(X - \bar{X})^2/N}$
$= 13.9/8$
$= 1.74$
$= 1.32$

Figure 12.4 Steps in the Calculations of the Standard Deviation

tempted to think that we should just add the scores now. But if I do that, the sum of the individual deviations from the mean will always be zero, or close to it, as you can see in the "Check" at the bottom of the deviation column in Figure 12.4. No matter how many times you do this, the deviations from the mean in all instances will always total close to zero. It may be off a little bit from zero due to rounding, but the figure will always hover around that value.

In order to prevent the sum of zero, there's a mathematical principle that says we can square values without changing the relationship between the values so long as we square everything. So that is the third step of the formula: squaring the individual deviations from the mean. Now, if we add all those individual squared deviations (the fourth step), we will not get zero; in fact, as you see in Figure 12.4, the sum of the squared deviations is 13.9 squared years (years^2). You might be asking yourself what a "squared year" is—and that's a good question. But before we address that, there's another issue.

The standard deviation is supposed to be a summary statistic, like an average, that describes how individual scores vary in relation to the mean, but we have a value (13.9) that looks at *all* the scores together. In order to bring the statistic back to a number that would address an individual value in the distribution, we need to divide the sum of the squared deviations by the sample size, or we calculate the average squared deviation of each case. By doing so, we end up with a value of 1.74 squared years. This value is called the *variance*. Like the standard deviation, the variance measures the variability of a distribution (hence the name), but it does so as the average *squared* deviation of each case from the mean, which is not intuitive to most of us. In other words, the variance in this instance *is* measured in squared years, but I really have no idea what a squared year is.

To make the units more intuitive, the last step of the standard deviation calculation takes the square root of this average deviation. Therefore, in the last step, we learn that the standard deviation of the distribution of years in prison for robbery is 1.32 years. Taken together, we say that in this sample, the average years in prison for robbery is 1.74 years and the standard deviation is 1.32 years.

What does this mean? Well, the standard deviation by itself is only limitedly useful, and, in larger distributions (e.g., 200 or more observations), it can be useful in describing where certain proportions of the sample, such as 68 percent or 95 percent, lie. However, for most purposes, the standard deviation is useful when comparing the variability across different groups, such as men and women, or whites and racial minorities, or attorneys and paralegals, or senators and state representatives. For example, let's say I looked at the years in prison for robbery for four different regions of the country and found that the standard deviation for years in prison for robbery for prisoners in the southeast was 1.32, in the northeast it was 0.56, in the northwest it was 1.55, and in the southwest it was 2.34. I would then know that in the northeast, people get very similar sentences for robbery (it has the smallest standard deviation, therefore the least variation and the greatest similarity) and people in the southwest have greater variation in their sentence length for robbery.

It is also useful to use the standard deviation and the mean together to compare groups. For example, let's pretend that I am working for a funding agency and we decided that we are going to award "bonus" funding to the agency that illustrated that its new program (which we funded a year ago) was the most effective. There are three agencies and they each submitted monthly reports regarding how many people benefited from their program. The summary of those 12 reports for each agency is expressed in the following mean and standard deviations:

		Agency	
	A	B	C
$\bar{X}$ =	501.3	498.2	450.1
s =	4.3	2.3	5.1

Who would earn the reward of "bonus" funding? Well, the best way to determine this is to use the standard deviation in proportion to the normal curve. Remember, from Chapter 5 and the earlier brief comment, one standard deviation in both directions of the mean (the mean plus one standard deviation and the mean minus one standard deviation) covers about 68 percent of the scores or values in a distribution. Therefore, if I used this idea and added/subtracted one standard deviation from each respective mean, I would end up with the following ranges:

		Agency	
	A	B	C
Range:	497–505.6	495.9–500.5	445–455.2

So who would get the award? You may be tempted to think that Agency B would get it because it has the smallest standard deviation, which means that this agency was the most stable (least variable), and therefore the most consistent, in terms of the number of clients served. However, if you look at the ranges, you will see that Agency A actually deserves the bonus money. Why? Because even though it is not the most (or least) stable, since its standard deviation is the middle of the three, if you look at the corresponding ranges of scores, even at the low end of the 68 percent spread, the number of clients served is higher than that for the other two agencies. In other words, even when we take the mean (501.3) and subtract one standard deviation (4.3), we come up with a value of 497 (what's in the table at the low end of the range), which is *higher* than the low end of the other two agencies (495.9 and 445, respectively). This means that Agency A actually serves more clients, even though the number of clients served each month is more variable than that of Agency B, which has a mean number of clients served that is very close to Agency A and a smaller standard deviation.

Hence, measures of central tendency and dispersion frequently work hand in hand to give researchers a fuller understanding of the social phenomena under study. There is one other descriptive statistic that may be useful in trying to figure out a distribution without having to examine each score individually. That is the Z-score.

Z-score

The standard deviation is useful for describing 68 percent (plus/minus one standard deviation in each direction of the mean) and 95 percent (plus/minus two standard deviations from the mean), but it is not very useful in trying to figure out where individual scores lie in the distribution. For example, returning to my social services agency example, what if I wanted to know roughly what percentage of months Agency A served more than 510 people? I only have a mean of 501.3 and a standard deviation of 4.3. I have no information about individual scores, even though I am interested in seeing how a particular individual score compares to the rest of the scores. The Z-score will help me answer this question.

People can use the Z-score to identify an individual score in the distribution of scores in terms of their standard deviations from the mean. This allows us to find the relative position of a score in a distribution, which is what I was discussing in the earlier example.

The second way we can use the Z-score is to compare two or more distributions or groups. Let me illustrate the first way Z-scores can be used. The formula for a Z-score is

$$Z = (X - \bar{X}) / s$$

where X is the individual score of interest, $\bar{X}$ is the mean, and s is the standard deviation. To determine the number of standard deviation units from the mean that 510 is in my social services agency example, my formula would look like this:

$$Z = (510 - 501.3) / 4.3 = 8.7 / 4.3 = 2.02$$

This means that the score of 510 is 2.02 standard deviation units from the mean. But what does that *mean*? To answer this, I'd have to look at a table of Z-scores that statisticians have already compiled (which means we don't have to do the work!). There is a Table of Z-scores in Appendix D, but I've recreated a small section of it here (Table 12.7) to illustrate how we can use it for our agency example. Notice that there are three columns. The Z-scores that we calculate from the formula I just presented are in the left column (Column A), the area between the Z-score and the mean are in the middle column (Column B), and area beyond the Z-score is in the right column (Column C). Z-scores are based on the normal curve and sometimes it helps to visualize them as such.

Figure 12.5 illustrates the Z-scores in generic terms. Remember, in a normal distribution of scores, the mean always divides the scores in half and is therefore equivalent in value to the median. (In other words, if you did the calculations for both the mean and the median, your answers would be the same.) The standardized score, or Z-score, for the mean

TABLE 12.7 Table of Selected Z-Scores

(A) Z	(B) Area Between Mean and Z	(C) Area Beyond Z
1.96	.4750	.0250
1.97	.4756	.0244
1.98	.4761	.0239
1.99	.4767	.0233
2.00	.4772	.0228
2.01	.4778	.0222
2.02	.4783	.0217
2.03	.4788	.0212
2.04	.4793	.0207
2.05	.4798	.0202

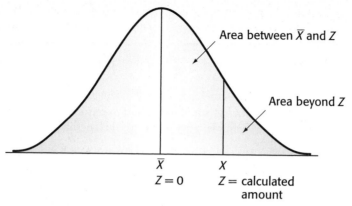

Figure 12.5 *Illustration of Normal Curves with Z-scores*

is 0. In Figure 12.6, we see that I have marked the mean value of 501.3 at the center and underneath it its corresponding Z-value of 0, which we essentially ignore. Now I want to know the percentage of months (or scores) in which Agency A served more than 510 people. So I have also marked the 510 on the normal curve and its corresponding Z-score of 2.02, which is the Z to which we refer when we just say Z, beneath it. I have also shaded the area of the normal curve to the right of the 510 because I want to know the number of months that the agency served *more* than 510 people. Therefore, the area to the right of the 510 is greater (and the area to the left is less than 510, which is apparent because the mean of 501.3 is less than 510 and lies to the left of it). If you compare Figures 12.5 and 12.6, you will see that shaded area is the area *beyond* Z because it is the area past Z and *not* the segment of the normal curve that lies between the mean and my score of 510. Remember, when we say Z we mean the Z-score that corresponds to our distribution score of inter-est—here, the Z that corresponds to the score 510. Therefore, I read down the left column of Table 12.7 until I find a Z-score of 2.02. Once I do, I read across to the third column which is the area beyond Z and I see that the number there is .0217. This number, .0217, refers to the proportion of the total area under the curve that lies beyond Z. I can make this number more intuitive by simply multiplying it by 100 to get a percent, and therefore I

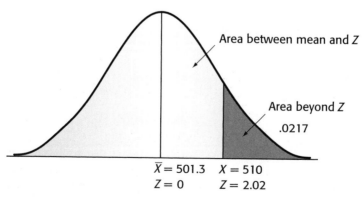

Figure 12.6 *Illustration of Z-score for Social Services Agency Example*

would say that 2.17 percent of the year Agency A served more than 510 clients. If I wanted to know the percentage of the year that Agency A served *between* 501.3 and 510 clients, I would read the middle column, which is the area between the mean and Z. If I wanted to know the percentage of the year that Agency A served *fewer* than 490 clients (not shown in Figure 12.6 because we are not calculating this Z-score), I would do the same thing as I did for the percentage of the year they served more than 510 clients, but everything would be on the left-hand side of the graph. This illustrates an important point. Since the mean divides the normal curve exactly in half, the proportions that correspond to the Z-scores are the same to the left of the mean as on the right. The sign of your Z-value that you obtain from the formula (in addition to the actual score you are looking at) will remind you what side of the mean your reference score lies. If the sign is positive, your score is higher than the mean; if it's negative, your score is lower than the mean. In Table 12.4, Z-scores don't have a sign, since the sign itself has no numerical meaning because the left and right halves of the normal curve are equivalent. In other words, it makes no difference if you are using the right or left half of the normal curve. The Z-value will be the same for scores which are the same standard deviation units from the mean. Try it. Draw and calculate the Z-score for the proportion of scores less than 490. You will see that the Z-score calculation produces the same Z-score it did for a score of 510, only negative.

Why bother converting individual scores to Z-scores? Why use the formula at all? The main reason is because Z-scores are *standardized,* which means that the unit of the scores—whether it's years, meters, crimes, or dollars—is no longer important. That essentially allows us to "ignore" the units and use the formula in all instances. Hence, by changing whatever units the original scores were measured by into standardized units, we can use different units that are equally valid in expressing distance no matter how the original scores were measured. When you stop and think about it, the Z-score formula is a relatively simple formula that allows researchers a lot of freedom in comparison.

Summary

To recap, one of the purposes of statistics is to summarize a lot of information (such as what the 2,000 people in our sample said about a variable) and to express that summary in a relatively few numbers. In this section we discussed various ways in which researchers can summarize the responses of all of their study participants regarding individual variables. We can use measures of central tendency to summarize what the typical response of a sample is and we can use measures of dispersion to see the arrangement or variation in responses relative to that central measure. We also learned that levels of measurement, a topic we spent so much time discussing in Chapter 4, have direct relevance at this stage of the research process because certain statistics can produce accurate results only for specific levels of measurement. For example, means should not be calculated for variables that are measured at the nominal level. The mean sex of 1.2 has no real meaning. Instead, a percent is more appropriate, and the finding that 36 percent of the sample were women is more telling than a mean.

We also learned that, at least for an individual variable, we can use the Z-score to find the relative position of any individual score of interest in a distribution. We can find the percentage of scores above and below a particular score, and we can also use Z-scores to find the percentage of scores that fall between two individual scores.

However, each of these statistics—measures of central tendency, measures of dispersion, and Z-scores—can summarize only what a sample of people said to *one* variable at a time. Hence, researchers refer to them as univariate or descriptive statistics. They cannot compare two variables simultaneously. In the next section, I will briefly discuss how researchers can use two or more variables to test hypotheses, as well as describe a sample.

■ Bivariate Statistics

Univariate statistics describe a sample and, depending on the way that sample was drawn, they may be used to describe a population as well. Researchers use bivariate and multivariate (*multivariate* means that the researcher is examining three or more variables simultaneously) statistics, on the other hand, primarily to *explain* a phenomenon. Therefore, researchers use bivariate and multivariate statistics to test hypotheses, to see if patterns found in a sample will hold true in a population, and to determine whether a difference between statistics is big enough to indicate that a relationship between variables really does exist.

The general principles I will discuss here for bivariate statistics also hold for multivariate statistics; however, the statistical formulas and interpretations for multivariate statistics are beyond the scope of this book, which aims only to give a basic foundational understanding of statistical tests. I will briefly elaborate on some specific issues of multivariate analysis in the next section; however, for now, let it suffice to say that the *principle* behind the logic of bivariate comparisons also generally holds for multivariate comparisons, even though the specific statistics for multivariate comparisons generally differ.

That being said, bivariate and multivariate statistics can address issues of either statistical significance or substantive significance. Researchers more formally refer to tests for statistical significance as *inferential statistics* because the goal of these statistics is to see whether researchers can generalize the findings in their sample to what may be going on in a population. To put this another way, with inferential statistics, researchers hope to infer what is going on in the population (which a researcher cannot directly observe) based on what they can directly observe in a sample selected from that population.

Let me briefly review a few points we covered in previous chapters that may help you grasp the meaning of inferential statistics. Remember that when researchers want to test hypotheses, they rarely can observe the entire population for which a hypothesis may apply. If I want to test the hypothesis that social sciences majors are more likely to get better grades in law school than are students with other undergraduate majors, I am not going to be able to survey all law students to learn their college majors and their law school grade-point averages. I am going to have to content myself with studying a *sample* of law school students and try to use that sample to make generalizations to all law school students. The first, and foremost, step in using a sample to study a population is to do a probability sample, which we discussed in Chapter 5. In fact, inferential statistics are based on the assumption that a researcher did probability sampling. Therefore, inferential statistics tell the researcher whether any relationship between variables (such as college major and law school GPA) found in a sample is likely to occur in the population. In this way, inferential statistics allow researchers to test hypotheses in a population (which researchers cannot observe) using subjects they can observe (a sample).

Researchers frequently consider findings to be statistically significant if the probability of error is less than .05. We've encountered some of this as well. Remember when we used confidence intervals to calculate how large a sample should be in Chapter 5? We said that one component in the confidence interval calculation for sample size was the amount of error one was willing to accept. If one wanted to be 95 percent confident of a relationship, the amount of error one is willing to accept is 5 percent, or a probability of .05. If someone wants to be 99 percent confident, then the probability of error is .01. Probability of error values are frequently called *p-values* for short, and sometimes researchers omit using a reference to the p-value at all and simply state something like: "Results were statistically significant at the .05 level." Any time a researcher discusses a .05 or .01 level, they are usually referring to the probability of error.

However, statistical tests do not always indicate that the observed relationship between two variables found in a sample will also be found in the population. For example, if we are comparing the level of racial tolerance between two groups, say men and women, we may see that the average score on a racial tolerance scale that ranges from 1 to 100 is 87.5 for women and 79.6 for men. Because these two numbers, 87.5 and 79.6, are different, does that mean that women are more racially tolerant than men? Not necessarily. If we do a statistical test, like a t-test, which I will discuss in a moment, and see that the probability of error is .07, that means that we can only be 93 percent confident that there is a relationship in the population. We want to be 95 percent confident or better to claim statistical significance, but here we cannot. Therefore, our conclusion would be that, despite the differences in percentages between men and women in our sample, there is no relationship between gender and racial tolerance in the population.

How can we say this if the two average scores are different? What inferential statistics tell the researcher whether those observed differences in the sample are "real" or likely due to chance? Think about it. What do you think is the probability that two groups will have the *exact same* score on any measure? Not very likely. Even if we gave the test to the same people a week later, it is likely that the average score on the retest at the second time point would be slightly different from the first—even for the same people. The point is that since we cannot expect scores to be exactly the same in order to illustrate that there is no difference between the groups, we need inferential statistics to tell us *how much difference* is necessary to assume that a real difference occurs. We cannot know that simply on our own.

Sometimes researchers stop here. They simply use inferential statistics to see whether a relationship between two variables is likely to occur in the population. However, many inferential statistics just tell the researcher whether there *is* a relationship between two or more variables in a population. These tests frequently to do not tell the researcher whether there is a *substantively significant* relationship between two variables. For example, I may find that there *is* a statistically significant relationship between gender and racial tolerance; however, a different statistical test for substantive significance may tell me that the degree of association (or effect) between these two variables is very small. If the association is very small, then there really is no relationship between the variables.

For example, suppose I sample 500 people and can conclude with 95 percent confidence that age and the amount of tax dollars someone was willing to contribute to social services programs was statistically related. This means that even though I studied only 500 people, in the larger population from which that 500 was drawn, say a population size of 2,500, I'm pretty confident (95 percent sure) that age and amount of tax dollars one is willing to pay for social services programs are also related. However, suppose I found that the measure of association, which researchers sometimes call a **correlation,** was only .11 on a scale of 0 (no relationship) to 1.00 (perfect relationship). This means that even though I have statistical significance (age and tax dollars *are* related in the population), I do not really have substantive significance because the degree of association is very small. Thus, I would report and conclude that although there *is* a statistical difference, the degree of association is so small as to make that statistical significance not very important (or not substantively significant).

I will refer to some of these points in the discussion that follows to further illustrate them. However, for now, I want to begin the very basic discussion of the actual statistics I can use to test both statistical and substantive significance.

Statistical or inferential significance

Because we live in a society in which people want to know exactly what they are getting, let me be clear about what I do and do not aim to do in these statistical discussions. As before, I will only highlight some common statistics used in the social sciences. My discussion is by no means complete or comprehensive. My goal is to give you the foundation to understand some of the more common and basic statistics you are likely to encounter or have to use. Any discussion that is more detailed is better suited for a class specifically on statistics. Now that I have the "legalese" of my goals covered, let's begin.

As with univariate statistics, not all inferential statistical tests are suitable for all levels of measurement. Furthermore, to throw another consideration in the mix, deciding on which inferential statistic to use generally depends on the level of measurement of the *dependent variable* only. The independent variable frequently tells the researcher how many groups are being compared. For example, I want to test the hypothesis that Christians are less likely to support the death penalty than are members of other religions. In this hypothesis, the independent variable is religion and I might decide to measure religion as Christian, Jewish, and Other. The values for my independent variable tell me that I will be comparing three groups: (1) Christians, (2) Jews, and (3) Other religions. The dependent variable, view of the death penalty, I am measuring as support, undecided, do not support. It is not important *how* I reached these rankings of "support, undecided, do not support" for my discussion here. However, if this was a real research project, I'd have to have made sure that I explained that earlier in the research process as we discussed in Chapter 4.

For my hypothesis about religion and view of the death penalty, my dependent variable is measured at the ordinal level. "Support, undecided, do not support" show rankings, but I cannot quantify how much more support someone who answers "support" has relative to someone who is "undecided." There is no numerical value I can put on that difference. Probably the most common inferential statistic for dependent variables measured at the nominal or ordinal level is the chi-square.

Table 12.8 shows findings from my hypothetical sample regarding people's religion and their view of the death penalty. Conventionally, the independent variable reads down the columns and the dependent variable reads across the rows. The numbers in each cell are percents followed by the raw number of observations in parentheses. For example, 21 Christians, or 51.22 percent of them (21/41 multiplied by 100), do not support the death penalty. The totals at the end of each column and row are *marginals*, and they will be important in the calculation of chi-square. I will discuss guidelines for table presentations later in this chapter. For now, I just wanted you to be familiar with the general terms and the placement of the independent and dependent variables.

As an inferential test, the goal of the chi-square (and all inferential statistics) is to reject the null hypothesis. Just like in a court of law where a defendant is presumed innocent until proven guilty, in statistics, variables are presumed unrelated until "proven" otherwise. Now I realize that I began this book by saying that social sciences researchers shy

TABLE 12.8 View of the Death Penalty by Religion

View of Death Penalty	Religion			Totals
	Christians	Jews	Other	
Not Support	51.22% (21)	26.32 % (15)	10.17% (6)	42
Unsure	29.27% (12)	43.86% (25)	35.59% (21)	58
Support	19.51% (8)	29.81% (17)	54.29% (32)	57
Totals	41	57	59	157

away from the word *proven*, but I just used it here to follow the courtroom analogy. The point is that even though researchers have a research hypothesis that they *hope* is going to be supported, statistically, the formulas they use assume that there is no relationship between variables.

Researchers call this hypothesis of no relationship the *null hypothesis*. We discussed the null hypothesis briefly in Chapter 2 so I won't go over it again here, except to say that with regard to chi-square, the null hypothesis is always the same. The null hypothesis is one of independence, which, in this instance, means that classification in one variable (such as a specific religion) has no influence on classification in a different variable (such as view of death penalty). So the goal of the **chi-square statistic** is to reject this null relationship of independence and, in fact, show that, in this instance, broad religious affiliation *does* affect one's view of the death penalty.

To accomplish this, chi-square compares the observed cells obtained from a sample to what we would *expect* to see in those cells if the two variables were independent. The overall chi-square formula looks like this:

$$X^2 = \Sigma \left[(f_{observed} - f_{expected})^2 / f_{expected} \right]$$

where X^2 is the symbol for chi-square, Σ, as you've encountered before, stands for "sum of," $f_{observed}$ is the frequency observed in a specific cell, and $f_{expected}$ is the frequency one would expect if the variables were unrelated. What is the expected frequency for a cell? Before we can use this formula, we first need to calculate this value for each cell. We do this by the formula:

$$f_{expected} = [(\text{row marginal}) (\text{column marginal})] / \text{sample size}$$

Remember when I said that knowing the term *marginal* was important? Here's why. We need to calculate the expected frequency for each cell of the table. Any "box" that has information that corresponds to the intersection of two variables is a *cell*. Therefore, if you look back at Table 12.8, you will see that the "21" in the upper left box is a "cell" because it is the number of people who are "Christian" (as we can tell by the column heading) and who "support" the death penalty (as we can tell by the row heading). To calculate the num-

TABLE 12.9 Table of Expected Frequencies to Match Table 12.8

View of Death Penalty	Religion			Totals
	Christians	Jews	Other	
Not Support	10.97	15.25	15.78	42
Unsure	15.15	21.06	21.80	58
Support	14.89	20.69	21.42	57
Totals	41	57	59	157

ber of people (expected frequency) we would expect to be in this cell if religion and death penalty view are not related, we would do the following:

$$F_e \text{ (Christian, support)} = [(42)(41)] / 157 = 10.97$$

This means that if religion and death penalty view are not related, we would expect to see about 10.97 people in that cell. A couple of points are important here. First, the expected frequency is a theoretical entity in that it does not refer to real people per se. Therefore, the general practice is not to round to whole numbers, but instead to use two decimal places to the right of the decimal point. Second, although you may be tempted to think that 10.97 is very different from 21 and therefore the two variables "must" be related, do not be so quick to make that call. The chi-square statistic is a *sum* of all the cells, and if the resulting cells are very close, then the sum may not be large enough to assume that the difference is real. The expected frequency is calculated for each cell and the resulting table of expected frequencies is shown in Table 12.9.

Now you are ready to calculate the actual chi-square value. By comparing the cell values (observed frequencies) in Table 12.8 to the expected cell values in Table 12.9 in the formula, we get this:

$$X^2 = (21 - 10.97)^2 / 10.97 + (15 - 15.25)^2 / 15.25 + (6 - 15.78)^2 / 15.78$$
$$+ (12 - 15.15)^2 / 15.15 + (25 - 21.06)^2 / 21.06 + (21 - 21.80)^2 / 21.80$$
$$+ (8 - 14.89)^2 / 14.89 + (17 - 20.69)^2 / 20.69 + (32 - 21.42)^2 / 21.42 = 25.73$$

Well, what does this mean? On its own, not much. In order to make sense of the chi-square statistic, we need to compare the chi-square we calculated, sometimes called the *chi-square obtained* to a chi-square critical value. And, to do this, we first need to calculate the degrees of freedom for our bivariate relationship. A full discussion and implication of degrees of freedom is beyond my purposes here. For now, I will say only that the degrees of freedom are essentially the number of cells one has to know in any bivariate table in order to be able to calculate the remaining cells (Healey, 2005). The formula for degrees of freedom is:

$$df = (r - 1)(c - 1)$$

TABLE 12.10 Selective Critical Values of X^2 for Probabilities of Error Equaling .05 and .01

Degrees of Freedom df	Probability of Error .05	Probability of Error .01
1	3.841	6.635
2	5.991	9.210
3	7.815	11.341
4	9.488	13.277
5	11.070	15.086
6	12.592	16.812

where df stands for the degrees of freedom, r is the number of rows (not counting the marginals), and c is the number of columns (not counting the marginals). In our example, we have three rows (support, undecided, not support) and three columns (Christian, Jewish, Other); therefore, our degrees of freedom are $(3 - 1)(3 - 1)$ or $(2)(2) = 4$. We use the degrees of freedom to determine the appropriate chi-square critical value for either a 95 percent confidence level (probability of error = .05) or a 99 percent confidence level (probability of error =.01). Our chi-square obtained needs to be greater than the critical value in order to reject the null hypothesis that these two variables are independent, or unrelated. As with the Z-scores, you need to use a table to find the critical values for chi-square, and one appears in Appendix E. Table 12.10 shows a subset of a table.

The probability of error values are listed across the top of the table and the degrees of freedom are down the left column. As before, we are interested in probability of errors that are .05 or less, but the convention is just to look at the probability values of .05 and .01. Looking at the table for 4 degrees of freedom, we see that the chi-square critical value for a probability of error of .05 and 4 degrees of freedom is 9.488. Our chi-square obtained was 25.73, which is greater than that, therefore we can reject the null of independence and assume that religious affiliation and view of the death penalty are related in the population.

Since I can pass the chi-square critical at the .05 level, I will try to see if I can make the "bonus round," as I like to call it, and pass the critical value at the .01 level. If I can't, no big deal. I have established statistical significance at the .05 level and I'm happy with that, but if I can be even *more* confident of my results and pass it at the .01 level (which means I'm 99 percent confident that the observed differences between cells are not due to chance), then I make the "bonus round." The chi-square critical for .01 error level and 4 degrees of freedom is 13.277 and can I pass it? Yes. The number 25.73 is greater than 13.277, so I can say that I am 99 percent confident that I can reject the null of independence and state that there is a relationship between religion and view of the death penalty (meaning that the two variables are "dependent" on each other).

However, chi-square only tells you whether the variables are related in the population. It does not tell you *how* the variables are related. You may find that the variables are indeed related, but not in the direction you hypothesized. For example, you may find that, yes, religion and view of the death penalty are related, but contrary to your hypothesis, Christians are more likely to support the death penalty than are Jewish people. To see whether your hypothesis is supported, you need to calculate the percentages for each cell and then compare them. Is the percentage of Christians who favor the death penalty greater than that of Jews and people of other religions? If so, and if your chi-square passed the test of statistical significance, then your hypothesis is supported. If not, then your hypothesis is *not* supported even though there *is* a relationship between these two variables.

In our case, we can reject the null, but our hypothesis is *not* supported because the percentage of Christians who favor the death penalty (19.51 percent, Table 12.8) is less than that of Jews (29.81 percent) and people of other religions (54.29 percent). If your chi-square obtained is *less* than your chi-square critical, and therefore you find that there is no statistical relationship between religion and view of the death penalty, then calculating and interpreting the percentages in the table is not informative, because the lack of statistical significance tells you that any patterns in the table are likely due to chance alone.[*]

T-test and Z-scores

For dependent variables that are measured at the interval/ratio levels of measurement, the chi-square is going to be cumbersome. You are likely to have many rows and columns, which will make it unwieldy to read as well as threaten the integrity of the chi-square statistic itself. For dependent variables measured at the interval/ratio levels of measurement, there are three different statistics people use. The first, called an **independent samples t-test statistic,** is used when the independent variables have two values but the combined sample size is less than 100. The second, a *Z-score,* which is a variation of the Z-score we calculated earlier, is also used when the independent variable has two values, but in this case the combined sample size is greater than 100. The last, called an *Analysis of Variance,* or *ANOVA* for short, is used when the independent variable has three or more values. I'll discuss the ANOVA statistic in the next section. For now, let's focus on the *t*-test and Z-score.

The *t*-test, which is sometimes called the *student's t,* is generally used to compare sample means of two groups. If the groups are different, then the calculated *t* statistic will be significant. As with the chi-square, we need to compare the calculated *t*-statistic to a critical value that we find in a table. However, the degrees of freedom for a *t*-test are calculated

---

[*]There are some limitations with the chi-square. One of the main ones is that the chi-square statistic is not accurate for small sample sizes where a high percentage of cells have an expected frequency of less than 5. There is disagreement as to how many cells actually constitutes a "high amount" (Healey, 2002); however, whatever threshold you use (even if it is just one cell), if a researcher collapses the table to a 2 × 2 table, then he can use the Yate's correction for continuity version of the chi-square. This formula is slightly altered from the traditional chi-square formula and reads:

$$X_c^2 = \Sigma \left[\left(|f_o - f_e| - .5 \right)^2 / f_e \right].$$

I only mention it to (1) make you aware of a key limitation of chi-square and (2) let you know that that limitation *can* be addressed. The resulting interpretation is the same as for the traditional chi-square.

differently than that for a chi-square, and it has a somewhat different meaning than the degrees of freedom do for the chi-square.

There are different *t*-tests depending on the nature of the data. If the sample is large (more than 100 people across the two groups), then the *t* distribution is actually a lot like the Z distribution that we discussed earlier with Z-scores. Plus, the formula is somewhat different, as we will see. Likewise, if we are comparing proportions instead of means, the formula varies again, even though the logic behind the statistic is the same. Last, if we are looking at the same group at two different time points (for example, a pre- and posttest score), then we use yet a different formula. I know that mentioning all of these formulas is probably confusing. I do so only because even though the details of the formula varies, the idea *behind* all of them is the same. Namely, you compare two means (or proportions) to see whether they are significantly different, which would imply then that the groups are different in the population. For all of the statistics, you need to compare your obtained statistic (which you calculate) to a critical value (which you look up in a table).

For example, I may want to compare the reading scores between inner-city grade school students who attended an after-school reading program and their inner-city counterparts who did not. The goal of the program was improve the reading ability of inner-city children. Therefore, I hypothesized that inner-city children who attended the after-school reading program will have higher reading scores on a standardized test than will inner-city children who did not attend the reading program. My null hypothesis is that the two groups are equal, that there is no difference in reading scores between those who attended the program and those who do not. I can show my null and research hypothesis as such:

$$H_0: \mu_1 = \mu_2$$
$$(H_1: \mu_1 > \mu_2)$$

H_0 is my null hypothesis, where the 0 symbolizes no relationship, and H_1 is my research hypothesis, which is sometimes presented in parentheses to remind the reader that, statistically, it is *not* what is being tested, although substantively it is the hypothesis of interest. If you remember, in Chapter 3 I discussed the three directions a hypothesis can have: no direction (e.g., the variables are just different), greater than, and less than. The symbol > indicates that the reading scores from the population in which the first sample was drawn (those who attended the after-school program) is *greater* than the scores of those in the population from the second sample (those who did not attend the program). My resulting data are shown in Table 12.11.

In this scenario, I am comparing the mean reading scores of a small sample, since the total sample size is less than 100. Therefore, I am using the *t*-statistic (as opposed to the Z) and I am not studying the same people at two time points. (I am studying two different groups at one time point instead.) Therefore, the formula I will use is:

$$t_{\text{obtained}} = \left(\bar{X}_1 - \bar{X}_2\right) / \sigma_{\bar{X} - \bar{X}}$$

$$\text{Where } \sigma_{\bar{X} - \bar{X}} = \sqrt{(N_1 s_1^2 + N_2 s_2^2)/(N_1 + N_2 - 2)} \times \sqrt{(N_1 + N_2)/N_1 N_2}$$

The $\bar{X}$ as you well know by now, is the mean, the *s* is the standard deviation, and the *N* is the sample size. The subscripts 1 and 2 indicate the two groups. Therefore, $\bar{X}_1$ and s_1

TABLE 12.11 Reading Scores for Those Who Did and Did Not Attend the After-School Reading Program

Attended After-School Reading Program	Did Not Attend After-School Program
$\bar{X}_1 = 7.43$	$\bar{X}_2 = 5.50$
$s_1 = 0.75$	$s_2 = 0.25$
$N_1 = 15$	$N_2 = 16$

are the mean and the standard deviation, respectively, for one group. $\bar{X}_2$ and s_2 are the mean and the standard deviation, respectively, for the second group. It does not matter which group is the first or second.

Substituting all of my respective numbers, the formula produces the following:

$$\sigma_{\bar{X}-\bar{X}} = \sqrt{(15 \times .75^2 + 16 \times .25^2)/(15+16-2)} \ \times \ \sqrt{(15+16)/(15 \times 16)} = .57 \times .40 = .23$$

Therefore:

$$t_{\text{obtained}} = \left(\bar{X}_1 - \bar{X}_2\right) / \sigma_{\bar{X}-\bar{X}} = (7.43 - 5.50)/.23 = 8.39$$

The degrees of freedom are relevant for small samples (t statistic) but not for large samples (Z statistic). Since I have a small sample, my degrees of freedom are:

$$df = N_1 + N_2 - 2 = 15 + 16 - 2 = 29$$

There is not an easily intuitive way of explaining degrees of freedom in the short amount of space we have here, so I will defer that to a statistics course. At the risk of sounding repetitive, my goal here is just to give you a rudimentary understanding of *how* to use these statistics, not necessarily *why* they work the way that they do.

Before I continue with our *t*-test example, I have to make a few comments about one- and two-tailed tests. If my hypothesis specifies a direction of effect—for example, saying that children with the program will have *higher* levels of reading than those without the program—then that means that I am only interested in examining the upper half of the normal curve, as we see in Figure 12.7.

If I want to be at least 95 percent sure of my findings, that means I will accept only an error of 5 percent or, expressed in relation to the normal curve, a proportion of .05 under the curve. Since I am saying that I think one group is *greater* than another, I am only interested in the half of the normal curve that illustrates "greater," and therefore all of my error will be in that "one tail" of the normal curve. If, on the other hand, I did not specify *how* the two groups would differ and instead focused only on *whether* they differ, that means I don't make any implications as to whether a specific group is *higher* or *lower* than another. Hence, the difference can be in either direction, or at both ends of the normal curve, which is called a *two-tailed* hypothesis.

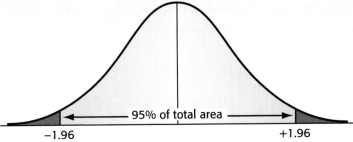

A. The two-tailed test, Z (critical) = ± 1.96

95% of total area

−1.96   +1.96

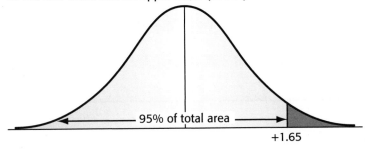

B. The one-tailed test for upper tail, Z (critical) = $+1.65$

95% of total area

+1.65

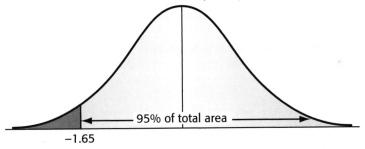

C. The one-tailed test for lower tail, Z (critical) = -1.65

95% of total area

−1.65

Figure 12.7 An Illustration of One- and Two-Tailed Tests for Statistical Significance at the Alpha = .05 Level

This has important implications for how to look up critical values. If I am doing a one-tailed test, then all of my error is together on one side of the curve and would be .05. If I am doing a two-tailed test, that means that my error is divided across both ends of the curve, so I would have .025 in each tail (.05 / 2 =.025). What does this mean in a practical sense? Well, once again, I need to use a table of critical values for the t-statistics to which I will compare my t-obtained. As before, I've included a selective table of critical values for the t-statistic (Table 12.12). A full table appears in Appendix F.

Table 12.12 shows that there are different critical values for t based on whether we have a one- or two-tailed test. For example, our data has 29 degrees of freedom and our hypothesis signifies a one-tailed test. Therefore, we are interested in the probability of error values that appear in the second row under "Level of Significance for a One-Tailed Test." The probability of errors presented in this partial table for a one-tailed test are .05, .025,

TABLE 12.12 Selective Table of Critical Values for the *t*-Statistic

	Level of Significance for a One-Tailed Test		
	.05	.025	.005
	Level of Significance for a Two-Tailed Test		
df	.10	.05	.01
26	1.706	2.056	2.779
27	1.703	2.052	2.771
28	1.701	2.048	2.763
29	1.699	2.045	2.756
30	1.697	2.042	2.750

and .005. If I want to be 95 percent sure, I have a probability of error of .05; and, since I have 29 degrees of freedom, if I match the column for probability of error of .05 for a one-tailed test with the row for degrees of freedom equaling 29, I see that my *t*-critical value is 1.699. To reject the null of no difference, my *t*-obtained has to be greater than my *t*-critical, and since 8.39 is greater than 1.699, I can reject the null and conclude, with 95 percent confidence, that the students who had the after-school reading program *did* score higher on their reading tests than did the students who did not have that program.

Why bother distinguishing between one- and two-tailed tests? Look at Table 12.12 again. If you look at the *t*-critical value for a probability error of .05 and a one-tailed test, you will see that it is, as I just said, 1.699. However, if you look at the second heading, for a two-tailed test, and find the probability of error level of .05, the corresponding *t*-critical for 29 degrees of freedom is 2.045, which is greater than 1.699. The benefit of using a one-tailed test is that it lowers the critical value, which means that, statistically, the null region threshold is less, and therefore it is easier, in a sense, to reject the null. That's the benefit of putting some theoretical thought into deciding on a one-tailed test as opposed to a two-tailed test whenever theoretically possible. It is easier to reject the null, and therefore find support for your hypothesis, when you have a one-tailed test.

Just for the sake of another illustration, I will also provide an example of how to compare means in large samples. Let's suppose that I did a study to assess life satisfaction among married and cohabiting couples. Higher scores indicate greater life satisfaction, and I hypothesize simply that the scores between the two groups will be different. Therefore, my null and research hypotheses are as follows:

$$H_0: \mu_1 = \mu_2$$
$$(H_1: \mu_1 \neq \mu_2)$$

The $\neq$ sign simply translates into "not equal" and signifies a two-tailed test.

TABLE 12.13 Life Satisfaction Scores for Married and Cohabitating Couples

Married Couples	Cohabiting Couples
$\bar{X}_1 = 12.4$	$\bar{X}_2 = 10.2$
$s_1 = 3.9$	$s_2 = 1.9$
$N_1 = 97$	$N_2 = 173$

The data for these results are shown in Table 12.13. Since I am not taking a stand in terms of how these scores differ, I am using a two-tailed test. Since my combined sample size is greater than 100, I am using the Z-score formula, and since I am looking at two groups of people at one point, I am not using the formula for related samples. Therefore, my formula is:

$$Z_{obtained} = \left(\bar{X}_1 - \bar{X}_2\right) / \sigma_{\bar{X}-\bar{X}}$$

$$\text{Where } \sigma_{\bar{X}-\bar{X}} = \sqrt{s_1^2 / (N_1 - 1) + s_2^2 / (N_2 - 1)}$$

Notice how the Z-obtained formula looks suspiciously like the *t*-obtained formula; the real difference is in the calculation of the denominator. Substituting our numbers, we calculate Z obtained to be:

$$Z_{obtained} = \left(\bar{X}_1 - \bar{X}_2\right) / \sigma_{\bar{X}-\bar{X}} = (12.4 - 10.2) / .42 = 5.24$$

where we calculated

$$\sigma_{\bar{X}-\bar{X}} = \sqrt{3.9^2 / (97 - 1) + 1.9^2 / (173 - 1)} = .42$$

We already encountered the table of Z-scores earlier in this chapter. If my probability of error is .05 and I have a two-tailed test, that means I have a probability of error of .025 in each of the tails (.05 / 2 = .025). Using Appendix D and looking in the column for an area *beyond* Z, which you will remember refers to the tail, for the value of .025, I see that the Z-score that corresponds to that value is 1.96. Therefore, my Z critical value, of which my Z obtained has to equal or be greater than in order to reject the null, is 1.96. The number 5.24 is definitely greater than 1.96, so I can reject the null and conclude with 95 percent confidence that life satisfaction is different for married and cohabiting couples. Remember, my research hypothesis says only that they are different, not *how* they are different, so my interpretation needs to be consistent with that. Also notice that, unlike for the chi-square and for the *t*-test, my Z observed can be greater than *or equal* to the Z critical. That is just a characteristic of the Z-score.

ANOVA

The *t*-test and Z-score formulas are useful when examining two groups; however, researchers frequently want to examine three or more groups instead. For example, if I wanted to compare Whites and African Americans, I could use the *t*-test or Z-score, depending on my sample size. However, what about if I wanted to compare Whites, African Americans, Hispanics, and Asian Americans? Technically, I could do a series of *t*-tests or Z-scores using two comparisons. However, that would require six different tests to capture all the unique pairings of two different racial groups, and each time I conduct a statistic, there is room for error (hence, the reason we use *probabilities of error*, or *p-values*). Therefore, if I did all of these two-group comparisons, I would have six different opportunities to introduce statistical error due to random chance. The ANOVA test, which stands for *analysis of variance*, removes this problem by doing *one* test, as opposed to six.

Basically, the ANOVA statistic compares the statistical means across three or more categories. This means that the dependent variable has to be measured at the interval/ratio level and that the independent variable has to have three or more answer categories (and is usually measured at the nominal or ordinal level). Logically, the ANOVA statistic argues that there should be more variation between groups (e.g., across the four racial categories) than within groups (e.g., among Whites alone or among African Americans alone).

One-way ANOVAs are the most common version of this statistic, in which only one independent variable is considered; however, some researchers can and do use two-way ANOVAs, which are a multivariate form of analysis that includes *two* independent variables (and, of course, one dependent variable). The actual calculation of the ANOVA statistic is more complex than the calculation of the other statistics I discussed, therefore I will not provide an example here. All I will say is that the ANOVA statistic is sometimes called the *F-statistic* or *F-ratio* because it uses the F-distribution, which is a variation of the *t* distribution and Z distribution that I have already discussed. Therefore, the ANOVA requires comparing the obtained, calculated, F-statistics (F observed) with a table of probabilities (F critical). Like the *t*-statistic, the F-statistic also involves degrees of freedom, but there are two here instead of one: one degree of freedom for the between-group comparison and one for the within-group comparison. As before, the relationship between the two variables is determined to be statistically significant if the F obtained is greater than the F critical.

■ Substantive Significance or Degree of Association

The previously mentioned statistics tell us only if we can expect, with any certainty, that the relationship between variables that we see in our sample are likely to be present in the population. Inferential tests for statistical significance do *not* tell the researcher *how much* the two variables are related. Statistical measures of association, however, do.

As with inferential statistics, measures of association vary according to the level of measurement for the variables. However, with measures of association, the independent and dependent variables do not provide different pieces of information to help determine the statistics. Instead, the level of measurement of *both* variables is important because with statistical measures of association, the statistic has to correspond to the lowest level of measurement. For example, if my independent variable is a nominal level of measurement (e.g., political party affiliation) and my dependent variable is ordinal (e.g., support for a specific candidate measured on a five-point Likert scale), then the measure of association has to be one of those appropriate for nominal levels of measurement because that is my lowest level of measurement. If both my independent and dependent variables are the same level of measurement, however (e.g., they are both ordinal), there is no problem. I would just use a statistic that corresponds to ordinal levels of measurement.

I will not go into detail about the actual calculation of each measure, as that is more appropriate for a statistics class, but I will briefly make some comments here so you are at least equipped to determine whether a researcher used the appropriate statistic, given the level of measurement for the dependent variable, and if the researcher made the appropriate interpretations of that statistic. Furthermore, I will not discuss the measures of association used for nominal levels of measurement or for ordinal levels of measurement that have few categories. There *are* statistical measures of association such as lambda, phi, and gamma, for these levels of measurement, but many researchers just use the chi-square measure. The calculation of the other possible measures, although simple, are more than I can go into here because they are not frequently used in research.

But wait, you may be wondering why I mentioned the chi-square statistic when we have already discussed this in inferential statistics. That's because the chi-square can be used in two ways. One way is as an inferential statistic, which, you are right, we discussed earlier. The other way is a descriptive measure of association. To use chi-square as a descriptive statistic, we just look at the value of the chi-square obtained that we calculated using the chi-square formula. The closer that value is to 0, the weaker the relationship. A chi-square value of (or very near) 0 means that the variables are independent and have no association at all. The higher the value, the stronger the association (Neuman, 1997).

However, there is a bit of a problem here. Although I said that the higher the chi-square obtained, the stronger the association between the two variables, this is somewhat subjective. A chi-square obtained value of 12.6 has no inherent meaning in and of itself. We know that a chi-square obtained of 12.6 indicates a weaker relationship than one of 20.6, but we can only interpret that statistic relative to another calculated chi-square comparison. In other words, we can best interpret the strength of a relationship between two variables with the chi-square obtained if we compare that chi-square to the chi-square of *another* bivariate relationship.

For example, if I am examining the strength of association between race and volunteerism and I have a chi-square obtained of 12.6, to interpret that, I might want to compare it to the chi-square I calculate for the relationship between employment status and volunteering, which let's say is 20.6. This means that there is a stronger relationship between employment status and volunteering than there is between race and volunteering. That's pretty much all that I can do, but it illustrates an important point.

At various times in this book, I have stressed that you always want to use the highest levels of measurement possible because it will lead to the more informative statistics. This is a good example. Nominal and ordinal levels of measurement (the latter which have few categories) are pretty low on the level of measurement scale. Hence, it is not surprising that their statistics are not as independently informative. In order to interpret them, we need to compare them to other calculated statistics; on their own, they have no real meaning.

That is not the case with ordinal levels of measurement that have many categories or with interval/ratio levels of measurement. For variables measured at any one of these levels, the measures of association that researchers frequently use *can* stand alone, which means that they *do* have inherent meaning on their own without needing to be compared to other statistics. For variables measured at the ordinal level (if there are many categories) or the interval/ratio level, many of the measures of association are interpreted either along a continuum that ranges from 0 (no association) to ± 1 (perfect association). The closer the score to 1 (positive or negative), the stronger the relationship, and the closer the score to 0, the weaker the relationship. The plus sign or the minus sign just indicates whether the variables are positively related (+) or negatively related (−).

For ordinal levels of measurement that have many categories, the most common statistical measure of association in the social sciences is *Spearman's rho*, which as I just said, ranges in value from 0 to ± 1. Without going into much statistical detail, the calculation of Spearman's rho involves ranking the values of the two variables under consideration for each person in the sample. Essentially, a plus sign means that the differences in ranking between the two variables matched exactly, whereas a negative sign would mean that the differences in the rankings were the exact opposite (for example, a person ranked highest on the one variable and the lowest on the other, and the person who ranked the second highest on the first variable was the second lowest on the second, etc.).

By the time we move up to interval/ratio levels of measurement, however, the measures of association are much clearer. The most common measure of association for interval/ratio levels of measurement is *Pearson's r*, which, like Spearman's rho, also ranges from 0 to ± 1 where 0 indicates absolutely no relationship and 1 indicates a perfect relationship. However, unlike Spearman's rho, the positive and negative signs of Pearson's r have inherent meaning. A positive sign means that as the values of one variable increase, so do the values of the second value (or as the values of one variable decrease, the values of the other variable decrease as well). In other words, a positive relationship means that the values of the two variables are moving together—they are either both increasing or both decreasing. A negative sign, on the other hand, indicates that as the values of one value increase, the values of the second value *decrease* (and vice versa), or that the two variables are moving in opposite directions.

In summary, measures of association tell a researcher how strongly two variables are related. They are most effectively used in conjunction with inferential statistics. If the researcher has used a probability sampling technique, inferential statistics tell a researcher whether any relationship between variables found in a sample is also likely to apply in the population. If inferential statistics suggest that a relationship between two variables does exist in the population, measures of association will tell the researcher how strong that relationship in the population is.

However, even if a researcher does *not* select a probability sample, measures of association can be useful on their own to tell the researcher the strength of relationship between two variables *in a sample*. In other words, measures of associations themselves make no inferences between a sample and a population. They just describe the strength of association between two variables in the sample—regardless of how that sample was selected. However, *if* the researcher did a probability sample and *if* inferential statistics suggest that any relationship found between two variables in the sample holds for the population, *then* a researcher can infer that the strength of association found in the sample will also hold in the population.

A summary of these common univariate and bivariate statistics appears in Figure 12.8.

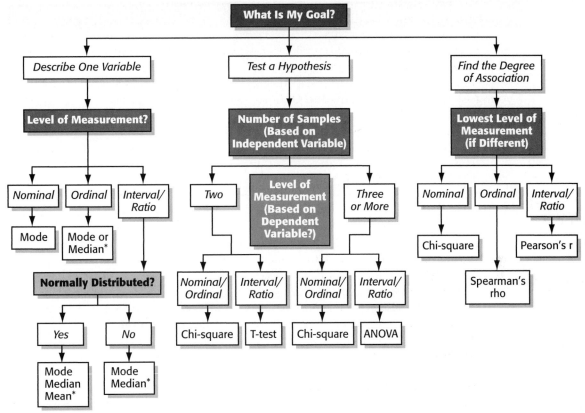

* This is generally the preferred statistic.

Figure 12.8 Flowchart for Selective Statistical Calculations

■ Multivariate Analysis

Very few social processes can be explained with one independent and one dependent variable. Researchers frequently use many independent variables to examine any particular dependent variable, and any time a researcher moves beyond a two-variable comparison, social scientists call that a **multivariate statistic.** Sometimes these additional variables are what researchers refer to as **control variables**, which means that they are additional variables that researchers think will affect the dependent variable. Therefore, researchers want to estimate the effect of the independent variable in light of or in addition to (in other words, *controlling for*) these other variables. Researchers can "control for" any number of variables, but I will just illustrate some of the basic issues of multivariate analysis by discussing how to control for only a third variable. In other words, I will simultaneously examine the effect of three variables: my independent variable, my dependent variable, and one control variable.

Multivariate analysis can be done with any level of measurement, but I will illustrate the issue here with variables measured at the nominal and low-level ordinal levels (meaning there are few answer categories). A thorough discussion of the accompanying statistics

TABLE 12.14 Voting Behavior by Income

Voting	Income		Total
	$60,000 and Under	Over $60,001	
Voted	55.1% (368)	60.9% (654)	1022
Did Not Vote	44.9% (300)	39.1% (527)	827
Total	668	1181	1849

for multivariate analysis is, as you have probably guessed by now, more appropriate for a statistics class. However, even with a simple tabular example, I can illustrate many points behind multivariate analysis. Let's suppose I wanted to examine the effect of income on voting, but I thought that a person's gender might also affect income. Table 12.14 shows the bivariate findings between income and voting.

Now let me introduce our control variable: gender. Let's suppose that I calculated the results shown in Table 12.15. What types of conclusions can we make from these two tables? Well, according to Table 12.14, there does not appear to be a strong difference in voting by income. The table suggests that people from higher incomes are slightly more likely to vote (60.9 percent) than are people from lower incomes (55.1 percent). However, if we look at Table 12.15, we see that the relationship between income and voting only holds for women. In other words, we see that (1) women are more likely to vote than are men regardless of income (they have the highest percent for having voted); (2) women who earn more money are more likely to vote (76.7 percent) than men who earn more money (31.0 percent); and (3) among men, men who earn *less* money are more likely to vote (47.0 percent) than are men who earn more money (31.0 percent). Thus, it appears that gender is an important variable to consider when examining the effects of income on

TABLE 12.15 Voting Behavior by Income Controlling for Gender

Voting	Men		Women		Total
	$60,000 and Under	Over $60,001	$60,000 and Under	Over $60,001	
Voted	47.0% (142)	31.0% (180)	65.6% (240)	76.7% (460)	1022
Did Not Vote	53.0% (160)	69.0% (401)	34.4% (126)	23.3% (140)	827
Total	302	581	366	600	1849

voting, since different patterns emerge when considering these three variables simultaneously as opposed to just considering the original bivariate relationship between income and voting.

Control variables are useful because they can further explain, or *elaborate*, the relationship between two variables. Because of this, comparison of tables that include controlling variables are sometimes called *elaboration tables*. Remember in Chapter 3 we discussed rival casual factors? I dubbed one type of rival casual factors "topical rival causal factors." These are factors that, through expertise, training, and a thorough reading of the literature, researchers suspect might influence the dependent variable. Therefore, the researchers include these measures in their research design so they can statistically *control* for them later. Well, now it's "later." There are a number of ways that the introduction of a third variable can shed light on the originally observed bivariate relationship. I will discuss three possible results of the introduction of a third variable, and these are presented in Figure 12.9.

The first possibility is that the introduction of a third variable will show that the relationship observed in the original bivariate relationship was *spurious*. This means that once the control variable is introduced, the original relationship the researcher noticed between the independent and dependent variables disappears or is seriously weakened. We can statistically test this, but that is not appropriate here. Even so, Figure 12.9 visually shows what may happen in such an instance. The original bivariate relationship, which is between social class (measured as "middle class" and "working class" for simplicity) and delinquency (measured as "delinquent" and "not delinquent"), is the table that appears at the top of the figure. If the relationship between these two measures was spurious, once the control variable, parental marital status, is added, the two subtables that result (since the control variable here has two values, married and not married, there is a separate table for each) will show no or little relationship. The first subtable shows a slight variation (45 percent and 55 percent in the first column, 55 percent and 45 percent in the second column), which is really no variation at all; and the second subtable (all 50 percents) shows no variation. Either of these or some similar variation will illustrate a spurious relationship. In this instance, the real relationship is between parental marital status and delinquency, and social class may have no effect.

The introduction of a control variable might also specify under what conditions the original bivariate relationship holds (hence, called *specification*), which is what is presented in the second outcome. We see this in the second set of bivariate relationships. When I introduced parental marital status as the control variable, we see that the original relationship between social class and delinquency holds *only* for those whose parents are *not* married. Sixty-five percent of the working-class juveniles whose parents were not married were delinquent compared to only 35 percent of the middle-class children with nonmarried parents. However, for those with married parents, we see that there is now *no* relationship between social class and delinquency. This means that the control variable of parental marital status specifies for what condition (here, for *what parental status*) the relationship between delinquency and social class applies. In this instance, both the independent and control variables have important effects on the dependent variable and both should be included in the analysis.

The third possible outcome is that the control variable will not add any information to the original bivariate relationship and will simply replicate it; this is called *replication*. In this situation, we see that the control variable of parental marital status has *no* real affect

Spurious Relationship: Original bivariate relationship disappears.

	Working Class	Middle Class		Married			Not Married	
				Working Class	Middle Class		Working Class	Middle Class
Delinquent	75	25	Delinquent	45	55	Delinquent	50	50
Not Delinquent	25	75	Not Delinquent	55	45	Not Delinquent	50	50

Specification: One table shows a stronger relationship than the other, thereby specifying under what conditions the original bivariate relationship holds. Here, the relationship between social class and delinquency is stronger for those who parents are not married.

	Working Class	Middle Class		Married			Not Married	
				Working Class	Middle Class		Working Class	Middle Class
Delinquent	75	25	Delinquent	55	50	Delinquent	65	35
Not Delinquent	25	75	Not Delinquent	45	50	Not Delinquent	35	65

Replication: Addition of a control variable does not really change or affect the original bivariate relationship.

	Working Class	Middle Class		Married			Not Married	
				Working Class	Middle Class		Working Class	Middle Class
Delinquent	75	25	Delinquent	74	30	Delinquent	75	20
Not Delinquent	25	75	Not Delinquent	26	70	Not Delinquent	25	80

Figure 12.9 Elaboration Tables: The Relationship between Social Class and Juvenile Delinquency Controlling for Parental Marital Status

on the bivariate relationship between social class and delinquency, therefore we would omit it from the analysis. It is not necessary.

Multivariate analysis, then, can help the researcher establish causality by statistically addressing topical rival causal factors. Multivariate analysis can also help the researcher obtain a better, fuller, more complete idea of what affects the dependent variable. Therefore, whenever possible, multivariate analyses should be used. There are both inferential statistical tests and measures of association that help the researcher statistically determine the role of variables other than the main independent variable of interest, as well as whether any observed relationships in the sample are likely to occur in the population (if the researcher did a probability sample).

Tables and graphs are ways researchers summarize their data for others to see. Sometimes, for example, when presenting evaluation findings to the general public, visuals can be an easier means of highlighting research findings than lengthy verbal explanations. After all, many of us have been socialized to dread the drone of someone reading numbers. As soon as we hear numbers rattling off someone's tongue, we tune out and ignore large hunks of that person's presentation. On the other hand, we've also become a very visual society. We spend hours in front of the television and computers, and many college professors now even use PowerPoint presentations to convey class material. So it's unsurprising that researchers recognize that visually summarizing research findings in tables and graphs may be a good way of conveying them to others, with the safety net of an accompanying written explanation for those who are less confident that they will read the tables or graphs accurately.

However, even with this recognition, students frequently admit to me that although they will look at graphs, they ignore tables when they see them in written reports because they're afraid that the tables will confuse them. However, with a little bit of practice, reading tables is not necessarily confusing and can actually save someone a lot of time. Being a skilled table reader also helps ensure that a person reading a research report will not be swayed by any hidden agenda or misinterpretation on behalf of the researcher—assuming, of course, that the reader is not making any mistakes either. So I'm going to present a fairly detailed explanation of how to read a table, followed by a briefer explanation of how to read some common types of graphs. By knowing how to read a table, you will, by default, have an idea of how to construct a table, because you will understand its basic components.

■ Table Construction and Reading

Cohabitation between romantic partners is relatively common today, yet despite its relatively high visibility, the act of cohabitation is still publicly viewed as a "nontraditional" behavior. Traditionally, couples wait until they are married before they establish a household together. Because of the cultural lag between cohabiting practices and the social view of cohabitation, Mitchell (2001, **AN 5616449**) decided to explore ethnocultural differences in views of cohabiting practices among Canadian couples. To gather her data, Mitchell used the Culture and Coresidence Study (1999–2000), which involves in-depth phone interviews. The study used a random sample of 1,907 young adults who identified themselves as being British, Chinese, Indo, or southern European origin and who were living in the Greater Vancouver Regional District (GVRD). The findings for Mitchell's study are presented in Table 12.16 and I'll use this table to illustrate the characteristics of a good table.

The first point to note in a table is the table's title. A good title will include a table number, in the event of more than one table being in the report, and it will tell the reader exactly what the researchers are studying. If the table is a bivariate comparison, it is conventional for the researcher to put the dependent variable first in the table title, followed by the independent variable. For example, a table title that reads "Table 1: Fear of Crime by Sex" would tell the reader that the dependent variable is fear of crime and the independent variable is sex. In Mitchell's example, the title tells us that the dependent variable is attitude toward cohabitation (since it appears first) and the independent variable is ethnocultural identity (since it appears second).

TABLE 12.16 Mitchell's Cohabitation Study

Table 1: Cross-Tabulation of Attitude toward Cohabitation by Ethnocultural Identity

Acceptability of Cohabitation	Ethnocultural Identity				
	British	Chinese	Indo	S. European	Total
Very acceptable	253 (64.7%)	89 (19.8%)	87 (17.9%)	157 (39.0%)	586 (33.9%)
Somewhat acceptable	100 (25.6%)	261 (58.0%)	98 (20.2%)	155 (38.5%)	614 (35.5%)
Somewhat unacceptable	17 (4.3%)	67 (14.9%)	26 (5.4%)	42 (10.4%)	152 (8.8%)
Very unacceptable	21 (5.4%)	33 (7.3%)	274 (56.5%)	49 (12.2%)	377 (21.8%)
Total	391 (100.0%)	450 (100.0%)	485 (100.0%)	403 (100.0%)	1.729 (100.0%)

Likelihood ratio $X^2 = 637.95$ (9 df), $p < 0.001$.

Source: Barbara A. Mitchell, "Ethnocultural Reproduction and Attitudes towards Cohabitating Relationships," Canadian Review of Sociology & Anthropology, 38 (4) (2001): 391–414. Reprinted by permission of The Canadian Sociology and Anthropology Association.

Second, tables also have each column and row subtitled, as well as the label of each category or value of the corresponding variable. In Mitchell's example, the columns, which read down, are subheaded as "Ethnocultural Identity" and the values of it are British, Chinese, Indo, and S. European. This table also illustrates another point: The independent variable generally reads down the column, and the dependent variable reads across the rows.

Third, tables should also include sample sizes and column and row marginals. If you remember, the column and row marginals report the total observations for each column and row value. The sample size may be included in the title, a footnote, or a tally at the lower right-hand cell of the table. In Mitchell's table, the sample size is 1,729 people and you can see that even without reading the body of the paper by looking in the lower right-hand side of the table.

Fourth, it is conventional for all percentages to be calculated with respect to the column total. A hint that lets you know that Mitchell did this is that the column percent totals all equal 100 percent. This means that the cell percentages were all calculated with respect to the column total that appears at the bottom of the column of the specific cell. Therefore, when we interpret this table, we say that 64.7 percent (calculated by dividing 253 by 391) of respondents who were British felt that cohabitation was "very acceptable." You may be tempted to use the total sample size as the denominator for calculating percents. Although it's not the convention in the social sciences, doing so is not incorrect *so long as* you alter your interpretation of the findings accordingly.

For example, if I use the total number of British respondents as the denominator for the first cell, then my resulting percent is *of the British respondents*. However, if I use the sample size of 1,729, then I have to alter my interpretation as follows: "14.6 percent *of my sample* is British and finds cohabitation to be 'very acceptable.' " Because I used the total sample size, my resulting percent has to be referenced by the values of *both* the independent and dependent variables simultaneously. Instead of saying, "64.7 percent of the British respondents find cohabitation to be very acceptable," I now need to say, "14.6 percent of my respondents are British and find cohabitation to be very acceptable." This is not incorrect, but it is not as intuitive for comparing group attitudes, which is the goal of the research. In other words, it is more direct to be able to say, "64.7 percent of the British respondents find cohabitation to be very acceptable, compared to 19.8 percent of the Chinese respondents." If I did the calculations with respect to the sample size instead of the relevant column size, I would have to say, "14.6 percent of my sample is British and has very favorable attitudes about cohabiting, whereas 5.1 percent of my sample is Chinese and feels the same." I am not clear in the second interpretation whether the difference is because of the different relative number of Chinese people or whether it's because of different views of cohabitation. The meaning of the latter interpretation is less clear and direct.

Fifth, if data are borrowed and reproduced from another source, such as the U.S. Census, for example, then the table also needs a footnote documenting the data source. Here, the source of the data is the actual survey that Mitchell described in the methods section of her research; therefore, she does not need to further cite it in the table itself. I, on the other hand, am using Mitchell's table in this book to illustrate how to read tables. Mitchell's table is not my own, therefore, I need to cite her work.

Last, if the table involves any inferential statistics, some notation of where statistically significant findings were present, and at what probability level of error, is important. Mitchell followed a common format of providing the statistical information at the bottom of the table in the form of the observed value of the statistic (here, chi-square, or X^2), the degrees of freedom (since it's relevant to the chi-square statistic), and the probability of error (here, less than .001, which means that she is 99.9% sure that the patterns found in the sample also apply to the population).

When tables include multiple variables, researchers will frequently use letters or asterisks to indicate statistically significant findings. For example, Hutton and Towse (2001, **AN 5202099**) presented a correlation matrix of reasoning ability, reading, and numerical skills in relation to short-term memory and working memory for a sample of 58 children ages 8 to 11. This matrix appears in Table 12.17. If you read the footnotes that appear under the table, you will notice that any correlation that has two asterisks beside it is statistically significant at the .01 level (which means that the probability of the findings being due to random chance are less than 1 percent) and any findings that have one asterisk have a probability of error level of 5 percent.

Therefore, if one knows how to read a table, one can learn, at a glance, (1) what the independent and dependent variables are, if that is relevant; (2) what the association between variables is (by looking at percents as in the first example and correlation values as in the second example); (3) what the sample size is; and (4) if inferential statistical information is presented (and not all tables have or need this), then one can easily see what relationships produced statistically significant findings.

TABLE 12.17 Hutton and Towse's Correlation Matrix

TABLE 3: Bivariate correlations between ability measures and memory tasks for all children

	Matrices	Reading	Number	STMF	STMB	STMASF	STMASB	WMF	WMB	TIME	AGE
Matrices		.52**	.62**	.43**	.53**	.55**	.52**	.53**	.55**	−.75**	.63**
Reading	.30**		.67**	.51**	.46**	.57**	.39**	.59**	.58**	−.56**	.50**
Number	.33*	.52**		.44**	.69**	.59**	.55**	.52**	.58**	−.71**	.68**
STMF	.36*	.45**	.38**		.42**	.29*	.34*	.76**	.47**	−.41**	.26*
STMB	.32*	.28*	.55**	.35*		.44**	.44**	.53**	.56**	−.45**	.50**
STMASF	.38**	.44**	.43**	.20ns	.27*		.65**	.37**	.30*	−.58**	.46**
STMASB	.34*	.21ns	.38**	.25ns	.28*	.54**		.43**	.48**	−.58**	.45**
WMF	.35*	.48**	.33*	.74**	.40**	.21ns	.28*		.71**	−.51**	.44**
WMB	.31*	.43**	.34*	.41**	.40**	.07ns	.31*	.62**		−.60**	.55**
TIME	−.57**	−.36**	−.49**	−.33*	−.20ns	−.42**	−.43**	−.33*	−.38**		−.65**

($n = 52$)

** Correlation is significant at the .01 level (2-tailed).

* Correlation is significant at the .05 level (2-tailed).

Type in italics represents correlation coefficients with age partialled.

Source: Una M. Z. Hutton and John N. Towse, "Short-Term Working Memory and Working Memory as Indices of Children's Cognitive Skills," *Memory, 9* (4–6) (2001): 383–394, by kind permission of Psychology Press, www.psypress.co.uk/journals.asp, 2006.

■ Graphs

Most computer programs are equipped to construct graphs with minimal effort on your part. I will discuss the three most common types of graphs here: the bar graph, the pie chart, and the line chart. As with tables, each graph needs a title and a graph number (if there is more than one graph); however, since graphs usually are univariate, there is no need to worry about the order of variable presentation (since univariate means that the graph only describes one variable).

Bar graph

Bar graphs are common graph forms in which the rectangle, or bar, height usually represents quantity or amount. Bar graphs are pretty easy to construct and to read. There are a few guidelines to keep in mind, however, when constructing bar graphs. First, the values of a variable are usually arranged along the horizontal axis, and the amounts, such as frequencies, ratings, and percents, are plotted along the vertical axis. Second, the horizontal

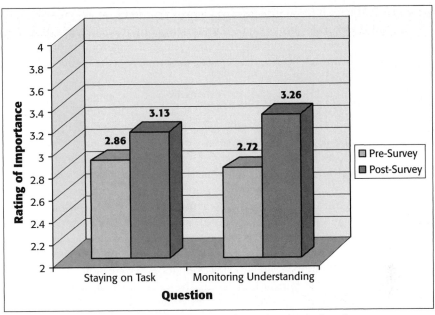

FIG. 5. Dimensions of collaboration students rated more important after pilot.

Figure 12.10 Yarnall and Colleagues' Graph

Source: Louise Yarnall, William R. Penuel, Jason Ravitz, Grahame Murray, and Barbara Means, "Portable Assessment Authoring: Using Handheld Technology to Assess Collaborative Inquiry," *Education, Communication & Information, 3* (1) (2003): 21. Reprinted by permission of Taylor & Francis Ltd. www.tandf.co.uk/journals.

and vertical axes should be labeled so someone reading the graph can determine what it is measuring at a glance. Furthermore, the values at each tic mark should be labeled as well. Tic marks are the little lines on the vertical or horizontal axis that tell the reader when another increment has started. For example, Yarnall, Penuel, Ravitz, Murray, Means, and Broom (2003, **AN 9756697**) did a pilot study to determine whether handheld computers helped measure the amount of learning students did in group work. These researchers tested a prototype software on student and teacher learning experiences and created a graph of one of their findings, which appears as Figure 12.10.

This bar graph actually addresses two questions: Do the students believe that they were able to stay on task while using the handheld computers and did they achieve a shared understanding (monitoring understanding)? Each of these questions is labeled on the horizontal axis, and the dependent variable, which is the mean rating score, is on the vertical axis. The mean rating score starts at 2 and increases by 0.2 for each tic. This is what I mean by labeling the values of the tics: the tics start at a value of 2 and proceed to 2.2, 2.4, 2.6, and so on, up to 4.0. The discussion of tics also illustrates an important third point—namely, that the starting point of measuring a variable that is numerical needs to be addressed. If these researchers did not let me know that their ratings started at 2, I would have probably assumed that they started at 0, which may have given me an entirely different interpretation of the ratings (2 being much higher than 0).

A fourth feature is to include a legend that identifies all variables and/or variable values in a graph. For example, in Yarnall and colleagues' graph, by looking at the labels on the X (horizontal) axis, you can see that there are two variables presented: "Staying on Task" and "Monitoring Understanding." By reading the legend on the right-hand side of the graph, you can see that the ratings of importance (dependent variable, Y axis) for "Staying on Task" varies between the presurvey (the lighter bar, as indicated in the legend) the and postsurvey (the darker bar). In this instance, the legend provides the reader with information as to what two groups are being compared for analysis.

A few final points are that it is helpful to extend the grid lines to the back of the bar graph, like Yarnall and colleagues did, and to actually include the dependent variable value that is depicted by the top of the bar. This latter point is especially relevant when reading three-dimensional bar graphs. Although three-dimensional bar graphs are definitely prettier than flatter, more traditional two-dimensional graphs, they can be difficult to interpret. For example, someone who is not familiar with reading bar graphs may be tempted to read the front-most line of the bar, which in the case of the second bar from the left would read about 2.95 (this is an estimate), which is different than the 3.13 that is depicted by the back line and noted by the researchers. Because bar reading may lead to incorrect data interpretations, three-dimensional bar graphs are not the most accurate from a research interpretation viewpoint. However, since they are more visually appealing and have almost become the standard, including the value of the dependent variable depicted so people correctly interpret your data is important. To summarize, to construct bar graphs:

1. Arrange variable values along the horizontal (X) axis and counts/frequencies/ratings along the vertical (Y) axis.
2. Label the horizontal and vertical axes.
3. Label the value of each tic mark, paying particular attention to labeling the values at which your tics start (such as "2" in Figure 12.10).
4. Extend the grid lines to the back of the bar graph.
5. Include a legend if more than one variable is being simultaneously examined.
6. If using a three-dimensional graph, include the value of each bar somewhere on the graph so it is easily evident to whoever is reading the graph.

Pie Chart

Probably the simplest type of graph, pie charts are circles (pies) whose pieces represent proportions or some variable or phenomena and total 100 percent. To construct a pie chart, make sure that each wedge, or piece of the pie, is labeled. This can be done by using different colored or patterned slices and a legend that tells the reader what each slice is by its color or pattern, or it can involve putting a label directly on the pie slice. Figure 12.11 is a general example of a pie chart.

The proportion or percent of the pie that each slice represents should also be included on the actual pie chart. Most people can't tell the difference visually between 26 percent and 30 percent and the wedges themselves just give a quick visual of which slice is more and less than others. As with bar graphs, three-dimensional pie charts are also popular, although making a pie chart three dimensional does not pose the interpretation challenges that a three-dimensional bar graph might. On the other hand, separating, or what is commonly called "exploding," the pie wedges is not a preferred method of presentation because if the wedges are not next to each other, it can be hard to interpret their relation to each other, especially if some wedges represent very small proportions (e.g., under 15%). To summarize:

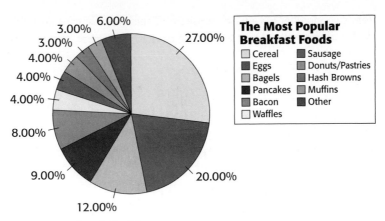

Figure 12.11 Sample Pie Chart

Source: Data from "What's for Breakfast, America?" *Scholastic News, 65* (14) (January 17, 2003). (**AN 9031952**). Chart created by author.

1. Label each wedge of the pie (preferably using a legend).
2. Label the proportion or percent of the pie that each slice represents.
3. Do not "explode" or separate the sections of the pie.

Line chart

Line charts are also a common and useful means of visually summarizing the data. Like a bar graph, line charts involve two axes, the X is the horizontal axis and the Y is the vertical axis. Each point on the graph shows the relationship between X and Y for a specific case. For example, Kaminski and Marvel (2002, **AN 7115058**) created a time-series graph, a specific type of line graph where the independent variable is a unit of time (e.g., a year, a month, etc.) depicting the rate of police homicides from the late 1800s to the late 1900s. This graph appears in Figure 12.12.

This graph very quickly alerts the reader that there were two periods in the past 100 years or so where police homicide rates were exceptionally high, the periods from 1918 to 1934 and from 1969 to 1981. Graphs like this can be very informative in suggesting history effects. Why might police homicide be high during these times? Well, although the graph is not sufficient evidence to create a concrete causal explanation, we do know by looking at those dates that from 1918 to 1934 was roughly the period of prohibition (and related gangster activity) and that the years from 1969 to 1981 were the beginning of the crack epidemic. Could there be a relation? Possibly, but further analysis would need to be done. However, the graph is a very strong and easy-to-read mechanism that would point us in the direction of looking for historical influences when explaining police homicide.

Line graphs can also suggest the strength of relationship between two variables. The steeper the line, the stronger the relationship; the flatter the line, the weaker the relationship. The more curvy the line, like we see in Kaminski and Marvel's research, the less linear the relationship. If the line makes a bell-shaped curve, we know that the data are normally distributed. Hence, line graphs can be very informative graphs that are relatively easy to construct.

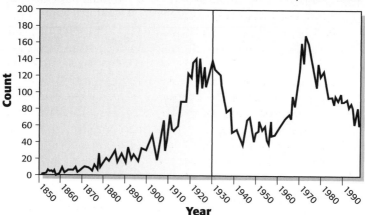

Figure 1: Number of Law Enforcement Officers Murdered, 1850–1998

Pre-1850 data are not shown as few police were killed from 1794–1849.
The years 1930–98 represent the period of the time-series analysis.

Figure 12.12 Kaminiski and Marvel's Data on Police Homicide

Source: Robert J. Kaminski and Thomas B. Marvel, "A Comparison of Changes in Police and General Homicides: 1930–1998," *Criminology, 40* (1) (2002). Reprinted with permission from the American Sociology of Criminology.

As I said, the X axis is labeled in some unit (here, it is time) and the Y axis is the count or percent. The value for each case is charted as a dot on the graph and then the dots are connected. Therefore, like the bar chart, it is important to make sure that the values of the X and Y axes are clearly marked and to include a legend if more than one line appears on the chart at a time. However, background grid lines are not really necessary in line charts because the purpose of a line chart is not necessarily to identify the value of a specific data point, but instead to look at the relationship across values, as depicted by the line. Since the shape of the line is the matter of concern, grid marks indicating specific point values are less important here than with bar graphs, which aim to provide estimates for specific points. Also, three-dimensional line graphs are possible, but they are not commonly used. To summarize, in order to construct a line graph:

1. Arrange variable values along the horizontal (X) axis and counts/frequencies/ratings along the vertical (Y) axis.
2. Label the horizontal and vertical axes.
3. Label the value of each tic mark, paying particular attention to labeling the values at which your tics start (such as "2" in Figure 12.10).
4. Include a legend if more than one variable is being simultaneously examined.
5. Connect the various data points, in order from left to right, to form a continuous line.

Cautions When Using Statistics

We have all heard the skeptical claim that people can "lie with statistics." Is it true? Can people get statistics to say anything that they want? The answer is yes and no. Statistics themselves don't lie per se, but if people use them incorrectly or if they hide information (for example, how a question was worded or how the sample was selected), then others may make incorrect assumptions—and therefore conclusions. What I will discuss here are some cautions and caveats when dealing with statistics.

The first issue to watch, both when doing your own statistics and when reading the statistics of others, is to make sure that the statistical tests are appropriate for the nature of the data. For example, a computer is stupid and most programs will run any statistic you ask of it. Therefore, if I ask SPSS (the Statistical Package for the Social Sciences, which is a common statistics package used among social researchers) to calculate a mean for the variable gender, the computer will happily do so. However, that mean will be essentially useless because gender is a nominal level of measurement and means are only appropriate for interval/ratio levels of measurement. Other data concerns include whether the data are normally distributed (which is an assumption behind some inferential statistics), whether the interpretations support the units of analysis (e.g., avoiding the ecological fallacy), whether the sample has been randomly selected, and how the question analyzed was worded.

A second caution is to always be wary of the relationship between statistical and substantive significance and to make sure that researchers do not ignore one of these and, consequently, overstate their findings. Remember, just because a relationship may be statistically significant, which means that it is likely to occur in the population if the sample was randomly selected (and should not even have been calculated if the sample was not), does not mean that the degree of association between the two variables is sufficiently large to be substantively significant. Researchers eager to find support for their hypotheses may intentionally or unintentionally overstate the importance of statistical significance regardless of substantive significance. Be wary of this.

A third issue is one that I did not address earlier but is important nonetheless. This is the issue of what researchers call Type I and Type II errors. **Type I errors** occur when researchers state that a relationship exists when, in fact, one does not. In other words, a researcher may conclude, based on a probability of error of .05 or 5 percent, that a relationship between two variables exists. In essence, the researcher is saying that he or she is 95 percent confident that the observed relationship exists in the real world. Type I error occurs when, contrary to the researcher's 95 percent confidence, the relationship does not hold. In other words, the 5 percent chance of error, in this particular instance, bore out.

We can use the courtroom as good analogy. In a court of law, a jury has to listen to evidence (hear the data) about a case and try to make conclusions (results) about what really happened. Since the jury members were not present at the crime, they will never have complete information as to what occurred (much like a researcher cannot study a complete population). They need to weigh the available evidence (the data), which is likely to have gaps and contradictions (no study is 100 percent perfect) to arrive at their best approximation of what actually occurred the night of the crime (results). A Type I error is akin to a jury thinking that an individual is guilty and convicting this person of the crime (a relationship between the individual and the crime exists) when, in fact, the individual is innocent (the individual did not commit the crime, hence there is no relationship). **Type II errors** are the opposite and occur when a researcher says that there is not a relationship when, in fact, there is. Going back to our jury analogy, a "Type II" error would occur when the jury found a person to be innocent (no relationship) even when that person really did commit the crime (a relationship).

You may be thoroughly confused by this, and that's not surprising. After all, we just read an entire book that discusses how to conduct a research design as accurately as possible and how to do statistical analyses of our data. Now I tell you that there is a risk of making the wrong conclusion regardless of all this, and you are probably wondering how you would even suspect when such an event occurred. You may be thinking "Well, maybe a 5 percent error, suggesting a 95 percent confidence, in my findings is actually too *low*. Maybe I should increase my confidence level to 99.99 percent and, correspondingly, accept only 0.01 percent error. That way, the chance that I'll commit Type I error, saying that there is a relationship when there really isn't, is only 1 in 10,000." But doing so actually increases your risk of Type II error—falsely saying that there is no relationship when in fact one may exist. Decreasing the error probability would likely do the opposite—decrease your chance of committing Type II error, while increasing your chance of committing a Type I error.

So what do you do? Your best line of defense is to make sure that you only do inferential tests on random samples, because, to some degree, these tests take into account sampling errors for random samples, but not for other types (Neuman, 1997). Besides that, relying on the conventional 95 percent as the base level of statistical significance (a probability of error, or alpha level, of .05) and 99 percent as the "bonus round" insulates you to some degree, since the scientific community has decided that the 95 percent threshold is the best statistical balance between Type I and Type II errors. However, using this threshold does not eliminate your risk.

The final piece of advice regarding this issue is to be wary of findings that are completely or mostly inconsistent with that of the rest of the literature, unless you can think of a sound methodological or theoretical reason for the noticeable difference. In other words, if your research regarding the success of treatment courts in helping drug addicts fight their addiction shows that treatment courts have very little success when the majority of the rest of the literature suggests the opposite, then you need to consider why your findings are so different. Is your study population drastically different from those in the rest of the literature (e.g., the other studies include drug addictions that are comparatively less difficult to break, such as marijuana and alcohol, whereas most of your sample is addicted to heroin)? Then perhaps you are "on to" a truly informative difference. However, if you cannot find any methodological (e.g., sample characteristics, drug court characteristics) or theoretical differences, then concluding that drug courts have no impact on helping addicts end their addiction puts you at risk of making a Type II error. When this occurs, simply come clean (no pun intended!). In the write-up of your results and discussion sections of the paper, note that a Type II error may be possible and why. This lets the reader decide how much weight to give to your findings.

The issues I have mentioned are by no means the only cautions to have when analyzing data; however, they are three of the most common. In fact, many of the comments I have made throughout this chapter serve researchers well not only when doing their own data analysis but also when reading the data analysis of others, as presented in the results section of published research.

Evaluating Written Research: Quantitative Results and Discussion Sections

The results section in quantitative research differs from that of qualitative research because the researchers focus on statistical or numerical data. That means that the reader is likely to be evaluating material found in tables or graphs in addition to the researchers' written interpretation. The following guidelines will help you.

1. **Is the results section a cohesive essay with the important findings highlighted?**

Even though researchers are likely to include graphs and/or tables in the results section, they should also include a written interpretation of those results in a cohesive essay form. The essay should not necessarily report on *all* of the findings, but it should highlight the findings that are the most relevant to the research hypotheses or goals.

2. **In the essay, does the researcher tie the results to the research hypotheses or goals stated in the introduction?**

The results section is where the researcher is finally able to get some answers. However, it helps the reader and the researcher if the researcher reminds us of what those questions and hypotheses were and how they relate to the data. Therefore, in the results section, the researcher needs to specifically connect the results to the original intent of the research. In the case of hypotheses, this involves specifically stating whether hypotheses were supported by the data. It is *not*, however, the place to discuss why results were what they were. That is reserved for the Discussion section. In the results section, a researcher should relate only the concrete findings to the research purposes or hypotheses.

3. **If there are tables or graphs, are they clearly presented?**

Tables and graphs are only going to be a useful summary if they are easy to read. Therefore, the techniques for table and graph construction that I mentioned earlier apply here. Are the titles of the tables informative? If it is a bivariate table, does the dependent variable come first in the title? Are percentages calculated with respect to the column marginals? If not, are they correctly interpreted in the results essay? Are the graphs easy to read? Are the relevant percents or other statistics noted in the graph?

Researchers do not need to explain the statistical tests in the table (or the text for that matter); therefore, if you do not know what a linear regression is and how to interpret one, that is not the researcher's fault. Therefore, your unfamiliarity with a statistic alone or how to read a statistical table is *not* an indicator of a poorly presented table. So how can you evaluate statistical tables that summarize statistics that are unfamiliar to you? You can't. The assumption in reading tables is that readers have some background knowledge enabling them to interpret the information present. Such is not the place for a researcher to provide a mini-tutorial on how to read this type of information. So if you encounter a table that has statistics you do not know how to interpret, the best course of action is to (1) find someone who *can* interpret that table or (2) withhold judgment about the correctness of the researcher's interpretation.

4. **Does the researcher present any descriptive statistics?**

Even if the goal of the research is to test hypotheses, researchers should present at least some descriptive statistics about the demographics of their sample. However, it is also useful, and a general strength, if researchers present the descriptive statistics for any variables that they will be using in inferential statistics. For example, if a researcher is conducting a pre- and posttest change in a variable, it is useful to present what those pre- and posttest scores were in addition to the results of any inferential statistics. Just presenting the percentage of change, without any reference to what the scores actually were, is poor style.

For example, a professor decides to offer an additional review session for the exam during the weekend. A 10 percent change in the average exam grades may be a lot more if a pretest score was 70 and a posttest score was 80 (a rough difference between a C- and a B-)

than if the pretest score was 40 and the posttest score was 50 (both failing grades, regardless of the review session).

5. Are the statistics appropriate for the level of measurement?

As I mentioned earlier, statistics can be run on any set of numbers; however, that does not mean that the numbers are the *right* numbers for the statistic. You can write any answer choices you want on a multiple-choice exam, but that does not mean that the answers you write are the *correct* ones. The reader serves as a double-check, so to speak, to make sure that the researcher is not making any careless (or less ethically, intentional) mistakes, especially so his or her hypothesis is supported. Readers, then, have the obligation to assess whether the researcher's choice of statistics is appropriate for the data—at least providing, as I implied in Point 3, that the reader has knowledge about the types of statistical tests used. If the reader agrees that the statistical choices are appropriate, all is well and good (at least with regard to this evaluation point). If not, that should lead the reader to question the merit of the research.

6. Are the conclusions the researcher draws appropriate for the statistical information?

Sometimes a researcher's hope to achieve a specific outcome (even researchers are happier with statistically significant findings as opposed to nonsignificant findings) may distort that researcher's interpretation of the data. For example, researchers may treat ambiguous findings as unambiguous, especially in the direction of the research hypotheses. Researchers may focus only on aspects of the findings that support their hypotheses and downplay or ignore those that do not. Or researchers may just focus on the statistical significance of findings, especially if they favor the research goal, and downplay any lack of substantive significance. Remember, one of the hallmarks about science as a means of gathering information is its objectivity, but science is done by people who are not always objective despite their best intentions. It is the role of the reader to be able to identify when objectivity has been violated.

7. In the discussion section, does the researcher briefly summarize the research purposes, methodologies, and key findings (in a nonstatistical manner)?

The results section is where rest of the research process "comes together." Essentially, it is a summary of what the research topic was, why the researcher was interested, what the hypotheses/purposes were, and what we learned. Since the results section contains all of the statistical data, it should not be repeated here. The discussion is simply a written, nonstatistical recap of the key findings. In fact, all of the findings discussed in the results section do not need to be individually mentioned here, either—just the key ones.

8. Does the researcher acknowledge any methodological or statistical weaknesses?

Students frequently get to the end of a research report, read the researcher's self-identified limitations, and then immediately discount the research as "flawed," "weak," or "useless." They figure that if researchers can spot problems, then there's probably even more problems that they have not spotted, and that the research, as a result, is seriously flawed.

This is not necessarily true. Perhaps more than anyone else, researchers realize the difference between ideal and "real" research. We try for the best conceptualizations, sample selections, survey questions, experimental designs, and so on, however, since we are human and since we do not have control over our social environment in most cases, there are bound to be limitations. No one can study *all* relevant people. We could always extend our study longitudinally if we had more money, but we frequently are strapped for funding. No matter how many assurances of confidentiality or anonymity, some people may provide "bogus" answers on a survey simply because they either don't believe the researcher or they want to "mess" with him or her. No research is, or ever was, perfect. But because of the steps that researchers take, if the research is done well, scientific research, even with its potential flaws, *still* is likely to produce more accurate and reliable information about our social world than the more common avenues of knowledge such as personal experience and tradition that I discussed at the beginning of this book.

Therefore, it is actually a characteristic of a *conscientious* researcher if the researcher identifies the limitations of his or her study up front in the discussion section. This serves to convey to the reader that the researcher realizes that the research is not perfect and is not trying to pass it off as such, but it also lets readers make their own conclusions *in light of* the stated limitations. Think of this as disclosure. The researcher tells the reader what some problems, in the researcher's opinion, are and the reader then gets to decide whether there were more problems than the researcher stated, whether the reader agrees with the researcher's stated problems (perhaps the reader does not feel that some are as important as the researcher may), and how the reader wants to interpret or use the findings as a result.

9. Are the implications of the research or suggestions for future research discussed?

Since no one study is the be-all and end-all of studies, researchers may provide suggestions for other researchers considering similar studies of the topic. If you remember from our discussion of topic selection, this suggestion for future research can be very useful to someone else. In applied research, the researcher may specifically state how the findings can be used by giving suggestions for program alteration or policy implementation. However, if the research is not applied, it is unlikely that the researcher will discuss implications, although doing so is not prohibited.

In sum, the guidelines for evaluating the written presentation of results and discussion sections are as follows:

1. Is the results section a cohesive essay with the important findings highlighted?
2. In the essay, does the researcher tie the results to the research hypotheses or goals stated in the introduction?
3. If there are tables or graphs, are they clearly presented?
4. Does the research present any descriptive statistics?
5. Are the statistics appropriate for the level of measurement?
6. Are the conclusions the researcher draws appropriate for the statistical information?
7. In the discussion section, does the researcher briefly summarize the research purposes, methodologies, and key findings (in a nonstatistical manner)?
8. Does the researcher acknowledge any methodological or statistical weaknesses?
9. Are the implications of the research or suggestions for future research discussed?
10. Overall, is the results section adequate?
11. Overall, is the discussion section adequate?

Box 12.1 gives you more practice with evaluating the results and discussion sections of written research.

In democratic countries, such as the United States and Great Britain, every time there is an election, there is an opportunity for education regarding civic social issues as each candidate tries to convince voters why his or her stance is best. Norris and Sanders (2003) were interested in how campaign information informed people about public affairs.

To study this, the researchers drew a quota sample of almost 900 people (480 actually were in this part of the study) in the Greater London area and conducted experiments where the researchers varied the medium of campaign information. Participants completed a short (15-minute) pretest questionnaire about their media habits, political attitudes, and personal background.

The researchers then randomly assigned participants to watch a 30-minute video compilation of television news, followed by the participants reading selected newspaper stories on off-line party web pages (which the researchers downloaded and edited into a dedicated site). Respondents subsequently complete a short (15-minute) posttest questionnaire.

Norris and Sanders conducted linear regression tests to predict which avenues of media had the greatest effect on civic education. Because the linear regression statistic is beyond a discussion of results for this section, I present only their pre- and posttest comparisons on whether participants learned *anything* after being exposed to campaign information.

In other words, instead of focusing on which aspect of campaign information is the most effective in educating the public, Norris and Sanders first establish whether campaign information *did* educate the public and it is those results that I present here. Of course, as always, you can find the complete article (including the regression results) on Research Navigator by using the access number ***AN 10466954.***

Learning about Party Policies and the Government's Record

Despite the barrage of media headlines on some of the key issues in the campaign, prior to the experiments the British public displayed widespread ignorance about party policies on Europe, asylum seekers, and taxation (see Table 1). About half the public could identify the Conservatives as the party proposing to keep the pound for the duration of the next parliament, to house new asylum seekers in reception centers, and to introduce the 8 billion pound tax cut. Even fewer (41%) knew that the Liberal Democrats proposed raising income tax, their most distinctive pledge in the election. More of the public (67%) were aware of Labour's baby bond pledge, with two thirds identifying this correctly as Labour policy, a surprising result in the sense that of all the issues under comparison, this had been given by far the least coverage in the mass media during the election and had received almost no attention in Labour speeches or campaign literature. . . .

But is there a group of irredeemable know-nothings in the British public, consigned forever to political ignorance about party policies? The answer is clearly negative. After relatively brief exposure to information in the media experiments. . . there were significant gains registered in eight out of eleven knowledge items, as measured by the mean change in correct answers from the pre-test to post-test among the pooled group of all those exposed to the learning experiments. The significance of the difference between the pre-test and post-test results was measured by paired sample *t* tests. For example, those who could identify the Conservatives as the party proposing housing new asylum seekers in secure reception centers jumped dramatically from half to three quarters of the public. Knowledge that Labour proposed baby bonds rose from 67% to 83%. . . .

Conclusions and Discussion

The question of the educational functions of election campaigns has been subject to extensive scrutiny. The bulk of the research in recent decades has been American, and this has usually, although not always, pointed toward the superior role of the print media as channels of

BOX 12.1   Evaluating Written Research, continued

TABLE 1 11-Point Political Knowledge Scores Before and After Exposure to Information Sources

	Pre-test Correct (%)	Post-test Correct (%)	Change (%)
House new asylum seekers in secure reception centers (Con)	49	76	+27***
Raise income tax (Lib Dem)	41	59	+18***
Create a baby bond saving fund for every child at birth (Lab)	67	83	+16***
Cut taxes by £8 billion (Con)	49	49	+10***
Keep the pound for the duration of the next parliament (Con)	52	61	+9***
Euro notes and coins are due to be introduced in most EU member states next year (T)	61	68	+7***
The government has removed the automatic right of asylum seekers to get cash benefits (T)	36	41	+5**
A record number of asylum seekers came to Britain last year (T)	78	84	+6***
The overall rate of crime has gone down since 1997 (T)	29	29	0 (ns)
The rate of unemployment in Britain has fallen during the last 12 months (T)	73	72	−0.5 (ns)
The basic rate of income tax has risen under Labour (F)	46	45	−0.6 (ns)

Note: The pre-test survey was prior to any experimental stimuli. The post-test was administered after the stimuli. Only respondents ($N = 389$) exposed to campaign learning experiments from any source are included, excluding the control group ($N = 91$). The significance of the difference between the pre-test and post-test groups was measured by paired-sample t tests. *True/false:* The percentage of respondents exposed to campaign information from any news source who could correctly identify whether the statement about the government's record was true or false. T = true, F = false. *Con/Lab/Lib Dem:* The percentage of respondents exposed to campaign information from any news source who could correctly identify the correct party advocating each policy. **$p < .01$; ***$p < .000$.

Source: Campaign Learning Study.

information rather than television news. Different reasons have been offered to explain the impact of print and television news on political knowledge. . . . We theorize that the structure of the news industry can have an important impact upon the typical contents of the major information sources like television news, newspapers, and party websites within each country, and therefore what the electorate can be expected to learn during campaigns from these sources. We sought to test this argument, particularly variations in levels of campaign learning according to the type of media and the prior knowledge of voters in the context of the last British election campaign. The major conclusions from this study are as follows.

BOX 12.1   **Evaluating Written Research, continued**

1. Campaign learning did occur. In the midst of the June 2001 British general election, despite extensive political news available on radio, television, current affairs programs, newspaper supplements, and the Internet, about half the public appeared unaware about some of the key issue features in party political debates, such as the stance of the Conservatives toward the Euro and their promise to cut taxes. Nevertheless, after relatively brief exposure to more information about these issues, interspersed by other election and non-election news, the public's issue knowledge rose significantly on eight out of eleven items. . . .

. . . We can conclude that despite the barrage of political commentary and election news, and the efforts by parties to convey their core message during the general election, in the pre-test survey the British public remained unaware of many basic issues at the heart of the campaign. But although many electors are "know-nothings," or at least "know-littles," under certain conditions, when exposed to more information, the evidence shows that the public *can* learn, quite a lot, quite rapidly, and from television news, party websites, *and* newspapers. . . . The real challenge for journalists, broadcasters and politicians—indeed, the challenge for civic engagement in general—is how to achieve this transformation in real life.

Source: Pippa Norris and David Sanders, "Message or medium? Campaign learning during the 2001 British general election," *Political Communication, 20* (3) (July 2003): 233. **(AN 10466954).** Reproduced by permission of Taylor & Francis Group, LLC, www.taylorandfrancis.com.

Critical Thinking Questions

1. Is the results section a cohesive essay with the important findings highlighted?

2. In the essay, does the researcher tie the results to the research hypotheses or goals stated in the introduction?

3. If there are tables or graphs, are they clearly presented?

4. Does the researcher present any descriptive statistics?

5. Are the statistics appropriate for the level of measurement?

6. Are the conclusions the researcher draws appropriate for the statistical information?

7. In the discussion section, does the researcher briefly summarize the research purposes, methodologies, and key findings (in a non-statistical manner)?

8. Does the researcher acknowledge any methodological or statistical weaknesses?

9. Are the implications of the research or suggestions for future research discussed?

10. Overall, is the results section adequate?

11. Overall, is the discussion section adequate?

Critical Thinking Discussion

1. Yes. The couple of paragraphs before the table describe some of the highlights of the material in the table in an easy to follow essay form.

2. Not quite. Since this table is not the "crux" of the research article (the main hypotheses are tested with linear regressions), but instead the foundation that precedes the rest of the analysis, Norris and Sanders do not tie the table to their research hypotheses. However, they do not *need* to do this. Their purpose is not to test whether people become educated about issues per se, but instead to examine *how* they become educated.

Before one discusses *how* something occurs, however, a person must first establish that it *does* occur. In other words, it would be pretty pointless for Norris and Sanders to discuss how media affects civic education if they first found out that the media had *no* effect on this education.

BOX 12.1   **Evaluating Written Research, continued**

Therefore, here they are simply establishing that, yes, the media do affect civic education and no tie to the introduction is necessary. (Note: However, in the more complicated linear regression discussions, they do concretely tie their research findings to their earlier stated goals and hypotheses.)

3. The table is very clear. The column headings tell us the pre- and posttest scores as well as the amount of change. The rows tell us each of the 11 test items regarding respondent political knowledge. The footnote gives the sample size, a mention of the statistical test used, a discussion of probability values and the source of the data. This is a very good table.

4. Descriptive statistics of the sample are present in the full text but not in this excerpt. However, the researchers *do* provide the descriptive statistics for the 11 items of knowledge by presenting the percent of the respondents (a frequency statistic) who got the answers right before the introduction of the media and after.

5. Percents are a ratio level of measurement and since there are two time periods where the same group is tested, Norris and Sanders's decision to used pooled *t*-tests is appropriate. You may be asking why they didn't use Z scores since their combined sample size is greater than 100. They could have; but since the *t* distribution becomes indistinguishable from the Z distribution for larger samples, using the *t* is essentially the same as using the Z.

6. Yes. Overall, people *did* (at least in the short term) become more knowledgeable about issues *after* they were exposed to the relevant media.

7. For the most part. They highlight the main findings of previous research, which they discussed in detail in their literature review (". . . The bulk of the research in recent decades . . . rather than television news. . . ."), their research goals ("We sought to test . . . variations in levels of campaign learning according to the type of media and the prior knowledge of voters . . . ."), and their main

findings (". . . Campaign learning did occur. . ."). They, however, did not summarize their sampling or experimental approach.

8. No, at least not in the discussion section. Throughout some earlier discussion of results (linear regression results, not shown) in the results section, they briefly mentioned some, but there was no mention of weaknesses in the discussion section, where such a discussion typically belongs.

9. Which method of campaign information is the most useful for educating the public about civic issues in and of itself is not an applied research topic, although it undeniably has clear implications for usage. Therefore, although the researchers would not necessarily *need* a discussion of implications for future use, having one would certainly be beneficial.

Norris and Sanders do not, however, present any real guidance. In fact, they just imply that using their findings in a real-life way would be a "challenge" for those involved in political campaigns to decipher. Since this is not directly an applied study, some discussion of future research direction should be present as well; however, this too is missing.

10. The results section is very well done. The tables are clear and complete, the essay presentation of results is clear, the statistics are appropriate for the data, and the statistics are appropriately interpreted. Overall, this is a very good example of a results section.

11. The discussion section is weaker. The researchers refer to their basic research goals and hypotheses, reiterate the link between their research and that which others have previously done, and summarize their main findings. However, they do not summarize their methodology; and, they do not discuss any weaknesses of their design, any implications for use or any directions for future research on this topic. Therefore, overall, this is a mediocre discussion section.

Key Terms

Alpha level (517)
Bivariate statistics (517)
Chi-square statistic (522)
Code sheet entry (525)
Coding (518)
Computer-assisted telephone interviewing (CATI) (526)
Control variables (567)
Correlation (553)

Direct-entry methods (526)
Distribution (540)
Frequency distribution (526)
Independent samples *t*-test statistic (558)
Mean (542)
Measure of central tendency (541)
Measure of dispersion (544)

Median (542)
Mode (542)
Multivariate statistic (567)
Optical scan sheet (526)
Probability of error (517)
Type I error (579)
Type II error (579)
Univariate statistics (515)

Review Questions and Exercises

1. *What measure of central tendency and dispersion are appropriate for the following variables:*

   a. *Support for a campus safety escort program at night measured as: strongly support, somewhat support, undecided, generally not support, strongly do not support*

   b. *Number of negative campaign advertisements airing on major television networks between 5:50 and 8:30 p.m. on a Monday night*

   c. *Parental marital status measured as: never married, married, separated/divorced, widowed*

2. *A scale measuring political attitudes ranges from 0 to 200, where a higher score indicates more liberal attitudes. If the average score on this scale among a sample of college sophomores is 135 with a standard deviation of 12, what percent of people scored:*

   a. *Higher than 160?*

   b. *Between 120 and 150?*

   c. *Less than 140?*

3. *I hypothesize that freshmen go out and "party" more so than sophomores. I conduct a simple random sample of 40 freshmen and 55 sophomores and obtain the following data regarding the number of nights a week they report "partying."*

Freshmen	Sophomores
$\bar{X} = 4.51$	$\bar{X} = 3.62$
$s = .67$	$s = .45$

   a. *Write a null and research hypothesis that summarizes this problem.*

   b. *Is my hypothesis supported at the .01 level? Why or why not? In other words, I want only a 1 percent chance of error in my interpretation.*

4. *A random sample of 200 college men and 200 college women were selected to see who they planned to vote for in the upcoming presidential election. Their results are as follows:*

	Women	Men	Total
Candidate A	40% (80)	53% (106)	186
Candidate B	60% (120)	47% (94)	214
Total	200	200	400

   a. *State the null and research hypothesis.*

   b. *Do men and women significantly differ in their support for the candidates? You want a probability of error level of at least .05. If so, how?*

5. *A sociology professor conducted a random sample of 500 people (300 men and 200 women) to assess their amount of charitable contributions during the winter holiday season. She found that women donated, on average, $175 (s = $57) and men donated, on average, $210 (s = $80). Are men more likely to donate to charitable organizations than women? You need to be at least 96 percent confident (yes, that's 96 percent, not a typo!) of your findings.*

a. Write a null and research hypothesis that summarizes this problem.

b. Is the hypothesis supported at the .01 level? Why or why not?

6. Evaluate the results and discussion sections in the following articles found on Research Navigator:

a. Alcohol abuse may aggravate HIV symptoms. (2004, April 5). Alcoholism & Drug Abuse Weekly, 16 (14), 1 p. (AN 12748547)

b. Igartua, Juan Jose, Cheng, Lifen, and Lopes, Orquidea, (2003, November). To think or not to think: Two pathways towards persuasion by short films on AIDS prevention. Journal of Health Communication, 8 (6), 16 pp. (AN 11763089)

Appendix A

Writing a Research Report

While reading the book, you may have been piecing together an idea of how a research report generally flows. If you have not begun reading the book, this may serve as a good general overview that will help you put the chapter information into context. Either way, this appendix serves as a brief overview of the various parts of a research report that are common in most social science research writing. Specific issues, such as heading formation and citation format, may vary based on the discipline (for example, there's APA format used in psychology and sociology and MLA used in other disciplines), so I am not going to cover those here. Rather, I am just going to give a brief overview of what the different parts of a research report are and what they entail. You can find more specific information regarding what to look for in each section throughout the book, since each chapter ends with a section entitled "Evaluating Written Research" that focuses on some guidelines for evaluating specific parts of a research report.

Organization of the Report

■ Title

Clearly, every research article is going to start with a title. That is the first piece of information researchers will use to see if a particular article is relevant to their interests. If I am interested in studying the effects of material employment on adolescent daughters' educational behavior, I am not going to bother reading an article that is titled "Reducing Crime among Juveniles: A Longitudinal Study of Innovative Reforms." Titles should be direct and informative. They do not need to be "cute" or attention getting unless someone manages to do so while also being direct and informative. Usually when writing a research report, a researcher may keep some general idea of a title in mind, but this is actually something that many researchers finalize at the *end* of the writing process, once they have a better sense of how their mental ideas translated into written words.

■ Abstract

Like the title, researchers frequently write this *after* the rest of the paper is done; however, when a paper is in final form, the abstract appears *before* the body of the paper and right after the title. Abstracts are brief, usually 150 to 200 words, summaries of the main points of the research. They frequently include a mention of the study purpose, who was sampled, the sample size, the method of observation, and some general (nonstatistical) findings. The reason researchers frequently write the abstract at the end of their writing process is because the abstract is probably the most important part of the article for conveying to others the general gist of the research, and it is what other researchers are likely to use, even more so than the title, to see if a specific report is relevant to their interests. A title may give readers a general idea of whether an article is relevant, but because titles are shorter than abstracts, they clearly can't contain enough relevant information to narrow the options of reading beyond very basic criteria.

■ Introduction and Literature Review

The abstract addresses the purpose of your research, but it is important to more fully explain that purpose in the beginning of the research report itself. Therefore, in the introduction, it is common practice to establish the general purpose of the research and its social importance. Generally, researchers address this in one to two paragraphs (although, if time and space permit, they can clearly make this section as long as they desire). The introduction does not necessarily have to be distinguishable from the literature review with subheadings, which is why I have the introduction and literature review grouped together here.

The literature review is where you put your research goals in context relative to what is already known based on other research. In the literature review, researchers discuss what other researchers have already learned about the general problem of interest, what they agree about regarding that problem, and where they disagree, as well. You may also use the literature review to indicate where gaps in knowledge exist and perhaps make an argument for how the *current* research about to be described in *this* report addresses that gap.

The point is: The literature review is not just a "book report" of what other researchers have found. It is an analysis. When writing the literature review, you should compare and contrast the existing research, critically evaluate it for gaps, and evaluate the methodological strengths and weaknesses of the existing research to try to explain the various findings and to argue how *your* research will fit with the existing knowledge. Therefore, even though you may have mentioned the social importance of the present topic in the introduction, in the literature review, you make the contribution of the present study to the world of social sciences even clearer.

Because this section obviously heavily relies on describing the work of others, writers have to be very careful about avoiding plagiarism. Another writers' words or ideas cannot be used without properly citing them. Again, the actual mechanics for *how* to cite material will vary slightly by discipline; however, anything borrowed verbatim needs to be in quotes and cited. Even ideas that one borrows and *rewords* or *summarizes*, a process known as *paraphrasing,* must be cited. In some disciplines, how one cites quoted and paraphrased information varies somewhat. Even if a couple of researchers express similar ideas or opinions, those ideas or opinions cannot be taken as common knowledge. Therefore, you still need to cite these people, simply by including all of the people in the citation.

For example, if three researchers are of the opinion that boot camps are no better than arrest for curbing juvenile delinquency (a highly debated issue despite the research), and I want to include their opinions in my literature review, I might write something like this:

> There is disagreement regarding the viability of boot camps for juveniles. Some researchers note that boot camps, although ideologically popular, are no more

effective in preventing juvenile recidivism than are more traditional methods like time in a detention center (Smith, 1998; Jones, 2003; Collins, 2004).

Here, I cited all three researchers who shared the same opinion about boot camps.

■ Theory and Hypotheses (if Applicable)

Not all research involves hypotheses. Exploratory or descriptive research may not; however, explanatory or evaluation research frequently does. If you have hypotheses that you are testing, the bridge between the literature review and the actual description of research methodologies usually consists of a discussion of the relevant theory to be tested and the hypotheses the researcher will use to test that theory. Sometimes the hypotheses are couched within the context of a paragraph; sometimes a researcher specifically identifies them by setting them a bit apart from the body of the paragraph and using the subheadings "Hypothesis 1," "Hypothesis 2," and so on.

Regardless of which format you use, you should always make it explicitly clear what your hypotheses are by somehow using the term *hypothesis*. After all, if you are using hypotheses, they are the crux or the "ultimate purpose" of your research. What you describe in the introduction is the general purpose, how you intend to address that purpose is your hypothesis. Therefore, anyone writing a research report needs to draw explicit attention to the hypotheses being tested.

■ Methodological Description

Granted, this is a research *methods* textbook, but it usually is not until about half-way through the writing process that a person actually gets to discuss the *methods* used for the study. So far everything else I have discussed has "set the scene," so to speak, by describing what we will be studying and how it fits into the context of the existing field knowledge. In this section, a researcher actually goes into detail about what he or she did to examine his or her research problem. This section usually entails a lot of information, such as a description of the study population and sample, the measures, and the method of observation. Because of the large amount of information frequently in this section, researchers sometimes use subheadings to alert the reader when a change in methodological focus occurs.

Regardless of whether you present this section as one large cohesive essay or use subheadings to distinguish the various parts, this is arguably the most important section of the entire research report. The worth of the scientific findings expressed in the next section heavily depend on the quality of how the data were gathered, which is described in this section. Therefore, to be able to follow the steps of the researcher and to assess data quality, the reader should be able to answer the following questions at the end of this section:

1. Who did the study? Who was the study population? How was the sample selected? Did the researcher use a probability or nonprobability technique? How many subjects are in the study? What are their demographics?
2. How did the researcher measure his or her concepts? What variables did the researcher use and how do we know that those variables are valid and reliable?
3. What was the method of observation? Was the study an experiment, a survey, a form of content analysis?

4. What were the exact steps the researcher took to collect the data? For example:
   a. What type of survey or experiment did the researcher do? A telephone survey? An anonymous questionnaire? A true experiment? A quasi-experiment?
   b. When were the data collected? Are the data cross-sectional or longitudinal?
   c. Where were the data collected? In a laboratory? In a city? What city?
5. Did the researcher discuss and address any ethical issues inherent in his or her design?

Knowing what the *reader* needs to be able to answer will help you ensure that the key information is present in your write-up. Also, keeping your write-up as specific as possible will help other researchers who use *your* study as part of *their* literature review and research design to replicate any parts they found particularly useful.

■ Analysis and Interpretation

Once the researcher has described the methodology in detail, he or she is ready to present the findings of the data analysis. In quantitative research, this section is likely to contain both some type of visual depiction of the data, such as tables and graphs, as well as a discussion of key findings and how they relate to the hypotheses in a cohesive essay format. Both a visual and an essay depiction of the findings are common because a reader can easily look at the visual depiction and form his or her own conclusions and then use the essay to either confirm or deny those conclusions. If you draw conclusions in the data (as expressed in the essay) different from what the reader did (as surmised by the tables or graphs), then the reader has to decide whether he or she correctly interpreted the information (and, for whatever reason, you did not) or whether he or she made a mistake.

Either way, a mismatch between a person's reading of a table, for example, and a researcher's written interpretation would lead a conscientious reader to reexamine the data-gathering strategies described in the previous section to determine whether the reader or the researcher made a mistake. This serves as a double-check, so to speak, which helps knowledgeable and careful readers get the most out of scientific research while minimizing the risks of being led astray.

Incidentally, when you (the researcher) analyze data, you are likely to conduct many different descriptive and inferential statistics. However, you do not necessarily present *all* of those statistical tests and calculations in the written report. Doing a variety of data analysis helps you obtain a fuller understanding of what was going on in your sample; however, it is likely to overwhelm the average reader. Therefore, present only the information that is directly relevant to the hypothesis or research purpose, and that which presents the clearest, most informative picture of what was going on in your sample. To make sure that it is clear to the reader why you selected the material to present that you did, it is useful to briefly state your rationale for a particular analysis (e.g., Why did you do an inferential statistic on gender and crime? Is it directly related to one of your hypotheses?), present the data relevant to it, and interpret the results (Was the hypothesis supported? Was the degree of association noteworthy?).

In this section you are telling the reader only what you found and how it relates to your research purpose or hypotheses. Researchers generally do not go into detail about *why* they found the results that they did. For example, if a hypothesis was not supported, generally you would not suggest why this was the case in this section. In this section, you state only the findings as they are.

■ Discussion and Conclusion

The discussion section usually serves as the summary of the entire research process. Therefore, it may begin with a reiteration of the research problem and the general methodological approach to studying the problem. Researchers should next highlight some of the key findings—both expected and unexpected. However, since these findings are summaries, they usually do not involve a reiteration of the specific statistics. For example, instead of reiterating that "71 percent of those who make charitable contributions only do so during the winter holiday," you might say, "The majority of people who make charitable contributions do so only during the winter holidays."

However, this section is not just a summary of everything a researcher did. It also includes some discussion as to the limitations of the study. Even if everything worked out exactly how you had hoped, no research is perfect, and therefore a discussion of study limitations should be present. This section also includes some discussion as to the general conclusions one can draw from this research and what significance these results have to the wider field. Also, it may include some suggestions for future research. Four factors—limitations, significance of findings for the field, general conclusions, and suggestions for future research—should be present, regardless of whether the study worked completely as intended or whether it did not (e.g., hypotheses were not supported).

If hypotheses (some or all) were not supported, you may use some of these issues to explain *why* these specific results were obtained. In other words, how did the limitations of the study perhaps influence the lack of statistical support for the theoretical hypotheses? If the study did work as you intended, you still need to discuss limitations; however, now those limitations may be couched in a way that suggests what direction future research can take.

For example, if the data were based on a probability sample of people in the eastern part of the United States, even if all of the hypotheses were supported, there may be reason to believe that people in the western part of the country may have different views. Therefore, it is not a fault per se that the study focused only on the eastern part of the country (researchers frequently limit their studies to manageable groups), but it is a limitation nonetheless, and we would have more confidence in the findings if *another* researcher (hence the direction for future research) tried to replicate the study in the western part of the country.

The biggest concern in the discussion section is that writers avoid generalizing beyond the data they have. If your sample is only from people in the eastern part of the country, you cannot generalize to "all" Americans, unless you have statistically established that these people in your sample are demographically (at least) similar to those people in the rest of the country. Therefore, in your attempt to make useful conclusions, don't overstate them.

The only sections that follow the discussion and conclusion section are any endnotes, references, and appendixes. Endnotes and appendixes are not in all articles, and if they are in an article, journals usually have explicit directions as to how they will be handled. The reference section is akin to a bibliography and is sometimes called a "Works Cited Page." I presume that by being in college, you are all familiar with the concepts of bibliographies; however, like the endnotes, journals are usually very explicit about what type of format (e.g., APA or MLA) they want bibliographies to be. Therefore, I will not discuss them here.

■ General Advice

Let me conclude by giving some general advice about writing a research report. In order to be familiar with the more specific styles of your discipline, a good first step to take is to examine some journal articles in your field to get a sense of the writing style and format common in that field. This is not necessarily "extra" research, as you need to read other published research for your literature review anyway. All I'm saying here is that in addition to reading the content of the published research for the relevant methodological and statistical findings regarding your topic of choice, also pay attention to the mechanics of the report. What sections are there? What citation format does the researcher use? What are the heading formats? In fact, many academic and trade journals have specific criteria for the format of their submissions. You can usually find this information at the journal's website, on the inside or back cover of a journal, or in the early or late pages of any journal edition. Reading different journal manuscript submission criteria and looking for commonalities is probably a good way of getting some general ideas for how to present your report.

Another important consideration is your audience; in other words, who will read your report? Early in my career, I was doing an evaluation of a local community program for which I had to write a report to submit to the government and I also had to submit a copy to a local judge who was in charge of the program. I worked hard on that report and produced (what I thought to be) an impressive 50-page report with detailed tables and methodological discussions. The judge in charge of the project called a meeting in his chambers with me and the senior team to discuss the report findings. When we entered his chambers, the judge very kindly looked at me and complimented me on the very "impressive looking" report and then smiled as he said, "So, to the rest of us, what does all of this really mean? After page 5 or 6 I started just flipping through the report."

At first, I was taken aback—after all, I had worked hard on this report and I knew the judge felt strongly about the program, so I was surprised that he just "flipped through" my report after a few pages. Then I realized that (1) the judge was a very busy man and probably had a lot of "reports" for other projects to read and (2) he was a *judge*, not a social sciences *researcher* and may have easily been bored after the first few pages of methodological discussion. On the other hand, a few months later, the project coordinator of the program received a call from the federal funding agency praising my report as one of the most detailed and easy-to-follow reports they had seen in awhile. Go figure.

The reason I gave you a glimpse into this initial "faux pas" on my part is to illustrate the importance of your audience. In the case of the federal grants person, that person was a skilled researcher who was comfortable reading research reports and was therefore pleased (and able to understand) my detailed methodological and analytical conclusions. For this person, I had identified the audience correctly. However, the judge was *not* a skilled researcher and reading my report must have been akin to me reading a legal contract or a deposition transcript. Without someone telling me what to look for in either of these legal documents, I would be lost. It was probably the same for the judge. He wanted to know the bottom line: What did I find and how can we use it?—and he wanted it in plain English. In this instance, I completely *missed* my audience.

As a result, I learned to write two reports. The "main" report for the funding agency that included all of the methodological and statistical detail, and a briefer "report" that flowed more like an executive summary (something like a cross between an abstract and a discussion section) and included only figures that highlighted the findings that would be the most useful to the judge.

Last, do not be afraid to write drafts. Students frequently hate the idea of drafts because they see it as extra work. Although it takes time to read and edit a written document in addition to the original writing, since research reports involve the synthesis of a lot of different parts, drafts are important to make sure that the flow of the paper is cohesive and that you make the point you intend.

Overall, research reports should start broadly in the introduction with a general discussion of the research purpose. The literature review serves to narrow the focus by putting it into context relevant to the other research that already has been done. By the time a person is done reading the literature review and the writer's critical analysis, he or she should have a clear idea of exactly *where* the researcher is going with regard to the broader research topic. The writer will explicitly state this with the research purpose or hypotheses, but the point I'm making is that if the literature if done well and has focus, by the time the writer does explicitly state the focus of this research, it will come as no surprise to the reader.

The methods section, then, is the "action section." It tells the reader exactly *how* the research purpose or hypotheses will be tested (the data gathered), and the results section tells the reader what the researcher found. Essentially, the research report is a story that starts off broadly and builds to a climax, which is the research results. The denouement, or "wind down," is the discussion section. This reminds the reader of the goals and key findings and then, once again, puts the specific study into a broader context by suggesting directions of future research and how the conclusions may be relevant to the field. In other words, there's a definite flow to a well-done research report; however, this flow is not likely to be achieved in the first writing.

In Appendix B, I provide one complete example of how to evaluate a written research article that unites most of the points from the individual chapters. Consequently, Appendix B may serve as additional help in writing a research report because by being aware of what one should see in a good research report written by *others*, one knows what to make sure is present in one's *own* research report.

Appendix B

Putting It Together: An Example of the Evaluation of an Entire Research Article

Throughout this book, the end of each chapter focuses on the evaluation of a specific part of a research report. In this appendix, I will illustrate an example of how to evaluate an entire written research report using the question guidelines from the relevant chapters for an article on the evaluation of school-based mental health services. Nabors and Reynolds (2000) studied 181 middle and high school students who were receiving mental health services (in addition to a control group of 113 students) to examine the relationship between treatment goals, time in therapy, and change in behavioral and emotional functioning for adolescents receiving school-based mental health services. Students can find the article I am using by looking up the article number **AN 3342001** on Research Navigator.

For this example, I have identified each part of the research report and the corresponding critical thinking questions in its own subheading. You may notice that the book involves separate critical thinking guidelines for surveys, experiments, evaluation research, field research, and so on. Most research involves only one of these methods of observation, and the Nabors and Reynolds research involved the evaluation of a program. Therefore, when it comes to the method of observation section, I will present *only* the guidelines for evaluation research, since other methods of observation, such as field research, for example, are not applicable.

Title

1. Is the title specific enough to differentiate it from other related topics?
   - Yes. It tells the reader that this is a program evaluation of mental health services for adolescents. It gives the topic, method, and general study population.
2. Do subtitles, if present, provide important information regarding the research?
   - Yes. The subtitle actually provides the method of observation—evaluation research.
3. Are the main variables expressed in the title?
   - Yes. They are treatment outcomes and receipt of school health-based services.
4. Are the terms in the title easily understood by most people?
   - Yes.
5. Does the title avoid any reference to the study's results?
   - Yes.

6. Overall, is this a good title? Why or why not?
   - Yes. It is direct, easy to understand at a glance, and does not imply any results prior to the reading of the study.

■ Abstract

(*Note:* In the HTML version of the text, the first paragraph is actually the abstract.)

1. Is the purpose of the research clear?
   - Yes. The purpose is stated in the third sentence.
2. Are the main points of the research methodology highlighted?
   - No.
3. Does the researcher highlight the main findings?
   - Yes. The researchers do this in the last four sentences of the abstract.
4. Overall, do you find this to be a strong abstract? Why or why not?
   - Generally, yes. The research methodology is not highlighted; however, we know from the title that it is evaluation research. It would have been nice, however, to have the sample sizes mentioned.

■ Introduction/Literature Review

1. Is the material presented in the literature review relevant to my research interests?
   - Since I did not establish a research agenda for this example, this question is not applicable.
2. Is the specific problem area identified in the first paragraph or two of the report?
   - If you read the HTML version of the text, the first paragraph is really the abstract (which is more clearly identifiable as such in the PDF format), and the second paragraph in the HTML format is really the beginning of the body of the article. This second paragraph establishes that the problem area is mental health services for adolescents. This is very vague, and that is appropriate at this early stage of the write-up.
3. Does the researcher establish the importance of the research problem?
   - The researchers establish the importance of mental health services for adolescents early in the article by stating the "positive" effects on youth and by implying that the said effects are avoiding sex, drug use, and violence. This early paragraph also establishes why paying particular attention to urban youth is important.
4. Has the researcher been appropriately selective in deciding what studies to include in the literature review?
   - It appears so. There are no strings of citations with three of more studies mentioned.
5. Is the research cited recent?
   - This article was published in 2000 and all of the research mentioned is from the 1990s—most from the mid to late 1990s, so the information is recent relative to the publication date.
6. Is the literature review critical?

- Somewhat. The authors state that more attention regarding community-based setting is necessary and that there is a gap in research regarding longitudinal studies of school-based mental health services for urban youth.

7. Is the researcher clear as to what is research, theory, and opinion?
- Not really. The researchers treat all opinions and research essentially the same—as fact. There are no clue words such as, "Some researchers *feel* . . ." or "Smith *argues* . . ." that suggest an opinion even though some of the views in the literature review are exactly that—opinion.

8. Overall, do you think this is an adequate literature review? Why or why not?
- Overall yes, this literature review is accurate. Except for not distinguishing research from opinion and for having only a moderately critical approach to existing studies (but not one that is completely missing or weak), this is a pretty good literature review. No article is going to be perfect—and few individual sections are likely to be perfect—and the weaknesses of the literature review in this article are relatively minor.

■ Operationalization

1. Is the conceptualization suitably specific?
- The main goal of the research is mentioned in the last paragraph before the "Methods" section. The researchers want to see whether clinician and adolescent ratings of behavioral and emotional functioning improved as a result of the therapy (and there are different types) and they want to see what variables are specifically related to improved outcomes. The researchers have more indirect goals as well, which include seeing the relationship between treatment goals and protective factors as well as what factors were related to attrition.

  Given these goals, the main concepts are behavioral functioning, emotional functioning, treatment goals, protective factors, and therapy type.

  The authors, however, do not explicitly state these concepts here, nor would they. Concepts are usually more indirectly stated when the researchers actually explain their operationalization, which relates to the next question.

2. Are conceptual/operational definitions presented and are they adequate?
- Yes they are presented in the subsection entitled "Measures," at least indirectly. What the researchers actually do is present their measures (as the subheading suggests) and *then* tell the reader the operational definitions by identifying what the measures address.

  For example, these researchers operationalize behavioral and emotional functioning using the Child and Adolescent Functional Assessment Scale (CAFAS) and the Youth Self-Report Form (YSR), both of which contain subscales that address either behavioral or emotional functioning. The CAFAS measures for behavioral functioning are the child's behavior in his or her school, home, and community; the child's behavior toward self and others; the child's self-harming behaviors; and substance use.

  Because we don't know exactly *how* this scale measures these (although the citations suggest where to find this information), these "measures" are actually the operational definitions. They still need answers to the question "What do I mean?"

to be ultimately understood. There are a lot of ways we could further operationalize children's behavior in their school, for example. The YSR measures for behavioral functioning are not directly described; however, the researchers do provide citations of other studies that use and address this scale, so one could follow the paper trail to see what operational definitions this scale uses.

3. Are the definitions productive?
   - Yes. Remember, researchers have limited space to set up their research problem, describe their methodologies, present their results, and analyze the meaning of those results. Therefore, it is perfectly acceptable to take shortcuts by citing other research that has the necessary information the authors do not have the space to include. These operational definitions, which the researchers present as measures, are very productive in giving me a sense of what factors these researchers are observing.

4. How many different dimensions are being measured at once? Are the various dimensions sufficient?
   - The CAFAS alone includes eight different scales, which essentially means that it addresses eight different dimensions. In fact, most of the measures in this research are different scales that generally include subscales, and each subscale addresses a dimension. Therefore, the research seems to adequately address many of the dimensions of adolescent problematic behavior. Furthermore, these researchers have established that these scales are widely used in the field. This gives me further confidence that the scales, and the dimensions they include, are sufficient.

5. Are the actual questions (or a sample of them) provided?
   - No, but as I've stated earlier, this is not unusual, and the researchers provide citations regarding where this material can be found.

6. Is the response format clear or, when not clear, does the researcher provide information on the response format? Is there any information on restrictions in respondents' response?
   - Given the answer to question 5, this is not applicable.

7. If the researcher is using a published instrument, does he or she cite sources where additional information can be found?
   - Yes.

8. Has the researcher avoided overstating the preciseness of the measurement?
   - Yes. The researchers state that the score for the CAFAS, for example, has "adequate psychometric properties" and cite three different studies that establish this claim.

9. Does the researcher provide some measure of reliability? What type of reliability is established? Do the measures indicate adequate reliability for your purposes?
   - Not directly, but once again, the researchers do so in the paper trail of citations they establish, so this is OK.

10. Does the researcher provide some measure of validity? What measures of validity are presented and are they adequate for your purposes?
    - Ditto number 9.

11. Overall, is the measurement appropriate and adequate, given the research purpose?
    - Given the large number of dimensions, the general acceptance in the field (as indicated by the citations), and the adequate tests of validity and reliability (again, as

presumably established in the research cited), these measures are definitely adequate.

■ Sampling

1. Does the research goal lend itself to generalization? Is the broad sampling method appropriate for the research goal?
   - The research goal is to evaluate *this* program, not necessarily to generalize these findings to other adolescents receiving mental health services. Therefore, probability sampling would not be necessary *if* the researchers studied the *population* of students receiving mental health services. In fact, a quick reading implies that that is exactly what these researchers did, but it is not.

     If you read the last paragraph in the "Methods" section, it states: "In the year this evaluation was conducted, clinicians provided services to 1,308 middle and high school youth. They conducted over 4,300 individual sessions; 1,300 group sessions; and 500 family sessions" (p. 178). Now we do not know whether the students who are in this research are the only ones receiving *this type* of school-based mental health services (the population) or if over 1,000 students are receiving the same school-based mental health services, but only 181 are studied by these researchers. This leaves the issue of sampling unclear.

     Furthermore, the authors give no indication of how they selected the 113 middle and high school students who served as the control group. This may be an issue (which will be relevant in a bit).

2. Does the researcher provide information regarding the study population? The sample?
   - Some. In the body of the paper, the researchers mention that the majority of the students were African American, but more detail on the 181 treatment students, presumably the population of students receiving mental health services, appears in Table 1. However, if you look at Table 1 and add up the sample sizes of the middle and the high school students, you will see that this table refers *only* to the students receiving mental health services (the numbers in footnotes a and b total 181). There is *no* description of the control group, and this is a serious omission because without it, we cannot be sure of any comparison made between those adolescents receiving mental health services and those not. What if the control group was predominantly white? Or male?

3. Is the exact sampling method (e.g., simple random, purposive) specified?
   (Remember, it is not sufficient for a researcher to simply state that a sample was selected "randomly.")
   - No sampling method is discussed at all. It may be that the researchers used the entire population of students at these schools, but they may not have (see question 1). Regardless, there is also no information on how they selected their control group, who "were recruited" for the study.

4. Is the sample size sufficient, given the research goals, the degree of accuracy the researcher desires, and the nature of the population studied? Given the nature of the research, is the sample size sufficient?
   - General rule of thumb would suggest that if the population is around 1,000, then the researchers need to sample about 40 percent of it, which would be around 400

students. However, that is an unwieldy sample size for a study of this type that examines the therapy of adolescents in detail and its effects on a large number of dimensions. Furthermore, if the researchers are not generalizing to a wider population, they would be less concerned with a large sample size.

The problem is that we just don't know. Since the researchers did not give any indication of doing a probability sample, we need to make sure that they do *not* try to generalize their findings beyond the 181 adolescents they studied; *and*, if they don't do that (meaning they don't generalize), then the sample size is less relevant.

5. If the researcher uses a probability sample, does he or she generalize the findings to the appropriate population? If the researcher uses a nonprobability sample, does he or she refrain from generalizing to a wider population?
   - They do not generalize their findings beyond a description of what *this* sample did. Therefore, the information missing in sampling is probably less relevant, with the exception of any comparisons between the control and treatment groups.
6. Overall, is the sampling appropriate?
   - Given that their goal was to describe only *this* sample of people and since that is all that they did, their sampling technique is less relevant here than it may be in other types of research. *However,* regarding any comparisons to the control group, these are very poorly done from a sampling perspective, because we know nothing about what the control group looked like (in terms of demographics) or how they were selected. Therefore, any comparisons between the adolescents receiving mental health services and the control group are suspect, because we have no means of evaluating whether the two groups are comparable.

■ Evaluation Research

(*Note:* Since the purpose of this research is to evaluate mental health services, only the questions pertaining to evaluation research are presented.)

1. What is the purpose of the evaluation presented?
   - The purpose is given in the last paragraph of the "Methods" section.
2. Is the nature of the program described in detail?
   - Yes. The treatment goals are described in detail in the "Participants" subsection, the nature of the School Mental Health Program (SMHP) is described in the "Introduction," and the researchers describe the clinicians who did and did not participate in the last paragraph in the "Participants" subsection.
3. Can the goals that the author presents be evaluated?
   - The dimensions on the subscales seem to adequately address behavioral and emotional functioning, which is what the researchers want to evaluate (the dependent variable) in relation to the therapy characteristics (independent variable). If we accept these scales as good measurements, then all of the goals can be evaluated.
4. What type of observation method is used? Is it appropriate, given the real-life restrictions of evaluation research?
   - The observational method is "observer as participant," which is a type of field research where the observer interacts with the participant, but the level of that interaction, *as it pertains to the research*, is less active. The observer does not, for

example, spend high amounts of time with the participants and does not participate in any of the participants' daily activities aside from designated "research" time.

Furthermore, in this example, the clinicians are gathering data for the researchers based on the mental health services rendered. In other words, the research is *secondary* in a way to the provision of mental health services. The services would be given with or without this research being done. Therefore, yes, in this type of setting, this approach is appropriate.

5. Is a control group used? If so, how has the researcher tried to show that it is equivalent to the experimental group? If not, does the researcher adequately explain its omission?
   - Yes, a control group is used, but as I've already stated, we have no information regarding whether it's equivalent to the experimental group or not. Furthermore, the researchers provide no explanation of the omission of this information.

6. How are people selected for program participation? Does this affect the interpretation of findings, and, if so, does the researcher discuss this?
   - We know nothing about how people were selected for program participation, nor do the researchers discuss how this may affect the interpretation of results. This can be a serious problem.

7. Are the results clearly explained?
   - I will address this in the "Results and Discussion" section.

8. Do the researchers describe who funded the research? Does this affect the interpretation at all?
   - The researchers state that the Agency on Healthcare Research and Quality funded this study. This is a third-party group, meaning that, although they clearly have an interest in the findings, they do not have a *vested* interest because it is not directly *their* program being studied. Therefore, the funding agency has no effect on the interpretation of the results.

9. Overall, is the evaluation method adequate?
   - For the most part. The goals, measures, and type of observation are all generally adequate. However, the lack of information regarding the control group is a noticeable limitation to this study. The before/after tests of the test group are not influenced by this lack of description, so that section is fine from an evaluation point of view. The only real concern is any comparisons between students who do receive the mental health services and those who do not.

■ Results and Discussion

1. Is the results section a cohesive essay with the important findings highlighted?
   - Yes. In fact, in the essay the researchers state that they only present models in which statistical significant relationships were present.

2. In the essay, does the researcher tie the results to the research hypotheses or goals stated in the introduction?
   - Yes. The basic goal is the measurement of behavioral and emotional functioning, which is the dependent variable; therefore, any discussion of the dependent variable essentially links the results to the research goal.

3. If there are tables or graphs, are they clearly presented?
   - Yes, they are clear.

4. Does the research present any descriptive statistics?
   - For the study group, yes, primarily in Table 1. There are no descriptive statistics, however, for the control group.
5. Are the statistics appropriate for the level of measurement?
   - Yes. The dependent variables are interval/ratio levels of measurement, therefore two group t-tests and regression formulas are appropriate.
6. If the relationships have statistical significance, but not substantive significance (meaning the measures of association are small), does the researcher note this?
   - The statistics that have statistical significance also have substantive significance.
7. Are the conclusions the researchers draw appropriate for the statistical information?
   - Yes.
8. In the discussion section, does the researcher briefly summarize the research purposes, methodologies, and key findings (in a nonstatistical manner)?
   - The researchers do not restate the research goals nor do they summarize the methodology. However, they do summarize their key findings. There are some percents present, but they are relatively rare.
9. Does the researcher acknowledge any methodological or statistical weaknesses?
   - For the most part. The researchers provide a detailed discussion about the potential research limitations (for example, how clinicians may have hindered the research efforts and "several other shortcomings"), however, they generally do not acknowledge any limitations in the selection of their treatment sample (which, if you remember from the sampling evaluation, was unclear). They do, however, recognize that the lack of random assignment for the control group may be problematic (although random assignment is not necessarily the same as random selection, which would be another problem).
10. Are the implications of the research or suggestions for future research discussed?
    - Yes, in the last sentence of the second last paragraph.
11. Overall, is the results section adequate?
    - Yes.
12. Overall, is the discussion section adequate?
    - Yes.

■ Ethics

1. Are the steps the researcher took to honor ethical responsibilities to individuals clear? Are they appropriate? Are they enough?
   - No information regarding this is presented.
2. If there were any findings (based on your readings of tables or other means of data presentation) that refuted the researcher's hypothesis, did he or she address these findings?
   - There were no explicitly stated hypotheses.
3. If any results were unexpected, did the researcher acknowledge this? Did the researcher discuss any explanations for the unexpected effects?
   - Yes. There were not many results they considered to be unexpected, but the relationship between having a father at home and attrition was one of them. They discuss this at length in their "Discussion" section.

4. Did the researcher adequately acknowledge the limitations of the research?
   - Yes. See question 9 in the "Results and Discussion" section.
5. Overall, has the researcher adequately fulfilled his or her ethical obligations?
   - This is less clear. There is no discussion on how the participants were ethically treated in the written report, but as I stated in Chapter 3 on ethics, this is not unusual (unfortunately), given the limited amount of pages that people have to write their reports.

■ Overall, Is This a Good Piece of Research?

On the surface, this research would appear to be very strong. It has a well-designed introduction, literature review, operationalization of measures, results section, and discussion section. However, the problems surrounding the sampling cannot be ignored because they are the foundation for which the result and interpretation lie. The goal of this research was not to generalize to other studies, therefore a lack of random sampling in and of itself is not the problem. The problem lies in understanding (1) whether the 181 study adolescents were a sample or a population; (2) if they were a sample, how did they compare to the study population? (after all, the researchers mention that over 1,300 adolescents are getting mental health treatment); (3) how the control group was selected; and (4) how the control group compares to the experimental group. The last two questions alone make any comparisons between the study and control groups suspect, regardless of the lack of random assignment that the researchers do recognize. The first two issues call question to the general interpretation, because a reader does not really know how to fit the context of the findings without knowing how the sample fits the population (or whether it *is* the population). It is fine if the sample is not representative of the population; however, if that is the case, a reader who might be using this information as the basis for his or her own program needs to know how this sample differs from the population.

The lack of a discussion of ethical issues is also a bit troublesome, but unfortunately, not unusual, so that alone would not cast too much doubt on these findings.

Therefore, I'd say that this study was a very useful tool in identifying some key measures for emotional and behavioral well-being among adolescents; however, I would be extremely cautious about any conclusions regarding the effectiveness of mental health services on adolescents.

My comments illustrate some important points. First, as I have stated, no research is perfect, and having some limitations in a section or having some entire sections be relatively weak is not necessarily enough to negate the entire article. There may still be some useful information in it. Second, not all sections are created equal. A poor introduction or abstract does not necessarily hurt the overall evaluation of a study; however, poor sampling design alone may be enough to do just that. Therefore, be careful in reading the research, and remember that the only absolute point of research is that nothing is absolute.

Appendix C

Table of Random Numbers

10480	15011	01536	02011	81647	91646	69179	14194	62590	36207	20969	99570	91291	90700
22368	46573	25595	85393	30995	89198	27982	53402	93965	34095	52666	19174	39615	99505
24130	48360	22527	97265	76393	64809	15179	24830	49340	32081	30680	19655	63348	58629
42167	93093	06243	61680	07856	16376	39440	53537	71341	57004	00849	74917	97758	16379
37570	39975	81837	16656	06121	91782	60468	81305	49684	60672	14110	06927	01263	54613
77921	06907	11008	42751	27756	53498	18602	70659	90655	15053	21916	81825	44394	42880
99562	72905	56420	69994	98872	31016	71194	18738	44013	48840	63213	21069	10634	12952
96301	91977	05463	07972	18876	20922	94595	56869	69014	60045	18425	84903	42508	32307
89579	14342	63661	10281	17453	18103	57740	84378	25331	12566	58678	44947	05585	56941
85475	36857	53342	53988	53060	59533	38867	62300	08158	17983	16439	11458	18593	64952
28918	69578	88231	33276	70997	79936	56865	05859	90106	31595	01547	85590	91610	78188
63553	40961	48235	03427	49626	69445	18663	72695	52180	20847	12234	90511	33703	90322
09429	93969	52636	92737	88974	33488	36320	17617	30015	08272	84115	27156	30613	74952
10365	61129	87529	85689	48237	52267	67689	93394	01511	26358	85104	20285	29975	89868
07119	97336	71048	08178	77233	13916	47564	81056	97735	85977	29372	74461	28551	90707
51085	12765	51821	51259	77452	16308	60756	92144	49442	53900	70960	63990	75601	40719
02368	21382	52404	60268	89368	19885	55322	44819	01188	65255	64835	44919	05944	55157
01011	54092	33362	94904	31273	04146	18594	29852	71585	85030	51132	01915	92747	64951
52162	53916	46369	58586	23216	14513	83149	98736	23495	64350	94738	17752	35156	35749
07056	97628	33787	09998	42698	06691	76988	13602	51851	46104	88916	19509	25625	58104
48663	91245	85828	14346	09172	30168	90229	04734	59193	22178	30421	61666	99904	32812
54164	58492	22421	74103	47070	25306	76468	26384	58151	06646	21524	15227	96909	44592
32639	32363	05597	24200	13363	38005	94342	28728	35806	06912	17012	64161	18296	22851
29334	27001	87637	87308	58731	00256	45834	15398	46557	41135	10367	07684	36188	18510
02488	33062	28834	07351	19731	92420	60952	61280	50001	67658	32586	86679	50720	94953
81525	72295	04839	96423	24878	82651	66566	14778	76797	14780	13300	87074	79666	95725
29676	20591	68086	26432	46901	20849	89768	81536	86645	12659	92259	57102	80428	25280
00742	57392	39064	66432	84673	40027	32832	61362	98947	96067	64760	64584	96096	98253
05366	04213	25669	26422	44407	44048	37397	63904	45766	66134	75470	66520	34693	90449
91921	26418	64117	94305	26766	25940	39972	22209	71500	64568	91402	42416	07844	69618
00582	04711	87917	77341	42206	35126	74087	99547	81817	42607	43808	76655	62028	76630
00725	69884	62797	56170	86324	88072	76222	36086	84637	93161	76038	65855	77919	88006
69011	65795	95876	55293	18988	27354	26575	08625	40801	59920	29841	80150	12777	48501
25976	57948	29888	88604	67917	48708	18912	82271	65424	69774	33611	54262	85963	03547
09763	83473	73577	12908	30883	18317	28290	35797	05998	41688	34952	37888	38917	88050

```
91567   42595   27958   30134   04024   86385   29880   99730   55536   84855   29080   09250   79656   73211
17955   56349   90999   49127   20044   59931   06115   20542   18059   02008   73708   83517   36103   42791
46503   18584   18845   49618   02304   51038   20655   58727   28168   15475   56942   53389   20562   87338
92157   89634   94824   78171   84610   82834   09922   25417   44137   48413   25555   21246   35509   20468
14577   62765   35605   81263   39667   47358   56873   56307   61607   49518   89656   20103   77490   18062

98427   07523   33362   64270   01638   92477   66969   98420   04880   45585   46565   04102   46880   45709
34914   63976   88720   82765   34476   17032   87589   40836   32427   70002   70663   88863   77775   69348
70060   28277   39475   46473   23219   53416   94970   25832   69975   94884   19661   72828   00102   66794
53976   54914   06990   67245   68350   82948   11398   42878   80287   88267   47363   46634   06541   97809
76072   29515   40980   07391   58745   25774   22987   80059   39911   96189   41151   14222   60697   59583

90725   52210   83974   29992   65831   38857   50490   83765   55657   14361   31720   57375   56228   41546
64364   67412   33339   31926   14883   24413   59744   92351   97473   89286   35931   04110   23726   51900
08962   00358   31662   25388   61642   34072   81249   35648   56891   69352   48373   45578   78547   81788
95012   68379   93526   70765   10592   04542   76463   54328   02349   17247   28865   14777   62730   92277
15664   10493   20492   38391   91132   21999   59516   81652   27195   48223   46751   22923   32261   85653

16408   81899   04153   53381   79401   21438   83035   92350   36693   31238   59649   91754   72772   02338
18629   81953   05520   91962   04739   13092   97662   24822   94730   06496   35090   04822   86774   98289
73115   35101   47498   87637   99016   71060   88824   71013   18735   20286   23153   72924   35165   43040
57491   16703   23167   49323   45021   33132   12544   41035   80780   45393   44812   12515   98931   91202
30405   83946   23792   14422   15059   45799   22716   19792   09983   74353   68668   30429   70735   25499

16631   35006   85900   98275   32388   52390   16815   69298   82732   38480   73817   32523   41961   44437
96773   20206   42559   78985   05300   22164   24369   54224   35083   19687   11052   91491   60383   19746
38935   64202   14349   82674   66523   44133   00697   35552   35970   19124   63318   29686   03387   59846
31624   76384   17403   53363   44167   64486   64758   75366   76554   31601   12614   33072   60332   92325
78919   19474   23632   27889   47914   02584   37680   20801   72152   39339   34806   98930   85001   87820

03931   33309   57047   74211   63445   17361   62825   39908   05607   91284   68833   25970   38818   46920
74426   33278   43972   10119   89917   15665   52872   73823   73144   88662   88970   74492   51805   99378
09066   00903   20795   95452   92648   45454   09552   88815   16553   51125   79375   97596   16296   66092
42238   12426   87025   14267   20979   04508   64535   31355   86064   29472   47689   05974   52468   16834
16153   08002   26504   41744   81959   65642   74240   56302   00033   67107   77510   70625   28725   34191
```

Appendix D

Area under the Normal Curve

Column (a) lists Z scores from 0.00 to 4.00. Only positive scores are displayed, but, since the normal curve is symmetrical, the areas for negative scores will be exactly the same as areas for positive scores. Column (b) lists the proportion of the total area between the Z score and the mean. Figure D.1 displays areas of this type. Column (c) lists the proportion of the area beyond the Z score, and Figure D.2 displays this type of area.

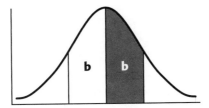

Figure D.1   Area between Mean and Z

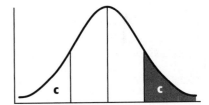

Figure D.2   Area Beyond Z

(a) Z	(b) Area between Mean and Z	(c) Area Beyond Z	(a) Z	(b) Area between Mean and Z	(c) Area Beyond Z
0.00	0.0000	0.5000	0.21	0.0832	0.4168
0.01	0.0040	0.4960	0.22	0.0871	0.4129
0.02	0.0080	0.4920	0.23	0.0910	0.4090
0.03	0.0120	0.4880	0.24	0.0948	0.4052
0.04	0.0160	0.4840	0.25	0.0987	0.4013
0.05	0.0199	0.4801	0.26	0.1026	0.3974
0.06	0.0239	0.4761	0.27	0.1064	0.3936
0.07	0.0279	0.4721	0.28	0.1103	0.3897
0.08	0.0319	0.4681	0.29	0.1141	0.3859
0.09	0.0359	0.4641	0.30	0.1179	0.3821
0.10	0.0398	0.4602	0.31	0.1217	0.3783
0.11	0.0438	0.4562	0.32	0.1255	0.3745
0.12	0.0478	0.4522	0.33	0.1293	0.3707
0.13	0.0517	0.4483	0.34	0.1331	0.3669
0.14	0.0557	0.4443	0.35	0.1368	0.3632
0.15	0.0596	0.4404	0.36	0.1406	0.3594
0.16	0.0636	0.4364	0.37	0.1443	0.3557
0.17	0.0675	0.4325	0.38	0.1480	0.3520
0.18	0.0714	0.4286	0.39	0.1517	0.3483
0.19	0.0753	0.4247	0.40	0.1554	0.3446
0.20	0.0793	0.4207	0.41	0.1591	0.3409

(a) Z	(b) Area between Mean and Z	(c) Area Beyond Z	(a) Z	(b) Area between Mean and Z	(c) Area Beyond Z
0.42	0.1628	0.3372	0.95	0.3289	0.1711
0.43	0.1664	0.3336	0.96	0.3315	0.1685
0.44	0.1700	0.3300	0.97	0.3340	0.1660
0.45	0.1736	0.3264	0.98	0.3365	0.1635
0.46	0.1772	0.3228	0.99	0.3389	0.1611
0.47	0.1808	0.3192	1.00	0.3413	0.1587
0.48	0.1844	0.3156			
0.49	0.1879	0.3121	1.01	0.3438	0.1562
0.50	0.1915	0.3085	1.02	0.3461	0.1539
			1.03	0.3485	0.1515
0.51	0.1950	0.3050	1.04	0.3508	0.1492
0.52	0.1985	0.3015	1.05	0.3531	0.1469
0.53	0.2019	0.2981	1.06	0.3554	0.1446
0.54	0.2054	0.2946	1.07	0.3577	0.1423
0.55	0.2088	0.2912	1.08	0.3599	0.1401
0.56	0.2123	0.2877	1.09	0.3621	0.1379
0.57	0.2157	0.2843	1.10	0.3643	0.1357
0.58	0.2190	0.2810			
0.59	0.2224	0.2776	1.11	0.3665	0.1335
0.60	0.2257	0.2743	1.12	0.3686	0.1314
			1.13	0.3708	0.1292
0.61	0.2291	0.2709	1.14	0.3729	0.1271
0.62	0.2324	0.2676	1.15	0.3749	0.1251
0.63	0.2357	0.2643	1.16	0.3770	0.1230
0.64	0.2389	0.2611	1.17	0.3790	0.1210
0.65	0.2422	0.2578	1.18	0.3810	0.1190
0.66	0.2454	0.2546	1.19	0.3830	0.1170
0.67	0.2486	0.2514	1.20	0.3849	0.1151
0.68	0.2517	0.2483			
0.69	0.2549	0.2451	1.21	0.3869	0.1131
0.70	0.2580	0.2420	1.22	0.3888	0.1112
			1.23	0.3907	0.1093
0.71	0.2611	0.2389	1.24	0.3925	0.1075
0.72	0.2642	0.2358	1.25	0.3944	0.1056
0.73	0.2673	0.2327	1.26	0.3962	0.1038
0.74	0.2703	0.2297	1.27	0.3980	0.1020
0.75	0.2734	0.2266	1.28	0.3997	0.1003
0.76	0.2764	0.2236	1.29	0.4015	0.0985
0.77	0.2794	0.2206	1.30	0.4032	0.0968
0.78	0.2823	0.2177			
0.79	0.2852	0.2148	1.31	0.4049	0.0951
0.80	0.2881	0.2119	1.32	0.4066	0.0934
			1.33	0.4082	0.0918
0.81	0.2910	0.2090	1.34	0.4099	0.0901
0.82	0.2939	0.2061	1.35	0.4115	0.0885
0.83	0.2967	0.2033	1.36	0.4131	0.0869
0.84	0.2995	0.2005	1.37	0.4147	0.0853
0.85	0.3023	0.1977	1.38	0.4162	0.0838
0.86	0.3051	0.1949	1.39	0.4177	0.0823
0.87	0.3078	0.1922	1.40	0.4192	0.0808
0.88	0.3106	0.1894			
0.89	0.3133	0.1867	1.41	0.4207	0.0793
0.90	0.3159	0.1841	1.42	0.4222	0.0778
			1.43	0.4236	0.0764
0.91	0.3186	0.1814	1.44	0.4251	0.0749
0.92	0.3212	0.1788	1.45	0.4265	0.0735
0.93	0.3238	0.1762	1.46	0.4279	0.0721
0.94	0.3264	0.1736	1.47	0.4292	0.0708

(a) Z	(b) Area between Mean and Z	(c) Area Beyond Z	(a) Z	(b) Area between Mean and Z	(c) Area Beyond Z
1.48	0.4306	0.0694	2.01	0.4778	0.0222
1.49	0.4319	0.0681	2.02	0.4783	0.0217
1.50	0.4332	0.0668	2.03	0.4788	0.0212
1.51	0.4345	0.0655	2.04	0.4793	0.0207
1.52	0.4357	0.0643	2.05	0.4798	0.0202
1.53	0.4370	0.0630	2.06	0.4803	0.0197
1.54	0.4382	0.0618	2.07	0.4808	0.0192
1.55	0.4394	0.0606	2.08	0.4812	0.0188
1.56	0.4406	0.0594	2.09	0.4817	0.0183
1.57	0.4418	0.0582	2.10	0.4821	0.0179
1.58	0.4429	0.0571	2.11	0.4826	0.0174
1.59	0.4441	0.0559	2.12	0.4830	0.0170
1.60	0.4452	0.0548	2.13	0.4834	0.0166
1.61	0.4463	0.0537	2.14	0.4838	0.0162
1.62	0.4474	0.0526	2.15	0.4842	0.0158
1.63	0.4484	0.0516	2.16	0.4846	0.0154
1.64	0.4495	0.0505	2.17	0.4850	0.0150
1.65	0.4505	0.0495	2.18	0.4854	0.0146
1.66	0.4515	0.0485	2.19	0.4857	0.0143
1.67	0.4525	0.0475	2.20	0.4861	0.0139
1.68	0.4535	0.0465	2.21	0.4864	0.0136
1.69	0.4545	0.0455	2.22	0.4868	0.0132
1.70	0.4554	0.0446	2.23	0.4871	0.0129
1.71	0.4564	0.0436	2.24	0.4875	0.0125
1.72	0.4573	0.0427	2.25	0.4878	0.0122
1.73	0.4582	0.0418	2.26	0.4881	0.0119
1.74	0.4591	0.0409	2.27	0.4884	0.0116
1.75	0.4599	0.0401	2.28	0.4887	0.0113
1.76	0.4608	0.0392	2.29	0.4890	0.0110
1.77	0.4616	0.0384	2.30	0.4893	0.0107
1.78	0.4625	0.0375	2.31	0.4896	0.0104
1.79	0.4633	0.0367	2.32	0.4898	0.0102
1.80	0.4641	0.0359	2.33	0.4901	0.0099
1.81	0.4649	0.0351	2.34	0.4904	0.0096
1.82	0.4656	0.0344	2.35	0.4906	0.0094
1.83	0.4664	0.0336	2.36	0.4909	0.0091
1.84	0.4671	0.0329	2.37	0.4911	0.0089
1.85	0.4678	0.0322	2.38	0.4913	0.0087
1.86	0.4686	0.0314	2.39	0.4916	0.0084
1.87	0.4693	0.0307	2.40	0.4918	0.0082
1.88	0.4699	0.0301	2.41	0.4920	0.0080
1.89	0.4706	0.0294	2.42	0.4922	0.0078
1.90	0.4713	0.0287	2.43	0.4925	0.0075
1.91	0.4719	0.0281	2.44	0.4927	0.0073
1.92	0.4726	0.0274	2.45	0.4929	0.0071
1.93	0.4732	0.0268	2.46	0.4931	0.0069
1.94	0.4738	0.0262	2.47	0.4932	0.0068
1.95	0.4744	0.0256	2.48	0.4934	0.0066
1.96	0.4750	0.0250	2.49	0.4936	0.0064
1.97	0.4756	0.0244	2.50	0.4938	0.0062
1.98	0.4761	0.0239	2.51	0.4940	0.0060
1.99	0.4767	0.0233	2.52	0.4941	0.0059
2.00	0.4772	0.0228	2.53	0.4943	0.0057

(a) Z	(b) Area between Mean and Z	(c) Area Beyond Z	(a) Z	(b) Area between Mean and Z	(c) Area Beyond Z
2.54	0.4945	0.0055	3.07	0.4989	0.0011
2.55	0.4946	0.0054	3.08	0.4990	0.0010
2.56	0.4948	0.0052	3.09	0.4990	0.0010
2.57	0.4949	0.0051	3.10	0.4990	0.0010
2.58	0.4951	0.0049	3.11	0.4991	0.0009
2.59	0.4952	0.0048	3.12	0.4991	0.0009
2.60	0.4953	0.0047	3.13	0.4991	0.0009
2.61	0.4955	0.0045	3.14	0.4992	0.0008
2.62	0.4956	0.0044	3.15	0.4992	0.0008
2.63	0.4957	0.0043	3.16	0.4992	0.0008
2.64	0.4959	0.0041	3.17	0.4992	0.0008
2.65	0.4960	0.0040	3.18	0.4993	0.0007
2.66	0.4961	0.0039	3.19	0.4993	0.0007
2.67	0.4962	0.0038	3.20	0.4993	0.0007
2.68	0.4963	0.0037	3.21	0.4993	0.0007
2.69	0.4964	0.0036	3.22	0.4994	0.0006
2.70	0.4965	0.0035	3.23	0.4994	0.0006
2.71	0.4966	0.0034	3.24	0.4994	0.0006
2.72	0.4967	0.0033	3.25	0.4994	0.0006
2.73	0.4968	0.0032	3.26	0.4994	0.0006
2.74	0.4969	0.0031	3.27	0.4995	0.0005
2.75	0.4970	0.0030	3.28	0.4995	0.0005
2.76	0.4971	0.0029	3.29	0.4995	0.0005
2.77	0.4972	0.0028	3.30	0.4995	0.0005
2.78	0.4973	0.0027	3.31	0.4995	0.0005
2.79	0.4974	0.0026	3.32	0.4995	0.0005
2.80	0.4974	0.0026	3.33	0.4996	0.0004
2.81	0.4975	0.0025	3.34	0.4996	0.0004
2.82	0.4976	0.0024	3.35	0.4996	0.0004
2.83	0.4977	0.0023	3.36	0.4996	0.0004
2.84	0.4977	0.0023	3.37	0.4996	0.0004
2.85	0.4978	0.0022	3.38	0.4996	0.0004
2.86	0.4979	0.0021	3.39	0.4997	0.0003
2.87	0.4979	0.0021	3.40	0.4997	0.0003
2.88	0.4980	0.0020	3.41	0.4997	0.0003
2.89	0.4981	0.0019	3.42	0.4997	0.0003
2.90	0.4981	0.0019	3.43	0.4997	0.0003
2.91	0.4982	0.0018	3.44	0.4997	0.0003
2.92	0.4982	0.0018	3.45	0.4997	0.0003
2.93	0.4983	0.0017	3.46	0.4997	0.0003
2.94	0.4984	0.0016	3.47	0.4997	0.0003
2.95	0.4984	0.0016	3.48	0.4997	0.0003
2.96	0.4985	0.0015	3.49	0.4998	0.0002
2.97	0.4985	0.0015	3.50	0.4998	0.0002
2.98	0.4986	0.0014	3.60	0.4998	0.0002
2.99	0.4986	0.0014	3.70	0.4999	0.0001
3.00	0.4986	0.0014	3.80	0.4999	0.0001
3.01	0.4987	0.0013	3.90	0.4999	<0.0001
3.02	0.4987	0.0013	4.00	0.4999	<0.0001
3.03	0.4988	0.0012			
3.04	0.4988	0.0012			
3.05	0.4989	0.0011			
3.06	0.4989	0.0011			

Appendix E

Distribution of Chi-Square Values

df	.99	.98	.95	.90	.80	.70	.50	.30	.20	.10	.05	.02	.01	.001
1	$.0^{3}157$	$.0^{3}628$	.00393	.0158	.0642	.148	.455	1.074	1.642	2.706	3.841	5.412	6.635	10.827
2	.0201	.0404	.103	.211	.446	.713	1.386	2.408	3.219	4.605	5.991	7.824	9.210	13.815
3	.115	.185	.352	.584	1.005	1.424	2.366	3.665	4.642	6.251	7.815	9.837	11.341	16.268
4	.297	.429	.711	1.064	1.649	2.195	3.357	4.878	5.989	7.779	9.488	11.668	13.277	18.465
5	.554	.752	1.145	1.610	2.343	3.000	4.351	6.064	7.289	9.236	11.070	13.388	15.086	20.517
6	.872	1.134	1.635	2.204	3.070	3.828	5.348	7.231	8.558	10.645	12.592	15.033	16.812	22.457
7	1.239	1.564	2.167	2.833	3.822	4.671	6.346	8.383	9.803	12.017	14.067	16.622	18.475	24.322
8	1.646	2.032	2.733	3.490	4.594	5.527	7.344	9.524	11.030	13.362	15.507	18.168	20.090	26.125
9	2.088	2.532	3.325	4.168	5.380	6.393	8.343	10.656	12.242	14.684	16.919	19.679	21.666	27.877
10	2.558	3.059	3.940	4.865	6.179	7.267	9.342	11.781	13.442	15.987	18.307	21.161	23.209	29.588
11	3.053	3.609	4.575	5.578	6.989	8.148	10.341	12.899	14.631	17.275	19.675	22.618	24.725	31.264
12	3.571	4.178	5.226	6.304	7.807	9.034	11.340	14.011	15.812	18.549	21.026	24.054	26.217	32.909
13	4.107	4.765	5.892	7.042	8.634	9.926	12.340	15.119	16.985	19.812	22.362	25.472	27.688	34.528
14	4.660	5.368	6.571	7.790	9.467	10.821	13.339	16.222	18.151	21.064	23.685	26.873	29.141	36.123
15	5.229	5.985	7.261	8.547	10.307	11.721	14.339	17.322	19.311	22.307	24.996	28.259	30.578	37.697
16	5.812	6.614	7.962	9.312	11.152	12.624	15.338	18.418	20.465	23.542	26.296	29.633	32.000	39.252
17	6.408	7.255	8.672	10.085	12.002	13.531	16.338	19.511	21.615	24.769	27.587	30.995	33.409	40.790
18	7.015	7.906	9.390	10.865	12.857	14.440	17.338	20.601	22.760	25.989	28.869	32.346	34.805	42.312
19	7.633	8.567	10.117	11.651	13.716	15.352	18.338	21.689	23.900	27.204	30.144	33.687	36.191	43.820
20	8.260	9.237	10.851	12.443	14.578	16.266	19.337	22.775	25.038	28.412	31.410	35.020	37.566	45.315
21	8.897	9.915	11.591	13.240	15.445	17.182	20.337	23.858	26.171	29.615	32.671	36.343	38.932	46.797
22	9.542	10.600	12.338	14.041	16.314	18.101	21.337	24.939	27.301	30.813	33.924	37.659	40.289	48.268
23	10.196	11.293	13.091	14.848	17.187	19.021	22.337	26.018	28.429	32.007	35.172	38.968	41.638	49.728
24	10.856	11.992	13.848	15.659	18.062	19.943	23.337	27.096	29.553	33.196	36.415	40.270	42.980	51.179
25	11.524	12.697	14.611	16.473	18.940	20.867	24.337	28.172	30.675	34.382	37.652	41.566	44.314	52.620
26	12.198	13.409	15.379	17.292	19.820	21.792	25.336	29.246	31.795	35.563	38.885	42.856	45.642	54.052
27	12.879	14.125	16.151	18.114	20.703	22.719	26.336	30.319	32.912	36.741	40.113	44.140	46.963	55.476
28	13.565	14.847	16.928	18.939	21.588	23.647	27.336	31.391	34.027	37.916	41.337	45.419	48.278	56.893
29	14.256	15.574	17.708	19.768	22.475	24.577	28.336	32.461	35.139	39.087	42.557	46.693	49.588	58.302
30	14.953	16.306	18.493	20.599	23.364	25.508	29.336	33.530	36.250	40.256	43.773	47.962	50.892	59.703

Source: Table IV of Fisher & Yates: *Statistical Tables for Biological, Agricultural and Medical Research*, published by Longman Group Ltd., London (1974), 6th edition (previously published by Oliver & Boyd Ltd., Edinburgh). Reprinted by permission of Addison Wesley Longman Ltd.

Appendix F
Distribution of *t*-Values

Degrees of Freedom (df)	Level of Significance for One-tailed Test					
	.10	.05	.025	.01	.005	.0005
	Level of Significance for Two-tailed Test					
	.20	.10	.05	.02	.01	.001
1	3.078	6.314	12.706	31.821	63.657	636.619
2	1.886	2.920	4.303	6.965	9.925	31.598
3	1.638	2.353	3.182	4.541	5.841	12.941
4	1.533	2.132	2.776	3.747	4.604	8.610
5	1.476	2.015	2.571	3.365	4.032	6.859
6	1.440	1.943	2.447	3.143	3.707	5.959
7	1.415	1.895	2.365	2.998	3.499	5.405
8	1.397	1.860	2.306	2.896	3.355	5.041
9	1.383	1.833	2.262	2.821	3.250	4.781
10	1.372	1.812	2.228	2.764	3.169	4.587
11	1.363	1.796	2.201	2.718	3.106	4.437
12	1.356	1.782	2.179	2.681	3.055	4.318
13	1.350	1.771	2.160	2.650	3.012	4.221
14	1.345	1.761	2.145	2.624	2.977	4.140
15	1.341	1.753	2.131	2.602	2.947	4.073
16	1.337	1.746	2.120	2.583	2.921	4.015
17	1.333	1.740	2.110	2.567	2.898	3.965
18	1.330	1.734	2.101	2.552	2.878	3.922
19	1.328	1.729	2.093	2.539	2.861	3.883
20	1.325	1.725	2.086	2.528	2.845	3.850
21	1.323	1.721	2.080	2.518	2.831	3.819
22	1.321	1.717	2.074	2.508	2.819	3.792
23	1.319	1.714	2.069	2.500	2.807	3.767
24	1.318	1.711	2.064	2.492	2.797	3.745
25	1.316	1.708	2.060	2.485	2.787	3.725
26	1.315	1.706	2.056	2.479	2.779	3.707
27	1.314	1.703	2.052	2.473	2.771	3.690
28	1.313	1.701	2.048	2.467	2.763	3.674
29	1.311	1.699	2.045	2.462	2.756	3.659
30	1.310	1.697	2.042	2.457	2.750	3.646
40	1.303	1.684	2.021	2.423	2.704	3.551
60	1.296	1.671	2.000	2.390	2.660	3.460
120	1.289	1.658	1.980	2.358	2.617	3.373
∞	1.282	1.645	1.960	2.326	2.576	3.291

Source: Table III of Fisher & Yates: *Statistical Tables for Biological, Agricultural and Medical Research*, published by Longman Group Ltd., London (1974), 6th edition (previously published by Oliver & Boyd Ltd., Edinburgh).

Glossary

Abstract: A very brief summary of the research that is usually 100 to 150 words long. Abstracts generally include a summary of the research problem, a brief description of the sample and sampling techniques, the general research design, and a basic overview of research findings.

Activities: In program or policy language, activities are what people do with the inputs they have. In other words, activities are the specific services a program offers.

Anonymity: Guaranteeing a respondent that the researcher will have no means of matching the respondent's answers to his or her identity.

Attribute: *See* Variable.

Axial coding: The second stage of the successive approximation method of qualitative data analysis, where the researcher organizes the code lists from the previous stage of open coding to compare the content within broadly coded themes.

Belmont Report: Ethical guidelines established by the National Commission for the Protection of Human Subjects that distinguishes the ethical responsibilities of the social sciences from biomedical research. This report establishes the three main social science ethical responsibilities to be respect for persons, principle of beneficence, and principle of justice.

Bivariate statistics: Statistics that assess or describe how two variables are related to each other.

Central limit theorem: When a large number of samples of sufficiently large size are drawn, the means of those samples will distribute themselves along the normal curve, with the midpoint of this curve approaching the true population parameter.

Closed-ended questions: Survey questions in which the researcher specifies predetermined answer choices from which respondents can select the one that best approximates their views or experiences.

Code sheet entry: The format of data entry where the coder reads a code sheet and types into a computer the corresponding numbers that appear.

Coding: The process of assigning numbers to the individual written responses or *values* to a question so that a computer can understand and analyze this information.

Cohort study: A form of longitudinal research that studies people who share a specific time characteristic (e.g., born in a certain year, graduated high school in a certain year). Each sample consists of people from the same cohort; however, the researcher draws a new sample from this cohort at every stage of the study.

Competent insider performance: In qualitative data analysis, this is a validity test that refers to the degree to which the researcher is accepted among the participants and determines whether the researcher provided enough information about the field to give outsiders a sense of the social context in which the study occurred.

Complete observer research: The researcher observes social behavior without becoming involved in any way.

Complete participant research: A method of qualitative field research where the researcher observes and interacts with the participants, but also actively seeks to manipulate the participants' activities.

Computer-assisted telephone interviewing: A method of interviewing where the interviewer or research assistants read the survey to a respondent from a computer and then directly enter that respondent's response into the computer.

Concepts: Abstract terms people use to describe reality. People may share general definitions or understandings of a concept, but because they are abstract, the specific interpretation of these concepts among many people may differ.

Conceptual definition: A working definition a researcher uses for a concept.

Conceptualization: The process of defining what a concept means.

Concurrent validity: A type of criterion validity where the researcher uses another, widely accepted measure, at the same time the researcher is using the variable of interest in order to validate his or her own measure of interest.

Confidence interval: The range of values within which researchers think the true population parameter lies.

Confidence level: How sure researchers are that their findings are not produced by chance or random error.

Confidentiality: An ethical issue where the researcher knows the respondent's identity, but guarantees that he or she will not reveal it in any publication of the research.

Construct validity: When researchers can show that their measure is related to other measures specified in a theory.

Contamination: When members of the experimental or control group learn of each other and this knowledge affects their behavior in the posttest.

Content validity: A validity test for whether the measure covers the full range, or all of the dimensions, of a concept's meaning.

Context effects: This occurs when the wording of a research question influences people's responses to subsequent questions.

Contingency questions: Questions that are answered only if the respondent answers a specific way to a previous question (a filter question). In other words, how a respondent answers this question is "contingent" on that respondent's answer to a previous question.

Control group: In an experiment, this is the group that does not receive the treatment or stimulus. This group serves as a comparison group to the experimental group.

Control variable: Variables that are extraneous to the main research question itself, but that need to be addressed (or "controlled") because they may have an effect on the dependent variable.

Convergent validity: When a measure is associated with other related measures in the same way.

Correlation: A statistical measure of how strongly two variables are related. Correlations frequently range from 0 to 1, where the closer to zero the weaker the relationship between variables, and the closer to one the stronger the relationship between variables.

Cost-benefit analysis: A form of evaluation research where program costs, such as staff wages and material costs, are compared to the program outcomes, such as taxpayer savings, measured in monetary terms.

Cost-effective analysis: A form of evaluation research where inputs (program costs) are estimated in monetary terms (similar to cost-benefit analysis), but outcomes are estimated in actual impacts, such as the number of families that are reunited.

Cover letter: The letter included with a mailed survey. It contains the general information about the survey and research study that is necessary to obtain informed consent and encourage people to participate.

Criterion validity: A type of validity that compares a researcher's chosen measure to some external criteria—whether it is another measure widely accepted in that particular field or a more directly observable criterion.

Debriefing: The process of explaining to research participants the purpose of the research, how the respondents may have been manipulated (e.g., in an experiment), answering any questions the respondents may have, and giving the respondents the right to withhold information after the fact *after* research has been completed and before any results are calculated or released.

Dependent variable: The effect in a causal relationship. The value of the depended variable "depends" or is influenced by the independent variable.

Descriptive statistics: *See* Univariate statistics.

Dimensions: A theoretical term used to describe clusters of concepts that together represent a broader, more complex concept.

Direct entry method: When a coder sits at a computer terminal with the raw method of observation (e.g., a survey) and directly enters the respondent's information from that survey or other observational method into the computer.

Direct notes: Detailed notes that the field researcher writes after he or she leaves the field for a while that are based on the jotted notes that the researcher took during the course of the day.

Discriminant validity: When scores on a measure are compared to measures of different, but related, concepts and the measure of interest behaves differently.

Discriminating: Items in an index or scale that add to the final scale measurement by distinguishing between high and low scores.

Distribution: All of the responses to a particular variable.

Double-barreled questions: Questions in which two or more questions are asked even though there is only one answer. A common identifier is the word *and* in a question where the "and" is used to ask two different questions, not to link two or more specific aspects of one question.

Double blind study: A form of research in which the researcher does not know which group is receiving an experimental treatment. This is done to avoid the threat to validity known as the "experimenter effect."

Ecological fallacy: When researchers draw conclusions about individuals when they study groups.

Ecological validity: In qualitative research this is the degree to which the social relationships and experiences that the researcher describes actually matches those of the participants.

Elements: The units a researcher is studying. Elements are similar to units of analysis, but elements are a sampling term and units of analysis refer to data analysis.

E-mail survey: A type of survey where the researcher sends a questionnaire to respondents through the respondent's electronic mail and the respondent returns the completed survey also through electronic mail.

Equivalence reliability: When several items are used to measure the same concept and they all produce the same result with all indicators.

Ethical relativism: The recognition that ethical guidelines, to some degree, specify what "ought" to happen in the course of social science research. Behavior that is ethical in one context may not be in another.

Exhaustive answer categories: Making sure that there is an answer choice for everyone. In nominal levels of measurement this can be accomplished by adding an "Other" category. In ordinal opinion questions, adding a "No opinion" or "Not applicable" category can accomplish this.

Experimental group: In an experiment, this group experiences the situation or stimulus that the researcher modified.

Experimental mortality: A threat to validity that may occur in longitudinal studies when a large proportion of members of an original sample or sample members with similar characteristics drop out of a study as time goes on.

Experimenter effects: A validity threat present in experiments where conscious or unconscious behavior on behalf of the researcher (as opposed to the independent variable) leads to a change in the dependent variable.

Face validity: The most basic validity test that measures whether the measure appears valid "on the face of it." In other words, determining whether the measure seems to make logical sense as an indicator of a concept.

Filter question: The first question in a series of questions that determines whether a respondent will continue to the next question or skip some questions and resume the survey at a later question.

Frequency distribution: A list of the number of observations for each value of a variable.

Gatekeeper: People who can help an outsider, such as a researcher, gain access to a setting by vouching for the researcher's presence.

Hawthorne effect: *See* Reactivity.

History effect: Events external to the research that can affect the results obtained.

Hypothesis: A statement that makes a causal connection between concepts that will be tested with empirical observation (research).

Ideal types: A term coined by Max Weber that refers to descriptions of abstract characteristics that, when taken together, create a complete ideal definition or description of a concept.

Ideology: Oversimplified explanations for social behavior that focus on one or a few variables to explain a social phenomenon. Ideologies are resistant to change and become entwined with moral, instead of empirical, arguments.

Independent variable: The "cause" in a causal relationship. It is the variable that produces the change in the dependent variable.

Indicator: *See* Operational definition.

Informed consent: Telling potential research subjects any and all information about the study that might influence their decision whether to participate.

Inputs: The resources, guidelines, and operating procedures that go into a policy or program.

Institutional review board: Review committees that are responsible for making sure that the benefits of a research project any potential costs to the participants and that the procedures used in the research methodology include adequate safeguards to protect the identify, safety, and general well-being of participants.

Instrumentation: A potential threat to validity that occurs when the measures used to observe concepts change during the course of the study.

Inter-observer reliability: A reliability test where more than one researcher observes and codes people, events, or environments. Agreement between the two researchers in their coding illustrates inter-observer reliability.

Internal validity: Determines whether some factor other than the independent variable produced the observed change in the dependent variable.

Interval measure: A variable whose answer choices are exhaustive, mutually exclusive, and have quantifiable distances between categories, but does not have a true zero point (any zero value is arbitrarily assigned).

Jottings: A type of field note that is short and temporary. These notes are designed to trigger the researcher's memory when he or she has the time to write more detailed notes.

Key informants: A member of a group that a researcher is studying who serves as a knowledgeable insider for the researcher. Key informants help the researcher gain access to other group members and understand the cultural context of the group or environment.

Latent content: Coding commonly used in content analysis that identifies the underlying meaning behind communication.

Literature review: A review of published research that tells a person what is already known about a topic, what research gaps need to be filled, and where researchers have found conflicting findings. A literature review serves to help researchers specify their specific research problem, gives them ideas for how to measure concepts, and provides ideas on how to design a method of observation.

Longitudinal research: Research that studies individuals at more than one time point.

Macro-theory: A theory that focuses on how the wider social structure affects groups.

Mailed self-report survey: A survey that a respondent receives in the mail along with a cover letter and a stamped self-addressed envelope. The respondent completes the survey on his or her own and returns it to the researcher in the stamped self-addressed envelope.

Manifest content: Coding commonly used in content analysis that involves counting or identifying the visible surface content of communication.

Matrix format: An efficient way of presenting several items that share the same answer choices. The answer choices are listed once across the top of a matrix and the questions sharing those choices are listed down the page. Then instead of repeating the same answer choices for each question, the respondent just checks or circles a corresponding space or number for each choice that is lined up under the response categories listed at the top of the question set.

Maturation: A concern in longitudinal research that occurs when participants' behavior changes, but the change may be due to the simple act of aging or because of the length of the study rather than due to the independent variable.

Mean: A statistic used for normally distributed interval/ratio levels of measure that measure the average response to a variable.

Measure of central tendency: Univariate, or descriptive, statistics that identify the typical, or central, response.

Measure of dispersion: Univariate statistics that summarize the spread, or variability, of a distribution.

Measurement: The process of observing concepts, as indicated by their operational definitions, and assigning some type of score or meaning to people's responses.

Median: A statistic used for ordinal or interval/ratio levels of measure that measure the middle response. Fifty percent of the distribution lies below this value and fifty percent lies above.

Member validation: A form of assessing the validity of qualitative data analysis in which the researcher presents his or her conclusions to the study participants to determine whether the researcher's conclusions match the interpretations of those in the study.

Meso-theory: A theory that tries link macro- and micro-levels of theory by simultaneously explaining broad social processes with people's experiences within those broad processes and how people's actions, in turn, affect broad social processes. As a form of theory, this is relatively rare.

Micro-theory: A theory that explains the social experience of individuals, smaller social groups, small segments of time, or small instances of space.

Mode: The most frequent response in a distribution.

Mutually exclusive: Survey answer questions are mutually exclusive when they have categories in which respondents can select one and only one response, unless directed otherwise.

Natural history validity: In qualitative data analysis this is the researcher's full explanation about how his or her study was conducted. It is the researcher's documentation of his or her methodological procedures, his or her actions during the experience, and his or her assumptions made during all phases of the experience (meaning before, during, and after).

Needs assessment: A form of evaluation research that tries to scientifically assess the degree of a social problem and the corresponding social need.

Negative case testing: A form of evaluating the validity of qualitative data analysis that involves examining the lists of themes and supporting points and reexamining the data to see if there is evidence of data and themes that counter those already found.

Nominal measure: A variable whose answer choices are exhaustive as well as mutually exclusive.

Nonreactive research: Research that examines the results of human behavior, as opposed to people's behavior or expressed views, and therefore the researcher has no direct or indirect contact with any people.

Nonspurious relationship: Establishing that the observed relationship between two variables is not due to (or caused by) a third variable.

Observer as participant research: In this type of research, the researcher makes his or her identity as a researcher known but only marginally interacts with the participants. The researcher does not partake in whatever activity he or she is observing with the participants.

Open coding: An early stage of the successive approximation method of qualitative data analysis where the researcher rereads field notes numerous times in order to find patterns in the data.

Open-ended questions: Survey questions that have no predetermined answer categories. Respondents are free to write their responses in their own words.

Operational definition: The definitions that indicate exactly what a researcher means by his or her concepts. They *indicate* what the researcher's concept is, therefore they are also sometime called "indicators."

Operationalization: The process of continually defining concepts until the researcher arrives at a definition that is directly empirically observable. It is the process of asking "What do I mean?" until the answer is clearly observable and understood by a variety of people without further explanation.

Ordinal measure: A variable whose answer choices are ranked, exhaustive, and mutually exclusive.

Outcome: In program evaluation this is the direct results of the specific accomplishments (and failures) of the program regarding client experiences and wider societal goals.

Output: In program evaluation, this is a description of program process or delivery. It is the same as a result.

Panel study: A longitudinal form of research in which the same people are studied across a span of time.

Paradigm: Loose theoretical models that organize people's thoughts about some phenomenon. A general point of view of related concepts or assumptions relevant to a theory. Groups of theories constitute paradigms.

Participant observation: A form of field research where the researcher makes his or her identity as a researcher known to subjects, but also interacts extensively with the subjects in their natural environment.

Periodicity: A problem for systematic samples that occurs when elements in a sampling frame are arranged in a cyclical pattern.

Personal notes: A form of field notes in which the researcher keeps notes about his or her personal feelings and experiences on a particular day.

Physical trace analysis: Studying the deposits or accretion of matter left by human behavior.

Plagiarism: A violation of a researcher's ethical responsibility to science that occurs when the researcher uses the work or ideas of another person without citing the source.

Population: A broad grouping of people from which researchers select a sample. In quantitative research, the sample is used to generalize findings to this larger group.

Population parameter: The value or attribute of a variable in the population. This figure is usually unknown and researchers use statistics to estimate it.

Predictive validity: A type of criterion validity where a measure's validity is judged by its ability of a measure to predict future behavior.

Pretest effect: A threat to validity that occurs when the administration of a pretest or a survey affects a later test or survey because participants have now been sensitized to the research information as a result of being tested.

Principle of beneficence: The ethical responsibility of a researcher to his or her participants to do good for them whenever possible.

Principle of nonmalefiscence: The ethical responsibility of a researcher to his or her participants not to cause the participants any physical, legal, psychological, or social harm as a result of the respondents' participation in the research.

Probability of error: The probability that a difference noticed between two or more groups does not signify a "real" difference in a statistical sense and essentially just occurred by chance.

Probability theory: Because the sample of the sampling means in random samples will arrange themselves along the normal curve, one standard error in either direction (plus or minus) of the mean of the sampling means will account for approximately 68 percent of the means samples drawn. Likewise, two standard errors in each direction will account for 95 percent of the means of the samples selected, and three standard errors in each direction will account for 99 percent of all the sample means selected. When researchers conduct one random sample, test statistics from that one sample have a 68 percent chance of falling within plus/minus one standard deviation of the sample mean, a 95 percent chance of falling within plus/minus two standard deviation of the sample mean, and a 99 percent chance of falling within plus/minus one standard deviation of the sample mean.

Probe: Follow-up questions a researcher asks in order to encourage respondents to give a specific level of information to a question or a fuller answer.

Problem formation: The identification or specification of a research problem.

Program process: Essentially this is the same as an activity. *See* Activities.

Proposal: A written plan submitted to a funding agency when requesting money to finance research or a program. This plan tells the potential funding agency what an applicant intends to do with any money awarded.

Proposition: A term used to describe a theoretical statement that links two or more concepts. Its counterpart is a hypothesis. *See* Hypothesis.

Qualitative research: Research aimed at an in-depth understanding of a social issue. It focuses on the nuances of behavior or experiences in a small group.

Quantitative research: Research aimed at trying to find statistical patterns or trends in a population based on the observation of a sample.

Random assignment: A condition in true experiments where the researcher randomly decides which subjects will be in treatment and control groups. Each subject has an equal and known probability in being in any particular group.

Random digit dialing: A method of sampling used for telephone surveys in which researchers obtain a list of area code exchanges numbers (the first three numbers in a phone number) and a computer randomly fills in the remaining numbers. Researchers then contact the people who the computer randomly selected via their completion of the telephone number.

Random selection: A form of sampling in which members of the study population have an equal, and known, probability of being selected for the sample.

Ratio measure: A variable whose answer choices are exhaustive, mutually exclusive, have quantifiable distances between categories, and have a true zero point.

Reactive research: Research in which the researcher has some level of involvement, directly or indirectly, with the subjects.

Reactivity: When research participants behave atypically because they know they are being observed by another person.

Recollection questions: Survey questions that ask participants about behavior that occurred in the past. Because human recall is questionable, these questions work best if the information asked is general and monumental.

Reductionism: Occurs when researchers are overly limited, either in terms of their variables or their units of analysis, and try to make conclusions about a broad range of human behavior. This is the mirror opposite of the ecological fallacy.

Reliability: Reliability is established when studies or measures produce consistent results in a variety of settings, times, or circumstances.

Representative reliability: Determination of whether an indicator produces the same results across different groups of people.

Research fraud: An ethical violation of a researcher's responsibility to science that occurs when a researcher invents or intentionally distorts information.

Researcher interpretation notes: A type of field note in which the researcher separately records his or her interpretations about a field observation. These notes should be kept separate from the other types of notes because later information may indicate that the interpretations were not actually accurate, and a researcher would not want to later mistakenly confuse interpretations with "facts."

Researcher-worker reliability: *See* Inter-observer reliability.

Response set: When all survey questions are written in the same direction, meaning that agreement or disagreement to all of the questions shows the same view of the hypothesis. To avoid response set patterns, researchers need to word survey questions where positive answers to some questions and negative answers to other questions would illustrate the same opinion regarding the research topic.

Result: In program evaluation, this is a description of program process or delivery. It is the same as an output.

Rival causal factors: Variables that are extraneous to the original independent/dependent relationship but actually account for the change in the dependent variable.

Sample: A subset of a population that researchers use in order to study that population.

Sampling interval: In a systematic sample, it is the interval the researcher uses to select a sample after finding a random starting point.

Secondary data analysis: Research that occurs when researchers analyze the data collected by other people.

Selection bias: When characteristics of the experimental and control groups or the sample and population differ so that the two groups being compared are not equal prior to the study.

Selective coding: The third stage of the successive approximation method of qualitative data analysis where the researcher has identified the major themes of the research and has to select which among those he or she will develop as the main themes or findings.

Skip question: In a contingency pattern of questions, skip questions are those that some respondents will not answer based on their previous answer to a filter question.

Skip pattern: The unanswered questions in a contingency format that result from a specific answer to a filter question. Not all respondents are necessarily going to experience skip patterns.

Social desirability bias: When participants give what they think is an acceptable or socially normative answer to a threatening or embarrassing research question in order to appear in a positive way to the researcher.

Split-half reliability test: The researcher divides a survey into two smaller instruments by randomly (either by the unscientific, but still random, method of flipping a coin or by the more scientific method of using a table of random numbers) separating the questions. Reliability is achieved if the two halves of the survey produce similar results.

Stakeholders: In program evaluation, stakeholders are the individuals or groups who have some specific interest in the program and concern for its outcomes.

Standard deviation: The square root of the sum of the squared differences between each individual test statistic from the sample mean. This measures the distribution of sample statistics.

Statistic: Any information that researchers directly obtain from a sample.

Statistical conclusion validity: A validity test that occurs when the data illustrate a pattern between two or more variables that the researcher theoretically expected to find.

Stratification variable: In stratified sampling, it is the variable used to separate a larger sample into smaller subsamples that are alike on a specific value of this variable.

Temporal reliability: Determination of whether a measure produces the same results if measured at different time periods.

Test-retest method: A means of assessing reliability where the researcher administers a measure more than once. If there is no reason to expect people's answers to that measure to change, then the responses should be the same at both time points.

Theory: A systematic, detailed means of explaining why a social phenomenon exists that recognizes the influences of a multitude of factors, is subject to change, and avoids moral arguments in favor of empirical arguments.

Treatment: In an experiment, this is what the researchers are manipulating. It is usually a value of the independent variable.

Trend studies: A type of longitudinal research where a researcher draws a new sample of people at different time points to examine the changes in a general population over time.

Type I error: This occurs when researchers state that a relationship exists between variables when, in fact, one does not. In other words, researchers erroneously reject the null hypothesis.

Type II error: This occurs when researchers state that a relationship does not exist between variables when, in fact, one does. In other words, researchers erroneously accept the null hypothesis.

Typology: A theoretical term for when researchers combine two or more simple concepts to create new concepts. For example, the combination of education, income, and occupation combine to form a typology for social class that ranges from upper middle class to the underclass.

Units of analysis: The people or things that a researcher is analyzing. There are generally four units of analysis: individuals, groups, organizations, and social artifact. Units of analysis are similar to elements, but elements are a sampling term and units of analysis refer to data analysis.

Univariate statistics: Sometimes also called descriptive statistics, these are statistics that summarize a sample or population one variable at a time.

Values: The answer options for a variable.

Variable: A means of measuring a concept where the answer choices can vary.

Web survey: A type of survey where the researcher has the questionnaire posted at a website and the respondent completes the survey at this website. Respondents are frequently e-mailed a link to the site.

Bibliography

Abel, Gillian; Plumridge, Libby; and Graham, Patrick. (2002). Peers, networks or relationships: Strategies for understanding social dynamics as determinants of smoking behaviour. *Drugs: Education, Prevention & Policy*, 9 (4), 325–338.

Alfred, Randall. (1976). The church of Satan. In Charles Glock and Robert Bellah (Eds.), *The new religious consciousness* (pp. 180–202). Berkeley: University of California Press.

Anderson, C. A., and Dill, K. E. (2000). Video games and aggressive thoughts, feelings, and behavior in the laboratory and life. *Journal of Personality and Social Psychology*, 78, 772–790.

Anderson, C. A., and Ford, C. M. (1986). Affect of the game player: Short term effects of highly and mildly aggressive video games. *Personality and Social Psychology Bulletin*, 12, 90–402.

Antecol, Heather, and Bedard, Kelly. (2002). The relative earnings of young Mexican, Black, and White women. *Industrial & Labor Relations Review*, 56 (1), 122–136.

Asch, Solomon. (1952). Effects of group pressure upon the modification and distortion of judgments. In Guy Swanson, Theodore M. Newcomb, and Eugene L. Hartley (Eds.), *Readings in social psychology*. New York: Holt, Rinehart and Winston.

Asch, Solomon. (1952). *Social psychology*. Englewood Cliffs, NJ: Prentice-Hall.

Aulette, Judy Root. (2002). *Changing American family*. Boston: Allyn and Bacon.

Ayidiya, Stephen A., and McClendon, McKee J. (1990). Response effects in mail surveys. *The Public Opinion Quarterly*, 54 (2), 229–247.

Ayoke, Oluremi B.; Härtel, Charmine E. J.; and Callan, Victor J. (2002). Resolving the puzzle of productive and destructive conflict in culturally heterogeneous workgroups: A communication accommodation theory approach. *International Journal of Conflict Management*, 13 (2), 165–196.

Babbie, Earl. (1995). *The practice of social research* (7th ed.). Albany, NY: Wadsworth.

Bachman, Ronet, and Schutt, Russell K. (2001). *The practice of research in criminology and criminal justice*. Thousand Oaks, CA: Pine Forge.

Baker, Kristan, and Donelly, Michelle. (2001). The social experiences of children with disability and the influences of environment: A framework for intervention. *Disability & Society*, 16 (1), 71–86.

Baptist, David A., Jr. (1986). The image of the Black family portrayed on television: A critical comment. *Marriage and the Family Review*, 10, 41–65.

Barber, Nigel. (2002). Plagiarism. *Encyclopedia of Ethics in Science and Technology*. Facts On File. *Science Online*. www.factsonfile.com.

Barnett, Cynthia, and Mencken, F. Carson. (2002). Social disorganization theory and the contextual nature of crime in nonmetropolitan countries. *Rural Sociology*, 67 (3), 372–394.

Barrie, Gunter. (1998). Ethnicity and involvement in violence on television: Nature and context of on-screen portrayals. *Journal of Black Studies*, 28 (6), 683–703.

Barton, A. J. (1958). Asking the embarrassing question. *Public Opinion Quarterly*, 22, 67–68.

Bates, Vernon L. (2000). The decline of a new Christian right social movement organization: Opportunities and constraints. *Review of Religious Research*, 42 (1) 19–41.

Bauman, Karl E.; Viadro, Claire I.; and Tsui, Amy O. (1994). Use of true experimental designs for family planning program evaluation: Merits, problems, and solutions. *International Family Planning Perspectives*, 20 (3), 108–113.

Beasley, Berrin, and Standley, Tracy Collins. (2002). Shirts vs. skins: Clothing as an indicator of gender role stereotyping in video games. *Mass Communication & Society*, 5 (3), 279–294.

Becker, Howard. (1953). Becoming a marijuana user. *The American Journal of Sociology*, 59, 395–403.

Benton, J. Edwin, and Daly, John L. (1991, Winter). A question order effect in a local government survey. *Public Opinion Quarterly*, 640–642.

Berg, Bruce. (1995). *Qualitative research methods for the social sciences* (3rd ed.). Boston: Allyn and Bacon.

Berg, Bruce. (2004). *Quantitative research methods for the social sciences* (5th ed.). Boston: Allyn and Bacon.

Bianchi, Suzanne M. (2000, November). Maternal employment and time with children: Dramatic change or surprising continuity? *Demography, 37* (4), 401–414.

Billings, Andrew C.; Halone, Kelby K.; and Denham, Bryan E. (2002). "Man, that was a pretty shot": An analysis of gendered broadcast commentary surrounding the 2000 men's and women's NCAA final four basketball championships. *Mass Communication & Society, 5* (3), 295–316.

Bishop, George; Hippler, Hans; Schwarz, Norbert; and Strack, Fritz. (1988). A comparison of response effects in self-administered and telephone surveys. In Robert Grooves (Ed.), *Telephone survey methodology* (pp. 321–340). New York: Wiley.

Boruch, R. F. (1975). On common contentions about randomized field experiments. In R. F. Boruch and H. W. Riecken (Eds.), *Experimental testing of public policy: The Proceedings of the 1974 Social Science Research Council Conference on social experiments*. Boulder, CO: Westview Press.

Bradburn, Norman M.; Sudman, Seymour; Blair, Ed; and Stocking, Carol. (1978). Question threat and response bias. *The Public Opinion Quarterly, 42* (2), 221–234.

Brasher, Holly. (2003). Capitalizing on contention: Issue agendas in U.S. Senate campaigns. *Political Communication, 20* (4), 453–172.

Breedlove, J. L. (1972). Theory development as a task for the evaluator. In E. J. Mullen and J. R. Dumpson (Eds.), *Evaluation of social intervention* (pp. 55–70). San Francisco: Jossey Bass.

Brewster, Zachary W. (2003). Behavioral and interactional patterns of strip club patrons: Tipping techniques and club attendance. *Deviant Behavior, 24* (3), 221–244.

Briggs, Chad S.; Sundt, Jody L.; and Castellano, Thomas C. (2003). The effect of supermaximum security prisons on aggregate levels of institutional violence. *Criminology, 41* (4), 1341–1376.

Broom, Michael. (2003). Portable assessment authoring: Using handheld technology to assess collaborative inquiry. *Education, Communication & Information, 3* (1), 7–56

Brown, Ivan. (1999). Embracing quality of life in times of spending restraint. *Journal of Intellectual & Developmental Disability, 24* (4), 299–309.

Bumpass, Larry L. (1997). The measurement of public opinion on abortion: The effects of survey design. *Family Planning Perspectives, 29* (4), 177–180.

Bureau of Justice Statistics. (1994). *Drugs and crime facts, 1994.* www.ojp.usdoj.gov/bjs/pub/pdf/dcfacts.pdf.

Campbell, D. T. (1969). Reforms as experiments. *American Psychologist, 24,* 409–429.

Campbell, Donald T., and Stanley, Julian C. (1963). *Experimental and quasi-experimental designs for research.* Chicago: Rand McNally.

Chambers, Sharon M.; Hardy, James C.; Smith, Brenda J.; and Sienty, Sarah F. (2003). Personality indicators and emergency permit teachers' willingness to embrace technology. *Journal of Instructional Psychology, 30* (3), 185–189.

Chaudry, Ajay. (2004). *Putting children first: How low-wage working mothers manage child care.* New York: Russell Sage Foundation.

Code of Federal Regulations. (1975, March 13). Title 45, A. Department of Health, Education and Welfare, General Administration, Part 46, Protection of Human Subjects. *Federal Registrar, 40,* 11854–11858.

Cook, Colleen; Heath, Fred; and Thompson, Russell. (2000). A meta-analysis of response rates in web- or Internet-based surveys. *Educational & Psychological Measurement, 60* (6), 821–837.

Cook, Thomas D., and Campbell, Donald T. (1979). *Quasi-experimentation: Design and analysis issues for field settings.* Chicago: Rand McNally.

Cook, T. D., Cook, F. L.; and Mark, M. M. (1977). Randomized and quasi-experimental designs in evaluation research: An introduction. In Leonard Rutman (Ed.), *Evaluation research methods: A basic guide.* Beverly Hills: Sage.

Cornell, Charles. (2003). How mentor teachers perceive their roles and relationships in a field-based teacher-training program. *Education, 124* (2), 401–412.

Coulson, David C.; Riffe, Daniel; Lacy, Stephen; and St. Cyr, Charles R. (2001). Erosion of television coverage of city hall? Perceptions of TV reporters on the beat. *Journalism & Mass Communication Quarterly, 78* (1), 81–92.

Cromwell, Paul, and Thurman, Quint. (2003). The devil made me do it: Use of neutralizations by shoplifters. *Deviant Behavior, 24* (6), 535–551.

Culen, Gerald R., and Volk, Trudi L. (2000). Effects of an extended case study on environmental behavior and associated variables in seventh- and eighth-grade students. *Journal of Environmental Education, 31* (2), 9–16.

Cummings, Jonathon N., and Robert Kraut. (2002). Domesticating computers and the Internet. *Information Society, 18* (3), 221–232.

Cummins, R. A. (1995). Assessing quality of life. In R. I. Brown (Ed.), *Quality of life for handicapped people.* London: Chapman and Hall.

Dammer, Harry R. (1992). *Piety in prison: An ethnography of religion in the correctional environment.* UMI Dissertation Information Service.

Darden, Donna K., and Worden, Steven K. (1996). "Cock-fighting: The marketing of deviance." *Society and Animals*, 4 (2), 211–213.

David, Matthew. (2002). Problems of participation: The limits of action research. *International Journal of Social Research Methodology*, 5 (1), 11–17.

Davis, Kingsley, and Moore, Wilbert E. (1945). Some principles of stratification. *American Sociological Review*, 10, 242–249.

Davis, Shannon N. (2003). Sex stereotypes in commercials targeted toward children: A content analysis. *Sociological Spectrum*, 23 (4), 407–425.

Dennis, Jancis. 2003. Problem-based learning in online vs. face-to-face environments. *Education for Health: Change in Learning & Practice*, 16 (2), 198–210.

Denzin, Norman K. (1989). *The research act*. Englewood Cliffs, NJ: Prentice-Hall.

Derbaix, Christian; Decrop, Alain; and Cabossart, Olivier. (2002). Colors and scarves: The symbolic consumption of material possessions by soccer fans. *Advances in Consumer Research*, 29 (1), 511–519.

Dill, K. E., and Dill, J. C. (1998). Video game violence: A review of the empirical literature. *Aggression and Violent Behavior: A Review Journal*, 3, 407–428.

Dillman, Don A. (2000). *Mail and Internet surveys: The tailored design method* (2nd ed.). New York: Wiley & Sons.

Dillon, Sam. (2003, April 30). Report finds number of Black children in deep poverty rising. *New York Times*.

Dingley, Catherine, and Roux, Gayle. (2003). Inner strength in older Hispanic women with chronic illness. *Journal of Cultural Diversity*, 10 (1), 11–23.

Douglas, Jack D. (1976). *Investigative social research*. Beverly Hills, CA: Sage.

Downey, Liam. (2005). The unintended significance of race: Environmental racial inequality in Detroit. *Social Forces*, 83 (3), 971–1008.

Durning, Alan. (1996). *The city and the car*. Northwest Environment Watch. Seattle: Sasquatch Books.

Elms, A. C. (1994). Keeping deception honest: Justifying conditions for social scientific research stratagems. In E. Erwin, S. Gendin, and L. Kleiman (Eds.), *Ethical issues in scientific research: An anthology* (pp. 121–140). New York: Garland. (Reprint of article first published in 1982.)

Emes, C. E. (1997). Is Mr. Pac Man eating our children? A review of the effect of video games on children. *The Canadian Journal of Psychiatry*, 42, 409–414.

Erikson, Kai T. (1970). A comment on disguised observation in sociology. In W. J. Filstead (Ed.), *Qualitative methodology* (pp. 252–260). Chicago: Markham.

Esterberg, Kristen. (2002). *Qualitative methods in social research*. Boston: McGraw-Hill.

Farley, Reynolds; Danziger, Sheldon; and Holzer, Harry J. (2000). *Detroit divided*. New York: Russell Sage Foundation.

Felson, Richard B. (1996). Mass media effects on violent behavior. *Annual Review of Sociology*, 22, 103–128

Fergusson, Ross. (2002). Rethinking youth transitions: Policy transfer and new exclusions in new labour's new deal. *Policy Studies*, 23 (3/4), 173–191.

Fontana, John. (2004, March 22). Survey: User annoyance grows along with spam. *Network World*, 21 (12), 86.

Ford, Thomas E. (1997). Effects of stereotypical television portrayals of African-Americans on person perception. *Social Psychology Quarterly*, 60 (3), 266–275.

Frey, Karin S.; Hirschstein, Miriam K.; and Guzzo, Barbara A. (2000). Second step: Preventing aggression by promoting social competence. *Journal of Emotional & Behavioral Disorders*, 8 (2), 102–113.

Gabris, Gerald T., and Ihrke, Douglas M. (2001). Does performance appraisal contribute to heightened levels of employee burnout? *Public Personnel Management*, 30 (2), 157–173.

Gans, Herbert. (1962). *The urban villagers*. New York: Free Press.

Garner, C. Alan. (2002, 2nd Quarter). Consumer confidence after September 11. *Economic Review* (Federal Reserve Bank of Kansas City), 87 (2), 5–26.

Geertz, C. (1988). This description: Toward an interpretive theory of culture. In R. Emerson (Ed.), *Contemporary field research: A collection of readings* (pp. 37–59). Prospect Heights, IL: Waveland Press.

Gilbert, Dennis, and Kahl, Joseph. (1993). *The American class structure: A new synthesis* (4th ed.). Homewood, IL: Dorsey Press.

Gjertsen, Lee Ann. (2000, September 12). Survey: People link insurance to getting bank loan. *American Banker*, 165 (175).

Glassner, Barry. (1999). *The culture of fear: Why Americans are afraid of the wrong things*. New York: Basic Books.

Goering, John M., and Ron Wienk (Eds.). (1996). *Mortgage lending, racial discrimination and federal policy*. Washington, DC: Urban Institute Press.

Gold, Raymond L. (1958). Roles in sociological field observations. *Social Forces*, 36, 217–223.

Gordon, Gerald, and Morse, Edward V. (1975). Evaluation research. *Annual Review of Sociology*, 1, 339–361.

Gordon, Jack. (2003). Internet is to college kids what water is to fish. *e-learning*, 4 (1), 9.

Gould, Andrew C. (2001). *Party size and policy outcomes: An empirical analysis of taxation in democracies. Studies in Comparative International Development*, 36 (2), 3–27.

Gowensmith, William N., and Bloom, Larry J. (1997). The effects of heavy metal music on arousal and anger. *The Journal of Music Therapy*, 34, 33–45.

Grant, Kathleen G., and Breese, Jeffrey R. (1997). Marginality theory and the African American student. *Sociology of Education*, 70 (3), 192–205.

Gratch, Amy. (2002). Teachers doing qualitative research: Examining school practices. *Educational Studies*, 33 (4), 422–436.

Greer, Jennifer D. (2003). Evaluating the credibility of online information: A test of source and advertising influence. *Mass Communication & Society*, 6 (1), 11–29.

Griffiths, M. (1999). Violent video games and aggression: Review of the literature. *Aggression and Violent Behavior*, 4 (2), 203–212.

Grossman, D. C.; Neckerman, H. J.; Koepsell, T. D.; Liu, P. Y.; Asher, K. N.; Beland, K.; Frey, K.; and Rivara, F. P. (1997). Effectiveness of a violence prevention curriculum among children in elementary school: A randomized controlled trial. *Journal of the American Medical Association*, 277 (20), 1605–1611.

Gubrium, Jaber F., and Holstein, James A. (1997). *The new language of qualitative method*. New York: Oxford University Press.

Gubrium, Jaber F., and Holstein, James A. (2002). From the individual interview to the interview society. In Jaber F. Gubrium and James A. Holstein (Eds.), *Handbook of interview research: Context and method* (pp. 3–33). Thousand Oaks, CA: Sage.

Guttman, Louis L. (1944). A basis for scaling qualitative data. *American Sociological Review*, 9, 139–150.

Gyasi Obeng, Samuel. (2000). Speaking the unspeakable: Discursive strategies to express language attitudes in Legon (Ghana) graffiti. *Research on Language & Social Interaction*, 33 (3), 291–320.

Hagan, Frank. (1997). *Research methods in criminal justice and criminology* (4th ed.). Boston: Allyn and Bacon.

Hallstone, Michael. (2002, Winter). Updating Howard Becker's theory of using marijuana for pleasure. *Contemporary Drug Problems*, 29 (4), 821–846.

Hamilton, Richard F., and Form, William H. (2003). Categorical usages and complex realities: Race, ethnicity, and religion in the United States. *Social Forces*, 81 (3), 693–715.

Hamm, Mark S. (1993). *American skinheads: The criminology and control of hate crime*. Westport, CT: Praeger.

Hammer, Joshua. (1992, October 26). "Must Blacks be bafoons?" *Newsweek*, pp. 70–71.

Harker, Richard. (2000, June). Achievement, gender and the single-sex/coed debate. *British Journal of Sociology of Education*, 21 (2), 203–219.

Harrell, A. V., and Wirtz, P. W. (1985). *The adolescent drinking index professional manual*. Odessa, FL: Psychological Assessment Resources.

Healey, Joseph F. (2005). *Statistics: A tool for social research* (7th ed.). Albany, NY: Wadsworth.

Henslin, James. (2003). *Sociology: A down to earth approach*. Boston: Allyn and Bacon.

Herek, Gregory M. (2002). Heterosexuals' attitudes toward bisexual men and women in the United States. *Journal of Sex Research*, 39 (4), 264–275.

Hershbein, Brad. (2003, 3rd Quarter). What is the deadliest job in America? *Regional Review*, 13 (3), 18–20.

Hirschhorn, N. (1999). *Shameful science: Four decades of the tobacco industry's hidden research on smoking and health*. www.globalink.org/tobacco/docs/secretdocs/0002verband.html.

Homan, R. (1991). *The ethics of social research*. London: Longman.

Houtzager, B., and Baerveldt, C. (1999). Just like normal: A social network study of the relation between petty crime and the intimacy of adolescent friendships. *Social Behavior & Personality: An International Journal*, 27 (2), 177–193.

Huberman, Michael, and Middlebrooks, Sally. (2000). The dilution of inquiry: A qualitative study. *International Journal of Qualitative Studies in Education*, 13 (3), 281–305.

Humphreys, Laud. (1970). *Tearoom trade: Impersonal sex in public places*. Chicago: Aldine.

Hunt, Geoffrey; Joe-Laidler, Karen; and MacKenzie, Kathleen. (2000). "'Chillin',' being dogged and getting buzzed": Alcohol in the lives of female gang members. *Drugs: Education, Prevention & Policy*, 7 (4), 331–354.

Hutton, Una M. Z., and Towse, John N. (2001). Short-term memory and working memory as indices of children's cognitive skills. *Memory*, 9 (4–6), 383–395.

Hyung-Jin, Woo, and Kim, Yeora. (2003). Modern gladiators: A content analysis of televised wrestling. *Mass Communication & Society*, 6 (4), 361–379.

Index Mundi. (2003). *CIA World Factbook*, updated January 1, 2003. www.indexmundi.com/g/r.aspx?c=bl&v=30.

Jankowski, Martin Sanchez. (1991). *Islands in the streets*. Berkeley: University of California Press.

Johnson, Brian R., and Warchol, Greg L. (2003). Bail agents and bounty hunters: Adversaries or allies of the justice system? *American Journal of Criminal Justice*, 27 (2), 145–165.

Joseph, Lee Rodgers; Nakonezny, Paul A.; and Shell, Robert D. (1999). Did no-fault divorce legislation matter? Definitely yes and sometimes no. *Journal of Marriage and the Family*, 61, 803–809.

Joynson, R. B. (1989). *The Burt affair*. New York: Routledge.

Kahn, Kim Fridkin. (1994). The distorted mirror: Press coverage of women candidates for statewide office. *The Journal of Politics*, 56 (1), 154–173.

Kalmijn, Matthijs. (1994). Mother's occupational status and children's schooling. *American Sociological Review, 59* (2), 257–275.

Kaminski, Robert J., and Marvell, Thomas B. (2002). A comparison of changes in police and general homicides: 1930–1998. *Criminology, 40* (1), 171–191.

Kasprisin, Christina Algiere; Boyle Single, Peg; Single, Richard M.; and Muller, Carol B. (2003). Building a better bridge: Testing e-training to improve e-mentoring programmes in higher education. *Mentoring & Tutoring: Partnership in Learning, 11* (1), 67–79.

Kelly, Kevin R., and Pulver, Chad A. (2003). Refining measurement of career indecision types: A validity study. *Journal of Counseling & Development, 81* (4), 445–455.

Kempinen, Cynthia A., and Kurlychek, Megan C. (2003). An outcome evaluation of Pennsylvania's boot camp: Does rehabilitative programming within a disciplinary setting reduce recidivism? *Crime and Delinquency, 49* (4), 581–606.

Klofas, John, and Cutshall, C. (1985). Unobtrusive research methods in criminal justice: Using graffiti in the reconstruction of institutional cultures. *Journal of Research in Crime and Delinquency, 22,* 355–376.

Kodrzycki, Yolanda K. (2001). Migration of recent college graduates: Evidence from the National Longitudinal Survey of Youth. *New England Economic Review,* 13–35.

Koegel, Paul. (1987). *Ethnographic perspectives on homeless and homeless mentally ill women.* Washington, DC: Alcohol, Drug Abuse, and Mental Health Administration, Public Health Service, U.S. Department of Health and Human Services.

Krysan, Maria. (2002). The residential preferences of Blacks: Do they explain persistent segregation? *Social Forces, 80* (3), 937–981.

Latané, Bibb, and Darley, John M. (1970). *The unresponsive bystander: Why doesn't he help?* Englewood Cliffs, NJ: Prentice-Hall.

Lauder, Matthew A. (2003). Covert participation observation of a deviant community: Justifying the use of deception. *Journal of Contemporary Religion, 18* (2), 185–197.

Lawson, Carole. (1985, June). Doctors cite emertic abuse. *American Anorexia/Bulimia Association Newsletter,* p. 1.

Lefly, Dianne L., and Pennington, Bruce F. (2000, May/June). Reliability and validity of the adult reading history questionnaire. *Journal of Learning Disabilities, 33* (3).

Lehrer, Evelyn L. (1999, December). Religion as a determinant of educational attainment: An economic perspective. *Social Science Research, 28* (4), 358–380.

Leo, John. (1999, May 3). When life imitates video. *U.S. News & World Report, 126* (17), 14.

Levine, John M. (1999). Solomon Asch's legacy for group research. *Personality and Social Psychology Review, 3* (4), 358–364.

Levine, S. Joseph. *Guide for writing a funding proposal.* www.learnerassociates.net/proposal/.

Levy, Paul S., and Lemeshow, Stanley. (1999). *Sampling of populations: Methods and applications* (3rd ed.). New York: Wiley.

Lofland, John. (1984). *Analyzing social settings.* Belmont, CA: Wadsworth.

Lofland, John, and Lofland, Lyn H. (1995). *Analyzing social settings* (3rd ed.). Belmont, CA: Wadsworth.

Lynch, Deirdre C.; Teplin, Sari E.; Willis, Stephen E.; Pathman, Donald E.; Larsen, Lars C.; Steiner, Beat D.; and Bernstein, James D. (2001). Interim evaluation of the rural health scholars program. *Teaching & Learning in Medicine, 13* (1), 36–43.

MacKenzie, Doris, and McCarthy, Belinda. (1990). *How to prepare a competitive grant proposal: A guide for university faculty members pursuing criminal justice research grants.* Highland Heights, KY: Academy of Criminal Justice Sciences.

Maidment, Jane, and Cooper, Lesley. (2002). Acknowledgement of client diversity and oppression in social work student supervision. *Social Work Education, 21* (4), 399–407.

Malmgren, Judith A.; Martin, Mona L.; and Nicola, Ray M. (1996). Health care access of poverty-level older adults in subsidized public housing. *Public Health Reports, 111,* 260–263.

Man So, Stella Lai. (2004). A comparative content analysis of women's magazine advertisements from Hong Kong and Australia on advertising expressions. *Journal of Current Issues & Research in Advertising, 26* (1), 47–59.

Marvasti, Amir B. (2004). *Qualitative research in sociology.* London: Sage.

Matthew, David. (2002, January–March). Problems of participation: The limits of action research. *International Journal of Social Research Methodology, 5* (1), 11–18.

McBride, Ron E.; Xiang, Ping; Wittenburg, David; and Shen, Jianhua. (2002). An analysis of preservice teachers' dispositions toward critical thinking: A cross-cultural perspective. *Asia-Pacific Journal of Teacher Education, 30* (2), 131–141.

McLeod, M. (1984). Women against men: An examination of domestic violence based on an analysis of official data and national victimization data. *Justice Quarterly, 1* (2), 171–193.

McMahon, Jennifer, and Clay-Warner, Jody. (2002). Child abuse and future criminality: The role of social service placement, family disorganization, and gender. *Journal of Interpersonal Violence, 17* (9), 1002–1020.

Meyer, Gary; Roberto, Anthony J.; and Atikin, Charles K. (2003). A radio-based approach to promoting gun safety: Process and outcome evaluation implications and insights. *Health Communication, 15* (3), 299–319.

Milgram, Stanley. (1974). *Obedience to authority: An experimental view.* New York: Harper.

Mitchell, Barbara A. (2001). Ethnocultural reproduction and attitudes towards cohabiting relationships. *Canadian Review of Sociology & Anthropology, 38* (4), 391–414.

Montemurro, Beth; Bloom, Colleen; and Madell, Kelly. (2003). Ladies night out: A typology of women patrons of a male strip club. *Deviant Behavior, 24* (4), 333–353.

Mooney, Margarita. (2003). Migrants' social ties in the U.S. and investment in Mexico. *Social Forces, 81* (4), 1147–1171.

Nabors, Laura A., and Reynolds, Mathew W. (2000). Program evaluation activities: Outcomes related to treatment for adolescents receiving school-based mental health services. *Children's Services: Social Policy, Research & Practice, 3* (3), 175–189.

National Center for Education Statistics. (1997, February). *1995 National Household Education Survey Questionnaire. NHES:95 Basic Screener and NHES:95 Adult Survey.* http://nces.ed.gov/nhes/pdf/quex/adulted/ae_95.pdf.

National Institute of Justice. (1997). *Boot camps for juvenile offenders.* Office of Juvenile Justice and Delinquency Prevention, U.S. Department of Justice. Cited in Office of Justice Programs. (1995). *Fiscal year 1995 corrections boot camp initiative: Violent offender incarceration grant program. Program guidelines and application Information.* www.ncjrs.org/pdffiles1/nij/197018.pdf.

National Vital Statistics Bureau. (2002). Table 3: Provisional number of marriages and divorces: Each state: December 2000 and 2001 and cumulative figures 1999–2001. www.cdc.gov/nchs/data/nvsr/nvsr50/50-14-12-03.pdf.

Neuman, W. Lawrence. (1997). *Social research methods: Qualitative and quantitative approaches* (3rd ed.). Boston: Allyn and Bacon.

Norris, Pippa, and Sanders, David. (2003). Message or medium? Campaign learning during the 2001 British general election. *Political Communication, 20* (3), 233–263.

Office of Juvenile Justice and Delinquency Prevention. (1978, June). *Evaluation issues.* Washington, DC: U.S. Department of Justice.

Orange, Carolyn M., and George, Amiso M. (2000). Child sacrifice: Black Americans' price of paying the media piper. *Journal of Black Studies, 30* (3), 294–314.

Pandey, Sanjay K., Hart, John; and Tiwary, Sheela. (2003). Women's health and the Internet: Understanding emerging trends and implications. *Social Science & Medicine, 56* (1), 179–192.

Parent, Dale G. (2003, July). Correctional boot camps: Lessons from a decade of research. *Series: Research for practice.* Washington, DC: National Institute of Justice.

Patterson, Janice H.; Collins, Loucrecia; and Abbott, Gypsy. (2004). A study of teacher resilience in urban schools. *Journal of Instructional Psychology, 31* (1), 3–12.

Patterson, Orlando. (1997). *The ordeal of integration: Progress and resentment in America's "racial" crisis.* Washington, DC: Civitas/Counterpoint.

Patton, Tracey Owens. (2001). "Ally McBeal" and her homies: The reification of White stereotypes of the other. *Journal of Black Studies, 32* (2), 229–260.

Pavetti, LaDonna; Derr, Michelle K.; Anderson, Jacquelyn; Trippe, Carole; and Paschal, Sidnee. (2001). Changing the culture of the welfare office: The role of intermediaries in linking TANF recipients with jobs. *Economic Policy Review* (Federal Reserve Bank of New York), *7* (2), 63–77.

Peltzer, Karl. (2001). Psychosocial correlates of healthy lifestyles in Black and White South Africans. *Social Behavior & Personality: An International Journal, 29* (3), 249–256.

Pena, Yesilernis, and Sidanius, Jim. (2002). U.S. patriotism and ideologies of group dominance: A tale of asymmetry. *Journal of Social Psychology, 142* (6), 782–791.

Peterson, Carla A.; Wall, Shavaun; Raikes, Helen A.; Kisker, Ellen E.; Swanson, Mark E.; Jerald, Judith; Atwater, Jane B.; and Wei Qiao. (2004). Early Head Start: Identifying and serving children with disabilities. *Topics in Early Childhood Special Education, 24* (2), 76–89.

Picket, Stephen. (2004, March 25). Neighborhood vote, in reality, a landslide against the Lake Ivanhoe. www.mycollegepark.com.

Plucker, Jonathan. (2003). The Cyril Burt affair. *Human intelligence.* www.indiana.edu/~intell/burtaffair.shtml.

Preski, Sally, and Shelton, Deborah. (2001). The role of contextual, child, and parent factors in predicting criminal outcomes in adolescence. *Issues in Mental Health Nursing, 22* (2), 197–206.

Pritchard, Colin, and Williams, Richard. (2001). A three-year comparative longitudinal study of a school-based social work family service to reduce truancy, delinquency and school exclusions. *Journal of Social Welfare & Family Law, 23* (1), 23–44.

Pritchard, David. (1986, Summer). Homicide and bargained justice: The agenda-setting effect of crime news on prosecutors. *The Public Opinion Quarterly, 50* (2), 143–159.

Probst, Tahira M. (2003). Exploring employee outcomes of organizational restructuring: A Solomon four-group study. *Group & Organization Management, 8* (3), 416–439.

Rasinski, Kenneth. (1989, Autumn). The effect of question wording on public support for government spending. *The Public Opinion Quarterly, 53* (3), 388–394.

Rennard, Barbara O.; Ertl, Ronald F.; Gossman, Gail L.; Robbins, Richard A.; and Rennard, Stephen I. (2000). Chicken soup inhibits neutrophil chemotaxis. *In Vitro, 118,* 1150–1157.

Richardson, Laurel. (1990). *Writing strategies: Reaching diverse audiences.* Newbury Park, CA: Sage.

Riedel, Marc. (2000). *Research strategies for secondary data: A perspective for criminology and criminal justice.* Thousand Oaks, CA: Sage.

Rives, Norfleet W., Jr., and Serow, William J. (1988). *Introduction to applied demography: Data sources and estimation techniques.* Sage University Paper series on Quantitative Applications in the Social Sciences, series no. 07-039. Thousand Oaks, CA: Sage.

Rodgers, Joseph Lee; Nakonezny, Paul A.; and Shell, Robert D. (1999). Did no-fault divorce legislation matter? Definitely yes and sometimes no. *Journal of Marriage and the Family, 61,* 803–809.

Roethlisberger, F. J., and Dixon, William J. (1939). *Management and the worker.* Cambridge, MA: Harvard University Press.

Rokeach, Milton. (1960). *The open and closed mind.* New York: Basic Books.

Ross, Catherine E. (2000). Neighborhood disadvantage and adult depression. *Journal of Health and Social Behavior, 41* (2), 177–187.

Rossi, Peter H., and Wright, James D. (1984). Evaluation research: An assessment. *Annual Review of Sociology, 10,* 331–352.

Sanders, Jimy; Nee, Victor; and Sernau, Scott. (2002). Asian immigrants' reliance on social ties in a multiethnic labor market. *Social Forces, 81* (1), 281–315.

Sawyer, H. G. The meaning of numbers. Speech before the American Association of Advertising Agencies, cited in Eugene Webb et al. (1961). *Unobtrusive measures.* Chicago: Rand McNally.

Schedler, Andreas. (2001). Measuring democratic consolidation. *Studies in Comparative International Development, 36* (1), 66–93.

Scheidet, Robert A. (2003). Improving student achievement by infusing a Web-based curriculum into global history. *Journal of Research on Technology in Education, 36* (1), 77–95.

Scherff, Andrew R., Eckert, Tanya L.; and Miller, David N. (2005). Youth suicide prevention: A survey of public school superintendents' acceptability of school-based programs. *Suicide & Life—Threatening Behavior, 35* (2), 154–170.

Schoen, Robert; Astone, Nan Marie; Rothert, Kendra; Standish, Nicola J.; and Kim, Young J. (2002). Women's employment, marital happiness, and divorce. *Social Forces, 81* (2), 643–663.

Schutt, Russell K. (2001). *Investigating the social world: The process and practice of research* (3rd ed.). Thousand Oaks, CA: Pine Forge Press.

Scully, Diana, and Marolla, Joseph. (1985). Riding the bull at Gilley's: Convicted rapists describe the rewards of rape. *Social Problems, 32* (3), 251–263.

Shannon, David M., and Bradshaw, Carol C. (2002). A comparison of response rate, response time, and costs of mail and electronic surveys. *Journal of Experimental Education, 70* (2), 179–193.

Sheehan, Eugene P., and DuPrey, Tara. (1999). Student evaluations of university teaching. *Journal of Instructional Psychology, 26* (3), 188–193.

Sherman, Lawrence. (1992). *Policing domestic violence: Experiments and dilemmas.* New York: Free Press.

Sherman, Lawrence W., and Berk, Richard. (1984b). The specific deterrent effects of arrest for domestic assault. *American Sociological Review, 49,* 261–272.

Sherman, Larry, and Berk, Richard. (1984a). *The Minneapolis domestic violence experiment.* Washington, DC: The Police Foundation.

Sherman, Lawrence W., and Smith, Douglas A., with Schmidt, Janell D., and Rogan, Dennis. (1992). Crime, punishment, and stake in conformity. *American Sociological Review, 57,* 680–690.

Shiloh, Shoshana; Sorek, Gal; and Terkel, Joseph. (2003). Reduction of state-anxiety by petting animals in a controlled laboratory experiment. *Anxiety, Stress & Coping, 16* (4), 387–396.

Simoni, J. M., and Cooperman, N. A. (2000). Stressors and strengths among women living with HIV/AIDS in New York City. *AIDS Care, 12* (3), 291–298.

Simpson, Brent. (2003). Sex, fear, and greed: A social dilemma analysis of gender and cooperation. *Social Forces, 82* (1), 35–52.

Smit, Filip; de Zwart, Wil; Spruit, Inge; Monshouwer, Karin; and van Ameijden, Erik. (2002). Monitoring substance use in adolescents: School survey or household survey? *Drugs: Education, Prevention & Policy, 9* (3), 267–175.

Smith, Judith R. (2002). Commitment to mothering and preference for employment: The voices of women on public assistance with young children. *Journal of Children & Poverty, 8* (1), 51–67.

Soloway, Irving, and Walters, James. (1977). Workin' the corner: The ethics and legality of ethnographic fieldwork among active heroin addicts. In Robert S. Weppner (Ed.),

Street ethnography, Vol. 1 (pp. 159–178). Beverly Hills, CA: Sage.

Sommers, Christian Hoff. (1994). *Who stole feminism?* New York: Simon and Schuster, pp. 11–12.

Soukup, Charles. (1999). The gendered interactional patterns of computer-mediated chatrooms: A critical ethnographic study. *Information Society, 15* (3).

Stack, Carol B. (1974). *All our kin: Strategies for survival in a Black community.* New York: Harper and Row.

Stanford University News Service. (1997). http://www2 .stanford.edu/dept/news/relaged/970108prisonexp.html.

Statistical Abstracts of the United States. (2003). Table No. 1066. On-time flight arrivals and departures at major U.S. airports: 2002. U.S. Department of Transportation, Aviation Consumer Protection Division. *Air Travel Consumer Report,* See http://airconsumer.ost.dot.gov.

Statistical Abstracts of the United States. (2003). No. 332. Background checks for firearm transfers: 1994 to 2001. U.S. Bureau of Justice Statistics, *Background Checks for Firearm Transfers, 2001,* Series NCJ 195235.

Statistical Abstracts of the United States. (2003). Table 695: Average earnings of full time year round workers by educational attainment: 2001. www.census.gov/prod/www/ statistical-abstract-03.html.

Stigler, James W.; Gallimore, Ronald; and Hiebert, James. (2000). Using video surveys to compare classrooms and teaching across cultures: Examples and lessons from the TIMSS video studies. *Educational Psychologist, 35* (2), 87–101.

Straus, Murray, and Gelles, Richard. (1986). Societal change and changes in family violence from 1875–1985 as revealed by a second national survey. *Journal of Marriage and the Family, 48,* 465–479.

Sudman, Seymour. (1976). *Applied sampling.* New York: Academic Press.

Szilagyi, Peter G.; Shenkman, Elizabeth; Brach, Cindy; La-Clair, Barbara J.; Swigonski, Nancy; Dick, Andrew; Shone, Laura P.; Schaffer, Virginia A.; Col, Jana F.; Eckert, George; Klein, Jonathan D.; and Lewit, Eugene M. (2003). Children with special health care needs enrolled in the State Children's Health Insurance Program (SCHIP): Patient characteristics and health care Needs. *Pediatrics, 112,* Supplement 2, 508–521.

Tanner, Julia; Cockerill, Rhonda; Barnsley, Jan; and Williams, A. Paul. (1999). Gender and income in pharmacy: Human capital and gender stratification theories revisited. *British Journal of Sociology, 50* (1), 97–118.

Thackrey, Don. *Proposal writer's guide.* Listed at the University of Michigan's research website, www.research.umich .edu/proposals/pwg/pwgcontents.html.

Thernstrom, Stephan, and Thernstrom, Abigail. 1997. *America in Black and White: One nation, indivisible.* New York: Simon & Schuster.

Thompson, Carol Y.; Young, Robert L.; and Burns, Ronald. (2000). Representing gangs in the news: Media constructions of criminal gangs. *Sociological Spectrum, 20* (4), 409–433.

Thorne, Barrie. (1993). *Gender play: Girls and boys in school.* New Brunswick, NJ: Rutgers University Press.

Thorpe, Lorna E.; List, Deborah G.; Marx, Terry; May, Linda; Helgerson, Steven D.; and Frieden, Thomas R. (2004). Childhood obesity in New York City elementary school students. *American Journal of Public Health, 94* (9), 1496–5000.

Tryon, Georgiana Shick. (2001). School psychology students' beliefs about their preparation and concern with ethical issues. *Ethics & Behavior, 11* (4), 375–394.

Tucker, W. H. (1997). Re-reconsidering Burt: Beyond a reasonable doubt. *Journal of the History of the Behavioral Sciences, 33* (2), 145–162.

Urban Institute. (2000). *A new look at homelessness in America.* Retrieved February, 1. www.urban.org.

U.S. Bureau of the Census. (1997). *Statistical abstracts of the United States* (117th ed.). Washington, DC: Author, p. 96.

U.S. Bureau of the Census. (2001). *Overview of race and Hispanic origin: Census 2000 brief.* www.census.gov/prod/ 2001pubs/c2kbr01-1.pdf.

U.S. Bureau of the Census. (2001). *Home computers and Internet use in the United States.* Current Population Reports. www.census.gov/prod/2001pubs/p23-207.pdf.

U.S. Census Bureau. (2001 March). *Overview of race and Hispanic origin: Census 2000 brief.* www.census.gov/prod/ 2001pubs/c2kbr01-1.pdf.

U.S. Census Bureau. (2002). *Current Population Survey, 2002 and 2003 Annual Social & Economic Supplements.* Table 1: Number in poverty and poverty rate by race and Hispanic origin: 2001 and 2002. www.census.gov/hhes/poverty/ poverty02/table1.pdf.

U.S. Census Bureau. (2002). Census 2000 Summary File 1, Matrices P17, P26, P27, P33, P34, and P35. Table QT-P10 Households and families. http://factfinder.census .gov/servlet/.

U.S. Census Bureau. (2002). Historical poverty tables. Table 18: Workers as a proportion of all poor people: 1978–2002. www.census.gov/hhes/poverty/histpv/hstpov18.html.

U.S. Bureau of the Census. (2003). *Current Population Survey (CPS), 2003 Annual Social & Economic Supplement* (ASEC).www.census.gov/hhes/poverty/poverty02/pov02hi .html.

U.S. Bureau of Labor Statistics. (2002, July). *National compensation survey: Occupational wages in the United States. Supplementary Tables.* www.bls.gov/ncs/ocs/sp/ncbl0540.pdf.

U.S. Department of Health and Human Services. (2003, March). *Ending chronic homelessness: Strategies for action.* Report to the Secretary's Work Group on Ending Chronic Homelessness. http://aspe.hhs.gov/hsp/homelessness/strategies03/ch.htm#ch2.

Van Deth, Jan W. (2003). Measuring social capital: Orthodoxies and continuing controversies. *International Journal of Social Research Methodology*, 6 (1), 79–93.

Van Eijck, Koen. (2001). Social differentiation in musical taste patterns. *Social Forces*, 79 (3), 1163–1186.

Van Maanen, John. (1982). Fieldwork on the beat. In John Van Maanen, James M. Dabbs, Jr., and Robert P. Faulkner (Eds.), *Varieties of qualitative research* (pp. 103–151). Beverly Hills: Sage.

Ven, Thomas Vander, and Cullen, Francis T. (2004). The impact of maternal employment on serious youth crime: Does the quality of working conditions matter? *Crime & Delinquency*, 50 (2), 272–292.

Ventis, W. Larry; Higbee, Garrett; and Murdock, Susan A. (2001). Using humor in systematic desensitization to reduce fear. *Journal of General Psychology*, 128 (2), 241–254.

Vogler, Kenneth E. (2002). The impact of high-stakes, state-mandated student performance assessment on teachers' instructional practices. *Education*, 123 (1), 39–56.

Waite, Linda J., and Gallagher, Maggie. (2000). *The case for marriage: Why married people are happier, healthier, and better off financially.* New York: Doubleday.

Wallin, E., et al. (2003). Alcohol prevention targeting licensed premises: A study of effects on violence. *Journal of Studies on Alcohol*, 64 (2), 270–277.

War Resister's League. *Where your income tax money really goes.* www.warresisters.org/.

Warren, Carol, and Karner, Tracy X. (2005). *Discovering qualitative methods: Field research, interviews, and analysis.* Los Angeles: Roxbury.

Weber, Max. (1913). *The theory of social and economic organization.* A. M. Henderson and Talcott Parsons, trans.; Talcott Parson, ed. Glencoe, IL: Free Press, 1947.

Webster, Jessica, and Tiggemann, Marika. (2003). The relationship between women's body satisfaction and self-image across the life span: The role of cognitive control. *Journal of Genetic Psychology*, 164 (2), 241–256.

What's for breakfast, America? (2003, January 17). *Scholastic News*, 65 (14), 3.

Wholey, J. S.; Scanlon, J. W.; Duffy, H. G.; Fukumoto, J. S.; and Vogt, L. M. (1970). *Federal evaluation policy.* Washington, DC: The Urban Institute.

Wholey, Joseph S. (1983). *Evaluation and effective public management.* Boston: Little, Brown.

Whyte, William Foote. (1955). *Street corner society.* Chicago: University of Chicago Press.

Whyte, William Foote. (1993). *Street corner society* (4th ed.). Chicago: University of Chicago Press.

Wilson, William Julius. (1987). *The truly disadvantaged: The inner city, the underclass, and public policy.* Chicago: University of Chicago Press.

Wight, Daniel, and Buston, Katie. (2003). Meeting needs but not changing goals: Evaluation of In-service teacher training for sex education. *Oxford Review of Education*, 29 (4), 521–544.

Wolcott, Harry F. (1995). *The art of fieldwork.* Walnut Creek, CA: AltaMira.

Woldoff, Rachel A. (2002). The effects of local stressors on neighborhood attachment. *Social Forces*, 81 (1), 87–117.

Wolfer, Loreen. (1998). Parenthood and marriage: Does maternal employment influence the timing of adult family transitions for daughters from different economic backgrounds? *Sociological Viewpoints*, 14, 39–62.

Wolfer, Loreen. (2001). Strengthening communities: Neighborhood watch and the non-urban elderly. *Crime Prevention and Community Safety: An International Journal*, 3 (3), 31–39.

Wolfer, Loreen T., and Moen, Phyllis. (1996). Staying in school: Maternal employment and the timing of Black and White daughters' school exit. *Journal of Family Issues*, 17 (4), 540–560.

Wolfer, Loreen. (2001a, May). The Lackawanna County Treatment Court: A descriptive analysis of early implementation. *Process Evaluation for January to March, 2001.* Research Report submitted to Lackawanna County District Attorney's Office. May 2001.

Wolfer, Loreen. (2001b, October). The Lackawanna County Treatment Court: A descriptive analysis of early implementation. *Process Evaluation for July to September, 2001.* Research Report submitted to Lackawanna County District Attorney's Office.

Wolfinger, Nicholas H. (2003). Parental divorce and offspring marriage: Early or late? *Social Forces*, 82 (1), 337–354.

Yammarino, Francis J.; Skinner, Steven J.; and Childers, Terry L. (1991). Understanding mail survey response behavior: A meta-analysis. *The Public Opinion Quarterly*, 55 (4), 613–639.

Yang, Shu Ching, and Lin, Wen Chaun. (2004). The relationship among creative, critical thinking and thinking styles in Taiwan high school students. *Journal of Instructional Psychology*, 31 (1), 33–45.

Yarnall, Louise; Penvel, William R.; Ravitz, Jason; Murray, Grahame; and Means, Barbara. (2003). Portable assessment authoring: Using handheld technology to assess collaborative inquiry. *Education, Communication & Information, 3* (1), 7–56.

Yarosz, Donald, and Barnett, William. (2001, January). Who reads to young children?: Identifying predictors of family reading activities. *Reading Psychology, 22* (1), 67–82.

Zabinski, Marion; Welfley, Denise; Pung, Meredith; Winzelberg, Andrew; Eldredge, Kathleen; and Taylor, C. Barr. (2001). An interactive-based intervention for women at risk of eating disorders: A pilot study. *Eating Disorders, 9* (3).

Zaehringer, Brent. (1998, July). *Juvenile boot camps: Cost and effectiveness vs. residential facilities.* Koch Crime Institute White Paper Report. www.kci.org/publication/white_paper/boot_camp/research_findings.htm.

Zekovic, Buga, and Renwick, Rebecca. (2003). Quality of life for children and adolescents with developmental dis-abilities: Review of conceptual and methodological issues relevant to public policy. *Disability & Society, 18* (1), 19–35.

Zhao, Dingxin. (1998). Ecologies of social movements: Student mobilization during the 1989 prodemocracy movement in Beijing. *The American Journal of Sociology, 103* (6), 1493–1529.

Zimbardo, Philip G. (1972). The psychology of imprisonment. *Society, 9,* 4–6.

Zimbardo, Philip G. (1999, July/August). Access to postsecondary education. *Gifted Child Today Magazine, 22* (4), 8.

Zimbardo, Philip G. (2002, October). Poll shows support for government monitoring of religion. *Church & State, 55* (9), 16–18.

Zimbardo, Philip G. Women make poor showing on boards. *Investor Relations Business, 8* (24), 5–7.

Index

coding, 518, 522–524
computer-assisted telephone interviewing, 526 (*see also* Survey research)
data:
    analysis (*see* Statistics)
    cleaning, 521, 526–527
    collapsing categories, 527–528
    entry, 525–526
    graphs, 574–578
    indexes and scales, 529–539
    tables, 554–555, 571–574
  direct entry method, 526
  evaluating written research, 580–587
  general definition, 13
  optical scan sheet, 526
  (*see also* Statistics)
Quota sample, 206, 209–211

R
Random digit dialing, 193–196
Range, 545
Reductionism, 115–116
Reliability, 148–154, 326, 365
  tests, 150–152
    inter-rater, 151–152
    split-half, 150–151
    test-retest, 150
  types, 149–150
    equivalence, 150
    representative, 149–150
    temporal, 149
  (*see also* Agency data; Content analysis; Field research; Qualitative research; Secondary data analysis; Survey research)
Representative reliability, 149–150
Research process (overview), 42–49

S
Sampling, 170–227, 233
  confidence interval, 176, 188, 215
  confidence level, 176, 188, 215
  convenience sample, 171
  elements, 173, 189
  error, 176, 203, 206
  evaluating written research, 217–226
  nonprobability sampling, 207–211, 344–345
    accidental sample, 208, 211
    convenience sample, 208, 211
    haphazard sample, 208, 211
    purposive sample, 208–209, 211

    quota sample, 206, 209–211
    snowball sample, 210–211, 345
    summary, 211
  population, 173–174
  population parameter, 176, 187
  probability sampling, 181–207
    central limit theorem, 181, 185–186
    cluster sample, 199, 202–207, 211
    normal distribution, 184, 186, 188
    periodicity, 195
    probability theory, 182, 186
    random digit dialing, 193–196
    sampling distribution, 184
    sampling interval, 194–196
    selection bias, 182
    simple random sample, 188–191, 211
    standard deviation, 187–188
    standard error, 181, 186–187
    stratified random sampling, 196–201, 211, 214
    summary, 191–193, 200–201, 211
    systematic random sampling, 191–195, 211
  sample size, 213–216
  sampling frame, 174–175, 189
  sampling units, 175–202
  selection of type, 212–213
  statistics, 175, 186
  study population, 174
  why sample, 172
Scales, 529–539
  Guttman, 533–539
  Likert, 529–533, 538
Secondary data analysis, 396–406
  advantages/disadvantages, 405–406
  appropriate topics, 397–398, 402
  considerations, 403–404
  ecological fallacy, 403
  ethics, 410
  gaining access, 389–399
  generalizability, 405
  measurement, 399–402
  quality, 399
  reliability, 405
  validity, 405
Simple random sample, 188–191, 211
Snowball sample, 210–211, 345
Solomon four-group design, 241–242
Spearman's rho, 566–567
Split-half reliability test, 150–151
Standard deviation, 187–188, 545–548
Standard error, 181, 186–187